OUT PLAYS

Also by Ben Hodges

The Commercial Theater Institute Guide to Producing Plays and Musicals (with Frederic B. Vogel)

Forbidden Acts: Pioneering Gay and Lesbian Plays of the Twentieth Century

Out Plays

LANDMARK GAY AND LESBIAN PLAYS
OF THE TWENTIETH CENTURY

Edited and with an introduction by
Ben Hodges

Foreword by Harvey Fierstein

Manufactured in the United States of America

Published by Alyson Books
245 West 17th Street, New York, NY 10011

Distribution in the United Kingdom by Turnaround Publisher Services Ltd.
Unit 3, Olympia Trading Estate, Coburg Road, Wood Green
London N22 6TZ England

First Edition: March 2008

08 09 10 11 12 13 14 15 16 17 a 10 9 8 7 6 5 4 3 2 1

ISBN: 1-59350-044-0
ISBN-13: 978-1-59350-044-3

Library of Congress Cataloging-in-Publication data are on file.
Cover design by Victor Mingovits
Interior design by Charles Annis

For David Lowry, Tim Deak, Carolyn Valentine Rapp, Gretchen Hall Kerr, Laura Hagan Hanson, Epitacio Arganza, and Wilson Valentin—my oldest friends, alternately players in, and audience to, the drama that is my life.

CONTENTS

ACKNOWLEDGMENTS

Thanks first and foremost to Richard Fumosa, editor at Alyson Books, who so enthusiastically and eagerly encouraged me to edit this anthology. Always a pleasure to work with, he was candid and supportive throughout the entire process

Buddy Thomas at International Creative Management and Eric Lupfer, Jack Tantleff, and Peter Franklin at William Morris Agency made what could have been an otherwise daunting permissions quest remarkably easy.

And the ever knowledgeable, courteous, and energetic staff of the New York Public Library at Lincoln Center—particularly the seasoned Jeremy McGraw—as well as the simultaneously effervescent and indomitable Sylvia Alicea, Edyie Wiggins, and Christina Nelson in the copy center, were all indispensable.

Finally, it is only because of the generous agreement of authors, or those who administer the estates of authors, that books of this kind get published, and permission to reprint seminal works such as these is often withheld. But I am forever grateful to the following for allowing me to be one of the few to whom they said yes: Beth Allen, Mart Crowley, Harvey Fierstein, Ron Fierstein, Shirley Knight Hopkins, Albert Innaurato, Terrence McNally, Paula Vogel, and Lanford Wilson.

To all of you who took the time to inquire, consider, and ultimately submit material for inclusion here, thank you. It is my sincerest wish that the publication of these works will once again celebrate their importance, and make them available again to those who can best ensure their longevity.

And to all of the below, who, whether it be on this project or for regularly supporting me so assuredly in ways large and small, you are thanked one and all: Epitacio Arganza; Rommel "Raj" Autencio; Jason Baruch and Sendroff and Baruch, LLP; Melina Bielefelt; Seth Barrish, Lee Brock, Eric Paeper, and The Barrow Group Theater Company/The Barrow Group School; Nicole Boyd; Nana Brunbage; Pearl Chang; Michael Che; Jason Cicci, Monday Morning Productions, and Summer Stage New York; Richard Cohen; Susan Cosson; Mart Crowley; Robert Dean Davis; Carol and Nick Dawson; Carmen Diaz; Diane Dixon; Craig Dudley; Sherry Eaker; Ben Feldman, Amy Luce, and Beigelman, Feldman, & Associates, P.C.; Lori Anne Larson and Farrar, Strauss, and Giroux, LLC; Marisa Kraus, Keegan Harris, and Smith and Krauss Publishers, Emily Feldman; Stanley Morton Ackert III and Gersen, Blakeman, and Ackert; Sarah Jo Hooker and Goddard College; Gerry Goodstein, the estates of the late Charles J. Grant Jr. and Zan Van Antwerp; Brad Hampton; Laura and Tommy Hanson; Richard M. Henderson Jr. and Jennifer Henderson; Richard M. Henderson Sr. and Patricia Lynn Henderson; Al and Sherry Hodges; Chi Hu; Charlie and Phyllis Hurt; Leonard Jacobs; Gretchen, Aaron, Eli, and Max Kerr; Jane, Lynn, and Kris Kircher; Tim Deak, Kim Spanjol, and The Learning Theatre Inc.; David Lowry; Joaquin Matias; Cecelia McCarton and the staff of the McCarton Center/The McCarton School; Michael Messina; Barry Monush and *Screen World*; Virginia Moraweck; Lucy Nathanson; Howard Sherman and the American Theatre Wing; Jason Bowcutt, Shay Gines, Nick Micozzi, and the staff and respective voting committees of the New York Innovative Theatre Awards; Petie Dodrill, Craig Johnson, Rob Johnson, Dennis Romer, Katie Robbins, Dean Jo Ann VanSant, Ed Vaughan, the late Dr. Charles O. Dodrill and the staff of Otterbein College/Otterbein

College Department of Theatre and Dance; William Craver and Paradigm; Hugo Uys and the staff of Paris Commune and Shag; John Philip; David Plank; Angie and Drew Powell; Kay Radtke; Carolyn, David, Glenna, and Jonas Rapp; Robert Rems; David Rothenberg; Kate Rushing; John Sala; Bill Schaap; Emmanuel Serrano; Hannah Richman Slosberg and Jason Slosberg; Charlotte St. Martin and the League of American Theatres and Producers; Professors Jake Barnes, Kevin J. Doyle, Linda Fisher, and Jon Romberg, as well as Christine Coiro, Betsy Gilligan, George Meresedis, Derek Pahigiannis, Debbie Placid, Charles Wilkes, Ashley Wissmiller, and the Seton Hall University School of Law Class of 2010; Susan Stoller; Martha Swope; Gretchen Smith and Southern Methodist University; Renée Isely Tobin and Bob, Kate, Eric, Laura, Anna, Foster, and Lucky Tobin; Bob Ost and Theater Resources Unlimited Inc.; John Willis, Scott Denny, Laura Viade, Michael Viade, Rachel Werbel, and the staff of *Theatre World* and the John Willis *Theatre World/Screen World* Archive; Peter Filichia, Tom Lynch, Kati Meister, Matthew Murray, and the board of directors of The Theatre World Awards Inc.; Harry Haun, Howard Kissel, Frank Scheck, Michael Sommers, Doug Watt, Linda Winer, and the voting committee of The Theatre World Awards Inc.; Martha S. LoMonaco, David Nochimson, and the Theatre Library Association; Elizabeth Williams, Jack Williams, Barbara Dewey, and the staff of the University of Tennessee at Knoxville; Wilson Valentin; Kathie Packer and the estate of the late Frederic B. Vogel; Anton Wagner; Sarah and Bill Willis; George Wilson; Shane and Bill Wolters.

FOREWORD

by Harvey Fierstein

Motorcycles rev and buck at the slow pace at which their leather-gloved mistresses progress down the street. The horns and drums of marching bands beat back the incessant pounding of disco blaring from dance-club uberspeakers. Smoke and laughter, screams of joy and protest, join in a cacophony that rises from the steaming summer asphalt, through throngs of drag tiaras, leather straps, happy-hands-at-home fashioned signs, bare breasts, and T-shirt messages, up over the glittered floats and rainbow balloons, to dance briefly with a hailstorm of confetti tossed by window-perched well-wishers before reaching into the cloudless sky and beyond. It's 1974, and the mass of humanity that is the Christopher Street Liberation Day Parade is exploding across the wide New York City boulevards of Thirty-fourth Street and Sixth Avenue. A very young version of myself is whirling in the ecstasy of belonging to this throng, when suddenly a woman on the sidewalk locks eyes with me. She's an elderly creature, with close-cropped nicotine-tinted gray hair, garbed in paisley-print cotton housecoat, Macy's shopping bags in one hand, purse tightly clutched in the other. She's caught behind the police barricade as if suddenly snatched in a fisherman's net. With guileless innocence, she looks into my eyes and asks, "Who are you people?"

What answer could I offer? "We are people who have sex with people of our own sex." If that ain't the lamest definition ever, then what is? So what are we? A race of people? A political movement? A culture? A subculture? A deviation from the norm? A subsection of the norm? As far as I can see, art offers the major evidence from which to form an answer.

History offers few records of homosexuals as a people. There are individuals who've left traces, but only extraordinary lives are remembered in histories, so what good are they at telling us who we everyday gays are? Anthropologists and sociologists guess at tracing our paths and patterns with sketchy paperwork. To them, we are footnotes. Even homocentric societies are filed away as oddities less worthy of serious study than practitioners of long-outmoded religions. Where are our records? Our lives seem to be evidenced only in the fecal materials of lawsuits, police files, and pornography. For most of history, our everyday lives were cloaked in shame and secrecy. Our heritage, our culture, our prized possessions have always been usurped by the greater heterosexual populace. Is Walt Whitman American or gay? How many school children sing "America the Beautiful" as a lesbian song? Does any textbook allow that the man who ended slavery in America was most likely homosexual? No. History and sociology teach us that the world is heterosexual and that only heterosexuality is important in forming society. Homosexuality is a factor only in the bedroom and has had no effect on law, society, or culture. That message is clear. So we are not going to find out who we are via history.

Can we find ourselves in books? As Joyce Carol Oates once said, "Speak truth at your own risk." Fiction gives us homosexual characters. Trashy dime-store novels have told stories of "the third sex" for generations. Tales of scandal, sex crimes, unbridled lust, and forbidden love certainly give evidence of our existence, but cannot tell us who we really are. According to that fiction, we are a bit of ornamentation in the architecture of society. These books would, in fact, be part of the folklore that keeps us closet bound, were it not for the fact that easily swayed minds don't feed on books. The dangerous third-sex message is therefore minimized.

Hollywood is an even bigger barrier to truth. It's big business aiming at the greatest world audience. So, while historically Hollywood has been filled with homosexuals, they mostly promised to pander to straight society before they were given the keys to their convertibles. Hooked on success, even the most politically aware seem to put away their gay stuff until they are established (which means forever), or they simply sell out gay truth by refusing to use gay actors, as if to do so would make their stories unpalatable. Several years ago, I did a survey and found that there had been seventeen gay characters in mainstream films that year. A gay or bisexual actor played not a single one of those characters. No. We are not going to find ourselves in Hollywood.

Television grinds under the same restrictions as movieland, but its lower bottom line and higher product output allow greater expression. Television has always been the gay Promised Land. I first glimpsed a real live homosexual on television. It was Allen Ginsburg on a talk show. There he sat in bearded glory, his lover placed at his feet in wifely repose, as he spoke about being a homosexual. Ginsburg was not the muscled fantasy of porn magazines or one of the shadow-dwelling creatures that populated the brittle pages of the cheap gay novels that had thus far been my key to our queendom. My world exploded. Here was homosexuality as normal. Television offered revolution. Unfortunately, TV is inherently a medium of fantasy. Created to be watched in the privacy of one's bedroom, it does best for its masters when delivering game shows, reality shows that have nothing to do with reality, and soap-opera drama. The pressure to keep masses of people tuning in every week for the newest shock leaves little room for expression of the everyday. On TV, we are usually the next-door neighbors who are good for a laugh, tragic victims, or heinous murderers. We are almost never whole people, so don't look for us there.

So, why would theatre offer us more?

I was comfortably ensconced in a first-class airplane seat, taking a ride home from Hollywood, where I'd just finished performing. It was 1985, and my very openly gay plays *Torch Song Trilogy* and *La Cage aux Folles* were reaching audiences on Broadway and on tour. I was minding my own business, perusing a magazine, when a booming voice pinned my skull to the headrest, "Where do you get off claiming to be the first person to play a homosexual onstage?" It was Academy Award-winning actor Eli Wallach pointing a bony finger and a sharp tongue toward my face. "Haven't you ever heard of the play *Staircase*? I was playing a homosexual when you were still in grade school."

"Yes," I replied. "But did you swallow?"

Well, that was enough to cement our friendship. Not only did I know about *Staircase,* I'd designed the set for a community-theatre production of it a few years prior. Plays like *Staircase, The Boys in the Band, The Children's Hour, The Haunted Host,* and *Falsettos* have been telling truths about our lives, leaving breadcrumbs to discover our private residences, and exposing our underbelly, for generations. Why theatre? Because it is the ultimate in artifice, it therefore demands the most stringent adherence to truth. Let's face it: Theatre is an act of faith. An audience of strangers gathers together in a darkened hall perfectly willing to suspend all disbelief. If an actor says, "Here in Tangiers . . ." the audience never questions that we have all been transported to Tangiers. Try that in a movie house. And any actor can tell you that stage demands an almost inhuman attention to truth. An actor has one shot at making the audience believe that every bit of his life is real. Screen actors get dozens of tries and only need to get each moment right once to provide the editor with material from which he will cobble to-gether a performance for that actor at a later time. And playwrights, having a small, well-educated, discriminating base audience to please, set out to express their human-ity instead of just lining their pocketbooks. Movies are about stories. Plays are ideas.

OK, here's the caveat: No work of art, not even the greatest, can represent an entire world. That would be an unfair expectation to put on any artist's shoulders. The *Mona Lisa* may be the greatest portrait ever painted, but it cannot express everything there is to say about being a woman, or even about being a Florentine businessman's wife in 1502. But digest the knowledge expressed in every portrait ever painted, and you might just start to get a fuller picture of what it means to be human. So too, in our liturgy of gay and lesbian drama, you will find portraits of people, but not portraits of *a* people. Still, look hard, and you will find us. We are there.

I have many more personal theories as to why theatre reeks of us, but my prejudices are extreme, and my arguments may sway you toward disagreement, in natural preser-vation of your own opinions, and, so, turn you away instead of toward this mother lode of information drama bears. I'll leave further conjecturing to others. The fact is, we do have honest gay and lesbian history in theatrical form, and it leaves a worthy record of our experience. Here, in this volume, you will find a bit. If you like what you find here, I beg you to seek more. It's out there and available to you. Read these plays. Produce them. Perform them. Let them enrich and nourish you. Let them inspire you. And, if you are so inclined, add to the canon with your own stories. We will all be better understood.

PREFACE

Out Plays marks the first time a concentrated anthology of the past forty critical years of gay and lesbian playes has ever been assembled. Prior to the late 1960s, plays containing gay and/or lesbian characters or subplots (rarely plots themselves) were understood only by audience members capable of decoding the secret language in which they were written. The exceptions were those in the 1920s like Mae West's *The Drag* and *Pleasure Man*—melodramas rife with every imaginable homosexual stereotype. West's plays guaranteed her between $70 and $100 a seat, as well a reputation as the P.T. Barnum of gay and lesbian theater history. But such exploitation was hardly a jumping off point for a serious study of gay and lesbian portrayals onstage, and that examination would have to wait another forty years.

Following the church and state sanctioned censorship of the 1930s and the postwar conservatism of the 1950s, the dialogue about what constitutes a *gay play* began in 1968, and in earnest, with the Off-Broadway debut of Mart Crowley's *The Boys in the Band*. At a time when homosexuality was still classified as a mental illness by the National Psychiatry Association (a designation it retained until 1973), *The Boys in the Band* first exposed the New York theatergoing public to realistic characters that were unmistakably—if not unapologetically—out of the closet.

Over the socially tumultuous decades that followed, the Stonewall Riots of the late 1960s, the equal rights activism of the 1970s, and the activism in response to the outbreak of AIDS in the 1980s, all propelled gays and lesbians into the national spotlight (with corresponding scrutiny) as never before. The parallel push for solidarity has not stopped at mere visibility (read *We're here. We're queer. Get used to it.*), and the latest battle is being played out in courtrooms across America as gays and lesbians argue that marriage is an equal right, not a *special* one. Correspondingly, the storytellers represented in this volume have served to educate students and theatergoers over the past forty years about gay and lesbian issues just as powerfully as their confederates on the front lines of protests (and in some cases while alongside them).

I chose to use a set of criteria for inclusion in this anthology that I hope will serve it well. All of the selected plays are notable for having explored gay or lesbian themes in a landmark way. All have had major New York American premieres, guaranteeing them an influential place in the pantheon of the genre. Finally, taken together and represented by gay and lesbian as well as straight writers, these plays are still powerful as testaments to the times in which they were written, and collectively serve as a tool to inform and instruct a contemporary audience.

I have included theatre reviews from the original New York productions in the introduction to the plays—some are surprising for the homophobia they so comfortably, if not consciously, demonstrate. But alongside the closed-minded and the condescending, there are also refreshingly nonjudgmental reviews by dispassionate and credible journalists who confined their criticism to the plays alone.

Out Plays traces the dramatic arc of the past forty years of a seminal and historical literary and social movement. These eight plays also include a range of theatrical genres: comedy, drama, romance, and farce. They remain vibrant and relevant not only as studies of gay and lesbian history, but also as testaments to art's irrepressible ability to persevere in the face of oppression, to collect and make audible the voices of unheard communities, and to deepen their understanding of them once they have developed a presence. These voices are due to be heard again, to be allowed to continue to assert an influence, and to assure the continued inspiration of a gay and lesbian identity in contemporary theater.

INTRODUCTION

It could be said that the curtain was finally fully and irreversibly raised on the presentation of gay life in the theatre when Mart Crowley's *The Boys in the Band* exploded onto the Off-Broadway stage in 1968. Crowley's own agent had discouraged him from attempting to mount the play, telling him the public would not be ready for it for at least five more years. Undeterred, Crowley sent it to the experimental Playwright's Unit, headed by producers Richard Barr and Charles Gnys, and a successful showcase production in January 1968 resulted in a quick move Off-Broadway.[1]

The Boys in the Band juggled stereotypes, but presented its all-gay cast of characters in vivid, explosive, emotional full-frontals (the real thing would have to wait), with all their human foibles exposed. But the stark contrast between the euphemistic and ambiguous themes in *Tea and Sympathy* in 1954 and Edward Albee's *The Zoo Story* in 1960 and the in your face portrayal of every aspect of gay life in *The Boys in the Band* could hardly have been more pronounced. The play was a harbinger of the tectonic shift about to occur in the gay community; it was a coming out party for gay and lesbian theater that ushered in the Stonewall era, and the iconic mark against which all future plays with gay themes would be compared. Critics were united in their assessment of the play's instant groundbreaking status:

> The play, which opened last night at Theater Four, is by far the frankest treatment of homosexuality I have ever seen on the stage. We are a long way from *Tea and Sympathy* here. The point is that this is not a play about a homosexual, but a play that takes the homosexual milieu, and the homosexual way of life, totally for granted and uses this as a valid basis for the human experience. Thus it is a homosexual play, not a play about homosexuality. (Clive Barnes, *The New York Times*)[2]

> All the once-forbidden words are there, and the action is highly explicit, but the play by Mart Crowley, now off-Broadway at Theater Four, doesn't strike me as a mere exercise in sensationalism . . . When I saw it last Thursday night at one of the previews, most of the spectators appeared to regard it as the merest of larks, and I think they were being unfair to it . . . Yet it is basically a sad and rather wistful play, it certainly has no truck with the theory that the third sex— "queens," "queers," and "fags" it prefers to call them—lead happy and carefree lives. (Richard Watts Jr., *New York Post*)[3]

> A couple of years ago, my colleague Stanley Kauffmann, in a perceptive but widely misunderstood essay, pleaded for a more honest homosexual drama, one where homosexual experience was not translated into false, pseudoheterosexual terms. This I think *The Boys in the Band,* with all its faults, achieves. It is quite an achievement. (Clive Barnes, *The New York Times*)[4]

Even many of those who were open to watching gays portrayed on stage did so with the expectation that the representation (and reality it was based on) must be a miserable one, and it is astounding from this purview to read critical jargon laced with derogatory epithets. This dichotomy underscores how new a phenomenon the examination of gays was in 1968, and how incapable or unwilling some of the most trained in dramatic criticism were to separate their analyses of gay and lesbian themes presented onstage from their own prejudices:

> Homosexuality—capitalized, boldfaced, and underlined—is the subject of *The Boys in the Band*. Mart Crowley's first play is a convincing study of limpwrist life, overbrimming with gasp-bait dialog and harshly candid situations. *The Boys in the Band* does, however, engender sympathy for a persecuted segment of the populace, and throws some dramatic light on the bleak world its members inhabit. (Richard Hummler, *Variety*)[5]

And to read some critics' summaries of *The Boys in the Band*, the play was as much a study of the cause and effect of the *disease* of homosexuality and those affected by it as *The Elephant Man* would later prove to be of elephantiasis:

> . . . *The Boys in the Band* was focused on the disease itself . . . In each character the neurosis takes a different form . . . With Peter White as the shocked "square" (who just may not be quite as sharp-cornered as he believes himself to be) and Robert La Tourneaux as a cowboy-costumed male version of a dumb female prostitute, these are the manifestations of neurosis which the playwright and his director, Robert Moore, combined with great skill into a harrowing stage portrait of the neurosis itself. (Otis Guernsey, *The Burns Mantle Theater Yearbook, The Best Plays of 1967–1968*)[6]

During a period when psychoanalysis—as well as gay character portrayals—were in their infancy in America, Crowley suddenly found himself a de facto spokesperson for gay men (and their neuroses) everywhere:

> Probably most homosexuals are unhappy . . . But that's because of stupid social taboos, not because of their state. I hope in a few years attitudes will change. There won't be the fear about blackmail, the hang-ups, the self-doubts. Michael needs his analyst, but he is aware of his problems. He's working them out gradually. (Frances Herridge, *New York Post*)[7]

Capable himself of psychoanalyzing his characters and clear on the amount of responsibility to be born by society in creating the bitterness exemplified by them, in writing what he considered an accurate representation of gay life, Crowley was himself capable of psychoanalyzing his characters and clear on the amount of responsibility to be borne by society in creating the bitterness exemplified by them, so he must must have been unprepared for his play to be reduced by so many to a study of a mental disorder. But he had unwitingly turned a searchlight onto the issues of gays, their treatment by the world at large, and the ensuing hell that his characters had lived in private as a result.

John R. Hopkins's *Find Your Way Home* echoed, or rather built on, much of Crowley's private and bitter banter, and although first appearing onstage in London at the Open Space Theater in 1970, did not make its debut in the United States until it opened at the Biltmore Theatre on Broadway in 1974. In a society that was just beginning to be exposed to openly homosexual relationships, comparisons to heterosexual ones were inevitable:

> The love triangle has become an eternal cliché. Does it make any difference when there is a homosexual relationship involved? I think it does . . . Here it is faced head-on. (Clive Barnes, *The New York Times*)[8]

Through an examination of the character of Alan Harrison—the archetypal closet case in *Find Your Way Home*, John R. Hopkins took as his subject matter what many in the mid-1970s were concerned with as the most frightening aspect of homosexuality— the threat that a *gay lifestyle* posed to heterosexual marriage. (It is a fear that has far from vanished in the intervening decades.) Hopkins goes beyond what in 1974 could easily have been main characters drawn (and were, a few decades earlier) as the stereotypes of an insidious gay interloper, a mentally ill husband, and a long suffering wife, offering instead a realistic portrait of the damage inflicted on all concerned by concealing the truth of one's true feelings—universal themes no matter the characters' sexuality. Still, Hopkins's theme was obscured by some reviewers' inability to separate the play from its subject matter:

> Sex could be given a serious setback by *Find Your Way Home,* which opened Jan. 2 at the Brooks Atkinson Theatre. Well, maybe that's a little exaggerated, but the John Hopkins drama does give the playgoer the urge to hurry home and have a nice, clean bath. A few people may be interested in and possibly even concerned with the characters in this study of a seemingly normal husband and father with an overpowering homosexual urge. It seems safe to assume, however, that the general public will be bored and perhaps more than slightly revolted. It's hardly a show to appeal to average audiences. (Hobe Morrison, *Variety*)[9]

It was perhaps inevitable that critics would view the watershed through the prism of their own heterosexuality. As much as critic Hobe Morrison considered himself an expert on *average audiences,* he similarly considers himself an expert on *normal husbands* and the *homosexual urge.* How his myopic evaluation of the presentation of homosexuality onstage looked in 1974 is also worth further review:

> *Find Your Way Home* seems weighted in a favor of the "honesty" of homosexuality, but the case is hardly convincing to a sexual square or "civilian." In fact, the negative flavor of the play even makes heterosexual love appear arid and unrewarding . . . (Hobe Morrison, *Variety*)[10]

Even those reviewers who did generally manage to review *Find Your Way Home* on its merits had their positive critiques couched in the prevailing sensibilities of the time. Critics who had cut their teeth on a new openness in the theatre manifesting itself through onstage nudity and sexual situations on Broadway recently like those in *Hair* and *Oh, Calcutta!* could not seem to manage the same tolerance when it came to gay relationships, even when they were of a more serious nature than their straight or bisexual counterparts. Clive Barnes of *The New York Times*, who generally pens a favorable review of *Find Your Way Home*, nevertheless offers the following caveats regarding its content:

It is the frankest discussion of homosexuality I have ever encountered in the theater, and the details it provides of homosexual acts may well prove repulsive to many Broadway theatergoers. And the language takes obscenity to new theatrical heights, or depths, whichever way you are counting. In some ways I think that a lot of this sexual detail is unnecessary, and possibly even prurient . . . (Clive Barnes, *The New York Times*)[11]

There was opposition to the subject matter in *Find Your Way Home* from homosexual as well as heterosexual corners—gay activists protesting that the portrayal of Julian Weston, Alan Harrison's gay lover, was less than sympathetic. But it took a neo-futuristic pioneer in psychology that had removed himself from the mainstream psychoanalytic community to accurately evaluate the groundbreaking nature of the play in a review for his own publication:

The play *Find Your Way Home* by John Hopkins, playing at the Biltmore Theater on Broadway, is a brilliant psychological statement of the problems of two homosexual lovers struggling to throw off the conventional social roles which society has assigned to them . . . The play is hard for some people to take. It makes reference to sexual acts in explicit and unvarnished language, and the problems of the characters are laid bare with an earthy and penetrating vision . . . People who oppose a work of art because it does not present a prettified view of gay life are book burners at heart . . . The critics are floundering even worse than the gay public relations people in their attempt to evaluate this play. The truth is that their critical capacities are overwhelmed by this exposure to a world that is alien to any view of life which they have permitted themselves to have. (Paul Rosenfels, *The Ninth Street Center Journal*)[12]

The fire that had been ignited six years earlier with *The Boys in the Band* would spread in many directions, and the seeds permanently planted onstage from the regrowth would become the standards by which gays and lesbians onstage and in society would be gauged for decades. New York audiences, in dozens of New York productions over the past seven years, had seen their share of gay trysts, tarts, and triangles. Now they were about to get inside what became the one of the most recognizable (and notorious) symbols of gay liberation in the1970s—the bathhouse.

Terrence McNally was coming off of his raucous 1973 hit *Bad Habits* when *The Ritz* opened on Broadway at the Longacre Theatre in January 1975. Over the next three decades, McNally would become one of the most prolific and celebrated playwrights writing about gay and lesbian issues of the late twentieth century, and his name would eventually become synonymous with the term *gay play*. He chose a farce as his first full-fledged foray into the new genre, an obvious—if not subtle—way to expose audiences to one of the most notorious facets of 1970s gay life.

Among other uses, the gay bathhouse as it existed in the mid-1970s was, if not a completely acceptable venue for a seasoned performer, at least a somewhat acceptable gig for an aspiring one. (After all, a real-life Bette Midler had recently been playing at clubs like the Continental Baths.) It was also a world that was as foreign to the average theatergoer as it was to the lead character in *The Ritz*, Gaetano Proclo, who accidentally stumbles into the establishment to hide out from a vindictive brother-in-law (in presumably the last place he would ever be found).

Before issuing what amounted to a mostly positive review of *The Ritz* for *Time* magazine, T. E. Kalem offered his evaluation of gay-themed plays over the preceding few years, and how *The Ritz* figured into it:

> In the past few seasons, "the love that dare not speak its name" has become one of the compulsive chatterboxes of the New York stage. Homosexuality surfaced as an acceptable theme with Mart Crowley's *The Boys in the Band*. This was followed by a number of dramas that waxed soulful on the ecstasy-torment of being gay or the purgative honesty (*Find Your Way Home*) of admitting gayness and acting upon it. Most of these plays were visual testimonials to bodybuilding exercises and auditory proof of acute self-pity but, for all their vibrations, no great shakes as drama. Now the cycle has gone far enough for Terrence McNally to reduce it to farce, a genre that depends on the humanly uninvolving mechanics of frivolity. (T. E. Kalem, *Time*)[13]

The Ritz did nothing to dispel the mystery of homosexuality to society at large. Clearly struggling to reconcile the outlandish representations of gay private life with the reality of their own, many theatergoers and reviewers were left questioning, if not the play itself, then the taste left in their mouth from the play and the real-life situations on which it was presumably based:

> [*The Ritz*] is a wildly wacky, uproariously funny comedy by Terrence McNally on a subject some people may find distasteful . . . The place swarms with virtually nude gays cavorting up and downstairs, in and out of doorways, scrambling under beds and propositioning each other in booby-hatch situations. Although it's all transparently absurd, it's packed with laugh lines and lunatic business, so the question of credibility is inconsequential—as to resemblance to actual life, it may be only slightly exaggerated. (Hobe Morrison, *Variety*)[14]

And Marilyn Stasio, writing for *Cue*, exhibits the kind of struggle to chart the various degrees of nontraditional sex roles that were emerging in society and exemplified onstage in *The Ritz*, playing as it was against a backdrop of the sexual revolution and the increasing complexity inherent in contextualizing onstage representations:

> Terrence McNally's new comedy is set in a gay bathhouse and features a garbage entrepreneur from Cleveland (straight, male), a Puerto Rican singer who burns to be a star (straight, female), a two-bit Mafioso (straight—but suspicious), a chubby-chaser (odd), and assorted denizens of the steam room (homosexual, but not gay). (Marilyn Stasio, *Cue*)[15]

As a farce, *The Ritz* marked the end of a rapid ten-year progression of gay subject matter through all forms of dramatic genres, confirming for some the stereotypical and mostly alien antics of gays in their private lives, and with AIDS about to put gay private life under a microscope, the play was soon to be relegated for a time to the most vilified quarters of the gay canon (although a revival opened on Broadway in October 2007, signaling a possible end to its exile).

With plays such as Albert Innaurato's *Gemini* in 1977 and Lanford Wilson's *Fifth of July* in 1978, however, the kind of gay characters who made appearances in plays during the early twentieth century as subordinates in the form of comic relief or peculiar oddities were now being portrayed as seriously struggling to come to terms with their sexual identities, confronting the difficulty that knowledge held for those wishing to fit into mainstream society. And after nearly a decade of being out (if not always proud), gay dramatists turned their attention from material based largely on the fringe of society—from the provocative representation of male prison life in John Herbert's *Fortune and Men's Eyes* in 1967 and the bathhouses in plays like *The Ritz*—to issues of understanding and acceptance both public and private. A paradigm shift was occurring in the evolution of gay and lesbian theatre, from the question raised by critics in the late 1960s of whether or not the stage was a suitable venue for the treatment of gay and lesbian issues at all, to a deepening examination and evaluation of the ramifications of what was beginning to take shape as a major movement in the theatre, exploring the human condition in ways that had never been done before.

Centering around main character Francis's internal struggle to understand the alienation he feels from his family and the world around him, Albert Innaurato's *Gemini* debuted in 1977 and ran for over four years at Broadway's Little Theatre. The deepening level of introspection was evident in the character of Francis, who even though questioning his sexuality, struggles to do so within the context of family, rather than in spite of it. Playwrights were no longer comfortable drawing marginalized characters who were closeted and angst-ridden on one hand and patently absurd on the other. A deepening self-examination was taking place in the theatre, and gay and lesbian writers were clamoring for acceptance and understanding from the world around them:

> The play pivots on the figure of Francis, broodingly but appealingly played by Robert Picardo, a Yale scholarship student who, though he has slept with a few girls and never with a man, is, until the very end, in doubt about his sexuality. He has been in love with, apparently made love to, during the last school year, a very pretty young heiress named Judith Hastings, who, with her brother Randy, turn up unannounced . . . Judith loves Francis, but suspects he is "queer." This central situation, though necessarily uncertain and uneasy, is set forth by Innaurato with the utmost decency and compassion. It is relieved by the humor and backyard eruptions of anger, joy, suicide threats, and such among, for the most part, the oldsters. The best written scene in the play joins these to sides of it, a discussion between the anxious Judith and father Fran's steady woman, Lucy, a widow who lives nearby. (Douglas Watt, *New York Daily News*)[16]

In comparing Innaurato's *Gemini* to his *The Transfiguration of Benno Blimpie*, which had also recently had an Off-Broadway opening, Mel Gussow, writing for *The New York Times*, points at the rising quandary faced by gays and lesbians coming of age in a world where traditions do not jibe with their own:

> The two plays share a sensibility, subject matter, and theme. In each we see obsessive characters formed and entrapped by family, background, and environment. (Mel Gussow, *The New York Times*)[17]

Still another reviewer illustrates the deepening self-understanding he was witnessing beginning to occur onstage in *Gemini*:

> During the play's process he learns that he is worthy of love, that he can be a

homosexual and a man too (one presumes the twins of the title). (Martin Gottfried, *New York Post*)[18]

Lanford Wilson was another in the generation of playwrights like Terrence Mc-Nally and Albert Innaurato who had seen firsthand the evolution of the gay rights movement and how it manifested onstage from the early improvisational days of the Café Cino in downtown Manhattan's West Village (considered the birth of the Off-Off-Broadway theatre movement), and culminating in the 1970s in regular Broadway and Off-Broadway productions relevant to a wider audience. Like Innaurato, Wilson was writing with a new naturalism that pervaded the theater in the late 1970s, with comparisons to Chekov in the accessibly conversational dialogue and easily relatable circumstances in which his characters found themselves. Opening at the Circle Repertory Company in New York City in 1978 and transferring to Broadway in 1980, Wilson's *Fifth of July* was groundbreaking precisely because gay lead character Kenneth's sexuality was *not* an issue. Wilson himself explains his reasons for this very calculated convention:

I had always intended to write a play where the two characters were lovers and that had absolutely nothing to do with the plot of the play. I have a feeling we're splintering like crazy. Audiences are wildly polarized just now. And want assurances and pats on the back and they want to be told that what they've invested their time with, like the sanctity of the home—they just don't want to be told that the sanctity of the home is a crock of shit. And in giving them a homosexual relationship that is working, we are saying that, in effect. I think the play is a threat to standardized living. The fact that no one wants to hear it is probably enough reason to say it. (*New York Theatre Review*)[19]

Actor William Hurt exemplifies how new the phenomenon was, feeling it necessary to qualify his character Ken's sexuality in an interview with writer William Carlton:

"Everybody has a glaring social problem but they don't dwell on them, they put their mangled lives behind them. It's not pat, it's full of subtleties," he says. "And the fact that my character is gay is not really important. (Hurt is not gay). "He's a human being." (William Carlton, *New York Daily News*)[20]

Gay writers like Wilson were beginning to demand and command not just a presence onstage and in society, but an equal one. And whatever Wilson's reasons for the sexuality component of his play taking a back seat to the plot, the lack of attention paid to it had the perhaps unanticipated effect of subtle but sure integration—a model for other playwrights and a cue for audiences that any fears of what the emergence of gays onstage or in society would mean might not be as real as they had imagined. And most critics' reviews, although making mention of characters' homosexuality in the *Fifth of July*, are notable for their lack of characterization of the gay portrayals:

As for Ken, he is both an English teacher who gets about on wooden legs (he enlisted for duty in Vietnam seemingly out of pique when Gwen and John ran off to Europe for fun without letting him know) and a homosexual whose lover of the same age, Jed, is mostly a background figure. (Douglas Watt, *New York Daily News*)[21]

It is remarkable that in 1980 and even with scores of gay plays characters appearing on the New York stage during the 1970s, that no overtly lesbian character had been seen onstage in a major New York theater production since Frank Marcus's *The Killing of Sister George* in 1966. Even more stunning, it had been since 1945 that an obviously lesbian character had appeared on the New York stage in a major production of a play written by a woman (Dorothy Baker's *Trio*—a stage adaptation of her novel of the same name).

Actress and playwright Jane Chambers had worked in television and penned several novels by the time her *Last Summer at Bluefish Cove* made its world premiere Off-Off Broadway in 1980 at the Gay Arts Center in New York, transferring five months later to the Actors Playhouse for an Off-Broadway run. The momentous occasion—however controversial—was not lost on reviewers of the time:

Chambers' piece, which had a brief Off-Off-Broadway run five months ago, is perhaps the first contemporary lesbian play to attempt mainstream theatre run. (Judy Thrall, *Back Stage*)[22]

What makes the plot far from standard, however, is the fact that the three couples are all women . . . While gay male relationships have been acknowledged by New York theater for a number of years, lesbianism has always been virtually taboo— certainly lesbianism as open, unashamed, and life-affirming as it is here. (Baker/Davidson, *New York Daily News*)[23]

Marilyn Stasio's comments below, however, offer a glimpse into the truth of the dearth of drama with lesbian subject matter and the craving for representations onstage of lesbian life that had been absent for so long:

NOTHING I'M going to say now will stop any Lesbian who saw *Last Summer at Bluefish Cove* six times from seeing it a seventh time. (Marilyn Stasio, *New York Post*)[24]

Perhaps the lack of exposure during the 1970s to lesbian characters onstage in comparison to the of surfeit of gay ones distracted reviewers as well as audience members from capably understanding the importance of the groundbreaking relationships they were witnessing onstage in *Last Summer at Bluefish Cove*. Frank Rich's review is indicative of the myopic attitude that still pervaded the time in which it was produced, notable for his misunderstanding that the women's movement of the 1970s—so responsible for increasing equality and opportunities for women—did not necessarily result in a corresponding increase in female same-sex partners (or the desire for them). His analysis reads as if lesbianism can be taken up or dropped whenever the urge strikes, as one would a hobby:

. . . Perhaps [Nyla Lyon, the director] and Miss Chambers sincerely thought they were creating a modern play about sexual choice . . . In "Bluefish Cove," homosexuality is not so much a passion as a red herring. (Frank Rich, *The New York Times*)[25]

If *The Boys in the Band* was the first *gay play*, then Harvey Fierstein's *Torch Song Trilogy* was the first gay play to bring home to audiences the challenges that gays and lesbians faced in gaining respect, acceptance, and understanding at home. With his widely acclaimed script and an indomitable tour de force performance, Harvey Fierstein made the most convincing case yet that gays had the same hopes and fears as everyone else. And for a vast community experiencing the same alienation from family as was Fierstein's character, Arnold Beckoff, his plaintive appeal to his mother for acceptance was resoundingly familiar.

> Ma, look: I'm gay. I don't know why. I don't think anyone does. But that's what I am. For as far back as I can remember. Back before I knew it was different or wrong . . . I know you'd rather I was straight, but I am not! (Harvey Fierstein, *Torch Song Trilogy*)[26]

By choosing a drag queen as the central character of his play, Fierstein's portrait could have been one easily painted with the same brush that colored such clichéd representations that had dominated gay characters for most of the century. But his deconstruction of Arnold Beckoff was an unprecedented and in-depth analysis of a man representing an archetype that had historically been relegated to the role of a tragic clown, revealing underneath that he, too, had the same triumphs and tragedies in his life as everyone else.

Fierstein's opus instantly distinguished itself from its obscured predecessors, and the reviewers of the time overwhelmingly agreed on the tectonic shift occurring in the portrayal of gay and lesbian characters in the theatre:

> Indeed, it is only in recent years that playwrights and authors have been able to deal openly with homosexual themes; in the past, such subjects were couched in metaphors and allusions, and characters who deviated from accepted norms of sexual propriety usually underwent conversion, died, or were condemned to lasting unhappiness. The homosexual was popularly portrayed as an effeminate clown, a corruptor of youth, or an out-and-out villain. Given this history, "Torch Song" clearly represents a radical achievement . . . (Michiko Kakutani, *The New York Times*)[27]

> Who would have ever thought that a play about a gay man and his relationships could appeal to a diverse audience? And, it does, first, because the feelings and emotions displayed—love, loneliness, jealously, insecurity—are universal ones. (Sherry Eaker, *Back Stage*)[28]

Not lost in the phenomenon that became *Torch Song Trilogy*, however, was the emerging nuance of gay and lesbian characters onstage of a sense of entitlement to the same middle class values as their heterosexual counterparts:

> Fierstein's hero Arnold is on a quest for two things. The first is love—true love. The second is acceptance from the world of his own homosexual preference. In fact, he doesn't really want acceptance, he wants respect, and the simple civilized right to structure his life along much the same patterns as his parents. (Clive Barnes, *New York Post*)[29]

But the scrutiny and suspiciousness of some reviewers still plaguing gay and lesbian writers was palatable:

Another standout of the off-Broadway year was Harvey Fierstein's *Torch Song Trilogy*, in which homosexuality is flaunted in the form of transvestism and then profoundly and movingly empathized in a network of family relationships . . . The theme was carried forward with a good deal of gay sexual gallows humor, but physical details of the experience were few, and except for one incident, restrained. (Otis Guernsey, *The Burns Mantle Theater Yearbook, The Best Plays of 1981–1982*)[30]

A contemporary read of Walter Kerr's review of *Torch Song Trilogy* in which he meticulously dissects Fierstein's dialogue reveals a more specific lack of understanding of gays and lesbians in society, and a general misunderstanding of the mask that gay and lesbians had donned in many different cultures for centuries:

But that self-mockery Mr. Fierstein delights in begins to pose problems as the performance now stands. It tends to become a permanent shield, concealing the man beneath it. Sometimes it is simply playful: two men on a telephone cooking up names for female singers, Kitty Litter, Bertha Vanation. Sometimes it is waspishly knowing: "I'm aging about as well as a Beach Party movie." Sometimes it makes "in" use of its homosexual background: "What's the matter—you catch your tongue on the closet door?" And sometimes it collapses on its own effort: speaking boastfully of all the "hims" he knows well, Mr. Fierstein includes "The Battle Him of the Republic." The quality of the jokes varies, but that's not the point. The point is that there's no knowing the joker. His defenses are, and remain, impenetrable. (Walter Kerr, *The New York Times*)[31]

Far from impenetrable, when the drag queen character of Arnold Beckoff occasionally chooses to remove his mask and reveal his true feelings, the departure from his usual modus operandi is all the more penetrating. Such routine misconceptions were discouragingly common to a gay and lesbian community that held an understandable expectation that the liberation movements of the 1970s would have brought an increased equity to such a historically persecuted minority. But Fierstein himself was under no illusions as to the tenor of the times:

A year of "Torch Song" on Broadway, has not, the playwright says, made it easier for the Arnolds of the world. "There's obviously no new acceptance of gay people. We just had the New Your City Gay Rights Bill defeated again. We can't get federal money for this epidemic of AIDS. The only newspaper articles I ever see, unless I'm blind, are the ones about a child being kidnapped by a band of gypsy homos. So obviously nothing has changed. True, he says, he is the first admitted homosexual to play the lead in a hit Broadway show, the author of the "first real gay play." But, he says, this is no major breakthrough: His audience, most of them liberal to begin with, often separates the play from its subject. (Jonathan Mandell, *Sunday News Magazine*)[32]

The prescient Harvey Fierstein, however, could only hint at what the specter of AIDS and the slow reaction to it by a newly conservative political environment would mean for the struggle for survival of gays and lesbians in America. First coming to public consciousness in 1982, the acronym AIDS was first assigned the disease in 1982—half way through the Broadway run of *Torch Song Trilogy*. The disease would bring gay and lesbian issues home in a way that could never have been expected, and the slow march forward of gays and lesbians during the fifteen years since the advent of *The Boys in the Band* suffered a giant step backward. The energy and attention that had been focused on gaining acceptance and understanding from the public suddenly became focused instead on fighting an insidious disease and trying to bring public attention to the plague that was about to ravish a demographic.

Robert Chelsey's *Nightsweat* ushered in the era of the AIDS play in 1984, and was quickly followed to the stage by Larry Kramer's *The Normal Heart* and William Hoffman's *As Is* a year later. Arriving on the stage as it did in 1991, Paula Vogel's *The Baltimore Waltz* was considered a second generation AIDS play, one that began to tell the story in an unconventional way. A metaphorical mystery tour of one woman's odyssey to understand her real life brother's death from AIDS, Vogel substitutes her real-life pain for his by crafting a play in which the main character suffers from the allegorical ATD (Acquired Toilet Disease). Her innovative approach was acknowledged:

> This is not only a rare AIDS play written by a woman, but also a rare AIDS play that rides completely off the rails of documentary reality, trying to rise above and even remake the world in which the disease exists. (Frank Rich, *The New York Times*)[33]

Vogel's effort accomplished the kind of cathartic exorcism from the demons that the gay and lesbian community and their families had been hopelessly suffering from for nearly ten years:

> The extraordinariness of Vogel's dramatic gesture comes from her personalizing the very essence of theater, which, as Richard Gilman once wrote, is "not pretending to be someone else, but imagining someone else as yourself." Taking her brother's fate on herself, she creates an event which at once healing in its effect and wildly resonant in its metaphors . . . Nothing more spiritually nurturing can take place on the contemporary stage. (Michael Feingold, *Village Voice*)[34]

Still, *The Baltimore Waltz* could not placate some reviewers inclined to dislike the subject matter no matter what the author's chosen vehicle:

> I daresay AIDS plays nowadays command Pavlovian adulation . . . (John Simon, *New York*)[35]

But the epidemic brought with it a strong and powerful reaction from the artistic community it was slowly decimating, and Vogel herself described the genesis for turning her real-life drama into one for the stage:

> Someone asked me recently why I wrote this play. I put my hands in front of that person's face and I said, "These were the hands that cleaned up my brother's body fluids and put his ashes in the ground. After that, these hands went to the computer." If that's not being able to testify from personal experience, I don't know what is. (Gerald Rabkin, *Theater Week*)[36]

From Mart Crowley's *The Boys in the Band* to Paula Vogel's *The Baltimore Waltz*, the years represented within these pages trace the arc of a dramatic movement born of societal alienation and writers' reaction to it. They also affected the times in which they were written as much as they were affected by them, with each successive generation influencing and inspiring the next. Let there be no mistake: There are still hurdles to be overcome and breakthroughs to be made. And with every new gay and lesbian play that hits the stage, our history is being written; and with it, a lot of great theater.

—Ben Hodges
New York, NY

NOTES

1. Interview with Mart Crowley, Frances Herridge, "'The Boys in the Band' Alters Author's Life," *New York Post*, April 22, 1968.
2. Clive Barnes, "Theater: 'Boys in the Band' Opens Off Broadway," *The New York Times*, April 15, 1968.
3. Richard Watts Jr. "A Birthday Celebration among the Homosexuals," *New York Post*, April 15, 1968.
4. Clive Barnes, "Theater: 'Boys in the Band' Opens Off-Broadway," *The New York Times*, April 15, 1968.
5. Richard Hummler, "'The Boys in the Band,'" *Variety*, April 17, 1968.
6. Otis Guernsey, *The Burns Mantle Theater Yearbook, The Best Plays of 1967–1968* (New York: Dodd, Mead, & Company, 1968), 21.
7. Interview with Mart Crowley, Frances Herridge, "'The Boys in the Band' Alters Authors' Life," *New York Post*, April 22, 1968.
8. Clive Barnes, "Theater: Homosexuality: Explicit 'Find Your Way Home' Is at Atkinson," *The New York Times*, January 3, 1974.
9. Hobe Morrison, "Show on Broadway," *Variety*, January 16, 1974.
10. Ibid.
11. Clive Barnes, "Theater: Homosexuality: Explicit 'Find Your Way Home' Is at Atkinson," *The New York Times*, January 3, 1974.
12. Paul Rosenfels, '"Find Your Way Home," by John Hopkins, reviewed by Paul Rosenfels,' *The Ninth Street Center Journal*, no. 2 (1974), http://64.233.169.104/search?q=cache:aKckaC1offQJ:www.ninthstreetcenter.org/J2Rosen.htm+%22Play+Find+Your+Way+Home%22&hl=en&ct=clnk&cd=1&gl=us, July 21, 2007.
13. T. E. Kalem, "Imps of the Perverse," *Time*, February 3, 1975.
14. Hobe Morrison, "Show on Broadway: 'The Ritz,'" *Variety*, January 22, 1975.
15. Marilyn Stasio, "Theatre: Farce in Baths," *Cue*, January 27, 1975.
16. Douglas Watt, *New York Daily News*, February 9, 1975.
17. Mel Gussow, "Theater: 'Gemini' Is Exceptional," *The New York Times*, March 14, 1977.
18. Martin Gottfried, "Innaurato's 'Gemini': Felt But Flawed," *New York Post*, March 14, 1977.
19. "Gay Theatre," *New York Theatre Review*.
20. William Carlton, "This Was No Quick Study," *New York Daily News*.
21. Douglas Watt, "'Fifth of July'—Plenty of Fireworks," *New York Daily News*, April 28, 1978.

22. Judy Thrall, "Capsule Reviews: 'Last Summer at Bluefish Cove,'" *Back Stage*, January 30, 1981.
23. Rob Baker and Bonnie Davidson, "'Last Summer,'" *New York Daily News*, December 22, 1980.
24. Marilyn Stasio, "Botched 'Bluefish' at Actors Playhouse," *New York Post*, December 26, 1980.
25. Frank Rich, "Theater: 'Bluefish Cove' Explores Summer Love," *The New York Times*, December 27, 1980.
26. Harvey Fierstein, *Torch Song Trilogy: Widows and Children First!* sc. 2.
27. Michiko Kakutani, "Fierstein and 'Torch Song': A Daring Climb from Obscurity," *The New York Times*, July 14, 1982.
28. Sherry Eaker, "'Torch Song Trilogy,'" *Back Stage*.
29. Clive Barnes, "'Song' of Love and Laughter," *New York Post*, July 15, 1982.
30. Otis Guernsey, *The Burns Mantle Theater Yearbook, The Best Plays of 1981–1982* (New York: Dodd, Mead, & Company, 1983), 21.
31. Walter Kerr, "'Torch Song Trilogy'—Self-Mockery as a Shield," *The New York Times*, June 27, 1982.
32. Interview with Harvey Fierstein, Jonathan Mandell, "Say Good Night, Arnold," *Sunday News Magazine*, May 1, 1983.
33. Frank Rich, "Play about AIDS Uses Fantasy to Try to Remake the World," *The New York Times*, February 12, 1992.
34. Michael Feingold, "Looking-Glass AIDS," *Village Voice*, February 18, 1992.
35. John Simon, "On Theater," *New York*, March 8, 1992.
36. Interview with Paula Vogel, Gerald Rabkin, "Playwright Paula Vogel," *Theater Week*, March 2–8, 1992.

OUT PLAYS

(left to right) Laurence Luckinbill (Hank), Keith Prentice (Larry),
Reuben Greene (Bernard), and Cliff Gorman (Emory) in the
Off-Broadway production *The Boys in the Band* (1968).
(Photograph reprinted with permission from the John Willis
Theatre World/Screen World Archive)

The Boys in the Band

BY MART CROWLEY

Introduction

Mart Crowley

The summer of 1967 changed my life forever. A decade earlier I'd graduated from the Speech and Drama Department of the Catholic University of America in Washington, D.C., and promptly tried to escape from my accent and my roots in Vicksburg, Mississippi, by moving to the Big Apple and "to go into the theatre." I had absolutely no idea which way I'd "go in"—designing scenery and costumes (for which I'd won several awards at C.U., one for *Billy Budd*, the collegiate debut of a very young, very blond Jon Voight), or acting (I went to some open calls, but I knew I was talent-free for treading the boards), or writing (I'd just co-written a revue skit for our annual original musical with my classmate, Jim Radomsky—later James Rado of *Hair* fame). One way or another, I was raring to go, and there's something to be said for clueless ambition.

It wasn't long before I actually got a job—not in the theatre, but on an independent film—as a production assistant on a three-week quickie, a remake of that old chestnut *The Last Mile*, starring Mickey Rooney. Other P.A. jobs in movies followed in rapid succession: Tennessee Williams's *The Fugitive Kind*, with Brando and Magnani, John O'Hara's *Butterfield 8*, with Elizabeth Taylor, and, finally, a step up, working for Elia Kazan's Newtown Productions as personal assistant to "Gadg" (Mr. Kazan, as I always called him to his face) on William Inge's *Splendor in the Grass*. One reason I got as close to Gadg as I did was because he taught me how to make a Greek salad for his lunch. I've forgotten how to do it now, but I sure was good at it then.

Simultaneously, I'd decided not to take the entrance exams for the scene design union. I knew I'd never be able to do the drafting requirements. I was about as good at math as I was at acting, and, besides, I didn't find the work truly fulfilling. So, I wrote a play. I found writing deeply fulfilling, although the play I'd written was hopeless. It was a closet drama, so to speak, in which a smart young southern woman (me), who's been living and working in New York, suddenly returns to her family, which is in some sort of crisis (mine always was), and falls for the bad boy from a good background, a horse trader on a plantation (actually, a certain graduate student at C.U., about whom I'd become dotty; he was from Rhode Island and had never seen a plantation; I'd later use him as the model for the character Larry in *Boys*). The play was called *Love in a One Horse Town*. Enough said. Anyway, I now knew what I wanted to do. But here I was, working in the movies, burning the well-known midnight oil on "spec" television scripts, and getting nothing but letters of rejection, if I got even those.

As *Splendor* was winding down, Gadg told me I'd better look for work because he was closing Newtown to go to Turkey to research his family for what was to become his film *America, America* three years later. Meanwhile, I'd become besotted with Natalie Wood, who was about to become a superstar and had already signed for the film version of *West Side Story*. Natalie liked me, too, and since she was to finish *Splendor* on a Friday night in Patchogue, Long Island, and start rehearsals for *West Side* the following

Monday morning at Goldwyn Studios in Hollywood, she had no time to pack up the sublet on Sutton Place South, which Bill Inge had arranged for her and her husband, the actor, Robert Wagner. Thus, she suggested I become *her* personal assistant, and that *I* see to the packing of the New York apartment and come to California just for the length of the *West Side* shoot, which turned out to be six months. (I stayed seven years.) Natalie well knew that I wanted to be a writer and that I had no professional representation, so she bargained with me by saying she'd introduce me to "some of the guys at William Morris." And, God bless her, she always kept her word, and I got my first agent.

By 1962 I'd written a screenplay for Natalie, and 20th Century Fox had bought it; the picture had a start date and I had an office on the lot and was getting memos from Darryl F. Zanuck. Natalie was to play a pair of identical twins who were so psychically close they thought they were the same person, until one fell for a guy named Jack. This freaked out the other sister, who realized she had incestuous leanings, and a yen for a lank-haired, poetry-reading dancer in a black leotard and lots of silver bracelets. Martin Manulis, the line producer, and I used to fall on the floor, aching with laughter at Zanuck's repeated inter-office commands to "take out the dykeisms." "Too many dykeisms." "*Still* too many dykeisms." How we roared over that word! Then the bottom fell out. Zanuck brought over a hot Parisian director for the picture, and it was instant hate with Natalie. In the last meeting that was to take place with the star, the director, the producer, the writer, and the costume designer (Edith Head), the director said to Natalie, "You were *good* in *West Side Story*, but in *my* film, you will be *great*." I looked at Edith, who'd been around a block or two, and I could tell, even through those coke-bottle glasses of hers, that it was over. Natalie confirmed my suspicion by suddenly looking at her watch and exclaiming, as if she were on camera, that she was late for another appointment. Perhaps it was for *Love with a Perfect Stranger*, her next film, at Paramount, not Fox. In any case, Natalie had another job, so did Edith, so did D.F.Z., and even the egomaniacal French director had another picture lined up, but no such luck for me. My brilliant career was over. So was my life, I thought. I was so devastated that I seriously considered killing myself. End of Round One.

Instead, I just drowned my sorrow in vodka to the point that Natalie paid for me to go to a psychiatrist. Meanwhile, I'd met Dominick Dunne, who was then the vice president of Four Star Television. (For the record, the four stars were David Niven, Charles Boyer, Ida Lupino, and Dick Powell, and, alas, I never clapped an eye on any one of them during my short tenure.) Nick offered me a six-month contract and the first order of the day was a project Bette Davis had agreed to when it was just an idea for a TV series. Now, she'd read the pilot script and was refusing to do it, and with good reason.

It was a Friday. Davis had said that if she did not get a rewrite she liked by Monday, she would definitely walk. Nick talked his boss, Tom McDermott, the president of the company, into giving me the task. McDermott had never heard of me, but had no other alternative, and so I stayed up for over forty-eight hours trying to make chicken salad out of chicken schiess.

To make a long story longer, I never left Four Star that weekend (the old Republic Studios). About six a.m. Monday morning, I staggered to the administration building and left the rewrite on Nick's desk, then somehow managed to drive to my apartment and collapse in bed. I never turned off the phone, but I never heard it ring. Repeatedly. Throughout the entire day. When I woke up, I called Dunne's office. Nick wanted to know where the hell I was. He said everyone had been calling for hours and hours. Davis wanted to meet me! He said he and McDermott had personally delivered the script to Davis at her Stone Canyon home where they were met by the stone-cold housekeeper who told them Miss Davis had said for them to wait in the foyer (on stiff straight-back chairs), while she read the rewrite behind the closed doors of her drawing room. Nick said he and Tom knew their bacon had been saved when they heard gales of laughter coming from an unmistakable voice behind the closed doors, which were then theatrically torn open by the diva, enunciating in her signature sing-song, "*Who . . . wrote . . . this? I want . . . to meett . . . himm!*"

Oh, no! I'd missed compliments, face to face, from the woman I'd watched (at the age of five) being stabbed to death at the end of *The Letter*. I was so inconsolable my mother lied to me all the way home, saying nothing really bad had happened to Bette, that it all was just play-acting. I was skeptical. I still am of certain methods of play-acting. But not in 1940, and certainly not from La Diva.

I was suicidal again. I was broke. I was washed up. William Morris said bye-bye. Nothing to do but sublet my apartment to a European who'd arrived to make a movie. I was about to stake out the sofa in a friend's place when the phone rang. It was my dear old pal, Diana Lynn (the droll brat sister in Preston Sturges's *The Miracle of Morgan's Creek*). She'd married Mortimer Hall, whose mother owned the *New York Post*, and they had four children, and a very posh lifestyle. Diana said she and Morty and their friends, Hope Lange and Alan J. Pakula, were taking their yacht through the Panama Canal to Nassau. They didn't want to have the children on the boat; the nanny would fly them down once the sailing party had arrived. Meanwhile, Diana told me the nanny was Swedish, the cook and butler were Chinese, and the gardeners and pool man were Hispanic, so "if somebody falls down the stairs and breaks a neck, there's no one to call a doctor in English." Could I house-sit/baby-sit for six weeks?

When I woke up in the guest bedroom of the faux-Georgian mansion on Tower Road, I stared at the Porthault toile upholstered walls and matching bed hangings and bed linens. I thought about Jack Lemmon living a couple of doors down the hill, and the David Selznick house at the top of Tower Grove. My God, was I ever in Hollywood! But would I ever make it in Hollywood? I knew the chances were about as bright as the sun, sinking in the Pacific like a lost cause.

There was a knock on my door and the butler brought me breakfast on a tray, and said the "cook" would like me to prepare the menus for the week. Diana had given me the key to the wine cellar (behind Morty's back), and told me to drink whatever I wanted, and to have as many people to dinner as I pleased. Thanks, I said. I thought it was a splendid opportunity for some rather grand paybacks. How civilized destitution can be.

But, oh, God, was I depressed. I couldn't get out of bed. The thought of no job. No agent. No prospects. And no shrink. So, what to do? I knew that I had to do *something* with this extraordinary free time during this extraordinary free ride. Six whole weeks. But then I realized the first week had almost gone past. Five weeks and a couple of days were left. The clock was ticking.

Still paralyzed under the Porthault duvet, I took out a yellow legal pad and started jotting down dialogue. I had a very vague idea for a play. I didn't really know what it was about. I didn't know who the characters were. All I knew was that all of the characters were men and that all of them were gay. I'd just read a Sunday *New York Times* piece, in the drama section, by the esteemed Stanley Kauffmann. It decried the coded plays of three of the most prominent playwrights of the day. They were all homosexual, so why couldn't they write plays with homosexual characters, instead of disguising them as women? I thought Mr. Kauffmann had a point. That smart, southern girl, working in the big city, was about to undergo sex-reassignment surgery.

After three or four days, having the yellow pages pile up, I decided to get up and go down to the library, unzip the Olivetti case and type up the talk. I recently discovered those very same pages, dated "8/8/67," which start at the top and go directly through the play to the end. There were no notes, and not much rewriting, just a lot of crossed-out material. Masses of it. It was a long play. Almost none of the characters had their final names: Arthur turned into Michael; Patrick turned into Donald; Teddy turned into Emory; and Max turned into Harold. "The Sailor" turned into "The Cowboy." There were a lot of titles. A few written down: *Somebody's Children* was one. Others were never written down. I remember thinking the whole thing would take place in a gay bar and I'd call it (what else?) *The Gay Bar.* But I couldn't have a mob scene on stage, so I moved it to a smart, 50s, East Side apartment. I was taken to a birthday party by my best friend, Howard Jeffrey, a master put-down artist and cynic, a talented dancer/choreographer who'd been Jerome Robbins's assistant on both the stage show and the film version of *West Side Story.*

Howard's friend, the birthday boy, was a very swish, very camp, fucking laugh riot! He reminded me of a director I'd worked for in summer stock, and I thought the two of them might combine to make a funny character. In fact, I thought the birthday party would make a good "hook" on which to hang the whole thing instead of the gay bar. I thought I might call it (what else?) *The Birthday Party.* However, shortly after, I read that Harold Pinter had written a new play called *The Birthday Party.* Pinter had gotten there first. Pinter had stolen my title. Just as Williams and O'Neill had gotten there first and stolen my southern territory and my wretched family history. How could I ever be original? Was I never, ever going to write something that didn't fall through or fail?

I remember the exact moment the final title came to me. I was lying in bed (this time late at night), staring up at a ceiling as blank as a blank sheet of paper. It's been written that I got it from the dialogue in the Garland/Mason version of *A Star Is Born.* Maybe I did, but if so, I am unaware of it. It's possible. Many lines from movies and plays and novels have seeped into my subconscious. In the scene where Mason's character, Norman Maine, gives Garland's character, Vikki Lester, a pep talk before her screen test, he reassures her of her talent, reminding her of a glorious after-hours jam session when she had no audience to please, saying: "Of course, you're scared! We all are. . . . Look—forget about the camera—it's the Downbeat Club at three o' clock in the morning—and you're singing for yourself, and for the boys in the band . . ."

I didn't have many dinner parties at the Hall's Tower Road house. I just had Natalie over a few nights and another good friend, Douglas Murray, an obsessive reader, a compulsive drinker, and a fierce critic. Doug would drive up to L.A. from Laguna to see his psychiatrist, after a hard day of professionally cleaning beach houses. He said he didn't have to think doing this sort of work, scrubbing, cleansing, no matter what its Freudian implication. And he could do it when and where he pleased, which gave him more time to devour the Laguna and Los Angeles public libraries. (In the play Laguna to L.A. became East Hampton to Manhattan.)

Bette was to play-act an interior decorator. Her character's only demand was that she live with her clients for two weeks prior to doing her magic, so that she could reflect their true personalities. (Can you imagine living with Bette Davis for more than a cab ride?) I wrote the part of her assistant specifically for the comic actor, Paul Lynde. I knew he'd be someone to give as good as he got, and I didn't see how the combination of the two could be anything less than hilarious. But the network wouldn't go for any traditional stock sissy (think Franklin Pangborn or Billy De Wolfe), and cast Mary Wickes in the part. Funny, but not as funny as Lynde would have been. Davis had worked twice before with Wickes and liked her, possibly not for her talent, but because Davis did not find the dry character actress with the eagle beak and receding chin a threat in any way.

Unfortunately, mostly, for me, in 1964, The Diva's performance off-camera and her intractable star behavior convinced Quaker Oats to cancel their sponsorship, and thus, the pilot, before it ever finished filming. Her old Warner Brothers work rhythm and her demands (Ernest Haller, who'd shot her in *Jezebel*, and who'd won an Academy Award for *Gone with the Wind,* was the lighting cameraman for this simple, half-hour sitcom) were not compatible with the budget and pace of shooting a weekly comedy for the small screen. *The Better Davis Show* was history, and my option at Four Star was not renewed. The point of all this, that the anxious twin from the Fox screenplay and the lethal-tongued assistant/sidekick in the Four Star pilot must have meant something, was rattling around in my brain that early on. Anyway, it didn't play. End of Round Two. Thoughts of suicide again. And I'm not kidding.

Round Three. I was hired to write a cockamamie original for Paramount. I was handed a title, *Fade In*, by the producer of an "A" feature western in pre-production, *Blue*, and told to write a "B" budget screenplay about a script girl on a real Paramount western, *Blue*, who falls in love on location in Knabe, Utah, with a local animal wrangler (shades of *Love in a One Horse Town!*). Both films were to be shot simultaneously. What did I care how silly and impractical it was? I had a cubbyhole on the lot in the "Betty Schaefer Memorial Writers' Building," a hallowed edifice to me ever since it was inhabited by Miss Schaefer (Nancy Olson), who stayed up nights, knocking out a script with Joe Gillis (William Holden) in *Sunset Boulevard*. I sat in Schaefer's old cubicle and wrote another script as bad as their source material (Gillis's *Dark Windows*) for their *Untitled Love Story*. The young, first-time director of *Fade In* quit and was replaced by a guy who brought in his crony to rewrite my original story and screenplay and I was fired.

For me, it wasn't "third time lucky." It was three strikes and you're out on your ass.

Doug would arrive at the Tower Road house after his sessions, frazzled, embittered about his family, talking a blue streak about what he'd said to his analyst. I'd make him a martini and he'd have a shower and change and we'd have dinner in the formal dining room, by candlelight, served by the Chinese couple. Afterward, we'd go in the library where we'd have coffee and Doug would put away almost a whole bottle of brandy. I'd read the pages I'd written during the week and he'd criticize them. "Oh, no, I'd never say that! I'd say . . ." and some gem would fall out of his mouth. After he'd been thoroughly oiled, he would hit the road for Laguna, never staying over. Why did he never get a D.U.I.? Why did he never kill himself? Or innocent drivers, or passengers, or pedestrians, or the odd quadruped?

On some of the nights in between Doug's weekly visits, I'd go down the hill to a gay bar in West Hollywood called, of all things, The Four Star. I kept seeing a very handsome, very preppy black guy. He didn't give me the time of day. Somehow I heard that his name was Bernard. He never knew mine.

I remember Nick Dunne's wife, Lenny, taking me to a very elegant, expensive dinner on my thirty-second birthday on August 21, at the chicest restaurant in Beverly Hills, the Bistro. I was disappointed that I'd not been able to finish the play while I was, at most, thirty-one. I remember being very depressed on turning thirty because nothing had worked out and I was, I thought, getting old. Now I was thirty-two and I'd only managed to finish Act One. Or, rather, where I thought the break in Act One should come. Later, I'd change the break to a bit further on, when I'd written some more material. But I was determined to finish Act One while I was still thirty-one, and so the curtain came down somewhere after the "straight" character had arrived. I wrote from morning to mid-afternoon when the older children would get home from school. Matthew, the eldest, who was eight or nine years old, would come into the library around three and say hello. He'd ask what I was doing. I said, oh, just writing a play.

I went to a party one night that Nick and Lenny Dunne gave for the visiting Royal Ballet company. It was at Nick and Lenny's summer rental in Malibu and everyone was doing "The Madison"—the ballet dancers, the A-list guests, and Mart Crowley, the failed writer. Nick asked me to go for a walk on the beach. It was "magic hour," and we rolled up our pants, took off our shoes, and went for a stroll. We passed a house Jane Fonda had rented, and I would later go to another party there. However, I didn't pay much attention that night. Nick said he was worried about me. I said I was fine, I was working. Nick asked what I was doing. I said, oh, just writing a play. Unlike Matthew Hall, Dominick Dunne asked me what it was about and I told him as much as I knew. I think we might have stopped walking because I remember Nick saying something in a somber voice, like, "I think it's great therapy that you're writing this play, Mart. But, listen, if it shouldn't go any further, if no one wants to do it, if it doesn't get produced . . . don't let it throw you. Do you know what I mean?" Yes, I knew what he meant. He thought I was losing my mind. Later, he wasn't the only one.

By the time the Halls came home, I'd written almost the entire play from beginning to end, straight through, non-stop. That is, with the exception of the last little scene between Arthur and Patrick (soon to be Michael and Donald). The play just came out of me; the exact same continuity that exists today. I can't explain it. I just know that I was very, very angry and in one hell of a hurry. I had done it all but the tag in five weeks.

I had to move out of the Hall's home and go back to my apartment. I had a little money from what the Hungarian actor had paid for the sublet. Since I didn't have an agent, I asked Natalie if she'd speak to her fiancé, Richard Gregson, who was an English talent agent and a producer. He was a partner in a company called London International. Richard set up a meeting with a woman who worked in the New York office. It was strictly a courtesy thing.

What happened after I'd put the play under my arm and set out for New York is another story, equally as long. Suffice it to say that I finished the last bit and changed the characters' names on Fire Island, after the Labor Day weekend when everyone had gone home. Houses were being boarded up and the Botel was fairly deserted at night. There were no more tea dances in the late afternoons. I never touched a drop during the entire time I worked on the play. Nothing from the Hall's wine cellar. Nothing at the Four Star Bar as I tried, unsuccessfully, to engage Bernard. And nothing on Fire Island as that unmistakable thing in the weather happened and you knew something had changed. It was late September 1967. It wouldn't be until Easter Sunday the following year that *The Boys in the Band* would premier, but my life had already changed, too, as irrevocably as the season had done. I remember being dry-mouthed and numb backstage on opening night, trying to swallow as I asked Robert Moore, the director, "Do you think they'll think it's funny?" And he replied, "Listen, they've been laughing at fags since Aristophanes, they're not going to stop tonight."

Not too long after all the noise, the play was published in hardback by Farrar, Straus and Giroux, no less. I sent a copy to Mrs. Mortimer Hall. The inscription read, "For dear Diana . . . Under whose roof, thatched, was this plot hatched. Thanks for the use of the Hall.—With my love, Mart."

—New York, 2007

For
Howard Jeffrey
and
Douglas Murray

The Boys in the Band was first performed in January 1968 at the Playwrights Unit, Vandam Theatre, Charles Gnys, managing director.

The Boys in the Band was first produced on the New York stage by Richard Barr and Charles Woodward Jr. at Theatre Four on April 14, 1968. The play was designed by Peter Harvey and directed by Robert Moore.

The original cast was:

MICHAEL	Kenneth Nelson
DONALD	Frederick Combs
EMORY	Cliff Gorman
LARRY	Keith Prentice
HANK	Laurence Luckinbill
BERNARD	Reuben Greene
COWBOY	Robert La Tourneaux
HAROLD	Leonard Frey
ALAN	Peter White

The play is divided into two acts. The action is continuous and occurs one evening within the time necessary to perform the script.

Characters:

MICHAEL	Thirty, average face, smartly groomed
DONALD	Twenty-eight, medium-blond, wholesome American good looks
EMORY	Thirty-three, small, frail, very plain
LARRY	Twenty-nine, extremely handsome
HANK	Thirty-two, tall, solid, athletic, attractive
BERNARD	Twenty-eight, Negro, nice-looking
COWBOY	Twenty-two, light-blond, muscle-bound, too pretty
HAROLD	Thirty-two, dark, lean, strong limbs, unusual Semitic face
ALAN	Thirty, aristocratic, Anglo-Saxon features

ACT 1

A smartly appointed duplex apartment in the East Fifties, New York, consisting of a living room and, on a higher level, a bedroom. Bossa nova music blasts from a phonograph.

Michael, wearing a robe, enters from the kitchen, carrying some liquor bottles. He crosses to set them on a bar, looks to see if the room is in order, moves toward the stairs to the bedroom level, doing a few improvised dance steps en route. In the bedroom, he crosses before a mirror, studies his hair—sighs. He picks up comb and a hair dryer, goes to work.

The downstairs front door buzzer sounds. A beat. Michael stops, listens, turns off the dryer. More buzzing. Michael quickly goes to the living room, turns off the music, opens the door to reveal Donald, dressed in khakis and a Lacoste shirt, carrying an airline zipper bag.

MICHAEL: Donald! You're about a day and a half early!

DONALD:

> *(Enters)*

> The doctor canceled!

MICHAEL: Canceled! How'd you get inside?

DONALD: The street door was open.

MICHAEL: You wanna drink?

DONALD:

> *(Going to bedroom to deposit his bag)*

> Not until I've had my shower. I want something to work out today—I want to try to relax and enjoy *something*.

MICHAEL: You in a blue funk because of the doctor?

DONALD:

> *(Returning)*

> Christ, no. I was depressed long before I got *there*.

MICHAEL: Why'd the prick cancel?

DONALD: A virus or something. He looked awful.

MICHAEL:

> *(Holding up a shopping bag)*

> Well, this'll pick you up. I went shopping today and bought all kinds of goodies. Sandalwood soap . . .

DONALD:

> *(Removing his socks and shoes)*

> I feel better already.

MICHAEL: . . .

> *(Producing articles)*

> Your very own toothbrush because I'm sick to death of your using mine.

DONALD: How do you think *I* feel.

MICHAEL: You've had worse things in your mouth.

(Holds up a cylindrical can)

And, also for you . . . something called "Control." Notice nowhere is it called hair spray—just simply "Control." And the words "For Men" are written about thirty-seven times all over the goddamn can!

DONALD: It's called Butch Assurance.

MICHAEL: Well, it's *still* hair spray—no matter if they call it "*Balls*"!

(Donald laughs)

It's all going on your very own shelf, which is to be labeled: Donald's Saturday Night Douche Kit. By the way, are you spending the night?

DONALD: Nope. I'm driving back. I still get very itchy when I'm in this town too long. I'm not that well yet.

MICHAEL: That's what you say every weekend.

DONALD: Maybe after about ten more years of analysis I'll be able to stay one night.

MICHAEL: Maybe after about ten more years of analysis you'll be able to move back to town permanently.

DONALD: If I live that long.

MICHAEL: You will. If you don't kill yourself on the Long Island Expressway some early Sunday morning. I'll never know how you can tank up on martinis and make it back to the Hamptons in one piece.

DONALD: Believe me, it's easier than getting here. Ever had an anxiety attack at sixty miles an hour? Well, tonight I was beside myself to get to the doctor—and just as I finally make it, rush in, throw myself on the couch, and vomit out how depressed I am, he says, "Donald, I have to cancel tonight—I'm just too sick."

MICHAEL: Why didn't you tell him you're sicker than he is.

DONALD: He already knows *that.*

(Donald goes to the bedroom, drops his shoes and socks. Michael follows)

MICHAEL: Why didn't the prick call you and cancel. Suppose you'd driven all this way for nothing.

DONALD:

(Removing his shirt)

Why do you keep calling him a prick?

MICHAEL: Whoever heard of an analyst having a session with a patient for two hours on Saturday evening.

DONALD: He simply prefers to take Mondays off.

MICHAEL: Works late on Saturday and takes Monday off—what is he, a psychiatrist or a hairdresser?

DONALD: Actually, he's both. He shrinks my head and combs me out.

(Lies on the bed)

Besides, I had to come in town to a birthday party anyway. Right?

MICHAEL: You had to remind me. If there's one thing I'm not ready for, it's five screaming queens singing "Happy Birthday."

DONALD: Who's coming?

MICHAEL: They're really all Harold's friends. It's *his* birthday and I want everything to be just the way he'd want it. I don't want to have to listen to him kvetch about how nobody ever does anything for anybody but themselves.

DONALD: Himself.

MICHAEL: Himself. I think you know everybody anyway—they're the same old tired fairies you've seen around since the day one. Actually, there'll be seven, counting Harold and you and me.

DONALD: Are you calling me a screaming queen or a tired fairy?

MICHAEL: Oh, I beg your pardon—six tired screaming fairy queens and one anxious queer.

DONALD: You don't think Harold'll mind my being here, do you? Technically, I'm *your* friend, not his.

MICHAEL: If she doesn't like it, she can twirl on it. Listen, I'll be out of your way in just a second. I've only got one more thing to do.

DONALD: Surgery, so early in the evening?

MICHAEL: Cunt! That's French, with a cedilla.

(Gives him a crooked third finger, goes to mirror)

I've just got to comb my hair for the thirty-seventh time. Hair—that's singular. My hair, without exaggeration, is clearly falling on the floor. And *fast*, baby!

DONALD: You're totally paranoid. You've got plenty of hair.

MICHAEL: What you see before you is a masterpiece of deception. My hairline starts about here.

(Indicates his crown)

All this is just tortured forward.

DONALD: Well, I hope, for your sake, no strong wind comes up.

MICHAEL: If one does, I'll be in terrible trouble. I will then have a bald head and shoulder-length fringe.

(Runs his fingers through his hair, holds it away from his scalp, dips the top of his head so that Donald can see. Donald is silent)

Not good, huh?

DONALD: Not the best.

MICHAEL: It's called, "getting old." Ah, life is such a grand design—spring, summer, fall, winter, death. Who*ever* could have thought it up?

DONALD: No one *we* know, that's for sure.

MICHAEL:

(Turns to study himself in the mirror, sighs)

Well, one thing you can say for masturbation . . . you certainly don't have to look your best.

(Slips out of the robe, flings it at Donald. Donald laughs, takes the robe, exits to the bath. Michael takes a sweater out of a chest, pulls it on)

MICHAEL: What are you so depressed about? I mean, other than the usual *everything*.

(A beat)

DONALD:

(Reluctantly)

I really don't want to get into it.

MICHAEL: Well, if you're not going to tell me, how can we have a conversation *in depth*—a warm, rewarding, meaningful friendship?

DONALD: Up yours!

MICHAEL:

> (*Southern accent*)
>
> Why, Cap'n Butler, how you talk!
>
> (*Pause. Donald appears in the doorway holding a glass of water and a small bottle of pills. Michael looks up*)

DONALD: It's just that today I finally realized that I was *raised* to be a failure. I was *groomed* for it.

> (*A beat*)

MICHAEL: You know, there was a time when you could have said that to me and I wouldn't have known what the hell you were talking about.

DONALD:

> (*Takes some pills*)
>
> Naturally, it all goes back to Evelyn and Walt.

MICHAEL: Naturally. When doesn't it go back to Mom and Pop? Unfortunately, we all had an Evelyn and a Walt. The crumbs! Don't you love that word—crumb? Oh, I love it! It's a real Barbara Stanwyck word.

> (*A la Stanwyck's frozen-lipped Brooklyn accent*)
>
> "Cau'll me a keab, you kr-rumm."

DONALD: Well, I see all vestiges of sanity for this evening are now officially shot to hell.

MICHAEL: Oh, Donald, you're so serious tonight! You're fun-starved, baby, and I'm eating for two!

> (*Sings*)
>
> "Forget your troubles, c'mon, get happy! You better chase all your blues away. Shout Hallelujah! C'mon get happy . . ."
>
> (*Sees Donald isn't buying it*)
>
> —what's more boring than a queen doing a Judy Garland imitation?

DONALD: A queen doing a Bette Davis imitation.

MICHAEL: Meanwhile—back at the Evelyn and Walt Syndrome.

DONALD: America's Square Peg and America's Round Hole.

MICHAEL: Christ, how sick analysts must get of hearing how mommy and daddy made their darlin' into a fairy.

DONALD: It's beyond just that now. Today I finally began to see how some of the other pieces of the puzzle relate to them.—Like why I never finished anything I started in my life . . . my neurotic compulsion to not succeed. I've realized it was always when I failed that Evelyn loved me the most—because it displeased Walt, who wanted perfection. And when I fell short of the mark she was only too happy to make up for it with her love. So I began to identify failing with winning my mother's love. And I began to fail on purpose to get it. I didn't finish Cornell—I couldn't keep a job in this town. I simply retreated to a room over a garage and scrubbing floors in order to keep alive. Failure is the only thing with which I feel at home. Because it is what I was taught at home.

MICHAEL: Killer whales is what they are. Killer whales. How many whales could a killer whale kill . . .

DONALD: A lot, especially if they get them when they were babies.

> (Pause. Michael suddenly tears off his sweater, throws it in the air, letting it land where it may, whips out another, pulls it on as he starts down the stairs for the living room. Donald follows)

Hey! Where're you going?

MICHAEL: To make drinks! I think we need about thirty-seven!

DONALD: Where'd you get *that* sweater?

MICHAEL: This clever little shop on the right bank called Hermès.

DONALD: I work my ass off for forty-five lousy dollars a week *scrubbing* floors and you waltz around throwing cashmere sweaters on them.

MICHAEL: The one on the floor in the bedroom is vicuña.

DONALD: I *beg* your pardon.

MICHAEL: You could get a job doing something else. Nobody holds a gun to your head to be a charwoman. That is, how you say, your neurosis.

DONALD: Gee, and I thought it's why I was born.

MICHAEL: Besides, just because I *wear* expensive clothes doesn't necessarily mean they're paid for.

DONALD: That is, how you say, *your* neurosis.

MICHAEL: I'm a spoiled brat, so what do I know about being mature. The only thing mature means to me is *Victor* Mature, who was in all those pictures with Betty Grable.

> (Sings à la Grable)

"I can't begin to tell you, how much you mean to me . . ."
Betty sang that in 1945. '45?—'43. No, '43 was *Coney Island,* which was remade in '50 as *Wabash Avenue.* Yes, *Dolly Sisters* was in '45.

DONALD: How did I manage to miss these momentous events in the American cinema? I can understand people having an affinity for the stage—but movies are such garbage, who can take them seriously?

MICHAEL: Well, I'm sorry if your sense of art is offended. Odd as it may seem, there wasn't any Shubert Theatre in Hot Coffee, Mississippi!

DONALD: However—thanks to the silver screen, your neurosis has got style. It takes a certain flair to squander one's unemployment check at Pavillion.

MICHAEL: What's so snappy about being head over heels in debt. The only thing smart about it is the ingenious ways I dodge the bill collectors.

DONALD: Yeah. Come to think of it, you're the type that gives faggots a bad name.

MICHAEL: And you, Donald, *you* are a credit to the homosexual. A reliable, hardworking, floor-scrubbing, bill-paying fag who don't owe nothin' to nobody.

DONALD: *I* am a model fairy.

> (Michael has taken some ribbon and paper and begun to wrap Harold's birthday gift)

MICHAEL: You think it's just nifty how I've always flitted from Beverly Hills to Rome to Acapulco to Amsterdam, picking up a lot of one-night stands and a lot of custom-made duds along the trail, but I'm here to tell you that the only place in all those miles—the only place I've ever been *happy*—was on the goddamn plane.

(Puffs up the bow on the package, continues)

Bored with Scandinavia, try Greece. Fed up with dark meat, try light. Hate tequila, what about Slivovitz? Tired of boys, what about girls—or how about boys and girls mixed and in what combination? And if you're sick of people, what about poppers? Or pot or pills or the hard stuff. And can you think of anything else the bad baby would like to indulge his spoiled-rotten, stupid, empty, boring, selfish, self-centered self in? Is that what you think has style, Donald? Huh? Is that what you think you've missed out on—my hysterical escapes from country to country, party to party, bar to bar, bed to bed, hangover to hangover, and all of it, hand to mouth!

(A beat)

Run, charge, run, buy, borrow, make, spend, run, squander, beg, run, run, run, waste, waste, *waste!*

(A beat)

And why? And why?

DONALD: Why, Michael? Why?

MICHAEL: I really don't want to get into it.

DONALD: Then how can we have a conversation in depth?

MICHAEL: Oh, you know it all by heart anyway. Same song, second verse. Because my Evelyn refused to let me grow up. She was determined to keep me a child forever and she did one helluva job of it. And my Walt stood by and let her do it.

(A beat)

What you see before you is a thirty-year-old infant. And it was all done in the name of love—what *she* labeled love and probably sincerely believed to be love, when what she was really doing was feeding her own need—satisfying her own loneliness.

(A beat)

She made me into a girlfriend dash lover.

(A beat)

We went to all those goddamn cornball movies together. I picked out her clothes for her and told her what to wear and she'd take me to the beauty parlor with her and we'd both get our hair bleached and a permanent and a manicure.

(A beat)

And Walt let this happen.

(A beat)

And she convinced me that I was a sickly child who couldn't run and play and sweat and get knocked around—oh, no! I was frail and pale and, to hear her tell it, practically female. I can't tell you the thousands of times she said to me, "I declare, Michael, you should have been a girl." And I guess I should have—I was frail and pale and bleached and curled and bedded down with hot-water bottles and my dolls and my paper dolls, and my doll clothes and my dollhouses!

(Quick beat)

And Walt bought them for me!

(Beat. With increasing speed)

And she nursed me and put Vicks salve on my chest and cold cream on my face and told me what beautiful eyes I had and what pretty lips I had. She bathed me in the same tub with her until I grew too big for the two of us to fit. She made me sleep in the same bed with her until I was fourteen years old—until I finally flatly refused to spend one more night there. She didn't want to prepare me for life or how to be out in the world on my own, or I might have left her. But I left anyway. This goddamn cripple finally wrenched free and limped away. And here I am—unequipped, undisciplined, untrained, unprepared, and unable to live!

(A beat)

And do you know until this day she still says, "I don't care if you're seventy years old, you'll always be my baby." And can I tell you how that drives me mad! Will that bitch never understand that what I'll always *be* is her son—but that I haven't been her baby for twenty-five years!

(A beat)

And don't get me wrong. I know it's easy to cop out and blame Evelyn and Walt and say it was *their* fault. That we were simply the helpless put-upon victims. But in the end, we are responsible for ourselves. And I guess—I'm not sure—but I want to believe it—that in their own pathetic, *dangerous* way, they just loved us too much.

(A beat)

Finis. Applause.

(Donald hesitates, walks over to Michael, puts his arms around him, and holds him. It is a totally warm and caring gesture)

There's nothing quite as good as feeling sorry for yourself, is there?

DONALD: Nothing.

MICHAEL:

(A la Bette Davis)

I adore cheap sentiment.

(Breaks away)

OK, I'm taking orders for drinks. What'll it be?

DONALD: An extra-dry-Beefeater-martini-on-the-rocks-with-a-twist.

MICHAEL: Coming up.

(Donald exits up the stairs into the bath; Michael into the kitchen. Momentarily, Michael returns, carrying an ice bucket in one hand and a silver tray of cracked crab in the other, singing "Acapulco" or "Down Argentine Way" or some other forgotten Grable tune. The telephone rings)

MICHAEL:

    (Answering it)

    Backstage, *New Moon.*

    (A beat)

    Alan? My God, I don't believe it. How *are* you? *Where* are you? In town! Great! When'd you get in? Is Fran with you? Oh. What? No. No, I'm tied up to-night. No, tonight's no good for me.— You mean, *now?* Well, Alan, ole boy, it's a friend's birthday and I'm having a few people.— No, you wouldn't exactly call it a birthday party—well, yes, actually I guess you would. I mean, what else would you call it? A *wake,* maybe. I'm sorry I can't ask you to join us—but—well, kiddo, it just wouldn't work out.— No, it's not place cards or anything. It's just that—well, I'd hate to just see you for ten minutes and . . . Alan? Alan? What's the matter?— Are you—are you crying?— Oh, Alan, what's wrong?— Alan, listen, come on over. No, no, it's perfectly all right. Well, just hurry up. I mean, come on by and have a drink, OK? Alan . . . are you all right? OK. Yeah. Same old address. Yeah. Bye.

    (Slowly hangs up, stares blankly into space. Donald appears, bathed and changed. He strikes a pose)

DONALD: Well. Am I stunning?

    (Michael looks up)

MICHAEL:

    (Tonelessly)

    You're absolutely stunning.— You *look* like shit, but I'm absolutely stunned.

DONALD:

    (Crestfallen)

    Your grapes are, how you say, sour.

MICHAEL: Listen, you won't believe what just happened.

DONALD: Where's my drink?

MICHAEL: I didn't make it—I've been on the phone.

    (Donald goes to the bar, makes himself a martini)

    My old roommate from Georgetown just called.

DONALD: Alan what's-his-name?

MICHAEL: McCarthy. He's up here from Washington on business or something and he's on his way over here.

DONALD: Well, I hope he knows the lyrics to "Happy Birthday."

MICHAEL: Listen, asshole, what am I going to do? He's *straight.* And *Square City!*

    ("Top Drawer" accent through clenched teeth)

    I mean, he's rally vury proper. Auffully good family.

DONALD: That's *so* important.

    (Same accent)

MICHAEL:

> *(Regular speech)*

> I mean, they look down on people in the *theater*—so whatta you think he'll feel about this *freak show* I've got booked for dinner?

DONALD:

> *(Sipping his drink)*

> Christ, is that good.

MICHAEL: Want some cracked crab?

DONALD: Not just yet. Why'd you invite him over?

MICHAEL: He invited himself. He said he had to see me tonight. *Immediately.* He absolutely lost his spring on the phone—started crying.

DONALD: Maybe he's feeling sorry for himself too.

MICHAEL: Great heaves and sobs. Really boo-hoo-hoo-time—and that's not his style at all. I mean, he's so pulled-together he wouldn't show any emotion if he were in a plane crash. What am I going to do?

DONALD: What the hell do you care what he thinks?

MICHAEL: Well, I don't really, but . . .

DONALD: Or are you suddenly ashamed of your friends?

MICHAEL: Donald, *you* are the only person I know of whom I am truly ashamed. Some people *do* have different standards from yours and mine, you know. And if we don't acknowledge them, we're just as narrow-minded and backward as we think they are.

DONALD: You know what you are, Michael? You're a *real* person.

MICHAEL: Thank you and fuck you.

> *(Michael crosses to take a piece of crab and nibble on it)*

> Want some?

DONALD: No, thanks. How could you ever have been friends with a bore like that?

MICHAEL: Believe it or not, there was a time in my life when I didn't go around *announcing* that I was a faggot.

DONALD: That must have been before speech replaced sign language.

MICHAEL: Don't give me any static on that score. I didn't come out until I left college.

DONALD: It seems to me that the first time we tricked we met in a gay bar on Third Avenue during your *junior* year.

MICHAEL: Cunt.

DONALD: I thought you'd never say it.

MICHAEL: Sure you don't want any cracked crab?

DONALD: *Not yet! If you don't mind!*

MICHAEL: Well, it can only be getting colder. What time is it?

DONALD: I don't know. Early.

MICHAEL: Where the hell is Alan?

DONALD: Do you want some more club soda?

MICHAEL: What?

DONALD: There's nothing but club soda in that glass. It's not gin—like mine. You want some more?

MICHAEL: No.

DONALD: I've been watching you for several Saturdays now. You've actually stopped drinking, haven't you?

MICHAEL: And smoking too.

DONALD: And smoking too. How long's it been?

MICHAEL: Five weeks.

DONALD: That's amazing.

MICHAEL: I've found God.

DONALD: It *is* amazing—for you.

MICHAEL: Or is God dead?

DONALD: Yes, thank God. And don't get panicky just because I'm paying you a compliment. I can tell the difference.

MICHAEL: You always said that I held my liquor better than anybody you ever saw.

DONALD: I could always tell when you were getting high—one way.

MICHAEL: I'd get hostile.

DONALD: You seem happier or something now—and that shows.

MICHAEL:

(Quietly)

Thanks.

DONALD: What made you stop—the analyst?

MICHAEL: He certainly had a lot to do with it. Mainly, I just didn't think I could survive another hangover, that's all. I don't think I could get through that morning-after ick attack.

DONALD: Morning-after what?

MICHAEL: Icks! Anxiety! Guilt! Unfathomable guilt—either real or imagined—from that split second your eyes pop open and you say, "Oh, my God, what did I do last night!" and ZAP, total recall!

DONALD: Tell me about it!

MICHAEL: Then, the coffee, aspirin, Alka-Seltzer, Darvon, Daprisal, and a quick call to LA.—Icks Anonymous.

DONALD: "Good morning, I.A."

MICHAEL: "Hi! Was I too bad last night? Did I do anything wrong? I didn't do anything terrible, did I?"

DONALD:

(Laughing)

How many times! How many times!

MICHAEL: And from then on, that struggle to live till lunch, when you have a double Bloody Mary—that is, if you've *waited* until lunch—and then you're half pissed again and useless for the rest of the afternoon. And the only sure cure is to go to bed for about thirty-seven hours, but who ever does that? Instead, you hang on till cocktail time, and by then you're ready for what the night holds—which hopefully is another party, where the whole goddamn cycle starts over!

(A beat)

Well, I've been on that merry-go-round long enough and I either had to get off or die of centrifugal force.

DONALD: And just how does a clear head stack up with the dull fog of alcohol?

MICHAEL: Well, all those things you've always heard are true. Nothing can compare with the experience of one's faculties functioning at their maximum natural capacity. The only thing is . . . I'd *kill* for a drink.

(The wall-panel buzzer sounds)

DONALD: Joe College has finally arrived.
MICHAEL: Suddenly, I have such an ick!

(Presses the wall-panel button)

Now listen, Donald . . .

DONALD:

(Quick)

Michael, don't insult me by giving me any lecture on acceptable social behavior. I promise to sit with my legs spread apart and keep my voice in a deep register.
MICHAEL: Donald, you are a real *card-carrying cunt.*

(The apartment door buzzes several times. Michael goes to it, pauses briefly before it, tears it open to reveal Emory, Larry, and Hank. Emory is in Bermuda shorts and a sweater. Larry has on a turtleneck and sandals. Hank is in a dark Ivy League suit with a vest and has on cordovan shoes. Larry and Hank carry birthday gifts. Emory carries a large covered dish)

EMORY:

(Bursting in)

ALL RIGHT THIS IS A RAID! EVERYBODY'S UNDER ARREST!

(This entrance is followed by a loud raucous laugh as Emory throws his arms around Michael and gives him a big kiss on the cheek.)
(Referring to dish)

Hello, darlin! Connie Casserole. Oh, Mary, don't ask.

MICHAEL:

(Weary already)

Hello, Emory. Put it in the kitchen.

(Emory spots Donald)

EMORY: Who is this exotic woman over here?
MICHAEL: Hi, Hank. Larry.

(They say, "Hi," shake hands, enter. Michael looks out in the hall, comes back into the room, closes the door)

DONALD: Hi, Emory.
EMORY: My dear, I thought you had perished! Where have you been hiding your classically chiseled features?
DONALD:

(To Emory)

I don't live in the city anymore.

MICHAEL: Here, I'll take those. Where's yours, Emory?

> *(To Larry and Hank, referring to the gifts)*

EMORY: It's arriving later.

> *(Emory exits to the kitchen. Larry and Donald's eyes have met. Hank has handed Michael his gift—Larry is too preoccupied)*

HANK: Larry!—Larry!

LARRY: What!

HANK: Give Michael the gift!

LARRY: Oh. Here.

> *(To Hank)*

Louder. So my mother in Philadelphia can hear you.

HANK: Well, you were just standing there in a trance.

MICHAEL:

> *(To Larry and Hank as Emory reenters)*

You both know Donald, don't you?

DONALD: Sure. Nice to see you.

> *(To Hank)*

—— Hi.

HANK:

> *(Shaking hands)*

Nice to meet you.

MICHAEL: Oh, I thought you'd met.

DONALD: Well . . .

LARRY: We haven't exactly met but we've . . . Hi.

DONALD: Hi.

HANK: But you've what?

LARRY: . . . *Seen* . . . each other before.

MICHAEL: Well, *that* sounds murky.

HANK: You've never met but you've seen each other.

LARRY: What was wrong with the way *I* said it?

HANK: Where?

EMORY:

> *(Loud aside to Michael)*

I think they're going to have their first fight.

LARRY: The first one since we got out of the taxi.

MICHAEL:

> *(Referring to Emory)*

Where'd you find this trash?

LARRY: Downstairs leaning against a lamppost.

EMORY: With an orchid behind my ear and big wet lips painted over the lipline.

MICHAEL: Just like Maria Montez.

DONALD: Oh, *please!*

EMORY:

(To Donald)

What have you got against Maria—she was a good woman.

MICHAEL: Listen, everybody, this old college friend of mine is in town and he's stopping
by for a fast drink on his way to dinner somewhere. But, listen, he's *straight,* so . . .

LARRY: *Straight!* If it's the one I met, he's about as straight as the Yellow Brick Road.

MICHAEL: No, you met Justin Stuart.

HANK: I don't remember anybody named Justin Stuart.

LARRY: Of course you don't, dope. *I* met him.

MICHAEL: Well, this is someone else.

DONALD: Alan McCarthy. A very close total stranger.

MICHAEL: It's not that I care what he would think of me, really—it's just that
he's not ready for it. And he never will be. You understand that, don't you,
Hank?

HANK: Oh, sure.

LARRY: You honestly think he doesn't know about you?

MICHAEL: If there's the slightest suspicion, he's never let on one bit.

EMORY: What's he had, a lobotomy?

(He exits up the stairs into the bath)

MICHAEL: I was super-careful when I was in college and I still am whenever I see him. I
don't know why, but I am.

DONALD: Tilt.

MICHAEL: You may think it was a crock of shit, Donald, but to him I'm sure we were
close friends. The closest. To pop that balloon now just wouldn't be fair to him.
Isn't that right?

LARRY: Whatever's fair.

MICHAEL: Well, of course. And if that's phony of me, Donald, then that's phony of me
and make something of it.

DONALD: I pass.

MICHAEL: Well, even you have to admit it's much simpler to deal with the world
according to its rules and then go right ahead and do what you damn well
please. You do understand *that,* don't you?

DONALD: Now that you've put it in layman's terms.

MICHAEL: I was just like Alan when I was in college. Very large in the dating
department. Wore nothing but those constipated Ivy League clothes and those
ten-pound cordovan shoes.

(To Hank)

No offense.

HANK: Quite all right.

MICHAEL: I butched it up quite a bit. And I didn't think I was lying to myself. I really
thought I was straight.

EMORY:

(Coming downstairs tucking a Kleenex into his sleeve)

Who do you have to fuck to get a drink around here?

MICHAEL: Will you *light* somewhere?

(*Emory sits on steps*)

Or I thought I thought I was straight. I know I didn't come out till after I'd graduated.

DONALD: What about all those weekends up from school?

MICHAEL: I still wasn't out. I was still in the "Christ-was-I-drunk-last-night syndrome."

LARRY: The *what?*

MICHAEL: The Christ-was-I-drunk-last-night syndrome. You know, when you made it with some guy in school, and the next day when you had to face each other there was always a lot of shit-kicking crap about, "Man, was I drunk last night! Christ, I don't remember a thing!"

(*Everyone laughs*)

DONALD: You were just guilty because you were Catholic, that's all.

MICHAEL: That's not true. The Christ-was-I-drunk-last-night syndrome knows no religion. It has to do with immaturity. Although I will admit there's a high percentage of it among Mormons.

EMORY: Trollop.

MICHAEL: We all somehow managed to justify our actions in those days. I later found out that even Justin Stuart, my closest friend . . .

DONALD: Other than Alan McCarthy.

MICHAEL:

(*A look to Donald*)

. . . was doing the same thing. Only Justin was going to Boston on weekends.

(*Emory and LARRY laugh*)

LARRY: Sound familiar?

(*To Hank*)

MICHAEL: Yes, long before Justin and I or God only knows how many others *came out*, we used to get drunk and "horse around" a bit. You see, in the Christ-was-I-drunk-last-night syndrome, you really *are* drunk. That part of it is true. It's just that you also *do remember everything.*

(*General laughter*)

Oh, God, I used to have to get loaded to go in a gay bar!

DONALD: Well, times certainly have changed.

MICHAEL: They *have.* Lately I've gotten to despise the bars. Everybody just standing around and standing around—it's like one eternal intermission.

HANK:

(*To Larry*)

Sound familiar?

EMORY: I can't stand the bars either. All that cat-and-mouse business—you hang around *staring* at each other all night and wind up going home alone.

MICHAEL: And pissed.

LARRY: A lot of guys have to get loaded to have sex.

>*(Quick look to Hank, who is unamused)*

>So I've been told.

MICHAEL: If you remember, Donald, the first time we made it I was so drunk I could hardly stand up.

DONALD: You were so drunk you could hardly *get* it up.

MICHAEL:

>*(Mock innocence)*

>Christ, I was so drunk I don't remember.

DONALD: Bullshit, you remember.

MICHAEL:

>*(Sings to Donald)*

>"Just friends, lovers no more . . ."

EMORY: You may as well be. Everybody thinks you are anyway.

DONALD: We never *were—really.*

MICHAEL: We didn't have time to be—we got to know each other too fast.

>*(Door buzzer sounds)*

>Oh, Jesus, it's Alan! Now, please, everybody, do me a favor and cool it for the few minutes he's here.

EMORY: Anything for a sis, Mary.

MICHAEL: That's *exactly* what I'm talking about, Emory. *No camping!*

EMORY: Sorry.

>*(Deep, deep voice to Donald)*

>Think the Giants are gonna win the pennant this year?

DONALD:

>*(Deep, deep voice)*

>Fuckin' A, Mac.

>*(Michael goes to the door, opens it to reveal Bernard, dressed in a shirt and tie and sport jacket. He carries a birthday gift and two bottles of red wine)*

EMORY:

>*(Big scream)*

>Oh, it's only another queen!

BERNARD: And it ain't the red one, either.

EMORY: It's the queen of spades!

>*(Bernard enters. Michael looks out in the hall)*

MICHAEL: Bernard, is the downstairs door open?

BERNARD: It was, but I closed it.

MICHAEL: Good.

>*(Bernard starts to put wine on bar)*

MICHAEL:

(Referring to the two bottles of red wine)

I'll take those. You can put your present with the others.

(Michael closes the door. Bernard hands him the gift. The phone rings)

BERNARD: Hi, Larry. Hi, Hank.

MICHAEL: *Christ of the Andes!* Donald, will you bartend, please?

(Michael gives Donald the wine bottles, goes to the phone)

BERNARD:

(Extending his hand to Donald)

Hello, Donald. Good to see you.

DONALD: Bernard.

MICHAEL:

(Answers phone)

Hello? Alan?

EMORY: Hi, Bernardette. Anybody ever tell you you'd look divine in a hammock, surrounded by louvres and ceiling fans and lots and lots of lush tropical ferns?

BERNARD:

(To Emory)

You're *such* a fag. You take the cake.

EMORY: Oh, what *about* the cake—whose job was that?

LARRY: Mine. I ordered one to be delivered.

EMORY: How many candles did you say put on it—eighty?

MICHAEL: . . . What? Wait a minute. There's too much noise. Let me go to another phone.

(Presses the hold button, hangs up, dashes toward stairs)

LARRY: Michael, did the cake come?

MICHAEL: No.

DONALD:

(To Michael as he passes)

What's up?

MICHAEL: Do *I* know?

LARRY: Jesus, I'd better call. OK if I use the private line?

MICHAEL:

(Going upstairs)

Sure.

(Stops dead on stairs, turns)

Listen, everybody, there's some cracked crab there. Help yourselves.

(Donald shakes his head. Michael continues up the stairs to the bedroom. Larry crosses to the phone, presses the free-line button, picks up receiver, dials information)

DONALD: Is everybody ready for a drink?

(Hank and Bernard say, "Yeah")

EMORY:

(Flipping up his sweater)

Ready! I'll be your topless cocktail waitress.

BERNARD: Please spare us the sight of your sagging tits.

EMORY:

(To Hank, Larry)

What're you having, kids?

MICHAEL:

(Having picked up the bedside phone)

. . . Yes, Alan . . .

LARRY: Vodka and tonic.

(Into phone)

Could I have the number for the Marseilles Bakery in Manhattan?

EMORY: A vod and ton and a . . .

HANK: Is there any beer?

EMORY: Beer! Who drinks beer before dinner?

BERNARD: Beer drinkers.

DONALD: That's telling him.

MICHAEL: . . . No, Alan, don't be silly. What's there to apologize for?

EMORY: Truck drivers do. Or . . . or wallpaperers. Not schoolteachers. They have sherry.

HANK: This one has beer.

EMORY: Well, maybe schoolteachers in *public* schools.

(To Larry)

How can a sensitive artist like you live with an insensitive bull like that?

LARRY:

(Hanging up the phone and redialing)

I can't.

BERNARD: Emory, you'd live with Hank in a minute, if he'd ask you. In fifty-eight seconds. Lord knows, you're sssensitive.

EMORY: Why don't you have a piece of watermelon and hush up!

MICHAEL: Alan, don't be ridiculous.

DONALD: Here you go, Hank.

HANK: Thanks.

LARRY: Shit. They don't answer.

DONALD: What're you having, Emory?

BERNARD: A Pink Lady.

EMORY: A vodka martini on the rocks, please.

LARRY:

(Hangs up)

Well, let's just hope.

(Donald hands Larry his drink—their eyes meet again. A faint smile crosses Larry's lips. Donald returns to the bar to make Emory's drink)

MICHAEL: Lunch tomorrow will be great. One o'clock—the Oak Room at the Plaza OK? Fine.

BERNARD:

(To Donald)

Donald, read any new libraries lately?

DONALD: One or three. I did the complete works of Doris Lessing this week. I've been depressed.

MICHAEL: Alan, forget it, will you? Right. Bye.

(Hangs up, starts to leave the room—stops. Quickly pulls off the sweater he is wearing, takes out another, crosses to the stairs)

DONALD: You must not work in Circulation anymore.

BERNARD: Oh, I'm still there—every day.

DONALD: Well, since I moved, I only come in on Saturday evenings.

(Moves his stack of books off the bar)

HANK: Looks like you stock up for the week.

(Michael rises and crosses to steps landing)

BERNARD: Are you kidding?—that'll last him two days.

EMORY: It would last *me* two years. I still haven't finished *Atlas Shrugged*, which I started in 1912.

MICHAEL:

(To Donald)

Well, he's not coming.

DONALD: It's just as well now.

BERNARD: Some people eat, some people drink, some take dope . . .

DONALD: I read.

MICHAEL: And read and read and read. It's a wonder your eyes don't turn back in your head at the sight of a dust jacket.

HANK: Well, at least he's a constructive escapist.

MICHAEL: Yeah, what do I do?—take planes. No, I don't do that anymore. Because I don't have the *money* to do that anymore. I go to the baths. That's about it.

EMORY: I'm about to do both. I'm flying to the West Coast—

BERNARD: You still have that act with a donkey in Tijuana?

EMORY: I'm going to *San Francisco* on a well-earned vacation.

LARRY: No shopping?

EMORY: Oh, I'll look for a few things for a couple of clients, but I've been so busy lately I really couldn't care less if I never saw another piece of fabric or another stick of furniture as long as I live. I'm going to the Club Baths and I'm not out till they announce the departure of TWA one week later.

BERNARD:

(To Emory)

You'll never learn to stay out of the baths, will you? The last time Emily was taking the vapors, this big hairy number strolled in. Emory said, "I'm just resting," and the big hairy number said, "I'm just arresting!" It was the vice!

(Everybody laughs)

EMORY: You have to tell everything, don't you!

(Donald crosses to give Emory his drink)

Thanks, sonny. You live with your parents?

DONALD: Yeah. But it's all right—they're gay.

(Emory roars, slaps Hank on the knee. Hank gets up, moves away. Donald turns to Michael)

What happened to Alan?

MICHAEL: He suddenly got terrible icks about having broken down on the phone. Kept apologizing over and over. Did a big about-face and reverted to the old Alan right before my very eyes.

DONALD: Ears.

MICHAEL: Ears. Well, the cracked crab obviously did not work out.

(Starts to take away the tray)

EMORY: Just put that down if you don't want your hand slapped. I'm about to have some.

MICHAEL: It's really very good.

(Gives Donald a look)

I don't know why everyone has such an aversion to it.

DONALD: Sometimes you remind me of the Chinese water torture. I take that back. Sometimes you remind me of the *relentless* Chinese water torture.

MICHAEL: Bitch.

(Hank has put on some music)

BERNARD: Yeah, baby, let's hear that sound.

EMORY: A drumbeat and their eyes sparkle like Cartier's.

(Bernard starts to snap his fingers and move in time with the music. MICHAEL joins in)

HANK: I wonder where Harold is.

EMORY: Yeah, where *is* the frozen fruit?

MICHAEL:

(To Donald)

Emory refers to Harold as the frozen fruit because of his former profession as an ice skater.

EMORY: She used to be the Vera Hruba Ralston of the Borscht Circuit.

(Michael and Bernard are now dancing freely)

BERNARD:

(To Michael)

If your mother could see you now, she'd have a stroke.

MICHAEL: Got a camera on you?

(The door panel buzzes. Emory lets out a yelp)

EMORY: Oh, my God, it's Lily Law! Everybody three feet apart!

(Michael goes to the panel, presses the button. Hank turns down the music. Michael opens the door a short way, pokes his head out)

BERNARD: It's probably Harold now.

(Michael leans back in the room)

MICHAEL: No, it's the delivery boy from the bakery.

LARRY: Thank God.

(Michael goes out into the hall, pulling the door almost closed behind him)

EMORY:

(Loudly)

Ask him if he's got any hot cross buns!

HANK: Come on, Emory, knock it off.

BERNARD: You can take her anywhere but out.

EMORY:

(To Hank)

You remind me of an old-maid schoolteacher.

HANK: You remind me of a chicken wing.

EMORY: I'm sure you meant that as a compliment.

(Hank turns the music back up)

MICHAEL:

(In hall)

Thank you. Good night.

(Michael returns with a cake box, closes the door, and takes it into the kitchen)

LARRY: Hey, Bernard, you remember that thing we used to do on Fire Island?

(Larry starts to do a kind of Madison)

BERNARD: That was "in" so far back I think I've forgotten.

EMORY: I remember.

(Pops up—starts doing the steps. Larry and Bernard start to follow)

LARRY: Yeah. That's it.

(Michael enters from the kitchen, falls in line with them)

MICHAEL: Well, if it isn't the Geriatrics Rockettes.

(Now they all are doing practically a precision routine. Donald comes to sit on the arm of a chair, sip his drink, and watch in fascination. Hank goes to the bar to get

another beer. The door buzzer sounds. No one seems to hear it. It buzzes again. Hank turns toward the door, hesitates. Looks toward Michael, who is now deeply involved in the intricacies of the dance. No one, it seems, has heard the buzzer but Hank, who goes to the door, opens it wide to reveal Alan. He is dressed in black tie. The dancers continue, turning and slapping their knees and heels and laughing with abandon. Suddenly Michael looks up, stops dead. Donald sees this and turns to see what Michael has seen. Slowly he stands up. Michael goes to the record player, turns it off abruptly. Emory, Larry, and Bernard come to out-of-step halts, look to see what's happened)

MICHAEL: I thought you said you weren't coming.

ALAN: I . . . well, I'm sorry . . .

MICHAEL:

(Forced lightly)

We were just—acting silly . . .

ALAN: Actually, when I called I was in a phone booth around the corner. My dinner party is not far from here. And . . .

MICHAEL: Emory was just showing us this . . . silly dance.

ALAN: Well, then I walked past and your downstairs door was open and . . .

MICHAEL: This is Emory.

(Emory curtsies. Michael glares at him)

Everybody, this is Alan McCarthy. Counterclockwise, Alan: Larry, Emory, Bernard, Donald, and Hank.

(They all mumble "Hello," "Hi")

Would you like a drink?

ALAN: Thanks, no. I . . . I can't stay . . . long . . . really.

MICHAEL: Well, you're here now, so stay. What would you like?

ALAN: Do you have any rye?

MICHAEL: I'm afraid I don't drink it anymore. You'll have to settle for gin or Scotch or vodka.

DONALD: Or beer.

ALAN: Scotch, please.

(Michael starts for bar)

DONALD: I'll get it.

(Goes to bar)

HANK:

(Forced laugh)

Guess I'm the only beer drinker.

ALAN:

(Looking around group)

Whose . . . birthday . . . is it?

LARRY: Harold's.

ALAN:

>   *(Looking from face to face)*
>
>   Harold?

BERNARD: He's not here yet.

EMORY: She's never been on time . . .

>   *(Michael shoots Emory a withering glance)*
>
>   He's never been on time in his . . .

MICHAEL: Alan's from Washington. We went to college together. Georgetown.

>   *(A beat. Silence)*

EMORY: Well, isn't that fascinating.

>   *(Donald hands Alan his drink)*

DONALD: If that's too strong, I'll put some water in it.

ALAN:

>   *(Takes a quick gulp)*
>
>   It's fine. Thanks. Fine.

HANK: Are you in the government?

ALAN: No. I'm a lawyer. What . . . what do you do?

HANK: I teach school.

ALAN: Oh. I would have taken you for an athlete of some sort. You look like you might play sports . . . of some sort.

HANK: Well, I'm no professional but I was on the basketball team in college and I play quite a bit of tennis.

ALAN: I play tennis too.

HANK: Great game.

ALAN: Yes. Great.

>   *(A beat. Silence)*
>
>   What . . . do you teach?

HANK: Math.

ALAN: Math?

HANK: Yes.

ALAN: Math. Well.

EMORY: Kinda makes you want to rush out and buy a slide rule, doesn't it?

MICHAEL: Emory. I'm going to need some help with dinner and you're elected. Come on!

EMORY: I'm *always* elected.

BERNARD: You're a natural-born domestic.

EMORY: Said the African queen! You come on too—you can fan me while I make the salad dressing.

MICHAEL:

>   *(Glaring. Phony smile)*
>
>   RIGHT THIS WAY, EMORY!

(Michael pushes the swinging door aside for Emory and Bernard to enter. They do and he follows. The door swings closed, and the muffled sound of Michael's voice can be heard. Offstage)

You son of a bitch!

EMORY:

(Offstage)

What the hell do you want from me?

HANK: Why don't we all sit down?

ALAN:. . . Sure.

(Hank and Alan sit on the couch. Larry crosses to the bar, refills his drink. Donald comes over to refill his)

LARRY: Hi.

DONALD:. . . Hi.

ALAN: I really feel terrible—barging in on you fellows this way.

LARRY:

(To Donald)

How've you been?

DONALD: Fine, thanks.

HANK:

(To Alan)

. . . Oh, that's OK.

DONALD:

(To Larry)

. . . And you?

LARRY: Oh . . . just fine.

ALAN:

(To Hank)

You're married?

(Larry hears this, turns to look in the direction of the couch. Michael enters from the kitchen)

HANK: What?

(Watching Larry and Donald)

ALAN: I see you're married.

(Points to Hank's wedding band)

HANK: Oh.

MICHAEL: Yes. Hank's married.

(Glaring at Donald)

ALAN: You have any kids?

HANK: Yes. Two. A boy, nine, and a girl, seven. You should see my boy play tennis— really puts his dad to shame.

DONALD:

> *(Avoiding Michael's eyes)*

> I better get some ice.

> *(Exits to the kitchen)*

ALAN:

> *(To Hank)*

> I have two kids too. Both girls.

HANK: Great.

MICHAEL: How are the girls, Alan?

ALAN: Oh, just sensational.

> *(Shakes his head)*

> They're something, those kids. God, I'm nuts about them.

HANK: How long have you been married?

ALAN: Nine years. Can you believe it, Mickey?

MICHAEL: No.

ALAN: Mickey used to go with my wife when we were all in school.

MICHAEL: Can you believe that?

ALAN:

> *(To Hank)*

> You live in the city?

LARRY: Yes, we do.

> *(Larry comes over to couch next to Hank)*

ALAN: Oh.

HANK: I'm in the process of getting a divorce. Larry and I are—roommates.

MICHAEL: Yes.

ALAN: Oh. I'm sorry. Oh, I mean . . .

HANK: I understand.

ALAN:

> *(Gets up)*

> I . . . I . . . I think I'd like another drink . . . if I may.

MICHAEL: Of course. What was it?

ALAN: I'll do it . . . if I may.

> *(Gets up, starts for the bar. Suddenly there is a loud crash offstage. Alan jumps, looks toward swinging door)*

> What was that?

> *(Donald enters with the ice bucket)*

MICHAEL: Excuse me. Testy temperament out in the kitch!

(Michael exits through the swinging door. Alan continues to the bar—starts nervously picking up and putting down bottles, searching for the Scotch)

HANK:

(To Larry)

Larry, where do you know that guy from?

LARRY: What guy?

HANK: *That* guy.

LARRY: I don't know. Around. The bars.

DONALD: Can I help you, Alan?

ALAN: I . . . I can't seem to find the Scotch.

DONALD: You've got it in your hand.

ALAN: Oh. Of course. How . . . stupid of me.

(Donald watches Alan fumble with the Scotch bottle and glass)

DONALD: Why don't you let me do that?

ALAN:

(Gratefully hands him both)

Thanks.

DONALD: Was it water or soda?

ALAN: Just make it straight—over ice.

(Michael enters)

MICHAEL: You see, Alan, I told you it wasn't a good time to talk. But we . . .

ALAN: It doesn't matter. I'll just finish this and go . . .

(Takes a long swallow)

LARRY: Where can Harold be?

MICHAEL: Oh, he's always late. You know how neurotic he is about going out in public.
    It takes him hours to get ready.

LARRY: Why is that?

(Emory breezes in with an apron tied around his waist, carrying a stack of plates, which he places on a drop-leaf table. Michael does an eye roll)

EMORY: Why is what?

LARRY: Why does Harold spend hours getting ready before he can go out?

EMORY: Because she's a sick lady, that's why.

(Exits to the kitchen. Alan finishes his drink)

MICHAEL: Alan, as I was about to say, we can go in the bedroom and talk.

ALAN: It really doesn't matter.

MICHAEL: Come on. Bring your drink.

ALAN: I . . . I've finished it.

MICHAEL: Well, make another and bring it upstairs.

(Donald picks up the Scotch bottle and pours into the glass Alan has in his hand. Michael has started for the stairs)

ALAN:

> *(To Donald)*

> Thanks.

DONALD: Don't mention it.

ALAN:

> *(To Hank)*

> Excuse me. We'll be down in a minute.

LARRY: He'll still be here.

> *(A beat)*

MICHAEL:

> *(On the stairs)*

> Go ahead, Alan. I'll be right there.

> *(Alan turns awkwardly, exits to the bedroom. Michael goes into the kitchen. A beat)*

HANK:

> *(To Larry)*

> What was *that* supposed to mean?

LARRY: What was what supposed to mean?

HANK: You know.

LARRY: You want another beer?

HANK: No. You're jealous, aren't you?

> *(Hank starts to laugh. Larry doesn't like it)*

LARRY: I'm Larry. *You're* jealous.

> *(Crosses to Donald)*

> Hey, Donald, where've you been hanging out these days? I haven't seen you in a long time . . .

> *(Michael enters to witness this disapprovingly. He turns, goes up the stairs. In the bedroom Alan is sitting on the edge of the bed. Michael enters, pauses at the mirror to adjust his hair. Downstairs, Hank gets up, exits into the kitchen. Donald and Larry move to a corner of the room, sit facing upstage, and talk quietly)*

ALAN:

> *(To Michael)*

> This is a marvelous apartment.

MICHAEL: It's too expensive. I work to pay rent.

ALAN: What are you doing these days?

MICHAEL: Nothing.

ALAN: Aren't you writing anymore?

MICHAEL: I haven't looked at a typewriter since I sold the very, very wonderful, very, very marvelous *screenplay*, which never got produced.

ALAN: That's right. The last time I saw you, you were on your way to California. Or was it Europe?

MICHAEL: Hollywood. Which is not in Europe, nor does it have anything whatsoever to do with California.

ALAN: I've never been there, but I would imagine it's awful. Everyone must be terribly cheap.

MICHAEL: No, not everyone.

(Alan laughs. A beat. Michael sits on the bed)

Alan, I want to try to explain this evening . . .

ALAN: What's there to explain? Sometimes you just can't invite everybody to every party and some people take it personally. But I'm not one of them. I should apologize for inviting myself.

MICHAEL: That's not exactly what I meant.

ALAN: Your friends all seem like very nice guys. That Hank is really a very attractive fellow.

MICHAEL: . . . Yes. He is.

ALAN: We have a lot in common. What's his roommate's name?

MICHAEL: Larry.

ALAN: What does *he* do?

MICHAEL: He's a commercial artist.

ALAN: I liked Donald too. The only one I didn't care too much for was—what's his name—Emory?

MICHAEL: Yes. Emory.

ALAN: I just can't stand that kind of talk. It just grates on me.

MICHAEL: What kind of talk, Alan?

ALAN: Oh, you know. His brand of humor, I guess.

MICHAEL: He can be really quite funny sometimes.

ALAN: I suppose so. If you find that sort of thing amusing. He just seems like such a goddamn little pansy.

(Silence. A pause)

I'm sorry I said that. I didn't mean to say that. That's such an awful thing to say about *anyone*. But you know what I mean, Michael—you have to admit he *is* effeminate.

MICHAEL: He is a bit.

ALAN: A bit! He's like a . . . a butterfly in heat! I mean, there's no wonder he was trying to teach you all a dance. He *probably* wanted to dance *with* you!

(Pause)

Oh, come on, man, you know me—you know how I feel—your private life is your own affair.

MICHAEL:

(Icy)

No. I *don't* know that about you.

ALAN: I couldn't care less what people do—as long as they don't do it in public—or—or try to force their ways on the whole damned world.

MICHAEL: Alan, what was it you were crying about on the telephone?

ALAN: Oh, I feel like such a fool about that. I could shoot myself for letting myself act that way. I'm so embarrassed I could die.

MICHAEL: But, Alan, if you were genuinely upset—that's nothing to be embarrassed about.

ALAN: All I can say is—please accept my apology for making such an ass of myself.

MICHAEL: You must have been upset, or you wouldn't have said you were and that you wanted to see me—*had* to see me and had to talk to me.

ALAN: Can you forget it? Just pretend it never happened. I know *I* have. OK?

MICHAEL: Is something wrong between you and Fran?

ALAN: Listen, I've really got to go.

MICHAEL: Why are you in New York?

ALAN: I'm dreadfully late for dinner.

MICHAEL: *Whose* dinner? Where are you going?

ALAN: Is this the loo?

MICHAEL: Yes.

ALAN: Excuse me.

> (*Quickly goes into the bathroom, closes the door. Michael remains silent—sits on the bed, stares into space. Downstairs, Emory pops in from the kitchen to discover Donald and Larry in quiet, intimate conversation*)

EMORY: What's-going-on-in-here-oh-Mary-don't-ask!

> (*Puts a salt cellar and pepper mill on the table. Hank enters, carrying a bottle of red wine and a corkscrew. Looks toward Larry and Donald. Donald sees him, stands up*)

DONALD: Hank, why don't you come and join us?

HANK: That's an interesting suggestion. Whose idea is that?

DONALD: Mine.

LARRY:

> (*To Hank*)

He means in a conversation.

> (*Bernard enters from the kitchen, carrying four wineglasses*)

EMORY:

> (*To Bernard*)

Where're the rest of the wineglasses?

BERNARD: Ahz workin' as fas' as ah can!

EMORY: They have to be told everything. Can't let 'em out of your sight.

> (*Breezes out to the kitchen. Donald leaves Larry's side and goes to the coffee table, helps himself to the cracked crab. Hank opens the wine, puts it on the table. Michael gets up from the bed and goes down the stairs. Downstairs, Hank crosses to Larry*)

HANK: I thought maybe you were abiding by the agreement.

LARRY: We have no agreement.

HANK: We *did*.

LARRY: *You* did. I never agreed to anything!

> (*Donald looks up to see Michael, raises a crab claw toward him*)

DONALD: To your health.

MICHAEL: Up yours.

DONALD: Up my health?

BERNARD: Where's the gent?

MICHAEL: In the gent's room. If you can all hang on five more minutes, he's about to leave.

(The door buzzes. Michael crosses to it)

LARRY: Well, at last!

(Michael opens the door to reveal a muscle-bound young man wearing boots, tight Levi's, a calico neckerchief, and a cowboy hat. Around his wrist there is a large card tied with a ribbon)

COWBOY:

(Singing fast)

"Happy birthday to you,
Happy birthday to you,
Happy birthday, dear Harold.
Happy birthday to you."

(And with that, he throws his arms around Michael and gives him a big kiss on the lips. Everyone stands in stunned silence)

MICHAEL: Who the hell are you?

(Emory swings in from the kitchen)

EMORY: She's Harold's present from me and she's *early!*

(Quick, to Cowboy)

And that's not even Harold, you *idiot!*

COWBOY: You said whoever answered the door.

EMORY:

(Quickly, to group)

But *not until midnight!*
He's supposed to be a *midnight cowboy!*

DONALD: He *is* a midnight cowboy.

MICHAEL: He looks right out of a William Inge play to me.

EMORY:

(To Cowboy)

. . . Not until midnight and you're supposed to sing to the right person, for Chrissake! I *told* you Harold has very, very tight, tight, black curly hair.

(Referring to Michael)

This number's practically bald!

MICHAEL: Thank you and fuck you.

BERNARD: It's a good thing *I* didn't open the door.

EMORY: Not that tight and not that black.

COWBOY: I forgot. Besides, I wanted to get to the bars by midnight.

MICHAEL: He's a class act all the way around.

EMORY: What do you mean—get to the bars! Sweetie, I paid you for the whole night, remember?

COWBOY: I hurt my back doing my exercises and I wanted to get to bed early tonight.

BERNARD: Are you ready for this one?

LARRY:

> (To Cowboy)

> That's too bad, what happened?

COWBOY: I lost my grip doing my chin-ups and I fell on my heels and twisted my back.

EMORY: You shouldn't *wear* heels when you do chin-ups.

COWBOY:

> (Oblivious)

> I shouldn't do chin-ups—I got a weak grip to begin with.

EMORY: A weak grip. In my day it used to be called a limp wrist.

BERNARD: Who can remember that far back?

MICHAEL: Who was it that always used to say, "You show me Oscar Wilde in a cowboy suit, and I'll show you a gay caballero."

DONALD: I don't know. Who *was* it who always used to say that?

MICHAEL:

> (Katharine Hepburn voice)

> I don't know. Somebody.

LARRY:

> (To Cowboy)

> What does your card say?

COWBOY:

> (Holds up his wrist)

> Here. Read it.

LARRY:

> (Reading card)

> "Dear Harold, bang, bang, you're alive. But roll over and play dead. Happy birthday, Emory."

BERNARD: Ah, sheer poetry, Emmy.

LARRY: And in your usual good taste.

MICHAEL: Yes, so conservative of you to resist a sign in Times Square.

EMORY:

> (Glancing toward stairs)

> Cheese it! Here comes the socialite nun.

MICHAEL: Goddamn it, Emory!

> (Alan comes down the stairs into the room. Everybody quiets)

ALAN: Well, I'm off . . . Thanks, Michael, for the drink.

MICHAEL: You're entirely welcome, Alan. See you tomorrow?

ALAN: . . . No. No, I think I'm going to be awfully busy. I may even go back to Washington.

EMORY: Got a heavy date in Lafayette Square?

ALAN: What?

HANK: Emory.

EMORY: Forget it.

ALAN:

(Sees Cowboy)

Are you . . . Harold?

EMORY: No, he's not Harold. He's *for* Harold.

(Silence. Alan lets it pass. Turns to Hank)

ALAN: Goodbye, Hank. It was nice to meet you.

HANK: Same here.

(They shake hands)

ALAN: If . . . if you're ever in Washington—I'd like for you to meet my wife.

LARRY: That'd be fun, wouldn't it, Hank?

EMORY: Yeah, they'd love to meet him—*her.* I have such a problem with pronouns.

ALAN:

(Quick, to Emory)

How many esses are there in the word pronoun?

EMORY: How'd you like to kiss my ass—that's got two or more *essessss* in it!

ALAN: How'd you like to blow me!

EMORY: What's the matter with your *wife,* she got lockjaw?

ALAN:

(Lashes out)

Faggot, fairy, pansy . . .

(Lunges at Emory)

. . . queer, cocksucker! I'll kill you, you goddamn little mincing swish! You goddamn freak! FREAK! FREAK!

(Pandemonium. Alan beats Emory to the floor before anyone recovers from surprise and reacts)

EMORY: Oh, my God, somebody help me! Bernard! He's killing me!

(Bernard and Hank rush forward. Emory is screaming. Blood gushes from his nose)

HANK: Alan! ALAN! ALAN!

EMORY: Get him off me! Get him off me! Oh, my God, he's broken my nose! I'm BLEEDING TO DEATH!

(Larry has gone to shut the door. With one great, athletic move, Hank forcefully tears Alan off Emory and drags him backward across the room. Bernard bends over Emory, puts his arm around him, and lifts him)

BERNARD: Somebody get some ice! And a cloth!

> *(Larry runs to the bar, grabs the bar towel and the ice bucket, rushes to put it on the floor beside Bernard and Emory. Bernard quickly wraps some ice in the towel, holds it to Emory's mouth)*

EMORY: Oh, my face!

BERNARD: He busted your lip, that's all. It'll be all right.

> *(Hank has gotten Alan down on the floor on the opposite side of the room. Alan relinquishes the struggle, collapses against Hank, moaning and beating his fists rhythmically against Hank's chest. Michael is still standing in the same spot in the center of the room, immobile. Donald crosses past the Cowboy)*

DONALD:

> *(To Cowboy)*

Would you mind waiting over there with the gifts?

> *(Cowboy moves over to where the gift-wrapped packages have been put. Donald continues past to observe the mayhem, turns up his glass, takes a long swallow. The door buzzes, Donald turns toward Michael, waits. Michael doesn't move. Donald goes to the door, opens it to reveal Harold)*

Well, Harold! Happy birthday. You're just in time for the floor show, which, as you see, is on the floor.

> *(To Cowboy)*

Hey, you, *this* is Harold!

> *(Harold looks blankly toward Michael. Michael looks back blankly)*

COWBOY:

> *(Crossing to Harold)*

"Happy birthday to you,
Happy birthday to you,
Happy birthday, dear Harold.
Happy birthday to you."

> *(Throws his arms around Harold and gives him a big kiss. Donald looks toward Michael, who observes this stoically. Harold breaks away from Cowboy, reads the card, begins to laugh. Michael turns to survey the room. Donald watches him. Slowly Michael begins to move. Walks over to the bar, pours a glass of gin, raises it to his lips, downs it all. Donald watches silently as Harold laughs and laughs and laughs)*

Curtain
End of Act 1

ACT 2

A moment later. Harold is still laughing. Michael, still at the bar, lowers his glass, turns to Harold.

MICHAEL: What's so fucking funny?
HAROLD:

> *(Unintimidated. Quick hand to hip)*

> Life. Life is a goddamn laff-riot. You remember life.

MICHAEL: *You're stoned.* It shows in your arm.
LARRY: Happy birthday, Harold.
MICHAEL: You're stoned and you're late! You were supposed to arrive at this location at approximately eight-thirty dash nine o'clock!

> *(To Harold)*

HAROLD: What I *am*, Michael, is a thirty-two-year-old, ugly, pockmarked Jew fairy— and if it takes me a while to pull myself together and if I smoke a little grass before I can get up the nerve to show this face to the world, it's nobody's goddamn business but my own.

> *(Instant switch to chatty tone)*

> And how are *you* this evening?

> *(Hank lifts Alan to the couch. Michael turns away from Harold, pours himself another drink. Donald watches. Harold sweeps past Michael over to where Bernard is helping Emory up off the floor. Larry returns the bucket to the bar. Michael puts some ice in his drink)*

EMORY: Happy birthday, Hallie.
HAROLD: What happened to *you?*
EMORY:

> *(Groans)*

> Don't ask!

HAROLD: Your lips are turning blue; you look like you been rimming a snowman.
EMORY: That piss-elegant kooze hit me!

> *(Indicates Alan. Harold looks toward the couch. Alan has slumped his head forward into his own lap)*

MICHAEL: Careful, Emory, that kind of talk just makes him s'nervous.

> *(Alan covers his ears with his hands)*

HAROLD: Who is she? Who was she? Who does she hope to be?
EMORY: Who knows, who cares!
HANK: His name is Alan McCarthy.
MICHAEL: Do forgive me for not formally introducing you.

HAROLD:

> *(Sarcastically, to Michael)*
>
> Not the famous college *chum.*

MICHAEL:

> *(Takes an ice cube out of his glass, throws it at Harold)*
>
> Do a figure eight on that.

HAROLD: Well, well, well. I finally get to meet dear ole Alan after all these years. And in black tie too. Is this my surprise from you, Michael?

LARRY: I think Alan is the one who got the surprise.

DONALD: And, if you'll notice, he's absolutely speechless.

EMORY: I *hope* she's in *shock!* She's a beast!

COWBOY:

> *(Indicating Alan)*
>
> Is it his birthday too?

EMORY:

> *(Indicates Cowboy to Harold)*
>
> *That's* your surprise.

LARRY: Speaking of beasts.

EMORY: From me to you, darlin'. How do you like it?

HAROLD: Oh, I suppose he has an interesting face and body—but it turns me right off because he can't talk intelligently about art.

EMORY: Yeah, ain't it a shame.

HAROLD: I could never *love* anyone like that.

EMORY: Never. *Who could?*

HAROLD: *I* could and *you* could, that's who could! Oh, Mary, she's *gorgeous!*

EMORY: She may be dumb, but she's all yours!

HAROLD: In affairs of the heart, there are no rules! Where'd you ever find-him?

EMORY: Rae knew where.

MICHAEL:

> *(To Donald)*
>
> Rae is Rae Clark. That's R-A-E. She's Emory's dyke friend who sings at a place in the Village. She wears pinstriped suits and bills herself "Miss Rae Clark—Songs Tailored to Your Taste."

EMORY: Miss Rae Clark. Songs tailored to your taste!

MICHAEL: Have you ever heard of anything so crummy in your life?

EMORY: Rae's a fabulous chanteuse. I adore the way she does "Down in the Depths on the Ninetieth Floor."

MICHAEL: The faggot national anthem.

(Exits to the kitchen singing "Down in the Depths" in a butch baritone)

HAROLD:

> *(To Emory)*
>
> All I can say is thank God for Miss Rae Clark. I think my present is a super-surprise. I'm so thrilled to get it I'd kiss you, but I don't want to get blood all over me.

EMORY: Ohhh, look at my sweater!

HAROLD: Wait'll you see your face.

BERNARD: Come on, Emory, let's clean you up. Happy birthday, Harold.

HAROLD:

> *(Smiles)*

> Thanks, love.

EMORY: My sweater is ruined!

MICHAEL:

> *(From the kitchen)*

> Take one of mine in the bedroom.

DONALD: The one on the floor is vicuña.

BERNARD:

> *(To Emory)*

> You'll feel better after I bathe your face.

EMORY: Cheer-up-things-could-get-worse-I-did-and-they-did.

> *(Bernard leads Emory up the stairs)*

HAROLD: Just another birthday party with the folks.

> *(Michael returns with a wine bottle and a green-crystal white-wine glass, pouring en route)*

MICHAEL: Here's a cold bottle of Pouilly-Fuissé I bought especially for you, kiddo.

HAROLD: Pussycat, all is forgiven. You can stay. No. You can stay, but not all is forgiven. Cheers.

MICHAEL: I didn't want it this way, Hallie.

HAROLD:

> *(Indicating Alan)*

> Who asked Mr. Right to celebrate my birthday?

DONALD: There are no accidents.

HAROLD:

> *(Referring to Donald)*

> And who asked *him*?

MICHAEL: *Guilty again.* When I make problems for myself, I go the whole route.

HAROLD: Always got to have your crutch, haven't you?

DONALD: I'm *not* leaving.

> *(Goes to the bar, makes himself another martini)*

HAROLD: Nobody ever thinks completely of somebody else. They always please themselves; they always cheat, if only a little bit.

LARRY:

> *(Referring to Alan)*

> Why is he sitting there with his hands over his ears?

DONALD: I think he has an ick.

(*Donald looks at Michael. Michael returns the look, steely*)

HANK:

(*To Alan*)

Can I get you a drink?

LARRY: How can he hear you, dummy, with his hands over his ears?

HAROLD: He can hear every word. In fact, he wouldn't miss a word if it killed him.

(*Alan removes his hands from his ears*)

What'd I tell you?

ALAN: I . . . I . . . feel sick. I think . . . I'm going to . . . throw up.

HAROLD: Say that again and I won't have to take my appetite depressant.

(*Alan looks desperately toward Hank*)

HANK: Hang on.

(*Hank pulls Alan's arm around his neck, lifts him up, takes him up the stairs*)

HAROLD: Easy does it. One step at a time.

(*Bernard and Emory come out of the bath*)

BERNARD: There. Feel better?

EMORY: Oh, Mary, what would I do without you?

(*Emory looks at himself in the mirror*)

I am not ready for my close-up, Mr. De Mille. Nor will I be for the next two weeks.

(*Bernard picks up Michael's sweater off the floor. Hank and Alan are midway up the stairs*)

ALAN: I'm going to throw up! Let me go! Let me go!

(*Tears loose of Hank, bolts up the remainder of the stairs. He and Emory meet head-on. Emory screams*)

EMORY: Oh, my God, he's after me again!

(*Emory recoils as Alan whizzes past into the bathroom, slamming the door behind him. Hank has reached the bedroom*)

HANK: He's sick.

BERNARD: Yeah, sick in the head. Here, Emory, put this on.

EMORY: Oh, Mary, take me home. My nerves can't stand any more of this tonight.

(*Emory takes the vicuña sweater from Bernard, starts to put it on. Downstairs, Harold flamboyantly takes out a cigarette, takes a kitchen match from a striker, steps up on the seat of the couch, and sits on the back of it*)

HAROLD: TURNING ON!

(*With that, he strikes the match on the sole of his shoe and lights up. Through a strained throat*)

Anybody care to join me?

(Waves the cigarette in a slow pass)

MICHAEL: Many thanks, no.

(Harold passes it to Larry, who nods negatively)

DONALD: No, thank you.

HAROLD:

(To Cowboy)

How about you, Tex?

COWBOY: Yeah.

(Cowboy takes the cigarette, makes some audible inhalations through his teeth)

MICHAEL: I find the sound of the ritual alone utterly humiliating.

(Turns away, goes to the bar, makes another drink)

LARRY: I hate the smell poppers leave on your fingers.

HAROLD: Why don't you get up and wash your hands?

(Emory and Bernard come down the stairs)

EMORY: Michael, I left the casserole in the oven. You can take it out anytime.

MICHAEL: You're not going.

EMORY: I couldn't eat now anyway.

HAROLD: Well, *I'm* absolutely ravenous. I'm going to eat until I have a fat attack.

MICHAEL:

(To Emory)

I said, you're *not going.*

HAROLD:

(To Michael)

Having a cocktail this evening, are we? In my honor?

EMORY: It's your favorite dinner, Hallie. I made it myself.

BERNARD: *Who* fixed the casserole?

EMORY: Well, *I* made the sauce!

BERNARD: Well, *I* made the salad!

LARRY: Girls, please.

MICHAEL: Please *what!*

HAROLD: Beware the hostile fag. When he's sober, he's dangerous. When he drinks, he's lethal.

MICHAEL:

(Referring to Harold)

Attention must *not* be paid.

HAROLD: I'm starved, Em, I'm ready for some of your Alice B. Toklas's opium-baked lasagna.

EMORY: Are you really? Oh, that makes me so pleased, maybe I'll just serve it before I leave.

MICHAEL: *You're not leaving.*

BERNARD: I'll help.

LARRY: I better help too. We don't need a nosebleed in the lasagna.

BERNARD: When the sauce is on it, you wouldn't be able to tell the difference anyway.

(Emory, Bernard, and Larry exit to the kitchen)

MICHAEL:

(Proclamation)

Nobody's going anywhere!

HAROLD: You are going to have schmertz tomorrow you wouldn't believe.

MICHAEL: May I kiss the hem of your schmata, Doctor Freud?

COWBOY: What are you two talking about? I don't understand.

DONALD: He's working through his Oedipus complex, sugar. With a machete.

COWBOY: Huh?

(Hank comes down the stairs)

HANK: Michael, is there any air spray?

HAROLD: Hair spray! You're supposed to be holding his head, not doing his hair.

HANK: *Air* spray, not *hair* spray.

MICHAEL: There's a can of floral spray right on top of the john.

HANK: Thanks.

(Hank goes back upstairs)

HAROLD: Aren't you going to say "If it was a snake, it would have bitten you"?

MICHAEL:

(Indicating Cowboy)

That is something only your friend would say.

HAROLD:

(To Michael)

I am turning on and you are just turning.

(To Donald)

I keep my grass in the medicine cabinet. In a Band-Aid box. Somebody told me it's the safest place. If the cops arrive, you can always lock yourself in the bathroom and flush it down the john.

DONALD: *Very cagey.*

HAROLD: It makes more sense than where I *was* keeping it—in an oregano jar in the spice rack. I kept forgetting and accidentally turning my hateful mother on with the salad.

(A beat)

But I think she liked it. No matter what meal she comes over for—even if it's breakfast—she says, "Let's have a salad!"

COWBOY:

(To Michael)

Why do you say I would say "If it was a snake, it would have bitten you"? I think that's what I *would* have said.

MICHAEL: Of course you would have, baby. That's the kind of remark your pintsize brain thinks of. You are definitely the type who still moves his lips when he reads and who sits in a steam room and says things like "Hot enough for you?"

COWBOY: I never use the steam room when I go to the gym. It's bad after a workout. It flattens you down.

MICHAEL: Just after you've broken your back to blow yourself up like a poisoned dog.

COWBOY: Yeah.

MICHAEL: You're right, Harold. Not only can he not talk intelligently about art, he can't even follow from one sentence to the next.

HAROLD: *But he's beautiful.* He has *unnatural* natural beauty.

(*Quick palm upheld*)

Not that that means anything.

MICHAEL: It doesn't mean *everything.*

HAROLD: Keep telling yourself that as your hair drops out in handfuls.

(*Quick palm upheld*)

Not that it's not *natural* for one's hair to recede as one reaches seniority. Not that those wonderful lines that have begun creasing our countenances don't make all the difference in the world because they add so much *character.*

MICHAEL: Faggots are worse than women about their age. They think their lives are over at thirty. Physical beauty is not that goddamned important!

HAROLD: Of course not. How could it be—it's only in the eye of the beholder.

MICHAEL: And it's only skin deep—don't forget that one.

HAROLD: Oh, no, I haven't forgotten that one at all. It's only skin-deep and it's *transitory* too. It's *terribly* transitory. I mean, how long does it last—thirty or forty or fifty years at the most—depending on how well you take care of yourself. And not counting, of course, that you might die before it runs out anyway. Yes, it's too bad about this poor boy's face. It's tragic. He's absolutely cursed!

(*Takes Cowboy's face in his hands*)

How can *his* beauty ever compare with *my* soul? And although I have never seen my soul, I understand from my mother's rabbi that it's a knockout. I, however, cannot seem to locate it for a gander. And if I could, I'd sell it in a flash for some skin-deep, transitory, meaningless beauty!

(*Alan walks weakly into the bedroom and sits on the bed. Downstairs, Larry enters from the kitchen with salad plates. Hank comes into the bedroom and turns out the lamps. Alan lies down. Now only the light from the bathroom and the stairwell illuminate the room*)

MICHAEL:

(*Makes sign of the cross with his drink in hand*)

Forgive him, Father, for he knows not what he do.

(*Hank stands still in the half darkness*)

HAROLD: Michael, you kill me. You don't know what side of the fence you're on. If somebody says something pro-religion, you're against them. If somebody denies God, you're against *them*. One might say that you have some problem in that area. You can't live with it and you can't live without it.

(Emory barges through the swinging door, carrying the casserole)

EMORY: Hot stuff! Comin' through!

MICHAEL:

(To Emory)

One could murder you with very little effort.

HAROLD:

(To Michael)

You hang on to that great insurance policy called The Church.

MICHAEL: That's right. I believe in God, and if it turns out that there really isn't one, OK. Nothing lost. But if it turns out that there *is*—I'm covered.

(Bernard enters, carrying a huge salad bowl. He puts it down, lights table candles)

EMORY:

(To Michael)

Harriet Hypocrite, that's who you are.

MICHAEL: Right. I'm one of those truly rotten Catholics who gets drunk, sins all night and goes to Mass the next morning.

EMORY: Gilda Guilt. It depends on what you think sin is.

MICHAEL: Would you just shut up your goddamn minty mouth and get back to the goddamn kitchen!

EMORY: Say anything you want—*just don't hit me!*

(Exits. A beat)

MICHAEL: Actually, I suppose Emory has a point—I only go to confession before I get on a plane.

BERNARD: Do you think God's power only exists at thirty thousand feet?

MICHAEL: It must. On the ground, I *am* God. In the air, I'm just one more scared son of a bitch.

(A beat)

BERNARD: I'm scared on the ground.

COWBOY: Me too.

(A beat)

That is, when I'm not high on pot or up on acid.

(Hank comes down the stairs)

LARRY:

(To Hank)

Well, is it bigger than a breadstick?

HANK:

>*(Ignores last remark. To Michael)*

>He's lying down for a minute.

HAROLD: How does the bathroom smell?

HANK: Better.

MICHAEL: Before it smelled like somebody puked. Now it smells like somebody puked in a gardenia patch.

LARRY: And how does the big hero feel?

HANK: Lay off, will you?

>*(Emory enters with a basket of napkin-covered rolls, deposits them on the table)*

EMORY: *Dinner is served!*

>*(Harold comes to the buffet table)*

HAROLD: Emory, it looks absolutely fabulous.

EMORY: I'd make somebody a good wife.

>*(Emory serves pasta. Bernard serves the salad, pours wine. Michael goes to the bar, makes another drink)*

>I could cook and do an apartment and entertain . . .

>*(Grabs a long-stem rose from an arrangement on the table, clenches it between his teeth, snaps his fingers and strikes a pose)*

>Kiss me quick, I'm Carmen!

>*(Harold just looks at him blankly, passes on. Emory takes the flower out of his mouth)*

>One really needs castanets for that sort of thing.

MICHAEL: And a getaway car.

>*(Hank comes up to the table)*

EMORY: What would you like, big boy?

LARRY: Alan McCarthy, and don't hold the mayo.

EMORY: I can't keep up with you two—

>*(Indicating Hank, then Larry)*

>—I thought you were mad at him—now he's bitchin' you. What gives?

LARRY: Never mind.

>*(Cowboy comes over to the table. Emory gives him a plate of food. Bernard gives him salad and a glass of wine. Hank moves to the couch, sits, and puts his plate and glass on the coffee table. Harold moves to sit on the stairs and eat)*

COWBOY: What is it?

LARRY: Lasagna.

COWBOY: It looks like spaghetti and meatballs sorta flattened out.

DONALD: It's been in the steam room.

COWBOY: It has?

MICHAEL:

(Contemptuously)

It looks like spaghetti and meatballs sorta flattened out. Ah, yes, Harold—truly enviable.

HAROLD: As opposed to you, who knows so much about *haute cuisine.*

(A beat)

Raconteur, gourmet, troll.

(Larry takes a plate of food, goes to sit on the back of the couch from behind it)

COWBOY: It's good.

HAROLD:

(Quick)

You like it, eat it.

MICHAEL: Stuff your mouth so that you can't say anything.

(Donald takes a plate)

HAROLD: Turning.

BERNARD:

(To Donald)

Wine?

DONALD: No, thanks.

MICHAEL: Aw, go on, kiddo, force yourself. Have a little *vin ordinaire* to wash down all that depressed pasta.

HAROLD: Sommelier, connoisseur, pig.

(Donald takes the glass of wine, moves up by the bar, puts the glass of wine on it, leans against the wall, eats his food. Emory hands Bernard a plate)

BERNARD:

(To Emory)

Aren't you going to have any?

EMORY: No. My lip hurts too much to eat.

MICHAEL:

(Crosses to table, picks up knife)

I hear if you puts a knife under de bed it cuts de pain.

HAROLD:

(To Michael)

I hear if you put a knife under your chin it cuts your throat.

EMORY: Anybody going to take a plate up to Alan?

MICHAEL: The punching bag has now dissolved into Flo Nightingale.

LARRY: Hank?

HANK: I don't think he'd have any appetite.

(Alan, as if he's heard his name, gets up from the bed, moves slowly to the top of the stairwell. Bernard takes his plate, moves near the stairs, sits on the floor. Michael raps the knife on an empty wineglass)

MICHAEL: Ladies and gentlemen. Correction: Ladies and ladies, I would like to announce that you have just eaten Sebastian Venable.

COWBOY: Just eaten *what?*

MICHAEL: Not *what*, stupid. *Who.* A character in a play. A fairy who was eaten alive. I mean the chop-chop variety.

COWBOY: Jesus.

HANK: Did Edward Albee write that play?

MICHAEL: No. Tennessee Williams.

HANK: Oh, yeah.

MICHAEL: Albee wrote *Who's Afraid of Virginia Woolf?*

LARRY: Dummy.

HANK: I know that. I just thought maybe he wrote that other one too.

LARRY: Well, you made a mistake.

HANK: So I made a mistake.

LARRY: That's right, you made a mistake.

HANK: What's the difference? You can't add.

COWBOY: Edward who?

MICHAEL: ·

> *(To Emory)*

How much did you pay for him?

EMORY: He was a steal.

MICHAEL: He's a ham sandwich—fifty cents anytime of the day or night.

HAROLD: King of the Pig People.

> *(Michael gives him a look. Donald returns his plate to the table)*

EMORY:

> *(To Donald)*

Would you like some more?

DONALD: No, thank you, Emory. It was very good.

EMORY: Did you like it?

COWBOY: I'm not a steal. I cost twenty dollars.

> *(Bernard returns his plate)*

EMORY: More?

BERNARD:

> *(Nods negatively)*

It was delicious—even if I did make it myself.

EMORY: Isn't anybody having seconds?

HAROLD: I'm having seconds and thirds and maybe even fifths.

> *(Gets up off the stairs, comes toward the table)*

I'm absolutely desperate to keep the weight up.

(Bernard bends to whisper something in Emory's ear. Emory nods affirmatively and Bernard crosses to Cowboy and whispers in his ear. A beat. Cowboy returns his plate to the buffet and follows Emory and Bernard into the kitchen)

MICHAEL:

(Parodying Harold)

You're *absolutely* paranoid about *absolutely* everything.

HAROLD: Oh, yeah, well, why don't you *not* tell me about it.

MICHAEL: You starve yourself all day, living on coffee and cottage cheese so that you can gorge yourself at one meal. Then you feel guilty and moan and groan about how fat you are and how ugly you are when the truth is you're no fatter or thinner than you ever are.

EMORY: Polly Paranoia.

(Emory moves to the coffee table to take Hank's empty plate)

HANK: Just great, Emory.

EMORY: Connie Casserole, no-trouble-at-all-oh-Mary, D.A.

MICHAEL:

(To Harold)

. . . And this pathological lateness. It's downright *crazy.*

HAROLD: Turning.

MICHAEL: Standing before a bathroom mirror for hours and hours before you can walk out on the street. And looking no different after Christ knows how many applications of Christ knows how many ointments and salves and creams and masks.

HAROLD: I've got bad skin, what can I tell you.

MICHAEL: Who wouldn't after they deliberately take a pair of tweezers and *deliberately* mutilate their pores—no wonder you've got holes in your face after the hack job you've done on yourself year in and year out!

HAROLD:

(Coolly but definitely)

You hateful sow.

MICHAEL: Yes, you've got scars on your face—but they're not that bad and if you'd leave yourself alone you wouldn't have any more than you've already awarded yourself.

HAROLD: You'd really like me to compliment you now for being so honest, wouldn't you? For being my best friend who will tell me what even my best friends won't tell me. Swine.

MICHAEL: And the pills!

(Announcement to group)

Harold has been gathering, saving, and storing up barbiturates for the last year like a goddamn squirrel. Hundreds of Nembutals, hundreds of Seconals. All in preparation for and anticipation of the long winter of his death.

(Silence)

But I tell you right now, Hallie. When the time comes, you'll never have the guts. It's not always like it happens in plays, not all faggots bump themselves off at the end of the story.

HAROLD: What you say may be true. Time will undoubtedly tell. But, in the meantime, you've left out one detail—the cosmetics and astringents are *paid* for, the bathroom is *paid* for, the tweezers are *paid* for, and the pills *are paid for!*

> (*Emory darts in and over to the light switch, plunges the room into darkness except for the light from the tapers on the buffet table, and begins to sing "Happy Birthday." Immediately Bernard pushes the swinging door open and Cowboy enters carrying a cake ablaze with candles. Everyone has now joined in with "Happy birthday, dear Harold, happy birthday to you." This is followed by a round of applause. Michael turns, goes to the bar, makes another drink*)

EMORY: Blow out your candles, Mary, and make a wish!

MICHAEL:

> (*To himself*)

Blow out your candles, *Laura.*

> (*Cowboy has brought cake over in front of Harold. He thinks a minute, blows out the candles. More applause*)

EMORY: Awwww, she's thirty-two years young!

HAROLD:

> (*Groans, holds his head*)

Ohh, my God!

> (*Bernard has brought in cake plates and forks. The room remains lit only by candlelight from the buffet table. Cowboy returns the cake to the table and Bernard begins to cut it and put the pieces on the plates*)

HANK: Now you have to open your gifts.

HAROLD: Do I have to open them here?

EMORY: Of course you've got to open them here.

> (*Hands Harold a gift. Harold begins to rip the paper off*)

HAROLD: Where's the card?

EMORY: Here.

HAROLD: Oh. From Larry.

> (*Finishes tearing off the paper*)

It's *heaven!* Oh, I just love it, Larry.

> (*Harold holds up a graphic design—a large-scale deed to Boardwalk, like those used in a Monopoly game*)

COWBOY: What is it?

HAROLD: It's the deed to Boardwalk.

EMORY: Oh, gay pop art!

DONALD:

> (*To Larry*)

It's sensational. Did you do it?

LARRY: Yes.

HAROLD: Oh, it's super, Larry. It goes up the minute I get home.

(Harold gives Larry a peck on the cheek)

COWBOY:

(To Harold)

I don't get it—you cruise Atlantic City or something?

MICHAEL: Will somebody get him out of here!

(Harold has torn open another gift, takes the card from inside)

HAROLD: Oh, what a nifty sweater! Thank you, Hank.

HANK: You can take it back and pick out another one if you want to.

HAROLD: I think this one is just nifty.

(Donald goes to the bar, makes himself a brandy and soda)

BERNARD: Who wants cake?

EMORY: Everybody?

DONALD: None for me.

MICHAEL: I'd just like to sleep on mine, thank you.

(Hank comes over to the table. Bernard gives him a plate of cake, passes another one to Cowboy and a third to Larry. Harold has torn the paper off another gift. Suddenly laughs aloud)

HAROLD: Oh, Bernard! How divine! Look, everybody! Bejeweled knee pads!

(Holds up a pair of basketball knee pads with sequin initials)

BERNARD: Monogrammed!

EMORY: Bernard, you're a camp!

MICHAEL: Y'all heard of Gloria DeHaven and Billy De Wolfe, well, dis here is Rosemary De Camp!

BERNARD: Who?

EMORY: I never miss a Rosemary De Camp picture.

HANK: I've never heard of her.

COWBOY: Me neither.

HANK: Not all of us spent their childhood in a movie house, Michael. Some of us played baseball.

DONALD: And mowed the lawn.

EMORY: Well, *I* know who Rosemary De Camp is.

MICHAEL: You would. It's a cinch you wouldn't recognize a baseball or a lawn mower.

(Harold has unwrapped his last gift. He is silent. Pause)

HAROLD: Thank you, Michael.

MICHAEL: What?

(Turns to see the gift)

Oh.

(A beat)

You're welcome.

(Michael finishes off his drink, returns to the bar)

LARRY: What is it, Harold?

(A beat)

HAROLD: It's a photograph of him in a silver frame. And there's an inscription engraved and the date.

BERNARD: What's it say?

HAROLD: Just . . . something personal.

(Michael spins round from the bar)

MICHAEL: Hey, Bernard, what do you say we have a little music to liven things up!

BERNARD: OK.

EMORY: Yeah, I feel like dancing.

MICHAEL: How about something good and ethnic, Emory—one of your specialties, like a military toe tap with sparklers.

EMORY: I don't do that at birthdays—only on the Fourth of July.

(Bernard puts on a romantic record. Emory goes to Bernard. They start to dance slowly)

LARRY: Come on, Michael.

MICHAEL: I only lead.

LARRY: I can follow.

(They start to dance)

HAROLD: Come on, Tex, you're on.

(Cowboy gets to his feet but is a washout as a dancing partner. Harold gives up, takes out another cigarette, strikes a match. As he does, he catches sight of someone over by the stairs, walks over to Alan. Blows out match)

Wanna dance?

EMORY:

(Sees Alan)

Uh-oh. Yvonne the Terrible is back.

MICHAEL: Oh, hello, Alan. Feel better? This is where you came in, isn't it?

(Alan starts to cross directly to the door. Michael breaks away)

Excuse me, Larry . . .

(Alan has reached the door and has started to open it as Michael intercepts, slams the door with one hand, and leans against it, crossing his legs)

As they say in the Deep South, don't rush off in the heat of the day.

HAROLD: Revolution complete.

(Michael slowly takes Alan by the arm, walks him slowly back into the room)

MICHAEL:. . . You missed the cake—and you missed the opening of the gifts—but you're still in luck. You're just in time for a party game.

(They have reached the phonograph. Michael rejects the record. The music stops, the dancing stops. Michael releases Alan, claps his hands)

. . . Hey, everybody! Game time!

(Alan starts to move. Michael catches him gently by the sleeve)

HAROLD: Why don't you just let him go, Michael?

MICHAEL: He can go if he wants to—but not before we play a little game.

EMORY: What's it going to be—movie-star gin?

MICHAEL: That's too faggy for Alan to play—he wouldn't be any good at it.

BERNARD: What about Likes and Dislikes?

(Michael lets go of Alan, takes a pencil and pad from the desk)

MICHAEL: It's too much trouble to find enough pencils, and besides, Emory always puts down the same thing. He dislikes artificial fruit and flowers and coffee grinders made into lamps—and he likes Mabel Mercer, poodles, and *All About Eve*—the screenplay of which he will then recite *verbatim*.

EMORY: I put down other things sometimes.

MICHAEL: Like a tan out of season?

EMORY: I just always put down little "Chi-Chi" because I adore her so much.

MICHAEL: If one is of the masculine gender, a poodle is the *insignia* of one's deviation.

BERNARD: You know why old ladies like poodles—because they go down on them.

EMORY: *They do not!*

LARRY: We could play B for Botticelli.

MICHAEL: We *could* play *Spin* the Botticelli, but we're not going to.

(A beat)

HAROLD: What would you like to play, Michael—the Truth Game?

(Michael chuckles to himself)

MICHAEL: Cute, Hallie.

HAROLD: Or do you want to play Murder? You all remember that one, don't you?

MICHAEL:

(To Harold)

Very, very cute.

DONALD: As I recall, they're quite similar. The rules are the same in both—you kill somebody.

MICHAEL: In affairs of the heart, there are no rules. Isn't that right, Harold?

HAROLD: That's what I always say.

MICHAEL: Well, that's the name of the game. The Affairs of the Heart.

COWBOY: I've never heard of that one.

MICHAEL: Of course you've never heard of it—I just made it up, baby doll. Affairs of the Heart is a combination of both the Truth Game and Murder—with a new twist.

HAROLD: I can hardly wait to find out what that is.

ALAN: Mickey, I'm leaving.

(Starts to move)

MICHAEL:

(Firmly, flatly)

Stay where you are.

HAROLD: Michael, let him go.

MICHAEL: He really doesn't *want* to. If he did, he'd have left a long time ago—or he wouldn't have come here in the first place.

ALAN:

(Holding his forehead)

. . . Mickey, I don't *feel* well!

MICHAEL:

(Low tone, but distinctly articulate)

My name is Michael. I am called Michael. You must never call anyone called Michael Mickey. Those of us who are named Michael are very nervous about it. If you don't believe it—try it.

ALAN: I'm sorry. I can't think.

MICHAEL: You can think. What you can't do—is leave. It's like watching an accident on the highway—you can't look at it and you can't look away.

ALAN: I . . . feel . . . weak . . .

MICHAEL: You are weak. Much weaker than I think you realize.

(Takes Alan by the arm, leads him to a chair. Slowly, deliberately, pushes him down into it)

Now! Who's going to play with Alan and me? Everyone?

HAROLD: I have no intention of playing.

DONALD: Nor do I.

MICHAEL: Well, not everyone is a participant in *life*. There are always those who stand on the sidelines and watch.

LARRY: What's the game?

MICHAEL: Simply this: We all have to call on the telephone the *one person* we truly believe we have loved.

HANK: I'm not playing.

LARRY: Oh, yes, you are.

HANK: You'd like for me to play, wouldn't you?

LARRY: You bet I would. I'd like to know who you'd call after all the fancy speeches I've heard lately. Who would you call? Would you call me?

MICHAEL:

(To Bernard)

Sounds like there's, how you say, trouble in paradise.

HAROLD: If there isn't, I think you'll be able to stir up some.

HANK: And who would *you* call? Don't think I think for one minute it would be me. Or that one call would do it. You'd have to make several, wouldn't you? About three long-distance and God only knows how many locals.

COWBOY: I'm glad I don't have to pay the bill.

MICHAEL: Quiet!

HAROLD:

> *(Loud whisper to Cowboy)*
>
> Oh, don't worry, Michael won't pay it either.

MICHAEL: Now, here's how it works.

LARRY: I thought you said there were no rules.

MICHAEL: That's right. In Affairs of the Heart, there are no rules. This is the goddamn point system!

> *(No response from anyone. A beat)*
>
> If you make the call, you get one point. If the person you are calling answers, you get two more points. If somebody else answers, you get only one. If there's no answer at all, you're screwed.

DONALD: You're screwed if you make the call.

HAROLD: You're a *fool*—if you screw yourself.

MICHAEL: When you get the person whom you are calling on the line—if you tell them who you are, you get two points. And then—if you tell them that you *love* them—you get a bonus of five more points!

HAROLD: Hateful.

MICHAEL: Therefore you can get as many as ten points and as few as one.

HAROLD: You can get as few as none—if you know how to work it.

MICHAEL: The one with the highest score wins.

ALAN: Hank. Let's get out of here.

EMORY: Well, now. Did you hear that!

MICHAEL: Just the two of you together. The pals . . . the guys . . . the buddy-buddies . . . the he-men.

EMORY: I think Larry might have something to say about that.

BERNARD: Emory.

MICHAEL: The duenna speaks.

> *(Crosses to take the telephone from the desk, brings it to the group)*
>
> So who's playing? Not including Cowboy, who, as a gift, is neuter. And, of course, le voyeur.
>
> *(A beat)*

Emory? Bernard?

BERNARD: I don't think I want to play.

MICHAEL: Why, Bernard! Where's your fun-loving spirit?

BERNARD: I don't think this game is fun.

HAROLD: It's absolutely hateful.

ALAN: Hank, leave with me.

HANK: You don't understand, Alan. I can't. You can . . . but I can't.

ALAN: Why, Hank? Why can't you?

LARRY:

> *(To Hank)*
>
> If he doesn't understand, why don't you explain it to him?

MICHAEL: *I'll* explain it.

HAROLD: I had a feeling you might.

MICHAEL: Although I doubt that it'll make any difference. That type refuses to understand that which they do not wish to accept. They reject certain facts. And Alan is decidedly from The Ostrich School of Reality.

(A beat)

Alan . . . Larry and Hank are lovers. Not just roommates, *bed*mates. *Lovers.*

ALAN: Michael!

MICHAEL: No man's still got a *roommate* when he's over thirty years old. If they're not lovers, they're sisters.

LARRY: Hank is the one who's over thirty.

MICHAEL: Well, you're pushing it!

ALAN: . . . Hank?

(A beat)

HANK: Yes, Alan. Larry is my lover.

ALAN: But . . . but . . . you're married.

(Michael, Larry, Emory, and Cowboy are sent into instant gales of laughter)

HAROLD: I think you said the wrong thing.

MICHAEL: Don't you love that quaint little idea—if a man is married, then he is automatically heterosexual.

(A beat)

Alan—Hank swings both ways—with a definite preference.

(A beat)

Now. Who makes the first call? Emory?

EMORY: You go, Bernard.

BERNARD: I don't want to.

EMORY: I don't want to either. I don't want to at all.

DONALD:

(To himself)

There are no accidents.

MICHAEL: Then, may I say, on your way home I hope you *will* yourself over an embankment.

EMORY:

(To Bernard)

Go on. Call up Peter Dahlbeck. That's who you'd like to call, isn't it?

MICHAEL: Who is Peter Dahlbeck?

EMORY: The boy in Detroit whose family Bernard's mother has been a laundress for since he was a pickaninny.

BERNARD: I worked for them too—after school and every summer.

EMORY: It's always been a large order of Hero Worship.

BERNARD: I think I've loved him all my life. But he never knew I was alive. Besides, he's straight.

COWBOY: So nothing ever happened between you?

EMORY: Oh, they finally made it—in the pool house one night after a drunken swimming party.

LARRY: With the right wine and the right music there're damn few that aren't curious.

MICHAEL: Sounds like there's a lot of Lady Chatterley in Mr. Dahlbeck, wouldn't you say, Donald?

DONALD: I've never been an O'Hara fan myself.

BERNARD: . . . And afterwards we went swimming in the nude in the dark with only the moon reflecting on the water.

DONALD: Nor Thomas Merton.

BERNARD: It was beautiful.

MICHAEL: How romantic. And then the next morning you took him his coffee and Alka-Seltzer on a tray.

BERNARD: It was in the afternoon. I remember I was worried sick all morning about having to face him. But he pretended like nothing at all had happened.

MICHAEL: Christ, he must have been so drunk he didn't remember a thing.

BERNARD: Yeah. I was sure relieved.

MICHAEL: Odd how that works. And now, for ten points, get that liar on the phone.

(A beat. Bernard picks up the phone, dials)

LARRY: You *know* the number?

BERNARD: Sure. He's back in Grosse Pointe, living at home. He just got separated from his third wife.

(All watch Bernard as he puts the receiver to his ear, waits. A beat. He hangs up quickly)

EMORY: D.A. or B.Y.?

MICHAEL: He didn't even give it time to find out.

(Coaxing)

Go ahead, Bernard. Pick up the phone and dial. You'll think of something. You know you want to call him. You know that, don't you? Well, go ahead. Your curiosity has got the best of you now. So . . . go on, call him.

(A beat. Bernard picks up the receiver, dials again. Lets it ring this time)

HAROLD: Hateful.

COWBOY: What's D.A. or B.Y.?

EMORY: That's operator lingo. It means—"Doesn't Answer" or "Busy."

BERNARD: . . . Hello?

MICHAEL: One point.

(Efficiently takes note on the pad)

BERNARD: Who's speaking? Oh . . . Mrs. Dahlbeck.

MICHAEL:

(Taking note)

One point.

BERNARD: . . . It's Bernard—Francine's boy.

EMORY: *Son*, not *boy*.

BERNARD:. . . How are you? Good. Good. Oh, just fine, thank you. Mrs. Dahlbeck . . .
is . . . Peter . . . at home? Oh. Oh, I see.

MICHAEL:

(Shakes his head)

Shhhhiiii . . .

BERNARD:. . . Oh, no. No, it's nothing important. I just wanted to . . . to tell him . . .
that . . . to tell him I . . . I . . .

MICHAEL:

(Prompting flatly)

I love him. That I've always loved him.

BERNARD:. . . that I was sorry to hear about him and his wife.

MICHAEL: No points!

BERNARD:. . . My mother wrote me. Yes. It is. It really is. Well. Would you just tell him I
called and said . . . that I was . . . just . . . very, very sorry to hear and I . . .
hope . . . they can get everything straightened out. Yes. Yes. Well, good night.
Goodbye.

(Hangs up slowly. Michael draws a definite line across his pad, makes a definite
period)

MICHAEL: Two points total. Terrible. Next!

(Michael whisks the phone out of Bernard's hands, gives it to Emory)

EMORY: Are you all right, Bernard?

BERNARD:

(Almost to himself)

Why did I call? Why did I do that?

LARRY:

(To Bernard)

Where was he?

BERNARD: Out on a date.

MICHAEL: Come on, Emory. Punch in.

(Emory picks up the phone, dials information. A beat)

EMORY: Could I have the number, please—in the Bronx—for a Delbert Botts.

LARRY: A Delbert Botts! How many can there be!

BERNARD: Oh, I wish I hadn't called now.

EMORY:. . . No, the residence number, please.

(Waves his hand at Michael, signaling for the pencil. Michael hands it to him. He
writes on the white plastic phone case)

. . . Thank you.

(A beat. And he indignantly slams down the receiver)

I do wish information would stop calling me "Ma'am"!

MICHAEL: By all means, scribble all over the telephone.

(*Snatches the pencil from Emory's hands*)

EMORY: It comes off with a little spit.

MICHAEL: Like a lot of things.

LARRY: Who the hell is Delbert Botts?

EMORY: The one person I have always loved.

(*To Michael*)

That's who you said call, isn't it?

MICHAEL: That's right, Emory Board.

LARRY: How could you love anybody with a name like that?

MICHAEL: Yes, Emory, you couldn't love anybody with a name like that. It wouldn't look good on a place card. Isn't that right, Alan?

(*Michael slaps Alan on the shoulder. Alan is silent. Michael snickers*)

EMORY: I admit his name is not so good—but he is absolutely beautiful. At least, he was when I was in high school. Of course, I haven't seen him since and he was about seven years older than I even then.

MICHAEL: Christ, you better call him quick before he dies.

EMORY: I've loved him ever since the first day I laid eyes on him, which was when I was in the fifth grade and he was a senior. Then, he went away to college and by the time he got out *I* was in high school, and he had become a dentist.

MICHAEL:

(*With incredulous disgust*)

A dentist!

EMORY: Yes. Delbert Botts, D.D.S. And he opened his office in a bank building.

HAROLD: And you went and had every tooth in your head pulled out, right?

EMORY: No. I just had my teeth cleaned, that's all.

(*Donald turns from the bar with two drinks in his hands*)

BERNARD:

(*To himself*)

Oh, I shouldn't have called.

MICHAEL: Will you shut up, Bernard! And take your boring, sleep-making icks somewhere else. *Go!*

(*Michael extends a pointed finger toward the steps. Bernard takes the wine bottle and his glass and moves toward the stairs, pouring himself another drink on the way*)

EMORY: I remember I looked right into his eyes the whole time and I kept wanting to bite his fingers.

HAROLD: Well, it's absolutely mind-boggling.

MICHAEL: Phyllis Phallic.

HAROLD: It absolutely boggles the mind.

(*Donald brings one of the drinks to Alan. Alan takes it, drinks it down*)

MICHAEL:

(*Referring to Donald*)

Sara Samaritan.

EMORY: . . . I told him I was having my teeth cleaned for the Junior-Senior Prom, for which I was in charge of decorations. I told him it was a celestial theme and I was cutting stars out of tinfoil and making clouds out of chicken wire and angel's hair.

(A beat)

He couldn't have been less impressed.

COWBOY: I got angel's hair down my shirt once at Christmastime. Gosh, did it itch!

EMORY: . . . I told him I was going to burn incense in pots so that white fog would hover over the dance floor and it would look like heaven—just like I'd seen it in a Rita Hayworth movie. I can't remember the title.

MICHAEL: The picture was called *Down to Earth*. Any *kid* knows that.

COWBOY: . . . And it made little tiny cuts in the creases of my fingers. Man, did they sting! It would be terrible if you got that stuff in your . . .

(Michael circles slowly toward him)

I'll be quiet.

EMORY: He was engaged to this stupid-ass girl named Loraine whose mother was truly Supercunt.

MICHAEL: Don't digress.

EMORY: Well, anyway, I was a wreck. I mean a total mess. I couldn't eat, sleep, stand up, sit down, *nothing*. I could hardly cut out silver stars or finish the clouds for the prom. So I called him on the telephone and asked if I could see him alone.

HAROLD: Clearly not the coolest of moves.

(Donald looks at Alan. Alan looks away)

EMORY: He said OK and told me to come by his house. I was so nervous my hands were shaking and my voice was unsteady. I couldn't look at him this time—I just stared straight in space and blurted out why I'd come. I told him . . . I wanted him to be my friend. I said that I had never had a friend who I could talk to and tell everything and trust. I asked him if he would be my friend.

COWBOY: You poor bastard.

MICHAEL: SHHHHHH!

BERNARD: What'd he say?

EMORY: He said he would be glad to be my friend. And anytime I ever wanted to see him or call him—to just call him and he'd see me. And he shook my trembling wet hand and I left on a cloud.

MICHAEL: One of the ones you made yourself.

EMORY: And the next day I went and bought him a gold-plated cigarette lighter and had his initials monogrammed on it and wrote a card that said "From your friend, Emory."

HAROLD: Seventeen years old and already big with the gifts.

COWBOY: Yeah. And cards too.

EMORY: . . . And then the night of the prom I found out.

BERNARD: Found out what?

EMORY: I heard two girls I knew giggling together. They were standing behind some goddamn corrugated-cardboard Greek columns I had borrowed from a department store and had draped with yards and yards of goddamn cheesecloth. Oh, Mary, it takes a fairy to make something pretty.

MICHAEL: *Don't digress.*

EMORY: This girl who was telling the story said she had heard it from her mother—and her mother had heard it from Loraine's mother.

(To Michael)

You see, Loraine and her mother were not beside the point.

(Back to the group)

Obviously, Del had told Loraine about my calling and about the gift.

(A beat)

Pretty soon everybody at the dance had heard about it and they were laughing and making jokes. Everybody knew I had a crush on Doctor Delbert Botts and that I had asked him to be my friend.

(A beat)

What they didn't know was that I *loved* him. And that I would go on loving him years after they had all forgotten my funny secret.

(Pause)

HAROLD: Well, I for one need an insulin injection.

MICHAEL: *Call him.*

BERNARD: Don't, Emory.

MICHAEL: Since when are you telling him what to do!

EMORY:

(To Bernard)

What do I care—I'm pissed! I'll do anything. Three times.

BERNARD: Don't. *Please!*

MICHAEL: I said call him.

BERNARD: Don't! You'll be sorry. Take my word for it.

EMORY: What have I got to lose?

BERNARD: Your dignity. That's what you've got to lose.

MICHAEL: Well, *that's* a knee-slapper! I love *your* telling *him* about dignity when you allow him to degrade you constantly by Uncle Tom–ing you to death.

BERNARD: *He* can do it, Michael. *I* can do it. But *you can't* do it.

MICHAEL: Isn't that discrimination?

BERNARD: I don't like it from him and I don't like it from me—but I do it to myself and I let him do it. I let him do it because it's the only thing that, to him, makes him my equal. We both got the short end of the stick—but I got a hell of a lot more than he did and he knows it. I let him Uncle Tom me just so he can tell himself he's not a complete loser.

MICHAEL: How very considerate.

BERNARD: It's his defense. You have your defense, Michael. But it's indescribable.

(Emory quietly licks his finger and begins to rub the number off the telephone case)

MICHAEL:

(To Bernard)

Y'all want to hear a little polite parlor jest from the liberal Deep South? Do you know why *Nigras* have such big lips? Because they're always going "P-p-p-p-a-a-a-h!"

(The labial noise is exasperating with lazy disgust as he shuffles about the room)

DONALD: Christ, Michael!

MICHAEL:

(Unsuccessfully tries to tear the phone away from Emory)

I can do without your goddamn spit all over my telephone, you nellie coward.

EMORY: I may be nellie, but I'm no coward.

(Starts to dial)

Bernard, forgive me. I'm sorry. I won't ever say those things to you again.

(Michael watches triumphant. Bernard pours another glass of wine. A beat)

B.Y.

MICHAEL: It's busy?

EMORY:

(Nods)

Loraine is probably talking to her mother. Oh, yes. Delbert married Loraine.

MICHAEL: I'm sorry, you'll have to forfeit your turn. We can't wait.

(Takes the phone, hands it to Larry, who starts to dial)

HAROLD: Well, you're not wasting any time.

(To Larry)

HANK: Who are you calling?

LARRY: Charlie.

(Emory gets up, jerks the phone out of Larry's hands)

EMORY: I refuse to forfeit my turn! It's *my turn*, and I'm taking it!

MICHAEL: That's the spirit, Emory! *Hit that iceberg—don't miss it! Hit it! Goddamn it!* I want a smash of a finale!

EMORY: Oh, God, I'm drunk.

MICHAEL: A falling-down-drunk-nellie-queen.

HAROLD: Well, that's the pot calling the kettle beige!

MICHAEL:

(Snapping. To Harold)

I am not drunk! You cannot tell that I am drunk! Donald! I'm not drunk! Am I!

DONALD: *I'm* drunk.

EMORY: So am I. I am a *major drunk.*

MICHAEL:

>*(To Emory)*

>Shut up and dial!

EMORY:

>*(Dialing)*

>I am a major drunk of this or any other season.

DONALD:

>*(To Michael)*

>Don't you mean shut up and *deal*?

EMORY: . . . It's ringing. It is no longer B.Y. Hello?

MICHAEL:

>*(Taking note)*

>One point.

EMORY: . . . Who's speaking? Who? . . . Doctor Delbert Botts?

MICHAEL: Two points.

EMORY: Oh, Del, is this really you? Oh, nobody. You don't know me. You wouldn't remember me. I'm . . . just a friend. A falling-down drunken friend. Hello? Hello? Hello?

>*(Lowers the receiver)*

>He hung up.

>*(Emory hangs up the telephone)*

MICHAEL: Three points total. You're winning.

EMORY: He said I must have the wrong party.

>*(Bernard gets up, goes into the kitchen)*

HAROLD: He's right. We have the wrong party. We should be somewhere else.

EMORY: It's your party, Hallie. Aren't you having a good time?

HAROLD: Simply fabulous. And what about you? Are you having a good time, Emory? Are you having as good a time as you thought you would?

>*(Larry takes the phone)*

MICHAEL: If you're bored, Harold, we could sing "Happy Birthday" again—to the tune of "Havah Nageelah."

>*(Harold takes out another cigarette)*

HAROLD: Not for all the tea in Mexico.

>*(Lights up)*

HANK: My turn now.

LARRY: It's my turn to call Charlie.

HANK: No. Let me.

LARRY: Are *you* going to call Charlie?

MICHAEL: The score is three to two. Emory's favor.

ALAN: Don't, Hank. Don't you see—Bernard was right.

HANK:

>*(Firmly, to Alan)*
>
>I want to.
>
>*(A beat. Holds out his hand for the phone)*
>
>Larry?
>
>*(A beat)*

LARRY:

>*(Gives him the phone)*
>
>Be my eager guest.

COWBOY:

>*(To Larry)*
>
>Is he going to call Charlie for you?
>
>*(Larry breaks into laughter. Hank starts to dial)*

LARRY: Charlie is all the people I cheat on Hank with.

DONALD: With whom I cheat on Hank.

MICHAEL: The butcher, the baker, the candlestick maker.

LARRY: Right! I love 'em all. And what he refuses to understand—is that I've got to *have* 'em all. I am *not* the marrying kind, and I never will be.

HAROLD: Gypsy feet.

LARRY: Who are you calling?

MICHAEL: Jealous?

LARRY: Curious as hell!

MICHAEL: And a little jealous too.

LARRY: Who are you calling?

MICHAEL: Did it ever occur to you that Hank might be doing the same thing behind your back that you do behind his?

LARRY: I wish to Christ he would. It'd make life a hell of a lot easier. Who are you calling?

HAROLD: Whoever it is, they're not sitting on top of the telephone.

HANK: Hello?

COWBOY: They must have been in the tub.

MICHAEL:

>*(Snaps at Cowboy)*
>
>Eighty-six!
>
>*(Cowboy goes over to a far corner, sits down. Bernard enters, uncorking another bottle of wine. Taking note)*
>
>One point.

HANK: . . . I'd like to leave a message.

MICHAEL: Not in. One point.

HANK: Would you say that Hank called? Yes, it is. Oh, good evening. How are you?

LARRY: Who the hell *is* that?

HANK: Yes, that's right—the message is for my roommate, Larry. Just say that I called and . . .

LARRY: It's our answering service!

HANK: . . . and said . . . I love you.

MICHAEL: *Five points!* You said it! You get five goddamn points for saying it!

ALAN: Hank! Hank! . . . Are you crazy?

HANK: . . . No. You didn't hear me incorrectly. That's what I said. The message is for Larry and it's from me, Hank, and it is just as I said: *I . . . love . . . you.* Thanks.

(*Hangs up*)

MICHAEL: Seven points total! Hank, you're ahead, baby. You're way, way ahead of everybody!

ALAN: Why? . . . Oh, Hank, why? Why did you do that?

HANK: Because I do love him. And I don't care who knows it.

ALAN: Don't say that.

HANK: Why not? It's the truth.

ALAN: I can't believe you.

HANK:

(*Directly to Alan*)

I left my wife and family for Larry.

ALAN: I'm really not interested in hearing about it.

MICHAEL: Sure you are. Go ahead, Hankola, tell him all about it.

ALAN: No! I don't want to hear it. It's disgusting!

(*A beat*)

HANK: Some men do it for another woman.

ALAN: Well, I could understand *that*. That's *normal*.

HANK: It just doesn't always work out that way, Alan. No matter how you might want it to. And God knows, nobody ever wanted it more than I did. I really and truly felt that I was in love with my wife when I married her. It wasn't altogether my trying to prove something to myself. I did love her and she loved me. But . . . there was always that something there . . .

DONALD: You mean your attraction to your own sex.

HANK: Yes.

ALAN: Always?

HANK: I don't know. I suppose so.

EMORY: I've known what I was since I was four years old.

MICHAEL: Everybody's always known it about *you*, Emory.

DONALD: I've always known it about myself too.

HANK: I don't know when it was that I started admitting it to myself. For so long I either labeled it something else or denied it completely.

MICHAEL: Christ-was-I-drunk-last-night.

HANK: And then there came a time when I just couldn't lie to myself anymore . . . I thought about it but I never did anything about it. I think the first time was during my wife's last pregnancy. We lived near New Haven—in the country. She and the kids still live there. Well, anyway, there was a teachers' meeting here in New York. She didn't feel up to the trip and I came alone. And that day on the train I began to think about it and think about it and think about it. I thought of nothing else the whole trip. And within fifteen minutes after I had arrived I had picked up a guy in the men's room of Grand Central Station.

ALAN:

(Quietly)

Jesus.

HANK: I'd never done anything like that in my life before and I was scared to death. But he turned out to be a nice fellow. I've never seen him again and it's funny I can't even remember his name anymore.

(A beat)

Anyway. After that, it got easier.

HAROLD: Practice makes perfect.

HANK: And then . . . sometime later . . . not very long after, Larry was in New Haven and we met at a party my wife and I had gone in town for.

EMORY: And your real troubles began.

HANK: That was two years ago.

LARRY: Why am I always the goddamn villain in the piece! If I'm not thought of as a happy-home wrecker, I'm an impossible son of a bitch to live with!

HAROLD: Guilt turns to hostility. Isn't that right, Michael?

MICHAEL: Go stick your tweezers in your cheek.

LARRY: I'm fed up to the teeth with everybody feeling so goddamn sorry for poor shat-upon Hank.

EMORY: Aw, Larry, everybody knows you're Frieda Fickle.

LARRY: I've never made any promises and I never intend to. It's my right to lead my sex life without answering to *anybody*—Hank included! And if those terms are not acceptable, then we must not live together. Numerous relations is a part of the way I am!

EMORY: You don't have to be gay to be a wanton.

LARRY: By the way I am, I don't mean being gay—I mean my sexual appetite. And I don't think of myself as a wanton. Emory, you are the most promiscuous person I know.

EMORY: I am not promiscuous at all!

MICHAEL: Not by choice. By design. Why would anybody want to go to bed with a flaming little sissy like you?

BERNARD: Michael!

MICHAEL:

(To Emory)

Who'd make a pass at you—I'll tell you who—nobody. Except maybe some fugitive from the Braille Institute.

BERNARD:

(To Emory)

Why do you let him talk to you that way?

HAROLD: Physical beauty is not everything.

MICHAEL: Thank you, Quasimodo.

LARRY: What do you think it's like living with the goddamn gestapo! I can't breathe without getting the third degree!

MICHAEL: Larry, it's your turn to call.

LARRY: I can't take all that let's-be-faithful-and-never-look-at-another-person routine. It just doesn't work. If you want to promise that, fine. Then do it and stick to it. But if you *have* to promise it—as far as I'm concerned—nothing finishes a relationship faster.

HAROLD: Give me Librium or give me Meth.

BERNARD:

> (Intoxicated now)

> Yeah, freedom, baby! Freedom!

LARRY: You gotta have it! It can't work any other way. And the ones who swear their undying fidelity are lying. Most of them, anyway—ninety percent of them. They cheat on each other constantly and lie through their teeth. I'm sorry, I can't be like that and it drives Hank up the wall.

HANK: There is that ten percent.

LARRY: The only way it stands a chance is with some sort of an understanding.

HANK: I've tried to go along with that.

LARRY: Aw, *come on!*

HANK: I agreed to an agreement.

LARRY: Your agreement.

MICHAEL: What agreement?

LARRY: A ménage.

HAROLD: The lover's agreement.

LARRY: Look, I know a lot of people think it's the answer. They don't consider it cheating. But it's not my style.

HANK: Well, *I* certainly didn't want it.

LARRY: Then who suggested it?

HANK: It was a compromise.

LARRY: Exactly.

HANK: And you agreed.

LARRY: I didn't agree to anything. You agreed to your own proposal and *informed me* that I agreed.

COWBOY: I don't understand. What's a me . . . mena-a . . .

MICHAEL: A ménage à trois, baby. Two's company—three's a ménage.

COWBOY: Oh.

HANK: It works for some.

LARRY: Well, I'm not one for group therapy. I'm sorry, I can't relate to anyone or anything that way. I'm old-fashioned—I like 'em all, but I like 'em one at a time!

MICHAEL:

> (To Larry)

> Did you like Donald as a single side attraction?

> (Pause)

LARRY: Yes. I did.

DONALD: So did I, Larry.

LARRY:

> *(To Donald, referring to Michael)*

> Did you tell him?

DONALD: No.

MICHAEL: It was perfectly obvious from the moment you walked in. What was the song and dance about having seen each other but never having met?

DONALD: It was true. We saw each other in the baths and went to bed together, but we never spoke a word and never knew each other's name.

EMORY: You have better luck than I do. If I don't get arrested, my trick announces upon departure that he's been exposed to hepatitis! One more shot of gamma globulin and my ass'll look like a pair of colanders!

MICHAEL: In spring a young man's fancy turns to a fancy young man.

LARRY:

> *(To Hank)*

> Don't look at me like that. You've been playing footsie with the Blue Book all night.

DONALD: I think he only wanted to show you what's good for the gander is good for the gander.

HANK: That's right.

LARRY:

> *(To Hank)*

> I suppose you'd like the three of us to have a go at it.

HANK: At least it'd be together.

LARRY: That point eludes me.

HANK: What kind of an understanding do you *want!*

LARRY: Respect—for each other's freedom. With no need to lie or pretend. In my own way, Hank, I love you, but you have to understand that even though I do want to go on living with you, sometimes there may be others. I don't want to flaunt it in your face. If it happens, I know I'll never mention it. But if you ask me, I'll tell you. I don't want to hurt you, but I won't lie to you if you want to know anything about me.

BERNARD: He gets points.

MICHAEL: What?

BERNARD: He said it. He said "I love you" to Hank. He gets the bonus.

MICHAEL: He didn't call him.

DONALD: He called him. He just didn't use the telephone.

MICHAEL: Then he doesn't get any points.

BERNARD: He gets five points!

MICHAEL: He didn't use the telephone. He doesn't get a goddamn thing!

> *(Larry goes to the phone, picks up the receiver, looks at the number of the second line, dials. A beat. The phone rings)*

LARRY: It's for you, Hank. Why don't you take it upstairs?

> *(The phone continues to ring. Hank gets up, goes up the stairs to the bedroom. Pause. He presses the second-line button, picks up the receiver. Everyone downstairs is silent)*

HANK: Hello?

BERNARD: One point.

LARRY: Hello, Hank.

BERNARD: Two points.

LARRY: . . . This is Larry.

BERNARD: Two more points!

LARRY: . . . For what it's worth, I love you.

BERNARD: Five points bonus!

HANK: I'll . . . I'll try.

LARRY: I will too.

>(Hangs up. Hank hangs up)

BERNARD: That's ten points total!

EMORY: Larry's the winner!

HAROLD: Well, that wasn't as much fun as I thought it would be.

MICHAEL: THE GAME ISN'T OVER YET!

>(Hank moves toward the bed into darkness)

Your turn, Alan.

>(Michael gets the phone, slams it down in front of Alan)

PICK UP THE PHONE, BUSTER!

EMORY: Michael, don't!

MICHAEL: STAY OUT OF THIS!

EMORY: You don't have to, Alan. You don't have to.

ALAN: Emory . . . I'm sorry for what I did before.

>(A beat)

EMORY: . . . Oh, forget it.

MICHAEL: Forgive us our trespasses. Christ, now you're both joined at the goddamn hip! You can decorate his home, Emory—and he can get you out of jail the next time you're arrested on a morals charge.

>(A beat)

Who are you going to call, Alan?

>(No response)

Can't remember anyone? Well, maybe you need a minute to think. Is that it?

>(No response)

HAROLD: I believe this will be the final round.

COWBOY: Michael, aren't you going to call anyone?

HAROLD: How could he? He's never loved anyone.

MICHAEL:

>(Sings the classic vaudeville walk-off to Harold)

"No matter how you figger,
It's tough to be a nigger,

(Indicates Bernard)

But it's tougher
To be a Jeeeew-ooouu-oo!"

DONALD: My God, Michael, you're a charming host.

HAROLD: Michael doesn't have charm, Donald. Michael has counter-charm.

(Larry crosses to the stairs)

MICHAEL: Going somewhere?

(Larry stops, turns to Michael)

LARRY: Yes. Excuse me.

(Turns, goes up the stairs)

MICHAEL: You're going to miss the end of the game.

LARRY: You can tell me how it comes out.

(Pauses on stairs)

MICHAEL: I never reveal an ending. And no one will be reseated during the climactic revelation.

LARRY: With any luck, I won't be back until it's all over.

(Turns, continues up the stairs into the dark)

MICHAEL:

(Into Alan's ear)

What do you suppose is going on up there? Hmmm, Alan? What do you imagine Larry and Hank are doing? Hmmmmm? Shooting marbles?

EMORY: Whatever they're doing, they're not hurting anyone.

HAROLD: And they're minding their own business.

MICHAEL: And you mind yours, Harold. I'm warning you!

(A beat)

HAROLD:

(Coolly)

Are you now? Are you warning *me*? *Me*? I'm Harold. I'm the one person you don't warn, Michael. Because you and I are a match. And we tread very softly with each other because we both play each other's game too well. Oh, I know this game you're playing.

I know it very well. And I play it very well. You play it very well too. But you know what, I'm the only one that's better at it than you are. I can beat you at it. So don't push me. I'm warning *you*.

(A beat. Michael starts to laugh)

MICHAEL: You're funny, Hallie. A laff riot. Isn't he funny, Alan? Or, as you might say, isn't he amusing? He's an amusing faggot, isn't he? Or, as you might say, freak. That's what you called Emory, wasn't it? A freak? A pansy? My, what an antiquated vocabulary you have. I'm surprised you didn't say sodomite or pederast.

(A beat)

You'd better let me bring you up to date. Now it's not so new, but it might be new to you—

(A beat)

Have you heard the term "closet queen"? Do you know what that means? Do you know what it means to be "in the closet"?

EMORY: Don't, Michael. It won't help anything to explain what it means.

MICHAEL: He already knows. He knows very, very well what a closet queen is. Don't you, Alan?

(Pause)

ALAN: Michael, if you are insinuating that I am homosexual, I can only say that you are mistaken.

MICHAEL: Am I?

(A beat)

What about Justin Stuart?

ALAN: . . . What about . . . Justin Stuart?

MICHAEL: You were in love with him, that's what about him.

(A beat)

And *that* is who you are going to call.

ALAN: Justin and I were very good friends. That is all. Unfortunately, we had a parting of the ways and that was the end of the friendship. We have not spoken for years. I most certainly will not call him now.

MICHAEL: According to Justin, the friendship was quite passionate.

ALAN: What do you mean?

MICHAEL: I mean that you slept with him in college. Several times.

ALAN: That is not true!

MICHAEL: Several times. One time, it's youth. Twice, a phase maybe. Several times, *you like it!*

ALAN: IT'S NOT TRUE!

MICHAEL: Yes, it is. Because Justin Stuart *is* homosexual. He comes to New York on occasion. He calls me. I've taken him to parties. Larry "had" him once. *I* have slept with Justin Stuart. And he has told me all about *you.*

ALAN: Then he told you a lie.

(A beat)

MICHAEL: You were obsessed with Justin. That's all you talked about, morning, noon, and night. You started doing it about Hank upstairs tonight. What an attractive fellow he is and all that transparent crap.

ALAN: He *is* an attractive fellow. What's wrong with saying so?

MICHAEL: Would you like to join him and Larry right now?

ALAN: I said he was attractive. That's all.

MICHAEL: How many times do you have to say it? How many times did you have to say it about Justin: what a good tennis player he was; what a good dancer he was; what a good body he had; what good taste he had; how bright he was—how

amusing he was—how the girls were all mad for him—what close friends you
were.

ALAN: We . . . we . . . were . . . very close . . . very good . . . friends. *That's all.*

MICHAEL: It was *obvious*—and when you did it around Fran it was downright
embarrassing. Even she must have had her doubts about you.

ALAN: *Justin . . . lied.* If he told you that, he lied. It is a lie. A vicious lie. He'd say
anything about me now to get even. He could never get over the fact that *I*
dropped *him.* But I had to. I had to because . . . he told me . . . he told me
about himself . . . he told me that he wanted to be my lover. And I . . . I . . .
told him . . . he made me sick . . . I told him I pitied him.

(*A beat*)

MICHAEL: You ended the friendship, Alan, because you couldn't face the truth about
yourself. You could go along, sleeping with Justin, as long as he lied to himself
and you lied to yourself and you both dated girls and labeled yourselves men
and called yourselves just fond friends. But Justin finally had to be honest
about the truth, and you couldn't take it. You couldn't take it and so you
destroyed the friendship and your friend along with it.

(*Michael goes to the desk and gets address book*)

ALAN: No!

MICHAEL: Justin could never understand what he'd done wrong to make you cut him
off. He blamed himself.

ALAN: No!

MICHAEL: He did until he eventually found out who he was and what he was.

ALAN: No!

MICHAEL: But to this day he still remembers the treatment—the scars he got from you.

(*Puts address book in front of Alan on coffee table*)

ALAN: NO!

MICHAEL: Pick up this phone and call Justin. Call him and apologize and tell him what
you should have told him twelve years ago.

(*Picks up the phone, shoves it at Alan*)

ALAN: NO! HE LIED! NOT A WORD IS TRUE!

MICHAEL: CALL HIM!

(*Alan won't take the phone*)

All right then, *I'll dial!*

HAROLD: You're so helpful.

(*Michael starts to dial*)

ALAN: Give it to me.

(*Michael hands Alan the receiver. Alan takes it, hangs up for a moment, lifts it
again, starts to dial. Everyone watches silently. Alan finishes dialing, lifts the
receiver to his ear*)

. . . Hello?

MICHAEL: One point.

ALAN: . . . It's . . . it's Alan.

MICHAEL: Two points.

ALAN: . . . Yes, yes, it's *me*.

MICHAEL: Is it Justin?

ALAN: . . . You sound surprised.

MICHAEL: I should hope to think so—after twelve years! Two more points.

ALAN: I . . . I'm in New York. Yes. I . . . I won't explain now . . . I . . . I just called to tell you . . .

MICHAEL: THAT I LOVE YOU, GODDAMNIT! I LOVE YOU!

ALAN: I love you.

MICHAEL: You get the goddamn bonus. TEN POINTS TOTAL! JACKPOT!

ALAN: I love you and I beg you to forgive me.

MICHAEL: Give me that!

> (*Snatches the phone from Alan*)

> Justin! Did you hear what that son of a bitch said!

> (*A beat. Michael is speechless for a moment*)

> . . . Fran?

> (*A beat*)

> Well, of course I expected it to be you! . . .

> (*A beat*)

> How are you? Me too. Yes, yes . . . he told me everything. Oh, don't thank *me*. Please . . . Please . . .

> (*A beat*)

> I'll . . . I'll put him back on.

> (*A beat*)

> My love to the kids . . .

ALAN: . . . Darling? I'll take the first plane I can get. Yes. I'm sorry too. I love you very much.

> (*Hangs up, stands, crosses to the door, stops. Turns around, surveys the group*)

> Thank you, Michael.

> (*Opens the door and exits. Silence. Michael slowly sinks down on the couch, covering his face. Pause*)

COWBOY: Who won?

DONALD: It was a tie.

> (*Harold crosses to Michael*)

HAROLD:

> (*Calmly, coldly, clinically*)

> Now it is my turn. And ready or not, Michael, here goes.

(A beat)

You are a sad and pathetic man. You're a homosexual and you don't want to be. But there is nothing you can do to change it. Not all your prayers to your God, not all the analysis you can buy in all the years you've got left to live. You may very well one day be able to know a heterosexual life if you want it desperately enough—if you pursue it with the fervor with which you annihilate—but you will always be homosexual as well. Always, Michael. Always. Until the day you die.

(Turns, gathers his gifts, goes to Emory. Emory stands up unsteadily)

Oh, friends, thanks for the nifty party and the super gift.

(Looks toward Cowboy)

It's just what I needed.

(Emory smiles. Harold gives him a hug, spots Bernard sitting on the floor, head bowed)

. . . Bernard, thank you.

(No response. To Emory)

Will you get him home?

EMORY: Don't worry about her. I'll take care of everything.

(Harold turns to Donald, who is at the bar making himself another drink)

HAROLD: Donald, good to see you.

DONALD: Good night, Harold. See you again sometime.

HAROLD: Yeah. How about a year from Shavuoth?

(Harold goes to Cowboy)

Come on, Tex. Let's go to my place.

(Cowboy gets up, comes to him)

Are you good in bed?

COWBOY: Well . . . I'm not like the average hustler you'd meet. I try to show a little affection—it keeps me from feeling like such a whore.

(A beat. Harold turns. Cowboy opens the door for them. They start out. Harold pauses)

HAROLD: Oh, Michael . . . thanks for the laughs. Call you tomorrow.

(No response. A beat. Harold and Cowboy exit)

EMORY: Come on, Bernard. Time to go home.

(Emory, frail as he is, manages to pull Bernard's arm around his neck, gets him on his feet)

Oh, Mary, you're a heavy mother.

BERNARD:

(Practically inaudible mumble)

Why did I call? Why?

EMORY: Thank you, Michael. Good night, Donald.

DONALD: Goodbye, Emory.

BERNARD: Why . . .

EMORY: It's all right, Bernard. Everything's all right. I'm going to make you some coffee and everything's going to be all right.

(Emory virtually carries Bernard out. Donald closes the door. Silence. Michael slowly slips from the couch onto the floor. A beat. Then slowly he begins a low moan that increases in volume—almost like a siren. Suddenly he slams his open hands to his ears)

MICHAEL:

(In desperate panic)

Donald! Donald! DONALD! DONALD!

(Donald puts down his drink, rushes to Michael. Michael is now white with fear, and tears are bursting from his eyes. He begins to gasp his words)

Oh, no! No! What have I done! Oh, my God, what have I done!

(Michael writhing. Donald holds him, cradles him in his arms)

DONALD: Michael! Michael!

MICHAEL:

(Weeping)

Oh, no! NO! It's beginning! The liquor is starting to wear off and the anxiety is beginning! Oh, NO! No! I feel it! I know it's going to happen. Donald!! Donald! Don't leave me! Please! Please! Oh, my God, what have I done! Oh, Jesus, the guilt! I can't handle it anymore. I won't make it!

DONALD:

(Physically subduing him)

Michael! Michael! Stop it! Stop it! I'll give you a Valium—I've got some in my pocket!

MICHAEL:

(Hysterical)

No! No! Pills and alcohol—I'll die!

DONALD: I'm not going to give you the whole bottle! Come on, let go of me!

MICHAEL:

(Clutching him)

NO!

DONALD: Let go of me long enough for me to get my hand in my pocket!

MICHAEL: Don't leave!

(Michael quiets down a bit, lets go of Donald enough for him to take a small plastic bottle from his pocket and open it to give Michael a tranquilizer)

DONALD: Here.

MICHAEL:

>*(Sobbing)*

>I don't have any water to swallow it with!

DONALD: Well, if you'll wait one goddamn minute, I'll get you some!

>*(Michael lets go of him. He goes to the bar, gets a glass of water and returns)*

>Your water, your Majesty.

>*(A beat)*

>Michael, stop that goddamn crying and take this pill!

>*(Michael straightens up, puts the pill into his mouth amid choking sobs, takes the water, drinks, returns the glass to Donald)*

MICHAEL: I'm like Ole Man River—tired of livin' and scared o' dyin'.

>*(Donald puts the glass on the bar, comes back to the couch, sits down. Michael collapses into his arms, sobbing. Pause)*

DONALD: Shhhhh. Shhhhhh. Michael. Shhhhhh. Michael. Michael.

>*(Donald rocks him back and forth. He quiets. Pause)*

MICHAEL: . . . If we . . . if we could just . . . not hate ourselves so much. That's it, you know. If we could just *learn* not to hate ourselves quite so very much.

DONALD: Yes, I know. I know.

>*(A beat)*

>Inconceivable as it may be, you used to be worse than you are now.

>*(A beat)*

>Maybe with a lot more work you can help yourself some more—if you try.

>*(Michael straightens up, dries his eyes on his sleeve)*

MICHAEL: Who was it that used to always say, "You show me a happy homosexual, and I'll show you a gay corpse"?

DONALD: I don't know. Who was it who always used to say that?

MICHAEL: And how dare you come on with that holier-than-thou attitude with me! "A lot more work," "if I try," indeed! You've got a long row to hoe before you're perfect, you know.

DONALD: I never said I didn't.

MICHAEL: And while we're on the subject—I think your analyst is a quack.

>*(Michael is sniffling. Donald hands him a handkerchief. He takes it and blows his nose)*

DONALD: Earlier you said he was a prick.

MICHAEL: That's right. He's a prick quack. Or a quack prick, whichever you prefer.

>*(Donald gets up from the couch, goes for his drink)*

DONALD:

>*(Heaving a sigh)*

Harold was right. You'll never change.

MICHAEL: Come back, Donald. Come back, Shane.

DONALD: I'll come back when you have another anxiety attack.

MICHAEL: I need you. Just like Mickey Mouse needs Minnie Mouse—just like Donald Duck needs Minnie Duck. Mickey needs Donnie.

DONALD: My name is Donald. I am called Donald. You must never call anyone called Donald Donnie . . .

MICHAEL:

(Grabs his head, moans)

Ohhhhh . . . Icks! Icks! Terrible icks! Tomorrow is going to be an ick-packed day. It's going to be a bad day at Black Rock. A day of nerves, nerves, and more nerves!

(Michael gets up from the couch, surveys the wreckage of the dishes and gift wrappings)

Do you suppose there's any possibility of just burning this room?

(A beat)

DONALD: Why do you think he stayed, Michael? Why do you think he took all of that from you?

MICHAEL: There are no accidents. He was begging to get killed. He was dying for somebody to let him have it and he got what he wanted.

DONALD: He could have been telling the truth—Justin could have lied.

MICHAEL: Who knows? What time is it?

DONALD: It seems like it's day after tomorrow.

(Michael goes to the kitchen door, pokes his head in. Comes back into the room carrying a raincoat)

MICHAEL: It's early.

(Goes to a closet door, takes out a blazer, puts it on)

DONALD: What does life *hold?* Where're you going?

MICHAEL: The bedroom is ocupado, and I don't want to go to sleep anyway until I try to walk off the booze. If I went to sleep like this, when I wake up they'd have to put me in a padded cell—not that that's where I don't belong.

(A beat)

And . . . and . . . there's a midnight mass at St. Malachy's that all the show people go to. I think I'll walk over there and catch it.

DONALD:

(Raises his glass)

Well, pray for me.

MICHAEL:

(Indicates bedroom)

Maybe they'll be gone by the time I get back.

DONALD: Well, *I* will be—just as soon as I knock off that bottle of brandy.

MICHAEL: Will I see you next Saturday?

DONALD: Unless you have other plans.

MICHAEL: No.

>*(Turns to go)*

DONALD: Michael?

MICHAEL:

>*(Stops, turns back)*

>What?

DONALD: Did he ever tell you why he was crying on the phone—what it was he *had* to tell you?

MICHAEL: No. It must have been that he'd left Fran. Or maybe it was something else and he changed his mind.

DONALD: Maybe so.

>*(A beat)*

>I wonder why he left her.

>*(A pause)*

MICHAEL: . . . As my father said to me when he died in my arms, "I don't understand any of it. I never did."

>*(A beat. Donald goes to his stack of books, selects one, and sits in a chair)*

>Turn out the lights when you leave, will you?

>*(Donald nods. Michael looks at him for a long silent moment. Donald turns his attention to his book, starts to read. Michael opens the door and exits)*

End of Act 2
End of Play

Jane Alexander (Jacqueline) and Lee Richardson (Alan)
in the 1974 Broadway premier of *Find Your Way Home*
at the Brooks Atkinson Theatre.
(Photograph by Martha Swope, reprinted with permission from the
John Willis Theatre World/Screen World Archive)

Find Your Way Home

BY JOHN R. HOPKINS

Find Your Way Home was produced on Broadway by Rick Hobard. It opened at the Brooks Atkinson Theatre, New York City, N.Y. on January 2, 1974 with the following cast:

JULIAN WESTON	Michael Moriarty
DAVID POWELL	John Ramsey
ALAN HARRISON	Lee Richardson
JACQUELINE HARRISON	Jane Alexander
DIRECTED BY	Edwin Sherin
SETTING BY	William Ritman
LIGHTING BY	Marc B. Weiss
COSTUMES BY	Theoni V. Aldredge

ACT I

A small flat in a large town in the south of England.

The main room of the flat is medium-sized, on the ground floor of the house, an old house, with high, decorated ceilings. Down right the long, angle-shaped window overlooks a run of large gardens, back to back, stretching a barrier against the traffic noise from the main coast road, which runs past the front of the house.

The room is furnished with the dreary and conventional cheap furniture common to furnished flats. It is only rescued from total depression by a variety of personal touches.

A footlocker sits down right. In the nook in front of the window stands a dining table with a straight chair at the end of it and another at the upstage end. An armoir with Julian's sweater and other clothes in it stands against the right wall. At a right angle to this and going upstage is the kitchen area. This consists of a small counter with two open shelves on the downstage side. The first shelf has magazines on it and the bottom shelf holds tan place mats. There is a sink next to this and an icebox with a counter on top next to the sink. On this counter is a dish drainer and an electric tea kettle. A dish cloth is draped over the tap in the sink and a dish towel is on the downstage end of the counter. A wastebasket is on the floor between the armoir and the counter. There are two cabinets with three shelves each on the kitchen wall. Dishes, cups and saucers, glasses, silverware and coffee as well as other kitchen things are in them. There is a dripolator coffee pot near the tea kettle. Upstage center is the door into the hall which leads to the front door. On the wall opposite the kitchen is a mirror and two coat hooks above it. At right angles to this wall is the door to the bathroom. Next to this door is a photomontage of faces on the wall. Some of the faces are famous actors and film stars, singers. Some of the faces have been cut roughly out of newspapers and a very few stare out of glossy photographs, smiling and posed. The faces are jumbled together without recognizable pattern. Some of the photographs are pinned to the wall. Some of them are stuck there with Scotch tape. A bed has been pushed against this wall, using the wall as a substitute bed-head. Two pillows with grey covers, two grey sheets, and a brown blanket lie under a blue print bedspread. At the foot of the bed is a blanket chest with two clean blue pillow covers and two clean blue sheets. Julian's white socks are also there. At right angles to the montage wall is a mirror. At right angles to this is another wall with a table in front of it. On this table sits a small alarm clock and a lamp. In the middle of the stage left wall is a fireplace with a gas heater in it. On the mantel sit two speakers for the stereo. Over the mantel hangs a mirror. Upstage of the fireplace are shelves filled with a wide range of books. Some of them are hardback; art books, illustrated books about the great houses of England, books on the history of costume design. There are also shelves filled with paperback books, which look almost brand-new. One shelf holds a stereo unit with records on the upstage side of it. There are also some records on the floor in front of the shelves. Downstage of the fireplace is a small table with a lamp and ashtray on it. Downstage of this table is an old straight-back armchair. Down center there is a chair, contemporary in design, luxurious and obviously an addition to the furniture the landlady has provided. It has a footstool in front of it. A small round table with an ashtray and matches is on the right side of the chair. The room is lit mainly from these table lamps, a lamp that hangs over the bed and a chandelier that hangs from the ceiling center. Holiday posters with sun-bright vistas of golden sky and blue sea are pinned to the walls of the room, interspersed with pop art posters in psychedelic designs. Everything is tidy and, within the compass of the room, comfortable.

It is eight o'clock in the evening.

There is a rock LP playing on the record player. On the upstage end of the dining table, a mat has been placed with a dinner plate on it. There are crumbs on the plate as well as a knife, fork, spoon and rumpled paper napkin. There are crumbs on the table as well.

Julian Weston is lying on the floor in front of the fire, his arms crossed on his chest, his body stretched straight and rigid.

Weston is twenty-three years old, just below average height, slender, with very blond hair.

Slowly, Weston raises his head and shoulders, tucking his chin down against his chest. When he feels his stomach muscles pull tight, he holds the position for a silent count of eight and then lowers his head and shoulders to the floor.

WESTON: Love! Darling, you don't know the meaning of the word.

> *(David Powell is sitting in the leather chair. Powell is thirty years old. He has broad shoulders and a tough, slender physique. He has thick-growing, brown hair cut relatively short. He is wearing an open-necked shirt and brown corduroy pants)*

> "Wham, bam and thank you, mam!"

> *(The telephone starts to ring. Weston lowers himself slowly to the floor and rolls on to his side looking up at Powell. Powell smiles amiably at Weston)*

> You're a lazy bastard.

> *(The telephone is on the floor downstage end of the bed. Weston picks up the receiver)*

> Hello.

> *(Silence. Weston picks up the telephone and carries it to left of the center chair. He puts the receiver against Powell's ear)*

POWELL: Can't hear . . .

> *(Powell seems to produce words from a distance, reluctantly, with a visible effort)*

WESTON: Listen. Listen carefully . . .

> *(Silence)*

POWELL: Still can't . . .
WESTON: Breathing?
POWELL:

> *(Harshly)*

> Nothing.
WESTON: Probably frightened him off. Silly bitch!

> *(Puts the receiver against his ear and listens)*

> Oh, well. 'Bye, love.

> *(Silence. Weston shakes his head, crosses to chest, puts phone on floor, sits on chest and then looks coldly along the length of Powell's legs, up at his face)*

POWELL:

> *(Quietly)*

> You can look, baby—but you mustn't touch.

(Silence)

WESTON: Cheap and nasty, aren't you?

POWELL: You want to change the record?

WESTON: I didn't say you should move in, you know. I had a sort of more temporary arrangement in mind.

POWELL:

> *(Quietly)*
>
> You ask people in—you want they should take care of you, when it's dark and you're afraid—you can't just—you know?—when it's got light again and you're not frightened any more—tell them 'out'. You going to change the record?
>
> *(Silence)*

WESTON: When I went off to work this morning I sort of thought—you might—well, have something to do—somewhere to go?

POWELL: No.

WESTON: You don't work?

POWELL: I don't work.

WESTON: How d'you keep—the wolf from the door?

POWELL: I don't—if I can help it. This is comfortable. Really—the most . . . comfortable—chair I think I've ever sat in—had the pleasure . . .

> *(Silence)*
>
> Hmm.

WESTON: Yes, it is.

POWELL: How d'you afford—something . . .

> *(Silence)*
>
> Present?

WESTON: Yes.

> *(Rises, crosses to stereo, moves needle to another band, turns volume control up, turns into the room)*

POWELL: Someone—loves you a lot—giving you presents—fancy presents like this.

> *(The sound is loud)*
>
> Hey, Julie—no. Let's have something gentle—you know—peaceful.

WESTON:

> *(Harshly, crosses downstage)*
>
> You don't like this—get up—get off your fat backside—find something you do like. For God's sake, David—you make me sick.
>
> *(Powell sits forward and swings his legs off the foot stool, onto the floor. Half-laughing)*
>
> David?
>
> *(Powell rises. Weston backs away as Powell walks forward)*

I didn't mean—hey!—you know me—you know—er—nothing personal—right?

(Powell *stands watching* Weston *following his movement around the room staring at him*)

Well—like you said—things to do!

(He *crosses down to center table, picks up ashtray, crosses to trash can, empties tray, returns it to table*)

Lots of things—must keep busy—yes? Busy hands make light work—or something—the devil finds hands for idle work—hands, knees and up your daisy!

(Powell *walks to the record player and bends forward, takes needle off record, cutting off the sound in mid-phrase. He rests his hands on the downstage shelf, letting his head roll forward onto his chest*)

Here.

(*Crosses downstage of* Powell)

Let me.

(*Takes the stub of the cigarette carefully from* Powell's *fingers*)

What you do with your mind—that's your business.

(*Pressing the stub flat in the ashtray on the downstage left table*)

My furniture—that's something else.

(Powell *reaches out suddenly and catches hold of* Weston's *arm. He holds it tightly, backs* Weston *to below chest, the fingers pressing into the flesh and marking it white.* Weston *watches* Powell *calmly, without showing visible reaction to the pain*)

Well? If you don't want the goods—you know?—don't muck 'em about.
POWELL: You bother me, Julie. All the time—fussing—you bother me.
WESTON: You bore the shit out of me.

(*Silence*)

POWELL: You want to fuck?
WESTON: Not particularly.

(*Silence*)

And now—if you don't mind—
POWELL: It's colder. Isn't it getting colder?
WESTON:

(*Harshly*)

Will you let go!

(Powell *lets go of* Weston's *wrist.* Weston *crosses above center chair to dining table*)

POWELL:

(Quietly)

Times—and you like to be hurt.

WESTON: Ha!

POWELL: I was reading about that—people—hurting you.

WESTON: Reading? Reading what? What d'you mean?

POWELL: Int'resting. All that stuff. Better than books.

(Silence. Weston *opens the door of the armoir and crouches in front of it. He reaches into the armoir and pulls out a folder. He looks at the mass of notebooks stacked inside it)*

WESTON: You bitch. You rotten, filthy bitch. You cunt!

POWELL:

(Crosses to center chair, knee on upstage arm)

You don't have secrets—I mean—there isn't anything you have to hide. It's like—I've been inside your head. Inside your body—now—inside your head.

WESTON:

(Shuts armoir door)

You must've known—surely!—reading—couldn't you see? I didn't mean anyone should read . . .

POWELL: I wanted you last night. Tonight!—The way I feel tonight—what I know about you—what happens—thinking . . . If you didn't mean anyone should read it—how come you wrote it all down. Couldn't you just as well remember—keep it in your head?

(Weston crosses, sits on foot locker, holding folder close)

WESTON: I didn't mean anyone should read it.

POWELL:

(Crossing below armoir)

Someone—you wanted someone to read it. Maybe not me . . .

WESTON: Not you.

POWELL: No—maybe not, but someone—yes?

(Silence)

Julie?

(He crosses and kneels beside Weston *and puts an arm across his shoulders, pulling him close towards him, holding him tight)*

I'm sorry, Julie.

(He rubs a hand down Weston's *arm, comfortingly)*

You have to understand—reading those books—it seemed like a chance to know you—get to know you—and I couldn't stop myself . . . I've watched you—days and weeks. You must've seen me—you must've known. Didn't you

know? Days—and I've wanted just to come and knock on your door—nights—
the nights weren't any easier. And then—last night . . .

WESTON:

> *(Cold, pulls away, crosses to below armoir)*

Last night, darling—I needed something warm in bed with me—something
beside me—something I could touch—reach out and touch—if I woke in the
night and I was scared—something—there—in the darkness—anything,
darling—man, woman or dog.

> *(Crosses to bed, puts folder under mattress. Then rises, facing* Powell*)*

You think I'm going to let you fuck me? I mean—now! What are you?
Some sort of raving maniac! I wouldn't let you fuck me—as long as you live—
one thing you have to know—you'll never—ever, ever, ever—get into me
again.

POWELL:

> *(Rises, crosses below armoir)*

Don't fight me, Julie. Not tonight. Couldn't it be gentle? I mean—last
night—we did that whole thing . . .

WESTON:

> *(Right of chest)*

Do you want to know about last night? You talk like it was something
special. Darling—I've had more satisfaction eating an over-ripe banana—
sucking on a stale blood orange. Truthfully, I've had fellas make you look like
a girl.

> *(Powell* crosses to above center chair, reaching for *Weston* who crosses below
> center chair to right of it. Powell* turns toward him)*

You don't coordinate too well. Must be all those nights—thinking about
me—having yourself—sitting in your dark and dirty little room—chasing me
around your dark and dirtier little mind.

POWELL:

> *(Lunges at* Weston, *between center chair and footstool, loses his balance and falls
> across small table center knocking it over. He rolls onto the floor downstage right)*

Come here.

WESTON:

(Below armoir)

Go fuck yourself!

(Silence. Powell rolls onto his back)

Silly bitch!

(Above center chair)

Go away—will you? Please! You want to get into me—you'll have to do
better than that.

POWELL: I've been into you already—remember?

WESTON:

> (Picks up table and replaces it, picks up ashtrays and matches and puts them on table)

Doesn't establish property rights. Is that what you thought? Darling—if I can't do any better—if the best I can expect—the rest of my life . . .

> (The doorbell rings)

I'll shoot myself in the head. Will you please get up and get the hell out of here?

> (The doorbell rings again. Weston crosses up center)

I'm not—if you'll pardon the expression—playing hard to get—just—I want you to get out—go home—have yourself—you're not having me.

> (Walks to the door, opens it, exits. Silence. Powell stands up, pulling at his trousers and generally making himself more tidy. He crosses down left center. Weston appears in doorway, looks in. Turns back to hall, enters and stands right of the door. Quietly)

Come in.

> (Weston steps back from the door and watches Alan Harrison walk into the flat. Harrison is forty-seven years old. He smiles easily, a smile which protects the eyes from showing too much pain, the face from seeming too vulnerable.
> Powell watches Harrison as He walks into the room.
> Harrison sees Powell and stops. He glances around at Weston quickly and then looks back at Powell)

HARRISON: I'm sorry. I didn't mean to disturb you—er—interrupt anything.

WESTON:

> (Casually)

You know my brother, don't you?

HARRISON: No, I don't think . . .

WESTON:

> (Crossing, closing door, crossing right of bed)

Surely?

POWELL: No. We've never met. I'd certainly remember.

WESTON: Well—Davy . . . this is Alan Harrison—a friend of mine—an old friend. I haven't seen him . . .

> (Silence)

How long is it?

HARRISON: I don't think it's so very long. Six months—maybe—a little longer.

WESTON: Longer. Almost a year.

HARRISON: Is it? Well—if you say it is—I imagine . . .

WESTON: Almost a year.

> (Harrison looks at Powell, glances at center chair, crossing to dining table)

HARRISON: You've changed things around—haven't you?—moved the furniture . . .

WESTON: Yes.

HARRISON: I thought so. I wasn't sure . . .

WESTON: A year is really quite a long time—can be—a long time.

POWELL:

(Smiling)

Julian's really quite the little homemaker, isn't he? I don't know how he can afford all these expensive things.

WESTON:

(To Harrison)

Are you staying? How long are you staying?

HARRISON: I don't know.

POWELL: Would you like something to drink?

WESTON: There isn't anything to drink.

POWELL: I can go out.

HARRISON: No—thank you—really. It doesn't matter.

WESTON: Take off your coat. Sit down.

POWELL: Yes. Make yourself comfortable. How is it out there? Still raining?

HARRISON: No. It's quite pleasant. A little heavy—I think perhaps it might . . .

WESTON: You should get home, Davy—before it starts.

POWELL: I don't mind the rain. It's good for the complexion. Isn't that what they say?

HARRISON: You don't live here?

POWELL: Oh, no. I'm just visiting. Keeping an eye on my baby brother. Seeing he doesn't get into trouble.

(The telephone rings)

I'll get it.

(He sits down on chest and picks up the receiver. He listens for a moment, and then looks up at Weston)

I think it's for you.

(He holds the receiver out to Weston. Weston takes the receiver and puts it to his ear.
Harrison watches the Two Men standing together, sensing the understanding between them, controlled and invisible, but clearly present in their attitudes)

WESTON: You must have the wrong number. There's no one living here called—what did you say?—Wilkinson!

(He looks at Powell)

Sorry.

(Puts the receiver back on the telephone. Powell puts his hand on Weston's hand. Weston sits on his heels)

POWELL:

(To Weston)

I thought he said Weston.

(*To* Harrison)

I could've sworn.

WESTON: He didn't.

POWELL: Easy enough mistake to make. It was such a bad line—I could hardly hear him.

(*To* Harrison)

Very breathy voice.

WESTON: Davy—why don't you tell Dad I'll look in this weekend—some time this weekend.

POWELL: That's a promise?

WESTON: Yes—a promise.

POWELL: I'll tell him.

(He *releases* Weston's *hand*)

WESTON:

(*Rising, cross above center chair*)

Not the whole weekend.

POWELL: He'll be so pleased.

WESTON: Tell him that—so he won't be disappointed.

POWELL: You know how much he looks forward to you coming.

WESTON: He shouldn't expect more than he can have from me.

POWELL: It's the only pleasure he has left.

WESTON: For God's sake, Alan—will you sit down? If you're staying—I mean—are you staying?

(Harrison *shakes his head in doubt*)

POWELL: All this family gossip. I'm afraid it's very boring.

HARRISON: I thought your father was dead?

POWELL: No. What made you think—Dad! He wouldn't like to know—Julian—did you say . . .

HARRISON: I thought you told me.

WESTON: Mum—I told you—Mum's dead. A couple of years ago that was. Dad's all right.

POWELL: Never better.

(*Rises*)

Goodbye, Mr. Harrison. I wish I could stay longer, but I can see Julian wants you all to himself. Got things to talk about. A year—did you say it was a year?

(*Crossing to* Weston)

A lot can happen in a year. A person can change in a year—almost completely. I mean—sometimes—you might hardly recognize them—

(*Hand on* Weston's *shoulder*)

Meeting them again.

(Weston *takes* Powell's *hand off shoulder.* Powell *hangs on*)

WESTON: I'll see Davy to the door—yes? I won't be a minute.
HARRISON: Plenty of time.
POWELL:

> (Abruptly)

That's a promise—about the weekend?
WESTON: A promise.
POWELL:

> (Smiling)

One thing about Julian—never breaks a promise. Always know—if he makes a promise, he's going to keep it.
WESTON: Yes.
HARRISON: Goodbye.
POWELL:

> (To Harrison)

Enjoy yourself.

> (To Weston)

We'll be thinking about you—

> (To Harrison)

Dad and me.

> (Weston opens the door and the Two Men walk out of the flat. Silence. Weston walks into the flat. He stands in the doorway for a moment, and then shuts the door behind him)

WESTON:

> (Up center)

I thought you said—when I saw you last—didn't you say—I'd never see you again?
HARRISON: No. I said—I would never see you again.

> (Silence. Smiling)

There is a difference.
WESTON:

> (Harshly)

Either way—what are you doing here now? What do you want?
HARRISON: I want to see you.
WESTON:

> (Crossing above center chair)

You didn't think—would I want to see you? You didn't ask yourself . . .
HARRISON: Yes.
WESTON: You could have phoned.
HARRISON: I thought—if I phoned . . .

WESTON: I might say—no? I might—just possibly—tell you—go to hell?
HARRISON: Yes.
WESTON: Right. Damn' right!

> *(Silence. Quietly)*

> Go to hell.

HARRISON: Yes.
WESTON: You're so understanding. You always were. Sort of a bloody sponge! Let them say—anything—it's only right—everybody's right—mea culpa—yes? Bastard!

> *(Silence)*

> Can't you sit down? I mean—if you're going to stay? How long can you stay?

HARRISON: That's up to you.
WESTON:

> *(Violently)*

> Oh, for God's sake! How can you say—look—if it's up to me—now—bloody go now—and don't come back. Don't come crawling in here with all this humble shit! You went away. You said—end—dead end. Goodbye—once more, good night—you said that. You said—remember?—it isn't possible.

> *(Quietly)*

> Didn't you say that?

> *(Abruptly)*

> Didn't you?

HARRISON: Yes, I did.
WESTON: Will you sit down?

> (Harrison *walks deliberately across downstage to a dingy, brown leather chair downstage of the fireplace)*
> *(Laughing)*

> Oh, God—dear God! You're too much. Altogether—you know?—too bloody much. Do you know what that does—

> *(Crosses to chest)*

> D'you have any idea? "I mustn't take anything for granted"—right?

> *(Sits on chest)*

> "I mustn't sit in my own chair. He might think . . ." You're so noble. Has anyone told you? Understanding—like I said before—reticent and sensitive—like five elephants in ten pairs of hob-nail boots. Sit in your own chair, will you?

> *(Silence. Harrison *walks across to door, hangs coat and hat on hook, crosses to the chair and sits down on it)*

> You look tired.

HARRISON:

> *(Smiling)*

> Older?

WESTON: Yes—older, I suppose. Tired. Working too hard?

HARRISON: No.

> *(Silence)*

> Why did you leave the firm?

WESTON: What did you expect me to do?

HARRISON: I don't want to feel you had to leave—because—you and I—because . . .

WESTON: Oh, my love—your battered, beautiful, bleeding heart! I would have left long before, if it hadn't been for you. Most of the time I hated the place and everybody working there. What was I? Sort of a glorified office boy—right? Do this—do that—fetch the tea, lad—shit!—and get anything wrong—like I'd raped the Mother Superior. Didn't I ever tell you? Anyway, I've got a much better job now.

HARRISON: What's that?

> *(Silence)*

WESTON: I don't want to talk about it.

HARRISON: Why not? Where are you working? What're you doing?

WESTON: Most of the time, love—I mean—my main preoccupation—waiting for Mr. Right to come along—riding his great, white charger, wearing his silver, shining armour and waving his ten foot lance eagerly in my direction. What I do is my affair entirely and nothing to do with you.

HARRISON: No.

WESTON: What are you doing here?

HARRISON: I came to see you.

WESTON:

> *(Silence)*

> You want to go to bed?

> You always did. Hardly inside the door and it was—"Take off your clothes— get into bed"—and getting out again—"Sorry, love—can't stay long tonight— they're expecting me home early."

> *(Silence. Harrison takes out cigarette and lighter)*

> How are they all at home? I should have asked. How very forgetful of me! What's-her-name—your loving, forgiving wife—how is she?

HARRISON:

> *(Lights cigarette)*

> Jackie . . .

WESTON:

> *(Harshly)*

> I know what her name is.

> *(Silence)*

HARRISON: She's well.

WESTON: And the children—how are they?

HARRISON: They're all right.

WESTON: Were they happy—getting you back? No, of course not. They didn't ever know you'd left—right? 'Course you didn't leave—physically—leave!—did you? That's the important thing. Presence—physical presence—never mind where the head is—where the thoughts go—the body—walking into the house at night—playing with the kids—sitting at dinner—in front of the telly—lying in bed—maybe—fucking—yes?

HARRISON: I wanted to leave them. I thought I could. I wasn't as strong—I wasn't—strong enough.

WESTON: You left me.

HARRISON: I thought I was.

WESTON: I think—it took strength—didn't it? Leaving me?

HARRISON: It was so easy.

WESTON: Bastard!

HARRISON: Isn't it always easy—running away?

WESTON: Oh, yes—I remember. Christ Almighty—yes! You're going to explain to me, aren't you—why it was easy—leaving me—difficult—going back to them—and why you had to do the difficult thing—right? You bloody martyr-saint!

> (Rises, crosses center)

I have to understand—accept—it was easy to leave me—you—are going to make me understand. You—go fuck yourself!

> (Crossing, sits on bed.)
> (Silence)

You always make me feel stupid—in bed and I make you feel good—then—you can be generous. You can show me—love. You can give—and not explain—make me understand all the giving means—to you—to me—the meaning! I don't give a shit!

> (Silence)

I have changed. Things—have changed. I'm not sure there's any place for you here. I don't think it exists any more. I think it was smashed—I think—we questioned too much—smothered—whatever it was—love—and now—there's nothing left. Truthfully, I think you should just go away.

> (Silence. Harrison puts cigarette out, rises, crosses right of center chair to up center)

HARRISON: Can I tell you something—first—before I go? I will go—if you want me to—if you send me away.

WESTON: That isn't fair.

HARRISON: I came to say something I didn't say that night—something I couldn't say. It was bad enough already.

WESTON: Yes.

HARRISON: I didn't want to make it worse by telling you I needed time to think. I needed time—to find out if I had to stay with them—if I could stay with them—and if I couldn't—then—what else to do.

WESTON: You didn't say anything about thinking.

HARRISON: No.

WESTON: You went away. You didn't tell me you might come back—when you'd had
time to think.

HARRISON: I didn't know.

WESTON: I would have waited.

HARRISON: I couldn't ask you to wait . . .

WESTON: I wish you had.

HARRISON:

(Crosses toward Weston)

. . . until I knew—until I was certain . . .

WESTON:

(Quietly)

Oh, God.

HARRISON: . . . I couldn't.

(Silence)

WESTON: You should've—really, love—that's what you should have done.

(Rises, crosses to kitchen, glass and Scotch bottle from cabinet)

I need a drink.

HARRISON:

(Counter-crosses left)

There's something else I want to say.

WESTON: Couldn't it wait? I'm having a certain amount of trouble accepting the story
so far—much more excitement—I might just faint away. You know how
susceptible I am to stories of mystery and suspense.

(Drops Scotch bottle into trash can)

HARRISON: Now—I am certain.

(Silence)

I wanted to tell you.

WESTON:

(Crossing, leans against side of armoir)

You're certain?

HARRISON: Yes.

WESTON:

(Brightly)

Well—that only leaves me to ask . . .

(Shakes his head)

I don't want to know.

(Silence)

HARRISON: Certain about what?

(Crossing toward Weston*)*

I want to live with you. Live here—with you—live anywhere.

WESTON: No. You can't—Christ! Oh, Christ!

HARRISON:

(Crossing and reaching out for Weston*)*

Julie!

*(*Weston *pulls away from* Harrison, *stumbling backwards)*

WESTON: Get away from me.

(He crosses below armoir to upstage of upstage chair in nook. Angrily)

Do you know what you're saying? God in heaven—it isn't—happening. I don't believe . . .

(Silence)

Live with me?

HARRISON: Yes.

WESTON: Damn you!

(He brings his hands up to his mouth and starts to cry)

HARRISON:

(Helplessly, crossing below armoir)

Please—Julie—I didn't mean . . .

(He walks hesitantly towards Weston*)*

WESTON:

(Crossing below to stereo)

Don't come near me. Don't—most of all!—don't touch me.

(Silence)

HARRISON: Shall I go away?

WESTON: I don't want you to go away.

HARRISON: I can come back. We can talk tomorrow. I don't want to upset you.

WESTON: Did you think—I suppose . . . Yes, you did. You thought I'd be just enchanted. Fall into your arms with shrill squeals of delight. Isn't everyone simply ravished when you walk into their dreary lives?

HARRISON:

(Smiling)

I thought you'd be happy, rather than sad.

WESTON: Time passes, Alan.

(Crosses below to dining table)

People have to live the best way they can.

(*Picks up plate, napkin, silver, glass, mat, and crosses to kitchen. Puts mat on bottom counter of shelf, glass on counter, silver in sink, wash plate, put in drainer*)

I don't think it's very practical, love. No—I don't think it's a good idea—you—moving in here. For one thing—my landlady would never approve. She gives me a pretty hard time as it is. And you—anyway—I hardly seem to know you. Just the other day, I was trying to remember what you looked like. I got you confused with a whole bunch of other people.

(*Brightly, crosses left of armoir*)

Sorry about that—still—it's better you know the worst—rather than go on—hoping. The best thing—truthfully—very much the best thing—we should say—goodbye—and forget this whole thing happened.

HARRISON:

(*Coldly*)

How do you plan to forget it? You haven't done too well so far—forgetting.

(*Crosses below* Weston *to left of him*)

It's almost a year. You keep saying it is and I'm sure you're right. It's as clear now as it was then—

(*Grabs* Weston's *wrists*)

clear and painful—isn't it?

WESTON:

(*Controlled*)

Let go of me.

HARRISON: Why won't you even let yourself consider the possibility of my living here—living with you?

WESTON: You're hurting my wrists.

HARRISON: Is there someone else? Was he really your brother? Your father is dead. I'm sure he is. You told me he was.

(*Silence*)

Is he your brother?

WESTON:

(*Pushing Harrison left*)

Brother—sister—distant cousin from Australia—what the hell difference does it make. I said he's my brother. As far as you're concerned—he is.

(*Breaks away, crosses to table. Silence*)

You have changed. You hurt me. You were angry—maybe—jealous?—and you hurt me.

HARRISON: Why can't we talk?

(Weston *puts his hands to his face*)

WESTON:

Julie?

(Seriously, crossing downstage)

I can't trust you, love. You went away. You said you wouldn't—all the same—you did.

HARRISON:

(Crossing right of center chair)

I tried to explain.

WESTON: I know—and you were very fair. You could've written a letter—phoned.

(He crosses to kitchen)

You came and told me. 'Course, you would. That's part of the thing—

(Switches kettle on, puts coffee from cabinet into dripolator)

your whole thing—

(Harrison crosses, sits in center chair)

a man stands straight—takes his medicine—faces up . . . I didn't understand. I hurt a lot—and I cried—after you left. I used to cry all the time.

(Laughing)

It got ridiculous. Buses and trains—restaurants—

(He crosses with dish cloth to table, sits in upstage chair, wipes crumbs off table)

once—I was home—talking to my mother—I started to cry. I said I'd lost my job. I was worried about the rent. She gave me a couple of quid—patted me on the head and told me—"Don't worry." Poor old thing. I wanted to tell her—"Alan's left me. Gone back to his wife." Oh, God! Everything there was—I gave it to you—and you went away—and I didn't have it any more. I couldn't give it to anyone else—d'you understand? I gave it to you—that—whatever it is—inside thing—truthful—me thing—you don't even know you have. Left on your own—trying with someone else—you find—it doesn't happen—nothing happens. He's all the way inside you—everything's the same—seems to be the same—the noises in your head—the anger—all the struggling—violence—only—you don't feel—there isn't—love.

(Rises, crossing to sink)

I used to cry all the time.

(Shakes out dish cloth)

Isn't that ridiculous?

(Mocking. Dish cloth down on counter. Turns kettle off)

Oh, you! God help us!

(Pours water from kettle into dripolator)

You're a push-over for any sob story. You watch the old movies on the telly—yes? Leslie Howard—painting his last great masterpiece—

(Acts this out up center)

struggling against blindness, insanity—and the men taking away all the furniture.

(Grabs dish towel from counter, puts it on his head, crosses left of center chair, kneels)

Merle Oberon beside him—her arms outstretched—"Don't take the canvas. Leave him the canvas. At least . . ."

(Chin in hand, leaning on chair arm)

Or was it Ronald Colman? You stand up when they play the National Anthem—right? Stand in line to wave at the Queen—all those good things! You really believe Mary Magdalene went straight after He died—

(Rises, crosses to sit on chest, dish cloth in lap)

didn't go back on the game? All this—you know—it's just—will I go to bed with you? I will. I want to. I like going to bed with you. We can get into bed and make love. When it's dark—you go home—and no regrets. Something good we can both remember—and no regrets.

(Smiling)

Like the song says.

(Silence)

I promise I won't expect—afterwards—you won't have to stay.

(Abruptly)

Alan—for God's sake! How bloody noble do I have to be? You want me—yes?

HARRISON:

(Harshly)

No.

(Doorbell buzzes. Silence. Doorbell buzzes. Weston rises, exits front door. Harrison rises. Weston enters, picks up dripolator from counter)
(Crossing to door)

I think I'd better go, Julie.

WESTON:

(Crosses with dripolator to table)

God knows what that was all about! Some crazy lady—thought she wanted this flat.

HARRISON: We can't talk. We don't even seem . . . I don't think we even like each other very much.

WESTON:

(Crossing to kitchen)

Did you have anything to eat?

(Silence—cream, sugar, cup, saucer, spoon to table)

No—you didn't. Oh, well—that's your bad luck. Davy ate just about everything I had—including tomorrow's lunch.

HARRISON:

(Takes hat from hook)

Is he your brother?

(Silence)

Sorry. I shouldn't ask.

WESTON: No. He's not my brother.

HARRISON: Is he important?

WESTON: He's so unimportant—he hardly exists.

HARRISON: He was here.

WESTON:

(Sits in downstage chair, pours coffee)

He was here last night as well—for the first time. Tonight—for the last time. If you'd come around just that bit sooner, love—he might not have been here at all.

HARRISON: I couldn't come back any sooner.

WESTON: No.

(Smiling)

Well . . .

HARRISON: And the weekend? Something—you promised—for the weekend.

WESTON: So—I'll break a promise.

(Smiling)

I'm not that bloody special, love—I can't break a promise.

HARRISON:

(Hangs hat back on hook)

Why did you lie?

WESTON: Why d'you think?

HARRISON:

(Crosses downstage)

You didn't want me to know?

WESTON: Right! Abso-bloody-lutely-right! Give the man a prize. Any prize from the bottom shelf—if you'll pardon the expression!

HARRISON: What difference does it make—knowing or not knowing—why should you care?

WESTON: Pride. There is such a thing . . . I'd rather . . .

(Crosses below to fireplace)

Christt!

HARRISON:

(Crossing by dining table)

What? What is it?

WESTON: I'm defending myself. Bringing out excuses—all the justifications . . .

HARRISON: There's no reason . . .

WESTON:

(Harshly)

I know that!

(Silence)

How long is it you've been here—and already . . . How do you do that? What is it—makes me feel so guilty? Instant guilt! You make me feel I've committed sins I've never even heard of. Everything—a sin—deliberately done to hurt you—bruise your sweet sensitive soul. God in heaven—are you so pure?

HARRISON: You don't have to defend yourself.

WESTON: Have you been faithful? Forget what's-her-name?

(Crosses center)

I don't count her.

(Silence)

Male or female? Most likely female. Some dolly at the office. New—since I was there—right? Looked at you twice and read the signs all wrong? Thought you wanted her—the silly bitch—and not the all-consuming nothingness between her legs.

(Crosses above center chair)

Did you tell what's-her-name? No—of course not! Why should you? It wasn't anything you meant to last. No reason you should hurt—I know you—if it isn't going to last—if there's no danger she'll find out—surely, it's better—what the eye can't see . . . What did you tell the dolly? Did you tell her—"This is to do with me, love—nothing to do with you?" Did you say— "If I was more honest—I'd stay home and have myself—but that's so nasty, furtive, guilty and sordid—and this sweet, ugly sickness—having myself in you . . ."

HARRISON: No, Julie—don't . . .

WESTON: ". . . this is the game—part of the game . . ."

HARRISON:

(Crosses above center chair)

Please!

WESTON: ". . . I'll use you—and you—use me . . ."

HARRISON: Don't do this—to us.

WESTON:

(Anguish)

Stop me. Make me stop. I love you.

(Silence. Quietly)

Alan—I love you. I've been angry for so long and I was never angry. Lonely—yes—and sometimes—lost—not angry—with this almost uncontrollable desire to hurt—to torture—even kill! The times I've killed you—wanted to destroy—and always in such hideous . . .

(Silence. He crosses downstage left chair, sits)

Why did you go away?

HARRISON:

(Quietly)

I ran away, Julie—mostly from myself.

(Silence)

If what you are disgusts you—the man you are—how can you live with any hope of being—knowing—happiness—or peace? No—you can only punish—prove to yourself—yes—I am disgusting. There is some satisfaction . . .

(Silence)

I thought it was meant. I thought—this is the man you are—the life you've made—and now—accept it. What did you expect? What right have you—has anyone!—expecting the life they want—perhaps—think they deserve?

(Smiling)

I caught myself thinking—if I'm so special—and I am!—how is it no one sees? I lived ten years—and every day lies, deceit—and endless little insincerities. I had affaires—pathetic, cruel affaires. Women, at first—then girls—because the women asked—expected—more than I could give them— time and consideration—and the girls—they didn't take it seriously. They had the time to pass—and passing it with me—it wasn't painful—sometimes boring, I suppose—but there were compensations. I always bought them presents—and they didn't know I wasn't really there—I wasn't ever there. Any more—I think—than Jackie knew. There was excitement—running from bed to bed—a sense of power—able to have—no—not any woman I might choose— but I was careful and I chose without much risk they would refuse and so— could tell myself—with anyone I chose.

(Silence)

Much more important—sleeping with strangers—I could make an answer to the question—why—with my wife—with Jackie—why don't I feel desire— why can't I make myself enjoy—why?—and in all the other beds—thinking of her—I could tell myself—if anyone's at fault, it surely isn't me.

(Silence)

I played so many games with truth I lost all sense of honesty. Business trips—late dinners—

(Crosses above to left of center chair)

entertaining guests in town—visiting executives—I had a madness in my head. I never told the truth to anyone—

(Silence)

Once—I arranged an evening on my own—with all the same elaborate mechanism—time to think—time—to step back and look at this whole distorted pattern of reality. I found—there was no one in my life I trusted. No one I could let come close—no one could even understand—no one who knew the simple basic fact—my life—everything—was part of this same lie—this slight—but central!—divergence from the truth. I had contrived an absolute aloneness for myself. Why did I go away?

(Crosses, sits on chest)

You have to understand, love—at that time—truthfully, I thought—That was the life I wanted—and most of the time—enjoyed it—It was a sort of death—but locked inside—keeping my head down and my eyes closed—I was happy—and why not! What's so much better here?—out here!—and I'm not happy—more alone—and all the time—aware!

(Silence)

I did come here tonight—thinking we could make love—and right away—before we talked—before—anything!—make love. That was the fantasy—blanking out thought—and all consideration—just—the memory of every night we spent here.

(Weston rises, crosses to Harrison, hand to Harrison's head, caressingly)

WESTON: We could do that. Why don't we? There's no reason why we shouldn't. Couldn't we, Alan—make love?

HARRISON: How do I make you feel guilty? You always seem to me—so innocent.

(The telephone starts to ring. Harrison rises, crosses and sits in center chair. Weston sits on chest, picks up phone)

WESTON: Hello.

(Silence)

I'm sorry, love. You must have the wrong number . . . That's all right. Goodbye.

(Puts the receiver down)

Bloody telephone! You remember days you get a right number.

HARRISON: You get your share of wrong ones.

WESTON: Yes.

HARRISON: Was it Davy?

(Silence)

WESTON:

(Harshly)

No, it wasn't Davy.

(Stands up, crosses up center)

If it had been Davy—I would've said—get stuffed and knotted—will you? Stop messing me about.

(Viciously)

Go fuck yourself!

(Silence)

HARRISON: I'm sorry.
WESTON:

(Bitterly)

You're allowed. The whole charade was pretty stupid. I don't know why—suddenly—it was so important you should think he was my brother—something—anything—but not—well—what he was.
HARRISON: Thank you.
WESTON:

(Crosses to bed, sits)

Oh, no—now—that's taking chivalry too far—thanking me . . .
HARRISON: If it meant that much . . .
WESTON: D'you know what this party needs? Booze! I know that's what I need.
HARRISON: I thought you said there isn't a drink in the house?
WESTON: The pubs are open. Love—would you go down to the local? Buy us a bottle of scotch.
HARRISON:

(Feet on footstool)

Do I have to? I don't want to move. It's warm here and I'm comfortable.
WESTON: Lazy—that's what you are.
HARRISON: I suppose—I don't feel much like a drink myself . . .
WESTON: Selfish—and lazy!
HARRISON: If you insist . . .

(Rises, crosses up center, hat and coat from hook, crosses downstage putting coat on)

Julie—you're glad—yes?

(Silence)

WESTON: Yes.
HARRISON: Why don't I want to go?
WESTON:

(Rises, helps Harrison with coat)

I'm sorry he was here.

HARRISON: I won't be long.

WESTON: Alan, I'm not innocent, you know.

HARRISON: It'll be all right.

WESTON: The night you left—after you left . . .

(Silence. Briskly)

I'll tell you all about it some time—if you really want to hear. Go and buy the scotch.

HARRISON: Tell me about it.

WESTON: Here. You'll need a key.

(Taking keys from pocket, hands them to Harrison)

HARRISON:

(Harrison pulls the door open, looks at Weston, walks out of the flat pulling the door shut quietly behind him. Weston looks around the flat. Silence)

Thanks.

WESTON:

(Muffled)

After you left—

(Weston crosses to door, light switch off. Strips sheets and blankets off bed. Reaches for switch—turns on lamp over bed. Sits on bed)

I walked for an hour—longer—I don't know exactly. I went to your house. I stood on the street and watched. The lights went out downstairs. I saw you go to bed—and when you switched the light out in your bedroom—then—I went away.

(Silence)

I sat in a cafe. It was one o'clock. A man spoke to me—asked—was I on my own—and I said—yes, I was. We sat for a while and talked and he said—would I go with him? We left the cafe and we walked together—talking—he was talking—and he said—would I let him fuck me? I loved you, Alan.

(Silence)

We went into a park and—yes—I let him fuck me. It was cold and the grass was very wet. He held me—with his hands around my neck. He hurt me—pushing into me. His nails tore the skin across my neck. He talked and told me all the things he'd do—but he came quickly and there wasn't time. He left me then. He went away. He didn't speak to me.

(Silence. Weston pushes himself forward across the bed and stands up. He reaches to pick up the blankets. He stands in the middle of the room, holding them in his arms, pressed against his chest)

I couldn't go back home. I asked a friend—did he have a room? Could I sleep there—maybe on the couch? Come on—he said—of course there's room—No reason we should make you sleep in there—he said—the fire's gone out and it's so bloody cold. You come and sleep with me. I couldn't let him fuck me—and he said—what do you think this is, love? You sleep here—you pay the rent. I took him in my mouth. He came—and went to sleep. I stayed there—but I couldn't sleep—and in the morning—soon as it was light—I went away.

(*Pulls one blanket free and spreads it clumsily across the bed. He kneels beside the divan, fumbling with the blanket, trying to push it straight*)

Why did you leave me? Why did you go away? It's your fault—your fault! God in heaven—why did you let me? I didn't want to do those things. I didn't want to let them fuck me. They were strangers. I didn't know their names. Why weren't you here to stop me, Alan? If you'd been here . . .

(*Pushes himself to his feet and turns away from the bed. He stumbles across the room towards the record-player and starts record*)

They were all friends—good friends—I knew them—really quite well—and they said—"Julie—we're having a party. You're the guest of honour"—and they laughed. I went to the party with them, and of course there wasn't any party. It was a game they were playing with me, and I knew. Love—I knew it was a game. I always knew! I knew what they had planned and that was my game— played against them—knowing—and letting it happen anyway. They had this plan to rape me. Two of them holding—two of them watching—one of them— and I laughed. What did they think—what was there left to rape? They thought they were so wicked—pulling off my clothes—dissolute—depraved! "Shit, darling—I've been fucked" I said "in dirty lavatories—but men would just as soon fuck sheep. I've been spread across tables in transport cafes . . . fucked in the dark by frightened little men . . . fucked in broad daylight—nearly torn in half . . ."

(*The sound blasts out of the twin speakers.*
The door of the flat opens and Harrison *walks into the room, carrying a paper bag with a Scotch bottle in it. He pushes the door shut behind him. He walks to counter, puts bag down, crosses to stereo, lifts arm off record, crosses to* Weston. *Silence*)

HARRISON: What is it, Julie? For God's sake—what happened?
WESTON: Love me, Alan—please—make love.

(Weston *crosses to* Harrison. *They embrace*)

Curtain

ACT II

One hour later.

The room is almost dark.

The only lights on are the lamp over the bed, the lamp on the U.L. table and the lamp on the D.L. table.

Harrison is sitting in the chair, with his legs stretched across the foot stool. He is wearing a shirt and trousers. The shirt is open at the neck.

Weston is sitting on the bed, in his bathrobe, holding a pillow.

Silence.

WESTON: Love—

HARRISON: Yes.

WESTON: Since I left home I've always lived in rooms—hideous furnished rooms—like this.

HARRISON:

> *(Crosses up center to mirror)*

> What's wrong with this?

WESTON: I want to live in some place really nice—some place belongs to me—

> *(Smiling)*

> belongs to us—yes?

HARRISON: Yes.

WESTON: I'd like to make a home for you.

> *(The doorbell rings)*

> Oh, for pity's sake! Do I have to answer?

HARRISON: Will they go away?

> *(Crosses to upstage window)*

WESTON: I don't know.

> *(Silence. The doorbell rings again. Weston rises, crosses toward up center door)*

> I'll have to answer. Can't let them wake my landlady—at this time of night!

HARRISON: Put something on your feet.

WESTON:

> *(Mocking, crosses to bathroom door, exits)*

> Yes, Dad.

HARRISON:

> *(Crosses below armoir)*

> If it's someone you know . . .

WESTON:

112

(Off)

It better be someone I know. A stranger—I might just punch in the mouth.

(Weston enters)

What sort of time is this for strangers!

HARRISON:

(Crosses center)

If you want to ask them in . . .

WESTON: I don't.

(The doorbell rings again.
Weston *crosses to up center door, turns on lights)*

Bloody persistent, aren't they? Really—you think I'd ask anyone . . .

(Silence)

Oh, love.

*(Weston *shakes his head and walks out of the flat.*
Harrison *crosses to down left armchair, picks up tie from back, puts it on, crosses to stereo, turns it down.*
The sound of the front door being closed.
Harrison *turns to look across the room at the door, as it is pushed open.* Weston *enters, stands right end of armoir. Jacqueline Harrison *walks into the flat, stands up center.*
Jackie *and Harrison *stare at each other across the room)*
(Closes door behind Jackie, then crosses to sink)

She absolutely insisted you were here, Alan.

HARRISON: Jackie. What are you doing?

JACKIE: I followed you.

(Silence)

WESTON: Mrs. Harrison—wouldn't you like to sit down? You must be so tired—
standing out there half the night. I know how exhausting that can be.

*(Jacqueline Harrison is *forty-two years old)*

Let me take your coat?

JACKIE: No.

WESTON: Suit yourself.

HARRISON: I don't understand, Jackie. Followed me?

JACKIE: Who is he? What is happening?

(Violently crosses downstage)

You don't understand!

WESTON:

(Blandly)

My name's Julian Weston. You two know each other already, don't you?

(Silence)

JACKIE:

(To Julian; *quietly)*

Julie.

WESTON: My friends call me Julie—yes. It's sort of sweet, don't you think?

JACKIE:

(To Harrison)

Julie?

WESTON: No. I'm Julie. That's Alan.

JACKIE:

(Shouting)

Julie!

WESTON: Please—do you mind—Don't make too much noise. My landlady . . .

JACKIE:

(Crosses below chest)

He is Julie? He wrote those letters?

(Silence)

WESTON: Letters?

JACKIE:

(Desperately)

Did he write those letters?

HARRISON: Yes.

JACKIE: I read them.

WESTON: My letters? You read my letters?

(Harrison walks towards Jackie and She backs quickly away from him, stumbling against the foot stool. She falls heavily across it and rolls on to the floor.
Harrison crouches beside Jackie, reaching to take hold of her)

JACKIE:

(Screaming)

Get away from me. Get away!

WESTON: Why did you let her read my letters? Why didn't you keep them safe?

(Silence)

JACKIE:

(Viciously, gathering herself together)

I thought at least you had a woman here. I didn't realise . . .

HARRISON:

(Reaches for her again)

JACKIE:

(Here—let me help you.

(Rises, crosses away right)

Don't touch me. Filth! You are—filthy!

WESTON:

(At center chair)

I have a feeling, love—this could be sort of ugly.

(Brightly)

Tell you what—why don't we—right away now—all of us—pull ourselves together? Stop behaving like children. Remember where we are—and—God is always watching!—all those good things—and before we start this—stop! Why don't we do that?

JACKIE: You've been—to bed together?

WESTON: Could we do that?

JACKIE: You've been—what do you call it—surely not!—making love?

WESTON: No, we couldn't.

JACKIE: Is that what you've been doing?

WESTON:

(Crosses behind Harrison)

Darling—if you can't get it—don't knock it.

HARRISON:

(Crosses, gets coat from down left chair, crosses to Jackie)

Jackie—why don't you let me take you home?

JACKIE:

(Harshly. Backs away to dining table)

When I want to go home, I'll find my own way—thank you very much.

HARRISON: I don't see the point—staying here to fight.

JACKIE: Will it upset him? Is he sensitive—easily bruised?

WESTON:

(Crosses down left center)

Alan—you can't just walk out of here.

HARRISON:

(Upstage of Jackie)

Be reasonable, Julie . . .

WESTON: You can't do that.

HARRISON: Try to understand.

WESTON: No.

HARRISON: I'll just take Jackie home.

WESTON: You won't come back.

HARRISON: Don't be ridiculous.

WESTON: You won't.

HARRISON: I have to talk to her. I can't talk here—with both of you . . .

JACKIE:

    (To Harrison)

Do I make you feel uncomfortable?

WESTON:

    (Crosses left of foot stool)

It would've been all right—yes?—if you'd found him with a girl?

JACKIE: It would have been more normal. It's always been a girl before.

WESTON: How do you know?

HARRISON:

    (Harshly)

No—come on—will you? Stop it!

WESTON: Act like a gentleman—nice and polite? I'm not a gentleman—I'm not a man at all. Ask her. She'll tell you.

JACKIE: You make me feel sick!

    (Harrison turns upstage)

WESTON:

    (Crosses downstage)

Why? What's so special 'bout the way you fuck? You get it in the front. I get it in the back. Sometimes—a bit of both—and so do you. What makes it normal—done to you—makes it so shameful—when it's done to me?

HARRISON:

    (Crosses below to left of foot stool)

Julie—shut up!

WESTON:

    (Crosses above center chair to right of it)

You take him in your mouth—right? Something he expects—and if you won't—maybe he'll go find someone else who will. Why—when you do it— good—and when I do it—evil, sick—depraved? I didn't ask you to come here.

    (Turns to Harrison, crosses up left)

I didn't ask you to come back. Why don't you—yes!—if you want to—go away!

JACKIE: Is he always this hysterical?

WESTON:

    (Above center chair)

You let her read my letters.

HARRISON: I didn't.

WESTON: I wrote them to you.

HARRISON: I wouldn't let anyone read your letters.

JACKIE: I should hope not. From a girl—they're pretty sickening to read—but from a man—disgusting!

HARRISON: Jackie—please?

(Crosses to stereo, turns it off)

WESTON:

(Crosses right center)

I make you sick? You make me vomit blood! I know the life he has with you. I know the things you do to him. You think he hasn't told me?

JACKIE:

(Quietly)

One thing—obviously—you don't know. How much he hates a scene.

WESTON: I know how much he hates you. Each time he comes here—each time we make love—he tells me—what it's like with you. How nothing happens—just—the fantasies he makes inside his head.

HARRISON: You make me feel ashamed.

WESTON:

(Harshly)

You're going back with her.

HARRISON:

(Crosses up center)

Whatever I do—how can that justify—trying to destroy—saying things—deliberately to hurt . . .

WESTON:

(Laughing. Crosses toward Harrison)

I couldn't put a mark on her—much less destroy. She'd have to take me seriously—admit I might exist. She'd have to hear the things I say.

JACKIE: I can hear quite clearly.

WESTON:

(Crosses above center chair)

No—you're reacting to a new idea—Alan can fuck a fella. You don't see me—certainly, don't hear—just all the clutter in your head—screaming and shouting—"How can he do this to me? How can he make me feel so dirty? How can he put himself—inside . . ." Have you got that far? Or is it still—"What sort of idiot does this make me—loving him—going to bed with him—letting him fuck me—and all the time he wanted—this!"

(Silence. Gently)

Is that more like it?

HARRISON:

(Crosses downstage to foot stool)

Jackie—I'll take you home.

WESTON: I've been there, darling—every time he went from me to you—back into your bed—I had to think—"He'll fuck her. Yes—of course he will. He has to." I told myself—he couldn't want to—very likely I was wrong.

HARRISON:

(Sits on foot stool)

What good does it do—talking like this?

WESTON: Because I'm stupid—and not sensitive at all—I put myself through all the messy business of your—making love. Is that what you still call it? After all this time!

HARRISON: Julie—you must stop.

WESTON:

(Crosses above Harrison)

I want to save you, Alan. Presumptuous of me—yes, I know—

(Kneels left of Harrison)

and if I can't—maybe—protect a little. When she gets you out of here, she'll be so sympathetic. She'll say—"Darling, you're sick—a little bit insane"—no—some much kinder word. Unbalanced! Meaning the same thing—out of your bloody mind! She'll take you to a doctor and they'll try to cure you—'cause they don't want to think—they can't let themselves believe—you love me 'cause you love me . . . and the making love—something we do because it makes us happy.

(Rises, crosses above Harrison to above center chair)

Look at her, love—she thinks we have some sort of orgy here—and do forbidden things! She thinks you want to fuck me 'cause it'd be different—sick—perverted—some new kind of thrill! She thinks it can be cured—with help—and the love of a good woman!

(Sits center chair)

You won't make anything clear—taking her away—talking to her—telling her where you both went wrong and why it's better you should separate—she knows all that.

(Rises, crosses left of Harrison)

Christ Almighty, Alan—aren't you here? You're separated. Maybe you haven't told each other—you've been separate for years.

(Embraces Harrison)

She has to know—you are in love with me—not 'cause I'm a fella—'cause you are in love.

(Silence)

JACKIE:

(Calmly)

Alan—I think he's asking you a question.

(Silence)

WESTON: Why do you want him back?

JACKIE: Has he ever left?

WESTON: Didn't you tell her?

JACKIE: Isn't it obvious? He hasn't told me anything.

WESTON: You came here and you didn't—

> *(Rises, crosses up center)*

what are you doing here?—you didn't tell her?

> *(Harrison puts head in hands)*

JACKIE: I simply thought you were a girl—another girl—and this time—for many personal and private reasons I won't discuss with you—I couldn't let him—get away with it.

WESTON: You followed him?

JACKIE: One of your letters told me where you lived—another had your name—a note I found—your telephone number.

WESTON: You looked at everything?

JACKIE: Everything I could find.

> *(Silence)*

WESTON:

> *(Crosses above center chair, hand on back of it)*

Is this the way you always carry on? Playing at amateur detective? Catching them—in flagrante delicto—yes? Taking him home again—his tail—between his legs?

JACKIE:

> *(Crosses below armoir)*

It isn't—fucking—what you do together. You want to think it is—you want to call it that—all right, it isn't.

WESTON:

> *(Quietly)*

No.

JACKIE: He—uses you. He . . .

> *(Silence)*

WESTON: Buggers me? Yes. Unless you would perhaps prefer to use some more refined and technical expression? Sodomy? You want to use these words—you have to say them with a little less concern—more casual, darling—

> *(Backs Jackie to table)*

'cause they are the truth of what we do together and they say more clearly what it means—to put yourself inside another human being—taking him— yes—and using him—for your own satisfaction. Is that what he does to you?

> *(Crosses up center)*

That's what he does to me. It gives him pleasure and it makes me glad. I want him—using me.

HARRISON:

(Desperately)

I want this all to stop.

WESTON:

(Crosses to center chair, sits)

How do you think it will then? Do you anticipate—an act of God!—in His mercy—reaching down to take you up—out of this "earthly travail"? You and Christ—Moses—and Isaiah!

JACKIE: Did you think you could walk out tonight and—what?—write me a letter! I'm not coming home again. Give my love to the children.

WESTON: You ran away.

HARRISON: I wanted time.

JACKIE: Is that what you wanted? Coming here?

WESTON:

(Crosses down left chair)

You took time—leaving me—then—you had your time to think—and decided to come back.

JACKIE:

(Crosses right of foot stool)

Time to think? Think about what? Leaving a family you've had for twenty years? How long did you take—thinking about that?

WESTON: A year—almost.

JACKIE: Thinking—about you? And all that time—he hasn't had affairs? Really—you think! There's one at least I know about—and if there's one, then you can take my word—there's plenty I don't know about. Give himself time to think! He doesn't give himself the time to change his shirt and clean his shoes.

WESTON: You should have told her.

HARRISON:

(Violently; rises; crosses above to table)

I should have left her fifteen years ago, when I was first unfaithful. Don't tell me what I should have done!

JACKIE:

(Upstage left turn, watching Harrison)

Fifteen years ago?

HARRISON: If I'd had any sense, I would have left you then. I knew I would. I knew— some day . . .

JACKIE:

(Purse on center chair, crosses down right center)

Why didn't you leave me? If you wanted to—why didn't you ask me— God!—I would have told you quick enough—go—yes—go away. D'you think I wanted you to stay—out of pity—because I had the children to bring up?

HARRISON: Yes—the children.

JACKIE:

(Harshly)

No! Don't blame the children.

HARRISON: Betty was only one year old.

JACKIE: What is she now? Sixteen. A ripe old age to see her father turning queer.

HARRISON: And Michael—four.

JACKIE: You think he's ready now? You've decided he can cope. Nineteen years old— able to deal with anything. His father—leaving home—setting up house with a homosexual not much older than he is himself. You do intend to live together?

WESTON: Yes, we do.

JACKIE: Alan?

HARRISON: I couldn't leave them.

JACKIE: You could leave me!

WESTON: He already had.

JACKIE: Are you saying—all this time—you stayed with me, because of the children?

HARRISON: I could only think—how young . . .

JACKIE: Bastard!

HARRISON: . . . defenceless . . .

JACKIE:

(Crosses to Harrison)

You couldn't imagine living on your own. You never have—how could you face it then? Alone! In six months you'd be mad—or dead.

HARRISON: I am alone.

JACKIE:

(Turns downstage)

Alan—please! You'll have us all in tears.

WESTON: You bitch!

JACKIE:

(Looks at Weston. Then)

You never let yourself be on your own for more than twenty minutes—any day in your whole life.

WESTON: Look—if you really want to take each other through your dismal marriage—day by day—apportioning praise and blame—I would much rather you went home.

JACKIE: Would you like to see the letters Alan wrote to me?

(Crosses above center chair to below chest)

Just ordinary letters—written with ordinary love and foolishness. Nothing like the passion, violence and near hysteria you write about in yours. Would you like to see the—loving kindness—there can be between two people— friends for more than twenty years—and how much more between a man and woman who have been through that same intoxication you can write about so well?

(Silence. Crosses upstage of Weston)

121

Would you like to see how much affection Alan has for me?

(*Silence*)

At best you share him with me—at worst—because of me—you'll lose him. It isn't easy—breaking the habits of more than twenty years. You think he won't remember? You think he won't regret? Some things—

(*Left center area*)

he must regret. How well can you cook? I cook really well. You keep your home quite tidy. Do you like to walk? Can you entertain yourself—he spends so many nights at work. Obviously—some of those nights he'll spend with you. He won't need to go elsewhere, will he? There's such a plentiful supply at home. But—only some—he does work hard—and he won't be able to take life easy now. With two homes to support—the children at their most expensive age. Happily—there won't be any more.

(*She turns to face him. Viciously*)

Of course, he won't come back to me. Perhaps, I wouldn't have him.

(*Silence*)

He can't stay here with you. You're the excuse he needs to leave me—his "grand amour!" He'll make you accept the guilt he cannot even recognize—and when he does—you think he'll stay? Surely—much easier—go on to someone else. Leave all the guilt with you and run away again. At his age—forty-seven—forty-eight next month—can he change completely—make himself into another man—and start again? Living with some other woman—just the guilt would cripple him—with you—the shame—contempt—disgust on people's faces—you think he won't despair?

WESTON: Go away. Alan—take her away.

JACKIE: Excitement has always been his one great stimulant—the novelty—the first infatuation. How long can you excite him? He does get bored. Have you had long enough to find out how easily? Have you had time to talk? What can you talk about? Except to tell each other how much you are in love—how brave, courageous—noble—you both are. All for love—and the world . . . You think he never was in love with me? Is that what he told you? He loved me—not only when we married—years after that and he still loved me. After his affairs began—

(*Crosses upstage of* Weston)

he still made love to me—still wanted me. You think he wasn't violent? Is that what he told you? He used to beg me—"Jackie—take me in your mouth."

HARRISON: You think I'm still the man you married.

JACKIE: No. I watched him

(*Crosses to center chair, handkerchief from purse*)

come to pieces some ten years ago. I make the best of what small fragments I have left.

WESTON: I'd like you to continue this conversation in the peace and privacy of your own home. I've had enough.

(Rises, crosses to bathroom door)

I'm tired. I'd like to go to bed. Shut the door quietly as you leave. I want you both to go away.

JACKIE:

(Quietly)

I was unfaithful once. It wasn't too successful. He didn't even like me. He didn't like you either.

WESTON: Please—will you go away?

JACKIE:

(Crosses above center chair to right center)

I think that's how we came to go to bed.

WESTON: Alan!

JACKIE: We had so much to talk about.

WESTON: There's no point hanging on. There's nothing left. Why don't you just go home?

JACKIE: We spent the evening quietly. We talked. He took me out to dinner. It was all so ordinary.

HARRISON:

(Sits at table)

I want to stay here.

WESTON:

(Opens bathroom door)

It was a nice idea, love. It didn't work.

JACKIE: When he took me home—funny—it seemed so natural—going to bed with him. Was he so very clever—or was I—so inexperienced? Of course, I wanted him to love me.

WESTON: Before I get to screaming at you, Alan—will you go away?

(Silence. Jackie looks at Weston. Weston exits)

JACKIE: When I woke up later, he was asleep. I couldn't think why there was a face I didn't recognise—I couldn't understand—lying on the pillow next to me. I thought I must be dreaming. In my mind—when I was unfaithful—thinking about it—then, it was so fierce—explosive—uncontrolled—and this—it didn't even seem important. How can you tell one from any other, if it's always just the same?

(Silence. Weston enters, gets socks from chest, sits chest, puts on socks)

Why don't we go home?

(Picks up purse)

HARRISON: I want to stay here.

JACKIE: I don't think you should. I don't think it's very sensible. I'm tired. Can't we go home?

HARRISON: Why did you follow me?

JACKIE: I want to help you.

HARRISON: You couldn't let me go.

JACKIE: Really—do you want me to?

HARRISON: Would you believe me—if I told you—yes, I do?

JACKIE:

(Calmly)

If there was any reason why I should—yes—I'd believe you.

WESTON:

(Puts on shoes)

I think you should at least give it some thought. He might not be so careless next time—leave you so many clues. Let him go again—you might not find him quite so easily.

JACKIE: He wanted me to find him.

WESTON: Come and fetch him home? Yes—I think perhaps you're right. Still— maybe—another time.

JACKIE:

(To Julian)

He won't come back to you.

WESTON: Darling—I wouldn't have him if he did. I'm much too good for him.

(Rises, crosses to armoir, gets sweater, puts it on.
Jackie *counter-crosses below foot stool)*

It's sort of cold. I think I'll take a sweater. If that's the life you settle for, old love—must be the life you deserve—right? Don't we always get what we deserve?

(Silence. Crosses to up center door, keys from counter, hat from hook)

I'm going out. I'd rather you weren't still here when I get back. Oh—and switch the lights out. Somehow I feel I'm making some sort of exit—which is ridiculous. I mean—this is where I live—it was a nice idea. Take him home and keep him safe. If you can't stop him—nobody else can.

*(Weston *walks out of the flat and pulls the door shut quietly. Silence)*

JACKIE: Some time ago I knew you were having an affair. As a matter of fact, I wanted to ask you—I mean—if anyone could help—you were unhappy—and I thought—

(Embarrassed)

probably I could help you—if you'd just talk about it.

HARRISON: Talk to you about it?

JACKIE:

(Abruptly)

You were hardly keeping it a secret! Moping about the house. Betty asked me what was wrong. You think I couldn't guess. I've been married to you . . .

HARRISON:

> *(Harshly)*
>
> Yes, I know how long.
>
> *(Silence. Crosses above to down left center)*
>
> I didn't want to talk about it.

JACKIE: And then—last week—either it was starting up again—or there was someone else—something—and I had to stop it.

HARRISON: You went to my desk and searched through all my papers.

JACKIE: You think I liked doing that?

HARRISON: I don't know. You did it.

JACKIE: I didn't want to find the bloody letters!

HARRISON: . . . A little while ago . . . I would have said it was impossible.

JACKIE: Yes—impossible. Well—I was younger—and I had a lot more hope.

> *(Silence)*
>
> Why didn't you leave me? I could have brought the children up. Why did we have the children? Fifteen years ago! You must have known you meant to be unfaithful long before.

HARRISON: I never meant to be unfaithful.

> *(Silence)*

JACKIE: Would he mind—d'you think I could have a drink?

HARRISON: I didn't set out—

> *(Harrison crosses to kitchen, two glasses from cabinet, scotches from the bottle on the counter. Jackie puts purse on center chair, crosses to fireplace, takes coat off and puts it in down left chair)*
>
> for God's sake!—what d'you think?—one day I made up my mind—I'm going to be unfaithful. I didn't think—in a million years—I couldn't imagine . . .

JACKIE: It isn't difficult, is it? I've always understood it's something anyone can do. Anyone gets married in the first place. It doesn't count, does it—if you aren't married? That isn't being unfaithful, is it? What is that called?

> *(Silence. Harrison crosses to Jackie)*
>
> If it was so difficult for you—
>
> *(Smiling)*
>
> I can believe it was!—you must have thought a lot about it. Knowing you . . .
>
> *(Harrison turns downstage. Mocking.)*
>
> I'm not supposed to say that. Sorry. Let's say I've never met you. I'll make no assumptions. I'll simply tell you how you seem to me—tonight—as if I met you—tonight.
>
> *(Jackie drinks some of her scotch)*

One thing—you don't seem queer.

(*Silence*)

Why did we have the children?

HARRISON: You—had the children.

JACKIE: You didn't want them?

HARRISON: I didn't think I had a choice.

JACKIE:

(*Angry*)

God in heaven!—

(*Silence. Quietly. Crosses to* Harrison)

Really—you didn't want them? Would you rather—now—they didn't exist?

HARRISON: They do exist.

JACKIE: Yes—but if we hadn't . . .

HARRISON: We did.

(*Silence*)

JACKIE:

(*Softly. Crosses above to right of center chair*)

Yes. Something you can be thankful for—you don't have to get a divorce. Save yourself a lot of money—and save me the . . . He won't insist you marry him?

(Harrison *crosses to fireplace, glass on mantel*)

Sorry!

(She *drinks some of her scotch*)

You see—if I once let myself—if I begin to take this—any of this—seriously—I might begin to scream—

(*Crosses, sits chest*)

You went to bed with him. You did—make love—to him. It could be rather funny. Can't you hear them—"Poor Jackie—did you know? Her husband left her for another man." Isn't that funny? I think it has a certain quality—you might say—surprise. Would you say—surprise?

(*Silence*)

Alan!

(Harrison *walks to* Jackie. She *presses herself against* Harrison, *putting her arms around his back.* Harrison *accepts the embrace awkwardly*)

Sit down. Please—will you?

HARRISON:

(*Sits next to* Jackie)

If you knew I was unfaithful . . .

JACKIE:

    (Quickly)

    I didn't know.

HARRISON: You had a pretty good idea.

JACKIE:

    (Quietly)

    Yes.

HARRISON: Why didn't you throw me out?

JACKIE: I thought it was probably my fault. I never was much good in bed. It didn't seem—well—altogether fair I should blame you entirely—and anyway—I never thought . . .

    (Silence. Smiling. Leans towards him)

    You've got a kind face, sir. Give a poor girl a kiss.

    (Silence. Pulls back)

    Actually, you've got rather a silly face. Sweet, of course. Look—you don't have to sit there—if you don't want to. God forbid—you should do anything . . .
    (She drinks some of her scotch. Rises, crosses above to below armoir)
    I thought this would help. Funny—you want to know something? It doesn't help a bit. What's on the telly?

    (Silence. Crosses right of center chair)

    Somehow—I never thought you'd get around—to leaving. I thought you needed me—and what you couldn't find in bed with me—you were taking care of that.

HARRISON: How could you accept—how could you do that—to yourself?

JACKIE: Yes—I was quite surprised.

    (Silence. Abruptly)

    It wasn't my immediate reaction.

    (She looks at her empty glass. Turns toward kitchen)

    Shall I have another?

HARRISON: I don't think so.

JACKIE:

    (Turns downstage)

    At first—I thought—I'd kill you—then—I'd kill myself. All rather melodramatic, I'm afraid. Then—I thought—go away some place—just disappear—and then—I'd take the children, bag and baggage, leave you, find a place to live and make a life for them—and then—do nothing.

    (Crosses down right center)

    I was wrong! I stood out there tonight more than an hour—watching this house. I dodged round corners, hid in the darkness. Sometimes I felt an idiot—sometimes—I felt ashamed.

(Silence. Crosses to kitchen, refills glass, crosses down right center)

I really would quite like another drink. What kind of thing is that? Running after your husband—to find out where he goes! Ask him—if you want to know. That's what normal people do. People who talk to each other—trust each other.

HARRISON: I trusted you.

JACKIE:

(Violently)

Never to make a fuss. Keep a safe distance from the awkward question. Yes—you trusted me! I stood and watched you walk into this house. I didn't try to stop you. I watched the windows—every window was a bedroom and you were making love—and I was—watching. The pictures in my mind! Always with a girl, of course. I didn't know then what was really going on—and just as well! I would have thrown up in the gutter—seeing all the pictures he put in my mind. Why did he do that, Alan?

(Silence. Crosses above center chair, sits upstage arm)

You think we'll all just go away. Keep quiet long enough and let us talk— we'll all get bored and leave you—and then, the noise will stop? Alan—the noise is in your mind. It isn't us.

(Silence)

I know some things about you. More than twenty years?

(Puts glass down on small table)

Even I can understand a little of the pain. I can't help take it all away. Once—I thought I could. I was so arrogant when I married you.

(Abruptly)

I had the feeling—as I walked into this room—now—you've done this and you can't go back. You can never be the same—quite the same person. This is a thing the woman you thought you were could not have done—and so—you're not that woman. Do you understand what I'm saying?

(Jackie rises, crosses and sits next to Harrison, takes his hands in hers)

I can change—Alan—I can be anything you want me to be. If there's hope. There is—isn't there? Hope? Some hope?

HARRISON: I should have left you long ago. I didn't have the strength—and—yes, I was frightened.

(Harrison tries to release his hands. Jackie holds on to him tightly)

JACKIE: You're not—you can't—leave me? I wasn't asking—will you stay with me? You are—you're going to—stay with me?

HARRISON: Jackie—it doesn't make any sense. I told you—

(Desperately. Rises)

how many times . . .

JACKIE:

> (*Violently*)

> Once!

> (*Silence. Rises*)

> You have to say it once—and clearly. So I hear the words. So I know I didn't—misunderstand—and let you go—when you really meant to stay— just—wanted me to ask.

HARRISON: Why does it have to be so painful?

JACKIE: Pulling people into pieces—isn't that always—painful? God in heaven! What do you want me to do? Send you away with a kiss on the forehead—a pat on the bottom? I have got feelings.

> (*Jackie lets go of* Harrison's *hands and turns away from him, laughing. Crosses center*)

> I didn't say that! Did you hear what you made me say? Alan—this is ridiculous! What are we doing in this dreadful room? Are you going to live here? You'll go raving mad.

> (*Jackie crosses up center and gestures at the psychedelic pop art posters*)

> Is that the kind of thing he likes?

HARRISON:

> (*Crosses down left*)

> Jackie—for pity's sake!

JACKIE:

> (*Harshly*)

> I don't have any pity. Alan—I hope he takes you—really breaks you into bits. Why should I pity you?

HARRISON:

> (*Smiling*)

> Do you have to hate me?

JACKIE:

> (*Crosses right center*)

> Does it matter? Do you care?

> (*Silence. Slowly*)

> I suppose you do. You'll have to see me—coming to collect the children— yes—you wouldn't want to meet me—hating you. I suppose—if I don't greet you—smiling—sweetness and light—you won't ever come to see us. Still—it's not for long. I mean—right now—Michael's old enough—you can meet him for a drink—a meal. Betty . . .

> (*Silence*)

> I'm not sure I want you seeing too much of her. I'll have to think about it.

(Quietly)

If you're going to leave us—live this extraordinary life—that's your decision. Betty's still a child. I have to think for her. I'm not sure it's a good idea she should see you very often—if at all. When people hear about this—well—they're bound to talk and I think that's enough for the child to cope with. Her friends at school . . .

(Silence)

I shall divorce you, Alan. I don't want to have your name—not any more. You'll have to support me—and the children, of course—you'd do that anyway. But I can't start to work again. It's been too long and I'm feeling rather old. I think—perhaps—we'll move. I don't want to go on living in that house. What plans have you made? Are you going to live here? I presume you'll leave the firm. You won't want to face . . .

(Silence. Crosses down center)

There won't be many of your friends you'll want to see. Still—I don't suppose you care. Not many of them you like. Most of them—business friends—and you won't need them, when you leave the firm. Starting a new life! You'll find new friends. In a way—I have to admire you—at your age— making this break. If you'd really thought about it—then—I might admire you.

HARRISON: I've thought about it.

JACKIE:

(Crosses to Harrison)

You can't do this. You can't leave me on my own. I can't manage, Alan—all on my own. What can I do? Tell me—please—what do you want me to do? You always said—making love to me—the world just went away—you said—and everything was silent. It can be like that—surely—it can—if you'll help me.

(Jackie puts an arm around his neck and pulls Harrison's face down towards her. She kisses him fiercely. Urgently)

Tell me—what shall I do?

(Whispering)

What would you like me to do? There's isn't anything—Alan—you can ask and I won't do for you. I want to make you happy. Ask me—please—my darling—what shall I do? I only want to make you happy.

(Harrison pulls his face away, turns downstage. Jackie hits him on upstage shoulder)

Don't do that! Is it so disgusting? Does it offend you—kissing me? You made love to me three nights ago. Did it make you sick? Did you think of him when you were making love to me—is that how you made yourself—able—to make love? . . .

(Silence. Harshly)

If you can't fuck the one you want to fuck—you can at least think about him . . . You are queer aren't you? I suppose you always were.

(Crosses below chest)

Christ!—what sort of idiot . . . Did you ever make love to me—days when you made love to him?

(Silence)

All the nights you couldn't make love—I blamed myself. I wasn't attractive—clever enough—I didn't know how to make you want me—how to seduce you! The times I went to sleep—knowing I was so inadequate a lover, I couldn't even make my husband hard. No wonder then you couldn't satisfy me. The years we've been married and you never left me really satisfied.

HARRISON:

(Quietly)

You came to bed smelling of children. You made love to me like a mother—comforting a child who made unreasonable demands—which had to be endured. One night I wanted to make love. I put my arms around you—kissed you—and you said—"Darling—before we start—will you just see—is Betty still asleep? She's been so odd today, I think she must be coming down with 'flu'." I was halfway on top of you—and you said . . . The bed has never lost the smell of children. All your clothes—your body—the smell sticks to you. It has since they were born and you said—"I don't want any help. We can't afford it—anyway, I want to do it all myself."

JACKIE: Was that wrong?

HARRISON: We could afford it.

JACKIE: Doing it myself—was that wrong? Why didn't you tell me?

HARRISON: Why didn't you ask me? Eight years—talking to babies—when did you talk to me? Jackie—you dressed them—undressed them—walked with them in the park. You nursed them and your breasts still smell of milk. You changed them—held the messes in your hands. Smell your hands. Can you . . . on your hands—can you smell?

(Silence)

The children are more secure now than I have ever been. They sleep in the dark. They hide in tiny cupboards. They run to strangers. I needed so much more than them. I needed you—and they had you—and couldn't let you go. Why should they? Children need their mother—and their mother . . . The trouble is—of course—I look human like any other man—a reasonable and rational—adult, human being—able to cope with all his problems—buying a house—paying the bills—making the money for you all to spend—giving you presents—asking—

(Abruptly)

love me. When was it ever quiet enough for you to hear? Where was the understanding—help—I needed? Love and tenderness.

(Silence)

I knew it was foolish, weak—unmanly. I couldn't admit everything—each day of my life—frightened me to tears—and I couldn't even cry.

(Silence)

131

JACKIE:

(Hesitantly)

I love you.

HARRISON: I know—yes—of course.

JACKIE:

(Step toward Harrison)

If you could've told me . . . Alan—if you could have said you felt—left out—you felt—I was neglecting you . . .

HARRISON:

(Quietly)

I did say—Jackie—I told you—almost every day. You couldn't hear.

(Smiling)

The children make more noise than Clapham Junction. How could you hear?

JACKIE:

(Vehemently)

I can't—Alan—please! Don't make me say—I could've kept you—we'd still be—together—if the children—if I hadn't . . . I love them. They are the best of me.

HARRISON:

(Crosses to Jackie)

I don't want you to say that. I don't think it's true. They're very probably— the best of me.

JACKIE:

(Jackie *pushes her hand through* Harrison's *arm and links her two hands around it)*

It's almost over. Michael's grown up—with his own life. I hardly ever see him—he's so busy. Betty—she wants to leave school next year and get a job. They'll both of them live away from home. We'll be on our own again.

(Goes into Harrison's *arms)*

We didn't always have the children. We were happy then. We can—I know we can—Alan—can't we—be happy?

HARRISON: Pretend it's 1953. Pretend—we just got married and we're twenty. Live all kinds of lies—because we can't cope with what we are—what we've made ourselves?

(Harrison holds her away. Softly)

Is that what you want to do?

JACKIE: How do you intend to cope? Hiding yourself in everlasting, short and furtive love affairs! How long will this one last? How long have any of them—and you came back—always!—you came back to me.

HARRISON: I never left you.

JACKIE: You haven't left me now.

HARRISON: You—haven't let go.

(Silence)

JACKIE:

(Harshly)

You want to leave me.

(Jackie *lets go of* Harrison *and steps back*)

That's all it is. You've decided—and nothing's going to stop you. You won't even let yourself think what you're doing—to me—to the children.

(Shouting to Harrison*)*

You can't leave me. Don't you understand? Twenty years now! More than half my life! You belong to me.

(Silence)

HARRISON: I don't love you.

JACKIE:

(Harshly)

Alan—you haven't loved me for fifteen years. You stayed with me. What's so different—now—why do you have to love me?

HARRISON: I love him.

JACKIE:

(Backs away)

Aren't you just a bit too old—talking about love—telling yourself—I am in love—and that makes anything I do—all right—justified—in the eyes of heaven—sacred! What am I doing? Begging you to stay!

(Crosses center)

Christ—if you were a man—halfway mature—

(Viciously)

Michael is more grown up than you are—more a man.

(Silence)

HARRISON: Jackie—please. Go home.

JACKIE: You're going to stay here?

HARRISON:

(Crosses to fireplace)

Yes.

JACKIE:

(Crosses to down left chair, picks up coat, crosses to center chair, putting coat on)

You'll find love and tenderness with him? With all the anger—ugliness—he has inside—you expect him to be gentle—understanding?

HARRISON:

> *(Crosses to down left chair)*

> I don't want to talk about him.

JACKIE:

> *(Smiling)*

> No. What shall I tell the children?

HARRISON: I'll come and see them. I think I should tell them myself—don't you?

JACKIE: What will you tell them?

HARRISON: We're going to live apart.

> *(Silence)*

JACKIE:

> *(Picks up purse)*

> We will see each other? You don't intend—we never meet again?

HARRISON: I'll come and see the children. You'll be there?

JACKIE:

> *(Crosses right of chair, finishes drink. Quietly)*

> Yes.

HARRISON: There's a lot of things we have to talk about.

JACKIE: I suppose there are—yes—what about your clothes? What shall I do with them? Have you brought anything?—did you pack a suitcase?

> *(Anger)*

> Did you?

HARRISON: No.

JACKIE: Just what you're wearing? Oh, love—not even a clean shirt.

HARRISON: I haven't thought—I didn't—think . . .

JACKIE:

> *(Crosses above center chair)*

> Will we be friends?

HARRISON: I don't know.

JACKIE:

> *(Crosses up center. Abruptly)*

> Why did you wait so long?

HARRISON: I'm sorry.

JACKIE: Before you knew me—you must have known—eventually . . .

HARRISON:

> *(Smiling)*

> How could I know—before I knew you?

JACKIE: When you were a child—didn't you—play—with other boys? Didn't you know? Is it possible—you can be queer and not know? Live so long . . .

HARRISON:

(Quietly)

I don't know.

JACKIE: Well—you really had me fooled!

(Silence)

When will you see the children?

HARRISON: Tomorrow?

JACKIE:

(Opens door)

Saturday? Yes—all right. I'll see they both stay home. I won't be there. Will you manage?

(Harrison nods his head)

This is even smaller than the flat we used to live in. How will you survive?

(Silence)

You'll let me go? You won't even try to stop me? I keep expecting . . .

(Jackie turns and walks out of the flat.
She leaves the door open.
Silence.
The sound of the front door, as it opens and then closes.
Harrison stands for a moment, then walks toward the door.
He stares at the photo-montage on the wall.
Harrison steps forward, kneels on the bed and reaches to tear the faces off the wall.
Harrison murmurs angrily to himself, grunting with the effort, exerting himself violently, tearing his fingernails across the photographs, rasping them down the wall)

Curtain

ACT III

Harrison sits in center chair, smoking. Silence. The door opens quietly. Harrison listens expectantly. Powell looks in.

POWELL: Hello. Are you still here?
HARRISON: Hello.

(Silence)

POWELL:

(Closes door)

Where's Julie? Gone and left you—all on your own?

(Crosses above center chair)

You've been having sort of a busy night down here.

(Powell looks at the scraps of torn photographs and smiles)

Cleaning house?

(Harrison crosses to up left chair, puts on jacket.
Powell glances around at Harrison, takes picture off wall)

I always thought it was a bit tactless—keeping all those photographs—pinning them up where anyone can see them. When will Julie be back? You do expect him to come back?
HARRISON:

(Sits up left chair, cigarette from packet, relights from old cigarette)

I don't know. Yes, I do.
POWELL:

(Sprawls on bed)

Are you going to move in with Julie? Good thing if you did. He shouldn't be left on his own. Some of us—I think we're probably better—on our own. Julie—gets into all sorts of trouble.

(Silence)

I'm not his brother. Did he tell you?
HARRISON: Yes.
POWELL: Must have been pretty obvious. You're clever enough to know when you've interrupted—

(Smiling)

something. No point trying to kid you. I could've told him that—the silly bitch!—and I hardly know you.

(Rolls on tummy)

You were talking sort of loud. One time—I thought I heard a woman's voice. Was there a woman here? Is that what you were fighting about? Do you like to make it with women as well?

(Sits up, leans on elbow)

I make it with women. Not too often—just—when I have to.

(Harrison *rises, crosses down left, puts old cigarette out in ashtray*)

It's not so bad. Sometimes I could almost say I enjoy it. 'Course, if they make a lot of fuss—try and take you over—then you have to show them—make it clear—you know? Are you serious about Julie?

(Silence)

You don't have a whole lot to say for yourself.

HARRISON:

(Crosses to fireplace)

I think perhaps it would be better if you came back tomorrow. Talk to Julie in the morning.

POWELL: I'm coming back tomorrow. I have a date with Julie. He's spending the weekend with me. Don't you remember? You were here.

(Silence. Smiling)

Sorry 'bout that! First come—if you'll pardon the expression—first served.

(Pats bed)

Come and sit here. Come on. I'd much rather talk to you. I think you're sort of interesting.

(Silence. Lies back)

I could've been angry, you know—the way you interrupted—making Julie throw me out—but—I'll forgive you. I'm not jealous. Share and share alike—that's what I say. Don't be greedy. Something I saw once written on a bus—

(Holds arms up toward ceiling)

"If you've had some—smile."

(Sits up)

I've had some—and I'm smiling.

(Silence)

Do you want to fuck?

(Harrison *puts cigarette out*)

You think Julie's good—

(Powell *swings legs over, sits left of bed*)

I'll show you things that make Julie look an amateur.

(Powell *rises, crosses behind* Harrison, *holds him on his upper arms*)

If you're frightened Julie might come back—we can go up to my room. Darling—don't be shy. I'll tell you what I like to do . . .

(Harrison *turns quickly, lunges at* Powell, *and sends him staggering back upstage. Laughing*)

I like enthusiasm, darling . . .

(Harrison *lunges after* Powell, *reaching for his throat. They fall on to the bed*)

. . . this is ridiculous!

(*Suddenly,* Powell *is frightened. He tries to pull himself free, clawing at* Harrison's *hands*)

You're choking me.

(Harrison *tightens his grip on* Powell's *throat. Incoherent sounds rasp out of his throat. Gasping*)

Let go. Let—go. Please . . .

(*Violently, desperately,* Powell *swings his arms up against* Harrison's *arms and breaks the hold* Harrison *has on his throat.* Powell *falls on to the floor and rolls away. He scrambles up on to his feet, lunging towards the armoir.* Powell *faces* Harrison, *who rises, crosses left center*)

What the hell d'you think you're doing? You could've killed me.

HARRISON:

    (*Quietly*)

I wanted to kill you.

POWELL: Why? 'Cause I touched you? 'Cause I wanted you to fuck? What is it, darling—saving yourself for Julie?

    (Harrison *starts for* Powell)
    (*Reading*)

Are you going to behave? Couple of things I want to show you.

(*Crosses to armoir, opens door*)

Things might interest you.

(*Crosses to bed, gets folder, dumps stuff out of it*)

Things about Julie. Starting life together—you shouldn't have any secrets. Isn't that what they say? I'll tell you a couple of Julie's secrets. Would you like that? No—I don't think you will. I'm going to tell you anyway. There's so much I don't really know where to start.

(Powell *takes a notebook*)

I'll give you a taste. You can read the rest of it yourself. I think you'll enjoy it more. I spent a very happy morning—some of it is sort of wild—if you like that kind of thing. A lot of it I don't understand. Some of it simply doesn't make any sense. The bits I like . . .

(Powell reads quickly down a page. Reading)

"A spade—with a handle fourteen inches long." In all fairness, darling—I should tell you—I haven't read them carefully. It's just pot luck. I don't know them well enough to find the best stuff all the time.

(Reading)

Young man seeks interesting part-time occupation. There's a telephone number—650-5372.

(Looks at phone, then at Harrison)

If you don't like the food at home, eat out occasionally. Put yourself in my place, you'll enjoy it. I'll make your body beautiful—no apparatus required—no discrimination.

(Silence.
Harrison crosses to down left chair)

Goes on for half a page!

(Powell reads quickly down the page. Crosses below chest)

The man was awkward, hesitant. I opened the door. He almost turned away. It was ridiculous . . . I thought—at least—knowing he's come to fuck—all he has to do is pay—

(Harrison sits down left chair)

at least he'll be decisive.

(Reading. Crosses down left center)

Loving in the night of dying.

(Turns the page, reading)

Naturally—he assumed—I had all the experience. I would take control—seduce him. Offering all manner of mysterious delights. Five pounds down—and rapture guaranteed. I pulled the curtains—asked—what shall I do? What do you like? I thought—he's bound to notice—I don't even know the words. He wanted me to take off all my clothes . . . He wanted just to look at me, he said. At first—he wanted just to look. He began to get excited—and then—he took control. It was as I imagined it would be. No feeling—it wasn't my body—no guilt—I belonged to him—no self—I didn't exist.

(Silence. Turns pages, looking)

I thought he'd give us some more detail.

(Turns the page. Reading. Turns downstage)

When the punishment is shame and there is no shame—how can the punishment begin? How can it ever end?

(Powell *turns the pages quickly. Crosses to up left chair, brings it close to* Harrison, *sits. Reading*)

November 18th. The telephone woke me. A fat man. Almost impotent. Made me sick. My face so close to the flaccid, dead heaviness, of his thighs. The belly mound. Once. He wanted to stay. 3:30 P.M. A young man. Tall and dark. Big. Frightening. Twice. 5 P.M. A businessman, I think. Lonely. Excited. Middle-aged. He wanted me to fuck him. The silly bitch. Once. Pages of this.

(*Reading*)

Pretty one. Waiting on the road. We talked. Went home with him. Strange— and sad—he cried a lot. Oh, mother—he was so my own, own brother.

(*Throws book to* Harrison)

What the hell is that!

(*Rises, crosses to bed, searches for another book, finds it*)

I wish I could find the one I was reading this morning. It's sort of interesting, isn't it? Somehow—you wouldn't expect Julie—doesn't seem tough enough.

(*Silence*)

Are you listening, darling? I wouldn't want you to miss anything.

(*Smiling. Crosses to small chair*)

I could have you now. You wouldn't even try to stop me.

(*Puts chair back upstage*)

Funny—'cause now—I don't really want you.

(Harrison *holds the notebook in his hands, his arms hanging loosely in front of him.* Powell *crosses and sits center chair, one foot on foot stool. Reading*)

December 27th. I haven't spoken to anyone now for three days. I've been sitting here in my room. I read for a while. Most of the time—nothing. It has been very quiet. At five o'clock today the telephone rang. I didn't answer. Doesn't that make you want to cry? The silly bitch! I was here that whole bloody Christmas.

(*Looks at* Harrison. *Then—reading*)

Gordon was filthy to me all night. Kept laughing at me. Told stories about me to his friends. Told them all the things he made me do. After we finished dinner—he showed some pornographic films. He sent me to the bedroom with a friend of his—an old man—told me—"I want him to enjoy himself. Julie—he's a very dear old friend of mine." He could hardly make it. I was there almost an hour—and then, he said—"Yes—it was all right. Nothing to make a lot of fuss about, dear boy." Gordon said—'Julie—you should have tried a little harder. Now—I shall have to punish you'—and he hit me with a cane. He made me take off all my clothes and he hit me with a cane. He hit me . . .

(Half-smiling)

Sort of party you read about—and never get invited to. Darling, that isn't all. That isn't half. Wait 'til I find . . .

(Powell turns the page and reads quickly down it. Reading)

After the other men went home, Gordon kissed me—said—would I be gentle with him—take off his clothes—wash him and oil him—powder—put him to bed. "All the excitement, Julie—now—I feel so tired. We won't make love tonight." He reached to pat my face and said—"You were such a good boy tonight. Behaved yourself quite beautifully"—and I pushed my thumbs into his eyes. I forced my nails through the soft, staring wetness—into his head. His blood—the obscene jelly of his brains—spilled on my hands. I threw him off the bed. I put my foot down on his stomach—walked on his chest. I felt the bones break—splintering—underneath my feet. I pushed my heel hard into his mouth. I felt his teeth drive deep into my flesh. I knelt beside him— whispered what I would do before I would let him die. I cut across his stomach—opened his body—thrust the knife inside.

(Silence. Powell puts book down on foot stool, rises, walks to counter, gets a drink. Silence. Powell crosses to table, sits. The door opens and Weston walks into the flat. He stops abruptly)

WESTON:

(Up center)

Dear God in heaven! What's been going on? What have you been doing?

(Harrison looks at Weston, holding the notebook against his chest. Weston looks at the notebooks on the bed, the photographs torn from the wall and the general confusion in the room)

POWELL: Hello, Julie.

(Weston turns and looks across the room at Powell, who is holding a glass of scotch)

I was wondering when would you get back.

(Silence. Weston looks at Harrison)

WESTON:

(Shuts door)

If you want to read it, love—don't let me stop you.

POWELL: We've already looked at quite a lot of them.

WESTON:

(Crosses center)

Alan?

(Harrison half-turns away from Weston and opens the notebook)

POWELL: We've been entertaining ourselves—waiting for you—

WESTON:

> (*To* Powell)

> Was that your idea?

POWELL: Of course it was. He didn't know anything about them. I thought—starting out together—you shouldn't have secrets from each other. Gives you such an unfair advantage. Don't you think?

WESTON: Was it a lot of fun?

POWELL: Full of surprises.

WESTON: I can imagine.

POWELL: Lot of things I missed the first time through.

WESTON:

> (*Crosses by bed*)

> Did you—was that . . .

> (Weston *gestures at the ruined photomontage and the scattered scraps of photographs*)

> . . . your idea too?

POWELL: That was your friend's idea. I got here in time to stop him pulling the whole place to pieces. You should be thankful.

WESTON:

> (*Harshly*)

> Davy—go home—will you? Get the hell out of here!

POWELL: Miss all the fun?

WESTON: Darling—the fun starts when I get hold of you and cut your balls off—I mean—cut them off! I can imagine things to do with you that'd make anything you read sound like a fairy tale.

> (Harrison *begins to read aloud from the notebook*)

HARRISON: ". . . stranger here. We haven't seen you before." He was a small man and he wore a faded, almost yellow overall. He smiled. I think he was embarrassed. I think he plays his game of jokes and camaraderie, because he cannot make another way to deal with the endless story of disease, decay and degradation. He wrote my name and told me to sit down. He smiled at me. There was contempt inside the smile—disgust—if I wanted to look—and if I didn't—it was there anyway.

> (*Reading*)

WESTON:

> (*Turns to* Harrison)

> Read it all, love.

> (Weston *crosses to* Harrison *and takes the notebook.* Weston *turns the page, looks at the words written on the page. Crosses to chest, sits*)

> (*Reading*)

"Yes—it sounds like gonorrhea. Let's have a look."

(Powell *crosses right center*)

He was a very young man, detached, professional, not at all involved. I unzipped my trousers, showed myself to him. What did he see? "I think well have a test. There's not a lot of doubt." He turned away and wrote on bits of paper. "Wash your hands." He gestured with his head. He didn't look at me. The water in the tap ran very hot—scalding my hands. I held them in the water.

(*Silence. Turns page*)

Talking—to ask—asking—to know . . . knowing—to understand and hoping—hoping—hoping. Looking—to see . . . listening—to hear . . . touching—to feel and holding—holding—holding. Searching—to find . . . finding—to have . . . having—to keep and loving—loving—loving.

(*Glances at* Harrison)

He looked through a microscope—he looked at me—smeared across a narrow piece of glass. He looked inside me. What did he see? He made me bend across a high, hard couch and punched a hypodermic needle into my buttock—into my body—into my rotting soul—and shame—I was ashamed.

POWELL: Yes.
WESTON:

(*Smiling*)

Does that make you sick? Darling—that doesn't begin to tell you what it was like! I've done things that would really turn your stomach. I've been to bed with you. I've touched you. I've let you touch me. Think about that. If anything is going to make you sick!

(*Rises, turns to* Powell)

Have you any idea, darling—just how bad you smell? Has no one ever told you? Standing in the same room makes me want to take a bath in disinfectant. Your clothes stink. Don't you ever wash? Do you have any idea how ugly you are? Kissing you is like swimming underwater in a sewer. Anyone goes to bed with you—he's got to be pretty desperate.

POWELL: You went to bed with me.
WESTON: Darling—last night—I would have fucked a pig.

(*Starts to laugh*)

POWELL: You vicious, degenerate—evil . . .
WESTON

(*Calmly*)

You cock-sucking, mother-fucking cunt.

(*Silence*)

Does that give you some idea, darling—how I feel about you? What sort of chance you have—hanging about—hoping to get into me?

POWELL: I don't want to—get into you! You're diseased. You're—depraved . . .

WESTON: Right. All those good things.

POWELL: If I'd known . . . if I'd had any idea . . .

WESTON: You're in no danger, darling. The good doctors cured me—and I've been a lot more careful since. Until last night, of course. Nothing I've done this year I regret so much as letting you in here last night—letting you—fuck me.

POWELL:

> (Powell *walks out of the flat*. Weston *shuts the door, puts hat on hook. Silence*)

> You won't get another chance.

WESTON: Oh, love.

> (*Silence.* Harrison *rises, crosses to foot stool takes book and tears it. Crosses to bed, tears up books and papers. Takes folder and book, crosses to table tearing folder and book.* Weston *walks forward center*)

HARRISON:

> (*Harshly, leaning on table*)

> Stay there, Julie. Stay where you are. Stay away.

WESTON: I don't know what else I'm going to say. Some of the things I wrote—if it helps you—

> (*Abruptly*)

> —the worst things—anger at you—and hatred, all of that—they didn't happen.

HARRISON: Ugliness.

WESTON: I can't start defending all the things I've done.

> (*Angrily*)

> I don't have to. It's none of your bloody business. You weren't here.

HARRISON: I don't know—with all the words—Julie—all the pictures . . .

WESTON:

> (*Crosses to below chest*)

> Nobody says you have to stay. I don't want you—staying—if it means you punish me for everything I've done. I want to send you away. If I didn't love you—Christ!—I know I should. You have to understand—reading those things sickens—and disgusts you—reading! They happened to me. It's possible I manage pretty well—punishing myself. Do you want to go?

HARRISON:

> (*Turning*)

> I want this—not to have happened.

WESTON: Coming here tonight?

HARRISON: Finding you—with him—fighting with you—and Jackie—all the bitterness—reading . . .

> (*Silence. Sit table*)

> It has happened.

144

WESTON: You made it happen.

HARRISON: I did all kinds of things tonight—leaving the house. I told myself—I'm doing this for the last time—walking down the stairs—listening to the sounds around the house—the gramophone playing in Betty's room—doors opening and closing—kitchen noises—cars on the street outside. I've lived in that house for eleven years. I've made a lot of changes—made it my house—you wouldn't recognize the house I bought—and now—pulling open the front door—for the last time—I thought.

WESTON:

(Crosses, sits in chair, center)

Coming here tonight—was that supposed to be some sort of ending?

HARRISON: Leaving it all behind—yes—walking away . . .

WESTON: How could it be? In your head—maybe. Did you think she'd just—let you go? Wish you good luck and wave! You didn't even tell her you were leaving.

HARRISON:

(Angrily)

I couldn't tell her. Until I saw you—I didn't know myself.

WESTON: You didn't leave home just to live with me? You didn't? I mean—if you did—hadn't you better think about it? How long do you think this is going to last? I won't be a comfort to you in your old age.

(Rises, crosses away left)

There's nothing I hate more than old, painted queens—

(Picks up papers)

—and you're a whole lot older, love—than I am. Twenty years? You haven't worn particularly well. You haven't taken care of yourself. You've lost your hair. You're getting soft. And smoking the way you do! How long will your heart put up with that? What d'you think—I'm going to spend my life nursing an old man? Anyway, you'll soon get bored with me. I'm sort of stupid, when you get to know me. I'm not really meant to live with people, I've decided. Something happens in my head—I expect . . . all sorts of idiotic things. It takes a lot of strength—living with me—and you're not very strong. I'm not sure you've got the strength to make it—being queer. You meet a lot of funny people.

(Crosses above center chair)

You don't intend we sit here the rest of our lives—the two of us—together!

(Puts papers into trash can)

Doesn't that sound sort of draggy?

(Crosses to armoir, takes off sweater, hangs it up, shuts door)

Another thing—you could easily go back to girls. You've had a lot of practise. Since you can make it either way—it's easier with girls—easier to live—you know? People don't look at you so funny—with your arm around a girl—even a fella—old as you.

(Silence. Crosses right center)

You might go back to her. It's not impossible. You told each other some home truths tonight. Is that so bad? Could be the making of a great relationship. A little while—you might fall in love. I'm an incurable romantic.

(Harshly, crosses to fireplace)

Why don't you get out of here? If you're going to sit there—looking at me—Christ!—I can do without that. Accusing! What right have you—accusing me?

(Crosses down left center)

You think—what?—I failed you? All that stuff—and you can only see—I failed you? You set some bloody sort of standard and I'm supposed to live—you're not here to help me—love me—keep them all away—still—I'm supposed . . . Because you condescend to love me—not to live with me—at a safe distance—love me—in your head—where no one else can see—not even me! Listen—you failed me tonight. You let her scream at me. You didn't stop her. You didn't try. I made you feel ashamed! I'm supposed to let her walk in here—say what she likes—scream at us? She called our making love—filthy! You wouldn't stand up for yourself—leave alone take care of me. I thought you were some special sort of thing. I thought you had decided to leave her, because your life with her was nothing. I thought—you came here, because you loved me. I didn't understand—you had this picture in your head—some romantic dream of life with me—and tenderness—beauty! You can't come here—running away from her—using me. I won't survive, love—when you run away from me. I've cut off from you—for this moment—free—I can let you go. I want you to go.

(Silence. Crosses, sit in down left chair)

It would be easier. I could rest then—be the person I am—not have to try and be this person you have in your crazy head—this—innocent.

HARRISON: When you first went to bed with me, you knew so much about making love—you couldn't have been innocent. I never thought you were.

WESTON: We wouldn't have gone to bed together if I had been innocent.

HARRISON: I meant—without deceit. You tell the truth. I haven't told the truth to anyone in twenty years. I lived deceit and lies, as naturally as smiling. I wanted to escape. I thought perhaps I could.

(Smiling)

I'm not sure, if I'd known this whole night had to happen—I'm such a coward—I would most likely have stayed where I was.

(Bitterly, crosses above chair)

A strong man wouldn't have done all this. Only someone selfish—knowing what he wanted—disregarding other people's pain—his own responsibility—not looking any way but straight ahead—knowing if he looks around—he has to stop.

(Silence)

I used you, Julie. Leaving—I had to go somewhere—go—to someone. I wasn't ready—to go nowhere—on my own.

WESTON: I'm glad you came here.

HARRISON: I shan't go back. There's nothing there.

WESTON: I'm sorry I said those things. I didn't mean them. I was so terrified—knowing you'd read that stuff.

HARRISON: I could have stopped that happening to you. I can only think—

WESTON:

> *(Hesitantly)*

> It didn't happen to me, love—not all of it. I went out and made it happen.

HARRISON: I shall have trouble sometimes, when I think about it—

> *(Silence, crosses, sits on foot stool)*

> I may want to hurt you.

WESTON: I know that. Christ! Whatever happens—one thing—right? You don't go away. It's worth it, love—I mean—

> *(Laughing)*

> —speaking for myself, you understand—

> *(Doubtful)*

> Isn't it worth it? That's what this is all about—yes? Staying together—being together—and no lies.

> *(Abruptly)*

> Some lies—aren't there always—and—some pain—but not so much—and maybe—less and less—Love—I don't want to hurt you. I'm not angry anymore. I just have to know—right? Staying—you really are—and loving—whatever happens. We'll tidy all this mess tomorrow—yes?

HARRISON: Tomorrow—I have to see the children.

> *(Silence)*

> I can't think of Betty crying. I tell myself—she doesn't really care. She'll hardly notice I'm not there. I can't think—tomorrow—when I tell her—she might cry.

WESTON: Oh, love—my love.

> *(Silence)*

> Curtain

Rita Moreno (Googie), Jerry Stiller (Carmine), and Jack Weston
(Gaetano) in the 1975 Broadway premier of Terrence McNally's
The Ritz, at the Longacre Theatre.
(Photograph reprinted with permission from the
John Willis Theatre World/Screen World Archive)

The Ritz

BY TERRENCE MCNALLY

For Adela Holzer

The Ritz was originally performed at the Yale Repertory Theatre. It opened January 20, 1975, at the Longacre Theatre in New York City. It was produced by Adela Holzer. It was directed by Robert Drivas. Scenery and costumes designed by Michael H. Yeargan and Lawrence King. Lighting designed by Martin Aronstein. The production stage manager was Larry Forde. The assistants to the director were Tony DeSantis and Gary Keeper.

The Cast
(In Order of Appearance)

ABE	George Dzundza
CLAUDE PERKINS	Paul B. Price
GAETANO PROCLO	Jack Weston
CHRIS	F. Murray Abraham
GOOGIE GOMEZ	Rita Moreno
MAURINE	Hortensia Colorado
MICHAEL BRICK	Stephen Collins
TIGER	John Everson
DUFF	Christopher J. Brown
CARMINE VESPUCCI	Jerry Stiller
VIVIAN PROCLO	Ruth Jaroslow

The Patrons

PIANIST	Ron Abel
POLICEMAN	Bruce Bauer
CRISCO	Richard Boccelli
SHELDON FARENTHOLD	Tony deSantis
PATRON IN CHAPS	John Remme
PATRON FROM SHERIDAN SQUARE	Steve Scott

The time of the play is now.
The place of the play is a men's bathhouse in New York City.
The people of the play are:

GAETANO PROCLO	He is in his early 40's, balding and stout.
CHRIS	He is in his early 30's with a big, open face and features.
MICHAEL BRICK	He is in his mid-20's, very rugged and very handsome.

CARMINE VESPUCCI	He is in his 40's, balding and stout.
CLAUDE PERKINS	He is in his 40's and quite lean.
TIGER	He is in his early 20's, wiry and has lots of curly hair.
DUFF	He is in his early 20's, wiry and has lots of curly hair. In fact, he looks a lot like Tiger.
ABE	He is in his 50's and stocky.
THE PATRONS	They come in all sizes, shapes and ages.
GOOGIE GOMEZ	She is in her 30's and has a sensational figure.
VIVIAN PROCLO	She is in her early 40's and stout.
MAURINE	She's in her mid-40's and very thin.

ACT ONE

The house curtain is in, the house lights are on and the overture from Rossini's "Tancredi" is playing as the audience comes in. The house goes black. In the darkness we hear the sounds of the Rosary being recited. Occasionally a stifled sob over-rides the steady incantation of the prayers.

Priests and Relatives. Hail Mary, full of grace, the Lord is with thee. Blessed art thou amongst women and blessed is the fruit of thy womb, Jesus. Holy Mary, Mother of God, pray for us sinners now and at the hour of our death. Amen.

> *(Underneath all this, the funeral march from Verdi's "Nabucco" is heard. The lights have revealed* Old Man Vespucci's *death bed.* Relatives *and* Family *are grouped around him, all in silhouette. Kneeling to his right is Carmine. Kneeling to his left is* Vivian. *They are weeping profusely.)*

CARMINE: Poppa . . . !

VIVIAN: Poppa . . . !

> *(The death rattles are beginning.* Old Man Vespucci *feebly summons the others to draw close for his final words.)*

AUNT VERA: *Aspetta! Aspetta!*

COUSIN HORTENSIA: Sshh! Speak to us, Poppa!

AUNT VERA: Give us your blessing, Poppa!

COUSIN HORTENSIA: One final word, Poppa!

AUNT VERA: *Un poccita parole*, Poppa!

VIVIAN: Give us your blessing, Poppa!

OLD MAN VESPUCCI: Vivian.

VIVIAN: Yes, Poppa?

OLD MAN VESPUCCI: *Vieni qua.*

VIVIAN: Yes, Poppa.

OLD MAN VESPUCCI: Get Proclo.

VIVIAN: Get Proclo, Poppa? Yes, Poppa. He's coming. The plane was late from Cleveland. He'll be here for your blessing.

> (Old Man Vespucci *dismisses his daughter with a hand gesture.*)

OLD MAN VESPUCCI: Carmine, my son.

CARMINE: Yes, Poppa. I'm here, Poppa.

OLD MAN VESPUCCI: Get Proclo.

CARMINE: Get Proclo, Poppa?

OLD MAN VESPUCCI: Get Proclo. *Qui brute. Qui boce, Tha botania!* Kill him! Kill him! Kill him! Kill the son of a bitch!

VIVIAN: Proclo is my husband, Poppa!

OLD MAN VESPUCCI:

> *(Finally mustering all the strength he can, he raises himself up.)*

GET PROCLO!!!

> *(He falls back dead.)*

RELATIVES:

(Simultaneously.)

Aaaaaiiiieeeee!

AUNT VERA: *Poppa è morto!*

PRIEST: *In nomine patris et filii et spiritu sancti requiescat in . . .*

(*The lights fade on the death bed. At the same time, the sound of a pounding drum is heard. It leads directly into a lively rock orchestral. The lights come up, revealing activity inside The Ritz behind scrims. The main thing we see are doors. Doors and doors and doors. Each door has a number. Outside all these doors are corridors. Lots and lots of corridors. Filling these corridors are Men. Lots and lots of men. They are prowling the corridors. One of the most important aspects of the production is this sense of men endlessly prowling the corridors outside the numbered doors. The same People will pass up and down the same corridors and stairways over and over again. After a while, you'll start to think some of them are on a treadmill. Most of them are dressed exactly alike; i.e., they are wearing bathrobes. A few men wear towels around their waists. Every so often we see someone in bikini underwear or an additional accoutrement, such as boots or a vest. The number of men, referred to from now on as the* Patrons, *can vary, but* EACH ACTOR *must be encouraged to develop a specific characterization. Even though they seldom speak, these various* Patrons *must become specific, intetgral members of the cast. We also see* Tiger *and* Duff, *two attendants. They are sweeping up and making beds. Over the music, we hear announcements.*)

ABE:

(*Over the loudspeaker.*)

217 coming up, Duff! . . . Tiger, they're out of soap in the showers! On the double! And check the linens and robes on the third floor. . . . Just a reminder that every Monday and Thursday is Buddy Night at the Ritz. So bring a friend. Two entrances for the price of one.

(*The lights dim, and the entrance area is flown in. The inner door and Abe's booth are moved on from left and right. The center scrim flies as the lights come up bright, and we are in the admissions area of The Ritz. The various* Patrons *will pay, check their valuables, receive a room key and then be buzzed through the inner door adjacent to the booth. One* Patron *has just finished checking in. As he is buzzed through the door, we see* Abe *announce his room number over a loudspeaker.*)

274! That's 274 coming up, Duff!

(*The* Patron *disappears. The phone on Abe's desk rings, and he answers.*)

Hello, the Ritz. No, we don't take reservations!

(*He hangs up, as Another Patron enters.*)

PATRON: Good evening.

ABE: Yeah?

PATRON: Nasty night.

ABE: Is it?

PATRON: I'm one big puddle.

ABE: Well watch where you're dripping. I just had that floor mopped.

PATRON: I'd like a room, please.

ABE: That's ten bucks. Sign the registration book and check in your valuables.

> (The Patron *begins the check-in procedure.* Claude Perkins *has entered from the outside. He is wearing a raincoat over rather ordinary clothes. He carries a bag from Zabar's Delicatessen and has a Valet Pack slung over one shoulder. He gets in line behind the* Patron.)

PATRON: You're dripping.

CLAUDE: What?

PATRON: I said, you're dripping.

CLAUDE: Of course I'm dripping. It's pouring out there.

PATRON: Well try not to. They don't like you dripping here.

> (He starts for the door.)

See you.

> (He is buzzed through.)

CLAUDE: I hope not.

ABE:

> (Over the loudspeaker.)

376! That's room 376! Coming up, Duff!

CLAUDE: That's a good floor for that one. Nobody goes up there.

ABE: Well look who's back. Hello, stranger.

CLAUDE: Hello, Abe.

ABE: I thought you'd sworn off this place.

CLAUDE: I thought I had, too.

ABE: You got homesick for us, right?

CLAUDE: I didn't have much choice. I don't speak Spanish, so the Continental is out. The Club Baths are just too far downtown, I'm boycotting the Beacon, Man's Country's had it and I've been barred from the Everard.

ABE: You've been barred from the Everard?

CLAUDE: They'll regret it.

ABE: Nobody gets barred from the Everard. How'd you manage that?

CLAUDE: There was this man there.

ABE: A fat man, right?

CLAUDE: Fat? He was the magic mountain. He drove me into one of my frenzies. I went berserk and I kicked his door in. So they threw me out and told me never to come back. I was willing to pay for it. I just wanted to talk to him.

ABE: Pick on somebody your own size, why don't you, Claude?

CLAUDE: I wouldn't like that. How much do you weigh?

ABE: Forget it.

CLAUDE: Are you up to 200 yet?

ABE: Forget it!

CLAUDE: When you get up to 200 come and knock on my door.

ABE: Forget it!

CLAUDE: Couldn't we just install a weigh-in station here?

ABE: I said forget it!! You want to check that?

CLAUDE: It's my costume for the talent show.

(He is heading for the door, still carrying the Valet Pack and Zabar's shopping bag.)

It's good to be back, Abe. I'm feeling strangely optimistic this evening.

ABE: Just don't kick any doors in.

CLAUDE: I hope I don't have to.

(Claude is buzzed through the door.)

ABE: 205! Coming up! That's 205!

(Gaetano Proclo comes dashing in. He is carrying a suitcase and a big box of Panettone, the Italian bakery specialty. He is wearing a wet raincoat, a cheap wig, a big bushy moustache and dark glasses. He goes directly to Abe.)

PROCLO: Can you cash a check for me? It's on Ohio State National.

ABE: What do I look like? A teller in a bank?

PROCLO: You don't understand. I've got a cab waiting. I'll be right back. That's why I got into the cab in the first place, to go somewhere, and it's to here I've come.

(Sounds of a horn blowing.)

You hear that? That's him!

ABE: You got a traveler's check?

PROCLO: No.

ABE: Travelers are supposed to have traveler's checks.

PROCLO: Well this traveler doesn't. We left Cleveland in a hurry. Traveler's checks are for people who plan!

(More honking.)

There he goes again!

ABE: I'm sorry.

PROCLO: Look, I've got all the identification in the world. Driver's license, Social Security, Blue Cross, voter registration, Rotary Club . . . What about my business card? "Proclo Sanitation Services, Gaetano Proclo, President." That's me.

ABE: You got a credit card?

PROCLO: I don't want credit, I want cash!

ABE: N—o, buddy.

PROCLO: Oh come on! Do I look like someone who would try to pass a bad check?

(A realization.)

Why of course I do!

(He takes off his dark glasses.)

There! Now can you see me?

(More honking.)

Oh all right!

(He removes his moustache.)

Now are you satisfied?

ABE: I don't make the rules here.

PROCLO: Wait! Wait!

> (He takes off his wig.)

Everything else is real.

ABE: I'd like to help you out, mac, but—

PROCLO: Then do it! Do it!

ABE: Hey, calm down.

PROCLO: The only thing that's gonna calm me down is *you* cashing my check. My brother-in-law is a maniac and he's going to kill me tonight. If you don't let me in there I'm going to be a dead person. Please, mister, you are making a grown man cry. I'm begging you. It's a matter of life and death!

> (More honking.)

ABE: I shouldn't really be doing this but . . .

PROCLO: You are a good man . . .

ABE: Abe.

PROCLO: Abe. I'm gonna have a novena said for you when I get back to Cleveland. What's your last name? Abe what?

ABE: Lefkowitz.

PROCLO: I'm *still* gonna have that novena said for you!

> (More honking. Chris has entered from the outside. He wears jeans, a blue nylon windbreaker, and a bright purple shirt. He carries an overnight bag. Also, he is wearing a policeman's whistle and a "popper" holder around his neck.)

CHRIS: Does anybody have a cab waiting?

PROCLO: What?

CHRIS: Is that your cab out there?

PROCLO: Oh yes, yes it is!

CHRIS: Well you've also got one very pissed off driver.

PROCLO:

> (To Abe.)

Can you cash this for me now?

> (To Chris.)

How pissed off is he?

CHRIS: On a ten scale? Ten.

> (More honking.)

PROCLO: Christ!

> (Proclo is fumbling with the money and heading for the door.)

Keep an eye on those for me, will you?

CHRIS: Sure thing.

> (Proclo hurries out. Chris looks at the suitcase and the Panettone.)

Planning a big night of it, honey?

> (To Abe.)

I had a friend who tried moving into the baths.

ABE: What happened?

CHRIS: He died from a lack of sunshine. He died happy and blind, but he still died.

ABE: We missed you last week.

CHRIS: How do you think your customers felt? I'm a legend in my own lifetime.

(Yelling into Abe's microphone.)

Try to hold out, men! Help is on the way!

ABE: Hold your horses, Chris.

CHRIS: That's all I've been holding all week.

ABE: You wanna sign in?

CHRIS:

(While he writes.)

How's that gorgeous son of yours?

ABE: You're too late. He's getting married.

CHRIS: That's terrific. Give him my love, will you?

ABE: Sure thing, Chris.

CHRIS: Does he need anyone to practice with?

ABE: He's been practicing too much. That's why he has to get married.

CHRIS: Compared to me, Abe, she'd have to be an amateur.

(He returns the registration book.)

ABE: Ronald Reagan! Aw, c'mon, Chris!

CHRIS: You know, he used to be lovers with John Wayne.

ABE: Sure he was.

CHRIS: Right after he broke up with Xavier Cugat.

ABE: People like you think the whole world's queer.

CHRIS: It's lucky for people like you it is.

PROCLO:

(He comes rushing back in.)

He can't change a ten! Do you believe it? New York City, one of the great cities of the world, and this driver I have can't change a ten!

CHRIS: They still don't take anything over a five.

PROCLO: In Cleveland even a paper boy can change a ten!

CHRIS: Did I ever have you?

PROCLO: What?

CHRIS: I've got a rotten memory that way. You never used to live in Rego Park?

PROCLO: No!

CHRIS: 'Cause you look like someone I knew once who was from Rego Park.

PROCLO: I'm afraid not.

CHRIS: He was a large man like you and he was in ladies' shoes, I remember.

PROCLO: Well I'm from Cleveland and I'm in refuse.

CHRIS: I guess not then. Sorry.

PROCLO: That's perfectly all right.

(He hurries back out.)

CHRIS: A gay garbageman!

ABE: You never can tell.

CHRIS: That's true. I mean, look at me. If you just saw me walking down the street, you'd think I was a queen.

(Chris *blows his whistle as he is buzzed through the door.*)

All right, men! This is a raid! Up against the wall for a short-arm inspection!

ABE: 240! Two-four-oh! She's here, boys!

(*A young man has entered from outside. His name is* Michael Brick. *He is neatly dressed in a trench coat and hat. He looks like a classic detective. He steps up to the admissions booth.*)

MICHAEL: I'd like a room please.

(*The first time we hear* Michael's *voice we are in for a shock. It is a high, boy soprano-ish treble. A timbre totally incongruous with his rugged physique.*)

One of your private rooms. How much is that?

ABE: You want what?

MICHAEL: A room, please. I was told you have private rooms.

ABE: Yeah, we got rooms.

MICHAEL: Then I'd like one, sir. How much is that?

ABE: How long?

MICHAEL: Is what, sir?

ABE: How long do you want it for?

MICHAEL: Three or four hours should be sufficient for my purposes.

ABE: I don't care what your purposes are: twelve's our minimum.

MICHAEL: All right, twelve then, sir.

ABE: That's ten bucks. Sign in and I'll take your valuables.

MICHAEL: Tell me something. Has a balding, middle-aged fat man come in here recently?

ABE: I don't believe what just came in here recently.

MICHAEL: Think hard. I'll repeat his description. A balding, middle-aged fat man.

ABE: We got all kinds inside. Fat, thin, short, tall, young, old. I can't keep track.

MICHAEL: Well I guess I'll just have to go in and see for myself, sir.

ABE: I guess you will. You're not a cop, are you?

MICHAEL: I'm a detective, sir. Michael Brick. The Greybar Agency. Our client wants the goods on him and I'm just the man to get them. I've never failed a client yet. What do I do now?

ABE: Through there and up the stairs. Someone'll show you your room.

MICHAEL: Thank you, sir.

ABE: Let me give you a little tip, Brick. Stay out of the steam room.

MICHAEL: Why, sir?

ABE: It gets pretty wild in there.

MICHAEL: Oh, I can take it, sir. In my line of work I get to do a lot of wild things. This is my first seduction job. Wish me luck.

ABE: With that voice, you'll need it.

(Michael *is buzzed through the door and is gone.*)

101 coming up! That's one-oh-one! Oh boy!

(Googie Gomez *comes into the admissions area, protecting herself from the rain with a wet copy of* Variety. *She is carrying a wig box and wardrobe bag.*)

GOOGIE: No rain, he tells me! No rain, he says! No rain! That fucking Tex Antoine! That little maricon! I'd like to pull his little beard off! One spot on this dress and I'm finished! The biggest night of my life and it's pissing dogs and cats.

PROCLO:

(*Who has entered behind Googie.*)

That's cats and dogs.

(Googie *has been so busy worrying about rain spots on her dress she really hasn't noticed* Proclo *yet. When she does, there is a marked change in her behavior and vocabulary.*)

GOOGIE: Joe Papp! Hello, Mr. Papp. It's a real pleasure to meet you. I seen all your shows. Uptown, downtown, in the park. They're all fabulous. *Fabulosa!* And I just know, in my heart of hearts, that after you see my show tonight you're going to want to give me a chance at one of your wonderful theatres. Uptown, downtown, in the park. I'll even work the mobile theatre. Thank you for coming, Mr. Papp. Excuse me, I got a little laryngitis. But the show must go on, si?

PROCLO: My name isn't Papp.

GOOGIE: You're not Joe Papp?

PROCLO: I'm sorry.

GOOGIE: But you are a producer?

PROCLO: No.

GOOGIE: Are you sure?

PROCLO: Yes.

GOOGIE: That's okay. I heard there was gonna be a big producer around tonight and I wasn't taking any chances. You never know. It's hard for me to speak English good like that.

(*A new outburst.*)

Aaaaiiieee! My God, not the hairs! *Cono!*

(*Her hands are hovering in the vicinity of her head.*)

Okay. Go ahead and say it. It's okay. I can take it. Tell me I look like shit.

PROCLO: Why would I want to say a thing like that to such an attractive young lady?

GOOGIE: You boys really know how to cheer a girl up when she's dumps in the down.

(*She gives* Proclo *a kiss on the cheek.*)

My boyfriend Hector see me do that: *ay! cuidado!* He hates you *maricones,* that Hector! He's a ball breaker with me, too, mister. You know why you're not a producer. You're too nice to be a producer. But I'm gonna show them all, mister, and tonight's the night I'm gonna do it.

(Googie *is moving towards the door.*)

One day you gonna see the name Googie Gomez in lights and you gonna say to yourself "Was that *her*?" And you gonna answer yourself "That was her!" But you know something, mister? I was *always* her. Just nobody knows it. *Yo soy Googie Gomez, estrellita del futuro!*

(Googie *is buzzed through the door and is gone.*)

PROCLO: Who the hell was that?

ABE: Googie.

PROCLO: I thought this was a bathhouse.

ABE: It is.

PROCLO: A *male* bathhouse!

ABE: It is.

PROCLO: Then what's she doing in there?

ABE: Googie sings in The Pits.

PROCLO: The pits? What pits?

ABE: The nightclub.

PROCLO: You've got a nightclub in there?

ABE: We've got a nightclub, movies, TV, swimming pool, steam room, sauna, massage table, discotheque, bridge, amateur night and free blood tests every Wednesday.

> (Proclo *turns at the sound of* Maurine *entering behind him from outside. She is wearing a duffel coat with the hood up, pants and tall rubber rain boots. No chic dresser,* Maurine. *She seems deep in concentration and takes no notice of* Proclo *as she moves towards the door.*)

How'd it go today, Mo?

> (Maurine *just shrugs. She is buzzed through the door and is gone.*)

PROCLO: I don't even want to *think* what she does.

ABE: Mo's just our accountant.

PROCLO: I asked that cab driver to bring me to the last place in the world anybody would think of looking for me.

ABE: You found it.

PROCLO: Except everybody in the world is already in there. I need calm, privacy, safety tonight.

ABE: So stay in your room and keep your door locked.

PROCLO: Don't worry. I will. How much is that?

ABE: Ten dollars.

PROCLO:

> (*He looks at the registration book.*)

Ronald Reagan!

ABE: You can write John Doe for all I care. Just so long as we get some kind of a name down there.

PROCLO: Any name at all? Oh, Abe, I'm gonna speak to the Pope about getting you canonized!

> (*Reads what he's written.*)

"Carmine Vespucci, Bensonhurst, Brooklyn."

ABE: Who's that?

PROCLO: My maniac brother-in-law who was going to kill me tonight!

ABE: What did you do to him?

PROCLO: I got born and I married his sister.

ABE: That's all?

PROCLO: Just my whole life.

(Proclo *gathers his suitcase and* Panettone, *ready to enter now.*)

ABE: Do you mind if I ask you a personal question?
PROCLO: The man who just saved my life can ask me anything.
ABE: You ever been in a place like this?
PROCLO: Oh sure. We got a Jack LaLanne's in Cleveland.

(*The door is buzzed and* Proclo *goes through.*)

ABE: 196! That's one-nine-six coming up, Duff. Oh boy, oh boy, oh boy!

(*While Abe is speaking, the lights will fade on the admissions area and another rock orchestral comes up. The admissions area and the scrims are flown. Other lights are coming up and we are in the interior of The Ritz. On the lower level we see Tiger sweeping up. Chris enters behind him.*)

TIGER: Hey, Chris.
CHRIS: Hi, Tiger.
TIGER: What took you so long? They called your number ten minutes ago.
CHRIS: I was in the boutique.
TIGER: What'd you buy?
CHRIS: A red light bulb for my room and this month's VIVA.
TIGER: You don't need a red light bulb.
CHRIS: And I hope I don't need this month's VIVA. Much action tonight?
TIGER: With you here I'm sure there will be.
CHRIS: Slow, hurrh?
TIGER: Real dead, so far.
CHRIS: Don't worry, honey, I'll shake this place up good.
TIGER: If anybody can it's you.
CHRIS: The thing that no one understands about me is that sex is just my way of saying hello.
TIGER: Yeah, but you want to say hello to everybody you meet.
CHRIS: Don't you?
TIGER: I work here!
CHRIS: I wish I did.

(*They go.* Claude Perkins *has come up to the wandering and lost* Proclo. *The moment* Claude *lays eyes on him, we hear an immediately recognizable love theme.*)

CLAUDE: Hello, there.
PROCLO: Hello.
CLAUDE: What seems to be the problem?
PROCLO: I can't seem to find my room.
CLAUDE: Well you just come with me.
PROCLO: Why thank you. That's very kind of you.

(*They leave together as the music surges. On the upper level we see* Duff. Chris *comes up the stairs and pokes his head into the steam room.*)

CHRIS: Guess who!
DUFF: Hey, Chris.

CHRIS: Hi, Duffie.

DUFF: 240 again?

CHRIS: And it better be clean! Last time they were having a crab race on the sheets.

DUFF: I did it myself, first thing when I came on.

(He opens the door with Chris' key.)

CHRIS: Home sweet home! If these walls could talk . . . !

DUFF: They don't have to.

CHRIS: I've spent some of the happiest hours of my life in this room.

DUFF: I know. We've all heard you.

CHRIS: When are we gonna get together, you cute little hump?

DUFF: I don't know. Ask Tiger.

CHRIS: That means "forget it". Out! Out! I've got a busy night ahead of me, I hope.

(Calling out loudly.)

There will be an orgy beginning in room 240 in exactly four minutes! That's an orgy in room 240 in exactly four minutes!

(He goes into his room and closes the door. We have been watching Claude lead Proclo to his—that is, Claude's—room. Claude has followed Proclo in and has closed the door.)

PROCLO: Are you sure this is 196? I think this is someone else's room. Look, see the clothes?

CLAUDE: You'll never guess what I made for dinner tonight, so I'm just going to have to tell you.

PROCLO: I beg your pardon?

CLAUDE: A nice rich ground pork meat loaf with a mozzarella cheese center, gobs of mashed potatoes swimming in gravy, carrots floating in butter and for a salad, avocado chunks smothered in Roquefort dressing. Could you just die?

PROCLO: I could just . . . ! I don't know what I could just!

CLAUDE: And then: Dutch Chocolate layer cake with two big scoops of Baskin-Robbins mocha walnut ice cream and a fudge malted.

PROCLO: It sounds delicious.

CLAUDE: You could've been there.

PROCLO: I was in Brooklyn watching Bowling For Dollars. Now if you'll excuse me, I'll—

CLAUDE: Wait!

(He is rummaging in his shopping bag.)

You want a bagel with lox and cream cheese?

PROCLO: No, thank you. I've eaten.

CLAUDE: An eclair? Some homemade brownies? I know! A corned beef on rye with a dill pickle!

PROCLO: Really, I'm not hungry.

CLAUDE: How much do you weigh?

(He is blocking his way.)

PROCLO: What?

CLAUDE: Your weight! 210? 220?

PROCLO: 226.

(Claude *has started to undulate, dance almost, and move towards* Proclo.)

CLAUDE: JELLY ROLL BABY
YOU'RE MY JELLY ROLL MAN . . .

(*Singing in a low, sexy growl.*)

PROCLO: I think there is some confusion here.
CLAUDE: JELLY ROLL CUPCAKE
I'M YOUR JELLY ROLL FAN . . .
PROCLO: In fact, I *know* there is some confusion going on in here.
CLAUDE: YOU GOT THE ROLL
AND I GOT THE SOUL
THAT STRICTLY ADORES
PAYING JELLY ROLL TOLL. . . .

(Claude *is still singing as he pulls* Proclo *towards him and they collapse heavily on the bed.*)

PROCLO: Stop it! Please! You're hurting me!
CLAUDE: I'm hurting *you?*
PROCLO: Help! Help!

(Tiger *has been seen running along the corridor and uses his pass key now to come into the room. A small crowd of* Patrons *starts forming in the corridor outside the room.*)

TIGER:

(*Pulling* Proclo *off* Claude.)

Okay, fat man! Leave the little guy alone! What are you trying to do? Pull his head off?

(*He takes* Proclo's *key.*)

Let me see your key. 196! Now get down there and don't cause any more trouble. What do you think this is? The YMCA?

(*He puts* Proclo's *suitcase in the corridor and turns back to* Claude.)

I'm sorry, sir. It won't happen again.

CLAUDE:

(*He is moaning happily.*)

I certainly hope not.
TIGER: Get down there, man!

(*He goes.*)

PROCLO: He ought to be locked up!

(*The crowd of* Patrons *are all looking at* Proclo.)

Hello. Whew! I just had quite a little experience in there. I think that guy's got a problem. People like that really shouldn't be allowed in a place like this.

(*Stony silence from the* Patrons.)

What unusual pants. They look like cowboy chaps.

PATRON IN CHAPS: They are cowboy chaps.

PROCLO: I was just thinking I thought they looked like cowboy chaps. Well, gentlemen, if you'll excuse me, and let me get out of these clothes. Bye. Nice talking to you.

(Proclo *beats an embarrassed retreat down the stairs. The group of* Patrons *will slowly disband.* Chris *opens the door to his room, sticks his head out and yells.*)

CHRIS: Okay, boys, room 240! Soup's on, come and get it!

(*He goes back into his room.* Michael Brick *has appeared in the area of a pay telephone. He dials a number and waits.*)

MICHAEL: Hello, Bimbi's? Is this the bar across the street from The Ritz? There's a Mr. Carmine Vespucci there. I've got to speak to him. It's urgent.

ABE:

(*Over the loudspeaker.*)

Tiger! Duff! The linen people are here. On the double!

MICHAEL: Mr. Vespucci? My name is Michael Brick. I'm with the Greybar Detective Agency. You hired my partner to get something on a Mr. Gaetano Proclo, only my partner's sick so I'm taking over the case for him. I'm calling you from The Ritz. I just got here. Now let me see if I've got his description right. A balding middle-aged fat man? That's not much to go on, but I'll do my best.

(Googie *enters. She likes what she sees.* Michael *covers the receiver.*)

It's terrible here, sir. You have no idea. One of those transvestites is standing right next to me. Now you just stay by the phone in that bar across the street and I'll get back to you.

GOOGIE:

(*Vamping him.*)

Ay, que cosa linda!

MICHAEL: I can't talk now. I think he's surrounding me for unnatural things.

(Michael *hangs up, gives* Googie *a horrified look and hurries off.*)

GOOGIE: Hey *chico*, I was just gonna talk to you!

(*Tiger enters.*)

Tiger, is he here yet?

TIGER: Who?

GOOGIE: Who? What do you mean who? There is only one *who* I am interested in you telling me about! Listen, you told me there was gonna be a big producer here tonight. I dress special. I do the hairs special. If you're lying to me, Tiger . . .

TIGER: Can't you take a little joke?

GOOGIE: My career is no joke. Nobody's career is never no joke.

TIGER: I was just trying to build you up.

GOOGIE: I tell you something and I mean this: You ever hear of instant laryngitis? No producer be out there tonight and that's what I got—instant laryngitis—and you and Duff are gonna do the show alone. Those are my words, they are from the heart and I am now officially sick!

TIGER: Googie!

(Googie *rasps an answer and leaves,* Tiger *following her.* Proclo *comes wandering into view, still carrying his suitcase and still shaken from his experience with Claude.*)

PROCLO: This place is like a Chinese maze.

(Duff *comes out of one of the rooms.*)

DUFF: Are you 196?
PROCLO: Something like that.
DUFF: I meant your room.
PROCLO: So did I.
DUFF: Follow me.

(He leads *Proclo to the room.*)

196. Here it is.

(Duff *has opened the door for him.* Proclo *goes into the room. It is a shambles from the previous occupant. He calls out into the corridors.*)

Hey, Tiger! Room 196! On the double!
PROCLO: You're kidding. Tell me you're kidding.
DUFF: What did you expect?
PROCLO: I don't know. A room maybe. A normal size room.
DUFF: You should see some of the rooms they could've put you in.
PROCLO: You're telling me they come even smaller?
DUFF: Half this size.
PROCLO: Does Mickey Rooney know about this place?
DUFF: You got far out taste, mister.
PROCLO: Vespucci. Carmine Vespucci. What's your name?
DUFF: Duff.
PROCLO: It's good to see you, Duff.
DUFF: How do you mean?
PROCLO: I was beginning to think this place was a little too esoteric for my tastes, if you know what I mean. Like that guy up there with all the food.
DUFF: I think it's something to do with the weather. Rainy nights always bring out the weirdos.
PROCLO: They shouldn't let people like that in here. It'll give this place a bad name.
DUFF: This place already has a bad name.

(Tiger *has arrived with a mop and a change of linen. The room will be very crowded with the three of them and* Proclo's *luggage.*)

TIGER: We're both up shit creek again.
DUFF: Who with this time?
TIGER: I told Googie there'd be a producer out front tonight.
DUFF: Maybe there will be.
TIGER: I promised her. No producer, she's not going on. She's locked in her dressing room with instant laryngitis.

PROCLO: She told me she was feeling better.

TIGER: You know Googie?

PROCLO: I met her downstairs. She thought I was a producer. She's very colorful.

TIGER: Right now she's also very pissed off.

DUFF: Let me talk to her.

PROCLO: Not so fast, Duff. What about slippers?

DUFF: Slippers?

PROCLO: Slippers. For your feet.

DUFF: Where do you think you are? Jack LaLannes? Slippers!

(Duff *leaves as* Tiger *continues to clean* Proclo's *room and make up his bed.*)

PROCLO: I always thought they gave you slippers in a bathhouse. I mean, you could catch athlete's foot in a place like this.

TIGER: You're lucky if that's all you catch.

(*Trying to make up the bed.*)

Excuse me.

PROCLO: I'm sorry.

(*He stands.*)

Looking at you two, I think I'm seeing double.

TIGER: He's Duff. I'm Tiger.

PROCLO: How are people supposed to tell you apart?

TIGER: They don't usually. Just try to stay out of 205 this time.

PROCLO: What's in 205?

TIGER: That room I had to pull you out of. You could hurt someone doing that.

PROCLO: Now just a minute! I thought that guy was taking me to my room! You don't think I went in there because I wanted to?

TIGER:

(*Dawning on him.*)

You trying to tell me he's a chubby chaser?

PROCLO: A chubby what?

TIGER: Someone who likes . . .

(*He gestures, indicating great bulk.*)

PROCLO: You mean like me?

TIGER: You're right up his alley.

PROCLO: I knew someone like that once. I just never knew what to call him. "Get away from me, Claude!" was all I could come up with. A chubby chaser! That's kind of funny. Unless, of course, you happen to be the chubby they're chasing. Room 205. Thanks for the tip. I'll avoid it like the plague.

DUFF:

(*He has returned and is knocking loudly on the door.*)

Fifteen minutes!

PROCLO: Oh my God!

TIGER: Relax!

(*He opens the door.*)

166

DUFF: Come on, Tiger. Show time!

TIGER: What happened?

DUFF: Googie's Mr. Big is here. He's going to be sitting ringside for the first show tonight.

TIGER: How'd you manage that?

DUFF: I didn't. But with a little help from our friend here . . . !

PROCLO: Hey, now just a minute!

DUFF: Aw, now come on, Mr. Vespucci! Give two down and out go-go boys with aspirations for higher things a break.

PROCLO: I don't want to get involved with anything.

DUFF: All you have to do is listen to her act.

PROCLO: I don't want to listen to her act.

DUFF: I don't blame you, but that's not the point.

PROCLO: I'm not a producer.

DUFF: Googie's not really a singer.

TIGER: Come on, what do you say?

PROCLO: What if she finds out?

DUFF: That's our problem.

TIGER: Leave everything to us.

PROCLO: I came here to lay low.

TIGER: Man, you can't lay any lower than Googie's nightclub act.

DUFF: Come on, we gotta change.

TIGER: You're a prince, Mr. . . .

DUFF: Vespucci.

TIGER: An honest-to-God prince.

PROCLO: Thank you, Duff.

TIGER: He's Duff. I'm Tiger.

(They run off. Proclo closes the door and shakes his head.)

PROCLO: Seclusion! Is that asking so very much, God? Simple seclusion? I must be crazy! Allowing them to tell her I'm a producer!

(Michael Brick is seen outside Claude's door, which is ajar. He sticks his head into the room.)

MICHAEL: Excuse me.

CLAUDE: I'm resting.

MICHAEL: May I come in?

CLAUDE: I said I'm resting.

MICHAEL: I'm looking for someone.

CLAUDE: I told you I'm resting.

MICHAEL: That's okay. I just want to ask you—

CLAUDE: What do you need? A brick wall to fall on your head? "Resting!" It's a euphemism for "not interested"! Skinny!

(Claude slams the door in Michael's face. Michael. knocks on another door.)

MICHAEL: Excuse me. May I come in?

(Michael starts into the room, then comes rushing out.)

Oh, I beg your pardon! Excuse me, may I come in? Thank you very much.

(He goes into another room. The door closes. There is a beat and again he comes rushing out.)

Oh, my goodness!

(Michael's mother never told him there would be nights like this. He steels himself and enters the steam room. On the swing of the door, he is back out and gone. Proclo has nearly finished changing when there is a knock on his door. He quickly puts his wig back on.)

PROCLO: Yes?
CLAUDE: Are you there?
PROCLO: Who is it?
CLAUDE: Room service.
PROCLO: Who?

(He opens the door a crack, sees Claude and slams it.)

Go away!
CLAUDE: I've got a box of Hershey bars.

(He begins throwing bars of candy through the transom.)

PROCLO: I said go away!
CLAUDE: Peter Paul Mounds, Milky Ways . . .
PROCLO: I know what you are now!
CLAUDE: I can make you very happy!
PROCLO: You're a chubby chaser!
CLAUDE: I know.
PROCLO: Well stop it!
CLAUDE: How?
PROCLO: I don't know!

(Proclo waits, listens.)

Are you still there?
CLAUDE: I'm never leaving.
PROCLO: You can't stand out there all night. This is my room and that's my door to it. Now go away or I'll call Tiger and Duff.
CLAUDE: I'm not doing anything.
PROCLO: You're making me nervous.
CLAUDE:

(He thinks, then sings.)

LOVE YOUR MAGIC SPELL IS EVERYWHERE . . .

(He thinks.)

CAN'T HELP LOVING DAT MAN OF MINE . . .

(He thinks.)

THEN ALONG CAME . . .

(He stops singing.)

Who? Then along came who?
PROCLO: Vespucci.
CLAUDE: VESPUCCI!

(An inspiration.)

I JUST MET A BOY NAMED VESPUCCI! AND SUDDENLY THAT NAME . . .

(Proclo stops moaning and comes up with a plan.)

PROCLO: Okay, you win. What room are you in?
CLAUDE: 205.
PROCLO: All right, you go back to 205. I'll be right up.
CLAUDE: Promise?
PROCLO: On my mother's grave!

(He is crossing his fingers.)

Just get away from that door! 'Cause if you're still standing out there when I come out of this room, the deal is off.
CLAUDE: And if you're not up in my room in five minutes . . .
PROCLO: What?
CLAUDE: I'll find you.
PROCLO: And?
CLAUDE: You don't want to make me do anything rash, do you, Mr. Vespucci?
PROCLO: Oh no, oh no!
CLAUDE: Five minutes then. Room 205. If you're not up there, I'm gonna come down here and break your knees. Don't push your luck with Claude Perkins.

(He goes. His name seems to have struck a distant bell for Proclo.)

PROCLO: Claude Perkins. It can't be the same one. Claude Perkins. That's all I need. He's dead. He has to be dead. Claude Perkins.

(Proclo opens the door and looks out. No sign of Claude. Without realizing it, he shuts the door behind him and locks himself out.)

Oh no! Come on, will you? Open up. Damn!

(Calling off.)

Boys! Boys! You with the keys! Yoo hoo! Yoo hoo!

(Proclo is suddenly aware of a Patron who is just looking at him and smiling.)

Hello. Just clearing my throat. Ahoo! Ahoo! Too many cigarettes. Ahoo! Hello there. I hear the Knicks tied it up in the last quarter.
PATRON: Crisco.
PROCLO: What?
PATRON: Crisco oil party.
PROCLO: Crisco oil party?
PATRON: Room 419. Pass it on.
PROCLO: Pass what on?
PATRON: And bring Joey.

PROCLO: Who's Joey?

PATRON: You know Joey. But not Chuck. Got that?

PROCLO: Crisco oil party. Room 419. I can bring Joey but not Chuck.

PATRON: Check.

PROCLO: What's wrong with Chuck?

(Patron *whispers something in* Proclo's *ear. Proclo's eyes grow wide. He can't wait to get out of there.*)

Chuck's definitely out! If you'll excuse me now . . . !

(*He starts moving away. The* Patron *leaves.* Proclo *is pacing in rapid circles.*)

Now wait a minute. Wait a minute. Stay calm. Be rational. Don't get hysterical. All he did was invite you to a Crisco oil party, whatever the hell that is, and told you to bring Joey. Of course, I don't know Joey, and I don't think I want to, and not to bring Chuck because Chuck—. It can't be one of those places. I mean, one or two weird people do not a you-know-what make. People are just more normal in Cleveland.

CHRIS:

(*Leaning out of his room.*)

Telephone call for Joe Namath in room 240. Long distance for Mr. Joe Namath in room 240!

PROCLO: Well *there!* You see? I knew I wasn't a crazy person!

(*Proclo is heading towards* Chris' *room.*)

There's just no way Broadway Joe could be a you-know.

(*On his way, he composes a speech to himself.*)

Mr. Namath? Excuse me. I wonder if I might trouble you for an autograph. It's not for me. It's for my 12-year-old, Gilda. Say, did you hear the Knicks tied it up in the last quarter? Mr. Namath?

CHRIS:

(*From inside his room.*)

No, don't! . . . I can't! . . . Oooo! . . . Aaaa! . . . Oh my God! . . . Do it, do it! . . . Yes! Yes!

(*He puts down the magazine he was thumbing through.*)

If that doesn't get those queens up here nothing will.

PROCLO:

(*Knocking on* Chris' *door.*)

Mr. Namath?

(Chris *comes out of his room and sees* Proclo.)

You're not Joe Namath.

CHRIS: Neither are you.

PROCLO: I thought you were Joe Namath.

CHRIS: It's the lighting.

PROCLO: I was praying you were Joe Namath.

CHRIS: I don't blame you.

PROCLO: I mean, you just had to be him!

CHRIS: Eating your heart out, honey?

PROCLO: I don't know what I'm doing.

CHRIS: Join the club. It's like some strange heterosexual gypsy curse has been put on this place tonight. How's the orgy room doing?

PROCLO: I haven't—.

CHRIS: The steam room?

PROCLO: No.

CHRIS: The pool? The sauna? The dormitory?

PROCLO: Sorry.

CHRIS: Well no wonder you haven't made out.

PROCLO: I don't want to make out.

CHRIS: Who are you trying to kid? This is me, sweetheart, your Aunt Chris.

(He starts pounding on closed doors.)

Fire drill! Everybody out for fire drill!

(A door opens. A Patron looks out.)

I'm sorry. I thought this was the powder room.

PATRON: We're busy.

CHRIS: You like this one?

(To Proclo.)

PROCLO: No!

CHRIS: Neither do I!

PATRON: I said we're busy!

(He slams the door.)

CHRIS: You've got my son in there. Tell him his mother wants to see him.

PATRON:

(From behind the door.)

Buzz off!

CHRIS: One mark on that boy's body, Wanda, and I'm calling the police!

(To Proclo.)

Well I tried.

PROCLO: Really. I don't want you to do anything for me.

CHRIS: You're not going to believe this line, but "You're new around here, aren't you?"

PROCLO: I'm afraid so.

CHRIS: I never forget a face and I've seen a lot of faces in this place. Some people think I'm a sex maniac. They're right. If I don't get laid at least twice a day I go home and beat my dog. Here's hoping for you, Jeanette!

(He offers a "popper" to Proclo, who shakes his head no.)

It's fantastic stuff. I got it from this queen I know who just got back from a hairdresser's convention in Tokyo. He does Barbara Streisand's hair, so they gave him the Gene Hersholt Humanitarian Award.

(*He laughs and backslaps* Proclo.)

Come on, I'll show you around.

PROCLO: That's all right. I was just going back to my room.

CHRIS: Come *on!* I don't do this for everyone. I'm an expert guide. A lesser person would charge for this sort of tour.

PROCLO: There's something I better tell you.

CHRIS: Sweetheart, relax, you're not my type. I just want to help you find yours.

(*To a* Snooty Patron *who is walking by.*)

Hi.

(Snooty Patron *turns his back.*)

We said hello.

(Snooty Patron *turns his back some more.* Chris *turns to* Proclo, *gives him an eye signal and starts talking to him in a very loud voice.*)

Do I know her? Darling, she is what is known as a Famous Face. She's out cruising 24 hours a day. She must live in a pup tent on Sheridan Square. If I had a nickel for every pair of shoes she's gone through . . .

(Snooty Patron *finally turns around and glares at him.*)

Margaret Dumont! I thought you were dead!

SNOOTY PATRON: There's a reason some of us don't ride the subways and I'm looking right at him.

(*He huffs off.*)

CHRIS: Is that supposed to mean me?

(*After him.*)

Screw you, honey!

(*To* Proclo.)

One thing I can't stand is a queen without a sense of humor.

(*After him.*)

You can die with your secret!

(*To* Proclo.)

PROCLO: I have to tell you something. I'm afraid I'm not a . . . Miserable piss-elegant fairy.

(*He will try to convey something with his hands.*)

CHRIS: You're not gay?

PROCLO: No.

CHRIS: Then what are you doing here?

PROCLO: That's what I'd like to know.

CHRIS: Baby, you're very much in the minority around here.

PROCLO: That's what I'm afraid of.

CHRIS: Or maybe you're not and that's why I'm having such rotten luck tonight. What are you? A social worker or something?

PROCLO: You mean *everybody* here is . . . ?

CHRIS: Gay. It's not such a tough word. You might try using it some time.

PROCLO: Nobody is . . . the opposite?

CHRIS: I sure as hell hope not. I didn't pay ten bucks to walk around in a towel with a bunch of Shriners.

PROCLO: What about Tiger and Duff?

CHRIS: What about them?

PROCLO: I thought they were normal.

CHRIS: They are normal. They've also been lovers for three years.

PROCLO: I'm sorry. I didn't mean it like that.

CHRIS: Yes, you did.

PROCLO: Yes, I did.

CHRIS: I'll tell you something about straight people, and sometimes I think it's the only thing worth knowing about them. They don't like gays. They never have. They never will. Anything else they say is just talk.

PROCLO: That's not true.

CHRIS: Think about it.

PROCLO: I'm sorry. I didn't know what I was getting into when I came in here tonight. I'm in trouble, I'm scared and I'm confused. I'm sorry.

CHRIS: That's okay.

PROCLO: You're gonna think I'm crazy but somebody is planning to kill me tonight. My own brother-in-law.

CHRIS: Are you putting me on?

PROCLO: I wish I were. And if Carmine caught me in a place like this he'd have *double* grounds for murder.

CHRIS: What do you mean?

PROCLO: My brother-in-law. For twelve years I was the butt of every sissy joke played at Our Lady of Perpetual Sorrow. It was a good name for that place. And then, when I married his only sister . . . ! They're very close, even for Italian brothers and sisters, and you know what they're like.

(He clasps his hands together.)

Cement! Except for Vivian, Vivian's my wife, that whole family's always hated me. At our wedding, her own mother had a heart attack while we were exchanging vows. Vivian said "I do" to me and Mamma Vespucci keeled right over in the front pew.

CHRIS: It's kind of funny.

PROCLO: Not when it happens to you. Yesterday, at their own father's funeral even, Carmine had all the relatives giving me that look.

CHRIS: What look?

PROCLO: That look.

(He gives a look.)

CHRIS: I would've laid him out.

PROCLO: That's you.

CHRIS: Why didn't you?

PROCLO: The truth? I'm scared to death of him. I guess I always have been.

CHRIS: Maybe that's why he always hated you.

PROCLO: "Get Proclo." Those were their father's dying words. Do you believe it? This far from his Maker and all he can say is "Get Proclo."

CHRIS: Get Proclo?

PROCLO: That's me. With their father dead now, there's a lot of money involved that Carmine would love to screw me out of. And I'm not so sure it's particularly clean money. Carmine can chase me all over town but this is one night he's not gonna "Get Proclo."

CHRIS: And you picked a gay baths to hide out in?

PROCLO: I didn't pick it exactly. I asked my cab driver to take me to the last place in the world anybody would think of looking for me.

CHRIS: Don't worry, you found it.

PROCLO: Only now I've got a chubby chaser and someone who thinks I'm a producer after me.

CHRIS: Listen, it beats someone like your brother-in-law trying to kill you. Why don't you just stay in your room and try to get some sleep?

PROCLO: Sleep!

CHRIS: Strange as it may seem, no one's gonna attack you.

PROCLO: Someone already has.

CHRIS: Beginner's luck! Standing around out here like this, you're just asking for it. Go to your room.

PROCLO: I can't! I locked myself out!

CHRIS: Well try and find Tiger and Duff. They'll let you in. Now if you'll excuse me, darling, I want to try my luck in there. Us B-girls work better solo.

PROCLO: See you.

CHRIS: See you.

(He throws open the door to the steam room and blows the whistle.)

Hello, everybody, my name is June! What's yours?

(He is gone. Proclo *is alone. He stands undecided for a moment but we can see that his curiosity is getting the better of him. He opens the door to the steam room and peers in. He goes in. The door closes. There is a long pause. The stage is empty. And at once,* Proclo *comes bursting out of the steam room. You have never seen anyone move as fast. He comes tearing down the stairs and runs into* Duff.*)*

PROCLO: The key to 196, quick!

DUFF: You're supposed to wear it.

PROCLO: I know!

DUFF: What's the matter?

PROCLO: Just let me in, please.

DUFF: Try to hang onto your key from here on out, okay?

PROCLO: Believe me, I'll make every effort.

(He is admitted.)

Thank you.

DUFF: The show's about to get started.

PROCLO: Fine, fine!

> *(Puffing for breath.)*

DUFF: You won't be late?

PROCLO: Of course not!

DUFF: Googie's all keyed up.

PROCLO: So am I, so am I!

DUFF: Thanks a million for helping us out like this, Mr. Vespucci.

PROCLO: Tell me something, you and Tiger are . . . lovers?

DUFF: Three years. I think that's pretty good, don't you?

PROCLO: It's terrific.

DUFF: I better get ready. See you downstairs!

> *(He goes, closing the door.)*

PROCLO: I wouldn't go down there and see her act for a—? *Her* act? Of course! I knew there was something funny about that Gomez woman. She's not a woman! Female impersonators . . . chubby chasers . . . B-girls . . . Baby Junes! When I grow another head is when I'm gonna leave this room!

> *(He sits on the bed, exhausted. Where to go now? What to do? His eyes go to the Panettone. He looks a little more cheerful. Meanwhile, Michael has raced back to the area of the telephones and dialed a number.)*

MICHAEL: Bimbi's? Oh! Mr. Vespucci. Michael Brick. No one fits your description. It's pretty hard getting the goods on someone you've never seen. And you didn't tell me about that steam room.

> *(We see Googie entering. She sees Michael. She stops. She eavesdrops.)*

If you need me I'm at 929-9929. And I'm in room 101. 101!

GOOGIE: Room 101!

MICHAEL: He's here again.

> *(Michael hangs up and hurries off.)*

GOOGIE: I'll be there, *chico*. Googie's gonna straighten you out between shows.

> *(She turns to Proclo's room. Proclo is eating his Panettone when she knocks on the door. He jumps.)*

Guess who, Mr. Vespucci?

> *(More knocking. Proclo tries to ignore it but it is very urgent. Finally he goes to the door and opens it a crack. A fatal mistake.)*

PROCLO: Now wait a minute!

GOOGIE: I know what you're going to say.

> *(She barges in and closes the door.)*

PROCLO: You couldn't possibly!

GOOGIE: I don't believe in bugging producers just before they catch your act, so I just want to tell you one thing. In my second number, "SHINE ON HARVEST MOON", the orchestra and me sometimes get into different keys, but if you know that it won't matter. Other than that, the act is fabulous and I just know you're gonna love it.

PROCLO: I'm sure of it!

GOOGIE: You know what *guapo* means? Handsome.

PROCLO: Me? Oh, no, I'm ugly. I'm very, very ugly.

GOOGIE: With a face like that, you could've been an actor. You still could. It's never too late. Look at Caterina Valente or Charo or Vicki Carr.

PROCLO: Of course they're *real* women.

GOOGIE: Oh no!

PROCLO: They're *not?*

GOOGIE: Plastic Puerto Ricans. I am the real thing. You are the real thing and I knew you were in show business.

PROCLO: Me?

GOOGIE: I knew I'd seen you someplace.

PROCLO: I was in the Cleveland Little Theatre Masque and Mummer's spring production of "THE SOUND OF MUSIC", but I'd hardly call that show business.

GOOGIE: Oh yeah? What part?

PROCLO: It was really more of a walk-on.

GOOGIE: I was in that show.

PROCLO: You were in "THE SOUND OF MUSIC"?

GOOGIE: Oh sure.

PROCLO: Where was this?

GOOGIE: Broadway, the Main Stem, where else?

PROCLO: The original cast?

GOOGIE: I was more original than anyone else in it. They fired me the first day of rehearsal, those bastards. They said I wasn't right for the part.

PROCLO: What part was that?

GOOGIE: One of those fucking Trapp kids. But you know what the real reason was, mister?

PROCLO: They found out what you really were?

GOOGIE: Seymour Pippin!

PROCLO: Who?

GOOGIE: Seymour Pippin! If there's one man in this whole world I was born to kill with my own two hands it is Seymour Pippin. You want to hear something funny? If you didn't have all that hair you would look a lot like him and I would probably fly into a rage and tear all your eyes out! I never forget that face and I never forgive. He was the company manager and if there is one thing worse than a producer or a press agent, it is a company manager! Where was I?

PROCLO: Somewhere in "THE SOUND OF MUSIC."

GOOGIE: Ah si! But I fix them. I picket that show till they was crazy. I picket, I picket, I picket. Every night! They couldn't stop me. I picket that show every night until I got a part in "CAMELOT."

PROCLO: You were in "CAMELOT", too?

GOOGIE: Oh sure.

PROCLO: That's a wonderful show.

GOOGIE: It's a piece of shit.

PROCLO: Oh, they fired you from that one, too?

GOOGIE: Sure they fired me! What do you expect? Thanks to Seymour Pippin I get fired from everything.

PROCLO: I can't imagine why.

GOOGIE: You see this face? It's a curse!

(She is moving in for the kill. Proclo is backing off, horrified.)

PROCLO: Keep away!

GOOGIE: Don't fight it, *chico!*

PROCLO: Believe me, you won't be happy! I won't be happy! You're making a terrible mistake.

GOOGIE: I am suddenly all woman.

PROCLO: No you're not. You're someone with a lot of problems.

GOOGIE: Make me feel like a real woman, *chico.*

PROCLO: I can't help you out in that department! It's out of my hands.

GOOGIE: Kiss me!

(Sounds of an orchestra striking up.)

Oh shit! That's my music!

(She is dragging Proclo by the hand. She throws open the door.)

Come on, my Mr. Big Producer. You're gonna love my show. I got you the best seats. I see you ringside. We save the hanky-panky for later.

(Googie hurries off.)

PROCLO: Ringside! Hanky-panky! What am I doing here?

CLAUDE: Vespucci!

(He appears on the third level.)

PROCLO: It is the same Claude Perkins. We were in the Army together. Compared to those two, Carmine wanting to kill me is sanity!

(He rushes off, followed by Claude.)

CLAUDE: I warned you, Vespucci! You promised, I waited, and you didn't come!

(The music is building as the lights dim and the nightclub, complete with twinkle lights and mylar curtain, flies in.)

ABE:

(Over the loudspeaker.)

And now, on the great Ritz stage, direct from her record-breaking bus and truck tour with "FIDDLER ON THE ROOF", the sensational Googie Gomes! With Duff and Tiger, those amazing now-you-see-it, now-you-don't golden go-go boys!

(There is a roll of drums.)

Here's Duff.

(Duff runs on. Another roll of drums.)

Here's Tiger.

(Tiger *make a great entrance. Another roll of drums.*)

And here's Googie!

(Googie *bursts on and launches into her first number. She is very bad but very funny. It's the kind of number you watch in disbelief. Sincerity is what saves her. Such a lack of talent is appalling, yes, but it does come straight from the heart. Tiger and Duff are doing their best, too, they dance well enough and they look pretty good up there.*)
(*Whatever number Googie sings, you can be sure that it is the wrong one for her. So is the arrangement, her costume, the choreography, the lighting, the works. When the number ends, during the applause, we see* Proclo *run across pursued by* Claude. Googie, *followed by* Tiger *and* Duff, *goes after them.*)

GOOGIE: Hey, wait a minute! Where are you going? I was just gonna introduce you!

(*They are gone. Suddenly the figure of a very wet, very angry balding MIDDLE-AGED FAT MAN comes storming through the mylar curtain into Googie's spotlight.*)

CARMINE: I'm Carmine Vespucci of the Bensonhurst Vespuccis. I want a room in this here whorehouse and I don't want any shit.

(*There is a mighty roll of drums as Scarpia's Theme from Puccini's "TOSCA" is heard. A crack of cymbals. CURTAIN.*)

END OF ACT 1

ACT TWO

Carmine is seen coming along the corridor. He is still in street clothes. He looks all around and then knocks softly on the door of Michael Brick's room.

CARMINE: Brick? Are you in there, Brick? It's Vespucci. Don't open. I don't want anyone to see us. If you can hear me, knock once. If you can't, knock twice. Are you there, Brick?

(Michael *knocks once.*)

Good. Our signals are working. Now listen to me, have you seen that balding fat brother-in-law of mine yet?

(Michael *knocks twice.*)

What does that mean? No?

(Michael *knocks once.*)

Okay, I think I read you. Now I know he's in here somewhere. What I don't know is how you could miss him. He's a house. Listen, Brick, none of these fruits tried to pull anything with you, did they?

(Michael *knocks twice.*)

You can thank Our Blessed Lady for that. Meet me in 102 in fifteen minutes. Knock three times. Got that?

(Michael *knocks three times.*)

Not now, stupid, *then.* And you don't have to worry about him leaving this place, leaving it in one piece I should say. I got all my men outside. Ain't that great, Brick? Hunh?

(Michael *knocks once.*)

I knew you'd like that. Keep looking.

(Carmine *goes into his room, starts to undress. We will see him take out a revolver, a stiletto, and a pair of brass knuckles. From offstage,* Claude *calls.*)

CLAUDE: Vespucci!

(Proclo *appears on the third level and races into a room.* Claude *runs past the room and sees a* Patron.)

Say, have you seen a Vespucci go by?

(Proclo *leaves his hiding place and heads down to the second level.* Claude *yells as he follows him down the stairs and they disappear.*)

Vespucci! Vespucci!

(Googie *appears and pokes her head into* Proclo's *room.*)

GOOGIE: Where are you hiding, Mr. Vespucci?

(She disappears. Proclo *appears and starts down the stairs to his own room on the first level. Midway he crosses paths with* Tiger *and* Duff.)

TIGER: There you are!

DUFF: Why did you run away?

*(*Proclo *escapes and continues down to his room.* Tiger *and* Duff *disappear, looking for* Googie. *Meanwhile* Googie *appears in a corridor, now looking for* Claude.)

GOOGIE: Where is this person who ruin my act? Where is this skinny little man? I kill him!

(She disappears. Tiger *and* Duff *appear and criss-cross again.)*

TIGER: Googie! Googie!

DUFF: Googie! Googie!

(They are gone. As soon as Proclo *reaches his room,* Claude *comes down the corridor looking for him. He opens the door, but* Proclo *has hidden behind it.)*

CLAUDE: Vespucci!

(As he leaves, he shuts the door, revealing Proclo, *who quickly makes the sign of the cross and starts gathering his things. Meanwhile* Googie *has appeared down a corridor. She sneaks up on* Claude *and tears his robe off.)*

GOOGIE: Ah hah! *Cabron!*

*(*Claude *races off, pursued by* Googie, *who is in turn pursued by* Tiger *and* Duff.)

TIGER: Googie!

DUFF: Googie!

(They are all gone. Proclo *is in a terrific hurry. We can hear him muttering to himself as he frantically packs his bag.)*

PROCLO: I'd rather spend the night in Central Park in the rain than spend another minute in this place! They're all mad! I thought *I* had problems! If I ever get my hands on that cab driver, he's finished! So long, room, I won't miss you.

(He comes out of the room carrying his clothes, his suitcase and the box of Panettone. He slams the door.)

Hello, Cleveland!

(He sees a Patron *walking by.)*

Which is the way out of here?

PATRON: That way.

*(*Proclo *goes up the stairs to the second level, looking for an exit.* Claude *appears on a side balcony.)*

CLAUDE: Vespucci! Vespucci!

*(*Proclo *has made his decision: it's the steam room or else. He goes rushing in with his clothes, his suitcase and the Panettone.* Claude *leaps over the balcony in hot pursuit.)*

CLAUDE: I hope you know what a cul-de-sac is, because you're in one!

(He goes into the steam room. Now Googie *enters on the rampage. We see her tearing up and down the corridors,* Tiger *and* Duff *following, trying to calm her down.)*

GOOGIE: Where is this skinny little man who chase a producer out of my number? No one chases no producer out of Googie Gomez' number!

(She is pounding on doors. One of them is opened by the Patron in Chaps.*)*

PATRON IN CHAPS: Howdy, pardner.
GOOGIE: Don't howdy me, you big leather sissy!

(She pushes him back into the room.)

You think I don't know what goes on around this place? All you men going hee-hee-hee, poo-poo-poo, hah-hah-hah! I get my boyfriend Hector in here with his hombres and he kill you all!

(She is heading for the steam room.)

DUFF: You can't go in there!
TIGER: Googie, no!

*(*Googie *storms into the steam room,* Tiger *and* Duff *following. The door closes behind them. A moment later,* Googie *lets out a muffled yell.)*

GOOGIE: *Pendego!*

*(*Patrons *start streaming out.* Googie *comes right out after them. She has* Claude *firmly in tow.)*

There will be no more hee-hee-hee, poo-poo-poo, hah-hah-hah around this place tonight!

(She slings Claude *across the hall.)*

CLAUDE: You're hurting me!
GOOGIE: I'm just getting started!

*(*Tiger *and* Duff *attempt to subdue her.)*

CLAUDE: You could use a good psychiatrist, mister!
GOOGIE: What you call me?
TIGER: He didn't mean it!
GOOGIE: What you call me?
TIGER: Tell her you're sorry!
CLAUDE: I haven't seen such tacky drag since the Princeton Varsity Show!
GOOGIE: Tacky drag?
CLAUDE: Thirty years ago, sonny!

*(*Googie *has gotten herself into a good street fighting position by now. With a blood curdling yell she leaps for* Claude *and chases him off,* Tiger *and* Duff *close behind. The stage is bare for a moment. We hear* Claude *off.)*

CLAUDE: Help!

(From the yell, it sounds as if Googie's *got him. The steam room door opens and* Chris *comes out.)*

CHRIS: I'm going straight.

> (*Suddenly the steam room door slams open and* Proclo, *or what's left of him, staggers out. He is fully dressed, wearing the wig, dark glasses and moustache from his first entrance, and carrying his suitcase. He has visibly wilted. He doesn't seem to know where he is.*)

PROCLO: I don't believe this whole night.

CHRIS: Were you in there for all that?

> (Proclo *just nods.*)

> Where?

> (Proclo *just shrugs.*)

> You don't want to talk about it?

> (Proclo *just shakes his head.*)

> Why are you wearing your clothes?

PROCLO: I'm going to Central Park.

CHRIS: I thought you were going to stay in your room.

PROCLO:

> (*Blindly walking downstairs.*)

> I can't. I told Googie I was Carmine Vespucci. Claude thinks I'm Carmine Vespucci. Everybody thinks I'm Carmine Vespucci.

CHRIS: Well who are you?

PROCLO: Tonight I'm Carmine Vespucci.

CHRIS: I give up!

> (Chris *sees* Michael Brick *coming along a corridor.*)

> What have we here? Now this is a little more like it. Play it cool, Chris.

> (*He arranges himself attractively.*)

> If you don't mind, Mr. Vespucci, I'd like to try my luck with this one. Hey, Vespucci, I'm talking to you. Snap out of it!

MICHAEL: Are you Mr. Carmine Vespucci, sir?

CHRIS: You live around here, kid?

MICHAEL: No. I came in from Astoria. Are you Mr. Vespucci?

CHRIS: Say yes, say yes!

PROCLO: Yes!

MICHAEL: I'm Michael Brick. My room's right over here.

> (*He will start leading* Proclo *to his room.*)

CHRIS: Hi, I'm Chris. My room's right up there.

MICHAEL: Hi, Chris. How are you?

> (Michael *and* Proclo *have gone into* Michael's *room and closed the door.*)

> Am I glad to see you, Mr. Vespucci.

> (Chris *has been watching their encounter in envy and disbelief.*)

CHRIS: I don't date out-of-towners!

> (He starts to exit, but is stopped by the ring of the pay phone. He answers it with an enormous scream of frustration. He hangs up and disappears. A somewhat still dazed Proclo is sitting in Michael's room.)

MICHAEL: Now this is what I thought we'd do. Get under the bed.

PROCLO:

> (Beginning to cry.)

Another one!

MICHAEL: All right, stay there. We'll pretend you're him and I'm me and the real you is under the bed.

PROCLO:

> (Tears are really flowing.)

Only this one's the worst.

MICHAEL: Now get the picture. The lights are low, he's moving down the hallway and he sees me leaning against the door. I flex for him. Pecks and biceps are supposed to be a turn on. Don't ask me why. I catch his eye. I've got a cigarette dangling from my lips, I put one knee up, I wink, I kind of beckon with my head and finally I speak. "See something you like, buddy?" That's the tough guy approach.

PROCLO: Is that your own voice?

MICHAEL: Yes.

PROCLO: I mean, your real voice?

MICHAEL: Yes.

PROCLO: Your natural speaking one?

MICHAEL: Yes.

PROCLO: Thank you.

MICHAEL: Why? Does it bother you?

PROCLO: Oh no, no, no!

MICHAEL: Some people find it very irritating.

PROCLO: I can't see why.

MICHAEL: Me either. But of course I'm used to it. I've had it ever since I was a kid. I mean, I grew up and matured, only my voice didn't. Where was I?

PROCLO: The tough guy approach.

MICHAEL: Oh! And *then* . . . and this is where you're going to have to jump out—

PROCLO: I am having a nightmare.

MICHAEL: Very, very, very casually . . .

PROCLO: I can hardly wait.

MICHAEL: I thought I'd let my hand just kind of graze against my . . .

> (He hesitates, then whispers in Proclo's ear.)

PROCLO: I'm getting out of here!

MICHAEL:

> (Pulling him down.)

But you're going to have to help me catch your brother-in-law, Mr. Vespucci.

PROCLO: My brother-in-law?

MICHAEL: I haven't seen anyone who fits Mr. Proclo's description.

PROCLO: Proclo? My brother-in-law?

MICHAEL: The balding middle-aged fat man you hired me to catch.

PROCLO: Where do you know my brother-in-law from?

MICHAEL: I don't yet. That's why I called you at that bar across the street.

PROCLO: What bar?

MICHAEL: Where you and your men have this place surrounded so Mr. Proclo can't leave in one piece.

PROCLO: Who are you?

MICHAEL: Michael Brick, sir.

PROCLO: What are you?

MICHAEL: A detective.

> (Michael *is suddenly alerted by the alarm on his wristwatch.*)

> It's time!

PROCLO: For what?

MICHAEL: Get under the bed. He'll see you.

PROCLO: Who will?

MICHAEL: Your brother-in-law. He'll be here any second. Since I couldn't find Mr. Proclo I'm making him find me. I left a note by the Coke machines saying "Any middle-aged balding fat man whose initials are G.P. interested in a good time should meet me in Room 101 at midnight sharp." When he gets here you're gonna have to help me. You see, I'm not queer.

PROCLO:

> (*Already climbing under the bed.*)

> You could've fooled me.

MICHAEL: I'm right on top of you.

PROCLO: I can't tell you how comforting that is.

> (Chris *is seen moving along the corridors, playing "The Lady or the Tiger." He knocks softly at different doors, and finally on* Carmine's.)

CARMINE: I said knock three times!

CHRIS: He's being masterful with me already, the brute.

> (*He knocks three times.*)

CARMINE: That's more like it.

CHRIS: I think I'm in love.

> (Carmine *opens the door and pulls* Chris *violently into the room, slamming the door behind them.*)

CARMINE: Quick. Don't let anyone see you. Now let me get a look at you.

> (*He circles* Chris *appraisingly.*)

> I'm not a judge of fruit bait, but I guess you'll do.

CHRIS: Just cool it, sweetheart. This isn't the meat rack.

CARMINE: You can can the fag act with me, Brick. Now listen, I think I've come up with something. I know this sounds like the oldest stunt in the book, but I'm going to hide under your bed.

CHRIS: On the contrary, it's a first.

CARMINE: You never tried the old under-the-bed technique?

CHRIS: Not recently.

CARMINE: What kind of detective are you?

CHRIS: That's a good question, honey.

CARMINE: Can it, Brick, just can it. One thing I don't like is a wise guy. The only thing I don't like more is a queer wise guy. I'm calling the shots now and I'm getting under your bed.

CHRIS: Where am I supposed to be?

CARMINE: On top of it, stupid!

CHRIS: It sounds fabulous. Then what?

CARMINE: You know, do what you have to do.

CHRIS: What's that?

CARMINE: How should I know? Wiggle your fanny, shake your towel in his face.

CHRIS: Whose face?

CARMINE: My brother-in-law's, you dummy! The guy I hired you to catch! And then I pop out, catching you both in the act of fragrant delicto and whammo! I got him.

CHRIS: Your brother-in-law?

CARMINE: Who else? Jesus, you're like talking to a yo-yo.

CHRIS: Dumb and dizzy, that's me, darling!

> (In a very "butch" voice.)

Just a little more of that gay humor. Ho ho ho!

CARMINE: All right, now you go back to 101.

> (Chris desperately starts to leave.)

Not yet! If the coast is clear, whistle like this . . .

> (He whistles with two fingers.)

and I'll high tail it to your room and slide right under and we're in business. Got that?

CHRIS: Check.

CARMINE: It's about time.

CHRIS: Only I can't whistle.

CARMINE: Goddamnit, you can't whistle either?

CHRIS: Tell you what, Mr. . . .

CARMINE: Vespucci, Carmine Vespucci.

CHRIS: Carmine Vespucci . . .

CARMINE: Only don't call me that! He might hear us. I need a code name.

CHRIS: Evelyn.

CARMINE: Naw, I don't like Evelyn. Sounds effeminate.

CHRIS: How about Bunny?

CARMINE: Okay, Bunny.

CHRIS: All right then, Bunny, you get under *this* bed. That way I won't have to whistle and you won't have to high tail it to 101.

CARMINE: Maybe you're not so dumb after all, Brick.

CHRIS: Just to refresh my memory, give me his name again.

CARMINE: It's Proclo, Gaetano Proclo.

CHRIS: What did he do?

CARMINE: He married my sister! I told her. I pleaded with her. I was on my knees to her. "Viv, honey, marry this Proclo character and you're marrying to stick a knife in me." She loves him, she tells me. Well I hate him, I tell her. I've always hated him. He's not of the family. He's not like us. He don't belong in Poppa's business. But she wouldn't listen to me. And so what happens? Twenty years she thinks she's happily married, my sister, but the truth is it's twenty years she's been a martyr, that woman. My sister is a saint and she don't even know it. I'll tell you one thing: with Poppa gone now . . .

(He breaks into uncontrollable sobs.)

Poppa, God bless him . . . I ain't sharing Vespucci Sanitation Services and Enterprises, Inc., with no fairy!

CHRIS: Your brother-in-law is a fairy?

CARMINE: He's gonna be when I get through with him.

CHRIS: What are you going to do to him?

CARMINE: I'm gonna kill him!

CHRIS: Good!

CARMINE: You know what a *delitto di passione* is Brick? 'Cause you're gonna see one to-night. A crime of passion. An enraged brother catching his dear sweet sister's balding fat slob husband in an unnatural act with one of these fruitcakes around here! There's no court in the country that would convict me. Twenty years I waited for this night. You're looking at a man of great and terrible Italian passions, Brick.

CHRIS: I can see that, Bunny.

(He turns off the room lights.)

CARMINE: What happened?

CHRIS: That's how they do it here. Now get under the bed. I'm leaving the door open so he can come in. Once he gets here, you take it from there. I'm right on top of you. Now don't say another word.

(Chris has tiptoed out of the room, leaving the door ajar and Carmine *under the bed. He knocks on* Michael's *door.)*

MICHAEL: That must be your brother-in-law, Mr. Vespucci!

PROCLO:

(Ready to meet his Maker.)

I'm sure it is.

MICHAEL:

(Unlocking the closed door.)

Hold your horses, stud!

(He stretches out on the bed. We see Proclo's *face looking out from the foot of the bed.)*

It's open!

(Chris enters.)

See something you like, buddy?

CHRIS: You've got to be kidding.

MICHAEL: False alarm, Mr. Vespucci.

CHRIS: Where's your friend?

MICHAEL: He's under the bed.

CHRIS: Why not? Everybody else is. I always wondered what you straight guys did together. Now that I know, I'm so glad I'm gay. If you didn't have all that hair, I'd ask you if your name was Guy something.

PROCLO:

> (*Crawling out from under the bed.*)

> It is.

CHRIS: And you really do have a garbageman brother-in-law who's out looking for you, don't you?

PROCLO: Unh-hunh!

CHRIS: Well, the maniac is right across the hall and he's got a gun. I just thought I'd mention it.

MICHAEL: Now he's after you, Mr. Vespucci! And you didn't mention anything about a gun.

> (Googie *appears in the corridor and knocks on the door.*)

> I'm scared!

> (Chris *dives under the bed.*)

PROCLO: You're scared? Move over!

CHRIS: There's not enough room.

PROCLO: I can fit.

CHRIS: I was here first.

PROCLO: It's my brother-in-law!

CHRIS: It's my ass!

> (Michael *has opened the door a crack and peeked out. Now he slams it shut and dives under the bed from the other side.* Proclo *still hasn't managed to get under.*)

PROCLO: Where do you think you're going?

MICHAEL: It's not him, Mr. Vespucci!

PROCLO: Well who is it then?

MICHAEL: It's that transvestite again!

PROCLO: What are you talking about?

> (*The knocking is getting louder.*)

> Who's there?

GOOGIE: I know you're in there, *chico!*

PROCLO: Oh, no!

> (*He goes to the door and opens it.* Googie *comes flying in, closing the door behind her and clapping one hand over* Proclo's *mouth.*)

> Now, look—!

GOOGIE: Don't speak. Don't say nothing. Say one word and Googie's out on her ass. She's breaking every book in the rule doing this.

> (*She has pushed* Proclo *onto the bed and is lying on top of him.*)

You know why you don't like women? Because you never tried it, that's all. Or maybe you did and that's why. She was a bad woman. Forget her. Believe me, *chico*, itdon'thurt. It's nice. It's very nice. Just lie back and Googie's gonna show you hownice.

PROCLO: Look, I'd like to help you out—!

GOOGIE: Think of a tropical night! A beach.

PROCLO: What beach?

GOOGIE: The moon is shining on the sea and in the distance, over the waves, you hear music . . .

(*She sings.*)

BESAME, BESAME MUCHO!

(Proclo *is terrified. Almost involuntarily, under the bed,* Michael *and* Chris *join in singing. For several moments, there is almost a trio going between them, as* Googie *tries to take off* Proclo's *clothes.*)

GOOGIE, MICHAEL and CHRIS: COMO SI FUERA ESTA NOCHE
LA ULTIMA VEZ
BESAME, BESAME MUCHO
PIENSA QUE TAL VEZ MANANA
ESTARE LEJOS MUY LEJOS
DE TI.

PROCLO:

(*Suddenly,* Proclo *comes back to his senses.*)

This isn't going to work out, Mr. Googie!

GOOGIE: Mister?

PROCLO: There's just no way!

GOOGIE: Mister? You thought I was a drag queen? No such luck, *chico!*

PROCLO: You really are a miss?

GOOGIE: This is all real.

(*She has clasped his hands to her breasts.* Proclo *can't believe what he is feeling. His voice goes up at least an octave.*)

PROCLO: It feels real, it feels real!

GOOGIE: I just hope I'm gonna find me some *huevitos*.

PROCLO: What are *huevitos*?

GOOGIE:

(*Finding them under his raincoat.*)

Ay ay ay!

PROCLO: They're real, too!

GOOGIE: We're gonna make such a whoopee, *chico!*

PROCLO: Thank you.

GOOGIE: Thank you? You're gonna thank me.

PROCLO: The trouble is my brother-in-law is trying to kill me and there's someone under this bed.

GOOGIE: Oh no you don't! I'm not falling for that old hat and dance routine. You're not pulling no wool over my ears so easy.

PROCLO: I swear to God there is!

GOOGIE: Never try to shit an old pro, *chico*.

MICHAEL: He's not! There is someone under this bed.

CHRIS: Us! And if you two want to bounce around like that I'll gladly go back to my own room.

GOOGIE:

(*Leaping off the bed.*)

That's a rotten stunt, mister. I could lose my job for this. I told you: I threw wind in caution coming down here!

PROCLO: It's really very simple.

GOOGIE: I don't need no explaining. You rather make hee-hee-hee, poo-poo-poo, hah-hah-hah with that *maricon* you got hiding under the bed!

CHRIS: Two *maricons*, Googie!

GOOGIE: Who's that down there?

CHRIS: It's me, Chris.

GOOGIE: Hi, Chris. What are you doing down there?

CHRIS: I wish I knew.

MICHAEL:

(*Poking his head out now.*)

The reason we're under this bed—

GOOGIE: You!

MICHAEL: Now wait!

GOOGIE: Not only you got a fat boyfriend, you *maricon* hump—you got a mean one!

(*She is hitting* Michael *with the pillow.*)

MICHAEL: I'm not his boyfriend!

PROCLO: He's not!

MICHAEL: And I'm not gay!

GOOGIE: With a voice like that you're no straight arrow either.

MICHAEL: I was born with this voice.

GOOGIE: So was Yma Sumac. I saw you talking on the telephone and I said, "Googie, that boy could make your blood go boil."

PROCLO: I thought you said that about me.

GOOGIE: I say that about everyone.

(*Proclo is making an escape.*)

Where are you going?

PROCLO: Look, I'm just someone who's in a lot of trouble, lady.

GOOGIE: You're not staying for my second show?

PROCLO: I'm not a producer. It was all your two friends' idea. Now if you'd just let me get out of here—.

GOOGIE: Hey, now wait a minute!

PROCLO: Now what?

GOOGIE: Wait just one big fat minute!

(*She grabs for* Proclo's *wig. It comes off.*)

PROCLO: Hey!

GOOGIE: I thought maybe it was you!

PROCLO: Who are you talking about?

GOOGIE: Seymour Pippin! You don't fire Googie Gomez from no show and get away with it.

(She is trying to kill Proclo.)

You think I forget a face like yours, you bastard? I'm gonna tear your eyes out!

(Chris *and* Michael *will eventually subdue her.)*

CHRIS: It's not him, Googie.

MICHAEL: That's Mr. Vespucci.

GOOGIE: You promise?

PROCLO: I promise.

GOOGIE: I thought you was Seymour Pippin.

PROCLO: I wish I were.

GOOGIE: What do you know? I thought he was Seymour Pippin!

MICHAEL: Seymour Pippin!

(Carmine *has come out of his room and knocked on the door.)*

PROCLO: Oh my God!

(They all start scrambling for a place under the bed.)

GOOGIE: What about me?

CHRIS: That's my place!

MICHAEL: Hurry up!

GOOGIE: Suck your gut in!

PROCLO: I am!

GOOGIE: More!

PROCLO: Who is that?

CHRIS: Relax, mister. I told you: you're not my type.

PROCLO: Well just get your hand off my—

GOOGIE: It's okay! It's my hand.

MICHAEL: If it's him, Mr. Vespucci, just give me the word.

(Proclo, Chris *and* Googie *have somehow all managed to squeeze under the bed.* Michael *opens the door.* Carmine *storms in.)*

CARMINE: What the hell happened to you? You said you'd be on top! I've been under that damn bed so long I can hardly walk!

(As he turns he sees Michael *who has gone into his flexing routine.)*

MICHAEL: See something you like, buddy?

CARMINE: What the—?

MICHAEL: You new around here, mac?

CARMINE: You're not Brick! Where's Brick? What have you done to him?

MICHAEL: Lie down.

CARMINE: Get your hands off me!

(Michael *shoves* Carmine *onto the bed.* Googie *cries out.)*

GOOGIE: *Ay, cono!*

PROCLO: Sshh!

CARMINE: What the—?

MICHAEL: Relax.

CARMINE: Somebody's under there!

MICHAEL: Just stretch out on the bed, now.

CARMINE: What are you doing in here?

MICHAEL: Just relax: I'm trying to seduce you.

CARMINE: Get your hands off me, you goddamn Greek, or I'll lay your head open.

MICHAEL:

       (Pinning Carmine down.)

       Is it him, Mr. Vespucci?

PROCLO: Yes!

CARMINE: Vespucci? I'm Vespucci.

MICHAEL: Is it?

PROCLO: Yes, yes! It's him! It's him!

CARMINE: I know that voice!

       (He leans over the bed just as Googie rolls out.)

       What the hell is this? One of them goddamn transvestitites, sure you are!

GOOGIE: Seymour Pippin!

       (She is attacking Carmine, swatting him with a pillow.)

CARMINE: Fight fair, you faggot!

       (Michael knocks Carmine out with a karate blow.)

MICHAEL: Hi-ya!

       (Carmine falls onto the bed. Proclo groans.)

GOOGIE: Aw, shit! Why did you do that? I was gonna fix his wagon for him good!

MICHAEL: He's out cold, Mr. Vespucci!

PROCLO: Just get me out of here.

CHRIS: And we were just starting to have so much fun!

GOOGIE: You know something? This man is not Seymour Pippin either. He sure got a mean face though! I wonder who he is.

PROCLO:

       (He and Chris are up from under the bed now.)

       It's my brother-in-law.

GOOGIE: Is he in show business?

PROCLO: He's in garbage.

GOOGIE: A gay garbageman?

MICHAEL: You're sure it's him?

PROCLO: I'm afraid so.

GOOGIE: What are you two talking about?

MICHAEL: I'm a detective. Mr. Vespucci here hired me to get something on his brother-in-law Mr. Proclo there so Mr. Proclo doesn't inherit one half the family business.

PROCLO: So that's it.

       (He tries to strangle Carmine. The others hold him back.)

MICHAEL: Mr. Vespucci wanted to catch us together so he could commit a *delitto di passione*. What's a *delitto di passione*. Mr. Vespucci?

(*Again* Proclo *goes for* Carmine's *throat.*)

PROCLO: You're about to see one!

CHRIS: Hey, now take it easy! You can't do that!

PROCLO: *He* was going to!

MICHAEL:

(*He has been getting ready to photograph* Carmine *on the bed.*)

Look out now. You'll be in the picture.

CHRIS:

(*Primping his hair.*)

Picture? What picture?

GOOGIE:

(*Suddenly she grabs the camera.*)

Oh no! I see what you do! If that man want to be here, let him be here. What you care? I don't stand still for no blackmail! I tell Tiger and Duff what you do and you're out on your ass, big boy! Come on, Chris!

(*She goes with the camera.*)

CHRIS: Excuse me, but I promised Mark Spitz we'd do a quick ten laps around the pool.

(*He goes.*)

MICHAEL: Mark Spitz comes here, Mr. Vespucci?

PROCLO: I don't care!

MICHAEL: What should I do with him?

PROCLO: Kill him.

MICHAEL: I'm a private detective, Mr. Vespucci. I'm not a hit man.

PROCLO: You got something to tie him down with?

MICHAEL: Cuffs.

PROCLO: Hurry.

MICHAEL: Give me a hand with him, will you?

PROCLO: Can't you hit him again?

MICHAEL: That wouldn't be ethical, Mr. Vespucci.

PROCLO: Ethical? Your line of work and you're telling me what's ethical? Come on, let's get out of here.

MICHAEL: If you don't need me anymore, I want to find that Googie and get my camera back.

PROCLO: Fine, fine.

(Michael *goes.* Proclo *stands looking down at* Carmine *on the bed.*)

You blew it, Carmine. By the time you get out of this place I'll be back in Cleveland with Vivian and the kids.

(*He goes, leaving the door open. He passes into* Carmine's *room. We will see him gather up* Carmine's *clothes as he yells out.*)

Fat man in 101! Come and get it. Fat man in 101! He's all yours. Fat man in 101!

PROCLO:

(As he comes out of Carmine's *room, he sees* Tiger *in the corridor.)*

Duff.

TIGER: I'm Tiger.

PROCLO: Whatever! Burn these for me, will you?

TIGER: Burn 'em?

PROCLO: You heard me.

TIGER:

(Scooping up Carmine's *clothes.)*

You're sounding happy.

PROCLO: I'm close to feeling terrific!

TIGER: What happened?

PROCLO: I'm catching the next plane to Cleveland.

TIGER: Good luck.

PROCLO: You're too late. I've already got it!

(Tiger is gone. Proclo grabs his suitcase and starts to head off. The pay phone rings, and Michael *answers it.)*

MICHAEL: Hello? This is The Ritz. Michael Brick speaking. It's for you, Mr. Vespucci.

PROCLO: Who is it?

MICHAEL: Who is this? It's Mrs. Proclo, calling from that bar across the street.

PROCLO: Mrs. Proclo? My God, it's Vivian. Tell her I've left.

MICHAEL: I'm sorry but he just left, Mrs. Proclo. She doesn't believe me.

PROCLO: Tell her she has to believe you.

MICHAEL: He says you have to believe me. She says she's not staying there another minute. She's taking a man's hat and raincoat and coming right over here and nothing's going to stop her. Hello . . . hello?

(He hangs up.)

I didn't even get to tell her the good news.

PROCLO: What good news?

MICHAEL: That we got our man!

(Googie is coming along on her way to the night club.)

Miss Gomez?

GOOGIE: Don't Miss Gomez me now, *chico.* I got a show to do.

MICHAEL: I can explain about downstairs.

GOOGIE: I don't talk to no detectives.

MICHAEL: Then about my camera!

(They are gone.)

PROCLO: He'll kill me. She'll divorce me. My children will grow up hating my memory. Oh my God!

TIGER:

(He is passing.)

What happened?

PROCLO: I just ran out of luck! There's a woman trying to get in here. Keep her out.

TIGER: They don't let ladies in here.

PROCLO: It's my wife.

TIGER: Relax. She'll never get past Abe.

(He is gone.)

PROCLO: I did!

(He runs into his room. We see Claude come in behind him. Proclo doesn't. Yet. He sits on the bed and pants.)

CLAUDE: Your door was open.

PROCLO: What?

CLAUDE: I'm giving you one more chance.

(He starts to sing his song.)

JELLY ROLL BABY
YOU'RE MY JELLY ROLL MAN . . .

PROCLO: Please, I'm too weak.

CLAUDE: JELLY ROLL CUPCAKE
I'M YOUR JELLY ROLL FAN . . .

PROCLO: Look, this is a lot of fun, I can't tell you! I don't know about you, Claude, but I'm in terrible trouble.

CLAUDE: Claude!

PROCLO: I didn't say that.

CLAUDE: Wait a minute! Wait a minute! Guy! It's you, Guy!

PROCLO: Absolutely no.

CLAUDE: Gaetano Proclo, the fifth division, Special Services, the Phillipines.

PROCLO: I was 4-F. I never served.

CLAUDE: It's me, Claude! Claude Perkins.

PROCLO: Get away from me, Claude!

CLAUDE: That's right! "Get away from me" Claude! We had an act together. A trio with Nelson Carpenter. We pantomimed Andrews Sisters records. "RUM AND COCA COLA." Remember?

PROCLO: I don't know what you're talking about. I hate the Andrews Sisters.

CLAUDE: You hate the Andrews Sisters?

PROCLO: Look, I'm in desperate, desperate trouble, mister, and I wish you'd just go away.

CLAUDE: Just wait until I write Nelson Carpenter about this!

ABE:

(Over the loudspeaker.)

253 coming up! That's two-five-three. You're not going to believe what's coming up, boys!

PROCLO: Oh my God, it is Vivian!

CLAUDE: There are other fat fish in the ocean, Gaetano Proclo, and 253 just may be one of them.

PROCLO: Just don't touch 253, Claude!

CLAUDE: We'll see about that.

(He sweeps out. Proclo *returns to his room, sits on his bed, and holds his head despairingly. The* Patron in Chaps *walks in on the awakening* Carmine *in* Brick's *room.)*

PATRON IN CHAPS: Howdy, pardner. Handcuffs? Outta sight!

(He sinks to his haunches and just stares. Tiger, Duff, Googie *and* Michael *are running by. The Three Entertainers are dressed to go on.)*

GOOGIE: If I don't hit that note, cover for me.
DUFF: How?
GOOGIE: Take your clothes off! Anything!
MICHAEL: Miss Gomez!

(They are gone. Carmine *is starting to come around. The* Patron in Chaps *is still staring.)*

PATRON IN CHAPS: Far out! Far out!
CHRIS: Hi, girls!

(Pokes his head into the room.)

CARMINE: Brick!
CHRIS: Don't believe a word she says. She thinks she's a detective or something.
CARMINE: Who she? What she?
CHRIS: You she. And who do you think you are? Dale Evans?

(He starts to go.)

CARMINE: Let me out of here! I'll kill you!
CHRIS: I've got a date with 253.

(He is gone.)

CARMINE: Gaetano! Gaetano!

(The Patron in Chaps *runs off. On the second level we see* Vivian. *She is wearing a man's hat and raincoat over her black pants suit. She carries a shopping bag.* Chris *approaches her.)*

CHRIS: I had a hunch it would be bad, but nothing like this.

(To Vivian.*)*

Welcome to the city morgue.

*(*Vivian *recoils and lets out one of her giant sobs: an unearthly sound.)*

VIVIAN: AAaaaaaeeeeee!
CHRIS: Forget it, mister, that's not my scene!

(Opening the door to the steam room.)

Avon calling!

(He goes in. Claude *has approached* Vivian *in the corridor, and again the strains of the immediately recognizable love theme are heard the moment he sees her.)*

CLAUDE: Looking for 253?

> (Vivian *nods, stifling her sobs.*)

Right this way.

> (He *leads her to his own room, of course, carefully concealing the room number as they enter. He slams the door and starts to sing.*)

JELLY ROLL BABY
YOU'RE MY JELLY ROLL MAN . . .

> (Vivian *really lets out a big sob as he starts moving towards her.*)

Aaaaiiiieeeee!

> (No sooner does she scream than Vivian *faints dead away on* Claude's *bed. At that moment,* Carmine *manages to free himself from his handcuffs by banging the bed noisily on the ground.* Proclo, *in his room,* Carmine's *threats and* Vivian's *screams ringing in his ears, is literally quivering, as he softly calls out.*)

PROCLO: Help. Help. Help.

> (Carmine *is on the rampage. He shoots the lock off his own door. The door gives and he runs in.*)

CARMINE: My clothes! Somebody took my clothes!

> (He *runs out of the room, brandishing the revolver.*)

Okay, Gaetano! I know you're in here! I'm gonna find you if it's the last thing I do!

> (He *disappears. Meanwhile,* Claude *is trying to revive* Vivian.)

CLAUDE: All right, lie there like a beached whale.

> (No response from Vivian.)

Look, I'd love to stay here and play Sleeping Beauty with you but I've got to get ready for the Talent Contest.

> (He *starts getting his things together for his record pantomime act.*)

What's in the bag? You bring your own lunch?

> (He *is looking in* Vivian's *shopping bag.*)

ABE:

> (Over the loudspeaker.)

Just a reminder, boys and girls. It's amateur night at The Ritz.

CHRIS:

> (Coming out of the steam room.)

You can say that again!

CLAUDE: You've got to be kidding.

> (He *takes a long mink coat out of* Vivian's *shopping bag. He can't resist putting it on.*)

What becomes a legend most?

(Carmine comes storming up to Chris.*)*

CHRIS: Hi, Bunny. How's tricks?
CARMINE: You!

(He points his gun.)

CHRIS: Is that thing loaded?
CARMINE: And you're lucky I'm not using it on you. Now where is he?
CHRIS: Who?
CARMINE: My brother-in-law, you dumb dick!
CHRIS: He was just here.
CARMINE: And?
CHRIS: He went in there.

(He motions towards Claude's *room.)*

CARMINE: Well why didn't you say so?
CHRIS: I just did. You're really planning to shoot him?
CARMINE:

> *(Carmine starts for* Claude's *room.* Chris *hurries off in another direction.*
> Carmine *starts banging on* Claude's *door.)*

You if he's not in there!
CLAUDE: Who's that?
CARMINE: You know goddamn well who it is.

(Claude opens the door, takes one look at Carmine, *and starts his song.)*

CLAUDE: JELLY ROLL BABY
       YOU'RE MY JELLY ROLL . . .
CARMINE: What the—?

(He pulls his gun.)

Get out of here!

(Claude escapes, taking his clothes and Vivian's *mink with him.* Carmine *turns at
a moan from* Vivian *on the bed.)*

Okay, Gaetano, the jig is up!

(Then, realizing who it is.)

Viv! Vivian, baby. What have they done to you?

(He tries to revive her.)

Speak to me, Viv! Viv!

(Chris has come up to Proclo's *door.* Proclo *is slumped. He is too tired, too
defeated, to call for help anymore.)*

CHRIS: It's me, Chris! Open the door!

(Proclo does.)

That brother-in-law of yours means business.

197

PROCLO: Why can't he just find me and get it over with?

CHRIS: You're just going to sit there?

PROCLO: What's the use?

CHRIS: Hide somewhere.

PROCLO: I came here. He found me.

CHRIS: Wear a disguise.

PROCLO: I am!

(He tears off his wig and moustache.)

I thought you were mad at me.

CHRIS: I am but I prefer you alive to dead. I'm funny that way.

(Claude, wearing the mink, comes along the corridor.)

PROCLO: Claude!

CLAUDE: Oh, sure. Now you know me.

PROCLO: You've got to help me.

CLAUDE: I've got to get ready for the talent contest tonight.

PROCLO: My brother-in-law's here with a gun.

CLAUDE: So that's who that maniac is!

(Proclo, Claude and Chris go.)

CARMINE: Viv! Viv! Sis!

VIVIAN:

(Reviving.)

Where am I? Carmine!

CARMINE: What are you doing here?

VIVIAN: I couldn't stand being in that bar anymore.

CARMINE: Do you know what kind of place this is?

VIVIAN: It was horrible, Carmine. He wanted me to roll on him.

CARMINE: Who?

VIVIAN: I don't know. Some little thin man.

CARMINE: I'll kill him. I'll kill 'em all.

VIVIAN: I was afraid something terrible had happened. I asked myself what Gilda would do.

CARMINE: Gilda? Gilda's twelve years old.

VIVIAN: Not my Gilda. The one in "RIGOLETTO."

CARMINE: This isn't an opera, Viv.

VIVIAN: She disguised herself as a man for the man she loved and came to a place very similar to this one.

CARMINE: And then what happened?

VIVIAN:

(New sobs.)

She was stabbed to death!

CARMINE: You weren't stabbed. You were only rolled on.

VIVIAN: Take me home, Carmine, please.

CARMINE: Home? But he's here. I can prove it to you.

VIVIAN: I don't want proof. I just want to go back to Cleveland.

CARMINE: With a man like that?

VIVIAN: I don't care. He's my husband.

CARMINE: I'm gonna kill the son of a bitch when I find him.

VIVIAN: No killing, Carmine. I don't want killing.

CARMINE: All he's done to you.

VIVIAN: He hasn't done anything to me.

CARMINE: That's what you think. Now I want you to get out of here and take a cab back to Brooklyn. Leave that husband of yours to me.

VIVIAN: I'm not going!

CARMINE: Then stay in here and don't let anyone in.

VIVIAN: No!

CARMINE: This is between him and me, Viv!

VIVIAN: If you hurt him, I'll never speak to you again!

CARMINE: It's Poppa's honor that's at stake!

VIVIAN: Poppa's dead!

(This statement causes them both to collapse into sobs.)

CARMINE: Poppa! He's stained the Vespucci honor!

VIVIAN: Carmine, please!

CARMINE: It's like he peed on Poppa's grave!

VIVIAN: Aaaaaiiiiieee!

CARMINE: I'm thinking about Poppa, Viv. Believe me, it's not for me.

VIVIAN: What about me?

CARMINE: You, too. He peed on you, too. You've been dishonored, too, sister.

VIVIAN: Give me the gun.

CARMINE: What?

VIVIAN: Give me the gun. I'm going to kill myself.

CARMINE: Are you crazy?

VIVIAN: I want to die, Carmine. You've made me so crazy I want to kill myself.

CARMINE: It's him I'm going to kill.

(By this time, Vivian will have the gun. Suddenly, she becomes aware that her mink is missing.)

VIVIAN: Carmine! No, no!

CARMINE: What is it!

VIVIAN: No! . . . No! . . . No! . . .

CARMINE: What is it?

VIVIAN: My mink!

CARMINE: Your mink?

VIVIAN: It's gone. They've taken it. It was in here.

CARMINE: Why weren't you wearing it?

VIVIAN: I didn't want to get it wet. It cost 900 dollars.

CARMINE: I'll get your mink back, too.

VIVIAN: He gave it to me for our anniversary. Now I really want to kill myself.

CARMINE: I'll get your goddamn mink. Now let go of me.

VIVIAN: I'm coming with you.

CARMINE: You're staying here.

VIVIAN: I don't want him dead, Carmine.

CARMINE: It's not up to you. This is for Poppa!

(*He starts off.*)

Gaetano! Gaetano!

VIVIAN: Carmine!

(*But he is gone.* Vivian *runs out of the room and sees the* Snooty Patron.)

Stop him.

SNOOTY PATRON: Who?

VIVIAN: My brother. He'll kill him. You heard him. He's a violent man.

SNOOTY PATRON: Kill who?

VIVIAN: My husband. And my mink! They took my mink!

(Vivian *and the* Snooty Patron *disappear up a corridor.* Proclo, Claude *and* Chris *go running by on their way to the night club.*)

CHRIS: I don't know any Andrews Sisters numbers!

CLAUDE: Well fake it!

PROCLO: This will never work!

CLAUDE: He never really knew any either. Nelson and I carried you for years.

(Carmine *enters and comes face to face with* Chris *and the others.* Proclo *hides behind the mink coat as* Chris *blows his whistle.*)

CHRIS: He went up to the steam room, boss.

CARMINE: Thanks.

(*He heads upstairs.* Claude, Proclo *and* Chris *turn on their heel and run in the opposite direction.* Vivian *appears on the first level.*)

VIVIAN: Carmine, wait!

CARMINE: I said stay in there!

(*He continues toward the steam room.* Vivian *sees* Proclo *and his group just exiting.*)

VIVIAN: My mink! Stop, thief!

(*They are gone,* Vivian *in pursuit.* Carmine *runs into the steam room. This time all the* Patrons *come flying out.* Carmine *follows, brandishing his gun. They all run off. Music is heard offstage. It is a bad baritone singing the end of an operatic aria.*)

BAD BARITONE.

(*Singing, over the loudspeaker.*)

IL CONCETTO VIDISI
OR ASCOLTATE
COMEGLIE SVOLTO,
ANDIAM.
INCOMINCIATE!

(*This is the transition to the nightclub. The talent show is in progress. There is applause as* Googie *steps onto the stage.*)

GOOGIE: That was Tiny Naylor singing "The Prologue" from "PAGLIACCI". Bravo, Tiny, bravo. It's gonna be a close race tonight.

(*She consults a card.*)

Our next contestant is Sheldon Farenthold, song stylist, from Newark, New Jersey. Aren't we going to hear it for Newark? I know what you mean. Take it away, Sheldon!

(Sheldon *enters, encased in red balloons. He plays directly out front, thus making the audience in the theatre the audience in The Pits. During his number he will pop his balloons. What he will sing is a very old standard but done to a raunchy, burlesque beat. Suddenly, two groups of* Patrons, *one chased by* Carmine, *the other by* Vivian, *crisscross and disappear into the "backstage" area of the night-club.* Sheldon *shoots them a blinder but goes on performing like the good little trouper that he is.*)

SHELDON: Thanks a lot!

(When the number ends, Sheldon *takes his bows and goes.* Googie *steps forward into the follow spot.*)

GOOGIE: Thank you. You know, it gives me a real pleasure to emcee these amateur shows because I began as an amateur.

(Sounds of disbelief from the offstage band members.)

It's true! I didn't get where I am over night. Oh no, *chicos!* It took a long, long time. A star is born, that's true, I mean, you have "it" in the cradle or you don't, but she doesn't twinkle over no one night.

(She laughs at her own joke, then regains herself.)

Okay.

(Suddenly a group of Patrons, led by Sheldon *and his balloons, races across, chased by* Carmine. Googie *chooses to continue unflustered.*)

Our last contestant is Mr. Claude Perkins and partners recreating their famous Army act. Hit it, boys!

(MUSIC *is heard. It is a 40's sounding swing orchestra. A spotlight picks up* Claude *in his WAC uniform,* Proclo *in his wife's mink coat and a long blonde wig, and* Chris *in an elaborate make-shift gown made from sheets. The Andrews Sisters are heard singing one of their big hits.* Claude, Chris *and* Proclo *begin to pantomime to the record and jitterbug. At first,* Proclo *is all nerves and* Claude *does a Herculean job of covering for him. But as the number progresses, we see* Proclo *getting better and better as the act comes back to him. After a while, He's close to enjoying himself. Suddenly all of the* Patrons, *including poor* Sheldon, *balloons and all, with* Tiger *and* Duff, *are chased across the stage and into the house by* Carmine *and* Vivian. Chris *accidentally steps on* Proclo's *foot, but the number continues. The number is really building now.* Proclo *is boogying away like crazy. Suddenly* Carmine *fires a shot in the air. There is total pandemonium as the group of* Patrons *returns to the stage from the back of the house. They run into a big huddle.* Proclo *and* Claude *manage to lose themselves somewhere in the middle of the crowd.*)

CARMINE: Now everybody slow down! Nobody's going nowhere. And get some lights on. I want to see who I'm talking to.

(The follow-spot hits Carmine.)

Not on me! I want the room lights, you dumb fruit!

(All the lights come on.)

Okay, I want all the fairies in a line.

CHRIS: What about us butch types, boss?

CARMINE: Shut up, you.

CHRIS: It's me, Bunny, Brick.

CARMINE: You're fired. Get over there!

(He motions with his gun for Chris to form a line. He turns and sees Michael.)

I can't believe it. A good-looking, rugged boy like you.

MICHAEL: Believe what, sir?

CARMINE: I believe it. Get going.

GOOGIE: Wait a minute. All of this because some fat woman who lost her mink?

CARMINE: One more word out of you, you goddamn transvestitite and—.

GOOGIE: What you call me?

SHELDON: Careful, Googie.

GOOGIE: You make me see red, mister, and when I see red I tear you apart. Shit! You
    think I'm scared of a little gun?

(Carmine fires in the air again.)

That's okay, mister. You don't bother me, I don't bother you.

(She backs into the main group of Patrons.)

CARMINE: Okay, Cowboy. Your turn.

PATRON IN CHAPS: I don't know what your name is but you belong in Bellevue.

CARMINE: Who says?

PATRON IN CHAPS: A trained psychiatrist.

CARMINE: Get outta here!

(Duff and Tiger try to sneak up on Carmine.)

What are two? The Cherry Sisters?

DUFF: Up yours, mister.

CARMINE: Get over there. All right. The rest of you!

*(The Group crosses the stage, revealing Claude and Proclo, whose face is turned
    upstage. Claude approaches Carmine.)*

CLAUDE: You really know how to mess up an act, you know that, mister?

CARMINE: Christ, another one!

CLAUDE: I'm an entertainer. Pantomime acts are coming back, you'll see.

CARMINE: In the meantime, you're still a transvestitite. Move!

(Only Proclo remains now. Carmine is savoring every moment of his humiliation.)

I guess that makes it you. Look at you. I could vomit. Jesus, Mary and
Joseph! Is that her mink?

*(Proclo turns around. Not only is He wearing the mink and the Patty Andrews
    wig, He has added the dark glasses and the moustache. He nods.)*

Give it back to her.

(Proclo *shakes his head.*)

VIVIAN: I don't want it now. That's not Gaetano. I just want to go home.

CARMINE: Okay, Gaetano, the jig's up. Take that crap off. The wig, the glasses, the moustache, the mink. Everything. I'm giving you three.

(*To the others.*)

I want you all to meet my splendid brother-in-law, Gaetano Proclo.

MICHAEL: That's not Mr. Proclo! He is!

CARMINE: Who is?

MICHAEL: You are!

(Carmine *spins around.* Proclo *bites his wrist and grabs the gun. The others subdue* Carmine. *For a few moments he is buried as they swirl about him.* Vivian *just sobs hysterically.*)

CARMINE: Get your hands off me! This time you've really done it, Gaetano!

PROCLO: Shut up, Carmine.

CARMINE: Sure, you got some balls now, you're holding a gun.

PROCLO: Don't worry about my balls, Carmine.

CARMINE: I'm gonna kill you!

PROCLO: Keep him quiet. Sit on him. I don't want to hear that voice.

(Tiger, Duff *and* Chris *hold* Carmine *down and muffle his mouth, though* Carmine *will try* taaaaaaaaaaaaaao *get his two cents in during the conversation that follows.* Proclo *has approached* Vivian.)

PROCLO: Don't cry, Viv.

VIVIAN: Don't cry, he says. Look at him like that, telling me not to cry!

PROCLO: You want your coat back?

VIVIAN: I want to know what you're doing in it!

PROCLO: It was the only thing that fit.

VIVIAN: Aaaaiiiieeee!

PROCLO: Carmine was going to kill me!

VIVIAN: AAAAIIIIEEEE!

PROCLO: Vivian, please!

VIVIAN: My husband, the man in the mink coat! I can't wait to go to Bingo with you like that next week but I won't be there if God is merciful because I'm going to have a heart attack right here.

CARMINE: This is grounds for annulment, sis. I asked Father Catini.

VIVIAN: I don't want an annulment. I want to die. *Mi fa morire, Dio, mi fa morire!*

PROCLO: Is this what you wanted, Carmine?

CARMINE: You're finished, Gaetano.

PROCLO: I can understand you hating me as a brother-in-law but killing someone over a garbage company?

VIVIAN: *Un delitto di passione,* Carmine?

CARMINE: *Si! Un delitto di passione!*

VIVIAN: *Ma perchè?*

CARMINE: *Perchè* you're married to a flaming homo, that's *perchè!*

VIVIAN: Aaaaiiiieeee!

CARMINE: He came here tonight, didn't he?

PROCLO: A cab driver brought me here.

CARMINE: Because you told him to.

PROCLO: I never heard of this place.

CARMINE: You see that Vivian? Even a cab driver knows what a *fata* he is!

VIVIAN: I just hope you're not going to insist on mentioning this in confession.

PROCLO: Mention what?

VIVIAN: He knows your voice, Guy.

PROCLO: Who knows my voice?

VIVIAN: Father Bonnelli. He knows everyone's voice. For my sake, Guy, for the children's, don't tell him about this.

PROCLO: I wasn't planning to!

VIVIAN: You're going through a stage. Last year it was miniature golf.

CARMINE: This ain't like no miniature golf, Viv.

VIVIAN: I'll get over this. I get over everything. It's my greatest strength.

PROCLO: There's nothing to get over, then or now!

VIVIAN: Aaaaiiiieee!

PROCLO: Vivian, what do I have to do to convince you?

CARMINE: She is convinced! Cry your heart out, sis, it's all right. Carmine's here.

PROCLO: How the hell do you prove something like that to your wife? I give up. You win, Carmine. Let him go.

> (Tiger, Duff and Chris *reluctantly release* Carmine, *look at* Proclo, *and then leave.*)

CARMINE: Come on, sis, let's get out of here.

PROCLO: Vivian, wait!

CARMINE: Don't you even speak to my sister!

> (Proclo *stands there helpless.* Maurine *has appeared. She goes directly to* Carmine *and hands him a long sheet of figures.*)

MAURINE: Thirty-seven thousand five hundred on the week. The rain killed us tonight. And next week we got the Jewish holidays coming up. Good night, boss.

> (*She goes.*)

VIVIAN: Who was that?

CARMINE: Just a person.

VIVIAN: She called you boss.

CARMINE: A lot of people call me boss.

> (*He starts to eat the sheet of figures.*)

VIVIAN: Give me that.

CARMINE: It's not what you're going to think, Vivian.

VIVIAN: "Vespucci Enterprises, Inc. Carmine Vespucci, President." This is a statement!

CARMINE: I was going to tell you about it.

VIVIAN: We own this place?

CARMINE: Poppa'd done a lot of expanding while you were in Cleveland.

VIVIAN: We own this place, Guy!

CARMINE: He doesn't have to know the family business, Viv! Now come on, this isn't the place to talk about it.

VIVIAN: So you knew what kind of place this was!

CARMINE: So did he obviously. That's why he came here. I can't help it if we own it. It's just a coincidence.

VIVIAN: What kind of cab was it, Guy?

PROCLO: What?

VIVIAN: The one that brought you here.

PROCLO: I don't remember.

CARMINE: A fairy cab!

VIVIAN: Do you remember the name of the company?

CARMINE: The Fairy Cab Company! Fairy cabs for fairy passengers! Now come on, Vivian, let's get out of here. What do you care what kind of cab it was?

VIVIAN: Think hard, Guy. It's important.

PROCLO: It was an opera . . . Aida Cab!

VIVIAN: Aida Cab! We own that company!

PROCLO: We do?

VIVIAN: Carmine, did you tell that driver to bring Guy here?

CARMINE: Of course I didn't!

VIVIAN: What did the driver look like, Guy?

PROCLO: All I remember about him is his stutter.

VIVIAN: His stutter?

PROCLO: He stuttered and smoked pot.

VIVIAN: Cousin Tito! I should've guessed. It's going to be very hard to forgive you for this, Carmine.

CARMINE: What's to forgive! I don't want no forgiving!

VIVIAN: Now take the hit off him, Carmine.

CARMINE: Vivian!

VIVIAN: Take it off!

CARMINE: No!

VIVIAN: If you don't take it off, Carmine, I am gonna tell Frankie di Lucca about you muscling into the Bingo concession at the Feast of St. Anthony and then Frankie di Lucca is gonna put a hit out on you and you are gonna end up wearing cement shoes at the bottom of the East River and then there will be even more grief and less peace in our fucking family than there already is!

PROCLO: I am married to an extraordinary woman!

CARMINE: You wouldn't do this to me, sis!

VIVIAN: You know me, Carmine.

CARMINE: Vivian!

VIVIAN: I swear it, Carmine. *Lo giuro.*

CARMINE: *N on giura*, sis!

VIVIAN: *Lo giuro*, Carmine. *Lo giuro*, the Bingo and the cement shoes.

CARMINE: "Get Proclo." You heard Poppa.

VIVIAN: I've got Proclo, Carmine. Now take the hit off!

CARMINE: I'll lose face.

VIVIAN: Not under the East River!

CARMINE:

(*Writhing in defeat.*)

Aaaaiiieee!

VIVIAN: Now take the hit off him, Carmine! Is it off?

(He nods.)

On Poppa's grave?

(He shakes his head.)

I want it on Poppa's grave and I want it forever!

(He shakes his head.)

I'm calling Frankie di Lucca.

CARMINE: It's off on Poppa's grave!

VIVIAN:

(Finally breaking down.)

Poppa! All right, now I forgive you.

CARMINE: I told you: I don't want no forgiving.

VIVIAN: You already have it. And now I want to see you two forgive each other. *Il bacio del pace*, Carmine.

CARMINE: You gotta be kidding!

PROCLO: Over my dead body!

VIVIAN: I want you to kiss each other as brothers.

PROCLO: I wouldn't kiss him for a million dollars.

VIVIAN: That's exactly what it's worth, Guy.

PROCLO: I wouldn't kiss him, period.

VIVIAN: I want you to make your peace with Carmine.

PROCLO: Vivian!

VIVIAN: For me, Guy, for me.

PROCLO: I forgive you, Carmine. With a little luck nobody's gonna die in your family for a long, long time and we won't have to see each other for another twenty years. Just be sure to send the checks. Andiamo!

(By this time, all the Patrons will have gathered as an audience to the proceedings. Proclo opens his arms and moves towards Carmine for the kiss of peace.)

Hey!

CARMINE: Hey!

(They make a slow, ritual-like circle. Of course, both men do look rather ludicrous as they circle one another. Proclo in his wife's mink coat; Carmine in his bathrobe. Carmine hesitates.)

VIVIAN: Frankie di Lucca!

(The circling resumes. Just as they are about to kiss, Carmine gives Proclo a good punch in the stomach. But as Proclo bends over in pain, he knees Carmine in the groin. Carmine goes down. The others give a mighty cheer and congratulate Proclo.)

PROCLO:

(Amazed.)

I did it. I did it.

(Now jubilant.)

I won. I didn't fight fair but I won!

(To Carmine.)

You can go *va fangool* yourself, Carmine. People like you really do belong in garbage. People like me just marry into it. Get him out of here, men!

CHRIS: Bring her up to the steam room, girls!

(The others pounce on Carmine who is protesting mightily and carry him off.)

CARMINE: I'm coming back here and I'm gonna kill every last one of you fairies!

CHRIS: Sure you are, Nancy!

(It is a gleeful, noisy massed exit. It will be several moments that we can still hear Carmine yelling and the others cheering. Vivian has started to follow after them when Proclo stops her.)

PROCLO: Vivian!

VIVIAN: Where are your clothes? I want to go home.

PROCLO: I'm not leaving.

VIVIAN: Don't make any more waves in the family now, Guy.

PROCLO: It's the perfect time. If I don't do it now I never will. Your family's run herd on me since the day I met you. I'm sick of it. I'm sick of Carmine and Connie and Tony and Tommy and Sonny and Pipo and Silva and Beppe and Gina and your Aunt Rosa and Cousin Tito! I'm sick of all of them. The living and the dead. What am I? Some curse on a family? "Get Proclo." Those were your father's dying words!

VIVIAN: He was my father. I was his only girl. You expected him to like you?

PROCLO: Yes! Yes, I expect people to like me. I want people to like me. It's called self-esteem, Vivian. I'm talking about wanting things. And I do want things. I've always wanted things. I wanted so many things I didn't get I can't even remember them. I wanted to send Momma back to Italy before she died. I didn't have the money in those days.

VIVIAN: Not many eight-year-old boys do, Guy.

PROCLO: I want us to be terrific forever. I want to go on a diet. No, I want to *stay* on one. I want a boat. I want a brand new fleet of trucks. I want Proclo Sanitation services to be number *one* in Cleveland. I want people to stop calling me a garbageman. I want to be known as a sanitary engineer. I want to be honored as an ecologist! I want changes! I want changes! I want changes!

(He has exhausted himself.)

VIVIAN: I want to go back to Cleveland.

PROCLO: You know something? So do I.

(She goes to him and kisses his cheek. Claude enters with three trophies.)

CLAUDE: We won! We won!

(He hands one of the trophies to Proclo and heads upstairs.)

We won the talent contest! We won! God bless the Andrews Sisters! Chris! Chris, where are you?

CHRIS: In the steam room!

CLAUDE: We won!

CHRIS: We won?

(Claude joins Chris in the steam room with screams of joy.)

PROCLO: You see that, Viv? I never won anything in my whole life. That was Claude Perkins. We were in Special Services together.

VIVIAN: He seems like a nice person.

PROCLO: I wouldn't go that far, Vivian. To him I look like Tyrone Power.

VIVIAN: So did I. Now where are your things?

(They return to Proclo's room, where he will dress and pack. Googie comes storming on, followed by Tiger and Duff. She is dressed in street clothes and carrying all her belongings.)

TIGER: We're sorry, Googie.

GOOGIE: You build someone up like that and it's all a lie. Ay, that's a low down dirty trick to play.

TIGER: Look at it this way: one night there will be a Mr. Big out there and you'll be all keyed up for it.

GOOGIE: There ain't never gonna be no Mr. Big in this place. There ain't never gonna be me no more in this place neither. I quit.

DUFF: Come on, Googie, we adore you.

GOOGIE: You adore yourself.

(Michael appears.)

Would you believe it? They told me that Mr. Big was gonna be here tonight.

MICHAEL: Who's Mr. Big?

GOOGIE: Only the man you wait for all your life. Only the man who opens miracles. Only the man who can make you a star over one night. A producer, who else?

MICHAEL: My uncle is a producer, Miss Gomez.

GOOGIE: Oh yeah? What's he produce?

MICHAEL: Shows.

GOOGIE: Legitimate shows? I don't do no dirty stuff.

MICHAEL: Right now I think he's casting "OKLAHOMA" for a dinner theatre.

GOOGIE: "OKLAHOMA?" It's a stretch but I could do that part. You could get me an audition with him?

MICHAEL: Sure thing.

GOOGIE: You see? I had this hunch the whole evening. I got another show to do. I meet you in Bimbi's across the street. We run into my boy friend Hector and we tell him you're my agent.

(To Tiger and Duff.)

I see you two skunks later.

DUFF: I thought you quit.

GOOGIE: That's show business.

(She is gone.)

TIGER: You got an uncle who's in show business?

MICHAEL: Seymour Pippin. He's a producer.

DUFF: Forget it, mister.

TIGER: Come on, Duff.

(Michael, Tiger and Duff leave. Chris has entered.)

PROCLO:

    (*To* Vivian.)

    Are you ready?

CHRIS: I suppose you're wondering what happened to Bunny. We entered her in the Zinka Milanov look-alike contest. We're still awaiting the judge's decision. First prize is a gay guide to Bloomingdales.

VIVIAN: Who's he talking about?

PROCLO: Carmine.

VIVIAN: He said she.

CHRIS: We've called the 16th Precinct. They'll be right over for him.

VIVIAN: Oh, Guy, you've got to do something for him.

PROCLO: I will, Vivian. Thanks for the help back there.

CHRIS: Just let me know the next time you three are coming in. I want to be sure not to be here. I haven't had so much fun since the day they raided Riis Park.

PROCLO: If you're ever in Cleveland, Vivian makes a great lasagna.

CHRIS: Well, that's the best offer I've had all night.

PROCLO: Goodnight, Chris.

CHRIS: So long, boss.

    (*He heads back up to his room. We hear Googie offstage, singing a song from her third show.*)

ABE:

    (*On the loudspeaker.*)

    316 coming up! That's three-one-six, Duff!

PROCLO: Let's go.

VIVIAN: Guy, promise me you'll take good care of Carmine.

PROCLO: On Poppa's grave.

VIVIAN:

    (*A new outburst of grief.*)

    Poppa!

    (*She exits. Proclo calls off to her.*)

PROCLO: Not your Poppa's. Mine!

    (*As Proclo starts off, a Policeman races on. Proclo stops to watch with a contented smile. Chris blows his whistle, and the Policeman runs up to the steam room, where he finds Carmine, bound and gagged and dressed in a green brocade ball gown. Claude sees Carmine, too, and sings his "JELLY ROLL" song as he plays tug-o'-war with the Policeman over Carmine. Patrons are filling the halls. Duff and Tiger start making fresh beds. And Proclo just smiles.*)

CHRIS: Orgy! Orgy! Orgy in 240!

    (*The lights are fading. The play is over.*)

(left to right) Reed Birney (Randy), Jessica James (Bunny), Danny Aiello
(Fran), Robert Picardo (Francis), Anne DeSalvo (Lucille), and
Carol Potter (Judith) in the 1977 Broadway production of
Albert Innaurato's *Gemini*, at the Little Theatre.
(Photograph reprinted with permission from the
John Willis Theatre World/Screen World Archive)

Gemini

BY ALBERT INNAURATO

Characters

FRAN GEMINIANI	is forty-five, working class, boisterous, and friendly. He is slightly overweight, coughs a lot from mild emphysema.
FRANCIS GEMINIANI,	his son, is about to celebrate his twenty-first birthday. He is also plump, a little clumsy, is entering his senior year at Harvard.
LUCILLE POMPI	is Fran's lady friend, very thin, early forties, working class, but strives hard to act in accordance with her ideas of ladylike behavior and elegance.
BUNNY WEINBERGER,	the Geminiani's next-door neighbor, is a heavyset blowsy woman, about forty, once very beautiful and voluptuous, now rough talking and inclined to drink too much.
HERSCHEL WEINBERGER,	her son, is sixteen, very heavy, asthmatic, very bright, but eccentric. He is obsessed with Public Transportation in all its manifestations, and is shy and a little backward socially.
JUDITH HASTINGS,	Francis' classmate at Harvard, is a month or two younger than Francis. She is an exceedingly, perhaps even intimidatingly, beautiful WASP. She is extremely intelligent, perhaps slightly more aggressive than she should be, but is basically well meaning.
RANDY HASTINGS,	her brother, has just finished his freshman year at Harvard. Like Judith, he is a quintessential, very handsome WASP.

The play takes place on June 1 and 2, 1973. The latter marks Francis' twenty-first birthday.

212

ACT ONE

Scene 1: June 1, 1973. Early Morning.
Scene 2: That Evening.

ACT TWO

Scene 1: June 2, 1973. Morning.
Scene 2: That Evening.

The setting shows the backyards of two adjoining row houses in the Italian section of South Philadelphia. They are small, two-story, brick houses typical of the poorer sections of most big cities. In one house live the Geminianis, Fran and Francis, and in the other the Weinbergers, Bunny and Herschel. In the Geminiani yard is a fig tree, and along one side a high alley fence with a gate. The Weinberger yard contains an old ladder, a rusty, old tricycle, garbage cans, and a certain amount of general debris, and is also bounded by an alley wall, behind which is a high utility or telephone pole.

Gemini was first performed in a workshop production at Playwrights Horizons, and was later presented at the PAF Playhouse, Huntington, N.Y., before being produced by the Circle Repertory Company in New York City. On May 21, 1977, it opened at the Little Theatre, New York City, produced by Jerry Arrow and Jay Broad representing the Circle Repertory Company and the PAF Playhouse. It was directed by Peter Mark Schifter and had a setting by Christopher Nowak, costumes by Ernest Allen Smith, and lighting by Larry Crimmins, with the Broadway production being supervised by Marshall W. Mason. The cast in order of appearance was:

FRANCIS GEMINIANI	Robert Picardo
BUNNY WEINBERGER	Jessica James
RANDY HASTINGS	Reed Birney
JUDITH HASTINGS	Carol Potter
HERSCHEL WEINBERGER	Jonathan Hadary
FRAN GEMINIANI	Danny Aiello
LUCILLE POMPI	Anne DeSalvo

ACT ONE

SCENE 1

The sound of garbage men emptying the garbage in the alley. They are making an immense noise. It is just past dawn and they are banging lids, overturning cans, and yelling to one another.

Francis Geminiani appears at his bedroom window. He is dressed in a Tee shirt, his hair is wild, his glasses are awry. He has just been awakened and is in a rage.

FRANCIS: Shut up! Will you please shut up! Why aren't you men more civilized? Oh Jesus Christ!

> *(He sets a speaker on the window sill, and turns on full blast the final portion of Isolde's narrative and curse from Act 1 of* Tristan und Isolde. *Bunny Weinberger appears at the second floor window of her house. She is in a torn nightgown and faded robe, and is also in a rage)*

BUNNY: Francis! Francis! Why are you playing that music at six o'clock in the mornin'? You got somethin' against my gettin' a good night's sleep?

FRANCIS:

> *(Leaning out his window)*

Do you hear the garbage men?

BUNNY: Sure. They're just doing their job. That's the trouble wit you college kids—got no respect for the working man. Besides, I got an uncle out there.

> *(Shouts out to alley behind fence)*

Hi ya Uncle Jerry!

VOICE:

> *(From behind the fence)*

Hi ya, Bun!

BUNNY: How's your hammer hanging?

> *(Then to Francis)*

See, I got connections. You stick wit me kid, I'll get you a job.

> *(A knocking is heard at the front door of the Geminiani house)*

And now you got them knockin' at your door. You woke everybody up. Ain't you gonna answer it?

FRANCIS: I'm going back to bed.

> *(He takes the speaker off the sill)*

BUNNY: Good. Maybe we'll have some quiet.

> *(She disappears inside her bedroom. The knocking continues. The garbage men fade away. Francis has now put on a very quiet passage from Act IV of Verdi's I Vespri Siciliani. After a moment, a knocking is heard at the gate in the fence, the entrance*

to the Geminiani yard. Francis does not come to his window. More knocking. A
pause. Then a rolled up sleeping bag comes sailing over the fence, followed by a
small knapsack. Randy Hastings appears at the top of the fence. He climbs over and
jumps into the yard. He looks around. Suddenly a large knapsack, the kind that has
an aluminum frame, appears at the top of the fence. Randy takes it, and puts it
down on the ground. Next we see a rolled up tent, a second sleeping bag on the fence,
then a tennis racquet, and then Judith Hastings. She perches on top of the fence,
looks around, and then jumps into the yard. Randy has piled everything neatly
together in the middle of the yard. They are both in worn jeans and sneakers. They
circle about the yard, peeking into Bunny's part curiously. Judith notices the fig tree
and smiles. She knocks at the back door. No answer. Randy tries to open it, but it is
latched from the inside. He then peeks into the window Left of the door and sees
Francis sleeping in his room. He smiles at Judith, and they climb into Francis' room)

JUDITH and RANDY: Surprise! Surprise!

(The music stops. Francis leaps out of bed)

JUDITH:

(Inside the room)

Put your glasses on, it's Judith . . .
RANDY: . . . and Randy. What's the matter?
FRANCIS: What are you doing here?
JUDITH: Come to see you, of course—
FRANCIS: Why?
JUDITH: It's your birthday tomorrow, your twenty-first.

(At this moment, Herschel dashes out of the back door of his house and into the
yard. He hurls himself onto the rusty tricycle and making subway engine noises,
careens about the yard)

RANDY:

(Looking through screen door)

Francis, who's that?
FRANCIS:

(With Judith in kitchen window)

Herschel next door.
RANDY: What's he doing?
FRANCIS: Hey Herschel, what are you doing?
HERSCHEL: I'm pretending I'm a subway engine.
FRANCIS: Which one?
HERSCHEL: Three nineteen AA four six five AA BZ substratum two. Built in 1945, in
    April, first run on Memorial Day.
FRANCIS: Herschel is into Public Transportation.

(Bunny comes out of her house, still in the same torn and smudged nightgown and
housecoat. She has a quart beer bottle in one hand, and a cigarette in the other)

BUNNY: What the fuck's goin' on out here, hanh? Why you up so early?

(Herschel, making engine noises, heads right for her. She sidesteps the tricycle easily)

Jesus Christ, it's that engine you're goin' a see.

FRANCIS:

(From window, still with Judith. Randy has come out to get a better view)

Bunny, these are friends of mine from school. Judith Hastings and her brother, Randy.

(Indicates Bunny)

This is my neighbor, Bunny Weinberger.

BUNNY: I didn't know they had girls at Harvard.

FRANCIS: Judith is at Radcliffe.

BUNNY: This is my son Herschel. He's a genius. He's gotta IQ of 187 or 172, depending on which test you use.

(To Herschel, who is still careening about)

Stop that fuckin' noise! He's also got asthma, and he tends to break out.

HERSCHEL:

(To Randy)

You want to see my collection of transfers?

RANDY:

(With a shrug)

Sure.

(Herschel dashes into his house)

BUNNY:

(Looking after him)

Well, all geniuses is a little crazy. You kids look hungry, so damn skinny

(She is poking Randy in the stomach)

RANDY: Do you think so?

BUNNY: I guess you're scholarship students at Harvard, hanh? Although Francis is on scholarship you wouldn't know it to look at him. You wan' some breakfast?

JUDITH: That would be very nice.

(Bunny starts for her door)

FRANCIS: Get the roaches out of the oven first, Bunny.

BUNNY:

(Good-naturedly)

Oh, go fuck yourself. I ain't had a live roach in here in a year, unless you count Herschel, I think he's part roach. Whatayas want? Fried eggs and bacon alright?

RANDY: Sure.

BUNNY: He's normal, at least.

(She goes inside)

FRANCIS: So . . . you're just here for the day?

JUDITH: For the day? Some people go away to the beach from the city, we have come away to the city from the beach.

RANDY: Can you say that in French?

JUDITH:

(Coming out of the house)

Il ya des gens qui va . . .

FRANCIS:

(Interrupting)

How'd you get here?

JUDITH: We hitchhiked, of course.

FRANCIS: You rich people are all crazy. It would never occur to me to hitchhike.

JUDITH: That's because you couldn't get picked up.

RANDY: Come on, Judith, you can help me set up the tent.

FRANCIS:

(From his room, putting on his pants)

Tent?

RANDY: Sure. We always sleep outside. We could put it up under this tree. What kind is it?

JUDITH: Fig, idiot.

RANDY: What's a fig tree doing in your yard?

FRANCIS:

(Coming out of house, pants on, but barefoot)

You'll have to ask your father, he planted it. But look, I don't want . . . I mean . . . well, you see, it's my father. I mean you can't stay here. He doesn't like company.

RANDY: But I thought wops loved company.

(Judith hits him)

FRANCIS: Mafia.

JUDITH: The Mafia?

FRANCIS: You know, the Black Hand, Cosa Nostra, the Brotherhood . . .

RANDY: Your father's in the . . .

FRANCIS: Hit man.

JUDITH: Oh, come on!

FRANCIS: He offs Wasps. It was bred into him at an early age, this raving hatred of white Anglo-Saxon Protestants, they call them white people.

RANDY:

(Looks worried)

White people?

FRANCIS: He collects their ears after he murders them, he has a collection in his room . . .

(Starts picking up their camping equipment and hands it to Judith and Randy)

I'll tell you what, let's go to the bus terminal, I'll finish getting dressed, we'll put your stuff in a locker, I'll show you around, we'll take a few pictures, then you can go back later tonight. I'll get my camera.

(He runs inside)

RANDY: You mean we have to carry this junk around some more?

JUDITH:

(At Francis' window)

Why don't you come back with us—we've got plenty of room—mother will love you—you can cook for us.

FRANCIS:

(Appears at window)

I can't. I have a job.

RANDY: You can watch me work out.

JUDITH: Oh, Randy, grow up! I wanted to see you . . .

FRAN:

(Offstage)

Yo, Francis, you home!

FRANCIS: Oh, Jesus Christ!

(Randy is trying to escape for his life. Judith is holding him back)

FRAN:

(Offstage, yelling)

Yo, Francis, we're back!

(Fran unlocks the gate, which had a chain and padlock. He appears with an empty trash can, Lucille right behind him, holding three freshly-pressed shirts on hangers. Fran sets the trash can under his kitchen window, and then notices the visitors in his yard. Yelling into window)

You got company?

JUDITH:

(Hastily)

My name is Judith Hastings, and this is my brother Randy. We know Francis from Harvard.

FRAN: Oh yeah? I'm his dad. I didn't know Igor had friends. He just sits around all day, no job, nothin'. My name's Francis too.

(Turns to Randy)

But you can call me Franny, or Fran, or Frank.

(Turns to Judith)

And you can call me honey, or sweetness and light, or darling, whatever you like.

(Indicates Lucille, who is trying to blend into the fence, because she has been surprised in a housecoat)

This is Lucille.

LUCILLE: Oh, dear.

JUDITH: Well, we were just leaving.

FRAN: Leavin'? But you just got here, you can't leave.

LUCILLE:

(Attempting elegance)

Well, Fran, thanks for comin' over . . .

(She hands Fran his shirts)

Of course I was rather surprised, it's bein' so early, my dress.

BUNNY:

(Appears in her window)

Hi ya Fran.

FRAN: Yo Bun.

BUNNY:

(Sees Lucille)

I see you got The Holy Clam wit you. I'm cookin' breakfast.

LUCILLE:

(To Judith and Randy, still explaining)

And then I have to wash my hair . . .

BUNNY: Shut up, Lucille, you keep washin' it and it's gonna fall out, and not just your hair. Hey you kids, you wan' some oregano in these eggs?

FRAN: Why? They're still gonna be Irish eggs.

BUNNY: I gotta Jew name, but I'm Irish. Real name's Murphy.

FRAN: You still got roaches in that oven?

(Coughs from emphysema, then laughs)

BUNNY: You still got rats up your ass?

LUCILLE: Bunny!

(Then to Fran)

Stop smoking, hanh?

BUNNY:

(In her window, with a mixing bowl, singing)

"Oh I got plenty of nothin'
And nothing's got plenty of me
Got my butt
Got my boobs
Got my cup of tea
Ain't no use complainin'
Got my butt

Got my boobs
Got my boobs!"

(Dialogue continues over Bunny's song)

FRAN:

(To Randy and Judith)

You just get here?

JUDITH: You're sure you want us to stay?

FRAN: Whataya mean am I sure?

RANDY: We're Wasps . . .

FRAN: So? I'm broad-minded. Is that a tent?

RANDY: We like to sleep outside.

FRAN: You kids is all nuts, you know that? So put it up!

(Scratches)

LUCILLE:

(Setting up a lawn chair)

Stop scratching that rash.

FRAN: That's my fig tree, you know! I planted it.

LUCILLE:

(To Bunny, who is singing "Got My Boobs")

Bunny!

(She sits down. Bunny is now screeching her final "Got My Boobs." Lucille jumps up)

Bunny!

(Bunny laughs, and goes back to cooking. Lucille, with the situation under control, sits down for a chat)

So how do you do? My name is Lucille Pompi. I have a son at Yale and my daughter is a dental technician, she works at The Graduate Hospital, special shift, and my late husband . . .

FRAN: *Sta'zit'*, Lucille, these kids look hungry. You must be on scholarship at Harvard, though Francis is on scholarship you'd never know it to look at him. We got lots of food in, only thing that keeps him from jumpin' out the window when he's home.

(Indicating Francis' room. Coughs)

LUCILLE: Turn away from people when you cough, hanh?

(Randy and Judith are pitching the tent under the tree)

FRAN: We got brebalone and pepperoni, how 'bout some while horseshit finishes up the eggs? We also got pizzel. Francis loves them but I got a whole box hid.

JUDITH: Oh, I'm sure breakfast will be more than enough.

FRAN: But you don't understand. That's gonna be a Irish breakfast—that's a half a egg, a quarter slice a bacon . . .

(Scratches)

LUCILLE:

(Genteel)

The Irish mean well but they don't know how to eat.

(To Fran, genteel manner gone)

Don't scratch that rash!

FRAN: I'll get everything together.

JUDITH: I'll help you.

FRAN: Well, thank you sweetheart. What's your name again?

JUDITH: Judith.

(He lets her go in first and admires her figure. He shakes his head appreciatively and winks at Randy who winks back laughing. Randy continues pitching the tent)

LUCILLE:

(To Randy, after Fran and Judith have exited)

My son, Donny Pompi, is at Yale, he's a sophomore on the basketball team and in pre-med. He's on a Branford Scholarship. Do you know him?

RANDY: I go to Harvard.

LUCILLE: But he's at Yale. Wouldn't you know him?

RANDY: No, I go to Harvard.

LUCILLE: Is there a difference?

FRAN:

(Coming out of the kitchen, yelling)

Yo, Francis! Where's your manners? Was you raised in the jungle?

(Fran and Judith come into the yard, he is carrying, a typing table with a tray of food on it, and she has a cake and napkins)

Sometimes I wonder about him, his mother used to say when he was born he broke the mold, maybe she was right.

(Lucille starts serving, and repeating absentmindedly after Fran)

Now, we got here: Coffee cake . . .

LUCILLE: Coffee cake . . .

FRAN: Jelly donuts . . .

LUCILLE: Jelly donuts . . .

FRAN: Black olives, green olives, pitted black olives—they're easier to digest, chocolate-covered donuts—

(He holds one up)

—they're Francis' favorites so eat them first and save him some pimples—

(Lucille is embarrassed)

—brebalone, pepperoni, pizzel, biscuits, a fiadone Lucille baked last week and some hot peppers. Don't be shy.

(He gives Lucille a squeeze)

RANDY: Thanks.

FRAN: Yo, Francis! Where the hell are you?

BUNNY:

> (Enters carrying a huge tray of food)
>
> Here's breakfast.
>
> (She is followed out by Herschel, who is carrying a huge box. Bunny notices that the Geminiani tray is on a typing table, so she sets her tray on a trash can that is under her kitchen window, and drags the whole thing to the centre of the yard. She hands Randy a plate with a fried egg on it)

HERSCHEL:

> (To Randy)
>
> Here's my collection of transfers.

RANDY: Lot of them.

> (Sits down in front of tent to eat)

HERSCHEL:

> (Following Randy)
>
> Four thousand seven hundred and twenty-two. They start at eighteen seventy-three.

BUNNY: Biggest collection in the state outside of a museum. That's what my uncle works at the PTC told me.

HERSCHEL:

> (Opening one of the albums)
>
> These are from the old trolleys; they're my favorites, they're buried, you see.

FRAN: Yo, Francis!

FRANCIS: Jesus Christ in Heaven, I'm coming.

> (Inside, yelling)

FRAN: That's my Ivy League son.

FRANCIS:

> (Entering the yard)
>
> Lot of food.

FRAN: These kids gotta eat. Looka how skinny they are. You don' gotta eat, but that's all you do.

BUNNY:

> (About Herschel, who is gulping large quantities of food)
>
> This is another one. Looka him put that food away. Slow down!
>
> (Herschel chokes)
>
> Oh, oh, he's gonna have a asthma attack. I think he does it to punish me. You ever try to sleep with someone havin' a asthma attack in the next room? Drives you bananas.

(To Herschel, still gulping)

Take human bites for Christ' sake! Jesus, it's like a threshing machine: Varroom! Varroom!

FRAN:

(To Judith)

Don' be bashful we got plenty.

JUDITH: I'm not bashful.

FRAN: Eat then!

BUNNY:

(Lunges at Herschel with the fly swatter)

Slow down! The end of the world ain't for another twenty minutes.

(He slows down)

That's right.

(She looks at his neck)

Look at them mosquito bites. You been pickin' them? I says, you been pickin' them?

HERSCHEL: No.

BUNNY:

(Starts to beat him with the fly swatter)

I told you and I told you not to pick at them, they'll get infected.

FRAN:

(To Randy)

You got a appetite, at least.

JUDITH:

(Stands up, to Fran)

Egli è casa dapertutto.

FRAN:

(Not having understood)

Hanh?

FRANCIS: She's an Italian major at Radcliffe.

JUDITH:

(Very conversationally)

Questo giardin me piace molto. Il nostro camino non furo facile, ma siamo giovane e . . .

(They all look at her, puzzled)

LUCILLE: You see dear, that's Harvard Italian. We don't speak that.

FRAN: What did you say?

JUDITH:

(Very embarrassed, sits down)

Oh, nothing.

FRAN: You see, my people over there was the niggers. The farm hands, they worked the land. We're Abbruzzese; so we speak a kinda nigger Italian.

LUCILLE: Oh, Fran! He means it's a dialect.

BUNNY:

(Looking Fran over mock-critically)

Niggers, hanh? Let me look, let me look. Yeah, I thought so. Suspicious complexion.

(She grabs his crotch. Lucille scowls)

FRAN:

(To Bunny)

You're not eatin' as much as usual, Bun.

BUNNY: I'm eatin' light, got stage fright. Gotta go a court today.

FRAN: Yeah, why?

LUCILLE: Oh, Bunny, please, not in front of the kids!

BUNNY: That bitch, Mary O'Donnel attacked me. I was lyin' there, mindin' my own business, and she walks in, drops the groceries, screams, then throws herself on top of me.

FRAN: Where was you lyin'?

BUNNY: In bed.

FRAN: Who's bed?

BUNNY: Whataya mean: Who's bed? Don' matter who's bed. No matter where a person is, that person gotta right to be treated wit courtesy. And her fuckin' husband was no use; he just says: Oh, Mary! turns over and goes back to sleep. So's I hadda fend for myself. She threw herself on top a me, see, so I broke her fuckin' arm. Well, you woulda thought the whole world was fuckin' endin'. She sat there and screamed. I didn't know what to do. It was her house. I didn't know where nothin' was and she's a shitty housekeeper. So I shook her fuckin' husband's arm and said get the fuck up I just broke your fuckin' wife's arm. But he shook me off, you know how these men are, afta, so's I put on my slip, and I put on my dress and got the hell out of there. I'll tell you my ears was burnin'. That witch has gotta tongue like the murders in the Rue Morgue. Then, of all the face, she's got the guts to go to the cops and say I assaulted her. Well, I was real ashamed to have to admit I did go after Mary O'Donnel. She smells like old peanuts. Ever smell her, Lucille?

(Lucille shudders and turns away)

So's I gotta go to court and stand trial. But I ain't worried. I gotta uncle on The Force, he's a captain. Come on Herschel. Sam the Jew wan's a see his kid today.

(She picks up her tray)

LUCILLE:

(Not moving)

I'll help clean up.

JUDITH:

(Jumping up)

So will I.

BUNNY: Good, 'cause I gotta get ready to meet my judge. I'll show youse where everything is.

HERSCHEL:

(To Randy)

Do you want to see my collection of subway posters?

RANDY:

(After some hesitation)

Well, alright.

HERSCHEL:

(Following Randy into house, with his transfers)

I have eight hundred . . .

BUNNY:

(Holding door for Lucille)

Right this way, the palace is open.

(Fran and Francis are left alone)

FRAN: I didn't know your friends was comin'.

FRANCIS: I didn't either.

FRAN: They are your friends, ain't they?

FRANCIS: It isn't that simple.

FRAN: You kids is all nuts, you know that? It was that simple when I was growin' up. You hung out on the corner, see, and the guys you hung out wit was your friends, see? Never stopped to think about it.

FRANCIS: Those guys you hung out with were pretty quick to drop you when you had all the trouble with the bookies, and when mother left. You might say they deserted you.

FRAN: Yeah, yeah, you might say that.

FRANCIS: So then, they weren't friends.

FRAN: 'Course they was. People desert other people, don' make no difference if they're friends or not. I mean, if they wasn't friends to begin wit, you couldn't say they deserted me, could you?

FRANCIS: I guess not.

FRAN: Francis, this Judith, she's really somethin'. I didn't know you had the eye, you know?

FRANCIS: How was your trip to Wildwood?

FRAN: Well, Lucille had a fight wit Aunt Emma. That's why we came back. It was over water bugs. I didn't see no water bugs. But Lucille said they was everywhere. Aunt Emma thought she was accusin' her of bein' dirty. So we came back.

FRANCIS: Lucille is quite a phenomenon.

FRAN: She's good people, she means well. There ain't nothin' like a woman's company, remember that, my son, there ain't nothin' like a woman. You can think there is. I thought the horses was just as good; hell, I thought the horses was better. But I was wrong. But you gotta be careful of white women. I guess us dagos go afta them; hell, I went afta you mother, and she was white as this Judith, though not near as pretty. But you gotta be careful of them kinda women. A white woman's like a big hole, you can never be sure what's in there. So you be careful, even if she is a Italian major. What do you want for your birthday tomorrow?

(They start clearing the yard, folding the chairs, putting trashcans back in place, typing table back in the house)

FRANCIS: Not to be reminded of it.

FRAN: C'mon we gotta do somethin'. That's a big occasion: Twenty-one! I know what! You and your guests can have a big dinner out wit Lucille and me to celebrate.

FRANCIS: Oh, I think they'll have left by then.

FRAN: They just got here!

FRANCIS: Well, you know how these kids are nowadays, all nuts. They can't stand to be in one place more than a few hours.

FRAN: But they just pitched their tent under the fig tree, even. No, no, I think you're wrong. I think we're in for a visit. And I hope so, they seem like nice kids.

FRANCIS: Well, they're a little crazy; you know, speed, it twists the mind.

FRAN: Speed?

FRANCIS: Yeah, they're both what we call speed freaks. That's why they're so skinny.

FRAN: You mean they ain't on scholarship?

FRANCIS: They're on speed.

FRAN: Oh my God, them poor kids. They need some help. I'm gonna call Doc Pollicarpo, maybe he could help them.

(Randy comes out of Bunny's house, carrying heavy books)

RANDY: Herschel lent me his books on subways . . .

(He sets them down in front of the tent)

FRAN: You poor kid.

RANDY:

(Misunderstanding)

Well . . .

FRAN: No wonder you're so skinny.

RANDY: I'm not that skinny.

FRAN: Some other kid started you on it? Somebody tie you down and force it into your veins?

RANDY: What?

FRAN: Looka his eyes—that's a real strange color. I guess that proves it. You got holes in your arms too?

RANDY: What—why?

FRAN: Come here and sit down, you need rest, you need good food, have a black olive that's good for speed.

RANDY:

(Shocked)

Speed?

FRAN: And your sister too? That beautiful young girl on speed? It's a heart breaker. That stuff it works fast, that's why they call it speed.

(Francis nods in agreement)

You can see it rot the brain.

RANDY: But I'm not on . . .

(Looks at Francis, understanding. Francis shrugs)

FRANCIS: My father got it in his head you were on speed.

RANDY: I never touch it.

FRAN:

(Understanding)

Oh, yeah, let's make a fool of the old man.

(Yelling)

Yo, Lucille, get the hell out here.

(To Randy)

I'm sorry, young man, my son is a little twisted. His mother used to say when he came along he . . .

FRANCIS:

(Has heard this many times)

. . . when he came along he broke the mold.

FRAN:

(Yelling)

Lucille! I'm not gonna call you again.

LUCILLE: I'm here. And don't scratch that rash, makes it worse.

(Coming out)

FRAN:

(Yelling)

Yo, Bun, good luck wit the judge!

(To Lucille)

Come on.

(Heads toward the kitchen, turns back)

Randy, if you're gonna smoke pot out here, do it quiet.

LUCILLE: Oh, I'm sure he's too nice a boy to . . .

FRAN: Lucille, get inna house!

(Fran, with Lucille, enters house)

RANDY: What's all this about speed? That's what I call a sixties mentality.

FRANCIS: Where's Judith?

RANDY: Still cleaning up, I guess.

(Pulls out a box of joints)

Want some pot?

FRANCIS: Why'd you come? You could have given me some warning.
RANDY: We're not an atomic attack.

> (He starts boxing with Francis)

FRANCIS: You dropped in like one.

> (Randy starts doing push-ups)

What are you doing?
RANDY: I've been working out every day and taking tiger's milk and nutriment . . .
FRANCIS: What about "wate-on"?
RANDY: Overrated.

> (Rolls over on his back)

Hey, hold my legs.
FRANCIS: You want to play: "Sunrise at Campobello"?
RANDY: Smart ass, I want to do sit ups.

> (Francis kneels and gets a hold of Randy's feet. Randy starts doing sit ups)

FRANCIS:

> (Grunts)

One . . . Three . . . You weren't this bad last spring. Even though you did drag me to the gym once—I even had to take a shower—I stumbled around without my glasses, I couldn't see anything, my arms were out like Frankenstein's—they thought I was very strange.

> (He looks down at his arms)

My arms are getting tired—and what is this supposed to do?
RANDY: I'm tired of being skinny.

> (Still lying on the ground)

FRANCIS: You aren't that skinny.
RANDY: I'm grotesque looking. Look at my chest.

> (Lifts shirt)

I look like a new born duck. I want pectorals, I want biceps, I want shoulders. I want people to stop sniggering when they look at me.
FRANCIS: I don't snigger when I look at you.
RANDY:

> (Seriously)

You're my friend.

> (Francis rises, uncomfortable. Randy lights up a joint)

Is there a pool around here? I'd like to go swimming.
FRANCIS: That's a good way to get spinal meningitis. Look, Randy, don't you think I'm an unlikely choice for a jock buddy?

> (Judith comes out of the house, and joins them on the stoop)

JUDITH: Sorry that took so long, but Lucille didn't do anything, she just stood there and insisted I had to know her son. Hey, Francis, how are you going to entertain me? Is there a museum in walking distance of Philadelphia?

RANDY: That's low priority; we're going to the boat races.

JUDITH: Randy, why don't you simply realize you're pathetic, and stop boring intelligent people?

RANDY: And why don't you treat your hemorrhoids and stop acting like somebody out of Picasso's blue period . . .

(Bunny comes out of her house. She is wearing a very tight, white, crocheted suit, and carrying a plastic, flowered shopping bag. She is dressed for court)

BUNNY:

(Strikes a "stunning" pose)

How do I look?

RANDY: Like you can win the case.

BUNNY: You're sweet Give me a kiss for luck.

(Grabs and kisses him. Then yells)

Herschel!

(Back to Randy)

Look at his skin, look at his eyes; ain't anybody around here looks like you, honey. Like a fuckin' white sheik!

(Herschel enters from his house. He is dressed for a visit with his father, in an enormous, ill-fitting brown suit. He is munching on something)

Oh, Herschel. Come on.

(Brushes his suit roughly)

And look you, don' you go havin' no asthma attacks wit your father, he blames me.

JUDITH:

(Suddenly)

Herschel, Randy'll go with you; he wants to go to the park and study your subway books.

(She grabs one of the big books, and drops it in Randy's hands. Randy looks shocked)

HERSCHEL:

(Astounded and delighted)

Really?

JUDITH:

(Before Randy can speak)

And do you happen to have, by any chance, a map of the subway system? Randy was just saying how much he wanted to study one.

HERSCHEL: Yes!

(Digs in his pockets)

I have three. This one is the most up to date. You're interested—really interested?

RANDY: Well—I . . .

HERSCHEL:

(Grabbing his arm)

Come on, I'll walk you to the park!

(Drags Randy off down the alley)

I know the way and everything . . .

BUNNY:

(Yelling after them)

Don't fall down, Herschel, that suit costs a fortune to clean.

(To Judith and Francis)

Well, I'm off. Wish me luck.

JUDITH and FRANCIS:

(Smoking a joint)

Good luck.

BUNNY:

(Crosses to the gate)

I'll see youse later. I mean I hope I see youse later.

(She exits, crossing her fingers for luck. Judith passes the joint to Francis. She goes as if to kiss him, but instead, blows smoke in his mouth. He chokes)

FRANCIS: Did you come here to humiliate me?

JUDITH: What?

FRANCIS: What do you call coming here with your brother, climbing over the back fence, walking in on me, half-naked, unannounced? And then, Bunny, Herschel—the house is a mess—

JUDITH: That doesn't bother me, really. You oughtn't to be ashamed.

FRANCIS: Oh, I wish you hadn't come, that's all, I wish you hadn't come, you or Randy . . .

JUDITH: But why? I took you seriously, I took—everything seriously and then I hadn't heard—

FRANCIS: I didn't want any more of either of you.

JUDITH: Francis!

FRANCIS: Have you looked at me? I'm fat!

JUDITH: You're not fat!

FRANCIS: Then what do you call this?

(Makes two rolls of fat with his hands)

If I try I can make three—

JUDITH: You're crazy! What does that have to do with anything?

FRANCIS: No attractive person has ever been interested in me . . .

JUDITH: Well, maybe they thought you were a bore.

FRANCIS: "Love enters through the eyes," that's Dante . . .

JUDITH: And he liked little girls.

FRANCIS: Look, I don't know what you see when you look at me. I've made myself a monster—and tomorrow I'm to be twenty-one and all I can feel is myself sinking.

JUDITH: But Francis . . .

FRANCIS: Look, I don't want to discuss it now, not here, not with my father around the corner. Now I'm going into my room and play some music. Then I'm going for a walk. I would appreciate it if you'd strike your tent and gather up your things and your brother and leave before I return.

> (He goes into his room, and puts on some quiet music. Judith is left alone. Suddenly, Randy appears over the fence)

RANDY: This is very mysterious.

Blackout

SCENE 2

Scene the same. Later that day. It is early evening. During the scene night falls. Fran is cooking spaghetti in his kitchen. He is singing "Strangers in the Night." Randy is inside the tent.
Francis enters through the gate. Sees the tent. He slams the gate.

FRANCIS: They're still here.

FRAN:

> (From inside house)

Yo, Francis, is that you?

FRANCIS: Yes.

FRAN: I'm in the kitchen.

> (Francis goes inside)

Where have you been?

FRANCIS: Where is she now?

FRAN: In your room. Why don't you go in to see her?

FRANCIS: Didn't it ever occur to you that I don' want you to interfere . . .

FRAN:

> (Smiles)

"Strangers in the night . . ."

> (Francis goes into his room. Herschel comes bounding in from the alley)

HERSCHEL:

> (To Fran)

Hi. Where's Randy?

FRAN: In his tent.

> *(Yells)*

> Yo, Randy! You got company.

> *(Randy peeks out of the tent. Herschel sits down by the tent)*

HERSCHEL: Hi. I just got back from my father's. He wanted me to stay over but I faked a petit mal and he let me go.

RANDY: A petit mal?

HERSCHEL: You know, a fit. A little one. I stumbled around and I slobbered and I told him everything was black. He got worried. I told him I left my medicine back here, so he gave me money for a cab. I took the bus.

> *(Francis and Judith appear in window)*

> Like, I was wondering, would you like to come with me to, like, see the engine? It's not far from here. It's alright if you don't want to come, like, I mean, I understand, you know? Everybody can't be interested in Public Transportation, it's not that interesting, you know? So, like, I understand if you aren't interested but would you like to come?

RANDY:

> *(Who has gotten a towel and toilet case out of his knapsack)*

> Can we have dinner first?

HERSCHEL: You mean you'll come? How about that! I'll go and change—I'll be right back.

> *(He starts to run, trips over his own feet, falls, picks himself up, and runs into his house)*

JUDITH:

> *(From window)*

> I see you're about to be broadened.

RANDY: What could I do?

> *(To Fran in kitchen)*

> Mr. Geminiani!

FRAN:

> *(Appears in kitchen window)*

> Fran, it's Fran!

RANDY: Fran. Can I take a shower?

FRAN: Be my guest. You got a towel?

RANDY: Yes.

> *(He goes into the house)*

FRAN:

> *(Comes out, yelling)*

> Yo, Francis!

FRANCIS:

> *(He and Judith are right behind him)*

Jesus Christ, I'm right here.

FRAN: That's my Ivy League son. Look, once in a while when your lips get tired, go in and stir the spaghettis, hanh? I'm going to get Lucille.

FRANCIS: She lives around the corner, why can't she come over herself?

FRAN: Don' get smart and show some respect. She believes in the boogie man.

> *(He throws the kitchen towel in through the window, like he was making a jump shot)*

Yes! Two points!

> *(Holds up two fingers like cuckold's horns)*

"Strangers in the night . . ."

> *(He exits through the gate)*

JUDITH: Lucille and your father are—well, you know, aren't they?

FRANCIS: I don't know, they drink an awful lot of coffee.

JUDITH: Stimulates the gonads—

> *(She embraces Francis and kisses him. He looks uncomfortable)*

What's the matter?

FRANCIS: I'm sorry.

JUDITH: Sorry about what?

> *(He looks away)*

You know, I think you are an eternal adolescent, a German Adolescent, a German Romantic Adolescent. You were born out of context, you'd have been much happier in the forties of the last century when it was eternally twilight.

FRANCIS: Do I detect a veiled reference to *Zwielicht* by Eichendorf?

JUDITH: I took Basic European Literature also, and did better than you did.

FRANCIS: You did not.

JUDITH: I got the highest mark on the objective test: 98! What did you get?

> *(She laughs)*

FRANCIS:

> *(Bantering with her)*

My SAT verbal and achievement tests were higher than yours.

JUDITH: How do you know?

FRANCIS: I looked them up in the office. I pretended to go faint, and while the registrar ran for water, I looked at your file.

JUDITH:

> *(Entering into his game)*

I find that hard to believe; I had the highest score in the verbal at St. Paul's and also in the English Achievement Test.

FRANCIS: That's what it said alongside your IQ.

JUDITH:

> *(Taken aback in spite of herself)*

> My IQ?

FRANCIS: Very interesting that IQ. It was recorded in bright red ink. There was also a parenthesis, in which someone had written: "Poor girl, but she has great determination."

JUDITH: I find jokes about IQ's in poor taste.

FRANCIS: Then you are an adolescent, a German Adolescent, a German Romantic Adolescent.

JUDITH: And before this edifying discussion you were about to say: "Fuck you, Judith."

FRANCIS: Don't put it that way . . .

JUDITH: But more or less it was get lost, see you later, oh yes, have a nice summer— and maybe, just maybe, I'll tell you why later. You seem to want to skip that part, the why.

> *(She picks up the end of a garden hose, and points it at Francis like a machine gun, and with a Humphrey Bogart voice, says:)*

> Look, I came to see you, that's ballsy, now you've got to reciprocate and tell me why . . .

> *(She puts down the hose, and the accent)*

> Do I bore you? Do you think I'm ugly? Do I have bad breath?

FRANCIS: Oh, come on!

JUDITH: Hey, Francis, we're just alike, can't you see that?

FRANCIS:

> *(Indicates the house and yard)*

> Oh yeah.

JUDITH: Two over achievers. Really. I know my family is better off than yours; but we're just alike, and there was something last winter and now you're telling me . . .

FRANCIS: Look, I'm going to be twenty-one tomorrow. Well . . . I don't know what to say.

JUDITH: Is there a reason?

FRANCIS: I don't think I can say.

JUDITH: That doesn't make any sense.

FRANCIS: I think I'm queer.

JUDITH: Why don't we back up a bit. I said: "We're just alike et cetera," and you said you were going to be twenty-one tomorrow, and I looked at you with deep-set, sea-blue eyes, and you said . . .

FRANCIS: I think I'm queer.

JUDITH:

> *(Laughs)*

> Well, I guess we can't get around it. Do you want to amplify? I mean this seems like quite a leap from what I remember of those long, sweet, ecstatic nights, naked in each other's young arms, clinging to . . .

FRANCIS: We fucked. Big deal. That's what kids are supposed to do. And be serious.

JUDITH: I am serious. Is there a particular boy?

FRANCIS: Yes.

JUDITH: An adolescent, a German Adolescent . . .

FRANCIS: Not German, no.

JUDITH: Do I know him?

(Francis doesn't answer)

Reciprocal?

FRANCIS: It was just this spring. He began to haunt me. We became friends. We talked a lot—late in my room when you were studying. Well, I don't know, and you see—I've had, well, crushes before. I dreamed of him. It's not reciprocal, no, he doesn't know, but it became more and more obvious to me. I mean, I'd look at him, and then some other boy would catch my eye and I'd think—you see?

JUDITH: Well. I suppose I could start teaching you the secrets of make-up.

(Francis turns away, annoyed)

Well, how do you expect me to react? You seem to think I ought to leap out the window because of it. But it's like you're suddenly turning to me and saying you are from Mars. Well, you might be, but I don't see much evidence and I can't see what difference it makes. I'm talking about you and me, I and thou and all that. All right, maybe you do have an eye for the boys, well so do I, but you . . . you are special to me. I wouldn't throw you over just because a hockey player looked good, why do you have to give me up?

FRANCIS: I don't think that makes any sense, Judith. I mean, if I were from Mars, it would make a difference, I'd have seven legs and talk a different language and that's how I feel now.

(Judith embraces him)

Don't touch me so much, Judith, and don't look at me . . .

JUDITH: Then you're afraid. That explains, that fat and ugly nonsense and this sudden homosexual panic. You're afraid that anyone who responds to you will make demands you can't meet. You're afraid you'll fail . . .

FRANCIS: Good Evening Ladies and Gentlemen, Texaco Presents: "Banality on Parade!"

JUDITH: You're afraid to venture. That's why you've enshrined someone who doesn't respond to you, probably doesn't even know you're interested. If the relationship never happens, you are never put to the test and can't fail. The Over Achiever's Great Nightmare!

FRANCIS: That's crazy!

JUDITH: I bet this boy who draws you is some Harvard sprite, a dew-touched freshman . . .

FRANCIS: He was a freshman.

JUDITH: In Randy's class and that proves it. Look at Randy—what kind of response could someone like that have but the giggles? And you know that. You're afraid of commitment. And remember what Dante says about those who refuse to make commitments. They're not even in Hell, but are condemned to run about the outskirts for eternity.

(Francis, who has heard enough, has stuck his head inside Bunny's kitchen window, and brought it down over his neck like a guillotine. Judith now runs over to the fence, and starts climbing to the top)

Ed io che reguardai vidi una insegna che girando correva tanta ratta, che d'ogni posa me parea indegna . . . !

(She leaps off the fence. Francis runs to her aid)

FRANCIS: Judith! Jesus Christ!
JUDITH:

(As he helps her up)

You see? I ventured, I made the great leap and remained unscathed.

(Herschel runs out of his house, dressed in his old pants and torn sweat shirt, carrying one sneaker)

HERSCHEL: I heard a noise. Is Randy alright?
FRANCIS: Judith, you're alright?
JUDITH: Good as nude!

(Limps over to stoop and sits)

FRANCIS: Oh shit! I forgot to stir the spaghetti. Now they'll all stick together . . .

(Runs into the kitchen, runs out again)

You're sure you're alright?
JUDITH: Stir the spaghetti. We don't want them sticking together.

(Francis goes into the kitchen)

HERSCHEL: You're the one who fell?
JUDITH: You might put it that way
HERSCHEL:

(Sits down beside Judith. Puts on his other sneaker)

I do that. One time I fell while I was having an asthma attack. My mother called the ambulance. She has, like, an uncle who's a driver. They rushed me to the hospital. Like, you know, the siren screaming? That was two years ago, right before I went to high school. It was St. Agnes Hospital over Track 37 on the A, the AA, the AA 1 through 7 and the B express lines, maybe you passed it? I didn't get, like, hurt falling, you know. Still, my mother asked me what I wanted most in the whole world, you know? I told her and she let me ride the subway for twelve whole hours. Like, she rode them with me. She had to stay home from work for two days.

JUDITH:

(Crosses to tent, and gets a bandana out of her knapsack. She sits down, and starts cleaning her knee, which she'd hurt in leaping off the fence)

Why are you so interested in the subways?
HERSCHEL:

(Joins her on the ground)

Oh, not just the subways. I love buses too, you know? And my favorites are, well, you won't laugh? The trolleys. They are very beautiful. There's a trolley graveyard about two blocks from here. I was thinking, like maybe Randy would like to see that, you know? I could go see the engine any time. The trolley graveyard is well, like, I guess, beautiful, you know? Really. They're just there, like old creatures everyone's forgotten, some of them rusted out, and some of them on their sides, and one, the old thirty-two, is like standing straight up as though sayin', like, I'm going to stand here and be myself, no matter what. I talk to them. Oh, I shouldn't have said that. Don't tell my mother, please? It's, you know, like people who go to castles and look for, for, well, like, knights in shining armor, you know? That past was beautiful and somehow, like, pure. The same is true of the trolleys. I follow the old thirty-two route all the time. It leads right to the graveyard where the thirty-two is buried, you know? It's like, well, fate. The tracks are half-covered with filth and pitch, new pitch like the city pours on. It oozes in the summer and people walk on it, but you can see the tracks and you see, like, it's true, like, old things last, good things last, like, you know? The trolleys are all filthy and half-covered and rusted out and laughed at, and even though they're not much use to anybody and kind of ugly like, by most standards, they're, like, they're, well, I guess, beautiful, you know?

(Randy enters having finished his shower. He flicks his towel at Herschel)

RANDY: Hey, that shower is a trip. I should have taken my surf board.

HERSCHEL: Like, you should have used our shower, it's in much better shape, you know? Next time you want to take a shower, let me know.

JUDITH: Well, there's one cosmic issue settled.

RANDY:

> *(Crosses to kitchen window)*

Mmmmm. That sauce smells good.

FRANCIS:

> *(Appears in kitchen window)*

We call it gravy.

RANDY: When will it be ready?

FRANCIS: Soon.

> *(Disappears inside house)*

HERSCHEL:

> *(To Randy)*

Then we can go to the graveyard.

> *(Randy looks surprised)*

See, like, I decided it might be, well, more fun, if we saw all the dead trolleys, you know, and leave the engine for later.

RANDY: Whatever you say.

> *(Back to the window)*

Francis, look—is there something wrong?

FRAN:

> *(Offstage, yelling)*

Yo, Francis! We're here.

(Comes in from gate)

Hi kids.

(Going into house)

You stir that stuff?

FRANCIS:

(From inside)

Yeah.

(Randy gets a shirt out of his knapsack and crawls into the tent. Herschel starts crawling into the tent)

RANDY: Herschel . . . careful!
HERSCHEL: I'm careful.

(Inside the tent)

LUCILLE:

(Offstage)

Judith!
RANDY: Well, sit over there.

(Herschel plops down, blocking the entire entrance with his back. Lucille comes into the yard with a sweater and jacket. She approaches Judith)

LUCILLE: Judy, I brought you a sweater. I thought you might be chilly later tonight and I didn't know if you brought one with you.
JUDITH: Thank you.
LUCILLE:

(Puts sweater around Judith's shoulders)

It's real sheep's wool. My friend, Diane, gave it to me. Her daughter, Joann, is a model for KYZ-TV in Center City—special shift. She's a Cancer, so am I, that's why Fran says I'm a disease. My son, Donny, he's at Yale in pre-med, Branford Scholarship, I think he'll make a wonderful doctor, don't Yale make wonderful doctors?
JUDITH: I'm sure I don't know.

(Fran comes out with Francis. He is carrying a large fold-up metal table)

FRAN: Make yourself useful, Lucille. I got the table, go get the plates.
RANDY:

(Getting away from Herschel who is hovering around him)

I'll help set up.

(Lucille goes into the house, and returns with a tray, with plates, napkins, cutlery, glasses, bug spray, and a "plastic lace" table cloth)

FRAN: How was your shower?
RANDY: I expected to see seals and Eskimos any minute.

FRAN: At least you got out of the bathroom alive. There are beach chairs in the cellar, why don't you get them? Francis, show this young man where the beach chairs is in the cellar.

(Fran goes back into the house, Francis, Randy, and Herschel go past the house to the cellar, and Lucille starts setting the table)

LUCILLE: You know Judy, my daughter, she's a dental technician at The Graduate Hospital—special shift. She wanted to go to Yale, but she couldn't get in. She thought it was her teeth. They're buck. She said the woman looked at her funny the whole time at the interview. Now I told her she should just carry herself with poise and forget her teeth. Y'know what she said to me: how can I forget my teeth; they're in my mouth! Not a very poised thing to say. That's why she didn't get into Yale: No poise. That's why she ain't got no husband, either. Do the people at Yale think teeth are important?

JUDITH: I don't know anything about Yale.

LUCILLE: But what do you think?

JUDITH: Yes, I think teeth are very important for success in life.

(She is setting out cutlery)

At the prep school I attended they had us practice our bite three times a day.

LUCILLE:

(Politely, taken in)

Oh?

JUDITH: We would bite off a poised bite, and chew with poise, and then sing a C major scale whilst we swilled the food in our mouths. I could even sing songs whilst swilling food with poise. In fact, I once sang the first aria of the Queen of the Night while swilling half a hamburger and a bucket of french fries. . . . Of course, remaining utterly poised, or "pwased," as we say at Harvard.

LUCILLE: Oh.

(She walks around the table spraying insect repellent)

It kills them very quickly.

(Francis, Randy, and Herschel enter the yard with beach chairs and old kitchen chairs, which they proceed to set up)

RANDY:

(To Francis, continuing a conversation)

C'mon, Francis, what's going on?

FRAN:

(From the kitchen)

Yo, Lucille, give me a hand!

JUDITH: I'll be glad to help.

(Runs into the kitchen)

RANDY: Come on, Francis, I mean I'm three years younger than you—so tell me . . .

(Simultaneously, Lucille and Herschel approach Randy)

HERSCHEL: Would you like to see my models of the trolley fleet of 1926?

LUCILLE:

> *(Giving Randy a jacket)*

> I brought you one of my son's jackets, because I thought you might get cold later and I didn't know if you brought one wit you. My son's girl friend bought it for him at Wanamaker's.

> *(Fran and Judith come back out)*

BUNNY:

> *(Calling from inside her house)*

> Yo! Where is everybody?

FRAN: Yo, Bun! We're out here.

> *(Bunny comes stumbling out of her house. She has been drinking. She never stops moving, constantly dancing and leaping about, she cries out in war hoops and screams of victory)*

BUNNY: I won! I won! I wanna kiss from everybody but Lucille!

> *(She goes around kissing everyone, except Lucille. She gets to Randy)*

> Oh, you're such a honey bun, I could eat you.

> *(She kisses him, then grabs his crotch)*

> I'll skip Francis too.

RANDY: Wanna smoke, Herschel?

HERSCHEL: Sure.

> *(They sit down by the tent, Herschel sitting as far away from Bunny as possible)*

BUNNY: Break out the horsepiss, Fran!

> *(Fran goes into the kitchen for liquor)*

> Jesus Christ in Heaven, I won!

FRAN:

> *(Returns with bottle of Scotch)*

> How do you want it?

BUNNY: Straight up the dark and narrow path, honey.

> *(She takes a swig from the bottle)*

> You shoulda seen me in that courtroom, I told them all about it, that bitch didn't even have the decency to fart before throwin' herself on top of me. I coulda been ruptured for life, I says, and she's a Catholic, I couldn't believe it. Catholics got self-control.

LUCILLE:

> *(To Judith)*

Well, good Catholics have self-control. Sister Mary Emaryd, my friend, she used to work at Wanamaker's before she married Christ. She . . .

BUNNY:

> (To Randy)

That judge looked at me, let me tell you.

LUCILLE: She would allow herself to go the bathroom only twice a day.

BUNNY:

> (To Fran)

I felt twenty again.

LUCILLE:

> (To Judith)

She said: Urgency is all in the mind.

BUNNY:

> (To Randy)

I felt like a fuckin' young filly in heat. Look, honey, you ever see my boobies swayin'?

> (She sways them for Randy. He giggles)

LUCILLE:

> (To Francis)

I go to the bathroom more than that, yet I go to Mass every Sunday . . .

BUNNY:

> (To Randy)

You smokin' that killer weed, hon?

RANDY: Sure. You want some?

BUNNY: Don' need that shit. Don' need nothin' to get high, I'm high naturally. I was born floatin'.

> (She leans on table, almost knocking everything over)

Come and dance with me, baby.

> (She grabs a very reluctant Randy)

C'mon! "Flat foot floozie with the floy, floy . . ."

> (They start doing the jitterbug, and Randy bumps into Bunny, knocking the breath out of her)

Fuck you world! Fuck you Mary O'Donnel! Fuck you Sam the Jew! Fuck you Catholic Church! Fuck you Mom! I won! You shoulda seen them look at me, I felt like a fuckin' starlit. My boobies swayin', and when I walked to the stand I did my strut; my fuckin' bitch-in-heat strut. Come on, Lucille, can you strut like this?

> (She comes up behind Lucille, and "bumps" her. Lucille starts swearing in Italian. Bunny turns to Judith)

Come on, honey, what's your name, can you strut like this? I can fuckin' strut up a storm. My hips have made many a wave in their time, honey, many a wave! I sent out hurricanes, I sent out earthquakes, I sent out tidal waves from my fuckin' hips. Yo, Fran!

FRAN: Yo, Bun!

BUNNY: Remember when I was in that fuckin' community theatre down at Gruen Recreation Center?

FRAN: Seventeenth Street.

LUCILLE: Sixteenth and Wolf!

BUNNY: I played Sadie Thompson in that play. I let my hair grow down long. It was real long then, not dyed shit yellow like it is now. I fuckin' got hair like hepatitis now. I played that part! I hadda sheer slip on and my legs, Jesus Christ, my legs! I fuckin' felt the earth tremble when I walked, I played that bitch like Mount Vesuvius and the clappin', honey, the clappin'!

FRAN: You were a big hit, yep.

BUNNY: At the curtain call, I held my boobs out like this:

(She sticks out her chest)

. . . and they screamed, honey, those fuckin' grown men screamed!

(To Randy)

Feel 'em, honey, feel these grapes of mine.

(She puts Randy's hand on her boobs)

RANDY: Mrs. Weinberger!

BUNNY: They're still nice, hanh? I fuckin' won that case!

(She has to sit down)

Then I married Sam the Jew and bore Herschel. Look at the fruit of my loins, look, this is one of the earthquakes I sent out of my hips. Boom! Boom! When he walks you can hear him around the corner, but he's a fuckin' genius at least. He's got an IQ of 187 or 172, dependin' on which test you use, despite his father!

LUCILLE:

(This has been building up)

Che disgraziat'!

(She runs into the house followed by Fran)

BUNNY:

(Looking after Fran)

I coulda had . . . well, almost anybody, more or less. I coulda been a chorus girl, then I met Sam the Kike and that was that. He had the evil eye, that Hebe, them little pointy eyes. He'd screw them up like he was lookin' for blackheads, then, suddenly, they'd go real soft and get big. I was a sucker for them fuckin' eyes. He's a jeweller, called me his jewel. Sam the Jew. I smell like old peanuts!

RANDY:

> *(Offering her the joint)*

> Sure you don't want some?

BUNNY: No, honey, I got me some coke for a giddy sniff. I get it from my uncle on the force; he gives me a discount, he's a captain.

> *(She suddenly sees Herschel smoking behind the tent)*

> Hey, wait a minute! You been smokin' that shit? Herschel! Have you been smokin' that shit?

HERSCHEL:

> *(Butts the joint quickly)*

> No . . .

BUNNY: Don' you lie to me. Didn't I tell you never to smoke that shit? It'll fuckin' rot your brain and you'll be more of a vegetable than you already are. God damn you, I'll beat the shit outta you!

> *(She lunges for him)*

HERSCHEL:

> *(Scurrying out of her way)*

> Come on!

BUNNY: Come on???? Come on??? I'll come on, you fuckin' four-eyed fat-assed creep, I'll come on!

> *(She grabs the bottle of Scotch, and chases Herschel into the house. We see them in their kitchen window. She is beating the shit out of Herschel)*

> Twelve fuckin' hours! Twelve fuckin' hours I was in labor wit you, screamin' on that table and for what? To fuckin' find you smokin' dope?

> *(His asthma attack is starting)*

> That's right! Go ahead! Have a fuckin' asthma attack, cough your fuckin' head off! See if I care!

> *(She disappears inside the house. Herschel is at the window, gasping for air, until he realizes that she has gone. His asthma attack miraculously stops. He disappears. During Herschel's attack everyone on stage stares at him, horrified. Randy passes Judith the joint. She refuses it. Francis takes a toke, and passes it back to Randy. Bunny, inside her house, is heard singing at the out of tune piano. Offstage)*

> "Moon river wider than a mile
> I'm screwing up in style some day . . ."

> *(Fran and Lucille come in from the house. He has a big bowl of spaghetti, and she is carrying a very elaborate antipasto)*

FRAN:

> *(Sitting down at the head of the table)*

Well, I hope everybody's gotta appetite, 'cause there's enough to feed the Chinee army and ain't no room to keep it either.

LUCILLE:

(Sniffing the air)

I think the Delassandro's down the alley are burning their children's clothing again. That smell!

(Randy and Francis break up, and put out the joint)

FRAN: You all got plates, I'll serve. Francis you get the gravy pot, I'll pass the macs, we also got antipast'; made special by Lucille Pompi . . .

(Lucille simpers)

and Lucille Pompi's antipast' is a delicacy.

(He gives Lucille a hug. Francis arrives with the gravy pot. Fran is serving)

And here we got the gravy meat: Veal, sausage, lamb, meat balls, and brasiole.

(He passes plate to Judith)

JUDITH: Oh, that's too much!

FRAN: Your stomach's bigger than your eyes. We also got wine.
Francis!

(Randy snaps his fingers at Francis, as if to say: Hop to it. Francis goes into house for wine. Fran passes plate to Lucille)

Lucille?

LUCILLE: No thank you, Fran, I'll just pick.

(He passes the plate to Randy)

Randy?

(Lucille is busy making sure everyone is taken care of. Francis has returned and is going around the table pouring wine. Fran serves a plate to Francis)

Francis?

FRANCIS: I'm not so hungry tonight.

FRAN: Oh, we better get down on our knees, we've just witnessed a miracle.

(Keeping the plate for himself)

LUCILLE: Oh, Fran, don't blaspheme.

FRAN: Sure you don' wan' none, Lucille?

(Everyone is eating but Lucille)

LUCILLE: I'll just pick out of your plate.

(She then proceeds to pick a large piece of lettuce from Fran's plate and stuffs it in her mouth)

FRAN:

(To Randy and Judith)

You kids enjoying your stay?

(Lucille now gets a forkful of spaghetti from Fran's plate and proceeds to eat that)

This is your first time in South Philly, I bet. You ought to get Francis to take you around tomorrow and see the sights. Them sights'll make you nearsighted, that's how pretty South Philly is.

(Lucille has speared more lettuce from Fran, and he grabs her wrist)

Yo, Lucille, I'll get you a plate.

LUCILLE:

(She frees her hand, stuffs the lettuce in her mouth, and says:)

No, thank you, Fran, I'm not hungry.

(She notices something on Judith's plate, picks it, and eats it. Judith and Randy are amazed)

FRAN: Lucille! Let that kid alone and fill your own plate.
LUCILLE:

(With a full mouth)

Fran, I'm not hungry!

(She sees a tomato wedge on Randy's plate. She picks up her fork, and pounces on the tomato)

FRAN: Lucille!
LUCILLE: He wasn't going to eat that.
FRAN: How do you know?
LUCILLE: Look how skinny he is.

(Herschel appears in his doorway)

FRAN: Hi ya, Herschel.

(Everyone greets him)

You feel better?
HERSCHEL: I guess.
FRAN: Well, get a plate and sit down!
HERSCHEL: You don't mind?
FRAN: You're the guest of honor.

(Herschel comes down to the table, to the empty chair, and starts pulling it around the table, making Francis get out of the way, until he is next to Randy. Randy, Judith, and Lucille, who are all sitting on the long side of the table have to scoot over to make room for Herschel. He sits down next to Randy)

HERSCHEL:

(To Randy)

Can we still . . .
RANDY: Yeah, yeah, sure.

(Fran has piled spaghetti and sauce for Herschel. He is trying to pass the plate down to Herschel, but Lucille snatches it, gets a forkful of pasta, and then passes the plate on. Everyone, except Francis, is eating)

FRAN: Gonna be night soon. And tomorrow's my son's birthday. Seems like yesterday he was my little buddy, on the chubby side, but cute all the same, and tomorrow he's gonna be—what? Six? Gonna be a man tomorrow. Looka him squirm. Everybody hits twenty-one sooner or later, 'cept me, I'm still nineteen. Salute!

(They all lift their glasses in a toast and drink, except Herschel, who keeps shoveling it down)

Judith, look, you can see that fig tree wave in the wind if you squint. Francis, remember the day I planted it? I got the sledge hammer out of the cellar, people that was here before us left it, and I broke that concrete. His mother, she'd had enough of both of us, and took off headin' down south. She was like a bird had too much of winter. Met a nice Southern man.

LUCILLE: Protestant.

FRAN: They're married. Can't have kids though; she had a hysterectomy just before she left. It's a shame. She's good people and so's this man, she shoulda had kids wit him. He's real normal, nice lookin', don' cough like I do, don' get rashes neither, and to him, horses is for ridin'!

(He breaks himself up. Then starts to cough. Lucille is picking out of Judith's plate. Big forkful of spaghetti)

They'd have had nice kids. The kind that woulda made her happy. She's one of them people that like to fade inna the air. Don' wanna stand out. Francis and me, well, we stand out. Don't wanna, understand, but we talk too loud, cough, scratch ourselves, get rashes, are kinda big. You have to notice us. Don' have to like us but you gotta see us.

(Lucille pats Fran's cheek lovingly)

Well, his mother, she was good people and meant well, but she wasn't too easy wit us, she wanted a home in the suburbs, all the Sears and Roebuck catalogs lined up against the wall, and two white kids, just like her, white like the fog, kids you hadda squint to see. Well, this one day, she packed her bags, see, rented a big truck and took everything, even my portable TV.

(He laughs at the "joke")

I guess it'll be cool tonight. She left me, you see, she left me. So I come out here and smash that concrete. Next day I planted the fig tree. I went to the one guy in the neighborhood would give me the time of day, borrowed thirty dollars and bought this tree, the dirt, some fertilizer . . .

(Lucille's hand is in his plate again)

Jesus Christ in Heaven! Lucille! Would you fill your own plate and stop actin' like the poor relative??!

LUCILLE:

(She quickly stuffs food in her mouth)

Stop pickin' on me! I ain't actin' like the poor relative!

FRAN: Whataya call pickin' at his plate, then pickin' at my plate, then pickin' at his plate, then pickin' at her plate, for Christ' sake, hanh? Stop pickin'! Take! Take wit both hands, it's there, why you act like there ain't plenty when there is, hanh? What's the matter you???!!!!

(He has taken two enormous handfuls of spaghetti out of the bowl and dropped them into Lucille's plate)

LUCILLE:

(Screaming)

Eh! Sta'zit'!

FRAN:

(Shaking her plate under her nose)

Mangi taci' o—

LUCILLE:

(Stands up and screams at him)

Fongoul!

(She runs out of the yard)

FRAN: Jesus Christ! See you kids later.

(Yells)

Lucille, I was only kidding!

(Runs off after her)

HERSCHEL:

(Rising, to Randy)

I'm finished.

RANDY:

(With a sigh)

Alright.

(To Judith and Francis)

See you later.

(Herschel and Randy exit through the alley)

JUDITH:

(Rises, starts stacking)

I'll put the dishes in the sink.

(She suddenly drops the plates on the table)

It's Randy, isn't it?

BUNNY:

(Stumbles out of her house. She is in her robe and nightgown again)

Hi, you two. You got some more horsepiss? I'm out.

FRANCIS: I'll look, Bunny.

(Runs into his kitchen)

BUNNY: You look sort of peaked, hon, upset over somethin'? A man, maybe?

JUDITH: Maybe.

BUNNY: Well, take my advice and heat up the coke bottle; men ain't worth shit, not shit.

FRANCIS:

(Coming out with a bottle)

Here, Bunny.

BUNNY:

(Takes a slug of whiskey)

You're a saint, just a fuckin' saint.

(She collapses in a heap, completely out. Francis gets her under each arm, and Judith holds the door open. Francis starts dragging her back in. Bunny, coming to for a moment:)

Shit! Why am I such a whale? Why ain't a porpoise or a dolphin? Why do I gotta be a whale wit hepatitis hair?

FRANCIS: Come on, Bunny, I'll help you inside . . .

BUNNY: You're a saint, a fuckin' saint.

(They disappear inside Bunny's house. Francis returns immediately)

JUDITH: You and Randy . . . !

FRANCIS: Me and Randy nothing. He doesn't know a thing about it. He's been following me around all day asking why I won't look at him. What can I say? We were friends, and he can't understand . . .

(Randy and Herschel have re-entered from the alley)

Well, who can understand . . .

JUDITH: What about the trolleys?

HERSCHEL: A different guard was there. We can go tomorrow though, my friend'll be there.

RANDY:

(To Judith)

What's the matter?

JUDITH:

(To Francis, indicating Randy)

Just look at him.

(Peals of laughter)

And look at you.

HERSCHEL:

(To Randy)

It's early yet, would you like to see my books on ornamental tiles . . .

RANDY: Good night, Herschel.

HERSCHEL: I guess everybody can't be interested in . . .

RANDY:

(Pushes him inside, and closes the door behind him)

Good night, Herschel!

HERSCHEL: Good night, Randy.

(Disappears inside his house)

RANDY:

(To Francis and Judith)

Now, what's going on?

(Judith continues laughing)

Francis?

FRANCIS: Alright, Judith, why don't you just tell him?

JUDITH: And you don't want him told? What future is there for you if he doesn't even know? Happiness begins with knowledge, doesn't it?

FRANCIS: If it does, you are in a lot of trouble!

(Runs into his house, slamming the door)

RANDY: Hey look, this is unfair. What's going on?

JUDITH: I have discovered this fine day that I have a rival for the affections of one, Francis Geminiani.

RANDY: Oh yeah? I'm not surprised.

JUDITH: What?

RANDY: Well, Judy, you're kind of a bitch, you know. I mean, talking in Italian to his father and Lucille—nothing personal, I mean . . .

JUDITH: Well, you are a creep, aren't you?

RANDY: And I mean like forcing me to look at those subway books with Herschel, just so you could be alone with Francis. So who's this rival? Somebody from the neighborhood who can make good gravy?

(He is laughing, and crawling inside the tent)

JUDITH:

(Starts rubbing her hands together gleefully

Well, the person in question is in the yard right now, under the fig tree, and it isn't me.

RANDY:

(Pops his head out)

What?

Blackout

ACT TWO

SCENE 1

Scene the same. The next morning, about nine o'clock.

As the lights come up, Francis is seen in his window, staring at the tent. Judith is asleep in a sleeping-bag outside the tent, and Randy is inside.

Bunny comes out of her house, dressed in her ragged housecoat, she is disoriented and mumbles to herself. Francis sees her but says nothing.

She is carrying a brown paper bag. She disappears into the alley, and is next seen climbing up the telephone pole behind the alley wall. She has to stop every few rungs and almost falls off once or twice. Finally she gets to the top of the alley wall, still clutching the bag, shakes her fist at the heavens and makes to jump.

A dog is heard barking in the distance.

FRANCIS:

> *(Yelling from his window)*
>
> Hey, Bunny! What are you doing?

BUNNY:

> *(Peering in his direction, trying to bring him into focus)*
>
> Hanh?

FRANCIS: What are you doing?

BUNNY: Who's 'at?

FRANCIS: Francis next door. Come down, you'll hurt yourself.

BUNNY: What are ya, blind? You go to Harvard and can't tell I'm gonna jump?

FRANCIS: Bunny!

BUNNY: Shut up, Francis, I'm gonna splatter my fuckin' body on the concrete down there and don' wan' no interference. I thought it all out. My uncle's an undertaker, he'll do it cheap.

> *(Herschel sticks his head out the second story window of Bunny's house)*

HERSCHEL: Mom! What are you doing?

BUNNY: Herschel, don' look, it'll give you asthma.

HERSCHEL: Don't jump, Mom!

BUNNY: Herschel, I gotta favor to ask of you. If I don' die in jumpin', I want you to finish me off wit this.

> *(Waves the bag)*
>
> It's rat poison. Was Uncle Eddie's Christmas present.

HERSCHEL: Mom, please!

BUNNY: You didn't scratch them new mosquito bites, did you?

HERSCHEL: No. And I took my medicine and I used my atomizer and brushed my teeth, please don't jump.

BUNNY: Good, you keep it up. Don' wan' to be a mess at my funeral.

HERSCHEL: Funeral!

> (Pulls his head in, and runs out into the yard. Judith is awake and getting dressed. Randy comes out of the tent, a little confused by the noise. Francis has come out, and is trying to coax her down)

RANDY: What's going on?

HERSCHEL:

> (Arrives, puffing, in the yard. His pajamas are disgracefully dirty, as is his robe which is much too small for him)

Please, Mom, I'm sorry, I didn't mean to do it . . .

BUNNY: What?

HERSCHEL: I don't know, it must be something I did. I'll never have asthma again, I'll stop having seizures, I'll take gym class. Don't jump!

BUNNY:

> (Starts climbing higher, till she is about the height of the second story window)

Herschel, is that any way to act, hanh? Was you raised in the jungle? Show some dignity, you want the neighbors to talk?

HERSCHEL: I'll burn my transfer collection, I'll give up the subways . . .

BUNNY: Nah, that's alright, Herschel. You'll be better off in a home.

HERSCHEL: A home??!!!

> (He can hardly get the word out. He starts having an asthma attack)

BUNNY: Jesus Christ in Heaven, he's havin' an attack! Can't I even commit suicide in peace?

JUDITH: Should I call the police?

FRANCIS: Call Lucille. DE 6-1567.

JUDITH: DE 6-1567.

> (She runs into Francis' house)

RANDY: What about Herschel?

BUNNY: Get his fuckin' atomizer—it's in the third room on the second floor.

> (Randy runs into Bunny's house)

Jesus Christ in Heaven! And it's all for attention.

FRANCIS: What is, Bunny?

BUNNY: His fuckin' attacks! I read them books! It's all for attention, that all these kids want nowadays. I didn't get no attention when I was a kid and look at me? Am I weird? Nah! I didn't get no asthma, I didn't even get pimples.

JUDITH:

> (Appears in the kitchen window)

I get a busy signal.

FRANCIS: Busy? This time of day?

BUNNY: They think because they can fart and blink at the same time they got the world conquered.

FRANCIS: Did you get the number right?

BUNNY: That's all they want: attention!

JUDITH: DE 6-1567.

FRANCIS: Jesus! That's our number. It's DE 6-1656.

> *(Judith disappears inside the house. Randy appears in the second story window of Bunny's house)*

RANDY: I can't find the atomizer!

HERSCHEL:

> *(Gasping, on the ground at the foot of the wall)*
>
> By the bed, under all the Kleenex!
>
> *(Randy continues looking for it)*

FRANCIS: Come on, Bunny, climb down!

BUNNY: Education! That's these kids problems! Look at him—a fuckin' genius; and he looks like some live turd some fuckin' giant laid. Huff some more, Herschel . . .

> *(Climbing down to the top of the wall)*

RANDY:

> *(Running out of house)*
>
> I got it! I got it.
>
> *(Herschel grabs the atomizer. His attack subsides)*

BUNNY: They all oughta be put to work! That's what happened to me. Yeah! My mom put me to work when I was ten, singin' songs for pennies in the Franciscan monastery on Wolf Street!

> *(Judith comes back into the yard)*
>
> I hadda sing for everybody—them bums, them old ladies. Once some crazy old lady made me sing "Mein Yiddische Mama" six times—then gave me a five-dollar bill. Well, even though it's a Catholic place I figured, shit, make the money. So I learned "Bei Mir Bist du Shoen" for the next week and sang it—and they beat the shit outta me. If that wasn't a birth trauma, what was! I read them books, know all about it. I've hadda shit-filled life; feel like some turd stuck in the pipe so Herschel get your fat ass outta the way, you too, hon, or I'll crush youse!

FRAN:

> *(Offstage, yelling)*
>
> What's goin' on out here?

BUNNY: Yo, Fran!

FRAN: Yo, Bun!

BUNNY: I'm gonna jump!

LUCILLE:

> *(Running into the yard from gate, in hair curlers)*
>
> Che disgraziat'! Who's gonna clean it up, hanh?

FRAN:

> *(Follows Lucille in)*
>
> Whataya mean you're gonna jump?

BUNNY: Whataya mean, whataya mean? I'm gonna leap off this fuckin' wall and if that don' finish me, I'm takin' this rat poison and Herschel better move or I'm takin' him with me. Jesus Christ, can't even die without his havin' a attack.

> *(Fran and Francis half carry, half drag Herschel away from the wall, and lay him down on the stoop. He is screaming and kicking)*

You mean I gotta listen to that in Heaven?

LUCILLE: You ain't going to Heaven!

FRAN: Come on, be good and get down. You don't got no reason to jump!

BUNNY: I got reason, I got reason!

FRAN: Yeah, what?

BUNNY: Got nobody in the whole fuckin' world, I turned ugly, I got no money, I ain't got no prospects . . .

FRAN: That's been true of my whole life and you don' see me jumpin' off alley walls and takin' rat poison. Besides, it's Francis' twenty-first birthday today.

BUNNY: You mean there's gonna be a party?

FRAN: A big one!

BUNNY: Why didn't you say so, hanh? Get that friggin' ladder, I'm comin' down!

> *(Francis and Randy run to get the ladder that has been leaning against the fence. They set it up under the wall, and help Bunny climb down. Bunny, to Randy)*

You're so strong, hon, give me a kiss!

> *(Kisses him. Then she turns on Herschel, who is still wheezing and crying)*

You! Get in that fuckin' house! Makin' a spectacle of yourself wit them pajamas!

> *(She chases Herschel into their house. Much shaking of heads from the others. Everyone is very tense. Francis takes the ladder back to the fence)*

HERSCHEL:

> *(As he is running inside)*

What the fuck do you want me to do?

BUNNY:

> *(In her house continuing a diatribe against Herschel)*

And what's this I hear from your no good father? You had a fuckin' petit mal yesterday?!

HERSCHEL:

> *(In the house)*

No, I didn't!

BUNNY: Liar! Didn't I tell you to behave wit him?

> *(Sounds of her beating him)*

I told you to act normal.

HERSCHEL: Who could act normal with you for a mother?

(A sound like a piano falling over is heard from Bunny's house. A silence. Then suddenly, long surprised screams of pain from Herschel. Fran tries to hug Francis. Francis gets away. Bunny comes running out of her house to the stoop)

BUNNY: You guys wanna get a piano offa Herschel?

FRAN: What's the piano doin' on Herschel?

BUNNY: He gave me some lip and I threw it on him.

FRAN: Oh, alright.

(Kisses Francis)

Happy birthday my son.

(Fran and Francis run into Bunny's house)

BUNNY: Do you think I ruptured him for life?

(Bunny and Randy run into the house. Judith makes to follow, but Lucille stops her)

LUCILLE: Ain't ladylike to go in there.

JUDITH: Herschel might be hurt.

LUCILLE: If that kid ain't dead yet, he's indestructible.

(Noises from inside the house, of the piano being lifted)

He's always fallin' down stairs, gettin' hit by cars, gettin' beat up, havin' fits, gettin' asthma, throwin' up, comin' down with pneumonia. A piano ain't gonna hurt him.

(She sets a garden chair next to the tent)

Besides, that piano's out of tune, how much damage could it do?

JUDITH: This is crazy! All that noise and Bunny on the wall . . .

LUCILLE:

(Sits in chair)

Happens alla the time. That's why no neighbors stuck their heads out. We're used to it around here. Tessie across the street come back from the shore last Sunday and found this burglar in her cellar.

(Judith has gone in the tent to finish dressing)

Judy, she ties him to an old sofa, then, wit her sister, she shoves it down the front steps. Then she sets it on fire. We come back from church and there is this sofa on the front steps wit a screamin' man on it and flames everywhere. We call the fire engine. They hose the poor bastard down and rush him to the hospital. So this mornin' was mild, believe me.

(Judith is now sitting by the tent, putting on her sneakers)

Do you wanna come wit me to Wanamaker's and buy Francis a present? I have a employee's discount so you can buy him somethin' real nice for less. Or did you get somethin' already?

JUDITH: Not really—a few joke things. I don't think he's gonna think they're funny.

(She gets a brush and mirror out of her knapsack. Music is heard from Bunny's house. Bunny appears in her window, brushing her hair)

BUNNY: Yo, Lucille! We got the piano up. You wanna come in and sing?

LUCILLE: No, Bunny.

BUNNY: Well, I'm cookin' breakfast. You wan' some?

LUCILLE AND JUDITH: No thanks.

JUDITH: How is Herschel?

BUNNY: A little purple about the shins, but he'll survive. You sure you don' wan' some breakfast?

JUDITH: No thank you!

BUNNY: You should take some lessons from your brother.

(She disappears inside her house)

LUCILLE: What did she mean about your brother?

JUDITH: Everybody loves Randy—EVERYBODY it seems!

LUCILLE: Well, he's nice lookin', that's for sure. But I'm not crazy about him. I never warm up to white people much. You're an exception. You got poise. You have lovely teeth.

(From inside the house we hear:)

"I want a girl
Just like the girl
That married dear old dad
She was a pearl
And the only girl
That daddy ever had . . ."

(Dialogue continues over this)

JUDITH: They got Francis to play the piano, all those wrong notes.

LUCILLE: Why are you interested in Francis when you're so beautiful?

JUDITH: If I hear that once more, I'm going to stick my face in acid!

LUCILLE: But why? *Perchè?* What do you see in him?

JUDITH: Why are you interested in his father?

LUCILLE: I ain't got much choice. I'm not pretty. I'm a widow. Nobody wants a widow. It's like bein' an old sheet. I might be clean and kept nice but people can't help noticin' it's been used.

(Bunny is heard singing:)

"When Irish eyes are smilin'."

(Lucille continues over song)

So I put up wit Fran. He's good people, he means well. But you know, he coughs alla the time, eats too much, makes noises, you know he's got the colitis, and them rashes! Between coughin', scratchin' and runnin' to the bathroom, I'm surprised he's got so much weight on him. Oh, well, that's my life.

(Judith offers her the brush. She is about to use it, then discreetly pulls Judith's hair out of the bristles)

But, Francis? Like father like son, remember.

JUDITH: Oh, I don't know. We talked yesterday and I was up most of the night, thinking: why? All the possible bad reasons started cramming themselves into my head. Perhaps I have sensed it all along and I was attracted to Francis because he was . . .

(Stops herself)

Well, just because he's the way he is.

(From inside the house we hear:)

"For it was Mary, Mary
Plain as any name can be
For in society, propriety
Will say, Marie."

(Lucille speaks over this)

LUCILLE: You mean queer? Don't be shocked, I know what queer is.

(She turns her chair toward Judith)

I had a long talk wit my son, Donny, about it before he went off. He's at Yale, pre-med, Branford Scholarship. I warned him to be careful. My friend, Diane's husband, he's a foot doctor, they met in a singles bar, then got married because he had corns real bad, well, he told me, Yale puts out a lot of queers along wit the doctors and the lawyers. But Donny's got a girl friend, and though I think she's a pig, I guess it proves he's got some interest in the girls. But Francis? Well, Fran and me had a long talk. He's afraid for Francis. Well, I think Francis is. There ain't been no girls around here except to sell cookies. That's why Fran was so happy to see you, and wanted you to stay, even though you wanted to go. It's hard on a man to have a queer for a son. I mean, I guess Fran would rather he was queer than humpbacked or dead, still it's hard.

JUDITH: Well, I thought that might be why I was interested. He'd be safe then. But I don't think so. He and I are really alike, you see. Neither of us makes contact with people. We both goof a lot, but most of the time, that's all there is.

BUNNY:

(From inside her house)

Alright, I'm slingin' this shit on the table!

JUDITH: And there are other reasons. Just where I am, you know? I'm a romantic, I guess, and I assume there is something worth doing, that active is better than passive. But I feel on the edge of falling, or freezing.

LUCILLE:

(Shakes her head)

When I was your age—*madone . . . !*

JUDITH: Maybe it's harder for us, now. The war's over, no one much is ethnic anymore, there aren't many jobs. When there were marches and strikes and moratoriums, people didn't think much about the future, they were distracted, sort of a hippie bread and circuses idea.

LUCILLE:

> (*Nods her head, but she doesn't understand one word*)

Yeah.

JUDITH: No one had time to worry about how they'd live five years from now—it was all now. Everybody could be a hero, occupy a dean's office, publish his memoirs, have them serialized in *The New York Times*—

LUCILLE: Wit the small print!

JUDITH: And you have to wonder, all that energy, and that courage, was it just adolescence? Sometimes I'm afraid. Just afraid. Maybe we're at the end of the spiral which people once thought endless. Maybe it's running out. I don't want it to be over. Francis is afraid too. But together . . . I'm sorry, I'm not making any sense, I didn't sleep much.

LUCILLE: But you didn't buy him a birthday present.

JUDITH: Is that important?

LUCILLE: Vital. It's the gesture. Don' matter what it is but you got to make the gesture. It shows respect. It shows you're serious. No birthday present and he's gotta right to wonder if you mean it. It's like an outward sign. You just can't go around sayin': I need you, or I love you and then, ignorin' them on special occasions. That don' make no sense. So you buy them the birthday present, you send them the card, you go visit them inna hospital, you bake them the cake—you show them respect. *Cabisce?* Respect!

JUDITH: *Si.*

LUCILLE: *Bene.* All you can do is try and hope. That's how I got my husband, may God forgive him, and may he rest in peace. You really like Francis? Come on, you come wit me to Wanamaker's we buy Francis a present we cheer ourselves up.

> (*Fran comes out of Bunny's house*)

FRAN: Yo, Lucille!

LUCILLE: Judith and me's goin' ta Wanamaker's to buy Francis a present.

FRAN: See youse later, be good and be careful.

> (*Lucille and Judith exit through the gate. Francis comes racing out of Bunny's house*)

Yo, where you goin'?

FRANCIS: Nowhere.

FRAN: You got company.

FRANCIS: I didn't invite them.

FRAN:

> (*Embraces Francis*)

Happy birthday, son.

FRANCIS: Don't hang on me so much.

FRAN: What are you afraid of? You got somewhere to go you take some coin.

> (*Offers him some money*)

FRANCIS: I don't need any money.

FRAN: Well, take some more.

FRANCIS: I don't need any more.

FRAN: Take!

FRANCIS: I don't need it!!

FRAN: Look my son, I'm gonna give you a piece of advice I learned from the army, from dealin' wit your mother and from twenty years in the Printers' Union: Take! Take wit both hands, both feet and your mouth too. If your ass is flexible enough take wit that, use your knees and your elbows, train your balls and take! *Prend'—cabisce?* Somebody offers you somethin', you take it, then run . . .

(*Puts the money in Francis' shirt pocket*)

. . . but always say thank you first. And look, if there's ever anything, well, that conventional people, not like us Geminiani Italians—but other people might be ashamed of, don't ever be afraid to come to me, no matter how hard it is, I'll understand—understand?

FRANCIS: I don't understand.

(*Suddenly embraces his father*)

But I understand, okay?

(*Runs out through the gate*)

FRAN: Where you goin'?

FRANCIS: To buy some diet soda.

FRAN: That diet crap is gonna kill ya.

(*Randy comes out of Bunny's house, trailed by Herschel*)

RANDY: Where's Francis?

FRAN: He went to buy diet crap.

HERSCHEL: Maybe we'll pass him, you know, like on our way to the trolleys . . .

(*Grabs Randy's arm, and starts pulling him toward the alley*)

RANDY:

(*Freeing himself*)

Is there a pool around here? I'd like to go swimming.

FRAN: Yeah.

HERSCHEL: You promised!

FRAN: There's a Community Center about four blocks from here, Herschel can go with you. You can change here.

RANDY: Great.

(*Randy crawls into the tent to change. Bunny comes out of her house, eating a sandwich*)

BUNNY: Hey, Herschel, I thought you was draggin' Beau Brummel to the trolleys—

HERSCHEL: He wants to go swimming.

BUNNY: Why don't you go wit him?

HERSCHEL:

(*Under his breath*)

Fuck!

BUNNY: Where's the birthday boy?

FRAN: He took off.

BUNNY: Helluva way to treat company. Prob'ly went to buy a opera record.

RANDY:

> *(Still inside the tent)*

> He already has thousands.

FRAN:

> *(To Bunny)*

> Look, I got stuff to do, gotta buy Francis a birthday cake. Bun, you wanna come?

BUNNY: Sure, I could use a donut or two.

> *(They exit through the gate. Herschel picks up his tricycle)*

HERSCHEL: Randy, Randy!

RANDY:

> *(From inside the tent)*

> What?

HERSCHEL: Would you like to play trolley?

RANDY: How?

HERSCHEL: Just call ding, when I ask you to. Like . . .

> *(Pipes out)*

> Ding!

RANDY: Okay.

HERSCHEL:

> *(Careening around the yard like a trolley, making a lot of noise)*

> Ritner! . . . Now.

RANDY: Ding!

HERSCHEL: Good.

> *(Careens)*

> Tasker! . . . Now.

RANDY: Ding!

HERSCHEL: Dickinson! . . . Now.

> *(Silence)*

> Now. Oh, you missed that one.

> *(Randy comes of the tent, in a T-shirt and shorts)*

RANDY: Ding!

> *(Herschel is gaping at him)*

> Do you think I look weird?

> *(Herschel shakes his head "No")*

> I mean, skinny.

HERSCHEL: I think you look, like, you know—

RANDY: Yeah, yeah. But do you think my legs are too thin?

HERSCHEL: Oh, no!

RANDY: Boy, it's rough being this thin, you know, I've tried to put on at least ten pounds. I bought two quarts of this stuff called "Wate-On."

HERSCHEL:

> (Points to his stomach)

Oh yeah, like "weight on"—

RANDY: Putrid stuff. I drank a quart of it, tastes like milk of magnesia, I got sick for a week and lost ten pounds.

HERSCHEL: I tried to kill myself by drinking a quart of milk of magnesia once; but I didn't lose any weight.

> (Francis enters through the gate, drinking a diet soda. A tense moment between Francis and Randy)

RANDY: We're going swimming.

FRANCIS: I'll stay here.

RANDY: Okay, Herschel, let's go . . .

> (They start off, suddenly Randy staggers, clutches the air, twists about, acts dizzy, and falls to the ground. He is faking a petit mal)

HERSCHEL:

> (Very alarmed)

Randy, what is it?

FRANCIS:

> (Catching on)

Looks like a petit mal, Herschel.

HERSCHEL: No, no, that's epilepsy. Take your belt off!

FRANCIS: Why?

HERSCHEL: So he won't bite his tongue off. Give it to me!

> (Sticks belt in Randy's mouth)

I'll go get my medicine!

> (Rushes into his house)

RANDY:

> (Who has been writhing on the ground until now, suddenly sits up)

Are you a faggot?

> (Herschel comes running out with a bottle of medicine. Randy starts writhing again)

HERSCHEL: Here—you have to shake it first!

FRANCIS:

> (Shaking the bottle)

I think he'll need some valium too—

HERSCHEL: Good idea!

> (Runs into house, and reappears almost instantly)

Fives or tens?

FRANCIS: Fives should do it.

> (Herschel races into house)

RANDY:

> (Sits up, dropping the fit)

I mean homosexual—I mean, gay person—

HERSCHEL:

> (Racing back out)

We're out!

> (Randy fakes the fit again)

FRANCIS: Do you have any aspirin?

RANDY:

> (Mumbling unintelligibly)

Aspirin upsets my stomach!

FRANCIS: Aspirin upsets his stomach.

HERSCHEL: Tylenol?

FRANCIS: Tylenol?

RANDY: Tylenol!

HERSCHEL AND FRANCIS: Tylenol!

HERSCHEL: I'll go get some!

> (Races off through the alley)

RANDY:

> (He stands, dusts himself off, awkward pause)

When we talked and all that, you know in your room, were you just trying to make me?

FRANCIS: I don't know.

RANDY: I don't care that much, but it's worse being treated like you were laying a trap for me. And I didn't think you were gay—odd maybe. Have there . . .

> (He realizes how silly this is going to sound)

. . . been many before me?

FRANCIS: Well, starting in high school there was Max. He was a poet, a Libra, on the fencing team, short and dark, compact you might say, very dashing with his èpèes. Then there were George and Eliot, they were twins. Then, Sheldon Gold, briefly.

RANDY: How many did you sleep with?

FRANCIS: Sleep with? They didn't even talk to me.

RANDY: You never told them how you felt?

FRANCIS: Well, that's it, you see. I'm never sure how I feel, really.

RANDY: Have you ever had sex with a man?

(Francis shakes his head "no")

Were there girls before Judith?

FRANCIS: Well, there was Elaine Hoffenburg. She had braces.

RANDY: Braces on her teeth?

FRANCIS: Legs. I took her to the Senior Prom.

(Randy looks incredulous)

Well, I was no catch, either. I was very fat then. It wasn't too bad. Once she got enough momentum going, she could do a passable waltz. Then there was Luise Morely. Slightly pockmarked but pretty in a plain sort of way. We held hands through *The Sandpiper,* then we did it afterwards. It was my first time. Elaine had been willing, but it was a little hard getting her legs apart.

RANDY: Gross! I worked for months to get Nancy Simmons to go to the prom with me, then I got car sick on the way and threw up all over her; and you remember Roberta Hasserfluth, I broke up with her just as you and Judith got together, well, we decided we would do it, so we went to the drive in movie in Waltham. It was *The Four Stewardesses*—

FRANCIS: Wasn't that in 3-D?

RANDY: Oh, was it ever, we had to wear goggles and everything. Well, I bought this bottle of Mateus, see, and since I'd never bought wine before I forgot you needed a corkscrew. So I couldn't get it open, so there we are watching this dirty movie in the dead of winter, with this bottle of Mateus between my legs, trying to get it open with my car key—

FRANCIS: Well, did you ever do it?

RANDY: Too cold! I'm sort of a jerk with girls, but I like them. I like you too, you're my friend. But I don't think I'm in love with you. Does that mean you were in love with me?

(Francis shrugs)

I mean, Francis, has it ever occurred to you you might be suffering from homosexual panic.

FRANCIS:

(Snaps his fingers)

I knew I should have taken Psych. 101.

RANDY: I mean, it's true. It's really common in a competitive society.

FRANCIS:

(Shakes his head, irritated at being put on)

Oh, really.

RANDY: I'm serious. I mean, if you've never slept with a man, never laid a hand on me . . .

FRANCIS: Are you saying that if you were to strip right now and lie down inside that tent, I couldn't—well, do anything?

RANDY: Well, there's only one way to find out.

(Starts to strip)

FRANCIS: What are you doing? Randy, what are you doing?

RANDY: I'm stripping.

FRANCIS: Are you crazy? In front of me? Here?

(Francis makes a dash for his door, but Randy intercepts him. Randy stands in front of the door, blocking it. He looks around the yard, up at the windows, then unzips his fly)

Jesus Christ!

RANDY:

(Walks over to the tent)

I'll save the rest for inside the tent.

(Crawls inside)

FRANCIS: Jesus Christ! Oh Jesus . . .

(Holding his chin)

I didn't shave this morning.

(Francis is about to crawl into the tent, as Herschel comes bounding in from the alley)

HERSCHEL: How's Randy?

FRANCIS:

(Exasperated)

Jesus Christ, Herschel, he's dead!

HERSCHEL:

(Horror struck)

He is??!!

FRANCIS: Ten minutes ago; heart failure.

HERSCHEL: Are you sure? I mean, I faked a heart attack in gym class last month. Maybe he's faking. Call an ambulance!

FRANCIS: Damn it, Herschel, he's dead, now go away!

HERSCHEL: Can I see the body?

RANDY:

(Sticks his head out of the tent)

Hello, Herschel.

HERSCHEL: Randy! He said . . .

RANDY: I heard. Look, Herschel, Francis and I . . .

FRANCIS:

(Trying to stop him)

Randy!

RANDY: . . . are involved in a very serious ritual. We will both be drummed out of our exclusive clubs at Harvard if we don't do this.

HERSCHEL: Oh, heavy.

RANDY: Very. So Herschel, would you please go away and come back a little later?

HERSCHEL: Sure.

(He sets a little bottle of Tylenol in front of the tent, and starts for the alley. Randy throws the shorts out at Francis. Herschel turns back)

Like five minutes?

FRANCIS:

(Grabs the shorts, hides them behind his back)

Herschel, take a long walk!

(Herschel, dejected, exits out the alley. Francis hesitates, peers into the tent, and finally crawls inside. There is no movement for a few seconds, then Randy, wrapped in the sleeping bag, comes bounding out of the tent, followed by Francis)

Randy, what's the matter? What's the matter? Why did you strip if you didn't mean it? Were you bringing me on?

RANDY: No!

(Runs back into the tent)

FRANCIS: Is that what was going on this spring? Perhaps somewhere in some subconscious avenue of that boy-man mind of yours you sensed I had a vulnerable point and decided to make the most of it?

RANDY:

(From inside the tent)

I was seventeen fucking years old this spring—what's your excuse?

FRANCIS: Well, you're eighteen now.

RANDY:

(Coming out of tent, wearing jeans)

I liked you!

FRANCIS:

(Sarcastic)

Thanks!

RANDY: I really did.

FRANCIS: It's vicious of you.

RANDY: How?

FRANCIS: Because you did it all just to humiliate me—

RANDY: I really do like you. I mean, liking does exist, doesn't it? It doesn't have to include sex, or love, or deep need, does it?

FRANCIS: I don't know.

RANDY: I don't know either.

FRANCIS: I don't know either.

RANDY: Boy . . . you are really fucked up.

(He embraces Francis)

FRANCIS: I know.

(He puts his arms around Randy. Judith enters the yard from the gate carrying a large gaily wrapped box. She sees this embrace and lets out a surprised yell. The two jump apart, confused, and looking guilty)

RANDY: Judith!

JUDITH: You're disgusting!

RANDY: It's not my fault, he's older than I am!

JUDITH: He's younger than you are!

FRANCIS: Judith . . .

JUDITH:

>   *(Turns on him)*
>
>   And you!

FRANCIS: Now, look, Judith, it didn't have anything to do with sex!

JUDITH: Oh, no! I'm sure! Nothing you do has anything to do with sex! It's all a bring on, isn't it? You get to that point, and then, you're ugly, or you're fat, or you're gay! What did you use on him? That you were ugly, fat, and straight? Well, I'm on to you! Happy birthday!

>   *(She throws the box at Francis)*

FRANCIS: Act your age Judith!

JUDITH: Oh ho, act my age, act my age says this paragon of maturity, this pristine sage now come of age!

FRANCIS: It's hard to explain . . .

RANDY: That's right!

JUDITH: Hard? Hard to explain? What is? You're going to fuck my brother, that's very simple, that's the birds and the bees, that's Biology 1A. I thought I loved you. I thought I loved you!

>   *(Starts hitting Randy)*
>
>   I thought I loved him!

FRANCIS: Judith, will you please calm down.

JUDITH: And my mother told me never to trust fatties, they're self-indulgent. Go have a banana split!

RANDY: For Christ' sake, calm down!

JUDITH: I knew there was something suspicious in your wanting to come along. I bet the two of you were laughing at me, comparing notes, carrying on behind my back the whole time. Why, Francis, why would you do this to me?

FRANCIS: He was bringing me on, standing here with no clothes on, hanging onto me, what would you do?

JUDITH: Puke!

RANDY: Do you think I enjoyed it? Huh, tubby?

JUDITH:

>   *(To Randy)*
>
>   So you're a faggot too—won't the sophomore class be surprised?

RANDY: Why are you screaming at me, it's his fault!

FRANCIS:

>   *(Shaking his finger at Randy)*
>
>   It's your fault!

JUDITH: Oh, my God, it's love! M and M—mutual masturbation!

RANDY:

>   *(Angry)*

I thought I could help him, I should have known better, I can't help you—

(Shoves Francis. Herschel comes bounding in from alley)

HERSCHEL: Randy, your ceremony seems to be over, we can go see the . . .

RANDY:

(Screaming, runs into tent)

And I can't help you either, Herschel!

HERSCHEL: Francis . . .

FRANCIS: God damn it, Herschel, go away!

HERSCHEL: Oh, no, I did it again!

(Judith is on one side of the stage, talking to Francis, and Herschel is on the other side, talking to the tent)

JUDITH: And I was even out buying you a present!

HERSCHEL: I tried to be your friend, I don't know how . . .

JUDITH: And I was willing to be understanding.

HERSCHEL: I'm just stupid.

JUDITH: All those Callas records, and I hate her voice and her wobble!

FRANCIS: She only wobbles on the late recordings!

HERSCHEL: What did I do?!

JUDITH: And that Toti dal Monte, for Christ' sake, she sounds like a broken steam engine!

FRANCIS: Her mad scene is still the best on records!

HERSCHEL: It's just me!

JUDITH: And what about my mad scene?

HERSCHEL: I'm just retarded like they all say!

(He runs into his house)

RANDY:

(From inside the tent)

Shut up Judith!

JUDITH: Oh God, and I even came here bringing your beloved! And you kissed me, and you stroked me, and we held hands along the Charles River, and I thought: He's weird, he's pudgy, he likes Maria Callas, but he responds to me! What a laugh! That's funnier than *The Barber of Seville,* that's funnier than *The Girl of the Golden West—*

FRANCIS: Shut up, shut up, Judith, God damn it, act your age! You're like a fucking six-year-old!

JUDITH: And you? How old are you?!

(They are right in front of the Geminiani door. Bunny, Fran, and Lucille enter grandly from Fran's house, carrying a huge birthday cake and singing. They are wearing party hats. Bunny is running around, putting hats on Judith and Francis, and Randy, as he emerges from the tent. Fran has the cake on the same typing table that was used for breakfast. He also has a camera)

BUNNY, FRAN AND LUCILLE: "Happy birthday to you,
Happy birthday to you,

Happy birthday, dear Francis,
Happy birthday to you!"

FRAN: Happy birthday, my son!

(Snaps a picture)

LUCILLE: Come on, blow out the candles and cut the cake, it's too hot to wait.

BUNNY: There's only six candles, all we could find.

(Francis is about to blow them out)

LUCILLE: Come on, make a wish.

(He does. Fran takes another picture, and Francis blows out the candles. They all cheer and applaud. Judith and Randy are still stunned)

FRANCIS: Thank you. I would first like to thank my father, now that I am officially an adult, for teaching me how to dance and sing and cough and fart and scratch and above all how to treat a rash once it becomes visible to the general public, then I would like to thank my next-door neighbor Bunny . . .

(Fran snaps a photo of Bunny)

for demonstrating once and for all that motherhood ought to be abolished, along with drunks and whores, Lucille, for teaching me how to ruin the happiest occasion with one glance and the cheapest insect spray, and Randy, for providing us with living proof of the vacuity of American Higher Education, and then Judith, our brilliant, bubbly, and let's not forget, mature Italian major from Radcliffe will recite to us in her main-line Italian all the nonsense syllables of her upbringing and her recent reading. And I want you all to know precisely what I think of all this: this neighborhood, Bunny and Lucille, Randy and Judith!

(He rips into the cake with his hands and tears it apart, hurling pieces at Judith and the others. All duck away. After Francis has destroyed the cake, he runs off through the gate. Herschel stumbles out of his house, holding the bag of rat poison, powder all over his mouth)

HERSCHEL: I swallowed Uncle Eddie's rat poison!

BUNNY: My baby!

FRAN: Holy shit!

BUNNY:

(On her knees by Herschel)

My baby!

LUCILLE: Who's gonna clean it up, hanh?

Blackout

SCENE 2

Evening. Fran has a huge trash bag and is cleaning up the yard. Lucille is sitting on the divider between the two houses. Randy is finished packing. Their tent has been struck and is rolled up again.

LUCILLE: Rum and chocolate sauce everywhere—did he know how much it cost?

FRAN: Well, it was his birthday cake, if he wanted a throw it around, it's his right I guess.

LUCILLE: But it ain't his right to clean it up, hanh?

> *(She points to a piece of cake)*

Over there. Jesus, I'm sick and tired of cleanin' up afta people.

> *(Points again)*

Over here. Cleanin' up afta my brothers . . .

FRAN:

> *(Under his breath, still picking up)*

Your brothers . . .

LUCILLE: Afta pop . . .

FRAN: Afta pop . . .

LUCILLE: Then my mom got senile . . .

FRAN: Then mom . . .

LUCILLE: Then my husband . . .

FRAN: Your husband . . .

LUCILLE: Then Donny . . .

FRAN:

> *(Joking)*

Ain't he at Yale?

LUCILLE: Hanh? Of course he's at Yale, that's a stupid question, *ma stupidezza* . . .

RANDY: I'll see if Judith is ready.

> *(Runs into Bunny's house)*

FRAN: I hope Francis gets back soon—I think his guests are gonna leave any minute—

LUCILLE: Well, I'm surprised they stayed as long they did. Well, at least he didn't play so much opera music this weekend—all that screamin'—that's what I got against opera, Fran, ain't like real life.

> *(She tries to clean up some whipped cream with a Kleenex. Bunny enters from her house, depressed)*

BUNNY: Yo, Fran.

FRAN: Yo, Bun. How's Herschel?

BUNNY: Better and better, just ate all my leftovers.

FRAN: I guess they're gettin' ready to leave.

BUNNY: Yep.

LUCILLE:

> *(About Bunny, mean)*

E questa si chiama una madre?

FRAN: Lucille, take this bag in the house—tape up the top so nothin' gets in . . .

(Lucille takes the bag, and goes into Fran's house. He calls after her)

And put on the coffee!

BUNNY:

(Sits down on her stoop)

She could use a enema, lye and hot pepper!

(Looks at Fran)

Remember way back when, when we did it?

FRAN: Oh, Bun.

BUNNY: Oh, Fran! 'Sbeen a long time. I think it's time we did it again. Don't say it, you got Lucille! What's Lucille? Shit, she gotta get on the subway to get her hips movin'.

FRAN: You don' need me, Bun.

BUNNY: We was good together.

FRAN: How often? Five times the most? I remember the first time.

(He sits down beside her)

You remember? We forced Francis to take Herschel to the movies; it was *Lady and the Tramp*. They was that young, we could force them. Can you see the two of them together?

BUNNY: They was both so fat they probably took up a whole row between them.

FRAN: Didn't they have rashes too?

BUNNY: Nah, that was the third time. We forced Francis to take Herschel into Center City to buy calamine lotion.

(She puts her head on his shoulder. He looks up to his window, checking for Lucille)

FRAN: Why don't you give Sam a call?

BUNNY: He ain't interested.

FRAN: I bet you still like him.

BUNNY: You still like your wife?

FRAN: Sure, I married her, didn't I? We went together two years and were pretty happy until Francis came along. She wasn't the same after that. Oh well, she's gone. And now there's Lucille—at least she bakes good fiadone. And she's good people, even if she schives too much. I mean, what kinda choice I got? Hanh? Women today, they look at you, they see a man wheezin', coughin', goin' to the bathroom, scratchin', gettin' rashes, they take off. But Sam ain't attached yet—give him a call, fix yourself up, grow up a little—

BUNNY: Grow up a little? Like that was easy. Jesus, if only I didn't still act and feel nineteen. I look in the mirror and I know there's fat and wrinkles there, Jesus Christ do I know there's fat and wrinkles! Yet, I'll be damned if I don't still, somewhere in there, see this nineteen-year-old filly hot to trot and on fire for some kind of success in life!

(Looks at house, tricycle)

And look what I got—

FRAN: So Herschel's a little crazy, but he's gonna do wonders—

BUNNY: He's a fuckin' genius! Grow up a little. And what about Francis?

FRAN: Don't know, this Judith girl—

BUNNY: She seems to like him, hard as that is to believe, but I don't see much evidence of his liking her.

FRAN: No, I guess not, but kids nowadays, maybe they act different when they're goin' together—and maybe she isn't his last chance.

BUNNY: Don't kid yourself. Look, why don't you just ask him and save yourself years of wonderin' and never bein' sure . . . ?

FRAN: It's the hardest thing for a father to ask his son. Don' know why it should be, I know guys who . . . like . . . other guys who are regular, you know, in every other way. But you know, it's his life now, he's gonna pay the consequences for whatever he does . . . but still, I hope.

BUNNY: Well, I worry about Herschel too. But Jesus, I figure we're lucky if he lives to be twenty-one—

LUCILLE:

>   *(Appears in the doorway)*

>   Yo, Fran!

FRAN:

>   *(Gets away from Bunny)*

>   Yo, Lucille!

LUCILLE: I see the monster comin' down the street—

>   *(She goes back in)*

FRAN: Bunny, let's go inside, he won't want to see us right off—

>   *(They go into Bunny's house. Francis enters from the gate. He sees the packed knapsacks under the fig tree. After a moment, Judith enters from Bunny's house. She is wearing a skirt and blouse)*

JUDITH: Well . . . Azael has returned.

FRANCIS: Who?

JUDITH: Who else? The Prodigal!

>   *(Lucille comes out of Fran's house, carrying a coffee pot, and a new robe for Herschel. She sees Francis)*

LUCILLE: *Ma Sporcacione!*

>   *(She slams the door, and goes into Bunny's house)*

FRANCIS: Is everyone furious at me?

JUDITH: We have Bunny's uncle on the force waiting inside with handcuffs.

FRANCIS: Oh Jesus, you're at it again—

JUDITH: Well, to be serious, Lucille is making a novena to Saint Jude the Obscure, Patron Saint of the Hopeless and Pudgy who spoil their own birthday parties.

>   *(She gets a sweater out of her knapsack)*

>   Herschel took rat poison.

FRANCIS: Is he dead?

JUDITH: No more than ever. Bunny called her uncle on the ambulance squad and he was rushed to St. Agnes Hospital, across Track 37 on the A, the AA 1 through 7, and the B express lines, perhaps you've passed it? They cleaned up the yard as best they could, but you'll probably be finding birthday cake here and there for the next few months. Still the fall rains and the march of time should wash away all stains from your yard, your life, and these, the Days of our Youth! Thank you.

FRANCIS: And you're leaving.

JUDITH: You noticed! Maybe you aren't autistic. Yes, we're walking over to Broad Street, where we will get a cab to 30th Street Station, where we will take the 9:05 train to Boston, from there we're going to our summer home. We are not hitching, you'll notice, we've lost the stomach for it. Oh, by the way, happy birthday.

FRANCIS: Thank you.

JUDITH: I'm sorry.

FRANCIS: So am I.

(They are about to go to each other, when Randy comes out of Bunny's house)

RANDY: C'mon Judith. We have nineteen minutes to catch that train.

(Fran and Lucille come out of Bunny's house)

FRAN: So, Igor's back, hanh? I guess you kids is off.

(Randy and Judith are putting on their knapsacks and collecting their belongings)

RANDY: We're off!

LUCILLE: Goodbye!

FRAN: The way I see it, life is made up of hellos and goodbyes and forgivin' and forgettin'. So you two forgive and forget and come back, hanh? Even if Frankenstein ain't here, you're always welcome.

(Bunny comes out of her house with Herschel. He is wearing clean pajamas and a new bathrobe)

BUNNY:

(Sees Francis)

So, Igor's back, hanh?

(To Randy and Judith)

We wanted to see youse off, you're good people, you kids.

LUCILLE:

(To Judith)

If I give you Donny's number at Yale maybe you could get in touch with him this fall, he's nice, real good looking and athletic, and he ain't no party pooper neither.

(She gives Judith a slip of paper)

I have somethin' in the house for you.

(She goes inside)

HERSCHEL:

> *(To Randy, shyly)*

Like, if I promise to lose weight and get less weird, can we be friends?

RANDY: Sure, even if you gain and get weirder.

HERSCHEL: Like, don't lie to me, you know? Like, I understand if you aren't interested. But can I like, you know, write you letters?

RANDY: Oh sure. I'll give you our summer address, otherwise, just write me at Harvard.

> *(He writes address on a little piece of paper that Herschel had ready. Lucille returns with a plate wrapped in tin foil. The following three lines, are said at about the same time)*

JUDITH: C'mon Randy, let's go!

LUCILLE: C'mon Randy, you're gonna miss the train.

RANDY: See you, Herschel.

> *(Judith, Fran, and Lucille go out through the gate. They stand in the entrance saying final goodbyes. Randy, about to say goodbye to Francis, is grabbed by Bunny)*

BUNNY: Oh, honey bun, I feel like I've known you for years. Maybe I'm gettin' funny in the head, but I know a promising hunk when I see one.

RANDY: Thank you.

BUNNY: I'm gonna miss you.

> *(Randy smiles and tries to get away but she hangs on)*

JUDITH:

> *(Calling from the gate)*

C'mon Randy!

BUNNY: Be careful when you sit down on toilets, put paper there, you hear? And see that some people may be pretty, even if they got strange faces, and mean well, even if they act weird, and think of me once in a while, hanh?

> *(She kisses him)*

Goodbye!

> *(She goes into her house. Herschel and Randy shake hands, then Herschel, looking back sadly, blinking back tears, follows his mother into the house)*

RANDY:

> *(Goes to Francis)*

In the fall, right?

FRANCIS: Right.

> *(They shake hands)*

JUDITH: Randy!

RANDY: Listen, I was just trying to help, okay?

> *(Randy leaves. The goodbyes are heard from behind the fence. Francis is left alone)*

FRAN: Come back soon! Please!

(Francis goes into his room, and puts on a quiet, sad piece of music. Fran and Lucille come back into the yard)

Let's go to your place, hanh? Need some coffee.

LUCILLE: I got some nice cheese cake for you, Fran.

FRAN: Yeah? Sounds good.

(Yells to Francis)

Yo, Francis! We're goin' a Lucille's for coffee and cake. Wanna come?

(There is no answer)

Yo, Francis!

FRANCIS: God damn it, no!

(From his room)

FRAN: That's my Ivy League son.

(Fran and Lucille exit through the gate. Francis appears in his window. He is very agitated. The music is playing)

FRANCIS: Jesus Christ, what am I doing?

(Calls out)

Dad! Dad! Yo Dad!

(He runs out of the house, to the gate)

FRAN:

(Heard from offstage)

What is it?

FRANCIS: Give me some coin, I'm going to Boston!

(Runs back into his room)

FRAN:

(Running into yard)

Jesus Christ in Heaven! Yo, Bun!

(Bunny's lights go on. Francis turns off the music)

BUNNY:

(At her window)

Yo, Fran!

FRAN: Call your uncle on the ambulance service. We gotta get Francis to the train!

BUNNY: Holy shit!

(She goes to her telephone in the kitchen)

LUCILLE:

(Running into house)

I'll help you pack.

BUNNY:

(On the phone)

Hello, Uncle Marty, bring your fuckin' ambulance down, we gotta make a train!

HERSCHEL:

(Coming out of his house)

What's going on?

FRAN: Francis is going to Boston.

HERSCHEL: To see Randy?

BUNNY:

(Still on the phone)

Hello, Uncle Jimmy, send a fuckin' squad car down, we gotta make a train.

FRAN: Hey, Herschel! Catch them kids.

(Pushes him to the gate)

HERSCHEL: This way's quicker!

(Runs out through alley behind his house)

FRAN: And bring them back! I'm fuckin' outta money. Lucille!

(Yelling after him)

LUCILLE:

(In Francis' room, with a large laundry bag)

There ain't no clean clothes in here!

FRAN: You got some money, I'm out.

LUCILLE:

(Hurling coin purse out the window)

Look!

FRANCIS: Oh, I want to take my new records—Callas in *Parsifal*, 1950, and the 1955 *Norma!*

(Runs into his room)

FRAN:

(Going through change purse)

Jesus Christ, Lucille, all these pennies!

LUCILLE: For the tax!

FRAN: Yo, Bun!

BUNNY: Yo, Fran!

FRAN: We need some more money!

(Bunny comes out of her house, reaches into her bosom, and removes wad)

BUNNY: Here's the house money, take what you need.

(Sirens are heard in the distance, getting closer)

They're comin'!

(Francis runs out of the house, holding record albums)

You stick wit me, kid, I got connections!

(Hugs Francis, as Fran counts money)

Where's Gargantua?

FRAN: He went to get the kids.

(To Francis)

I think this is enough—

(Gives him money)

BUNNY: I hope he doesn't frighten them away!

LUCILLE:

(Runs out of the house with the laundry bag)

This is the best I could do—go to a laundromat when you get there!

(Francis takes bag, hugs her)

FRANCIS: Thanks everybody, I mean, thanks . . .

FRAN: Well, it's your birthday.

(Sirens increase. Herschel comes running in from the alley with Judith and Randy)

HERSCHEL: I got 'em! I got 'em!

FRAN: They're back!

(Francis embraces Judith. Sirens much louder)

BUNNY:

(At gate)

My uncle is here!

(The kids run out. The others watch at the gate)

FRAN:

(Checks his watch, then puts his arms around Lucille and Bunny)

I think they're gonna make it!

Blackout

Amy Wright (Shirley) and Jeff Daniels (Jed) in the 1978 Off-Broadway premier of Lanford Wilson's *Fifth of July*, at Circle Repertory Company. (Photograph reprinted with permission from the John Willis Theatre World/Screen World Archive)

Fifth of July

BY LANFORD WILSON

For Frank Anderson

THE TALLEYS

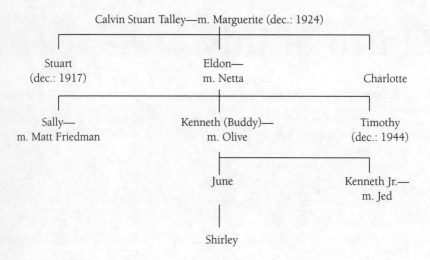

Calvin Stuart Talley—m. Marguerite (dec.: 1924)

Stuart (dec.: 1917)

Eldon— m. Netta

Charlotte

Sally— m. Matt Friedman

Kenneth (Buddy)— m. Olive

Timothy (dec.: 1944)

June

Kenneth Jr.— m. Jed

Shirley

Introduction

The genesis of *Fifth of July*, and what would develop into the Talley plays, occurred in about the same flurry of disorganized frustration as a distressingly large proportion of my work. In other words I was floundering, looking for any idea that would drive a wedge into this solid block of anger and dismay and alarm and, well, *frustration* I was experiencing at the complacent state of the country after the activism of the 60s and early 70s. For years soldiers had been returning from Vietnam to join the peace movement and tell us just how bad it was over there. The entire student body of the country, every artist I knew, had been either protesting or fleeing. And finally the war was over. It seemed to take years but America had finally finished pulling our troops the hell out of there. It was finally the admission of a tragic, immoral error. Statesmen, missing the point magnificently, tried to call our signing of a cease fire agreement a victory. We knew exactly what it was and didn't care as long as it was over. But then what often happens in defeat: The country seemed willing to forgive in order to forget and the war was all but forgotten, pushed under the rug. Our soldiers returned, many of them years later, from hospitals, to a cold shoulder and a psychiatrist, to group therapy and silence. Student protesters shut up, graduated, and started looking for good jobs. The air skillfully had been let out of the bell-bottomed balloon and it had sunk behind some hill, unnoticed. One almost had to admire the beautifully finessed betrayal of the peace movement. America has a way of turning something fine into bunk—or more likely into a buck. If African-Americans, finally in union, cry, "Black is beautiful," within a week it will be a new shade of lipstick. We had been singing "We Will Overcome" for years, but we had not overcome, we had been overcome, and I didn't know quite how it had been achieved.

To illustrate just how far we've traveled from meaningful activism, notice how quaint, old-hat, tiresome, and retrograde all that sounds now.

I was as content personally as I had been in a long time. I had a decent love life, the house I had bought and started to restore five years earlier was almost habitable, my work was being seen all over the country and still I felt—what? mislead, deceived. The life we had envisioned after the war had been degraded, dismissed; the well had been tainted. We had gone from Kennedy to Johnson to Nixon, through Watergate, to "I'm not a Lincoln, I'm a Ford." It's weird to be almost perfectly content and still seething. Oh, well . . .

One beautiful night my lover and I were walking around Washington Square Park. Maybe we had come from dinner or were on our way. He had been reading a book of Eskimo myths. (He was like that.) He was very serious as he told me, straight-faced, the story of an Arctic Hero who had saved the food supply of his family by a means so vile they couldn't eat it and so they had all starved to death. The story, if you look at it right, is hilarious. It is also perfectly ironic. And it occurred to me that night that it was also an apt metaphor for our involvement in that damn war. I wrote just that scene: the telling of the Eskimo myth. The impudent comments that are interpolated into Weston's telling of the story are roughly my thoughts as the myth was related to me that night. I had no characters, just the teller of the story and the listeners' rude remarks, about a three-page scene. I carried the notebook around for weeks. It also contained a scene that eighteen years later became scene two of *Sympathetic Magic*. I thought maybe the Eskimo scene took place in the friendly confines of the art department of an advertising agency I had worked for in Chicago. I believe I changed the locale because I thought John Lee Beatty, Circle Rep's brilliant set designer, would be completely uninterested in designing an art department. Now I almost wish I hadn't changed it, he would have designed a wonderful art department. The locale changed to Long Island; I had wanted to write something that took place there since I first saw the place. Maybe one of those big old houses. The characters (I still didn't know who they were) would be restoring the place, as I was restoring my house. I certainly knew about that. They would be building a garden, working on the land. The play would be one of restoration and commitment. Something the country sorely needed. I was almost surprised when I realized that the play had to be set in my hometown of Lebanon, Missouri. This had to be about the heartland. The house would not necessarily be in disrepair, but Jed would be a botanist and would be building a garden.

That summer I accepted the job of teaching a playwrighting course at Southampton College. I am not a teacher. The reason I write about teachers so often must be that I admire them enormously and think good teachers are the heroes of our time. There have been four who certainly were central to my life's path. I should have asked someone how to teach or at least had the sense to make a syllabus. On the first day I told the class everything I knew about playwrighting. And there was still half an hour left in the period. I don't know how I stuttered through that summer semester but I'm pretty sure I didn't fool anyone.

Among my students was a stunningly handsome man who had had both legs blown off AK (above the knee) in Vietnam. He walked with two aluminum crutches, clattering like a crab across the room. He was always late because it took him longer to get from class to class, and (maddeningly) he always took a seat by the windows—across the room from the door. The class was silent as he clanged cheerfully to his chair, hips flying out akimbo with each step, and sat with a great crash. Then he breathed a deep, exhausted sigh of relief and said, self-deprecatingly, describing what he must look like to the class, "Cha cha cha." He had a wonderful sense of humor and was a pretty darn good writer. The majority of the class was actually very talented. The only thing I felt bad about was their teacher.

One day I was given a lift home by a sweet, beautiful, tiny, infuriating pest of a girl who drove me crazy, usually standing at the back of the class:

TEACHER: Carey, would you care to sit down?
STUDENT: I can't I got this really bitchy rash on my ass that's killing me.
TEACHER: Well, you're driving me crazy fidgeting around back there.
STUDENT: That's your problem.

She was so flip and uninterested, staring out the window, chewing gum, playing with her hair, that I should have expected that her play, three pages, torn from a spiral notebook, written in faint pencil, would be the best work the class did all summer. Anyway, she drove me home. In the course of conversation, discussing the class, I said that David (I'll call him) was really a remarkably good-looking man. "Really?" she replied, "I've never looked at him. I don't think people like that like to be looked at."

That chilling remark was the beginning of *Fifth of July*. That was the wedge that finally split open the knot of all I had been feeling and had not known how to approach. Almost everything in the play can be traced to that ride home.

I took David out for coffee. I told him I wanted to write a play about someone who had come home injured. David had had his legs blown off in a land mine accident—

those devices our government currently maintains are essential to its security. He said the only other person who had asked him how he had been injured was a nurse in the hospital where he was stationed in England. They had been married now three years and were expecting their first child.

I told him I was thinking of making my character gay. He said, "Well, don't make him a downer, I'm so sick of angry, depressed, bitter vets in plays." I said I was sick of depressed gays in plays (one of them my own) and was thinking of the play as a comedy. One where the character's homosexuality was hardly mentioned, and was certainly not an issue. I promised to give him a lover as supportive and gorgeous as David's wife.

It had first been my intention to make the character of Kenneth quite effeminate: gestures so huge and sweeping that he was forever losing his balance and falling over. But in the writing it wouldn't happen. David's steady sense of humor and dignity and proportion kept asserting itself on my character. And one of the things he said frightened him the most was falling over backwards. "You're completely helpless and it's a bitch to get back up. You have to crawl to a big heavy chair for support, and it still isn't easy."

This play was written when Circle Rep was at its most glorious. Actors were in the office all the time; I almost never left. Much of the play was written with actors blabbing away in the room, all but looking over my shoulder. Everything seemed to feed the play, not just the energy of the office, and of people coming from one of Marshall's rehearsals, but when writing is going well, everything seems to pertain to your work. One of our board members was an accountant. He came to a meeting early, exhausted, saying what a weekend he'd had. His dad (also an accountant) had died three years ago and his mother had been carrying the ashes around ever since. They had finally gotten her to dump them in the lake. On the way back from the lake, walking to the car, she had a stroke. Not a big one, just a mild little stroke, but she'd been at the doctor's office all day. That went into the play that night and was the initiation of a nice offstage character named Matt Friedman (an accountant).

I wrote for specific actors in the company. Helen Stenborg, of course, and several I hadn't worked with before. My vet would be a newcomer to the company, Bill Hurt; his lover would be Jeff Daniels who had been so brilliant in *The Farm* the year before. Danton Stone had a moment, only a second, in *Mrs. Murray's Farm,* where he was momentarily confused. That had suggested someone I met in Woodstock; the guy was an actor but I met so many musicians there that I made my confused, bemused, character a composer. In the first draft I didn't have names for the characters. They were called Bill and Jeff and Danton and John—I never did come up with another name for the John Hogan character.

The first reading of the script was thrilling. The actors had known their characters for months, just waiting for me to finish the script. I had written Shirley for Amy Wright, an actress I had just talked to on the street, not a member of the company. She introduced herself and said she had played The Girl in *Hot L* the year before. I asked how she had been in it. She said she had been brilliant of course. She was so vibrant and exciting I knew I wanted her in my plays. She was probably twenty-two and Shirley was fourteen, but what the hell. All the other actors were deeply into their characters and playing the devil out of them on the first reading—Marshall had encouraged them not to try to act unless an impulse came to them and if that happened for God's sake go with it. Amy just read—dull words. I was watching her very closely as I was the only one in the company who knew her. Toward the end of the first act she looked around and seemed to realize that she wasn't showing Marshall (who didn't know her from Eve) or anyone else—anything. So she took a deep breath, glared daggers at me, cut loose, and just amazed everyone. She was so convincing in the part I'm afraid it cursed her with playing teenagers till she was well into her thirties. The part of Gwen had been written for Trish Hawkins. I wanted Trish in every play I wrote. I was crushed when she couldn't do it. Marshall and I thought we would have to go out of the company to replace her. We held auditions within the company first, but with low expectations. Nancy Snyder blew us totally away. She gave one of those auditions where the only thing to say is you've got the part, we don't need to read anyone else. We've been lucky with that role. When Nancy couldn't move to Broadway she was replaced by Swoozie Kurtz who won the Tony that year (deservedly) for best supporting actress.

All during rehearsals I kept working on the script. The focus was slightly off—Gwen was running away with the show, and I couldn't seem to tame her. It didn't matter; the play opened in late April and was repeatedly extended to run through the summer.

Almost two years later, more than a year after the play had been published, Gordon Davidson, Artistic Director of the Mark Taper Forum in Los Angeles, saw *Talley's Folly* and said he wanted to produce both the plays in rotating rep. He asked if there were any changes I wanted to make in *Fifth of July*. I first said no, but when I reread the play I realized immediately how to refocus it more toward Kenny, and to what I had been trying to say all along. Some of Gwen's funniest lines had to be sacrificed (a killer, that), but in the end it's closer now to what I was trying to say.

After every opening night at Circle Rep a crew cleared away the chairs and we had a party. A loud, dancing, lots-of-food-and-wine, party. One of our party regulars was the excellent director and critic Harold Clurman. Being a theater man and fond of the company, he felt nothing of partying with us all night then ripping our heads off in print. He always had a collection of girls around him who prompted him to tell fanciful stories and give impromptu lectures on aspects of the theater and art in general. On one of these openings Harold was talking about commitment. One of the girls said, "Lanford is writing a play about commitment." Harold said, "Oh, I don't care what a play is about, just so long as it's joyous!" A few months later, at another opening, I told him I was just about finished with my "joyous" play, but I wasn't certain how it would end. "It must end joyously!" he said, then grabbed my arm, and growled very seriously, "But what happened to the play you were writing about commitment?"

What a fine man he was, and what an inspiration. I promised myself the next comedy, the next "joyous" play I wrote, I would dedicate to Harold Clurman.

Original Production

Fifth of July was first presented by the Circle Repertory Company in New York City, on April 27, 1978. It was directed by Marshall W. Mason; the setting was by John Lee Beatty; costumes were by Laura Crow; lighting was by Marc. B. Weiss; the original song was by Jonathan Hogan; sound was by Chuck London.

The cast, in order of appearance, was as follows:

KENNETH TALLEY, JR.	William Hurt
JOHN LANDIS	Jonathan Hogan
GWEN LANDIS	Nancy Snyder
JED JENKINS	Jeff Daniels
JUNE TALLEY	Joyce Reehling

SHIRLEY TALLEY	Amy Wright
SALLY FRIEDMAN	Helen Stenborg
WESTON HURLEY	Danton Stone

(*Fifth of July* ran at Circle Repertory Company for 168 performances. For the last fourteen weeks Ken was played by Timothy Shelton.)

Fifth of July was subsequently presented by Jerry Arrow, Robert Lussier and Warner Productions, Inc. at the New Apollo Theatre, in New York City, on November 5, 1980. It was again directed by Marshall W. Mason; the setting was by John Lee Beatty; costumes were by Laura Crow; lighting was by Dennis Parichy; the sound by Chuck London; and the production stage manager was Fred Reinglas.

The cast, in order of appearance, was as follows:

KENNETH TALLEY, JR.	Christopher Reeve*
JED JENKINS	Jeff Daniels
JOHN LANDIS	Jonathan Hogan
GWEN LANDIS	Swoosie Kurtz
JUNE TALLEY	Joyce Reehling
SHIRLEY TALLEY	Amy Wright
SALLY FRIEDMAN	Mary Carver
WESTON HURLEY	Danton Stone

Characters

KENNETH TALLEY, JR.,	had both legs blown off seven years ago in the Vietnam War. He is 32, strong, good-looking and a touch cynical, but not deeply.
JED JENKINS,	25, his lover. Larger, stronger; an almost silent listener.
JUNE TALLEY,	34, Ken's sister.
SHIRLEY TALLEY,	14, her daughter.
JOHN LANDIS,	33, childhood friend of the Talleys.
GWEN LANDIS,	33, his wife. Racy.
WESTON HURLEY,	25, composer friend of Gwen and John. Listens late.
SALLY FRIEDMAN,	64, Ken and June's Aunt. Not really batty; preoccupied.

Scene

The Talley place, a farm near Lebanon, Missouri

Time

Act I: Early evening, Independence Day, 1977
Act II: The following morning

Later succeeded by Richard Thomas

ACT ONE

The set is the large sun porch/family room of a prosperous southern Missouri farmhouse built around 1865.

We see the wide doors to a hallway upstage, and a stairway going up. At one side, doors open to a porch that wraps around most or all of the house.

The room is furnished with two matching armchairs, tables, a desk. Ken sits at the desk. He is very hung over, and in this state tends to be blandly cynical.

He is listening to a small portable tape recording. The recording is of a boy who speaks with great hesitation, mangling words so badly nothing is intelligible to us. Ken listens, makes notes, rubs his eyes and head. There is the sound of distant firecrackers. Followed by dogs barking. Ken turns off the recording, realizes what the noise is, looks back to the recording, rewinds a bit of it, turns it on again.

Jed comes up onto the porch.

JED: Light's going, I'm about half blind.
KEN:

  (Turning the recording off.)

  What say?
JED: Don't stop. I have to go back down. I said the light's going; can't see a thing down there.
KEN: Where have you been hiding all afternoon?
JED: Aw, the stupid herb garden is going rank. The lavender's all over the thyme, the angelica's flopping all over the germander. Where are your two friends?

  (Jed enters house.)

KEN: John is showing Gwen his hometown, which should take about ten minutes.
JED: They came down to see me this afternoon. John was bragging about their garden in Carmel. It really pissed me off. I was throwing that lavender over my back, the whole garden smells like an English bathhouse. Check it out early. It'll be grown over by noon.

  (Kisses him.)

KEN: Holy God, you smell terrific.
JED: Come on, under that fragrance I'm as rank as a goat. You look like you're in great shape.
KEN: Oh, I'm fine. On a scale of one to ten, I'm about to show up on the chart any minute now.
JED: How much did you drink last night?
KEN: Much. You have no idea how little you missed by going to bed.
JED: That was the point.
KEN: You made that clear.
JED: I tried.
KEN: We wake you?
JED: Not me.

KEN: Even you. Even the dead. The little people in the wood. I didn't get to bed till five-thirty. All the birds were having fits. "Get the hell off that nest, get down into the garden and get me a bug." Got up at ten, that's six-thirty, seven-thirty—

JED: Four and a half. Did you eat?

KEN: I had coffee, I didn't even recognize it.

JED: You take your pills?

KEN: After last night my system would go into shock if I sent down one more chemical.

(Jed gets up.)

Yes, yes. I took my vitamins, I took my minerals, I took my protein and I took my birth control pill— Now, if only I had something to start it all moving. I've been up almost twelve hours, my heart hasn't beaten more than five times.

JED: You still feeling sorry for yourself?

KEN:

(Pause. Level.)

I wouldn't put it quite like that.

JED: How would you put it?

(Pause.)

It's been two weeks. You've had time to recover by now.

KEN: The incident to which you refer merely served as an illustration of something of which I've been aware for some time.

(They look at each other, mild Mexican standoff.)

JED: You get testy you start sounding like a bad textbook.

KEN: I'm not testy.

JED: What are you?

GWEN:

(Off.)

Honey, did you call that prick in Nashville?

JOHN:

(Off.)

Negative, we're taking dinner with him tomorrow at eight.

KEN: Did he say "negative"? Dear God.

JED: I'll close the door.

KEN: We'll talk tomorrow after they've gone.

JED: Could I have that in writing?

JOHN:

(Enters.)

Hey, Teacher. Oh, hi, Jed—you should have stayed up. We had a party last night.

JED:

(Still looking at Ken.)

GWEN:
　　　So I hear.

(Dead stop on porch.)

　　　Oh, God! I have never been at such peace in my life!

JOHN: We've been everywhere.

GWEN:

(Entering.)

　　　I want you to know this afternoon I have set your town on its ass.

JOHN: Don't kid yourself. Lebanon, Missouri, has been on its ass for a hundred and fifty years.

GWEN: I love the way you people live.

(Kisses Jed.)

JOHN: We brought back munchies for everybody.

JED: I have to go turn off the water.

(Sits on sofa, puts on shoes and socks.)

GWEN: Hey, I forgot to ask: What are the little red flags?

(As she hands out burgers and fries.)

JED: What little red flags?

JOHN: What little red flags?

GWEN: These sweet little red flags that are in rows all over the hill.

KEN: Oh, God! That's were Jed has planted his—hedges.

GWEN: Hedges.

JED: That's O.K. In five years you'll be able to see the plants.

GWEN: Honey, you think you've explained something to me, don't you? It's not that I'm slow; I'm just not horticultural.

KEN: He's making an English garden.

GWEN:

(To Jed.)

　　　You tell me.

JED: Each flag is where I planted a cutting.

GWEN: Yeah?

JED: A row of cuttings will grow into a hedge. The hedges will divide the garden into rooms.

GWEN: Rooms.

JED: Eventually the hedges will be held at seven feet tall; dividing the garden into different-sized spaces that are called rooms. And each room is treated differently—a pool or an herb garden, a rose garden, etc.

GWEN: And you're starting seven foot walls with plants I can't even see? You couldn't buy grown plants?

JED: Not the variety I want. I have to go turn off the water.

KEN: He baby-sat the cuttings all winter. Turned this sun porch into a greenhouse. He closed off the rest of the house, just lived in this room and the kitchen.

GWEN: You guys spent the winter here?

JED: I was here this winter. Ken was in St. Louis.

GWEN: Wait a minute. What am I hearing? What's the dirt?

KEN: I came down here three or four times.

JED: Twice.

KEN: Jed came up to St. Louis three or four times.

JED: Five. I'll be right back.

> (Exits.)

GWEN: What kind of lover sits down here alone all winter rooting hedges?

KEN: A botanical lover.

JOHN: Broke your heart, right? Don't forget we know you.

KEN:

> (Flattering himself.)

No . . . no, come on. I'm not as wild as we used to be.

GWEN: Oh, sure. Alone in St. Louis all winter.

KEN: Listen—Gwen—stop flying around.

> (They do rather.)

I've been thinking since you called. How serious are you about buying a place down here for your new studio?

GWEN: Oh, man, we have gotta have our own studio.

JOHN: The studios in Nashville bleed you dry. You wouldn't believe it.

KEN: I may have a proposition for you. If we could talk about this before Jed gets back up here.

JOHN: What's on your mind?

KEN: I know this place is a wreck, but actually any place you find would have to be completely rebuilt before you could use it for a recording studio wouldn't it?

JUNE:

> (Entering room from upstairs. Carries purse.)

I thought I heard you come back. So Kenny, are we doing this?

GWEN: Oh great. You haven't gone yet. I really made John burn rubber.

KEN: Gone where?

GWEN: You know. The funeral down by the river—Nommy yo-ho; Krisna yommy yommy—

KEN: No, no, soon.

GWEN: Good, because I'm coming along.

JUNE: Oh, sweetheart. You don't want to do that, really.

GWEN: Listen, Matt Friedman was very important to me too; I mean he really straightened me out. He was like a leveling influence. Like he told me not to take flying lessons. He kept trying to impress on me that I have a grave responsibility.

KEN: He didn't mean his, Gwen.

GWEN: You're quick. He was really pissed because Schwartzkoff, the bastard, appointed his wife's nephew to handle the trust. And if that's not nepotism, like by definition, I don't know what is.

KEN:

> *(To Gwen.)*

> Oh, that reminds me. You have a stack of phone calls. "While you were out."

JOHN:

> *(Crosses to Gwen.)*

> Later. Later. Honey, we got to get dressed if we're going to this shindig.

KEN: It's hardly a shindig.

JUNE: There's no reason for you two to—

GWEN:

> *(Looking out.)*

> Would you look at that fuckin' sunset!

> *(Wes enters from kitchen, exits upstairs.)*

KEN: Guaranteed every night.

JUNE: Aunt Sally doesn't show it, but she's really upset—

KEN: There's no reason for you to come.

JUNE: There's no ceremony.

JOHN: No, Gwen's got a real bug up her ass. She's been talking about it all afternoon.

GWEN: No Shit. Like I feel a responsibility, you know?

> *(Heads for stairs.)*

JUNE: There's no reason—

GWEN:

> *(Leaving, singing.)*

> Rock of Ages. Cleft—cleft for me. Let me hide.

> *(John gooses her. Gwen screams. Laughs. Shirley appears, sneaking after them. Yelps and runs off when she sees June.)*

JUNE: Shirley! Shirley!

> *(Gives up, gets pills out of purse.)*

> Why didn't you tell me those two were coming down here?

KEN: I believe I did.

JUNE: Don't get cute.

> *(Takes pill with wine.)*

KEN: They'll be gone tomorrow.

JUNE: I should have taken Shirley somewhere. Down to Branson for a couple of days.

KEN: How often do you see them?

JUNE: Every single year for the last five years they've showed up—always just happening to arrive on Shirley's birthday. Loaded down with presents.

KEN: Very subtle.

JUNE: Very cute.

KEN: Be thankful he doesn't come on Father's Day.

JUNE:

>*(Shirley might overhear.)*

Shhh! The walls have ears. She's playing Mata Hari today.

>*(Pause.)*

Oh, to hell with him. At least you've finally straightened yourself out.

KEN: Certainly not.

JUNE: In St. Louis you were never home when I called.

KEN: You don't have to look out for me any more, sis. I'm a big boy.

JUNE: Oh, sure. Running to every bar in town. I don't know what the hell you thought you were doing to yourself last winter.

KEN: Don't you?

JUNE: Oh, can the bitter and wise pose; I can't bear it. You're a lot better off back down here with Jed.

KEN: You were here two weeks ago. I think we all had a very graphic demonstration of the total fiasco it would be for me to stay here.

JUNE:

>*(Beat.)*

I beg your pardon?

KEN: There are a number of options open to me.

JUNE: Kenny, it is all settled.

KEN: Very well. It's all settled.

JUNE: You signed a contract. This is your life, Ken; this is one thing you're not going to crap out on.

JOHN:

>*(Entering from upstairs.)*

Yeah, babe. You said somebody called? Hey, babe. Look alive. I only have a sec.

KEN: What? Oh. Ah—what do you want first? A plasterer called. An Arthur Schwartzkoff called at eleven.

JOHN: What in the hell does he think he's doing? The man is crazy. You talked to him?

KEN: Not very coherently, I'm afraid.

JOHN: Damn. I told him not to call. If he did call not to leave his—

>*(Dialing.)*

Hey. I wheeled Gwen by the high school to see where you'll be teaching this winter.

JUNE: We were just talking about that.

JOHN: How about that new building? That's what we were campaigning for, remember? Ten years ago.

KEN: Fifteen, but who's counting?

JUNE: The old building collapsed.

JOHN: You're shittin' me. That finally fell in?

KEN: Unfortunately nobody was in it at the time.

JOHN:

(Phone.)

Operator, sorry to wake you up, doll—This is a credit card call. Card number 072-691-3037L. L . . . as in Love your lovely voice. Thank you.

(June crosses to sofa and sits. John notices them.)

Is this the only phone?

KEN: Sorry.
JOHN:

(Phone.)

Yeah, doll. This is Jack, he in? Goddamn, we are really missing each other today. Sure, have him call, but person-to-person. Right.

(Hangs up.)

JUNE: Boy, you're really becoming quite a magnate.
JOHN: Naw, naw, this is nothing. Leg work, busy work. It's nothing.
JUNE: Consisting mainly of keeping your wife at arm's length from the board of directors of her company.
JOHN: No, no, Gwen's cool. She just gets a little too enthusiastic sometimes.
JUNE: Then why all the clandestine phone calls?
GWEN:

(Off.)

Hey, John, what the hell's up?

JUNE:

(Yelling.)

Funny you should ask!

JOHN: Come on, lighten up. What are you doing?
JUNE: Well, I don't like it. We can see what's going on.
JOHN: There was only one thing I did that you ever liked.
GWEN:

(Off.)

Hey, John. What the hell's up.

JOHN:

(Sotto voce.)

Funny you should ask.

(Yelling.)

Comin', doll.

(Jed comes up on the porch.)

You said you had a scheme you wanted to talk over?

KEN: Uh . . . later.
JOHN: What's on your mind? 'Cause if it's what I think it is, we're definitely interested. We pulled up in front of the house, Gwen said this is the only place in the county that has the sort of layout we—

KEN: We'll talk, we'll talk. Good.

GWEN:

> *(Off.)*

> John, Goddamn it, shake a leg.

JOHN: Right with you, babe.

KEN: Later, okay?

JOHN: Sure, listen, we'll talk—I like it.

> *(Exits upstairs.)*

KEN: You ok?

JUNE: Yeah, I'm fine.

> *(Shirley enters and creeps up the stairs.)*

> Shirley!

KEN: Shirley, your mother is talking to you.

JUNE: Shirley, your uncle is talking to you.

> *(To Ken.)*

> What options?

KEN: I beg your pardon?

JUNE: You said you had a number of options open to you instead of staying down here to teach. As I recall you signed a contract.

> *(Jed enters.)*

KEN: Contracts are made to be broken, as is everything.

> *(To Jed, for June's benefit.)*

> There's no hurry, Jed. Gwen has decided she's coming with us.

JED:

> *(Entering.)*

> Oh, great.

KEN: They went up to change. I suppose into something black.

JED: You told them it wasn't formal?

KEN: I wouldn't presume.

JUNE: I saw them down in the garden with you this afternoon.

JED: Yeah. Gwen even pulled up what she thought was a weed.

JUNE: What did you think of John?

JED: He looks fine.

JUNE: Isn't he amazing? Somewhere there's a portrait of him that's really going to hell. You know he's running the whole copper business from your phone.

KEN: Behind Gwen's back.

JUNE: You can bet this new singing career he has her hyped on is just diversionary tactics.

KEN: Oh, I'm sure. That's all just so much . . . stardust.

JED: Smoke gets in your eyes.

KEN: I think given my choice between them now, I'd take her.

JED: Given my choice, I'd take hemlock.

JUNE: Oh, to hell with them both. Where's Aunt Sally? Is she ready at least?

KEN: Maybe not ready and willing, but probably able.

JUNE: I love being the villain in this. I'm really crazy about that.

> *(Off in the direction Shirley was last seen.)*

> Shirley!

> *(Shirley immediately sneaks on downstairs, out the door.)*

KEN: I'm going to bite that toe.

JED: What toe?

KEN: That toe. That toe. The big dirty one.

JED: They're only going to be here another twenty-one hours. I can hang in there if you can.

> *(Beat.)*

KEN: How could I ever have had the energy to live with those two?

JED: And June.

KEN: No, Gwen moved in, June moved out. Six months pregnant, big as a whale. Oh boy . . . all the old Berkeley days came back to wreck us last night. Reminiscences, and camaraderie, and everyone had an awful lot of "medicine." Snow rained like . . . snow. We called each other "man" and "cat," you would have vomited. I'll bet I said "dig it" five hundred times. It's a damned wonder we weren't down in the garden singing, "We Shall Overcome."

JED: I thought snow was heroin.

KEN: Oh, probably by now it is, but when we were very tired, we were very merry, we rode back and forth all night on the Sausalito ferry, snorting snow, snow was cocaine. And very dear even then.

JED: What does that matter to Gwen. She probably owns Peru or wherever it comes from.

KEN: She does not own Peru. She owns Montana and Colorado. Colorado owns Peru.

SALLY: All right, you wretch. I know you're in there somewhere. This is fair warning.

> *(Sally enters from downstairs carrying a macrame basket and a dried rose. She is looking for something.)*

KEN: Nothing has run through here in the last five minutes—unless you're looking for Shirley or June or Gwen or John . . .

SALLY: You haven't seen a roll of copper wire? The beast is being very difficult this evening.

> *(Hands rose to Ken.)*

> What does that feel like? Is that dry? I think that's perfectly dry.

KEN: Yes, that is perfectly dry and perfectly hideous-looking.

SALLY: The magazine said it would retain its color . . .

KEN: What color was it?

> *(Weston enters from upstairs, strumming his guitar.)*

SALLY:

> *(To Jed.)*

> *Have you seen a roll of copper wire?*

(*Sees Wes.*)

You haven't seen a roll of copper wire?

KEN: Darling, don't start anything now. We'll be leaving any minute.

SALLY: You're Wes Hurley, aren't you?

JED: Gwen's composer friend.

KEN: You met him last night, darling.

SALLY: I remember last night perfectly.

JUNE:

(*Entering from upstairs, to Weston.*)

Are they changing?

(*Weston stares at each in turn.*)

Gwen and John. Are they changing?

WESTON: Gwen and John.

KEN: Are they changing?

WESTON: How . . . do you mean . . . changing?

KEN: Clothes.

WESTON: Oh, wow, I had this whole metamorphosis thing going . . . I was reading this book about Kafka . . .

KEN: Gwen insists on coming with us tonight, so we are presumably waiting on them.

WESTON: I don't know. They shut the door.

(*He goes out to the porch.*)

KEN: That means that they're going at it. Every day in every way I'm getting stronger and stronger.

SALLY: How long are you all staying, Wes?

JED: Twenty-one hours.

SALLY: What kind of a visit is that?

KEN: This isn't a visit, it's a business trip—they're looking for a house down here.

SALLY: Oh, They aren't serious about a place in Missouri. Gwen could buy any house in the country.

KEN: Darling, if they think they're interested in a place down here, it's no business of ours.

JUNE: They want their own recording studio. Away from Nashville.

KEN: And God knows Lebanon is away from almost anything you could think of.

SALLY: I can't believe Gwen is seriously interested in a singing career.

KEN: Can you believe that John is interested in Gwen having a singing career?

SALLY: Oh, that is perfectly apparent. Well, everything changes, everyone's moving; I can't say I'm looking forward to it.

JUNE: You won't be alone; Mom and Dad are right next door.

SALLY: You remember how well we've always gotten along. Oh, I don't know why I let your father talk me into moving to some senior citizens enclave in California. Matt and I always hated retirement communities. Imagine choosing to live in the only neighborhood in the country that has a full one hundred percent unemployment.

JUNE: Mom and Dad love it.

SALLY: Well, I'm sorry. All those women in their ballet classes and craft classes, getting tangled up in their macrame. Even your mother. Did you get a basket from Olive for Christmas?

KEN: Ummmm.

SALLY: Yes, so did I. That sort of thing should really be left to the Indians. And I don't like the house.

KEN: You've hardly seen the house.

SALLY: No, it's too . . . big.

JUNE: Why are you buying it?

SALLY: Well, Buddy swears I'm lonely now that Matt's gone. Really he and Olive are just afraid of who might move in next to them.

KEN: This is undeniably true.

SALLY: But I don't love St. Louis any more, no one does.

KEN: There's nothing wrong with St. Louis.

JED: There's nothing right with it.

SALLY: The mayor on TV looks like he'd rather be the mayor of any other place on earth. And you aren't going to get anywhere with Shirley while I'm around.

JUNE:

> (Overlap.)

> Don't let that worry you.

SALLY: No, now, the two of you should be on your own.

> (Spots spool of tape.)

> Is that you? No, you're the green tape. I'll need you, too. How can people ever organize a hobby? It's just exhausting. Is it going to rain? I suppose they'll cancel the dance and the fireworks. Probably they'll move it to the Community Hall.

KEN: A fireworks display in the Community Hall?

JED: That'll be nice.

SALLY: I never liked fireworks. The smell of sulfur makes me sick. I wouldn't look very patriotic throwing up.

KEN: Oh, any honest reaction, I think.

> (Weston, on the porch, is playing a soft melody on the guitar.)

SALLY:

> (At the screen door.)

> It's gonna rain on Harley Campbell's funeral tomorrow. It must have rained every vacation we came down here. I don't know why Matt loved it. Everyone hated him. If it rained, he went fishing. Never caught a fish. I don't think he baited his hook. Loved every minute of it. Hated catching fish. Didn't want the responsibility. Sat in the rain and laughed like a moron. They all must have thought he was mad.

KEN: Don't be absurd; he was as sane as you.

JUNE: I really don't see any point in waiting for those two.

SALLY:

> (Looking out the door.)

> Where have they got to now? They came back from town.

KEN: They went into their room, shut the door, and are, we presume, going at it.

SALLY: Again? He certainly does try very hard to keep her occupied, doesn't he?

KEN: John has always known what side he was buttered on.

SALLY: You get the feeling the moment they're alone if she opens her mouth and doesn't sing, he sticks something in it. Was he like that when you lived with them?

JUNE: I didn't live with them, Kenny lived with them, and yes, he was like that.

KEN: June moved out; if you can't stand the heat, get out of the kitchen.

JUNE: The heat didn't bother me; it was the smell of all those burning cookies.

(Ken starts the tape recorder, the mangled words are heard again.)

I've been meaning to tell you that's really my favorite thing to listen to.

SALLY: Is there a moon tonight?

JED: Yeah, later.

JUNE: I think that and Mahler are in a class by themselves.

SALLY: He loved swimming naked.

KEN: Mahler? Loved swimming naked?

SALLY: Your Uncle Matt, darling.

KEN: This kid's name is Johnny Young. He's at the junior high. Wouldn't be in my class for years. And don't smirk, he's got an IQ of about 200. At noon tomorrow I'm supposed to tell this kid what I thought of his story.

JUNE: That's a story? I could tell you now.

KEN: It's kind of amazing. He's into the future.

JUNE: God, that entire Young family scared me to death. I'd walk a mile out of my way not to pass that house.

SALLY: Who did?

JUNE: You remember the Young brood. The church was always taking food baskets to them.

KEN: That they promptly sold.

JUNE: Four hundred white-haired children. All beautiful. All vacant as a jar.
A snaggle-toothed old crone out in the back yard, literally stirring a bubbling caldron. Grinning through the steam, cackling like a hen.

SALLY: She was making soap.

JUNE: Ummm . . . Sure, she was making soap. But out of what?

KEN: Oh, he's impossible.

JUNE: He certainly is.

(Ken turns it off. He gets up, taking a crutch in each hand, and crosses to another chair.)

KEN: He's more than likely a mathematical prodigy. No one here is qualified to judge. He communicates with scribbled messages. Half his problem is just tension. Fear of being anticipated. Everyone has cut him off as soon as they get the gist of what he's trying to say for so long that—

JUNE: Okay, okay.

KEN: He had almost no control over his entire vocal apparatus when we started. Nothing more than tension, really. He was simply terrified.

(He glares. She smiles.)

JED: Pissed his pants.

KEN: Not since that first time, actually.

JUNE: Oh, fine.

KEN: Entirely my fault. I couldn't understand the son-of-a-bitch was asking for permission to go to the john.

JUNE: You're terrific.
KEN: The patience of Job.
JUNE:

    (Exiting upstairs.)

    What a mother you would have been.
KEN: Was Job a good mother?
SALLY: June is being an awful tart, isn't she?
KEN: June is even more impossible with a straight man in the house than she is
    without one.
SALLY: I don't know why she had to come down here with me.
KEN: Oh, don't you. Three weeks ago as soon as she heard John was coming . . .
SALLY: That's over long ago, surely.
KEN: You know that, and I know that . . .
SALLY: But where would that get her?
KEN: Nevertheless.
SALLY: Well, it gives her focus. Poor June. You were always so bright and so popular,
    June was always rather "The Cheese Stands Alone."
KEN:

    (To Jed.)

    Is that the pest book?
JED: Mildew.
SALLY: Mildew? Not on the roses.
JED: Sally, bite your tongue.
SALLY: How to you know so much about gardening? Did you grow up on a farm?
KEN: No, darling, he has a Master's in botany.
JED: And no botanist has ever known anything at all about gardening, or there
    wouldn't be mildew on the phlox.
SALLY: Mildew on the phlox . . . What's the name of that novel?
GWEN:

    (Off.)

    No, I love it!
JOHN:

    (Off.)

    I'll kill her; you kidding me?

    (Entering, elated.)

    Hey, you sneak! Where is she? Hey, you know in Europe you could
have your eyes poked out for something like that? Caught the little twerp
at the window. You're really going to get it. She was up a tree looking in
the—
SHIRLEY: I certainly hope you aren't addressing me.

    (Appearing at the door.)

JOHN: How's that for innocence?
SHIRLEY: I have no idea—

(June enters down stairs, on landing.)

SHIRLEY:—what you are making
such a disturbance about, but
if you are alluding to me, there
are any number of low and
sniggling people who might
do something of that kind.

JOHN: You little sneak.
You peeper. If you don't watch
out, I'll tell it all. You could get
yourself in a pack of trouble.
That wasn't just snorting coke
and smoking dope like last night.

SHIRLEY: I have no memory of last night and I am a minor and not responsible for the
delinquency that so-called majors are leading me into.

KEN: What are you got up as?

JUNE: She makes about as good a drag as you would.

KEN: Anything is possible with a little taste and charm.

SHIRLEY: This is a beautiful gown that my great-grandmother wore when—

JUNE: She's been at Grandma's trunk in the attic.

(Gwen enters, wearing only a sheet.)

SHIRLEY: And you are a degenerate,
is what you are. Yes, I was
looking in the window and
I was smoking a cigarette and
I have never seen anything so
disgusting in my entire life. He
didn't even have his shoes off!
He didn't even have his pants
down! He was fully dressed and
Gwen was fully naked! And he
was performing cunnilingus all
over her and his face was all over
Mucus and it was the most
disgusting thing I've ever seen
in my life. And worse, worse,
worse, she was moaning and
groaning and he—he—he—was
reaching down with his own hand
and masturbating his own thing at
the same time. Himself! I have
never seen anything so unnatural
and warped in my young life! Ever!

JOHN: You are too much; and she was
also smoking a cigarette weren't
you? When did you start that?
And she was spying on a
private act, weren't you? I think
you ought to learn a lesson. I
think you should learn a thing
or two . . . You better watch it.
You're asking for it . . . You
watch it. You better just watch
it. You're gonna get it now.
That's it. You've had it.
(He continues.)

GWEN: Oh, I was! It was fantastic!
Oh, God, we were caught
in the act! It was too fantastic!
I looked back and saw this
face at the window. Oh,
shit, spies. No, audience! Oh, God,
how fabulous. And like,
wow, I really hit the moon.
I mean I came like a flash! I've
never come like that in such a
flash in my life. I just went
flash! Flash! All my blood, like,
just went flash! All through my
body. You were terrific! Shirley,
you gotta always be there!

*(John has continued saying "I'll get you for this. You just see. I'm gonna really get
you for this.")*

297

SHIRLEY:

> *(Yells when he would touch her.)*

> You just try it. You keep your dirty hands off me.

JUNE:

> *(Overlapping.)*

> John, Shirley, Shirley. You are going to rip that dress that does not belong to you. And you are forgetting that this evening is rather a sober occasion for some people if it isn't for you. Try for one night to respect Aunt Sally and Uncle Matt.

GWEN: Oh, shit. I forgot! I've got to dress. Don't anybody leave without me.

> *(Runs off upstairs.)*

SALLY: If he's waited over a year, he can wait a little longer.

JUNE: Sally, it cannot wait any longer.

SHIRLEY: I have just seen something that will warp my young mind and all you can think of is death and ashes. And I love Aunt Sally, whom I consider my mother, and Uncle Matt, who was the only father I ever had, a good deal more than—

JUNE: I'm gonna bust your ass for you, too, honey, if you try to dump that guilt trip on me.

SHIRLEY: I will not be a party to casting my dear granduncle's ashes into some filthy swimming hole, because I have more respect for his memory than that.

JUNE: I'm going to dump you in the river, which is something I should have done when I had the chance.

JOHN: You better watch that one. She's gettin' a little big for her pants, ain't you? How old are you now? How old are you?

JUNE: You wouldn't know, of course.

SHIRLEY: Age is the most irrelevant judge of character or maturity that—

JOHN: Yeah, yeah, how old are you?

JUNE: She's thirteen.

SHIRLEY:

> *(To June.)*

> I am eighteen years old,

> *(To John.)*

> and it is none of your business . . .

JUNE: She's thirteen.

SHIRLEY: If you must know, I'm seventeen.

JUNE: You are not seventeen, you cretin.

SHIRLEY: I am fifteen years old!

JUNE: She's fourteen.

> *(John picks Shirley up and carries her over his shoulder to the porch and slams the door on her. All through this, she is screaming: "Put me down, put me down, Rhett Butler, put me down.")*

JOHN:

(Smiles, turns back to the bedroom.)

You better watch that one.
Yeah?

(Exits to the bedroom upstairs.)

SHIRLEY:

(Comes back in, follows him to steps.)

I happen to, am going to be an artist, and an artist has no age and must force himself to see everything, no matter how disgusting and how low!

(Door slams offstage.)

WESTON:

(Pause.)

Far out.

KEN:

(Pause.)

I'm terribly sorry, Wes, what is it that's far out?
WESTON: The dude's been dead over a year?
SALLY: Oh, I know, I just don't get things done.
KEN: It isn't as though he'd spoil.
SALLY: No, the dear, he won't spoil.
SHIRLEY: Oh, God. Oh, my God!
JUNE: Will you please get out of that dress and stop trying to be the center of attention . . .

(Indicates bedroom.)

That was cute. Wasn't he cute?
KEN: We always thought so.
WESTON: He wanted you to scatter his ashes on the water?
JUNE: He said flush them down the toilet.
SALLY: Matt's wishes were never expressed.
JUNE: But we're taking him to the river. Better late than never.
KEN: It's hardly the Ganges, but you go with what you've got . . .
WESTON: Sure.
SALLY:

(To June.)

All he said was don't keep my ashes in a goddamned urn.
SHIRLEY: Oh, Jesus, God, I—ughh.

(Lights a cigarette in a long holder.)

SALLY: But one thing and another . . .
WESTON: Far out.
SHIRLEY: I cannot bear it. I am a spiritual person. I happen to . . .

JUNE: If you please . . .

(Takes cigarette from holder, stubs it out.)

SALLY: Well, of course the funeral home gave him to me in an enormous, blue, hermetically sealed urn with Matt Friedman in gold Old English lettering. I certainly took him out of that and put him in a box.

WESTON: Sure.

SHIRLEY: I cannot bear mature people calmly talking about cremation and death and ashes in a box. I cannot bear it.

SALLY: I open it up every day and give him a little air.

WESTON: Sure.

JUNE: Wes, don't start her off.

SHIRLEY: I cannot bear it.

SALLY: I dried a rose in him last week. Dried it very nicely, too. You know, Jed discovered this lost rose.

JED: Slater's Crimson China.

SALLY: Matt made a very good drying agent, too.

JUNE: He would have had a fit.

KEN: Actually, he might be put to better use spread around the rosebushes as fertilizer.

JED: Potash, absolutely. Prevents dieback.

KEN: Or John's ashes should be good for a quantity of potash, if you think about it . . .

JED: You cremate John and I'll happily spread his ashes.

SHIRLEY: I will absolutely *scream* if anyone says "ashes" one more time.

KEN: She will, too.

SALLY: I'm not at all happy about dumping him down at the boathouse. It looks too much like a shrine and Matt would hate that. But—we made love there the first time.

JUNE: Do we have to wait for those two?

SALLY: There's something wrong about it.

SHIRLEY: That's where they saw the UFO from.

SALLY: No, it was not. We were standing right on that porch when we saw the UFO.

WESTON: You've sighted UFOs here? I read this book about flying saucers.

JUNE: Don't start her . . . Wes, you read too much, concentrate on your music.

SALLY: We went out onto the porch. This was only our second date, mind.

WESTON: Sure.

SALLY: And we saw this silver flying thing . . . rise straight up from the river down there. Very slowly, till it was just over the trees. Just this huge litup top. And then it went off sideways—phettt! and was gone—just like nothing.

WESTON: Did it go "phettt!"?

SALLY: No. I went "phettt!" It didn't go anything.

JUNE: A marriage made in heaven, right?

WESTON: There's a saucer-shaped one and a cigar-shaped one. Only they think the cigar-shaped one is just the saucer-shaped one seen on an ellipse, like. Did it have a tail?

SALLY: No, no tail.

WESTON: Some of them have tails.

SALLY: This one didn't have a tail.

WESTON: Some of them don't have tails.

SALLY: This was one of the ones that didn't have a tail.

WESTON: Some of them don't have tails.

SALLY: Well, I mean to tell you, I wet my pants.

WESTON: Sure.

JUNE: You were lucky.

SALLY: I did. I wet my pants. Of course, we thought we were being invaded by the Japanese.

WESTON: Sure.

SALLY: We got on the telephone to the Civil Defense and they said to stay away from the area, don't go down there. Of course, we were down there in a minute.

WESTON: Sure.

SALLY: And, well, all the weeds and brush all along our riverbank were burned away. The place was still smoldering.

WESTON: Sure.

SHIRLEY: Probably they were burned by all kinds of radiation.

KEN: That would explain a good deal.

SALLY: And we ran all up and down the river, looking for spies, and listening, because that's what we thought it was. That they had landed Jap—Japanese troops.

WESTON: Sure.

SALLY: And by the time we had gone all the way to the boathouse we had to rest, and we talked and looked at the moon, and I'm afraid we got all involved with each other and forgot about the Japanese.

KEN: With wet pants? I'm sorry.

SALLY: Isn't that funny? I completely forget what I did about that. Of course, we had no idea what we had seen. It was years before anyone started talking about UFOs.

WESTON: Sure.

SALLY: But every time we came down here, every year after that, we went out to watch for them.

SHIRLEY: That's probably why Uncle Matt kept coming back down here instead of some place nice.

JUNE: Shirley, are you going to go or are you going to stay, because you can't go looking like that.

SHIRLEY: I have said repeatedly that I was staying here, and the sooner we get back to St. Louis and you stop acting like a mother the happier I'll be.

JUNE: Just a simple decision, we don't need the production number.

SHIRLEY: Unlike either of you, I do not have a single memory of the boyfriends I dated during the war in this one-horse burg.

JUNE: Where do you get the way you talk? I did not have "boyfriends," we did not go on "dates"; haven't you learned anything? She spends twenty-four hours a day in the queer movie house, watching Betty Grable reruns.

SHIRLEY: Betty Grable is the greatest star Missouri ever produced.

KEN: Oh, God. I'll bet that's true.

SHIRLEY: I would think one would know better than to proclaim her chastity to her illegitimate daughter.

JUNE: There is a world of difference between making love and teasing some basketball player after the junior prom.

KEN: June certainly never teased anyone.

(Gwen enters, dressed flamboyantly.)

Holy God.

JUNE: Oh, Good Lord!

> *(Over.)*

GWEN: I decided, if Shirley is wearing that, I'd let her set the tone.

JUNE: She isn't going, and she certainly isn't wearing that.

JED:

> *(To Ken.)*
>
> Be a minute; hold down the fort.
>
> *(Exits to upstairs.)*

SALLY:

> *(Overlapping.)*
>
> Now, where did you get to? You were here last night, and what did I do with you? It was hot—I know that.

KEN:

> *(Overlapping.)*
>
> Has anybody seen Aunt Sally's roll of copper wire?

GWEN: What brand? Copper's my business.

SALLY: What? Oh, yes, but no, darling, Uncle Matt. I can't seem to remember what I've done with his box of ashes.

KEN:

> *(Ken and June at the same time, overlapping.)*
>
> Don't say it!

JUNE: Please don't!

> *(Shirley screams.)*

WESTON:

> *(Pause.)*
>
> Far out.

GWEN: Oh, God, that's so great. I'd be a new person if I could do that. Ever since my shrink told me I should scream, I haven't been able to.

JUNE: Don't pay any attention to her. She's only trying to be the center of—oh, God, I sound exactly like Dad, don't I?

KEN: His voice was higher.

JUNE: Men and women aren't strong enough to have children. Trees should have children.

KEN: I'm afraid I can't help you, Aunt Sally. I haven't seen them.

SALLY:

> *(Overlapping.)*
>
> I only have to concentrate a moment. I had them last night, when it was so warm, and I took them up the bedroom, but I don't remember bringing him down this morning. I remember it was so hot.

KEN:

(Yelling upstairs.)

Jed! Hey, Jed!

GWEN: That's so wonderful.

JED:

(Off. Yelling.)

Yo!

GWEN: Jed is really butch, isn't he? Don't you love him?

KEN:

(Yelling.)

Listen. . . .

GWEN: I mean he's dull as dishwater, but he's so butch!

KEN:

(Yelling.)

Bring down Uncle Matt from Aunt Sally's bedroom when you come!

SALLY: No, darling, something tells me I didn't leave him up there. It was so warm, I was worried—

JED:

(Off.)

He's in the refrigerator.

SALLY: Oh, of course he is.

WESTON: Wow, that's really—

JUNE: Don't say it. One word.

WESTON:

(Mouth open, can't close it.)

I been reading this book about the Bermuda Triangle.

SHIRLEY: Oh, the Bermuda Triangle.

GWEN: Listen, forget it; it's a total rip-off. We went down there to try to disappear. Like we did everything you could think of to make ourselves conspicuous, you know? Not a fuckin' thing happened to us. Two solid months.

SHIRLEY: How long are you going to be in Nashville?

GWEN: Just a couple of weeks to line up a band. You want to come?

SHIRLEY: Yes!

(June starts to leave the room, to kitchen.)

SALLY: Where are you going?

JUNE: I'm . . . going to . . . the loo. You want to come?

SALLY: Just leave Matt in the refrigerator. He's fine there.

(June stops, stares.)

JUNE:

(To Ken.)

I'm only asking if we're doing this or not.

KEN: Don't push, don't force it.

JUNE: You're the original Will o' the Wisp.

SHIRLEY: The only place I've ever been for a vacation is Lebanon.

GWEN: Oh, shit. That's probably the pits, right? We were in Egypt, the guide stands in front of the Sphinx; he says, "For five thousand years the Sphinx had not given up her secret. Command her to speak but she remains silent." I said, you gotta be runnin' that up my ass, right?

KEN: Lebanon, Missouri.

SHIRLEY:

> (Overlapping.)

Here; you're there now.

GWEN: Oh, listen, no, this is the greatest place I've ever been. We walked down to the river, we were up on the hill; I've never seen such peace in my life.

SHIRLEY: Every place I've ever been has been peaceful.

GWEN: No shit; we're gonna move here.

SALLY: Oh, you are not.

KEN: Aunt Sally, darling.

GWEN: Hell yes, the whole bit; back to the land, it's John's hometown.

SALLY: John's dad moved to Miami ten years ago.

GWEN: He has great feelings for the place, though—and we got to have our own studio, see. Hey, John, damn it, come down here.

JOHN:

> (Off.)

What say, babe?

GWEN: Come down here. Hey Ken, how many rooms have you got?

JUNE: Nineteen, why?

> (John enters from upstairs.)

GWEN: Woo! You look great.

JOHN: Okay, I'm clean.

SHIRLEY: Don't touch me, I don't care.

JOHN: She's gonna really get it.

GWEN:

> (To Ken.)

We were talking about your proposition—

JOHN: Not now, doll—

GWEN: Oh, sure. We got to have our own place to record, see, 'cause the studios bleed you dry. You wouldn't believe it.

WESTON: Oh, wow, and she's . . .

JOHN: Gwen's got a little problem; we're working on . . . It runs into a lot of bread.

WESTON: She gets blocks.

JUNE: She gets what?

WESTON: Blocks. You know, like mental blocks.

JOHN: No, it all goes fine until they turn on the mikes.

KEN: Beautiful.

304

GWEN: Fuck it, it's not that bad.

JOHN: Listen, I thought it was cool.

WESTON: She freezes.

JOHN: It's nothing. She freezes. Her jaws clench up.

WESTON: You can't even pry them open with your fingers. We tried. It's really a bitch.

GWEN: Just to cut two sides I'm probably the only singer ever spent more money on the shrink than we did on the band.

JOHN: The band was really great, though.

GWEN: 'Cause they had decided I was just this rich bitch, you know, but like when we finally got it together and cut the tape they really flipped.

WESTON: But like she won't even listen to the demo.

GWEN: I don't want to hear it.

WESTON: Like she's got this real pain in her voice.

GWEN: Well, let's face it, like if I don't have pain in my voice, who would?

JOHN: There had to have been something to impress Jimmy King.

GWEN: Who's like the top manager in the business. They don't know Jimmy King.

JOHN: He wants to sign them both.

GWEN: Only thing he said I really should concentrate on this one thing.

JUNE: I'll bet.

GWEN: And like what happens to the copper business?

JOHN: One thing at a time, one thing at a time.

GWEN: Only I'm never sure which time to take what thing.

JOHN: You gotta learn to think about yourself.

GWEN: But wouldn't that be far out to have this really major career after you're already thirty-three years old and burned out?

JOHN: Nobody says you're burned—

GWEN: Everybody says I'm burned out. How can you take that many drugs and go through what I've gone through and not have your brains fried?

SHIRLEY: You are thirty-three years old?

GWEN: Isn't that gross?

SHIRLEY: How did you get burned out?

GWEN: Listen, I'm a real case, no shit. Like a year doesn't go by without me getting something terminal wrong with me.

WESTON: She's got this history of like medical milestone operations—

SHIRLEY: On, no.

GWEN: It's really crazy; I mean, I'm this fuckin' shell. They took everything out by the time I was twenty-five. You know, not all at once, one or two things at a time.

SHIRLEY: Oh, Lord . . . Can't you have children?

GWEN: Oh, please, that was like the first thing to go. If I didn't have this history of longevity in my family, I'd've been dead before I was ten.

WESTON: But like nobody in her family ever dies.

GWEN: Like you got to kill us off. Daddy's been like paralyzed, you know, for the last four years, with all these tubes and wires and all, but—I mean, like he's a Brussels sprout, but he's alive. It'd be really tragic, but you can't think about it without laughing, 'cause you know he had this stroke—

SHIRLEY: Oh. I cannot bear it.

GWEN: No, listen, it's far out. His face is all paralyzed, you know, but it's stuck in this real weird comic position. I mean even Arthur J. Schwartzkoff, who's like the most serious person I know, had to leave the room to keep from cracking up.

WESTON: She's got this real tragic history.

GWEN: Ask Wes.

WESTON: Her mother and her brother were killed in an airplane crash.

GWEN: Ronny, it was too bad; Mom was a bitch.

(Pause.)

I don't want to be a down or anything.

(Ken is pouring a glass of wine.)

JUNE:

(Takes bottle.)

Hey, don't start that again tonight.

KEN: You're right.

(Drinks.)

JUNE: This idiot was up to St. Louis all winter trying to kill himself—drinking himself blind—trying to prove what a swinger he is—till finally he managed to collapse in the street and wound up in the hospital. And now he's back in physical therapy.

KEN: I only go twice a week.

GWEN: Yeah, and—?

KEN: This nice dyke nurse tries to kill me. It's this game we play.

JOHN: I thought you were finished with all that.

GWEN: Why are you back in muscular therapy, creep?

KEN: Good God, no reason. Apparently I was walking wrong. I was walking with my arms instead of my stomach.

(Shirley presses the recorder.)

GWEN: Oh, God, I was gonna tell you. That's really weird to make love to.

KEN: Sorry, but it's really fascinating—

JOHN: You've got your work cut out for you, if this is one of your English students.

KEN: No, no. When I was in rehabilitation learning to walk, I worked with a couple of boys who had lost their ability to speak. Mac McConnell wanted me to work with this kid privately to see if I could help him.

JUNE: Johnny Young. Remember the Young brood?

JOHN: Jesus, forget I mentioned it.

KEN: He's too shy to talk to me. I gave him a tape recorder so he could tell me about himself, but instead he's filled the entire cassette with this amazing science fiction story about the future.

JOHN: When do you start back again?

JUNE: School starts the first Monday after Labor Day.

KEN: Start what?

GWEN: I think that is so far out to return to the fold like that. I mean it's parochial as hell, but it's so far out.

KEN: Oh, hardly. The profession has done very nicely without me for six years, I think it will survive a while longer.

JUNE: What the hell are you talking about?

GWEN: I thought that's what you were down here for. You were going back to your old high school.

KEN: I was never that interested in teaching.

SALLY: Oh, you were so.

GWEN:

(Overlapping Sally.)

You used to scream about it all the time.

JOHN: Hell you weren't, that was your mission, I thought.

JUNE: Kenny, it is quite settled.

JOHN: That guy said you were the best teacher Oakland ever had.

KEN:

(Suddenly unleashing his pent-up tension.)

Well once again Superfag's plans fail to materialize. Yes, I was quite happy leaving our cozy abode in Oakland each morning and walking briskly into the Theodore Roosevelt High School. Very "Good Morning, Miss Dove"; very "Good-bye, Mr. Chips." And—by prancing and dancing and sleight of hand, I actually managed to keep their little minds off sex for one hour a day. They became quite fascinated by trochees, thrilled by *Cyrano de Bergerac*. But now I'm afraid my prancing would be quite embarrassing to them.

JUNE: There was a little incident two weeks ago that has him running like a rabbit.

KEN:

(Almost angry.)

It is merely that as I slowly realized no accredited English Department was interested in my stunningly overqualified application, except the notoriously parochial hometown—

JUNE: Fine, that's where you belong.

KEN: —I became aware that what everyone was trying to tell me was—that teaching impressionable teenagers in my present state, I could only expect to leave quite the wrong impression. You have no idea how much noise I make falling down.

JOHN: Oh, bull. A big-deal war hero. They'd love you.

KEN: I don't think so. And though it seems incredible to us, they don't even know where Vietnam is.

JUNE: Why don't you just admit you're vain and terrified and face it instead of—

KEN: I have simply developed an overpowering distaste for chalk.

JUNE: Well, fine, teaching is the only thing you're prepared to do with your life, you obviously don't think that agrees with you anymore. What the hell do you see for yourself? Huh? What you got in mind to do with your life?

KEN: Just pack that away, all right?

(Yelling.)

Jed! come on. Let's go!

JUNE: What are you going to do down here then? 'Cause you sure as hell aren't going back to St. Louis this winter.

KEN: Jed and I might go to Greece; we might move to Spain. What the hell difference is it to you?

JUNE: Jed would love that. Have you dropped this on him?

KEN: *Not one word* about school to Jed! We will deal with that privately. Now that's it—no more!

GWEN: Well, listen, John and I were talking about your proposition, you know? The only thing was where would you and Jed go. Hell, if you're not going to be here, there's no hang-up is there?

KEN:

> (Over a bit.)

> Not now, doll, not now.

JOHN:

> (Over.)

> Later, babe.

GWEN: Why the hell is everyone being so circumspect? They'll have to know eventually— We haven't even talked price; hell, it may all be academic!

JOHN:

> (To Wes.)

> Come on, off your butt, we're gonna travel.

WESTON: Goin' where?

JOHN: We're gonna do the Matt Friedman gig; then we're gonna see my hometown's Fourth of July bash.

WESTON: No way.

GWEN: Honey . . . ?

JOHN: Big deal, get off your butt, get some air.

WESTON: I been getting air all day— I've never seen so much air in my life.

KEN: They don't have air in New Jersey?

WESTON: They got something, but it ain't air.

JOHN: He hasn't been home in two years.

GWEN: Honey, maybe I should stay here, 'cause Wes and me have to work, you know.

JOHN: No, we'll all go; we'll go on to the fireworks. You know if you don't go you'll be disappointed later.

GWEN: I just came here to see Kenny, I didn't bargain for funerals.

JUNE: It won't be like that at all.

JOHN: When you chicken out, you're always sorry later—

GWEN: Come on, I can't do it. I thought I could 'cause he was so nice, but I'm going to freak out. I just keep thinking about my daddy and my brother and I'm gonna freak. Tell me it isn't ashes. Tell me it's something else.

KEN: It's something else.

GWEN: No, no, you know, Johnny. Tell me it's something else. Make it better.

JOHN: Baby, you're thinking about your old man. You can't think about him. He's fine. The last time I saw him, he was—

GWEN: No, no, no, you're trying to change the subject; it's not gonna work to change the subject. You've gotta tell me it's something else.

JUNE: It's pickled peaches. We're going down to the river, we're going to have a picnic, we'll—

GWEN: —No, no, God, no, not something to eat! Tell me—oh, God, I'm going to freak out. I'm really gonna freak.

JOHN: Baby, you don't have to do a thing you don't want to.

KEN: Gwen. I do not know why you are carrying on. Have you seen that box? Have you seen it?

GWEN: No.

KEN: Well, you know while I was in the hospital I got all these presents from people who don't go to hospitals—you know that.

GWEN: People are such creeps! People are so candy-ass.

KEN: Well, you remember all the chocolates I got—

GWEN: We brought you a pound of peyote buttons, we didn't bring you—

KEN: But others, granted, less enterprising. You remember all those chocolates?

GWEN: Yeah, we sat on your bed and punched the bottoms out of them.

KEN: And half of them were something vile like—what was it you don't like?

GWEN: . . . maple.

KEN: I hate jelly chocolates.

GWEN: Oh, God, I hate jelly chocolates.

KEN: Well, that box is filled to the top with a six-year supply of jelly chocolates with their bottoms pushed in. And we are finally going to feed that crap to the fish.

GWEN: I hate it.

KEN: The fish will love it.

GWEN: Why don't you just throw them in the garbage?

KEN: It's against the law.

GWEN: Fuck 'em. Throw it in the garbage.

(Jed enters, from upstairs, in a suit.)

JOHN: We thought we'd make a party of it.

GWEN: So you go on to the party and Wes and I'll stay here.

(Screams when she sees Jed.)

JOHN: That's just Jed with clothes on and his hair combed. You know I'm not going to leave you. We go or we stay, I don't care.

GWEN: You come back for us after you've dumped the candy.

JUNE: Fine, now. Aunt Sally, can we do this?

SALLY: I'll go, June. Kenny said don't push me. You always push.

(Exits kitchen. June follows her Off.)

JOHN: They don't need this friction, honey, they're having a little problem.

GWEN: Well, I'm having a little problem, too. I don't believe for a minute it's candy in that box; I know perfectly well who's in there.

(Shirley enters from upstairs, wearing a different dress.)

Oh, that's fabulous.

SHIRLEY: I had it made for me in Paris.

(Phone rings. Jed gets up to answer it.)

KEN: That's long distance.

JOHN: I'll get it, it's gonna be for us.

JED: Please do.

(Has picked up the phone.)

JOHN: No, no, please.

JED: Hello? It's person-to-person.

(Hands phone to John, goes outside to the porch.)

JOHN:

(On phone.)

Yeah, hello.

(June re-enters from kitchen.)

JUNE:

(To Ken.)

She's talking to him, for God's sake.

KEN: Well, why not? Wouldn't you?

JUNE: She's talking into the refrigerator.

GWEN:

(Going to John.)

If that's the prick in Nashville, I want to talk with him.

JOHN: I've got it, I've got it. It's cool. Soon as I'm finished.

GWEN: Five fuckin' seconds.

JOHN: It's cool, it's cool.

GWEN: Well, Jesus, break my arm.

(Pause.)

Does anybody want a Quaalude? I'm really freaking out.

KEN: Darling, the town of Lebanon is not ready for you freaking out at their Independence Day celebration. That independent they aren't.

GWEN: Bullshit; if they can take you, they can take anything.

JUNE:

(To Ken.)

I don't know if Aunt Sally's going to do this tonight or not.

GWEN: You want me to talk to her?

KEN: No!

(To June.)

It's all up to her.

JUNE: You're the only person I know who can say "I'm not involved" in forty-five languages.

KEN: Seven or eight.

GWEN:

(To Shirley, who has Gwen's pillbox.)

Honey, you better not take one of those.

JUNE: Oh, let her have one.

SHIRLEY: I was merely trying to examine the pillbox.

GWEN: Yeah, but like one day you're trying to look at the box and the next day you're burned out and your hair won't hold a permanent.

(John hangs up the phone.)

You didn't hang up? I wanted to talk to him.

JOHN: No, it was just the engineer, checking our schedule.

GWEN: You haven't talked to Schwartzkoff, have you?

JOHN: Honey, it's the Fourth of July.

GWEN: Have you talked to Schwartzkoff?

JOHN: Everyone will be back to work tomorrow.

GWEN: Yeah, the creep. Every time I leave L.A., he calls the board. The last time I went to the hospital, I was having like my spleen stripped—

KEN: Hardly that—

GWEN: Well, who remembers, the son of a bitch called a meeting of the board to stab me in the back. He votes Daddy's stock, I can't vote it.

SHIRLEY: Stripped spleen?

KEN: Cassandra had it easy, you don't want to know.

GWEN: Cassandra? Oh, shit, don't you wish you knew all those myths? Like way down in some primordial place I've got this intuition that it's all in the myths, all the answers, if we could just get it together right.

WESTON: I was up in Canada, I got this book of Eskimo folk tales.

JUNE: Do you think we could go now, while nobody's freaking out?

JOHN: The Eskimos are in Alaska.

WESTON: No, they're both; they're in Canada, too. Did you know igloos aren't warm inside?

KEN: I hadn't thought about it before, but it makes sense.

WESTON: They're below freezing.

KEN: If it were above freezing, igloos would melt, wouldn't they?

WESTON: They have these blubber-oil lamps and these fur blankets and each other to keep themselves warm, and that's all.

JUNE: I'm sorry, I don't find that romantic at all.

GWEN: What's an Eskimo myth about?

WESTON: They're mostly about blubber. They're really these strange people. Like, they think very different from the way we think.

JOHN: I don't think I've ever been interested in the Eskimos, have you?

KEN: I don't think I have.

WESTON: There's this one folk story about this family. They had all this caribou meat stacked outside their igloo. Frozen, see. But it got so cold that their whole winter's supply of meat was frozen in one solid block of ice and none of the family could get at it. And they were all starving 'cause no one could break off any of this meat. So in a kind of last-ditch heroic effort this young Eskimo warrior goes outside and lets off this tremendous, powerful fart.

SHIRLEY: Oh, God.

WESTON: And thaws all the meat.

JUNE: That is very gross.

WESTON: But it stank so bad none of the family could eat it. And they all starved to death.

SHIRLEY: Oh, God.

KEN: This isn't, I hope, the basis for one of your songs.

JOHN: What kind of story is that supposed to be?

GWEN: I never heard that. Where did you hear that?

JUNE: That is gross.

WESTON: Isn't that gross?

JOHN: I mean, what kind of story is that?

WESTON: It's a folk story. I read it in this book.

JUNE: Even for an Eskimo.

JOHN: That isn't a folktale. Talley, have you ever heard a folktale like that?

KEN: Never. And I never wanted to.

WESTON: It is. That story has been handed down from father to son, generation to
    generation, verbally, for hundreds of years.

SHIRLEY: Oh, God.

KEN: That isn't a folktale, because there's no—

JOHN: What's the moral? There's no moral.

KEN: Exactly.

JOHN: Folktales have morals. There's no moral. There's no point . . .

WESTON: They couldn't eat the meat, so they starved to death.

JOHN: They were starving to death before he farted on the damn caribou meat.

WESTON: Well, then the moral is that that isn't the way to thaw caribou meat.

JOHN: No one could. It couldn't happen.

KEN: And if it could, it is not particularly beneficial.

JOHN: Heroic actions must have saving results.

WESTON: Who says?

KEN: It is the law of folktales.

JOHN: It's the law of heroes.

WESTON: Saving results for whom?

JOHN: For everybody. Like the little Dutch boy, for God's sake.

WESTON: Well, maybe these people are more realistic than the Greeks or the Dutch.

JOHN: It isn't realistic. It couldn't happen.

JUNE: And it's gross.

JOHN: And if it could happen, what do we learn from it? We have to learn something
    from a folktale.

KEN: That's a fable, but for the sake of argument.

WESTON: We learn that that isn't the way to thaw caribou meat.

JOHN: Who cares how to thaw caribou meat?

WESTON: The Eskimo cares! It's his staple diet!

JUNE: You are certifiable, you know that?

WESTON: I said it was this alien mind.

JOHN: This is the sort of thing you read in your own time.

KEN: Where did you find him, anyway?

WESTON: Skip it.

JOHN: No, you brought it up. I think it's very interesting. I mean the story is ridiculous,
    but the fact that you read it I find very interesting.

KEN: And retained it.

WESTON: Skip it. You obviously don't have the sensitivity to appreciate—

SHIRLEY: I have nothing but sensitivity and even I don't understand it.

WESTON: I thought it was a funny story to have been handed down from generation—

JOHN: I didn't find it funny at all. I see it as a tragedy. The entire family dies in the
    snow of starvation.

WESTON: They were dying already.

JOHN: That's what I said. It is a pointless, vulgar—

KEN: Scatological—

JOHN: —scatological story.

WESTON: I only thought it was interesting because it is a completely different culture.

JOHN: Wes, that isn't culture. That's hardship.

WESTON: No, no, it is. It's an alien culture. Like they call themselves "*The People*" and everybody else is "The *Other* People."

KEN: Wes, every people call themselves "The People," and everyone else is the other people.

WESTON: They have fifty different words for snow!

> *(Pause.)*

You don't think that shows a subtle mind?

KEN:

> *(Pause.)*

Wes, of course they have fifty different words for snow.

JOHN:

> *(Pause.)*

Their winters are fourteen months long.

KEN: They have nothing else to talk about.

JOHN: Snow is all there is.

KEN: They have to find some way to make it interesting.

JOHN: The Bedouins probably have fifty different words for sand.

WESTON: They probably do. They're a very interesting people.

> *(He slams out to the porch. Jed enters from porch.)*

KEN: They call themselves "The People" and . . .

JOHN:

> *(Yelling after him.)*

Wes, you know why you're not going to make a successful songwriter? Because you have too many interests.

GWEN: There's a song about syphilis, though; songs can be about anything.

SHIRLEY: You are so depressing.

> *(Jed hands Ken pill case, points to his watch.)*

GWEN: What are you taking?

KEN: We get these special little birth-control pills. In my condition we can't take chances.

JED: It's Percodan.

> *(Pours a glass of water from his watering can.)*

GWEN: That's like a horse-size painkiller.

KEN: We try to spice up our lives, what we can.

GWEN: Listen, when we heard that you were wounded, Kenny, I'll bet I never told you this—I called up, (I had to go right to the head of the damn Naval Hospital in Philadelphia). I didn't get off the phone till he told me Kenny's sexual performance would be in no way impaired.

KEN: Depends on what I'm expected to perform.

GWEN: Don't screw around, you know what I mean, your sexual performance . . .

KEN: . . . was absolutely in no way impaired; though we have had to cut out one show a night.

GWEN: I was so thankful, I went to church and actually lit a candle.

KEN: Appropriately.

SHIRLEY: I never intend to have sex in my life.

GWEN: Honey, it's not what you intend.

SHIRLEY: I am going to devote my life to art. The way Marie Curie devoted her life to science.

GWEN: Oh, science. I did that. I did.

JUNE: Darling, you didn't devote your life to science. You donated your body to science.

GWEN: Are those fireflies?

JUNE: Lightning bugs.

    (Gwen runs out to garden.)

JOHN: Who's Marie Curie?

SHIRLEY: She was only the only person to ever receive two Nobel Prizes for science.

JUNE:

    (With Shirley.)

    Two Nobel Prizes.

SHIRLEY: She was only the greatest scientist who ever lived.

JOHN: Okay, okay . . .

JUNE: Aunt Sally, can we go now?

JOHN: Sure, let's go. Gwen can stay with Wes and Shirley.

KEN: You don't have to stay with Gwen?

JED: No, he got his call from California. He doesn't have to hang around waiting for it any more.

SHIRLEY: I thought it was the engineer calling from Nashville.

JOHN: Come on, let's go. Before the squirt starts up again.

SHIRLEY: I am not starting up. I said I was going to be a great artist, which I have said repeatedly for the past solid year.

JUNE: With the emphasis on repeatedly.

SHIRLEY: And I am not a squirt!

JUNE: If I had it to do over again, I wouldn't give her to Aunt Sally. You live with a bat, you fly like a bat.

JOHN: You might have thought of that at the time.

SHIRLEY: I'm glad I was reared by Uncle Matt and Aunt Sally who had a true political and spiritual awareness and—

JUNE: Forget it. They did fine, you're doing fine; I'm doing fine.

JOHN: Yeah, but Matt's gone and Sally's going to California. You're gonna have her on your own, now: She's getting to that age when they start costing a lot of bread; a decent school, private tutors—

JUNE: Well, she'll just have to get along without the Sorbonne. Where was that bright idea ten years ago?

JOHN: You were out making a revolution, who could find you.

JUNE: I damn well did what I damn well had to do.

SHIRLEY: I don't think she was militant at all. I think you were just cross and angry.

GWEN: Are you kidding me? She was sensational.

JUNE:

> *(Shaken.)*
>
> You have no idea of the life we led.

GWEN: Really.

JUNE:

> *(With difficulty controlling herself.)*
>
> You've no idea of the country we almost made for you. The fact that I think it's all a crock now does not take away from what we almost achieved.
>
> *(Pause; then she runs upstairs; exits.)*

GWEN:

> *(To Shirley.)*
>
> Baby, you shouldn't—I mean, I think you're great, but you really don't tell someone that they aren't what they think they are. What's the profit?

SHIRLEY: Who?

GWEN: June was really something else. You would have been proud. It was her mom and dad made her send you to Sally.

SHIRLEY: I consider myself extremely lucky to have been raised by Sally and Matt.

GWEN: June was ready to carry you around like a flag. I mean, she was like Ma Barker or Belle Starr. She was really dangerous.

KEN: Mostly to herself.

GWEN: No, you don't know! Like they used to hitchhike to these rallies. I couldn't cut it. I couldn't bear the rejection. The first car passed me up, I was destroyed. I used to fly ahead and meet them. Also, I couldn't march 'cause I've never had a pair of shoes that were really comfortable.

JOHN: You were pretty good. She helped fire-bomb Pacific Gypsum, and it's her own company.

GWEN: One cocktail in the doorway of the building, broke about six windows.

SHIRLEY: And it was your own company?

GWEN: Oh, please, I was stoned. Who knew what we were doing? We were on TV, we were on the cover of *Time* magazine, it was a blast. Also it was such a crock, really. You go to an antiwar, end-the-war rally, right? You march to the White House.

JOHN: You take a taxi.

KEN: But nonetheless.

GWEN: Anyway. You get there. Five hundred thousand people, speaker's platforms, signs thick as a convention, everybody's high, we're bombed, the place is mobbed, everybody's on the lawn with their shirts off, boys, girls; they're eating chicken and tacos, the signs say: End the War, Ban the Bomb, Black Power and Gay Power and Women's Lib; the Nazi Party's there, the unions, demanding jobs, they got Chicano Power and Free the POWs and Free the Migrants, Allen Ginsberg is chanting Ommm over the loudspeakers, Coretta King is there: Jesus! How straight do you have to be to see that nothing is going to come from it? But don't knock your mother, 'cause she really believed that "Power to the People" song, and that hurts.

JOHN: It's all right, baby.
SHIRLEY:

>(Quietly determined.)

>I'm going to be the greatest artist Missouri has ever produced.

JOHN: Would that be so difficult?
SHIRLEY: The entire Midwest. What do you mean? There have been famous people—
world-famous people from—Tennessee Williams grew up in—
JOHN: Tennessee Williams is from Mississippi.
SHIRLEY: He may have been born there, but he grew up—
JOHN: And his people were from Tennessee, that's why—
SHIRLEY: He grew up not three blocks from where I live now! All his formative years!
JOHN: Okay, what do I know.
SHIRLEY: And Mark Twain. And Dreiser! And Vincent Price and Harry Truman! And
Betty Grable!

>(Gwen, Ken and John say "Grable" with her.)

>But me! Oh, God! Me! Me! Me! Me! I am going to be so great! Unqualified!
The greatest single artist the Midwest has ever known!

JOHN: Yes, yes, doing what?
SHIRLEY: Something astonishing! Just astonishing!
JOHN:

>(Overlapping.)

>In what field? What are you going to be?

SHIRLEY: A painter. Or a sculptor. Or a dancer! A writer! A conductor! A composer! An
actress! One of the arts! People will die. Certain people will literally have
cardiac arrest at the magnitude of my achievements.
JOHN: If you're going to be a dancer or a composer, you might matriculate into some
school before too much—
SHIRLEY: I will have you know that I intend to study for ten years, and then I will burst
forth on the world. And people will be abashed!
KEN: I don't doubt it for a minute.
SHIRLEY: Amazed!
GWEN: I think you're terrific.
SHIRLEY: Astonished! At my magnitude. Oh, God! Look! Is that she? Is that SHE? *Is that
she? Is it?* IT IS! IT IS SHE! IT IS SHE! AHHHHHHHHHHHHHHHHHHH!

>(She collapses on the floor. June enters from upstairs to landing.)

JOHN: She recognized herself on the street and fainted.
SHIRLEY:

>(Slowly getting to a sitting position; with great dignity.)

>She died dead of cardiac arrest and astonishment at the magnificence of my
achievement in my chosen field. Only Shakespeare, Michelangelo, Beethoven,
and Frank Lloyd Wright have risen to my heights before me.

JOHN: And Madame Curie.
SHIRLEY: Marie! Marie! She had a name of her own. Not Madame! Marie!

JUNE:

> *(Almost admiring.)*
>
> You are something else.

SHIRLEY:

> *(To John.)*
>
> And when I first achieved my first achievements I was eleven years younger than you are now.
>
> *(She sweeps to the front door and out to the porch. Sally enters from kitchen with an enormous chocolates box.)*

GWEN: Boy, if I had been like that.

SHIRLEY: Weston . . .

JUNE: Well, we're all here now.

KEN: Shhhh.

> *(They listen.)*

SHIRLEY:

> *(On the porch to Wes.)*
>
> As we'll be traveling to Nashville together, I don't want you to think I haven't noticed the way you look at me. But I believe in putting everything on the line, and I could never seriously consider marrying you, Weston Hurley. All her life until she was thirty-one and married Matthew Friedman, my Aunt Sally lived with the impossible handicap of being named Sally Talley. And if I married you, I'd be Shirley Hurley.
>
> *(She runs Off into the garden.)*

KEN: Aunt Sally, I see you've got Uncle Matt there in your lap. I don't think we should put this off.

SALLY:

> *(Long pause.)*
>
> They all hated him because he was a Jew. Your mother, your father, my folks, the whole damn town hated him.

JUNE: He kept coming back down here.

SALLY: Oh, nothing bothered him except when it bothered me. And if it didn't bother him, it didn't bother me. He liked young people. Shirley was a joy. He was terribly concerned about Gwen. He was very upset with Kenny for going to Vietnam and getting your legs blown off. But I know he was glad when you met Jed. People said he didn't love this country because he wasn't afraid to speak his mind.

JOHN: They say a lot.

SALLY: I think they were right. I don't think he loved this country a bit. He loved the countryside.

> *(Weston is heard on porch strumming "Anytime.")*

No, I'm sorry. I know you all liked him, and you don't mean to push, but I'm not going to dump Matt's ashes down in that rotting boathouse: We'd probably all break our necks anyway. Matt fell through those boards more than thirty years ago.

KEN: It doesn't really matter where, does it? Matt said he didn't want you to keep them, you know why—

SALLY: Kenny, I know what you're planning. Well, do it: The place belongs to you for what you can get from it, but I want you to know I'm damned angry with you. And if that's your scheme, then Matt doesn't belong here.

JUNE:

(To Sally.)

Darling, if you don't go tonight, you'll think of some reason to wait the whole year again.

KEN: Sally, it makes no difference to me, but Matt would—

SALLY: Altogether too many things make no difference to you all of a sudden, Kenny.

JED: A scheme?

SALLY: Exactly. And now he thinks he isn't interested in teaching anymore—He's talking about Spain and Greece—

KEN: Sally, damn it—

JED: That's okay, let him fantasize.

SALLY:

(To Jed.)

After all these people have gone to the dance, I want to talk to you. Now everybody go on.

JUNE: Sally, you can't take that box to California. They won't let you into the state.

SALLY: I don't want you to badger me. You people go dance. I'm going to get ready for bed.

(She exits to her bedroom.)

JUNE: Well, to hell with it.

GWEN: Is Sally a little—I mean, not that everybody isn't.

JED: She's all right.

JUNE: I don't intend to come here every year waiting for—I told Dad I'd get her to dump the damn ashes before she came out there, if I had to dump them myself.

(She storms outside to the porch.)

KEN: June!

JED: What scheme?

KEN: Nothing, nothing, we'll talk tomorrow.

JED: There's getting to be a pretty long list of things we're going to talk about tomorrow.

KEN: I know. *Later.*

JOHN: Hey, come on, the Lebanon band must be starting to boogie down across the river.

JED: I'm going to change if it's off for tonight.

KEN: Might as well.

GWEN: Oh, listen, about your place.

KEN: Darling . . .

GWEN: Well, Sally blew it, didn't she? Jed, if we put in an airstrip up on the hill, we wouldn't fuck up your garden, would we?

JED: No, not at all. But it takes twenty years for a garden to mature into anything; we only started three years ago; you don't have to follow through with it—do anything you want.

(Exits upstairs.)

GWEN: Hell, no, we can hire gardeners.

JOHN: Write down what you got in mind. We'll do it.

KEN: Hey, we'll talk.

JOHN: Hey, June.

(Jed is gone; June returns.)

JOHN: What say we check out the fairgrounds. The band's already started. Hey, look at this. Just the four of us. How about that.

JUNE: Son-of-a-bitch; together again.

GWEN: Oh, Jesus, I loved the four of us. That was like the greatest period of my life.

JUNE: Let's don't rerun that again. I couldn't take it.

GWEN: You should have stayed with us; we had like our own little commune . . . Then Kenny chickened out. John and I ended up by ourselves on that fucking European tour just like—not what we'd planned at all.

JOHN: Let's go celebrate. Come on.

JUNE: You three go on.

KEN: Not tonight. I've got to turn in. I've got to work tomorrow afternoon. I haven't exercised today. Not tonight.

GWEN: This is the last night we're here.

JOHN: I bet that really rips them up.

KEN: No, I'm just beat.

JOHN: Come on, June, let's go.

JUNE: You go on.

JOHN:

(To Gwen.)

Come on, babe, I want to show you the nightlife around here.

KEN: Crickets,

JUNE: Frogs,

KEN: Chiggers,

JUNE: Owls.

JOHN: You need a sweater, need a coat?

GWEN: No, I'm fine.

JOHN: You sure, now?

GWEN: I'm sure.

JUNE: We'll see you in the morning.

GWEN: Yeah, see you tomorrow.

JOHN: Hey, Wes, we're gone.

(Gwen and John exit.)

JUNE: Those two exhaust me.

KEN: Get over it.

JUNE: Easy said.

(*Looks at Ken for a long moment. Then gets up and turns off the light on Ken's desk. Sally reappears on porch, dressed in her nightgown and robe.*)

WESTON: Hey, Sally, what's happening?
SALLY: It didn't rain. There's even going to be a moon. Look at that sky.
JUNE: I'll see you in the morning.

(*She goes upstairs.*)

KEN: Good night.
SALLY: You haven't seen anything?
WESTON: Wasn't really lookin'.
SALLY:

(*To the sky.*)

We know you're up there. We won't hurt you. We want to see you.
WESTON: We'd like to talk with you.
SALLY: You can trust us.
WESTON: No shit.
KEN:

(*Gets up. Picks up his crutches.*)

With the stomach, not the arms.

(*Moves to the Center of the room.*)

Cha-cha-cha.
SALLY: Please show yourself to us again. We won't tell a soul!

(*Painfully Ken gets into a sitting position in the middle of the floor. He stretches out on his back to rest a moment. Then begins sit-ups. Jed enters from upstairs. Pause.*)

No. Not tonight.

(*To Weston.*)

Good night.

(*To Ken.*)

Good night, in there.

KEN:

(*Who has heard her.*)

Night doll; go to bed.
JED: Good night Sally.
SALLY:

(*To the sky.*)

Good night.

(*She goes off into the garden. Weston continues to play. Ken is panting very hard.*)

KEN:

> *(Exhausted.)*

> Oh, God . . . I'm just knocked out. I really . . . have done myself . . . in.

JED: So what do we do? You want to sell the house and run?

KEN: I can't teach those kids, Jed . . . We can't stay here . . . I can't walk into a classroom again . . .

> *(Jed picks him up, holding him in his arms. Leaning his head against him.)*

> I really have knocked myself out.

> *(Jed holds him for a moment, then carries him upstairs.)*

JED: Hang in there.

> *(Weston continues to play for a moment.)*

> Curtain

> End of Act One

ACT II

The porch. Jed is sitting in the sunshine, referring back and forth between two books, trying to compose a letter on a legal-size yellow pad. A bell tolls in the distance, five seconds between each deep, heavy stroke.

Shirley enters. She enjoys being alone with Jed for a moment. She looks out over the garden, quite forgetting that Jed does not see her there. She notices the bell.

SHIRLEY: Oh! Listen!

JED:

> *(Jumps a foot.)*

> Oh, God.

SHIRLEY: "Ask not for whom the bell tolls . . . It tolls for . . ."

JED:

> *(Overlap.)*

> It tolls for Harley Campbell.

SHIRLEY: Who?

JED: Your Aunt Sally went to the funeral. They ring the bell before the service and after the service.

SHIRLEY: Oh. Oh, God, now it sounds horrible. Oh, God, that's mournful.

JED: If the man made more than a hundred thousand a year and left a widow, they ring it all during the service as well.

SHIRLEY: We, of course, are the first.

JED: First?

SHIRLEY: To arise this morning.

JED: You're the last. You're up in time for brunch.

GWEN:

> *(Inside, on phone.)*

> What the fuck for, dial one?

SHIRLEY: Gwen is up?

JED: Yeah. And on the phone.

SHIRLEY: Uncle Kenny's up?

JED: Yeah, Sally and I had breakfast at seven and did a few things.

SHIRLEY: Like what?

JED: Never mind. And I drove her to church, woke up Ken, and we made an herbal anti-fungus concoction guaranteed to fail, and sprayed thirty-five phlox plants. With Wes's, uh . . . supervision.

SHIRLEY:

> *(Adjusts.)*

> Oh. Yes . . . I slept . . . fitfully. I tossed, I . . .

JED: Turned?

SHIRLEY: I had this really weird dream. I was being chased by a deer. All through the
woods, over bridges, this huge deer. What does a dream like that mean?

JED: Did he have antlers?

SHIRLEY: I don't remember. Why?

(Jed goes back to his books.)

JED: If you happen to dream about seven fat cows and seven lean cows, I know what
that one means.

SHIRLEY: I would never dream of a cow.

JED: Not a feisty young heifer? Jumping fences, trying to get into the corn?

SHIRLEY: Oh, please. I certainly hope you don't think of me like that! I am not a
common cow! I am a . . . flower, Jed. Slowly and frighteningly opening her
petals onto the spring morning. A trimu-a-timulus, a timu—an opening bud.

JED: A mimulus. You're probably a mimulus.

SHIRLEY: What's a mimulus?

JED: Mimulus is a wildflower. Pinkish-yellow, the monkey flower, they call—

SHIRLEY: No, not that one. Not a monkey flower! I am a . . .

JED: What?

SHIRLEY: Well not—I don't know. And it's important, too. But . . . I can *see* it. A nearly
white, small, single . . .

JED: What about an apple blossom? The first tree of spring to—

SHIRLEY: No, oh, God, no. And grow into an apple. A fat, hard, red, bloated, tasteless
apple? For some crone to bake in a pie for her ditchdigger husband to ear
without even knowing it? Oh, God. Never. I'm more than likely the
daughter of Che Guevara or Lawrence Ferlinghetti. My mother was very
promiscuous.

JED: So I've heard.

SHIRLEY:

(Thinks.)

I am a blossom that opens for one day only . . . and I fall. I am not
pollinared. It's too early for the bees. They don't find me. And I fade. Dropping
my petals one by . . . What kind of flower is that?

(He thinks a moment.)

A wild rose?

JED: No, you wouldn't flower till May at the earliest. There'd be bees lined up around
the block.

SHIRLEY: Well, *what?* Daisies are when?

JED: No.

SHIRLEY: Peony?

JED: There are some anemones . . . that bloom in March.

SHIRLEY: An anemone . . .

JED: The original ones are from Greece, so they're all claimed by heroes who fell in
battle and their blood seeped into the ground and anemones sprang up, but I
think they've found one or two somewhere else that haven't been claimed yet.

SHIRLEY: Do you have a picture of it?

JED: It's around; I'll look it up.

SHIRLEY:

> *(Hand on sleeve.)*

> Jed. Thank you. This is, you know, very important to me.

JED:

> *(Mock seriousness.)*

> Shirley. It's important to us all.

SHIRLEY: I know.

JED: We don't dwell on it because we try to spare you the pressure of all our expectations. We multitudes.

SHIRLEY: I know. But don't. Don't spare me. It makes me strong.

GWEN:

> *(Off, on phone.)*

> Yea, well screw you, too. I don't like the way you're handling this whole thing.

> *(Slams phone down.)*

KEN:

> *(Coming out.)*

> She hasn't been off the phone all morning. Your mother was up at the crack of ten and is baking bath buns.

JED: Bath buns?

SHIRLEY: Believe me, you don't want to know. God, when she gets domestic, there's no hope.

KEN: She speaks not with forked tongue.

JED: I'm no good at this; you'd better reconsider.

KEN: No way, do it yourself.

SHIRLEY: What are you doing?

JED: I'm trying to answer a letter.

KEN: I think there's a harpy in the bottom of our garden.

> *(Yelling.)*

> Yo! Aunt Sally!

SALLY:

> *(Offstage.)*

> I see you, I see you. Don't rush me.

KEN: She's at the roses again.

SHIRLEY: I retired late, of course, I was packing.

JED: Thought you were here for another two weeks.

SHIRLEY: I will probably return after only a few days; I can't imagine Nashville to hold anything of real interest.

KEN: I'm quite sure the City of Nashville is not ready for you.

JUNE:

> *(Offstage)*

> Outside, everyone outside. This is just the first batch.

KEN:

> *(To Sally.)*
>
> I thought you were going to Old Man Campbell's funeral . . .

SALLY:

> *(Entering.)*
>
> Oh, fine. Old Man Campbell. Imagine Harley Campbell being Old Man Campbell. No, no, I couldn't do it. That's the hottest place I've ever been in my life. The minister is mad at the whole congregation. They voted down a new air conditioner, so he shut the old one off and told them it broke. He's trying to sweat them out. They'll never give in. A good battle, especially if it's over money, brings out the stoic in them.

JUNE:

> *(In and out.)*
>
> This is just the first batch; another coming.

SHIRLEY: Gird your loins; Mom's making bath buns.

SALLY: Oh, dear. That's quite a walk.

KEN: Looks like it's done you in.

SALLY: Don't look at me.

KEN: Why didn't you call someone to pick you up?

JED:

> *(Overlapping.)*
>
> I could have—

SALLY:

> *(To Jed.)*
>
> I walked that road to school before even your mother was born.

KEN: You didn't know his mother. She could have been fifty. He might have been the— what's the expression?

JED: Last fruit on the tree.

KEN: I wasn't going to say that.

SALLY: I'm afraid I've done something very stupid, Jed.

JED: How's that?

SALLY: Never mind.

KEN: What are you two plotting?

SALLY: Never mind. What terrible houses they've built along the road. Windows right out to the street. I'd feel naked as a jay. Oh, dear.

KEN: Don't walk that again. There's always someone here to drive you.

SHIRLEY:

> *(With a letter Jed has received.)*
>
> That's very impressive. "Sissinghurst Castle. Property of the National Trust."

JED: Come on.

KEN: The lucky bastards.

SHIRLEY: Have you been there?

JED: Huh? Yeah.

KEN: Before we laid out the garden, we took a tour of the competition.

SHIRLEY: Is it fabulous?

JED: It's fabulous.

SHIRLEY: "Jed Jenkins, Esquire . . ."

JED: In other words, not Sir or Lord.

SHIRLEY: "First of all, we are writing to confirm the identification of your rediscovery of the Slater's Crimson China rose . . ."

KEN: Thank you so very much, though actually we did know that from the Royal Horticultural Society.

SHIRLEY: It's very exciting to have discovered a rose everyone thought was lost ages ago. How did it get here?

KEN: We assume someone planted it.

SHIRLEY: "Which bloomed in our test garden this summer and will be moved to a prominent position in the rose garden this autumn."

KEN: Do you love it? Only the greatest rose garden in the world.

SHIRLEY: How did they get it?

KEN: We sent it to them.

JED: They asked us for it.

SHIRLEY: "And second—" Should that be "second of all?"

KEN: Certainly not. Never.

SHIRLEY: "Second we would like to inform you that—"

GWEN:

(Entering, followed by Weston.)

Oh, God, would you feel that fuckin' sun? Don't let me fall asleep. I fry like a starfish.

(Flops down in the sun.)

SHIRLEY: "Second we would like to inform you that the Phyle-Hastings Nursery has—"

GWEN: I read that letter and they're so full of it.

SHIRLEY: If you please.

GWEN: Sorry. Hand me a cup.

SHIRLEY: ". . . Nursery has requested the honor of adding this rose to their catalogue so it can once again be propagated and grown as it deserves. You of course will be credited with this important rediscovery . . ."

JED:

(Embarrassed.)

Blah, blah, blah, blah.

GWEN:

(Overlapping.)

They are so full of it. No way, baby—

SHIRLEY:

(Overlapping.)

He rediscovered it, I don't know why not.

GWEN: You check with a lawyer before you sign anything. The limeys would as soon rip you off as look at you.

KEN: They did raise it, after all.

GWEN: Right, and lost it. Fuck 'em. They want it so bad they can pay for it. Not without a commission. Have you got Sweet 'n' Low? Oh, forget it.

SHIRLEY: How was the celebration?

GWEN: When?

SHIRLEY: The fireworks you went to last night?

GWEN: Oh, hey, I wanted to come back and get you. It was great. There—

SHIRLEY: They were pretty?

GWEN: —were these really—what? The fireworks? You've never seen anything so lame in your life.

KEN: Present company always excepted.

GWEN: There were these—

(Slaps him.)

—field hands—

KEN:

(Overlapping.)

You would strike a crippled fairy.

GWEN: These really randy, country Republican high school juniors drinking beer out of a paper sack.

SALLY: I remember.

GWEN: You've never seen a hornier

SHIRLEY: I would not have been interested.

GWEN: . . . collection of male brawniness in—oh, God, it was John and Kenny when we were in Berkeley. They were exactly the same randy farmhands when we first met.

KEN: Me? A farmhand? Son of my father who never farmed a day in his life?

GWEN: Yeah, and John's father was a dentist! They even look like you looked then. They still have long hair.

KEN: John and I moved in quite a different circle from your—

GWEN: You're such a snob.

KEN: We were quite a different social stratum from the horny river trash you're trying to associate with us.

GWEN: Horny. River. Trash! That's exactly what they were. And you were exactly like that.

(Hits his leg.)

Ouch!

KEN: Fiberglass! Light but strong.

GWEN: —You can't tell me you didn't drink beer out of a sack. You jerked off behind the same bushes they do.

KEN: I profess to have no memory of the bushes I jerked off behind.

JED: Very fickle.

KEN: Well, I warned you.

(John enters.)

GWEN: Honey, good, tell them. There was one blond stud—what was his name, you said you knew him.

JOHN: Jim Pendergast's little brother. Only he's assumed a very sinister style.

KEN: Decidedly unstable family.

GWEN: I don't care, he was gorgeous. Shirley would have loved him.

SHIRLEY: I don't think about men physically. I never have. I think about all people spiritually.

GWEN: I know, but you gotta get over that real quick.

(To John.)

Oh, baby, at noon our time you gotta call Schwartzkoff, because they're really screwing up. I don't care if we have to fly back to L.A. tonight, we have to straighten him out.

JOHN: He called here? Why didn't I hear—

GWEN: I called him, 'cause we hadn't heard from him and when he's silent for three days it means he's got something up—

JOHN: Honey, we got a recording session—

GWEN: I don't care. I have to think about one thing at a time. They aren't going to do what we want unless we really lean on him.

JOHN: He just panics. I told you it'll be all right. I'll worry about that. You worry about Nashville.

GWEN:

(Backing down a bit.)

No lie, though, he started in on the inner politics of Tasmania and the state wages precedent, and the whole song all over again. He's really not listening to us at all.

(June comes in with breakfast.)

JUNE: Here it is.

JOHN: I know. I'll talk to him. You worry about you.

GWEN: Lean on the son of a bitch. He doesn't have a leg to stand on.

KEN: Begging my pardon.

JOHN:

(To Ken.)

Hey, your name's going to be mud, too.

KEN: Why's that? Not that I mind. Kenneth Mudd.

JOHN: Mudd Talley, I think. We talked to Mac. Boy, he never changes.

GWEN: Oh, yeah, we talked to your boss. What a prick.

JUNE: Wouldn't you know he'd be there.

SHIRLEY: Who's Mac?

(Jed gestures inside. Sally shakes her head.)

JUNE: Mac McConnell; principal of the high school.

KEN: Superintendent, now.

JUNE: God, I hated him almost as much as he hated me.

GWEN: No, he said he'd like to see you while you're down.

JUNE: No way.

GWEN: It was John he hated. Said he suspected him of cheating on tests.

JOHN: You believe him still harping on that after ten years?

SHIRLEY: Why is Uncle Ken's name mud?

JOHN: He still thinks you're going to be teaching there this fall.

KEN: He's very mistaken.

JOHN: You ought to call him.

JED: What did you tell him?

JOHN: I'm not going to tell him nothing. Mac thinks you're happy as a pig in shit.

SHIRLEY: Please, I'm trying to eat Mother's cooking.

GWEN: He was very excited about one of his students returning to the fold.

KEN: The prospect excites me not at all.

JUNE: Sally, scrambled eggs, hot bath buns?

SALLY: No, thanks.

GWEN: Listen, who can know anything? When did we see you in New York?

JED: Three years ago.

GWEN: Was that three years ago? That was all you were talking about. Jed was going to build this garden, you were going to teach.

KEN: Don't start on that again.

JUNE: Actually, they had a little Fete to welcome the returning Vet two weeks ago—and Kenny was taken around to meet all his classes—

KEN:

(Overlapping.)

Yes, Jed and I visited that lovely new building. Dear old Mac was a little edgy about Jed, he couldn't quite put that together—

JED: I think he was coming pretty close.

KEN: Probably be thrilled. An opportunity to exhibit his liberal tolerance. But other than that, I found him quite pleasantly condescending, didn't you.

JED: No complaints. Said he liked gardens.

JUNE: And Ken had the pleasure of being introduced to the four classes he would be teaching this fall.

JED: Well, actually only three—

KEN:

(Annoyed.)

I begged off the fourth and went back to the car.

JED: Went in full of piss and vinegar, came out white as a sheet.

KEN: I just wasn't quite ready for them; or they certainly weren't ready for me. We don't have any milk out here, I can't drink—

GWEN: What did they do?

JED: He just overreacted.

KEN:

(Overreacting.)

I did not overreact! June, could you hand me my—crutches.

JUNE:

(Overreacting.)

No one had prepared them for him—Mac has always been about as tactful—

KEN:

(Biting.)

No, I think it was more a question of a sincere lack of rapport.

GWEN: A lot of messy questions, right?

KEN: No, I was quite prepared for the messy questions. Dry urbanity; humorous self-deprecation.

JED: The kids wouldn't look at him.

(Pause. Nobody looks up.)

KEN: Which God knows I should have been prepared for, but for some reason I was not.

JOHN: They were grossed out, for God's sake.

KEN: Well, if I had some deep-seated need to teach, trying to get at Johnny Young's speech problems will fulfill that quite nicely for a few more weeks.

GWEN: That's all too fuckin' humanitarian; I never trust that gig—it's creepy.

KEN: Not at all, the gimp leading the gimp; we form a very cozy symposium.

JOHN: So, do both.

JUNE: Came running back here.

KEN: Hardly running.

JUNE: Crawled into a closet.

KEN: Hardly a closet.

JUNE: And has been panic-stricken ever since.

WESTON:

(After a pause.)

Out of a paper sack?

GWEN: Yeah, passing these quart beer bottles in paper sacks. All very covert. None of them over seventeen. Strictly from twenty-four-hour hard-ons.

JOHN: The lucky stiffs.

KEN: Lucky now to get it up in twenty-four hours. Knock on wood.

(Hits his leg.)

WESTON: Knock on wood? Knock on wood?

GWEN: I thought you said they were fiberglass.

KEN: A technicality.

WESTON: Oh, shit.

SHIRLEY: If you please.

GWEN: Oh, you're too much. We told you Kenny had wooden legs from his Vietnam—

KEN: "Tour," we call it.

WESTON: Oh, wow.

KEN: Heavy, huh?

WESTON: Oh, wow. I thought you meant he could drink a lot of sake.

JOHN: That would be a hollow leg.

WESTON: No shit. How come?

KEN: Well, it was either accept their kind offer of a prosthetics device or find a position as a very cumbersome basketball.

SHIRLEY: Oh, no.

KEN: And I opted for a semblance of mobility.

JUNE: Unless you could handpick both basketball teams.

KEN: No, no, I've never liked being tossed around by a bunch of sweaty ectomorphs.

JUNE: I don't know. I always thought of John as a sweaty ectomorph.

KEN: Oh, please. That was many moons ago.

JUNE: Only fifteen years.

SHIRLEY AND WESTON: *Only* fifteen years?

JOHN: But those were pretty hot years back in Berkeley.

KEN: One had to move with the times.

> *(Jed goes into the house.)*

GWEN: It couldn't have been all that hot with Kenny. You were sleeping with June at the same time.

SHIRLEY: No! Oh, ugh! How could you. Oh, gwackk! You did it with him?

JUNE: I thought she was talking about me.

> *(To Shirley.)*

> Oh, shut up; you're too much.

JOHN: Everyone did it with June.

GWEN: Your mother was a bigger Pop-tart than I was.

KEN: Not at all, not till after you moved in and she started running with the—what do you call them?

SALLY: The wrong crowd, I think.

KEN: When we were in school here we used to sleep over and diddle each other.

JOHN: We were twelve years old.

SALLY: The two you?

JUNE: The three of us.

SHIRLEY: Oh, that's—

SALLY: It certainly is.

KEN: I'd been in love with you for years.

JOHN: You were not. That was just diddling.

KEN: Oh, yeah, remember the double date when you couldn't get Margy Majors to go all the way—

JOHN: One time. And I was drunk.

KEN: Well, I wasn't. I had planned it all week. I knew damn well you weren't going to get anywhere with Margy.

GWEN: Oh, God. Remember going all the way!

KEN: I must have been in love with you at least two years before we ran off to Berkeley. He was never out of this V-neck, sky-blue cashmere sweater, full of holes.

JOHN: Mostly from you poking your finger in them.

GWEN: He's ticklish.

JUNE: Very.

KEN: Well, then you discovered the Copper Queen.

GWEN: That would be me.

JUNE: Nobody said John didn't know a good thing when he saw it.

GWEN: Damn straight.

> *(Jed returns with milk and Ken's cane.)*

KEN: And they all lived happily ever after.

GWEN: Oh, I loved us then. I remember once we bought twenty dollars' worth of daffodils and your mother and I ran up and down on the Nimitz Freeway giving them to all the stalled drivers.

WESTON: Why?

GWEN: Why? June had decided they were wonderful.

JUNE: Unfortunately, they hated us. The traffic started moving; we nearly got run down.

KEN: You were decidedly before your time.

GWEN: That fuckin' war! Damn, it fucked us. It broke my heart when we weren't together. If only you'd come with us to Europe everything would have been so different. The whole idea was going off to escape from your draft thing. I'll never forgive you for chickening out on that.

KEN: I didn't chicken out; you were just afraid of the competition.

GWEN: You would never have been in Nam, you wouldn't have been injured; June wouldn't have gotten militant and estranged from us.

WESTON: I read this book. Like about war experiences in Nam? It said shock and dope were like common. In the goddamned reading room; Fairleigh Dickinson University.

KEN:

(To Shirley.)

I defy anyone to diagram that sentence.

WESTON: Really heavy.

KEN: The reading room at Fairleigh Dickinson was heavy? Vietnam was heavy or the book was heavy.

WESTON: You were there, man, I can't tell you.

KEN: Nothing was common except the American troops, and we were very common indeed.

WESTON: Like you're trying to be cool, but you still carry it around.

KEN: However awkwardly.

SALLY: Your mother was very proud that you went. I could have killed her.

KEN: Wasn't that interesting? I thought so, too. And ashamed that I came back.

SHIRLEY: Oh, that isn't true.

JUNE: The hell it ain't.   SALLY: Don't kid yourself.

WESTON: You still think about it.

KEN: I don't wake up screaming any more from visions of my buddies floating through the blue sky in pieces, if that's what you mean . . .

WESTON: Oh, shit.

KEN: Exactly that. The dream is more likely of some goddamned general moving down the row of beds in the hospital, handing our medals like aspirin. That's the first thing I saw when I regained consciousness.

JUNE: Beating the bushes for heroes.

SHIRLEY: Uncle Ken has five medals.

KEN: You may not be proud of that.

WESTON: What was the saving grace?

KEN: Beg pardon?

WESTON: You said a heroic action had to have a saving grace.

KEN: Silliest thing I ever heard of—

WESTON: Like with the Eskimo, you said there was no saving grace in—

KEN: Oh, Weston, doll, I'm all in favor of your Eskimo hero. I think he was a man among men. I completely blame the family. You see, if you had said that the warrior was flatulent on the walrus blubber . . .

WESTON: —caribou meat—

KEN: . . . Be that as it may, and it stank so bad that the family could hardly eat it, but they managed and survived, we could perhaps accept that as an unpleasant but not altogether vainglorious moment in the history of the Eskimo. I thought at the time that the family was too picayune for a myth.

WESTON: Oh.

KEN: See?

WESTON: Yeah.

KEN: Yeah. The family disappointed me deeply.

WESTON: So the saving grace—

KEN: —would have been surviving. Don't choke on it, don't turn up your nose, swallow it and live, baby.

WESTON: Even if it stinks, man.

KEN: Dig it.

WESTON: Right on.

KEN: They could have forever after been known as the family who bravely ate the fart-thawed meat and went on to become . . .

SALLY: —vegetarians.

JOHN: Baby, we gotta pack if we're going to hit the road by three this afternoon.

JUNE: That'll get you there by when?

JOHN: Five. We're driving to Springfield, hopping a plane.

JUNE: Oh, of course you are.

(Jed begins to sing: "Hit the road, Jack.")

SHIRLEY: I probably won't stay with you more than a few days; I can just crowd you in as it is.

GWEN: We go everywhere with an open-return ticket.

JUNE: This one is returning before she leaves.

SHIRLEY: There's nothing pressing this week.

JUNE: Can it.

SHIRLEY: What do you mean, can it?

GWEN: I thought you'd decided to let her come. Johnny, you said . . .

JUNE: The farthest thing from my mind. I wouldn't consider it.

GWEN: We'll take good care of her. Johnny promised me—

JUNE: No, not this time; another time.

SHIRLEY: What do you mean? You can't!

JUNE: Just cool it, because you're not going.

SHIRLEY: When have I ever had the opportunity to go some place? This could be the beginning of a whole new horizon for me.

JUNE: The one thing I can't bring myself to do is discipline the brat. I hated Mom for that.

SHIRLEY: Well, you had good reason!

JUNE: We'll discuss it some other time.

SHIRLEY: We won't discuss it at all!

(Storming out.)

I am twenty-one years old and I can do what I want to do!

WESTON: Am I going to have time to help with the cinders?

KEN: Sure.

JOHN: The what?

WESTON: Cinders. They got a problem in their garden. I'm gonna help them out.

JOHN: Yeah? Well, sorry, Jed, there goes the neighborhood. With Wes loose out there, that ought to do it.

WESTON: I helped them spray the—what was it?

JED: Phlox.

WESTON: The phlox for mold—

JED: Mildew.

WESTON: —for mildew this morning. This afternoon we got to get over to the school where Talley is going to teach . . .

KEN: . . . is not going to teach.

WESTON: —yeah, and get a load of cinders, and spread them around the—what was it?

JED: Penstemon.

WESTON: Gonna spread them around the penstemon, so the—what was it?

JED: Slugs.

WESTON: —so the slugs can't get at them. See, they got these soft vulnerable bellies—

JOHN: The penstemon?

WESTON: No, the—

> (To Weston.)

JED: Slugs.

WESTON: The slugs. They don't like to crawl over the cinders. You spread the cinders around the plant, it keeps them off it.

JOHN: That's . . . ingenious.

WESTON: Yeah, well, you can laugh, but I saw the damage they done just last night. When it's wet like it's been here, the—

JOHN: Slugs?

WESTON: —the slugs become this major problem. And see, we got to get it done before tonight, see, because they come out as soon as it gets dark. They don't like the light, see.

JOHN: Really.

WESTON: Sure.

JOHN: Why don't you put a light in the garden?

JED: Then the eggplant wouldn't set flower. It requires a period of six hours unbroken dark to set—

JOHN: Jed, you're going to tell me about photosynthesis.

JED: Photoperiod.

JOHN: I don't want to know about photosynthesis.

JED: Photoperiod.

JUNE: Oh, God . . .

JOHN: What?

JUNE: I was just imagining having a vulnerable belly, crawling over cinders.

WESTON: No, see, you can't think like that.

GWEN: Fuck it, kill 'em. They're ruining the garden.

WESTON: Right, you gotta be like cold-blooded and ruthless. Otherwise, you won't have any—what is it?

GWEN, JUNE, AND JOHN: Penstemon.

WESTON: Otherwise, you won't have any penstemon. They're really voracious. They eat six times their weight every night. I was reading one of Jed's books.

KEN: I wonder what a slug weighs.

WESTON: It didn't say.

KEN: Oh, well . . .

WESTON: We could catch one and weigh it.

KEN: Does anyone have something I could open a vein with?

WESTON: You know what they're trying to make here? What's the name of that garden
    in England? The one we didn't see.

JOHN: We didn't see any of them.

WESTON: The one we could have seen, though.

JOHN: I don't remember.

WESTON: Well, that's the one they're trying to make here.

SHIRLEY:

(Who has been standing in doorway.)

Sissinghurst Castle Gardens. They're a property of the National Trust.

WESTON: Isn't that far out?

GWEN: You know what would be even better? Just let it all go wild. Let whatever
    happens to grow all go wild.

JED: That would be one answer.

(The phone rings inside.)

GWEN: Oh, shit. That's Schwartzkoff calling back because I hung up on him.

KEN: It isn't long-distance.

GWEN: Yes, it will be. John, you talk to him. He just keeps saying the same thing
    to me.

KEN: It isn't long—

JOHN: Honey, you don't hang up on someone who's calling from the Coast—

(He goes into house to phone.)

GWEN:

(Yelling.)

I don't care. He was calling me capricious. I felt like showing him what
capricious was.

(To them.)

I will never be able to understand why I can't do what I please with my own
company.

JOHN: Ken, you or June, either one.

JUNE: I'll get it.

GWEN: It's like zero percent of the whole—conglomerate.

JOHN: We going swimming later?

JUNE: I can answer the phone all by myself.

JOHN: We've hardly had a chance to talk this whole visit.

JUNE: That really rips me up.

SHIRLEY: You own an entire company by yourself?

GWEN: Most of the like branches I own like nothing. Like six percent or fifteen
    percent. But Helena Copper is one hundred percent mine. Mom left it to me,

damn it. I was up there. Oh, God, they loved me. I made a speech, they just
went crazy. I told them what I wanted to do, no shit, they carried me around
the meeting hall over their heads, like a fuckin' astronaut.

KEN: What did you promise them?

GWEN: Oh, well, see the company makes all this money, but like the Surrogate won't
let me raise the—

(John is back, listening in the doorway.)

—salaries because of the labor situation in the state—

JOHN: In the industry.

GWEN: Is it the industry? Anyway, like, you remember when we read Marx? What
pissed Marx off was the owners making money off the workers, just because the
owners own the factory.

KEN: Exploitation of, yes—

GWEN: I may have failed economic philosophy, but I got that. Well, so I said I'd give
them a bonus after the year of all the profit. But they had to divide it evenly, file
clerks get as much as managers. They flipped.

SALLY: I'll bet.

KEN: Only what?

GWEN: Only Schwartzkoff, the bastard, is trying to take the profit from Helena Copper
and pay for—

JOHN: Capital improvements—

GWEN: Capital improvements in the other branches and claim there aren't any profits
this year.

KEN: And that surprises you?

JOHN: A hair illegal, but done all the time.

GWEN: Well, that really pisses me 'cause those people were great to us. They gave us a
picnic. We had pigs' feet. Wasn't it pigs' feet, John?

JOHN: It certainly tasted like pigs' feet to me.

GWEN: Come on! They were wonderful to us.

JUNE:

(Entering.)

Hold it a second. Gwen, excuse me.

(Alarmed but very firm.)

Aunt Sally.

SALLY: He went away. I didn't know where he had gone. I got tired of waiting for him.

JUNE: He was very upset when I told him you were here. He said for you to lie down.
He'll get here when he can.

SALLY: There is no reason for him to come here. And I'm fine where I am.

JUNE:

(Pause. To them.)

She passed out in church. They took her to Dr. Anderson's across the street
and she sneaked out on him.

SALLY: I did not. He always tries to take care of more than he can; giving everyone five
minutes. I waited as long—

JUNE: Would you please. He doesn't know. He hardly had time to examine her; she may have had a mild stroke, it might just be—

GWEN: June.

SHIRLEY: What?

SALLY: It was nothing of the kind! I merely blacked out. I do it all the time.

JUNE: When? When have you passed out before? Recently?

SALLY: When I was eleven.

JUNE: You should rest, inside. You can't tell the damage, if it was a stroke—

GWEN: June.

JUNE: Until she's been looked at.

GWEN: June.

SHIRLEY:

> *(Overlapping.)*

> Where's the doctor? Why didn't he come here?

JUNE: He'll be here as soon as he's free.

SHIRLEY: Free?

GWEN: June, you don't tell someone they have had a stroke. You say they've had a slight cerebral disturbance.

SHIRLEY: That sounds better?

GWEN: Daddy lapped it up. If they'd told him he had had a stroke, he would never have recovered.

JOHN: He didn't recover.

GWEN: John!

SALLY: It was very silly, very embarrassing. And when I woke up, I felt perfectly fine.

KEN: Don't talk. It's cooler out here. She's out of the sun.

JUNE: I don't know if she should be alone or lie down or—

SALLY: —I was sitting there listening to that stupid, vindictive Reverend Poole, and I looked over at that smug wife of his, always looking so pleased to have an occasion to show how easily she can cry. She was like that in school. You'd say, Francine, cry! And she'd burst into tears for you. And I looked at her and there were two of her. Sitting side by side. I just thought, Oh, my God, no. If there's one thing that Lebanon does not need it's another Francine Poole. And I was rubbing my eyes, trying to make one of her go away. Or both of her if possible. And I noticed that there were two Reverend Pooles giving that vacuous eulogy, and two pulpits and two caskets and it was just all too—much. And I got up to get the—hell out of there before there was two of me, and—

JUNE: She passed out in the aisle.

SALLY: Everyone must have enjoyed that. I woke up in Dr. Anderson's office, with him clucking at me, and I felt very rested. But there was only one of him. Wouldn't you know?

JED: Too bad. Town could use another Dr. Anderson.

KEN: Where's Dr. Cranefield?

JED: On vacation. Anderson's overloaded.

SALLY: Well, I wasn't going to wait all day for the man to tell me to go home. I wanted a glass of water, I still haven't had one.

> *(Shirley enters house to get a glass of water.)*

GWEN: Double vision is one of the symptoms of a—slight cerebral disturbance.

SALLY: I realized that while I was walking home. I had nurse's training during the war—

JUNE: Walked? You walked here from town?

SALLY: I didn't get in the least tired. No one has ever paid the slightest attention to me, so please don't now. I don't know how to cope with it. I'm sixty-one years old and I have a perfect right to have a stroke. I've suffered a trauma.

JUNE: You rest after something like that. You don't go for a five-mile hike.

SALLY: I came home slowly, June. It's only a mile and a half. I didn't go jogging.

JUNE: She's too much. I'm arguing with her. I'm killing her.

> *(Shirley brings Sally a glass of water. Sally takes a sip, and puts the flower she carries in the glass.)*

KEN: You really are too much.

SALLY: What a scandal to have ruined Harley's funeral. I looked for where he carved his initials on the pew, but I couldn't find it. Certainly the only mark he ever made on anything.

KEN: Would you please not talk. What do you do with her?

SALLY: We were engaged when we were kids, you know. I was certainly well out of that.

JUNE: Sally—

SALLY: His first wife and her kids and lawyer were on one side of the aisle and his second wife and her lawyer were on the other side, just glaring at each other. And both of them glaring at me.

> *(Laughs.)*

Oh, I shouldn't enjoy it, but it's the first time I've been in that church since I was fired from teaching Sunday school thirty-six years ago. God knows what everyone was calling me. Jezebel, I'd think. Married a Jew, thrown out of town, come barging back like a brazen huzzy.

KEN: Not Jezebel. Naomi, maybe.

JUNE: You were not thrown out of town.

SALLY: I was so! I was thrown out of town. Your father said Matt was a no-good Jew and was only interested in the bank. He never forgave Matt for making more money than he did.

KEN: Aunt Sally, please don't talk.

SALLY: Well, darling, with you all acting like everything I say might be the last word I utter, I want to be sure I get it all in.

JUNE: Sally, I absolutely forbid you to enjoy this.

GWEN: What's the point if you don't get off on it?

SALLY: Pino's made Harley look very waxy.

JUNE: Who did what?

SALLY: Pino's Funeral Home. They made Harley look very waxy. You remember Mrs. Farthing?

JUNE: No.

KEN: Taught algebra.

JUNE: She couldn't possibly still be alive.

SALLY: Oh, yes. She looked at poor waxy Harley and said she supposed death was something we none of us could avoid. But she looked like she thought she might have an angle.

JUNE: How can you tell? Fool that I am, I keep listening to her to see if she sounds normal. She's never sounded normal in her life.

SALLY: Well, don't listen to me. Matt didn't believe in death and I don't either . . .

KEN: I beg your pardon?

SALLY: There's no such thing. It goes on and then it stops. You can't worry about the stopping, you have to worry about the going on. Is that a hummingbird? Is that a bat?

JED: Where?

SALLY: No. Gone.

JUNE: Dr. Anderson said she left a candy box in his office.

KEN: Oh, God. You left Uncle Matt in the office?

SALLY: What are you talking about?

JUNE: The candy box.

SALLY: Well, that's as good a place for it as anywhere. Tell him to keep it.

JUNE: If he brings it back, I'll kill him.

SALLY: That's all taken care of.

KEN: How is "that" all taken care of?

SALLY: That is taken care of privately.

(Pause. Phone rings offstage.)

KEN: That one is long-distance.

JOHN: I'll get it.

GWEN: Oh, Jesus, that's going to be Nashville. I don't want to go to Nashville at all, man. I get more tense every minute.

WESTON: That won't happen again.

GWEN: No joke. Feel my back.

KEN: That won't happen; you'll relax, you'll feel fine.

GWEN: I just feel the tension creeping up my arms right to my jaws. My hands are like ice. Kenny, when could you be out, you know?

KEN: What, love?

GWEN: Like, if I'm gonna freak out till I have my own studio. Like, we could cancel this gig in Nashville, go back to L.A., and see what's eatin' Schwartzkoff while they're fixing up a place for us here and come back in August. What's it gonna cost me?

KEN:

(Overlapping.)

I've never built a recording studio, I really wouldn't—

GWEN: No, man, the place. What are you asking for it? What's your price? I mean, I don't do it, the company does it, but I should know what you're soaking us for.

JUNE:

(Almost amused.)

What on earth are you talking about?

GWEN:

(To Ken.)

Only I want to tell you right up front, I don't bargain. So you'll rip me off, but that's nothing new.

(Pause.)

Speak, damn it—we gotta catch a plane. What are you waiting for, some Arab to buy up the whole state? Copper money is as good as oil money. Daddy used to say that, only he was talking about . . . Rockefeller.

KEN: Maybe we should move this inside.

GWEN: I gotta find a place, Kenny; I can't fart around.

SALLY: We know what you're doing, you don't have to hide.

JUNE: Oh, my god; I have been blind and deaf!

JOHN:

(Entering.)

Hey, baby, you're going to have to talk to King, he won't tell me what's up.

GWEN: That's King? Calling here? What does he want?

JOHN: Some deal, some record company; the man's delirious.

GWEN: What record company—

JOHN: He won't tell me, he wants to talk to you. He's got someone lined up to be at the session. Talk!

GWEN: Did you call Schwartzkoff?

JOHN: He wasn't in. Take the call; he's a busy man.

GWEN: Oh, God, I'm going to look peachy with some record company in the studio, my shrink trying to pry open my mouth with his fingers.

JOHN: Would you take the goddamned call. Come on, Wes, move your butt.

SHIRLEY: I want to hear your tape before you leave. Apparently I won't be afforded the opportunity to—

GWEN: Listen, sure, anything you want as long as I don't have to hear it. Come on, I'm serious about this house. You talk it over. And like August, September.

JOHN: I know, we will.

(Weston goes inside.)

GWEN: No shit, it's what we been looking for.

(To John.)

Get a price. And find out when they can be out.

JOHN: I know, we will.

WESTON:

(On the phone.)

Yeah, man, what's happening.

GWEN: I got it.

(Goes into house.)

JOHN: Uh . . . I been setting up this thing with Jimmy King for three months; suddenly he won't talk . . .

KEN: Yeah . . . frustrating.

JED: About your place. Gwen's really got a hair up her butt.

SHIRLEY: Oh, dear.

JOHN: You tell her what you want for it?

JUNE: No, we were just getting to that.

JOHN: So what's the bite?

JUNE: In a word, no way.

JOHN: What's say?

JUNE: I'm not talking to you.

(To Ken.)

You are going to sell the Talley place to John and Gwen Landis for a recording studio?

KEN: It is not your decision, June.

JUNE: Do you know why he's doing this?

JOHN: I don't think you have anything to say about it, do you?

JUNE: Forget it. It isn't going to happen. No sale. No sale.

JOHN: Do the two of you own it?

JUNE: It doesn't matter who—

JOHN: Is the place yours to sell? You have the title; there're no leans on it, there're no mortgages? The place does belong to you?

KEN: Yes, of course.

JUNE: I'll sit on the road with a shotgun and we'll see how fast—

JOHN: I'd think you would have learned by now that that never got any of us anything we wanted.

KEN: Okay, okay, June—fine—stay out of it; it's no business of yours.

JOHN: So what's the bite?

KEN: I'll have to get a hundred seventy-five for the place.

JOHN: Jesus H. You don't want much. I tell you what. We'll give you a hundred and a quarter.

SALLY: For the Talley place? You're joking.

JOHN: For what's left of it. It'll take that much again to make it livable.

KEN: John, I don't own Helena Copper. I have this house; I want to guarantee a future for Jed and me—

JOHN: Listen, for all we care you can live here. We wouldn't be here more than three months a year. Jed can build his goddamned English garden.

JED: No thank you.

KEN: No, come on. I'm going to sell the place and never see it again. Jed? What do we need?

JED: We'll talk later.

JOHN: A hundred and a quarter, flat out. What's the problem?

KEN: You're really putting me on the spot here. We have over a hundred lilies Jed grew from seed two years ago; going to bloom this August. Gwen is talking about moving in tomorrow almost—

JUNE: You don't even like the place—Gwen wants to grow weeds—

JOHN: I love it, I always have.

JED: Yeah, but what do you care where you are, as long as there's a telephone.

JOHN: As it happens, Gwen wants this house. Whatever she wants is fine by me. Whatever makes me happy.

JED: I'm hip.

JOHN: Yeah, see, that's none of your business.

KEN: But, Jesus, John, the money you spend doing it. Come on, we're not blind. What are you buying, the whole record company now? How can you buy a—

JOHN: Oh, fuck, Talley. Stop being such a faggot. Look around you, wake up, for God's sake. You can buy anything!

SALLY: Not for a hundred and a quarter you can't.

JOHN: Okay, that was the wrong thing to say. Are you telling me you can't sell for that price.

KEN: I didn't say that.

JOHN: You can't sell to me for that price or you can't sell to anybody for that price? I'm not deaf to these insinuations and innuendoes that have been floating around.

   (Pause.)

KEN:

   (Level.)

   I was very angry when you took off for Europe without telling me, but that's long past.

JOHN: Don't dump that on me.

KEN: The three of us plan for six months to go to Europe to beat the draft, then Gwen drags you off a week ahead of schedule and you don't tell me, what the hell would you call it?

JOHN: No, I won't take that. You can't lay your goddamned fecklessness on me—I'm not responsible for anything that happened to you in—

KEN: Okay, forget it. Everyone loves you, everyone forgets everything. Nobody's dumping anything on you.

JOHN: What the hell would you call it? No. I told Gwen you changed your mind. I wanted me and my wife out of the whole steamy situation with both of you.

KEN:

   (Shocked.)

   You told her I changed my mind?

JOHN: Yeah. And we had a good cry and left in two days and how long did you stay in Oakland before you actually got called up? One month? Two months?

JUNE: Closer to three.

JOHN: So don't blame me. I thought you'd fag out. I thought you'd evade—go to Canada. I didn't think you'd join the damn Army. Why did you go, anyway? Did it have something to do with Gwen and me?

KEN: No.

JOHN: Now I hope everyone heard that.

JED: That's enough.

JUNE: It was just easier to let them take you.

KEN: I have never known why I went, and the question has crossed my—

JUNE: You sat on your butt and let them take you because it was easier than making a commitment; you let them make your commitment for you.

JOHN: Hey, baby, I'll tell you something. The first thing you learn in business is to talk about one deal at a time. Kenneth says he wants to sell the place. Now, I'll give you a hundred thirty, that's as high as I go.

SALLY: A hundred thirty-five.

JOHN: You bidding against me or are you trying to up the price?

SALLY: I'm bidding against you.

JOHN: A hundred forty.

SALLY: A hundred forty-five.

JOHN: A hundred fifty.

SALLY: A hundred fifty-five.

KEN: Aunt Sally, what the hell are you doing?

SALLY: Jed and I scattered Matt all over the rose garden early this morning. It didn't take ten minutes. You can sell the place to me, Kenny, if you've got to sell it; and I'll give it to Jed. If you can't stay here, Jed can. And you're not selling the Talley place for a hundred fifty thousand. I'm prepared to go to two hundred twenty-six thousand. You're a rich man, Kenny.

KEN: Jed.

JED: You go on to Greece; I've got work to do here.

KEN: Well, you're welcome to it. A hundred seventy-five, that's the price, John?

JOHN: Leave me out of this.

KEN: Sally? Take it or leave it.

SALLY: I'll take it.

KEN: You've got it. John, I'm sorry you've been outbid.

JOHN: I don't need this hassle. I came here to see June. I didn't come down here looking to buy the Talley place. That was your idea.

JUNE: Why? See me why?

JOHN: What? Oh, Jesus. Could we walk down away from here a minute?

JUNE: I don't think so.

JOHN: I just want to talk.

JUNE: Here I am.

JOHN: Then could Shirley go inside for a while?

SHIRLEY: Certainly not.

JUNE: I don't think you want to go into that right now.

JOHN: I don't have to enumerate the advantages for the kid.

JUNE: Advantages? What the fuck are—

JOHN: Gwen and I both love her. I don't want to seem cavalier—

KEN: Of course not.

JOHN: Just look at the situation. What she is and what we could offer her. Not permanently, just half the year. Just a few months a year—

JUNE: You're out of your mind. You have the balls. You have the balls—

JOHN: Come on, I don't think you want Shirley to—

SALLY: I knew goddamned well he didn't want the house. No, young man.

JUNE:

>   (Overlapping.)
>
>   I don't give a shit who hears it. Out. You better leave now, and you better never—never mention Shirley again.

KEN:

>   (Standing.)
>
>   You better watch what you say, buddy; you're leaving yourself open for one hell of a non-support suit—

JOHN: I have said nothing. I claim no responsibility.

JUNE: Some things you cannot buy, baby! Now leave.

JOHN: But if I wanted to take it to court, I could get her—Don't think I couldn't.

JUNE: You try it!

JOHN: All right, forget it; can it. You just by God remember you had the chance.
SHIRLEY: I will live in St. Louis with my mother.
JOHN: Fine, baby, it serves you right.
KEN: You're leaving now—
JOHN: You damn right we are.
GWEN:

> (Bursting into the porch, with Weston.)

> Holy shit, they want me! They want me! We're in! Oh, sweet Jesus! Columbia bought our tape! They're releasing the fucker in two weeks! Holy shit, they flipped out! The man is talking like retainers of five thousand a month for the first six months, then renegotiate. The man is talking like we're fuckin' stars.

WESTON:

> (Overlapping.)

> No shit, he's like sellin' it to us. We didn't have to say shit.

GWEN: Two weeks! Two weeks! He's going to have the fucking record on the air. On the motherfuckin' air waves.
WESTON: He wants it orchestrated, though, he wants strings. Whoever heard of strings in a—
GWEN: Damn straight. Violins, fuckin' cellos, the works. Lay it on me. Voice of pain! Shitfire.
KEN:

> (Overlapping.)

> Gwen, no, no, Gwen, you can't do it. We can't let John do this to you.

GWEN: Honey, this is a piece of cake, and me and Wes are hungry.
WESTON: She's good.
KEN: It doesn't matter if she's any good. It's all a sham. It's just something John has cooked up to keep you away from your business so he can—
JOHN: Hold it, now; enough. That's not true.
KEN: I wouldn't be a friend to you if I didn't tell you—it's a dream. It's not real.
JOHN: Shut up right now . . . Baby, that's wonderful.
KEN: Gwen has a responsibility to something more important—

JOHN: That's it. Come on, we're getting out of here—move it—
(Pushes him aside. Ken goes down flat on his back.)

> Oh, Jesus God, I forgot. I'm sorry, baby, I'm sorry. I forgot completely.

JED:

> (Goes to Ken.)

> Go on. Don't touch him. Leave. Move.

> (He grabs the garden shears, threatening.)

KEN: I'm not hurt! I'm not hurt! It's okay, Jed.
JOHN: I swear to God, I barely touched you!
JED: You take care of Gwen, I'll get him up!
KEN: I'm okay. Stop.

(A pause.)

JOHN: Listen. I'm your friend. If you know it or not . . .

(Exits into house upstairs.)

GWEN:

(To Ken.)

Boy, baby; with friends like you, huh?

KEN: Gwen, forgive me. It's none of our . . .

GWEN: John's doing nothing I don't know about. You think I'm blind? I gotta have John. And if he needs to wheel and deal behind my back, then he's welcome to it. With you flat on your back like a fuckin' turtle maybe you'll listen. You think you don't need Jed, you don't need to be useful—you'll sell the damn roof over your head to get out of facing yourself. You're on the edge of nowhere, baby, and you listen to me 'cause I *been* nowhere. Now are you gonna get to work or are you gonna lose it all? Huh?

KEN: I haven't worked out a syllabus, I haven't—

GWEN: You damn straight, we're all gonna have a busy summer. Fuckin' Columbia records. Come on, Wes, we gotta pack. Move your ass. Shirley, we're gonna listen to my tape.

(Exit, into house, upstairs.)

WESTON: John's gonna freak. This cat is a different cat from the one John set up for us. Columbia outbid the outfit John bought. She's really good, only John don't know yet.

JOHN:

(Offstage.)

Wes, move your tail.

WESTON: I got to go pack.

(Runs to the door. Stops. Politely.)

It was very nice meeting you.

(Exits into house, upstairs.)

KEN:

(As Jed starts to pick him up.)

Hold it a second.

(Ken pulls Jed down to him. A very long pause; Ken is nearly crying. Jed sits beside him, holding him.)

Jesus. That scares me.

(Fighting tears.)

Falling backwards is the one thing the guy always—

(Trying to joke.)

Jesus. I may never dance *Swan Lake* again.

(A pause. Jed rises and helps Ken to stand.)

JUNE:

(To Jed.)

You're quicker than you look.

SALLY: I've never been so scared in my life. And I'm sixty-four years old.

JUNE: I thought you were sixty-one.

SALLY: I've lied about that since I was twenty.

KEN: It's impossible. I haven't looked at my notes; I don't even know what textbooks are available anymore.

JED:

(Gets tape deck; gives it to Ken.)

Yeah, Gwen said you got a lot of work to do.

KEN: You know you're all going to pay for this.

(To Sally.)

How are you feeling?

SALLY: Much better.

JUNE: Oh, sure. Where's that damned doctor?

KEN: Should we drive her back down to the office?

SALLY: No, no. And you don't have time. You have to talk to the Young kid.

KEN: Oh, God, I'll have to call the Youngs and tell them I can't see Johnny this afternoon.

JUNE: No, you go on . . . I'll take care of Sally.

SALLY: Could you understand what the boy was talking about?

KEN: Oh, sure. It just takes listening to a couple times. You won't like it at all. He's into science and the future.

JUNE: Well, why not.

KEN: But he doesn't have much faith in Sally's spacemen. He's very positive and negative and decidedly eccentric . . . teleportation, space travel,

(Turns on cassette player.)

and this is the way it ends—

(He reads from his yellow pad at the same time.)

"After they had explored all the suns in the universe, and all the planets of all the suns, they realized that there was no other life in the universe, and that they were alone. And they were very happy, because then they knew it was up to them to become all the things they had imagined they would find."

(Turns off the cassette player. Weston come to the stairs, sits down, tuning his guitar.)

WESTON: Gwen? You're going to play our tape?

SALLY: You know, if I sold that mausoleum in California, I could dump an awful lot of money into this place. I was just thinking out loud.

KEN: I frankly don't think you should be moved from here.

SALLY: I'm much too ill to travel . . .

JED: Oh, that's out of the question.

WESTON:

> *(Through window.)*

> Hey, Sally, I want you to hear this. Shirley!

SALLY: I'm coming!

GWEN: June!

JUNE: God love her.

> *(Yelling.)*

> Coming.

WESTON: Kenny!

KEN: We hear you.

> *(June goes in. Gwen joins Weston; he plays the introduction to his song. Sally gets up.)*

> Are you okay?

SALLY: Well, I can walk.

KEN: You're beatin' me.

> *(Sally goes in to listen to them. Shirley and Jed and Ken sit on the porch. Shirley is crying quietly.)*

> What's wrong, doll?

SHIRLEY: I don't care. The important thing is to find your vocation and work like hell at it. I don't think heredity has anything to do with anything.

KEN: Certainly not.

SHIRLEY: You do realize, though, the terrible burden.

KEN: How's that?

SHIRLEY: I am the last of the Talleys. And the whole family has just come to nothing at all so far. Fortunately, it's on my shoulders.

> *(She gets up with the weight of the burden on her shoulders. Gwen and Weston begin to sing.)*

> I won't fail us.

> *(She goes into the house. Ken and Jed listen a moment.)*

KEN: We had to put in all those damn lilies. If they don't bloom, it's your ass. And you and Weston have got to get cinders this afternoon for the penstemon.

JED: Oh, God.

KEN: Well, maybe he'll write us a song.

> *(He gets up. Sighs. Picks up the portable recorder.)*

> I've got to talk to Johnny Young about the future.

> *(They look at each other a moment. The singers continue. Jed looks out over the garden, still seated. Ken begins to work his way toward the door. The music continues as the light fades.)*

> End of Play

Jean Smart (Lil) in the 1980 Off-Broadway premier of Jane Chambers's
Last Summer at Bluefish Cove at the Actors Playhouse.
(Photograph reprinted with permission from the John Willis
Theatre World/Screen World Archive)

Last Summer
at Bluefish Cove

BY JANE CHAMBERS

This play is lovingly and gratefully dedicated to IRENE TRAVIS without whom there would have been no production

Last Summer at Bluefish Cove was first produced by The Glines, opening February 13, 1980 at the Shandol Theatre, Manhattan, where it ran for twelve performances. Lawrence Lane, Executive Producer; Billy Blackwell, Producer; Directed by Harriet Leider; Sets by Tony Allicine; Lights by Debra Weiser; Stage Manager, Yvonne Fisher; Theme: "Impatient Heart" by Marcia Malamet and Peter Allen. In the cast were: Jean Smart (Lil,) Madelyn Albert (Eva,) Ellie Schadt (Kitty,) Aphroditi Kolaitis (Annie,) Madeline Welsing (Rae,) Janet Morrison (Rita,) Stephanie Rula (Sue,) Karen Sederholm (Donna.)

On June 3, 1980 *Last Summer* . . . opened at West Side Mainstage, Manhattan, as part of the First American Gay Arts Festival, produced by The Glines, for a limited run of eight weeks; it was extended an additional four weeks. Lawrence Lane, Executive Producer; Jerry Thomas, Producer; Directed by Nyla Lyon; Sets by Michael C. Smith; Lighting Design by Carol Sealey; Costumes by Joyce Ostrin; Production Stage Manager, Steve Zorthian*; Assistant Stage Manager, Sandra Sochngen. Theme Song, "Impatient Heart" by Marcia Malamet and Peter Allen. Publicity by FLT.

In the cast:

LIL	Jean Smart
EVA	Carolyn Cope
KITTY	Anita Keal**
ANNIE	Aphroditi Kolaitis
RAE	Madeline Welsing
RITA	Janet Morrison
DONNA	Karen Sederholm***
SUE	Stephanie Rula

Understudies: Mercedes Ruehl, Sandra Soehngen (*Replaced by Grant Brown; **replaced by Dolores Kenan; ***replaced by Elizabeth Wingate.)

On December 2, 1980, *Last Summer* . . . began previews at the Actors Playhouse, New York City. Produced by John Glines and Lawrence Lane presenting The Glines production. Opened Dec. 22, 1980; closed March 1, 1981. Director: Nyla Lyon; Sets: Reagan Cook; Lighting Design: Jeffrey Schissler; Costumes: Giva Taylor; Production Stage Manager: Paula Ellen Cohen*, Assistant Stage Manager, Laura Burroughs.

In the cast:

LIL	Diane Tarleton**
EVA	Susan Slavin

KITTY	Janet Sarno
ANNIE	Holly Barron***
RAE	Lauren Craig
RITA	Dulcie Arnold
DONNA	Robin Mary Paris
SUE	Celia Howard

Understudies: Holly Barron, Caroline Aaron, Lauren Craig, Margaret Ritchie, Carolyn Cope, Jane Chambers. (*Replaced by Peter Pope; **replaced by Jean Smart, Holly Barron, Caroline Aaron; ***replaced by Susan Blemhaert.)

ACT ONE

Early summer at Bluefish Cove, an isolated beach area near the city. In the foreground, there is a pebble beach. At the apron, a jutting rock rears its head above the sea, speckled with sea-weed and colonies of clutching mussels. Upstage, a flight of weathered wooden steps lead to a one-room rustic cabin with a living/sleeping area and a kitchenette. A door leads off the room to an unseen bathroom. There is also a door to a closet, upstage.

At rise, the cottage is dimly lit and our attention is focused on the rock and beach. A pair of rubber sandals and a well-worn workshirt are tossed carelessly at the foot of the steps. On the rock, barefoot, clad in worn cutoffs and frayed halter is Lil Zalinski, sitting (or standing) and squinting into the afternoon sun as she waits impatiently for a fish to bite. From her handling of the pole, we can see she is an experienced fisherwoman.

LIL: Come on, you mother, bite.

> *(Pause.)*

> I see you circling down there. Come on, sweetheart.

> *(She jiggles bait.)*

> Damn. You obviously don't know who you're dealing with here. I won the 1960 All American Girl Scout Fish-Off. I was the champeen. Sixteen bass and twelve blowfish. Of course I was just a kid then but I've gotten better with the years.

> *(She pulls in the line, checks the bait.)*
> *(Eva Margolis enters, unseen by Lil. Eva is walking quietly along the beach. She is dressed in proper resort clothing—everything about her says upper middle class. She watches Lil, unseen, with interest and amusement.)*

LIL:

> *(Wiggles line.)*

> If you were a person, you know what we'd call you? A C.T. You nuzzle the bait but you don't put out. Now, I'm going to try a different approach, it's called courting. You're going to love it. Here's how it goes. You're a terrific looking fish, you know that, sweetheart? You're a real knockout. Now, don't get me wrong, it's not just your body I'm after. I love your mind, your sense of humor, your intellect, your politics. . . . Aha, I'm getting your attention, huh? I respect you, darling. I love you. Now, bite, baby, bite.

> *(Eva who, unnoticed by Lil, has been listening, speaks.)*

EVA: I'd fall for that. It's a good line.

LIL:

> *(Surprised.)*

> Would you mind telling that to the bluefish?

> *(She notes that Eva is an attractive woman and turns on the charm.)*

I usually do pretty well with that line, I must be losing my touch.

EVA:

(*Not picking up on Lil's flirtatiousness.*)

Maybe you need to change your strategy.

(*She walks to water's edge and peers in at fish.*)

You could try caveman tactics. Hit it on the head with a stick.

LIL:

(*Still charming.*)

Not my style. I prefer a classier approach.

EVA:

(*Still innocent.*)

Have you tried poetry?

(*To fish.*)

"Shall I compare thee to a summer's day? Thou art more lovely and more temperate."

LIL:

(*Peers into water.*)

It's gone. Gone. You've driven that fish right back to the Atlantic.

EVA:

(*Shrugs.*)

As my mother always tells me, there are other fish in the sea.

LIL: That's a practical philosophy. Coldhearted but practical.

EVA: You're getting a bad sunburn. Is that your shirt? Better put it on.

(*Eva picks up Lil's shirt from the steps, tosses it to her. Lil takes this as a sign of interest from Eva but Eva is only being friendly and proceeds to exit down the beach.*)

LIL: Thanks.

EVA:

(*Going.*)

Don't lose heart. Maybe you'll catch that fish tomorrow.

LIL: Hey—

(*Eva turns.*)

I'm Lillian Zalinski. Everybody calls me Lil.

EVA: Eva Margolis. I'm the pink cabin for the summer.

(*She continues to leave.*)

LIL:

(*Trying to stop her.*)

Holly House. We call it Holly House. I'm in Crabapple, right up there. We've all been wondering who rented Holly House this season. The couple who had it the last two years split up. You're the only newcomer on the Cove this year, the other cabins are the same old gang. Are you alone?

EVA: Yes. The other cabins are all rented to couples?

LIL:

(Meaning herself.)

All but one.

EVA: I guess I'll have to get used to being odd man out.

LIL: More like New Girl In Town. You'll get lots of attention, I guarantee it.

EVA:

(Still misunderstanding.)

Well, I could use some attention. You're married, of course?

LIL: Not me. I'm the other one who's not a couple.

(Eva senses that Lil is not an ordinary person—that there is some subtext in this repartee but she can't identify it, so she asks:)

EVA: Are you one of those swinging singles I've read about?

LIL:

(Teasing.)

Well, that depends . . .

EVA:

(Thinking she's got it.)

I bet you're an artist—or a writer!

LIL: No. I used to sell time for a television station—but I'm taking the summer off.

EVA: You and I are the only singles?

LIL: That's right.

(Lil, of course, is pleased at that.)

EVA:

(Disappointed.)

Well, it's going to be a long summer. I hope you play chess.

(She starts to leave again.)

LIL: I hate it. I like to fish.

EVA: You can't fish at night.

LIL: I could fish at night but I prefer to do more interesting things.

(Eva still looks blank.)

Hey, would you toss me those sandals? This beach is murder on the feet.

(Eva brings her the sandals.)

You'll have to come to the opening of the season bash tonight. It's at my cabin, right up there. Music, food, booze, dancing.

(*Eva is trying to size* Lil *up.*)

EVA: Were you ever married?

LIL:

    (*Cavalierly.*)

    Oh, sure. Lots of times.

EVA: I was only married once. For twelve years.

LIL:

    (*Stunned.*)

    Twelve years? I had one that made it two years and eight months. Eight long months. Rae and Annie will approve of you. They've been together nine.

EVA: How many times were you really married?

LIL: Oh God, I don't know—a dozen? Who counts?

EVA: Come on. A dozen husbands?

LIL:

    (*Realizing.*)

    Husbands?

EVA: Husbands. You know the guy in the tuxedo, he's waiting at the altar when you come down the aisle.

LIL: Husbands.

EVA: Husbands.

LIL: How did you come to rent Holly House?

EVA: Oh, it was a godsend. I walked out on George on Wednesday, just packed the suitcases and left. It gave me such pleasure to leave him stranded with a paisley overnight bag and a Board of Directors meeting in Chicago the next day. He'd go naked before he'd carry a paisley bag into a Board of Directors meeting—no, he wouldn't go naked. He thinks he's underdeveloped—for all I know, he may be. I married him when I was still in college so my basis for comparison is limited. Is six inches small? This book I'm reading says size doesn't matter. It's all in how he uses it. Foreplay is everything—this book says. It's called *The Female Sexual Imperative*. It's written by a woman doctor. Have you read it?

LIL:

    (*Still stunned.*)

    I've seen it.

EVA:

    (*Enjoying this conversation.*)

    Well, you probably know everything that's in it, anyway. I can't believe I've gotten to be this old and I don't know anything.

LIL: How did you get Holly House?

EVA: I left George on Wednesday and drove until dark. I wasn't heading any place in particular, I was just leaving George. I wound up in the village over there and checked into the Holiday Inn. The desk clerk—he was one of those sweet young men, you know the kind—handed me the room key and I burst into tears. I realized that I was going to spend the night alone, away from home, for the first time in my life.

LIL: How did you get *here?*

EVA: To Bluefish Cove? Well, the desk clerk—actually, he was quite nice in spite of his predilections—he said there was a place right down the street where I could get a drink and not be approached by mashers, a place where mostly businesswomen went. . . .

LIL: He sent you to Molly Pitcher's?

EVA: And I met this nice lady at the bar—she's a real estate agent—

LIL: Margery Eaton.

EVA: She handles the rentals for Bluefish Cove. I suppose you know her.

LIL: Very well.

EVA: I told her I needed quiet, some place to get myself together—she was wonderful. She didn't question me or ask for references, she didn't even ask me if I had a husband or kids. She just took my money and handed me the lease. I think she's a feminist. She assumed I was in charge of my own life.

LIL: She assumed something, that's for sure.

EVA: And it's working out wonderfully. It's beautiful here—and maybe I'll make some new friends. This party tonight, it's at your cabin?

LIL:

> *(Quickly.)*

> But you don't have to come.

EVA: Oh, but I want to. I've been holed up in my cabin for days now reading *The Female Sexual Imperative.* A party tonight would be just perfect, Lil. It's time for me to make my debut as a single woman.

LIL:

> *(Trying to ease out gracefully.)*

> Eva, you might feel out of place.

EVA:

> *(Misunderstanding.)*

> Because I'm single? Well, you are, too. Of course, I've been married so long I've forgotten how to flirt—but then you said it's mostly couples here—still, somebody might have a single houseguest or a bachelor brother, you never know, we might get lucky. I don't even remember how to hold a conversation with a man.

> *(She sees that* Lil *is uncomfortable.)*

> I promise not to cut in on your territory.

LIL: Somehow I'm not worried about that. It's just a bunch of beach bums, just the residents of the Cove. It's no big thing.

EVA: It is to me. I'm going to a party—by myself! I feel like a teenager again. When I was in high school, my best friend Joan and I always had a pow-wow before going to a party—I would never have dreamed of picking out a dress—or a boyfriend—without getting Joan's approval first.

> *(Touching* Lil's *hand.)*

> This book is right. It is possible for grown women to be friends.

(She feels slightly awkward at the sudden closeness and turns to leave.)

Thank you, Lil. I'll see you tonight!

LIL:

(As Eva goes, Lil glances toward the cabin.)

Oh, dear. Oh, dear.

(Lights go down on the beach. Lil sits on the steps in the darkness and begins to clean fish quietly. We do not notice her because the lights go up in the cabin—there is music and chatter. Annie and Rae are dancing, Kitty paces as Rita watches. It is several hours later.)

KITTY: Damn Marge Eaton!

RITA: She might have been drunk.

RAE: I think she made a perfectly reasonable assumption.

ANNIE: Walks like a duck, talks like a duck, hangs out with ducks, must be a duck.

KITTY: How could Marge do this to me?

RAE: If you meet a woman in a gay bar, you naturally assume she's gay.

KITTY: This could ruin my career!

RAE: Annie has just as much to lose as you have, Kitty. Annie's famous, too.

ANNIE: Rae . . .

RAE: Well, you are, darling. Annie was famous when you

(Meaning Kitty.)

were still delivering babies at that clinic in Brooklyn.

KITTY: It's not the same thing. Annie's a sculptor.

RAE: Sculptress. We take pride in the feminine gender.

KITTY: Well, you shouldn't. It's diminutive. Sculptor is generic. And nobody cares who a sculptor . . .

RAE: Sculptress.

ANNIE: Honey . . .

KITTY: Who a sculptor goes to bed with.

RITA: Kitty is developing a new language. She's going to write a dictionary of nonsexist language.

KITTY:

(To Annie.)

Nobody cares who you go to bed with.

RAE: I do.

(Rae turns off the record player, busies herself in the kitchen. Annie tends the bar.)

KITTY: I have a new book coming out!

RITA: It's even better than *The Female Sexual Imperative.* It's called *Coming Together: The Search for Connubial Equality.* It's a play on words.

KITTY: I'm trying to liberate American women.

RITA: *Publisher's Weekly* gave her an award. "Literature's Most Credible Women's Libber."

ANNIE: Don't worry, Kitty. If your career blows up, we'll give you an award.

(She hands Kitty a drink.)

"Bluefish Cove's Most Incredible Dyke."

KITTY: It isn't funny. I'll lose my credibility.

ANNIE: Not to mention your royalties.

KITTY: I'm dependent on my royalties!

(About Rita.)

We're dependent on my royalties. I gave up a career in medicine, remember, to devote myself to The Movement.

RAE: Why is it every time Kitty says "The Movement," it sounds like a disturbance of the lower colon?

KITTY: I don't know why I come back here every summer—I don't know why I put up with the bunch of you—I'm dedicating my life to a worthy cause—

RITA: We didn't have to come here this summer. The Swedish government offered Kitty a grant to go there and write.

ANNIE: Kitty, m'dear, we are your old friends. We recognize that you gave up long gory hours in the operating room in order to make a million writing books; we recall how you sacrificed day after day of peering up dark vaginas with a penlight in order to become a national celebrity. Our hearts bleed for you when we see your handsome face on the cover of *Ms.* or tune into Phil Donahue and listen to you instructing American women to grab their sexuality—

RAE: No, honey. "Seize their sexuality," that's what she said on Donahue. "Seize your sexuality," she said. Some woman in the audience thought she was advocating masturbation.

RITA: She does advocate masturbation. There's a whole chapter on it in this new book.

ANNIE: We are aware of your achievements and cognizant of your sacrifices. We have watched you fall in and out of love, in and out of lust, in and out of hangovers, we have tolerated and accepted you when you were young, dedicated and struggling, we tolerate and accept you now that you are rich, famous and arrogant. Bluefish Cove is more than just a lesbian beach colony, Kitty, it's family. And that's why you keep coming back.

RITA: Kitty is not arrogant. She's brilliant.

ANNIE: She's both. And she depends on us to keep her from becoming totally obnoxious.

KITTY: I wouldn't take that from anybody else, you know.

ANNIE: I know. That's why I said it.

RAE: What are families for?

KITTY:

(Calling out to steps.)

Lil, how can you do this to me? My career is in jeopardy! A straight woman in Bluefish Cove. I can't believe it. Is nothing sacred any more?

ANNIE: Kitty, don't get in a snit and screw up this summer, huh? Have some consideration, will you?

(She nods toward the door where Lil sits outside.)

RAE: It's just one woman. One simple, little woman. She's not going to rent the Goodyear blimp and fly cross-country with a banner announcing that Dr. Kitty Cochrane is a lesbian.

KITTY: It only takes one person to start a rumor that can ruin a career.

ANNIE: Lil has the right to invite anybody she wants, anybody at all, to her own cabin for her own party.

KITTY: What difference does it make to Lil? She hasn't got anything to lose.

RAE: Kitty.

KITTY: I didn't mean it like that. I just mean—we're dealing with the rest of my life.

ANNIE: We're dealing with the rest of Lil's life, too.

RAE: We all agreed we were going to make this summer perfect. Nobody is going to fight—

ANNIE:

(To Kitty.*)*

—or fuck around.

RITA: Kitty never fucks around.

RAE: Love is blind.

ANNIE:

(To Kitty *and* Rita.*)*

Please, think about Lil.

RITA:

(Helpfully.)

Well, maybe it won't be so bad, Kitty. She is a straight woman. She'll be source material for your new book.

KITTY: Well, I can't see any other way of doing this: we'll all just have to pretend we're straight.

(Rae shakes her head helplessly. Annie, who has poured a drink for Lil, takes both glasses and heads for door, disgusted.)

ANNIE: I'm just about to give up on you, Kitty.

KITTY: I can say Rita's my cousin.

RITA: You could say I'm your secretary. I am your secretary.

KITTY: But, darling, she's bound to come into our cabin sometime during the summer and celebrities don't sleep in a double bed with their secretaries—but if you're my cousin—

RAE: Incest is preferable to being gay.

KITTY:

(To Rae.*)*

Annie could be your—sister-in-law. You can say you're divorced, which is true, you wouldn't have to lie, and you can say Annie's husband died valiantly in Viet Nam. Donna can say she's Sue's daughter.

RAE: I don't want to be around when you suggest that to Sue. Sue's slightly paranoid about that age difference, anyway.

RITA: But Kitty, we'd have to lie all the time. I mean, if the woman is living in Holly House, she's going to see us everywhere, every day, on the beach, at the picnic tables, in the glen, on the path . . .

RAE: Kitty, the woman may be straight but I haven't heard that she's retarded.

RITA: I don't know if we could carry it off, Kitty. Someone's bound to make a slip.

KITTY: Oh, shut up, Rita. I know that. They wouldn't do it, anyway. Nobody cares about my career! The whole thing is hideous and impossible.

(She wails and sinks into further depression.)

Sooner or later, it's your friends who do you in. My father used to say that.

(Lights dim on the cabin, up on beach. Annie has descended the steps and sits just above Lil.)

ANNIE: Need some help?
LIL: No thanks, I'm almost finished.
ANNIE: Why didn't you have them cleaned at the market?
LIL: How'd you know I didn't catch these?
ANNIE: I was looking out the window this afternoon when you came up the stairs with an empty bucket.
LIL: Don't rat on me. I have a reputation to uphold.
ANNIE: My lips are sealed.
LIL: Actually, I don't mind cleaning them. It releases my hostilities.

(Annie hands Lil the drink.)

Thanks. Has Kitty offended anyone yet?
ANNIE: Everyone. Right off.
LIL: Good. It's the opening of the season initiation. Kitty offends everyone, everyone puts Kitty in her place. Then we can settle in for the long, hot summer. Same thing, every year. When I lived with Kitty, it was a nightly ritual, putting Kitty in her place. She thrives on it, you know.
ANNIE: She's having a temper tantrum about your asking the straight lady to the party tonight.
LIL: I never would have if I'd known she was straight—but by the time I found out, it was too late. Well, she'll have to face it sooner or later—she might as well know right now, at the beginning of the season, she's smack in the middle of a bunch of dykes.
ANNIE: Kitty would prefer she never finds that out.
LIL: Kitty may change her mind when she sees her. She's nice looking.
ANNIE: I saw her. From the window.
LIL: Ah-ah.
ANNIE: Not me. I'm a married lady.
LIL: Maybe she'll turn out to be a nice, straight lady for Kitty to chase around after all summer. Kitty has never made it through a summer at Bluefish Cove without at least one side affair.
ANNIE: Not true. She never fooled around the two years she lived with you. You were the one who fooled around.
LIL: She called me an alley cat.
ANNIE: I remember. You had that fling with Donna. . . .
LIL: But I denied it. I swore, Girl-Scout's Honor, I hadn't laid a finger on Donna.
ANNIE: She didn't believe you. Kitty may be a pain in the ass but she's nobody's fool.
LIL: She set the answering machine to monitor and record. She bugged our goddam telephone.
ANNIE: And you, dummy, made a date to meet Donna at a motel—

LIL: Well, where else? She was living with Sue, I was living with Kitty—I'm too old to do it in the back of a car.

ANNIE: Didn't Kitty follow you to the motel?

LIL: Pounded on the door, made a complete ass of herself. Donna and I jumped out the window, bare-assed, with our clothes under our arms. Good thing we were on the first floor.

ANNIE: And Kitty never let you back in your apartment.

LIL: Never. Changed the locks and put my things out in the hallway like an Indian matriarch divorcing her husband.

ANNIE: You ever wish you'd stayed with Kitty?

LIL: It never would have worked.

ANNIE: It might have. I wouldn't have believed, nine years ago, that Rae and I would make it—but we have. And it's better now than it ever was.

LIL:

(Shrugs.)

I'm not a long-distance runner, Annie.

ANNIE: You were in love with Kitty.

LIL: Oh, for a minute, maybe. But I had a lust for freedom and she had a lust for fame and fortune. . . . Kitty's all right. Don't go so hard on her.

ANNIE: I'll try to remember that.

LIL: Someday sculptures by Anne Joseph will be in the Metropolitan and dedicated little art students will pry into your life, long-nosed intense professors will refer to you as the Master of Free Form. . . .

ANNIE: You think so?

LIL: I know it. And books by Dr. Kitty Cochrane will be on library shelves a hundred years from now. How long will your sculptures last?

ANNIE:

(Uneasily.)

Indefinitely.

LIL: Thousands of years. And Rae has two grown children and they'll have children. That's a kind of immortality.

(Pause.)

Alley cats just come and go.

(Lil *stands with the bucket and fish heads and bones, then runs down the steps onto the beach, tossing the fish remains against the rock, into the sea. Annie watches her with love and sadness.*)

ANNIE: Hey, Lil!

(Lil *looks up.*)

I love you.

LIL:

(Laughs and starts to climb the stairs.)

Don't you start that. We made a pact years ago in a dormitory room, never lovers, always friends.

ANNIE: I didn't mean that, dummy. I only meant you're my good buddy and I love you.

LIL: Come on, cut the crap. How many drinks have you had?

(Lights rise on cabin. Rae opens the door for them.)

RAE: I hope you didn't bring the heads and guts in with you.

LIL: Nope. Threw them in the sea. From the sea we come, to the sea we returneth. . . .

RAE: I don't mind cooking them but I sure hate to clean them.

(Rae takes fish, goes about preparing them.)

LIL:

(Patting Rae's ass.)

Just like a woman.

ANNIE: Watch that, buddy.

RAE: There's nothing more disgusting than a male chauvinist dyke.

(Lil and Annie go into living room.)

LIL:

(Approaching Kitty from behind.)

Don't tell me! Yes! It must be! It is! Dr. Kitty Cochrane, High Priestess of Feminism, right in my very own living room. May I have your autograph?

(Kitty looks at her coolly.)

Come on, Kitty.

RITA: She's upset that you invited that straight woman.

LIL: Eva? She's just a nice, naive little lady, Kitty. We're going to be a lot more upsetting to her than she is to us.

ANNIE: Ah, but she has invaded our secret Isle of Lesbos. The enemy is in our camp, a traitor moves among us. . . .

RITA: Kitty does have to be very careful.

LIL: She seems like a nice woman. She's all right, Kitty. It's going to be okay.

(Pause.)

Knock, knock, Kitty, can you hear me through the closet door?

KITTY: If this woman blows my cover, if she goes to the media and announces Dr. Kitty Cochrane is a dyke

(She wags her finger at Lil.)

do you know how David Susskind would love to get hold of that?

LIL: Deny it, Kitty. Deny everything. You're so good at that.

KITTY: The public is not ready. The public is still trying to accept the concepts of equal rights and the clitoral orgasm. It would be a catastrophe for me to come out of the closet now. It would be as incredible as if—Gloria Steinem announced her intention to marry—Marlo Thomas. The entire Movement would shudder and collapse.

RITA: Kitty is a figurehead, jutting boldly and courageously from the prow of the ship of human rights sailing through the treacherous sea of prejudice and ignorance. . . .

LIL:

> (*To* Kitty.)

> You didn't write that?

RITA: Yes, she did.

KITTY: I didn't use it. It was a first draft. Rita, how could you remember that?

RITA: I remember everything you write, Kitty. I have to type it four times. She does four drafts of everything.

LIL:

> (*To* Kitty.)

> I think I liked you better when you practiced medicine. You always looked so sexy in that white coat.

> (Lil, *tired, sits.*)

KITTY: How're you feeling, Lil?

LIL: Terrific.

KITTY: Really.

LIL: Don't start on me. You're not my doctor.

KITTY: You're under my supervision.

LIL: Bullshit. You have my records, that's all. I only agreed to that because my doctor wouldn't let me spend the summer out here otherwise. If I suddenly turn fuschia and collapse, do something. Otherwise, keep your distance, understand?

RITA: Kitty just wants to help you.

LIL:

> (*To* Kitty.)

> You don't even practice medicine any more.

RITA: She didn't go to Sweden this summer so she could stay here with you.

KITTY: Rita! That's not true, Lil. I never did like Sweden and I wouldn't miss a summer at the Cove for anything.

> (*She feels* Lil's *forehead.*)

> You're overdoing. You cannot stay on that beach all day. You can't take that much sun.

LIL: You try to take my pulse and I'll break your fingers. I 'm fine. I feel just fine.

> (Eva *is approaching on the beach.*)

RAE: Hey, here she comes.

ANNIE:

> (*Wiggling her eyebrows.*)

> Nice. Very nice. You always did have good taste, Lil.

RAE:

> (*To* Annie.)

> Get in here and butter this skillet before I break it over your head.

ANNIE: I love a possessive woman.

RAE: Well, you've got one.

> (*About* Eva.)

> She's skinny and she's got blue eyes—and if I catch you looking crocksided at her, I'll snatch you baldheaded.

EVA:

> (*Calling.*)

> Lil?

ANNIE:

> (*At the door.*)

> You've got the right place. Come on up.

RAE:

> (*To Annie.*)

> You're a married woman.

ANNIE: I can dream, can't I?

RAE: Skinny with blue eyes. Revs up her motor every time. Get in here.

> (*She hauls Annie in by her britches pocket. This is a game between* Rae *and* Annie. *They are devoted to each other.*)

EVA:

> (*At door.*)

> Lil?

> (*Lil, who shows evidence of being tired, goes to the door.*)

LIL: Hi, Eva.

EVA: I didn't hear much noise but I was too excited to wait. I've been dressed and ready for an hour.

LIL: Donna and Sue are late, as usual, but everybody else is here. Come on in.

EVA: Do I look all right?

ANNIE: I think you look terrific.

> (*To Rae.*)

> Doesn't she look terrific?

RAE: Wonderful.

KITTY:

> (*Inside, to Rita.*)

> I hope she doesn't introduce us by last names.

RAE:

> (*Wipes her hand on towel and extends it.*)

> I'm Rae. Welcome to Bluefish Cove. The Li'l Abner character here is Annie Joseph.

ANNIE: Hi. We've been looking forward to meeting you. Lil told us all about you.

LIL: Not all. I don't know everything.

ANNIE: Hey, what are you drinking? Besides being assistant chef, I'm also the official barkeep.

EVA: Scotch and water, do you have that?

ANNIE: Sure. Coming up.

LIL: Rita Sanderson, Eva Margolis.

EVA: Hi.

KITTY:

> *(Quickly.)*

> I'm Katherine.

EVA: Hello.

ANNIE: You want this Scotch heavy or light?

EVA: Oh, light, please, I'm not a big drinker. Did you say your name is Annie Joseph?

ANNIE: That's right.

EVA: Are you the sculptress?

KITTY: Sculp*tor.*

ANNIE: It doesn't matter. I make sculptures.

EVA: I took a class in art appreciation last year—we studied you.

ANNIE: Thank you.

EVA: I never met a sculptress

> *(She hesitates, anxious to please, and glances towards* Kitty's *back.)*

> —sculptor?—

> *(But* Kitty *doesn't respond.)*

> —before.

RITA:

> *(Being helpful.)*

> Sculptress sounds like she does a little less of it a little less well.

RAE: Bull!

KITTY:

> *(To Rae.)*

> We really need a new word altogether. We need to develop our own language.

EVA:

> *(To Kitty.)*

> You must be a feminist! I'm trying to become one. I'm reading that new book by Dr. Cochrane right now: *The Female Sexual Imperative.*

> *(Kitty has turned her face away from* Eva, *so* Eva *addresses* Annie.)*

> Have you read it?

ANNIE:

> *(To Lil.)*

> Do I have to answer that?

EVA: Oh, do. You'll love it. It'll change your life. I know most men get very uptight about their wives reading feminist literature—George nearly went wild when I bought this book by Dr. Cochrane. He said his secretary read it and got so uppity he had to fire her. And of course he blames Dr. Cochrane and her book for the fact I left him.

RAE: It wouldn't be the first time Dr. Cochrane's been blamed for a breakup.

EVA: But it's not true. It's really not. I would have eventually left, anyway. I mean, our marriage just wasn't working. We tried everything. We really did.

> (To Rita.)

> Have you read Dr. Cochrane's book?

RITA: Well, yes, I have.

EVA: She's wonderful.

RITA: She's marvelous.

EVA: I would have left George anyway but Dr. Cochrane's book made me feel good about it—as if it were a beginning, not an end.

KITTY: What a lovely thing to say.

RITA:

> (To Annie.)

> You see? She is a figurehead, jutting boldly and courageously from the prow of the ship of human rights.

EVA: She's the most important woman in the twentieth century, that's what I think. Kitty Cochrane is going to change the world.

ANNIE:

> (To Lil.)

> She can't hold out against this kind of flattery—I give her fifteen more minutes.

LIL: Fifteen more seconds. Bet you ten bucks.

EVA: If any of you haven't read the book, I'll let you have my copy when I'm finished. Just don't tell your husbands where you got it from. I'm in the last chapter now and I have savored every word. I'm telling you, you don't know what it is to be a woman until you've read Dr. Kitty Cochrane.

KITTY: I'm really thrilled the book has had such meaning for you.

LIL:

> (Nudges Annie.)

> See?

EVA: Oh, it has. It saved my life.

KITTY: Really?

EVA: Oh, yes.

LIL:

> (To Annie.)

> Watch this.

> (Kitty hesitates a moment.)

Now.

KITTY: I am Dr. Kitty Cochrane.

LIL:

(To Annie.)

Ten bucks. Fork over.

EVA:

(Stunned.)

Really?

RITA: But Kitty, you said . . .

KITTY: Rita, I have an obligation to my public.

EVA: How terribly exciting.

(Rae, who has missed much of the previous interchange because she was taking food out of the oven, rises, plates in hand.)

RAE:

(Handing out plates.)

Okay, group, soup's on.

EVA: But everybody's not here. . . .

RAE: Like I used to say to my kids, you get here on time or your plate goes in the oven.

EVA:

(To Rae.)

When is your husband coming?

RAE: My husband? Coming? Oh, he's not. He won't be here. We were divorced nine years ago.

EVA: Oh. What about your children?

RAE: What about them?

ANNIE: They're on their own. One of them's bumming around Oregon 'and the other one's in summer school in the city.

EVA: You have children, too?

ANNIE: No, I just feel like Rae's are half mine.

EVA:

(Befuddled.)

You're neighbors.

RAE: No, we live together.

EVA: Oh. I don't have children now. We had a son but—

(To Kitty, who is cringing.)

—you have children?

KITTY: Oh, no, I don't.

(Quickly.)

I delivered 273 of them, however, and what a glorious thing it is to bring new life into the world.

RITA: I almost had a baby once.

(Everyone stares at her, surprised.)

I was pregnant when I was in college. The boy was very considerate. He paid for the abortion. It was a little girl.

EVA: I used to want a little girl. I wanted her to look just like me. My immortality, I guess.

(To Kitty.)

Your book says a woman has the right to control her own body. My husband, George, thinks that's a mortal sin. George thinks a lot of things are mortal sins. Like the things you say in your book about marital sex—

(The lights are fading on that scene and coming up on the beach where Sue, *a homely woman in her mid-40s, is helping* Donna, *a beauty in her 20s, cross the rocky beach.* Sue *is obviously old money and wears frayed jeans and torn sneakers with the ease of the very rich.* Donna *is very conscious of her good looks. She's a flirt and a social climber and does both with charm.)*

DONNA: Wait, Sue!

SUE: Honey, I told you that you couldn't walk this beach in those sandals. If you'd wear sensible sneakers. . . .

DONNA: The sandals make my ankles look thinner.

SUE: If your ankles got any thinner, your feet would break off. Come on.

DONNA: The sandals are sexier. Too bad Gucci isn't imprinted on the back of them.

SUE: I could stamp Saks Fifth Avenue on your ass.

DONNA: I'd like to have a pair of these in white, too. Can we order them by phone?

SUE: On one condition. Don't flirt with Lil tonight.

DONNA: Flirt with Lil?

SUE: Don't look dumb. You always flirt with Lil.

DONNA: Oh, Sue.

SUE: Ever since you had that brief affair with her . . .

DONNA: I never had an affair with Lil.

SUE: Don't lie to me. Kitty told me all about it. You and Lil leaping out a motel window.

DONNA: Kitty made up that story.

SUE: Why would Kitty make up a story like that?

DONNA: I don't know but she did. Why on earth would I want Lil Zalinski when I've got you? I bet Lil never made more than fifteen thousand dollars a year in her whole life.

SUE: She's good looking. She's reputed to be dynamite in the sack. She had you once and dropped you like a hot potato. My baby doesn't like to get dumped.

DONNA: They have these sandals in blue, too.

SUE: Have a heart, will you?

DONNA: I saw a terrific denim pantsuit in Lord & Taylor.

SUE: Whatever you want, Donna, just don't flirt with Lil tonight. I may be a fool but I don't want to look like one. Leave me some pride, huh?

DONNA: Don't you even feel sorry for Lil? Don't you feel guilty? You're ten years older than she is and you're still healthy as a horse.

SUE: When you're born into my financial bracket, you feel sorry for everybody, guilty about everything—and you learn very quickly that you can't do a damn thing about other people's bad luck. Two pairs of sandals and a pantsuit, that's all you want? You have a tragic flaw, Donna. You never gamble for high enough stakes. I might have gone for a Mercedes.

(She pats Donna's rump.)

Keep moving, honey. We're late already. Go on.

DONNA:

(Climbing steps.)

YOO-HOO!

SUE:

(As they enter.)

Only an hour late, we're improving.

RAE: Come on in, your plates are in the oven.

ANNIE:

(To Eva.)

They're always late. Donna has to change clothes twenty times.

EVA: I changed clothes four times tonight, myself.

RAE: Sue McMillan, Donna Atterly, Eva Margolis. Eva's got Holly House this season.

SUE: Welcome. The two who had it last year fought nightly, kept the whole Cove in a state of crisis. I hope you're happily paired up with someone.

EVA: No, I'm not.

(Donna takes an interested look.)

SUE: Oh, dear. I was hoping for some peace and quiet.

RITA: Eva just broke up—

SUE: Well, we've all been through that—

RITA: With her husband. She's been married for twelve years.

DONNA: To a man?

EVA: What else?

(There is an awkward silence.)

Well, don't worry, I won't burden you with the boring details. Other people's divorces are a dull subject of conversation.

RAE: We were just discussing our children.

DONNA: Children?

RAE: Well, I do have two, you know.

EVA:

(To Donna.)

Do you have children?

DONNA: Me?

EVA: Well, I'm sure you will. You're young yet. Are you married?

DONNA: Married? Me?

ANNIE:

(To Donna.)

You're not married.

DONNA: No, I'm not married.

EVA: But your last name is different from your mother's.

DONNA: My mother?

LIL: She's not her mother.

DONNA: Sue? No, she's not my mother.

EVA: I'm sorry.

SUE: It's all right. It's an understandable mistake.

DONNA: You didn't think it was understandable when the maitre d' at Lutece said it. You nearly bit his head off.

EVA: I'm sorry. I just assumed . . .

SUE: Forget it. All right?

(She moves to the window, embarrassed.)

ANNIE: Honey, did you put coffee on?

DONNA:

(To Eva.)

Now see what you've done? She'll give me a hard time for the rest of the night.

EVA: I've apologized. I don't know what else to do.

DONNA: Well, it was a dumb thing to say.

LIL: Donna!

EVA: I thought it was a perfectly reasonable assumption. What is she, your aunt?

DONNA: Are you putting me on?

(To Lil.)

Where'd you find her?

KITTY:

(Quickly.)

I have a new book coming out. In the fall.

DONNA:

(To Eva.)

She's going to give me hell all night because of you.

RITA: Kitty's new book is really very exciting. I've read it, you know. I typed it.

DONNA: Jesus H. Christ.

(She glances toward Sue.)

RAE:

(Seizing the situation.)

Look how clear it is tonight. You can see Connecticut!

(She goes to window and puts her arm around Sue, comfortingly.)

I bet it's beautiful from the beach. Lil, why don't you take Eva down and show her the Connecticut skyline from the beach? Coffee will be another ten minutes.

LIL:

> (To Eva.)

> Would you like that?

EVA:

> (Anxious to get out of there.)

> Yes. Yes, I would.

DONNA:

> (To Eva.)

> You better get your act together or this summer is going to be a real mess.

ANNIE: Be careful on the steps, it's dark and those planks are older than both of you.

> (Lil leads Eva down the steps.)

KITTY:

> (Watching them go.)

> Dear God in Heaven.

ANNIE: Speak to her for us, Kitty. She listens to you.

KITTY: Sue, you've got to do something about her.

> (She means Donna.)

DONNA: About me? You better do something about her. Is Lil making it with her or what?

ANNIE: Poor Eva. She doesn't know what the hell is going on.

RAE: It must be awful for her.

DONNA: Awful for her? She hurt Sue's feelings.

SUE: Since when have you cared about that?

DONNA: I care. I've stuck around three years, I must care.

SUE:

> (Touched.)

> Come on then, give your old Mom a hug and kiss.

DONNA: Just a minute. I want to see what Lil's up to down there.

SUE: That's none of your business.

ANNIE:

> (Looking out the window.)

> That's what I'd say if they were doing something but they're not doing anything.

KITTY: Give Lil time.

RAE: I don't think that's what Lil has on her mind this summer.

ANNIE: Why not? If I were Lil, that's exactly what I'd have on my mind.

RAE: Kitty? Is she going to make it through the summer?

KITTY: The chemotherapy appears to have had a positive effect. There's no sign of new growth.

ANNIE: So she could get well and live for years.

KITTY: She could.

RITA: But, Kitty, you said that practically never happens, not with that kind of cancer. You said it moves so fast.

KITTY:

> (Snaps.)

> There is no indication of new growth at the present time.

RITA: But you said . . .

KITTY: It doesn't matter what I said, Rita. The practice of medicine is not an exact science. And I'm no expert in this field, don't ask me!

RITA: You are an expert, Kitty. You were an expert.

KITTY: Never.

RITA: It was your field of specialty!

KITTY: Don't tell me what I did, Rita!

RITA: You said you couldn't stand to watch people dying. You said you had to lie all the time and give people hope when you didn't think there was any.

KITTY: Rita, for God's sake!

RITA: These are your friends, Kitty, and they ought to know—she's not pushy and self-centered the way you think. She's kind and sensitive and caring. . . .

KITTY: Rita, Rita! What am I going to do with you?

RITA: I'm telling them because I love you.

KITTY: I know that! I just don't know how to shut you up!

RITA: She's angry at me that I told her secret.

RAE: It's not a secret, honey.

SUE: It's a charade. She wants us to play it with her, so we do.

DONNA: It's not all a charade. Kitty can be very pushy and self-centered. And mean. She can be very mean.

KITTY: And loud. I can be very loud. You can hear me clear through a motel room door.

DONNA: I haven't the foggiest notion what you're talking about.

RAE: Hold it! RING! Into your corners, ladies. We all agreed no fights this summer. We're going to make this summer perfect: this one's for Lil.

DONNA: What is she doing down there?

SUE: Will you get away from that window?

DONNA: I'm not flirting with her. I'm watching her.

SUE: Well, don't.

RAE: Hey, hey, take it easy, Sue.

DONNA: She can't help herself, she's menopausal.

KITTY:

> (Clinically.)

> Are you really?

DONNA: She has no interest in sex, she flies off the handle all the time.

RAE: According to Kitty's book, none of those symptoms come with menopause. That's an old wives' tale.

DONNA: Sue says she's menopausal, says it herself.

RAE: Kitty's book says . . .

SUE:

> (To Kitty.)

Fuck what Kitty's book says. How would Kitty know?

Have you *been* menopausal?

KITTY: Don't get so upset, Sue. There's nothing to get so upset about.

SUE: She makes me feel so completely inadequate.

DONNA: I don't make you feel any way—don't blame me for your own insecurities.

ANNIE:

(To Sue.)

Why do you continue to put up with that?

SUE: Because I love her.

DONNA: Do you really? Say that again. I like to hear you say that.

SUE: I can't. Donna, you're driving me crazy!

(Sue exits to bathroom.)

DONNA: Hey, *wait*! Sue! I was only kidding! Where's your sense of humor?

KITTY:

(At window, looking down at beach.)

I don't like the looks of that.

ANNIE:

(Looking, too.)

Naw, they're just talking.

KITTY: They've been talking too long. Straight ladies can be very dangerous. They tend to toy with our affections.

ANNIE: Well, you're certainly the expert on that subject.

KITTY:

(Starchily.)

Lil does not need to be toyed with this summer.

RITA: I had a college roommate like that. We'd make out all night and then she'd get up in the morning and babble on about how she loved her boyfriend. I thought for months I was hallucinating.

KITTY: I want this summer to be as pleasant and serene as possible.

ANNIE: Lil can take care of herself. She can. I think she can.

(Lights down on cabin, up on beach.)

LIL:

(As though concluding a description.)

. . . and to the left, that's the yacht basin. July 4th, they'll race, a hundred boats with spinnakers—it's really breathtaking.

EVA: You love it here, don't you?

LIL: It's my favorite place in all the world. I wish I'd found it sooner. This is only my fourth summer at the Cove.

EVA: Well, think of it this way. You have forty summers ahead of you. I think I'll head back to my cabin now. Thanks for inviting me.

LIL: It was awful for you, wasn't it? I'm sorry. The whole thing was just a terrible mistake.

EVA: I don't understand! I tried to be polite and sociable. I tried to say the right things. I've never felt so left out in my life. I might as well have been speaking another language.

LIL: You were speaking another language.

EVA: I thought I had it figured out—no men, no husbands—then Rae started talking about her children.

LIL: Lesbians have children, too. Some lesbians do.

EVA: I feel like such a fool. Why didn't you just tell me?

LIL: I couldn't. I couldn't just say, all the women in this cove are lesbians—because I don't have the right to make that kind of announcement for them. They have to make the decision to tell that themselves and everybody doesn't make the same decision at the same time—it's a mess, that's what it is, a mess. It's hard on us and it's hard on you. I'm sorry.

EVA: They're probably up there right now, laughing at what an idiot I made of myself.

LIL: No, nobody wanted to hurt you or embarrass you, Eva. I should never have invited you tonight—but at the time I asked you, I thought you were one of us.

EVA: You what?

LIL: It was a logical assumption. Marge Eaton has never, in recorded history, rented a cabin in Bluefish Cove to a heterosexual.

EVA: Never?

LIL: Bluefish Cove has been a gay women's haven for thirty years or more. These cabins were built by two elderly "maiden ladies"—that's what the locals called them. One of them's still alive in a nursing home, up island. Couple of years ago, a bunch of us drove up to see her. Annie took some photographs of the yacht race on the Sound and Rae brought her a bouquet of lavender. She never did understand who we were or why we were there. She kept staring at us and twice she looked around as though there were someone standing behind her and she said, "Elizabeth, I believe we have some company." Elizabeth was her lover's name, I guess. I don't know what will happen to the Cove when the old lady dies.

EVA: You could buy it. You could all get together and buy it.

LIL: Maybe Sue will buy it. She has the money to do it. Or Kitty.

EVA: I can't believe that Kitty Cochrane . . .

LIL: Yeah, well, don't talk about it, huh? It really could hurt her career.

EVA: George always claimed that women's libbers were a bunch of . . .

LIL: Dykes? Not all—but some. After all, dykes are women, too. I'll call Marge tomorrow. I'll explain to her and maybe she'll cancel your rental contract.

EVA: I don't know where else to go. I need a friend now. I'd wanted it to be you.

LIL: I'm not a vampire, for heaven's sake. I don't go around pouncing on pretty women. I know how to be friends. But you won't be comfortable here, Eva. You're out of place.

EVA: I'm out of place everywhere, Lil. I'm out of place here, in my marriage, in my life. And I'm terrified to be alone. I've never been alone.

LIL: Everybody's alone, Eva, sooner or later—we do all the important things alone.

EVA: Not me.

LIL: You're alone getting born, giving birth, dying. Oh, people may be standing around you, watching you, but you do the thing alone. You fall in love alone. Yes, you do. It's not like dancing the tango, two people don't fall in love in lockstep. One falls first, one falls later and maybe one never falls at all. You say Kitty's book changed your life—it didn't. It might have given you some courage but you're the one who changed your life, Eva. You rented the cabin, you spoke to me on the beach, you asked me to be your friend—you're not nearly so dependent as you think you are, Eva. Wherever you go this summer, I expect you'll do just fine.

EVA: Those women in your cabin tonight, they all seem so independent. And you, you don't need anybody. I admire that. You're not afraid of anything. George says women can't get along without men. Ha. I wish he could have seen what I saw tonight.

LIL: Eva, forget what you saw tonight, huh? Go back to your cabin, get a good night's sleep and I'll call Marge for you in the morning. Go on. Oh Jesus, don't start crying.

EVA: I'm not crying! I'm mad. I'm scared. You don't want me here and I don't know where to go . . . you were going to be my friend . . .

LIL: Eva, I am your friend. Everything's going to be just fine, you'll see. Now, go on. It's freezing out here. Good night.

> (*Reluctantly,* Eva *leaves.* Lil *watches, then turns and mounts stairs to cabin. Lights up in cabin.*)

ANNIE: Here she comes.

KITTY: Alone?

RAE: We'll, hey there. We were getting worried about you.

LIL: Sorry. She was pretty upset. This has been a stinking party, hasn't it?

DONNA: It's early yet. We can still party.

SUE:

> (*Exiting bathroom.*)

We're going home now, Donna.

DONNA: Why?

SUE: I'm tired. I'm menopausal!

DONNA: What a drag!

SUE: We'll see you on the beach tomorrow, okay? Donna?

DONNA: Lil, want to go sailing tomorrow?

SUE: Donna.

DONNA: You don't like to sail. It makes you seasick. Lil?

LIL:

> (*Her attention is toward the window.*)

I'll take a raincheck, Donna.

SUE: Donna, come on.

DONNA: If you change your mind, Lil . . .

SUE: Donna.

> (*They exit.*)

ANNIE: I'd like to strangle that kid. What a cunt.

KITTY: Annie! Never use a woman's genitalia as a derogatory word. What kind of feminism is that?

ANNIE: Kitty, m'dear, it has been my experience that in any group of men you will find a number of pricks. And occasionally, mind you, occasionally, in a group of fine upstanding women like ourselves, you will find a cunt. Donna is one. She wants Lil's body.

KITTY: She's had Lil's body.

ANNIE: Well, apparently she didn't get enough of it.

LIL: How could she? Kitty was breaking down the mote room door.

KITTY: She isn't good for you.

LIL: Don't worry. I can't be bothered. I haven't the energy or time.

RAE: That's the most sensible thing I've heard you say since I've known you.

> (Kitty *is preparing to leave.* Rita *follows suit.*)

KITTY:

> (At door.)

All right, gang. I'm going into town at ten a.m. tomorrow morning. If you want anything, write it down and attach cash. Last year, I managed to lose a lot of money. "Oh, Kitty, pick up some aspirin for me, will you?" "Toothpaste, we're nearly out of toothpaste." "Tampax, I forgot to get Tampax." This year, Rita's keeping track and I'm going to bill you.

LIL: Once a nitpicker, always a nitpicker; becoming famous hasn't changed you one damn bit.

KITTY: Last chance. Night all.

RITA: Thank you. It was a lovely dinner, Rae.

> (*They exit.* Rae *picks up the cups and stacks them in the sink.* Lil *stares out the window.*)

RAE: That Rita's got good manners. She's the only one who said how good the meal was, the only one. The rest of you bums just took it for granted.

ANNIE: I never take you for granted, love, never. My life with you is a glorious adventure.

RAE: Are you making that up?

ANNIE: My nights are rich with mystery, my dreams breathless with expectation.

RAE: You read that somewhere!

ANNIE: I think I read it in a Kitty Cochrane book.

> (Rae *smacks her with dishtowel.*)

On the other hand, maybe I overheard Lil saying that to Donna!

> (*Again, a smack.*)

ANNIE: Are you okay, Lil?

> (*Sees* Lil.)

LIL: Just tired.

ANNIE: Well, they told you to expect that, didn't they? Maybe you should take a nap in the afternoon.

LIL: I don't have time to take a nap.

ANNIE: Hey.

> (*She tries to comfort* Lil *but* Lil *brushes her off.*)

You like her, huh? I know you. Do I know you or do I know you? I know you. You like her, huh? Huh? Am I right? You like her! Uh-huh!

LIL:

(Laughs.)

Kind of.

ANNIE: See then? Who knows you? I know you. Nobody knows you like I do. Right?

LIL: Right.

ANNIE: I love you, good buddy.

LIL: You said that earlier. Don't get mushy.

ANNIE: I know. My loving you is not enough. But just the same, I do.

(Calls to Rae.)

Come on, ol' lady, we're going home. Don Juan here is plumb wore out.

RAE: All right, all right, I'm just finishing up.

ANNIE: You need anything, Lil?

LIL: Yeah. Time.

ANNIE: You really like her.

LIL: She needs somebody. So do I.

ANNIE: Well then?

LIL: No. Wouldn't work.

ANNIE: Never say never.

LIL: She's straight.

ANNIE: Maybe she is and maybe she isn't.

LIL: She is.

ANNIE: I thought Rae was, too. Married lady with chubby babies hanging on her skirt. Then she attacked me.

LIL: It's not the same thing. You could offer her a life together.

ANNIE: You don't know yet what you could offer her—it's not the quantity of time, Lil, it's the quality—and you've got lots of quality, my friend.

LIL: You know, the one thing I've always had going for me is I know who I am. I know who I am, what I am, and what I'm capable of doing. Most of the time, I actually know what I want.

ANNIE: And?

LIL: She doesn't. She doesn't know a thing about herself. I don't make brass sculptures that last forever. I never wrote a book or had a baby. I'd like to pass something on.

RAE:

(To Annie.)

Okay, hot shot, let's go.

ANNIE: We'll see you in the morning?

LIL: Thanks, both of you.

RAE: When you get to feeling better, you can cook for us and wash our dishes.

LIL: That's a deal.

ANNIE: Get some sleep, will you?

LIL: I'll try. I get tired but my mind won't stop. I don't want to waste time sleeping.

ANNIE: I bet you could work up a terrific erotic dream tonight. Now, I don't consider that a waste of time!

LIL:

> *(Grins.)*

You may be right about that.

ANNIE: Do I know you, huh?

LIL: Will you get outta here?

> *(They exit. Lil straightens up, unmakes the bed, sits on it, despondent. To herself.)*

It isn't fair.

> *(She examines Annie's sculpture on table, replaces it, lights a cigarette, then hurls the ashtray on the floor.)*

Goddammit.

> *(She bursts into tears and races into the bathroom.)*
> *(Lights slowly down on cabin, up on beach. A passage of time. Eva, wrapped in jacket and shivering against the sea breeze, enters. She looks up at the cabin and begins to mount the stairs. Lil, coming out of the bathroom, is startled by the knock.)*

LIL: Who is it?

EVA: I'm too upset to sleep.

LIL:

> *(Not going to door.)*

It's late, Eva. I'm very tired.

EVA: But I need to talk.

LIL:

> *(Reluctantly coming to door.)*

We'll talk tomorrow. Life doesn't look so damned dramatic in the sunlight.

EVA: Have you been crying? Your face is swollen.

LIL: Naw. Catching a cold or something.

EVA: Your eyes are puffy.

LIL: Probably an allergic reaction to the sun. I stayed on the beach too long this afternoon.

EVA: I warned you. Bet your shoulders are blistered.

LIL: No, they're fine.

> *(Eva touches Lil's shoulder; Lil winces.)*

EVA: See? You ought to put something on them. You have some Noxema?

LIL: No, Eva. I'm just fine. I'm terrific, wonderful. Good night.

EVA: It gets cold here at night, doesn't it?

> *(She shivers visibly.)*

That sea breeze. . . .

LIL: All right, Eva, but not for long. I've got to get some sleep.

> *(She lets her in. Lil keeps her distance. Eva sits awkwardly.)*

EVA: I used to talk to my little boy, Lenny, late at night like this. I'd sit by his bed and talk and he'd listen to me. He lived to be six years old. I taught him to read—he loved to read. He'd read to me out loud. I'd never been much of a reader myself, until Lenny came along. Then I started going to the library and bookstores to get books for him—and I'd pick up something for myself. In a way, you could say Lenny taught me to read. I think George thought he was somehow responsible for Lenny's heart. George thinks he's responsible for everything. He's not a mean man, he's just set in his ways. My mother wanted me to marry an adventurer—she was always dreaming about adventures. Going places no one else had gone, doing things no one had done—she never went anywhere herself, of course, it all happened in her mind. She wanted me to have adventures for her. And I haven't had a one. . . .

LIL: Oh, I'm sure you have, Eva. Coming to the party tonight was a kind of adventure, wasn't it? Maybe not a pleasant one, but—

EVA: I bet you have adventures all the time.

LIL: Don't make a heroine out of me, Eva.

EVA: But I admire you.

LIL: I've done a whole lot of things in my life which were not in the least bit admirable. Ask Kitty Cochrane, she'll give you an earful.

EVA: Were you and Kitty . . .

LIL: For a while.

EVA: But now, you're not . . .

LIL: It's not a time for me to make commitments. I was never much for making commitments, anyway.

EVA: How did you know you were?

LIL:

> *(Challenging her.)*

> What?

EVA:

> *(Forcing herself to say it.)*

> Gay.

LIL: I fell in love with a woman.

> *(Snaps.)*

> What is this, twenty questions?

EVA: I'm sorry—I just don't know anything about it and—

LIL: Okay. I knew very early, some people do. I knew when I couldn't take my eyes off my high school English teacher, when my knees quivered every time my chemistry lab partner brushed her elbow against mine. When I could hardly wait for double dates to end so my girlfriend and I could cuddle in her bed together and demonstrate to one another what the boys had done to us. I knew it didn't mean a thing to her—that when I touched her, she was pretending that I was a boy. But I wasn't pretending. She was the real thing for me. I didn't know there were so many others like me until I got to college and met Annie. Annie swears that she was born gay. She was playing doctor with little girls in kindergarten. She's never had the slightest heterosexual tendency.

EVA: So, it was you and Annie?

LIL: Oh, goodness, no. Never. Annie and I are best buddies. It was Annie who showed me the gay bars and restaurants, the gay resort areas—we gays are kind of like the hobbits—no matter how repressive earthlings get, we continue to thrive in Middle Earth. We're survivors. We straddle both worlds and try to keep our balance.

EVA: Kitty Cochrane's book says you can be bisexual. She says it's the most natural way to be.

LIL:

(Sardonically.)

She does, huh?

EVA: I'd really never thought about that before.

LIL:

(Knowing what is coming.)

Well, Kitty also claims a mature person should not expect their partner to remain monogamous, that jealousy is an immature response. And I'm here to tell you that what Kitty says and what Kitty does are not the same thing. Kitty is a very possessive lady.

EVA: You don't like her, do you? You're always putting her down.

LIL: Like Kitty? I adore Kitty. She's my good friend. I might poke a little fun at Dr. Kitty Cochrane, feminist soothsayer, but that's just a mask she wears. The real Kitty is an old-time friend of mine. We've been through a lot together. Kitty's all right. I can count on Kitty to come through.

EVA: Lil, were you ever attracted to a man?

LIL: Are you writing a book or what? It's after midnight!

EVA:

(Flustered.)

No, I'm just trying to . . .

LIL:

(Challenging.)

To what?

EVA:

(Quietly.)

To understand. You think I'm boring, don't you?

LIL: No. . . .

EVA: Just another runaway housewife.

LIL: I don't think you're boring, Eva. You're lonely, vulnerable, curious—and that combination scares the hell out of me.

(Lil smiles at Eva.)

EVA:

(Shyly.)

I thought about you ever since I saw you on the beach today—at the party tonight, I could feel you watching me. I thought I could.

(Lil shrugs, admitting it.)

I sensed something was happening between us, I mean, I've never felt this kind of thing with a woman and I didn't know how to . . . I don't know how to . . . I mean, I've never . . . I wasn't even sure, I'm not sure . . .

(Lil *begins to grin, watching* Eva *stammer through this.*)
(*Quietly smiling.*)

Are you just going to let me stand here and make a fool out of myself?

LIL: I'm not a curiosity, Eva. I'm not an experiment, not an adventure. On the other hand, I have never, repeat *never*, gone shopping with anybody for matching sheets and drapes at Bloomingdale's.

EVA: I understand.

LIL:

(*Touching her face.*)

Do you?

EVA:

(*Bravely.*)

I'm not as naive as you think I am.

LIL: You're not?

(Lil *touches* Eva *seductively.*)

EVA: All right, I am.

LIL: Uh-huh.

(*She guides* Eva *toward door.*)

Go home, Eva. It's late, I'm tired, I'll see you on the beach tomorrow. We'll spend the afternoon together on the beach, all right?

(*She touches* Eva's *lips with her fingers. Sighs.*)

My mother must have told me fifty times, never kiss on the first date.

EVA: You're a puritan.

LIL: No, but my mother is. This is the first time I've ever taken her advice. Goodnight.

(Eva *starts to descend stairs, looks back.*)

Goodnight, Eva.

(Lil *smiles as* Eva *exits, but the smile fades to anxiety as*)

Blackout

ACT TWO

(*Midsummer now.* Kitty, Rita, Rae *and* Donna *are sunbathing on the beach.* Donna *wears her useless sandals and a giant beach hat and the smallest possible bikini.* Rae, Kitty *and* Rita *wear ordinary bathing suits and are passing around a thermos of martinis.* Annie, *in ragged cutoffs and a shirt with the sleeves ripped out of it, is barefooted on the rock, fishing.* Sue *is with her.* Donna *struts back and forth, displaying her body and glancing up at the cabin with irritation.*)

DONNA: Don't they ever get out of bed?

RAE: Why don't you mind your own business?

DONNA: Well, they can't be doing it all the time. It's physically impossible.

RITA: Kitty says women are capable of many multiple orgasms. Men aren't but women are.

DONNA: Well, I think it's perverted. We've hardly seen Lil all summer.

RAE: It's Lil's summer. If she wants to spend it in bed, let her.

DONNA: Well, it isn't fair.

KITTY: You'd think it was fair enough if you were the one in bed with her.

> (Sue *turns and catches* Kitty's *eye. To* Sue.)

> Sorry.

> (Donna *climbs partway up the stairs, looking.* Sue *watches her.*)

ANNIE:

> (*To* Sue.)

> You deserve better than that, Sue.

SUE: Do I?

ANNIE: Yes. She uses you.

SUE: They all do. She's not the first pretty young thing I've kept. I don't expect she'll be the last.

ANNIE: You're a nice lady. You don't have to buy love.

SUE: I have never known, in fact, who loved me and who loved my bankbook—except with this one. I don't have to lie awake nights saying to myself, "But she said this," or, "She did this," and, "Maybe that does mean she loves me"—with Donna, I know exactly where I stand.

> (*Lightly.*)

> It hurts less that way, Annie.

KITTY:

> (*Calling to* Donna.)

> Come down from there, leave her alone.

DONNA: None of you are concerned about Lil.

> (*She comes down.*)

> You don't care whether you see her this summer or not. You don't care if you ever see her again.

RAE: Of course we care.

DONNA: Any day could be her last.

KITTY: Oh, don't be so dramatic, Donna. People in Lil's condition just don't keel over suddenly. She'll have adequate warning and so will we.

RAE: I saw them walking on the beach this morning. Lil looked fine, her color's good. And I don't know when I've seen her look so happy.

RITA: I saw Eva in the supermarket. She looks good, too. She was all excited about moving into Lil's apartment in the city—she said they'd signed a lease to take the cabin again next summer.

KITTY: She said what?

RAE: She hasn't told her!

KITTY: Why didn't you tell me that?

RITA: I told you I saw her.

KITTY: But you didn't tell me that.

RITA: You were writing. I didn't want to break your concentration.

RAE: Annie!

(Annie *leaps from rock to shore, turns to offer* Sue *a hand.*)

ANNIE: Yeah. I don't know what it is Lil does to catch fish off this rock but I don't seem to have any luck at all.

RAE: Did you know that Lil hasn't told Eva?

ANNIE: Hasn't told her what?

(*Pauses, realizes.*)

She hasn't?

KITTY: I understand it but I'm not happy about it. Lil's going through denial. It's natural—but in these circumstances—

ANNIE: I wouldn't tell her, either.

DONNA: I would—it would be so—romantic. Like Camille.

SUE: Will you shut up?

ANNIE:

(*To* Sue.)

Thank you. That's a step in the right direction, Sue.

RAE: But it isn't right, not to tell her. Eva ought to know.

ANNIE: As long as Lil feels good, I don't see why she has to tell her. Lil doesn't want to be looked on as a dying woman, for Christ's sake. Would you? She's in love, she feels wonderful, she wants to live. Leave her alone.

DONNA: You'd think she'd want to spend her last days with her friends. She just met Eva—she's known us for years.

ANNIE:

(*To* Sue.)

Will you do something about that brat before I drown her?

DONNA: I don't have to take that from you. I don't have to stand here and be insulted by a bunch of dykes.

ANNIE: Oh, and what are you, sweetheart, chopped liver?

DONNA: I'm bisexual. Or I could be if I wanted to. When we took that cruise to St. John's last year, I could have had every man on shipboard, couldn't I, Sue?

SUE: To tell the truth, dear, I thought you did.

DONNA: Well, I didn't! But nobody could blame me if I had. I certainly don't get any at home!

RAE: Donna!

DONNA:

>   *(To Annie.)*
>
>   You don't care about Lil. You're just going to let her stay up in that cabin with that stranger all summer long. She's going to die and we'll never see her again and you don't care. I'm going back to the cabin, Sue.
>
>   *(She hobbles off.)*
>
>   Sue? I'm going back to the cabin, aren't you coming?
>
>   *(No answer.)*
>
>   Sue!

SUE:

>   *(Not moving.)*
>
>   No. You're a big girl, Donna. You can get here to there alone.
>
>   *(Donna is stunned.)*
>
>   Go on.
>
>   *(Donna, puzzled and disgruntled, hobbles off.)*

ANNIE:

>   *(To Sue.)*
>
>   Good girl.

SUE: She's spoiled rotten. And I'm the one who spoiled her. She was a perfectly ordinary little girl from Brooklyn when I met her. Oh, she'd gone to modeling school but she worked as a trainee on the Information Desk at Bloomingdale's.

I was looking for the sale in Sportswear and she directed me first to Home Furnishings and then to Men's Outerwear and finally to Lingerie. She had a wonderful sense of humor about her inefficiency and never once apologized for sending me on wild goose chases all over the store. Donna was not always what she is now. I played a part in creating the monster. And like Dr. Frankenstein, I am somewhat reluctant to release my creation on the world.

>   *(Lights dim on beach, up in cabin. Eva is sitting on the unmade bed. She has a pad of paper in her lap; she is making a list. Lil is not in sight.)*

EVA: How big is your dining room?

LIL: What?

>   *(Sticking her head out the bathroom door, washing her face.)*

EVA: Your dining room?

LIL: *Our* dining room.

EVA: How big is it?

LIL:

(*Coming out, still scrubbing her face.*)

It's very tiny. Actually, it's not a dining room, it's an alcove. It's, oh, I don't know, about like—I don't know, honey, it's little.

EVA: Will it hold an oak table and six bentwood chairs?

LIL: Sweetheart, this is a very small apartment.

EVA: But I have so much gorgeous furniture. Do I have to leave it all for George?

(*Lil goes back to bathroom.*)

We can get a bigger apartment.

LIL:

(*Returning.*)

Honey, I can afford *this* apartment.

EVA: Well, I can get a job. Some kind of job. Can't I? Do you want me to work?

LIL:

(*From bathroom.*)

It's not what I want, Eva, it's what *you* want. What do you want?

(*Lil exits the bathroom, finished.*)

What do you want?

EVA: I wish you'd stop asking me that.

LIL: I don't want you to do anything to please me. Just please yourself.

EVA: But I don't know what I want. Except you. I want you. Always.

LIL:

(*Efficiently.*)

It may come as a big surprise to you, my darling, but there is more to life than—

(*Eva kisses her lightly, seductively, then moves away.*)

—uhhhh.

(*Lil follows. The following dialogue occurs during a slow-moving chase—Eva seducing, Lil reaching out, Eva moving away. It's a lovers' dance.*)

EVA: More to life than what?

LIL: Don't listen to me. I don't know what I'm talking about.

EVA: More to life than sex?

LIL: Some people say that but they lie. It's a pack of lies.

EVA: You mean love does make the world go round?

LIL: Oh, definitely.

EVA: Resolves all problems?

LIL: Absolutely.

EVA: Love conquers all?

LIL: No doubt about it.

EVA: My mother used to tell me, "Marry a rich man. Love doesn't pay the rent."

LIL: Your mother is a callous woman.

EVA: Will a six-foot couch fit in your living room?

LIL: *Our* living room.

EVA: Will it?

LIL: Honey, a six-foot person will hardly fit in that living room.

EVA: What am I supposed to do with all my furniture?

LIL: Sell it, store it, give it to George, give it to your mother, give it to the Salvation
Army, burn it, just stop talking about it, put that damn list away and come here.

EVA: My mother always told me to plan for the future.

LIL: I can see your mother and I are not going to get along.

EVA: We have so much future to plan for, Lil—so many years together, so many things
to do—do you ski?

LIL: Do I ski? I was the college downhill champion.

EVA: I'm the snowplow queen myself. You can follow my trail by the sitzmarks. But I
love it. Imagine riding beside you in a chairlift. I've always had a fantasy about
making love in a chairlift. Everybody on the mountain's craning their necks
looking but they can't get to me and my lover, we're isolated, out of reach,
oblivious to their stares and shouts, caught in the frenzy of our insatiable
desire. Want to try that?

LIL: Nope. You might have gotten away with doing that with George but if you and I
tried it, there'd be a sheriff waiting on the platform.

EVA: I never did it with George. George was never even in that fantasy.

LIL: But it was a man in the fantasy.

EVA: Well, I didn't know any better. Let's go to Switzerland and ski the Alps. And
Spain. You want to go to Spain? I've never been to Spain.

LIL: Nope. I don't want to go to Spain. They throw homosexuals in jail in Spain.
They'll take one look at the way my knees quiver when you look at me and
they'll put me in the hoosegow and throw away the key. Let's go to Amsterdam.
We can get married in Amsterdam.

EVA: Really?

LIL: Yep, we're nice and legal there, just like ordinary folks. Want to marry me?

EVA: Ah, you say that to all your girls.

LIL: I never said it before in my whole life. Girl-Scout's honor. It might make your mother
happy. She sounds like the kind of woman who doesn't want you to live in sin.

EVA: What am I going to tell her?

LIL: That you've left George.

EVA: I've already told her that. I called her the night I did it. She was hysterical for
twenty minutes but she got over it. She and George never got along. I'm sure
she's already called her friends to elicit names of suitable eligible men.

LIL: Tell her you have a roommate.

EVA: What if I tell her the truth?

LIL: Don't.

EVA: Why not?

LIL: Does she vote a liberal ticket? Did she march for civil rights? Did she protest the
war in Viet Nam? Did she boycott grapes and support the draft evaders?

EVA: No.

LIL: Don't tell her then. It's ten to one she'll disown you as a pervert.

EVA: She wouldn't.

LIL: Mine did. Just say you have a roommate and keep your mouth shut. Unless, of
course, you get off on verbal flagellation and suicide threats.

EVA: I don't want to have to lie to my mother. I've never lied to my mother.

LIL: Everybody has lied to their mother.

EVA: Well, not about anything important.

LIL: Annie's mother won't allow Rae in the house. Sue's brothers won't allow her to visit her nieces and nephews. Rita was trained to be a teacher, you know, junior high school math. Her father called the school board and reported her. My mother feigned a suicide attempt and then had a nervous breakdown. Her shrink finally convinced her that my sexuality was not her fault and now she has disowned me. She wipes her hands of me, she says. She says I have faulty genes and I'm a malicious pervert. I keep reading stories in the gay press about how eighteen-year-olds announce it to their families over Christmas dinner and everybody hugs each other and it's all hunky-dory. Well, maybe that happens to eighteen-year-olds but it's never happened to anybody I know. The only one I know who has remained unscathed by their family is Kitty Cochrane—and that's because she has remained safely inside the closet.

EVA: I don't want to lose my family—but I don't want to lie to them, either. I want them to share my happiness. I want them to know you and love you. . . .

LIL: Don't count on it, Eva. Don't tell them unless you're prepared to lose them. I don't think you should tell them anything at all, not yet. I mean, we're very new, you and me, and what if you change your mind, what if something happens—next year this time you could be married to some upstanding dentist in Westchester.

EVA: Lil! You don't mean that.

LIL: Why not?

EVA: I love you! This may have started out to be a summer fling but it's much more than that now—what's the matter with you?

LIL: I'm trying to be realistic, Eva. Things change, people change.

EVA: But you love me—you said you love me. Or is that just part of the game, part of the malicious perversion?

LIL:

(Embraces Eva)

I love you more than I have ever loved anyone. For the first time in my life, I understand why knights rode miles to slay a dragon for their lady's hand.

EVA:

(Half-crying, half-laughing.)

Lil.

LIL: And all those songs with "moon" and "June" and "croon," I thought they were pretty silly. Now, I'm whistling those tunes in the shower. Remember that song, "You're My Everything"? I used to hear that and say to myself, now what the hell does that mean, "You're my everything"? Nobody's anybody's everything. I was wrong.

EVA: Lil?

LIL: Yes, angel?

EVA: Are you ashamed of me? Do I embarrass you?

LIL: What?

EVA: You don't see your friends any more. Since I've been living here, you don't ever ask them over. I see them on the path and they ask how you are—they look at me funny as though I've taken you away from them.

LIL: I'd rather be alone with you.

EVA: At first I thought they didn't like me. And maybe you were embarrassed about me. That first party—it was awful. I know I made a bad impression.

LIL: Eva—I'm proud of you.

EVA: Do you know what tomorrow is?

LIL: Saturday?

EVA: It's our first anniversary. One month.

LIL: Oh, dear. If you cry because I forgot our first anniversary. . . .

EVA: Let's celebrate tomorrow night.

LIL: All right.

EVA: Invite your friends?

LIL: Not just the two of us?

EVA: We can't live in a vacuum forever. Besides, I want to show off. I want all your friends to see how much in love we are. I'm not such a dummy as they thought.

LIL: All right, you asked for it!

(She opens the door, runs partway down the steps.)

Hey gang! Hey, down there! We're throwing a beach party tomorrow night—steamed clams and crabs and lobsters! It's our first anniversary! Bring your own booze—

(The lights fade on the cabin and we hear the sound of a transistor radio on the beach. It's the night of the party, the beach is lit by moonlight. Donna, Sue, Rita and Kitty go to the edges of the stage, collecting driftwood for the fire. Lil joins Annie on the beach—they are laying the firewood. Rae climbs the stairs to help Eva prepare the party food in the cabin kitchen.)

LIL: Next year I'm going to buy some of that fire-starter, that stuff in cans. Trying to light a fire this big with drift and matches is an exercise in frustration.

ANNIE: I thought you were a Girl Scout, you got a merit badge in beach survival.

LIL: I did, I did, but I think I must have cheated—damned if I can remember how I did it.

ANNIE: You probably didn't do it at all. You charmed some little redhead into doing it for you.

LIL: That's not unlikely. That's how I passed Home Economics. Priscilla Miller, who could sew a seam straight as a ruler and fry an egg without breaking the yoke, lives forever in my grateful heart.

(She stands up, breathes the sea air.)

Annie, I feel terrific. I never felt so good in my whole life.

ANNIE: I'm glad, Lil. I'm happy for you. For both of you.

LIL: Doctors aren't infallible, you know. Sometimes these things just stop—the condition arrests itself, recedes, it goes away. When I was going to the clinic for chemotherapy, I met this woman whose tumor'd just stopped, disappeared, seventeen years ago. Then it came back—but she had a seventeen-year reprieve. It happens. She said she knew she couldn't die because she had to raise three kids—so she didn't die. And for seventeen years, until her kids were grown, she felt fine. It's all in having something to live for, Annie. I have Eva to live for now.

ANNIE: I've known you for a long time, Lil, and I don't think I've ever seen you in love before. Not like this.

LIL: It's never been like this. I didn't know it could be like this. Is it like this for you and Rae?

ANNIE: Well, probably not exactly—well, yes, I guess so. I mean, we're kind of passed that stage where we can't keep our hands off each other, thank goodness. You mellow out after a while, you know.

LIL: You mean the honeymoon ends.

ANNIE: Yeah—but that's when the good stuff starts.

LIL: Couldn't be any better than this. In ten years, we'll match notes, okay?

ANNIE: You haven't told Eva, have you?

LIL: She asked about the scar. I told her I had a hysterectomy. Which is true. She doesn't need to know any more than that—what more is there? I feel terrific. They told me I'd start having short-term pain. I haven't felt a thing. I'm telling you, Annie, it's gone. I know it is.

(Donna *approaches* Lil *with an armful of firewood.*)

DONNA: This is getting my shirt all dirty.

(Lil *takes the wood,* Donna *brushes at her shirt.*)

LIL: Come on gang, keep the driftwood coming.

SUE:

(*Depositing her load and collapsing on the beach.*)

Enough already!

RAE:

(*Out the cabin door.*)

Hey, we could use some help up here!

SUE: I volunteer! Anything to get out of this!

(*She gratefully climbs the steps.*)

KITTY:

(*Dumping driftwood.*)

I really think this is enough, Lil. We're cooking seafood, not signalling for rescue.

LIL: One more. One more armful.

KITTY: You overdo, Lil. You always overdo.

(Rita *is staggering up with her armload.*)

RITA:

(*To Kitty.*)

Is this it?

KITTY: She says one more.

(*Contemplates* Rita's *pile.*)

I'll take half of this, she'll never know the difference.

(*Lights down on beach, up in cabin.*)

SUE:

> *(Peering in pot.)*

> Jesus, that thing's alive!

RAE: They're all alive. That's how you cook them, alive.

SUE: Well, I know that, but I thought you drugged them or something first.

RAE: Nope. Right into the fire, alive.

SUE: I wish I hadn't seen it. It looked directly at me.

EVA: I take it you don't cook.

SUE: Only under duress. If push comes to shove, I can put a TV dinner in the oven.

EVA: Donna does the cooking?

SUE: Are you kidding? In the city, the cook does the cooking. When we travel, the hotel does the cooking and out here, we eat two meals a day at Molly Pitcher's.

RAE: Can you count to eight? Then count out the paper napkins, forks, spoons, glasses, paper plates—put them in that box and carry them downstairs.

> *(Sue grimaces and proceeds to do so.)*

EVA:

> *(To Sue.)*

> You travel all year round from place to place?

SUE: All my life. When I was growing up, it was Bar Harbor in the summer, a Massachusetts girls' school in the fall, Christmas in London, back to school for the winter, spring in Paris or Switzerland, back to Bar Harbor. There was a townhouse in the city we called home—my father lived there most of the time but the rest of us wafted in and out, on our way to somewhere else.

EVA: That's the kind of life my mother always said she wished that she could give me.

SUE: It was a nightmare.

EVA: I never went away to school. I went to a local college and lived at home. When George and I first married, we lived with his family for a year before we bought a place of our own. My mother was never crazy about George. She said that he was dull. If Lil were male, my mother would approve her as the perfect choice. We're going to travel, we're going to ski the Alps and Lil wants to take me to Amsterdam. Did you know you can get married in Amsterdam?

SUE: I thought you could get married anywhere.

EVA: A man and woman can get married anywhere. I mean Lil and me. We could get married in Amsterdam.

RAE: Whatever for?

EVA: Well, it would be kind of romantic.

SUE: For god's sake, don't tell Donna about it. She'd marry me, divorce me and wipe me out.

EVA: Oh, no she wouldn't.

RAE: Oh, yes she would.

EVA: Well, I'm glad I married George—I spent twelve years with him. If I'd just lived with him, if I didn't have a marriage contract, I wouldn't get a thing.

RAE: You may not get a thing. I didn't. Not one red cent. I put him through school, raised two kids, kept his house—now if he'd left me, I'd have had him by the short hairs. But I left him, see, and I left him for a woman. The only way he'd agree to let me keep the kids was if I forfeited my suit for child support. Annie's putting my kids through college.

EVA: But George and I bought that house together, we furnished it together, he made investments in the market for both of us.

RAE: In your name?

EVA: I don't know. George took care of those things.

RAE: Did he beat you up?

EVA: No!

RAE: Have a mistress?

EVA: Not that I know of—maybe.

RAE: Unless you can prove abuse or adultery, you're probably out of luck, sweetheart. At least in this state. You left him. And for heaven's sake, don't ever let him know you left him for a woman. Zilch. You'll get zilch.

EVA: But I never had to earn a living. George made good money. I don't know how to be anything but a housewife.

RAE: Me, either. And I'm good at it. I like to make a home, I like to shop, cook, clean. When my kids act up or Annie and I have a fight, I like to get down on my knees with a scrub-brush and wash that kitchen floor until it squeaks. It's a blasphemous thing to say in this age of Kitty Cochrane feminism, but I like creating an environment that's warm and pretty for the people I love.

EVA: Do your kids understand—about you and Annie?

RAE: Oh, we worried ourselves sick about that. We practiced just how we were going to tell the kids. Before we got up the courage to do it, they told us. They'd known it all along. My daughter went through a bad period about it when she was thirteen, fourteen—you know girls that age can't stand to be the least bit different—having a lesbian mother was an embarrassment, I guess. Even now, I'm not as close to her as I'd like to be—we get along all right but something's missing between us. My boy, it didn't phase him. He's a good kid, hair down to his ass but a mother can't have everything.

(She changes the subject abruptly.)

Okay, Eva, grab that pot, will you? And can you carry this box, too? Be careful with that, hold it upright.

EVA:

(Looking in box.)

What is it?

RAE: Get your nose out of there. It's a surprise.

EVA: It's a cake!

SUE:

(Looking.)

"Happy Number One. And Many More."

RAE: *And many more.*

EVA: Well, I should hope so. It's only a month. I expect us to stay together until we're ninety.

(They gather up the boxes and bags and start downstairs as the lights dim in the cabin and come up on beach. Donna is sitting on the stairs, watching. The others have finished preparing the fire.)

ANNIE: Fire's going good.

DONNA: At last.

LIL: You haven't done a thing to help.

DONNA: I did so. I carried wood.

SUE:

(Calls from above.)

Donna! I could use some help with this.

DONNA:

(Mimicking.)

"Donna," "Donna."

ANNIE: Give her a break, will you? She's damned nice to you. Show some appreciation.

DONNA: She doesn't want me to be nice to her, don't you know that? If I were nice to
her, she'd drop me in a minute.

(Donna goes to help.)

ANNIE:

(To Kitty.)

You understand that?

KITTY: Yes.

ANNIE: You would.

KITTY:

(As though from a textbook.)

Sue lacks self-esteem so she asks Donna to reinforce that she, Sue, is, in fact,
not worthy of receiving love. If Donna were to demonstrate affection for Sue, Sue
would feel betrayed and her emotional dependence on Donna would no doubt
cease. It's a classic interaction between neurotics—the symptoms vary from
battering to emotional flagellation. It is not infrequently found in parent/child
and employer/employee relationships as well as those of mates. In the case of
Donna and Sue, Donna, as the flagellator, also experiences guilt because she
does, in fact, harbor affection for Sue but she senses, accurately, that to
demonstrate that affection would jeopardize the game on which their
relationship is based. It is this guilt which causes Donna to act promiscuously as
in the case of Lil where Donna wishes Lil to punish her in the same way Donna
has punished Sue.

LIL:

(To Annie.)

I'm sorry you asked that.

ANNIE: Not as sorry as I am.

RITA:

(Who has been following this carefully.)

You mean that Donna wants Lil to beat her up?

KITTY: Emotionally, dear, emotionally.

RITA: Because she feels guilty because she's so nasty to Sue.

KITTY: That's right.
RITA: Well, why *is* she so nasty to Sue?

> (Kitty *opens her mouth to explain.* Annie *stops her.*)

ANNIE: Don't you say that again. I got a headache the first time.

> (*To* Rita.)

Donna is nasty to Sue because Sue's a sap and Donna's a cunt.

> (*She dares* Kitty *to challenge that.*)

KITTY: Well, I suppose that's another way of putting it.

> (*The others arrive on the beach and unload beside the fire.*)

LIL: Where's the beer? You forgot the beer!
RAE: I set it on the counter. The big red cooler. I thought you had it, Sue.
SUE: I thought Donna got it.
DONNA: I only carried what you handed to me, Sue. I'm not a mind reader.
EVA: I'll go back up.
LIL: No, I'll go, honey.
ANNIE: Oh, no you don't. I'll go.
KITTY:

> (*To* Lil.)

Let Annie go. That cooler's heavy.

LIL:

> (*Challenging her.*)

So what?
KITTY: Lil. Let Annie go.
LIL: No. I said I'm going.
ANNIE:

> (*Pushing her aside gently.*)

Out of the way, pal.

LIL:

> (*Seizing her.*)

I said I'm going.

> (*Meanwhile,* Eva *is completely bewildered by all this.*)

DONNA:

> (*Grabbing* Lil.)

Listen to Kitty, she's your doctor.
LIL: She's not my doctor. There's nothing wrong with me! Let me go, Annie.

> (Annie *looks at* Kitty.)

Don't do this to me, Kitty.

KITTY:

> (*To* Annie.)

Let her go.

(Lil *races up the stairs.*)

EVA: What was that about?

RAE: Rita? Give me a hand here, will you? Push back those coals, Annie, so we can
dump the clams in.

EVA:

(*To* Rae.)

What happened?

RAE:

(*Pats* Eva's *hand.*)

Nothing, honey, nothing happened. Sue?

SUE: Don't you ask me to pick up one of those evil-looking critters.

EVA:

(*Persistent.*)

Something happened but I didn't understand.

ANNIE:

(*To* Kitty.)

She swears she feels fine.

KITTY: Maybe she does.

ANNIE: She says being in love has cured her.

KITTY: Oh, Annie, I hope that's true. I really want to believe in miracles—I want a
miracle for her.

(Lil *appears at the top of the stairs with the cooler. She lifts it over her head and,
showing off, descends the stairs.*)

ANNIE: Jesus, Lil!

LIL: I'm an Amazon! I can lift bull elephants above my head. I can slay dragons to win
my lady's hand.

(Annie *starts to help her.*)

Don't, Annie, you'll upset my balance.

(Annie *stops. They all watch breathlessly as* Lil *successfully completes the steps
and presents the cooler at* Eva's *feet.*)

Voila!

(*She takes a deep bow. To* Annie.)

See?

(*To* Kitty.)

Now get the hell off my back.

RITA: She's only trying to help you!

LIL: I don't need her help.

(*But at that moment the abdominal pain strikes and bends her double.*)

ANNIE: Lil!

LIL: Don't touch me! I'm all right! I'm going to be all right!

> (It hits her again.)

> Eva!

> (Eva, bewildered, frightened, reaches out to Lil.)

> I'm going to be fine, Eva. It's nothing, really. I'm going to be just fine.

> (It hits again.)

KITTY:

> (To Annie.)

> Help me get her up the stairs.

> (They move to do so.)

EVA: What's wrong? What's the matter with her? Lil?

KITTY:

> (To Annie.)

> You get her shoulders.

> (As they straighten her up, Lil cries with pain.)

ANNIE: Take it easy, pal, we got you.

EVA: What's wrong? What are you doing to her?

LIL: Eva!

KITTY: Sorry, Eva, out of the way.

EVA: Lil!

> (As they carry Lil upstairs, the lights fade on the beach. There is a complete blackout and when the lights come up, one week has passed. On the stage is an open overnight case. Kitty and Lil's voices come from the bathroom.)

KITTY:

> (From bathroom.)

> Lil, listen to me.

LIL:

> (From bathroom.)

> You're wasting your breath, Kitty.

KITTY:

> (From bathroom.)

> Lil, you're stubborn as a mule.

> (During this, Annie comes out of closet where she has been hanging up Lil's nightshirt. She returns to open overnight bag and continues to unpack. She takes out robe and hangs it in closet, returns to take out slippers, toothpaste, etc.)

LIL:

> (From bathroom.)

KITTY:

Don't lecture me, Kitty.

(From bathroom.)

Put on your bathrobe.

(Out door, to Annie.)

Where's her robe?

(Annie hands it to Kitty.)

LIL:

(From bathroom.)

Go to hell.

KITTY:

(In bathroom.)

Put it on. You just got out of the hospital, for Christ's sake, Lil. You're going to lie down and rest if I have to tie you to the bed.

(Kitty, irritated, exits bathroom. To Annie.)

Can't you talk some sense into her.

ANNIE: I'm her best friend, not her keeper.

KITTY: She wants to go fishing.

LIL:

(From bathroom, hollers.)

I feel fine!

ANNIE:

(To Kitty *about overnight bag.)*

I'm unpacking this.

KITTY:

(Irritated.)

I see you are.

ANNIE: She said to unpack it.

LIL:

(Entering, wearing robe halfheartedly.)

I'm not going back to the hospital, Kitty.

(Annie unpacks cigarettes from bag and puts them tentatively on counter. Kitty reaches for them but Lil slaps her hand protectively across them.)

KITTY: You're self-destructive.

LIL: My lungs are fine. My lungs have always been fine. Pink and healthy as a baby's.

(Lil reaches for a drink.)

My liver's fine, too.

KITTY: Lie down, Lil. Please.

LIL: Stop trying to turn me into an invalid!

KITTY: Just *walked* out of the hospital. *Walked* out.

LIL: I'm an adult human being. I have a few civil rights left.

KITTY: Lil, you're not being reasonable.

LIL: Fuck reasonable! This is my body, my life. I'll decide what's going to happen to me.

ANNIE: Lil . . .

LIL:

> (*To* Annie.)

> Don't you start on me. You're supposed to be on *my* side.

KITTY: There are no sides. You need surgery.

LIL: Sure. I need surgery this month and I'll need it again next month and again in two months—you know the statistics, Kitty.

KITTY: It will prolong your life, Lil.

LIL: In a hospital bed? No thanks.

ANNIE: You could let them try the cobalt again. . . .

KITTY: You responded very well to chemotherapy last spring.

LIL: For six weeks I was nauseated all day, my hair started falling out, I broke out in blotches, I was so weak I could hardly get from one room to another—Annie and Rae were waiting on me day and night. . . .

ANNIE: We didn't mind!

LIL: I mind!

KITTY: But the treatments helped. You felt wonderful until last week on the beach. . . .

LIL: And I feel fine again now. Without operations, without treatments, I feel fine.

KITTY: Bullshit, Lil.

LIL: They've already got my ovaries, uterus, tubes—if I'm going, I'm going with my hair, guts, breasts, whatever I've got left. I'm going as a person, not a patient. I'm going wanting to live, not wishing I were dead.

KITTY: You are stubborn and bullheaded—and you won't let anybody help you! There's a part of you I've never reached, Lil. You always close the door!

LIL:

> (*Lightly.*)

> You and I were terrible together, Kitty. Just terrible. We competed with each other all the time. Our relationship was an exercise in "can you top this?"

KITTY:

> (*To* Annie.)

> She thought I was a coward when I stopped practicing medicine.

LIL:

> (*Lying, glances at* Annie.)

> No, I didn't.

ANNIE:

> (*Backing her up.*)

> She didn't.

KITTY:

> (To both of them.)

> I know.

LIL: Well, my mother always wanted me to marry a doctor.

ANNIE: And she thought you looked sexy in that white coat. I could never see it myself.

KITTY: Those two years with you, Lil, they were special.

LIL: Well, try to remember the good parts, will you?

KITTY: I don't ever want to forget beating on that door of that motel room. Every time I take myself seriously, I want to think of that. I must have looked like twelve kinds of a jackass.

LIL: You did.

> (To Annie.)

> She did.

> (They laugh together.)

KITTY:

> (Through the laughter, to Annie.)

> Don't let me forget that.

ANNIE: Count on it.

> (The laughter awkwardly peters out. A moment of silence falls.)

LIL:

> (Quietly.)

> How much time do I have left, Kitty?

> (Kitty can't answer. Annie turns away suddenly, about to cry. Lil puts her hand on Annie's shoulder. To Annie.)

> Don't you go soft on me. I need you now.

ANNIE:

> (Holding herself together.)

> I'm here. I'm right here.

> (Lil keeps her hand on Annie as though for support.)

LIL: Answer me, Kitty.

KITTY: What are you asking me, Lil? How long on your feet and pain-free?

LIL: Yes. I have to know. I have to plan.

KITTY: Lil, there's new growth. It could accelerate—or you could go into remission again.

LIL: Is that likely?

KITTY: It happens sometimes.

LIL: The worst that could happen, Kitty. The bottom line.

KITTY: Don't put me in this position, Lil.

LIL: Six months?

ANNIE: Answer her, Kitty.

KITTY: Less.

LIL: Three?

KITTY:

> *(Hedging.)*

> Maybe.

LIL: Six weeks of feeling good?

KITTY: At least.

LIL: Why is this happening to me, Kitty? Why isn't it happening to you or Annie or Rita or Rae? Why not Donna, why not Sue? Are you all so much worthier than I am? I'm in love—for the first time in my life, I feel totally alive. Damn you!

> *(She'd expected more time—she is stunned.)*
> *(Kitty is helpless.)*

ANNIE:

> *(To Kitty.)*

> Do something. Help her.

> *(But Kitty can't.)*

LIL:

> *(Seeing Kitty's helplessness.)*

> It's all right.

ANNIE:

> *(Angry.)*

> It's not all right!

LIL:

> *(Comforting Annie.)*

> I'm going to fish with you, my friend, out on that rock—we're going to smoke the best stuff we can buy—and every day, the first one to catch two blues buys lunch and drinks at Molly Pitcher's.

ANNIE:

> *(Trying to be light.)*

> I'm not much good at fishing.

LIL: I'll teach you all my tricks.

> *(To Kitty.)*

> And you, you never beat me in a game of poker yet.

KITTY:

> *(Trying to be light.)*

> That's because you cheat.

LIL: Me? The Girl Scout? Cheat? Eight o'clock tonight—I'm going to teach you how to fake. Quarters.

KITTY: Aw, Lil. *Pennies.*

LIL: *Quarters,* Kitty. Tightwad. Geez.

> *(To Annie.)*

> I'm offering her trade secrets and she's hassling me over quarters. Now I ask you, is that gratitude?

> *(During the above sequence, Rita, Rae and Eva enter. Eva is carrying a container of soup.)*

RAE: Don't slosh that. It's hot.

RITA: Her hands are shaking.

> *(She takes container from Eva. To Rae.)*

> Smells delicious.

> *(Onstage, Lil, Annie and Kitty are continuing their moment of closeness. As this scene on the beach concludes, they move awkwardly apart on stage.)*

RAE: Actually, it's very bland. Kitty said to make something easy on her stomach. They've got her on a lot of medication. Don't let her load it with salt.

EVA:

> *(Uncomfortably close to the stairs.)*

> I wish someone had told me. . . .

> *(Rae touches Eva supportively.)*

RITA: Would it have made a difference?

EVA: I don't know. It might have.

> *(She takes bowl from Rita and steps onto the stairs, calls.)*

> Lil!

> *(The group onstage responds immediately.)*

ANNIE:

> *(To Lil.)*

> Hey, it's Eva.

KITTY:

> *(Admitting Eva, Rae and Rita.)*

> It took you that long to open a can of chicken noodle?

RAE: I made it from scratch! Only the best for Lil.

KITTY: She could have starved while we were waiting.

> *(Eva sees Lil—they look at one another for a moment.)*

EVA: Soup. Rae made it for you.

> *(Eva puts it on counter.)*

LIL: Fuck Rae's soup.

> *(She opens her arms and Eva goes into them. They cling to one another.)*

RAE:

(*In response to* Lil's *line.*)

Gee, thanks.

RITA:

(*To* Lil.)

Welcome home.

(Rita *and* Rae *attempt to welcome* Lil, *touching her shoulder, kissing her cheek, but she's oblivious to them, her attentions are all on* Eva.)

RAE: Ditto.

(*But there is no response from* Lil.)

ANNIE:

(*Having stuck her finger in the soup.*)

This needs salt.

KITTY: She shouldn't have salt.

ANNIE:

(*To* Rae.)

It's too bland, honey, has no taste.

RAE:

(*Observing* Lil *and* Eva.)

Anybody get the feeling we're not wanted?

(*The others agree and they start to move out. As they go:*)

ANNIE:

(*To* Lil.)

Stay away from that soup, it's terrible.

KITTY: If you need me, Lil, I'll be on the beach.

RITA:

(*Calls.*)

She'll be in the cabin.

(*To* Kitty.)

You're going to bed. You've been at that hospital day and night.

KITTY:

(*Stubbornly.*)

I'll be on the beach, Lil.

RITA:

(*Lovingly.*)

Kitty, we haven't been alone together for a week. . . .

KITTY:

> *(Getting the picture.)*

> I'll be in the cabin, Lil.

ANNIE:

> *(As they exit, to Rae.)*

> Why don't we go to Molly Pitcher's and have lunch with Sue and Donna?

RAE: Because there's a pot of soup this big on the stove.

ANNIE: I was afraid of that.

> *(They are all offstage.)*

LIL:

> *(Holding Eva apart and looking at her.)*

> Well, I'm back. Fit as a fiddle.

EVA: You're going to be just fine.

LIL: Oh, yeah, I always said I could lick this thing.

EVA:

> *(Uncomfortable.)*

> Don't let the soup get cold.

LIL:

> *(Aware of Eva's discomfort.)*

> You didn't know you were getting damaged merchandise, did you? I'm sorry, Eva.

EVA: Stop that.

LIL: It changes everything.

EVA: No, it doesn't.

> *(But it does.)*

> Soon as you get to feeling better, we'll go to Europe just like we planned.

LIL: Sure.

EVA: We'll go to Switzerland—we don't have to ski.

LIL: I couldn't tell you.

EVA: I know.

> *(Pause.)*

> We can still ride the chairlift up the Alps.

LIL: I just couldn't tell you.

EVA: Tiny villages sparkling in the snow. . . .

LIL:

> *(Sharply.)*

> There's no snow in Switzerland this time of year.

EVA:

> *(Forging ahead.)*

> We'll go to Amsterdam then. Maybe Rae and Annie will come with us.
> Somebody has to give me away.

LIL: Nobody can give you away, Eva. You don't belong to anybody but yourself.

EVA: You're upset. You're not feeling well.

LIL: I feel fine. Alley cats recover very quickly.

EVA: We'll travel for a while, then maybe rent a cottage in New England this fall—we can go to the movies and read books together—I can read your favorite books to you—

LIL: Do yourself a favor, Eva. Leave me.

EVA: You don't mean that.

LIL: I do. I bet I've had a hundred women in my life—what makes you think I'd want to spend the rest of my life with you? And your memories of George and your goddam furniture and your uptight mother?

EVA: Lil, don't.

LIL: I want to do some living before I die.

(She goes to door.)

Hey, anybody down there? Where's Donna? I want to see Donna!

(She turns to Eva coldly.)

Get out of here, Eva. Get out of my life.

(Eva doesn't budge.)

EVA: That's always worked for you, hasn't it? One act of bravado and you're off the hook.

(Lil is stunned.)

You have to catch the biggest fish, take every card game, seduce all the women you encounter—as long as you're winning, Lil, you're just fine. But when things get difficult, you leap out the motel window. We love each other, Lil. That's a commitment.

LIL:

(Quietly.)

Next summer, someone else will be standing at this window watching a July sunset—and Rae and Annie will be sitting over there, sipping drinks, and they'll say to this stranger at the window—"Beautiful sunset, huh? Lil, loved that view. She thought God put that rock down there for her. When she stood on it with the surf pounding against it, spraying salt so high that she could taste it on her lips, she was Queen of Bluefish Cove."—I can't say goodbye to that beach out there, Eva. I can't say goodbye to Annie or to Kitty. How can I say goodbye to you?

(Lil goes to Eva, lets Eva hold her. Eva is now the strong one.)
(As the lights dim to black, we hear Kitty and Rita's voices.)

RITA: The wind's so strong. I had no idea it got so cold along the beach.

KITTY: Well, we've never had the occasion to be out here in late fall.

RITA: Pull that scarf around your neck, darling, I don't want you to catch cold. You start the promotion tour for your new book next week and it would be disastrous if you developed laryngitis.

KITTY: What would you think if I were to open up my office again. . . .

RITA: You mean go back to practicing?

KITTY: Lil always felt that I was copping out.

> *(The lights are now up on the cabin and the beach. Kitty and Rita, dressed for winter, walk to the stairs; Rae, also dressed for winter, sits on the stairs. Annie stands on the rock, looking out too sea. Rita and Kitty mount the stairs.)*

RAE:

> *(Glancing at her watch.)*

> I guess it's over now in Michigan. The service was at one o'clock.

RITA: I don't understand how they could take her. She wanted to be buried here.

KITTY: They're her family, honey. They have the legal right.

RITA: Her mother and father had disowned her.

KITTY: Well, they did fly here and stay by her at the end.

RITA: Stay by her? They guarded her from us.

> *(At the top of the stairs, they enter the cabin and begin to stack boxes and fold clothing for packing. Eva enters from the bathroom, carrying a box.)*

SUE: I don't know what to do with all this stuff. Toothpaste, aspirin, bubblebath—

EVA: I promised Marge Eaton we'd clear this place out. Just put it over there, Sue.

KITTY: Lil asked me to give these clothes to the women's center. Some of them are pretty raggedy.

RITA: You can't give that workshirt to anybody. It's torn in half a dozen places.

KITTY: Well, throw it away then.

EVA: No.

> *(She takes it.)*

> I'd like to have that.

RITA: We could store these toiletries in our cabin for the winter—it's a shame to throw it all away.

SUE: What about this tackle box?

EVA: She wanted Annie to have that.

RITA: I'll take it down to her.

> *(She goes downstairs.)*

EVA: I wonder who'll have this place next summer?

KITTY: How about you, Eva?

EVA: I don't think so, Kitty. I couldn't afford it, anyway.

KITTY: You can always visit us.

EVA: I hope I'll be working next summer. I finish that office management course in January, thanks to Sue.

KITTY: If I open my practice again, I'll need an office manager.

EVA:

> *(Gratefully.)*

> Thanks. I've filled out applications for several big corporations with offices in Europe. I'd really like to travel.

> *(Smiles.)*

> Have some adventures.

KITTY: She loved you very much.

EVA:

> *(Pulling herself together.)*

> I know.

KITTY:

> *(Changing the subject.)*

> I expected to see Donna here today.

SUE: I don't think she knows, Kitty. I don't know where to contact her.

KITTY: That was the healthiest thing you ever did, Sue.

SUE: If you say so.

EVA:

> *(Looking around.)*

> Well, I think that's it. We can start carrying it down.

SUE:

> *(Calls.)*

> Hey, Rae, Rita, let's go.

> *(Rae and Rita come upstairs and take bundles from Kitty. One by one, they begin to come down the stairs, arms loaded. Annie is squatting by Lil's tackle box, picking out the lures. As others come down the stairs, she leaps to the rock, holding one lure in her hand.)*

RAE: What is that, honey?

ANNIE: It's her favorite lure. She always used it for the bluefish.

> *(Puts lure in tackle box.)*

> Next year, we're going to build a barbeque pit down here. It'll be our summer project.

RAE: My summer project is going to be to lie in the sun with my feet up.

KITTY: I don't know how much time I'll be able to spend out here next year—if I open up my practice, I'll have office hours weekdays—

RITA: I think I'll hate it when you're on call, you'll be tired all the time.

SUE: I wouldn't miss a summer at Bluefish Cove for anything—it somehow puts my whole year in perspective.

> *(They are off now except Annie and Rae. They look up at Eva in cabin.)*

RAE: You coming, Eva?

EVA:

> *(Lowering blinds.)*

> Yes, I'm coming.

ANNIE: You need a hand?

EVA: No thanks, Annie. I can make it by myself.

> *(She lowers the blind between herself and audience. Rae and Annie exit, knowing Eva will soon follow.)*

> Blackout

Harvey Fierstein (Arnold) and Estelle Getty (Mrs. Beckoff) in
the 1979 Off-Broadway production of Harvey Fierstein's
Torch Song Trilogy at La Mama E.T.C.
(Photograph reprinted with permission from the
John Willis Theatre World/Screen World Archive)

Torch Song Trilogy

BY HARVEY FIERSTEIN

THE INTERNATIONAL STUD

International Stud was first presented by La Mama E.T.C. on February 2, 1978 with the following cast:

LADY BLUES	Diane Tarleton
ARNOLD	Harvey Fierstein
ED	Steve Spiegel

Directed by Eric Concklin
Musical Direction by Ned Levy
Costumes by Mardi Philips
Lighting by Joanna Schielke
Production Stage Manager: B.J. Allen
The production subsequently played at The Player's Theatre with Richard Dow as Ed and Lee Evans as Stage Manager.

There is a gay bar in New York City called "The International Stud." It boasts a pool table, pinball machine and the jumpingest backroom in town. I dearly dedicate these plays to all who made it their home.

I wish for each of them the courage to leave it when they can, and the good sense to come back when they must.

Characters

ED REISS	Thirty-four, very handsome; masculine with a boyish charm.
ARNOLD	Twenty-four (going on forty). A Kvetch of great wit and want.
LADY BLUES	

Synopsis of Scenes

1. January. Arnold, backstage of a nightclub.
2. February. Ed in "The International Stud" bar.
3. June. Ed and Arnold in their respective apartments.
4. September. Arnold in "The International Stud" bar.
5. November. Ed and Arnold backstage.

Lady Blues
Before scene I and between each of the following scenes, Lady Blues appears on a separate set, atop a grand piano, dressed in period, and sings a 1920s or 30s torch

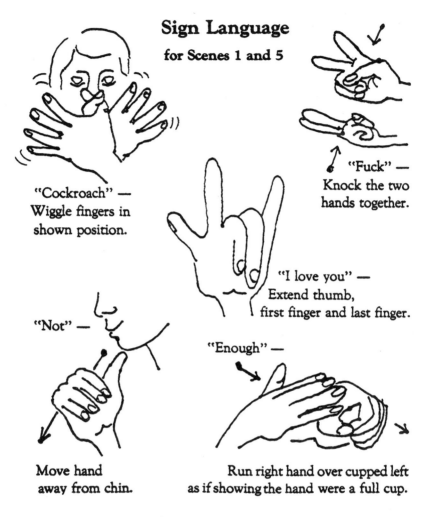

Sign Language
for Scenes 1 and 5

"Cockroach" —
Wiggle fingers in
shown position.

"Fuck" —
Knock the two
hands together.

"I love you" —
Extend thumb,
first finger and last finger.

"Not" —

"Enough" —

Move hand
away from chin.

Run right hand over cupped left
as if showing the hand were a full cup.

song in the manner of Helen Morgan or Ruth Etting. The choice of songs I leave to the director, as they should highlight the values of each particular production. They should not comment on the action as much as conjure it . . .

SCENE 1: ARNOLD

The play is performed against a black cyclorama with as little actual scenery as possible. Up-stage center the grand piano sits on its platform raising the singer high above the action. Downstage of her, on either side, are three-foot high platforms which will be the two apart-ments. Each has a chair, table and telephone. Arnold's chair is worn and comfortable, Ed's is new and straight. Downstage center stands the "Stud" platform. It is just large enough for one person to stand comfortably, raised two feet from the stage. Left of it is a larger platform, 6'×8', which holds an arm chair and vanity table. It is the dressing room. As the lights come down on Lady Blues after her opening song the sounds of a music box are heard softly. The lights rise on the backstage platform revealing Arnold in full drag applying a false eyelash to his face. He turns off the music box . . . The lash slips out of place . . .

Damned Elmer's glue! Just let me finish emasculating this eye and I'll be right with you.

(Fixes it. Poses in the mirror.)

Gorgeous, huh? Use your imagination, it's still under construction.

I think my biggest problem is being young and beautiful. It is my biggest problem because I have never been young and beautiful. More importantly, I will never be young and beautiful. Oh, I've been beautiful. And God knows I've been young. But never the twain have met. Not so's anyone would notice anyway. A shrink acquaintance of mine believes this to be the root of my attraction to a class of men most subtly described as old and ugly. But I think he's underestimating my wheedles. See, an ugly person who goes after a pretty person gets nothing but trouble. But a pretty person who goes after an ugly person gets at least cab-fare.

I ain't sayin' I never fell for a pretty face, but when *"les jeux sont faits"* . . . give me a toad with a pot of gold and I'll give ya three meals a day. 'Cause honeys, ain't no such thing as a toad when the lights go down. It's either feast or famine. It's the daylight you gotta watch out for. Face it, a thing of beauty is a joy 'till sunrise.

I never push Lady Luck myself. I got, what'choo call a extra-sensory sense about such things. If I really like a guy I automatically wake three minutes before him. Giving me just enough time to unsucker my pucker, reinstate my coif, and repose my repose so's his eyes upon waking conjure images by Jove and Lana Turner; guaranteeing my breakfast if not his real phone number.

Here's another hint to all present presently unattached. You can cross any man off your dance card who A: Discusses his wonderful relationship with his mother. B: Discusses his wonderful relationship with his shrinker. Or C: Refuses to discuss his wonderful relationship with his mother or shrinker. See, a guy who's got that kind of confidante is in what I call a "state of confession." And experience has sorely taught me, you can never be more to a man in such a state than subject matter for their conversations . . .

Not that I got anything against analysis, I don't. I think it's a great way to keep from boring your friends. But what's good for the bored just ain't so for the bed, if you get my drift. See, when there's trouble in Paradise you got two possible M.O.'s. Pull back or push in. But pull back when he's got a professional shoulder to lean on and the entire effect of losing you is shot. Try pushing and you've bought yourself two for one. Push hard enough, and you'll find yourself visiting him Sundays at the "Happy Home For The Bewildered."

Now, I ain't sayin' you should only date sane men (I don't want to krill off all the fish in the polluted sea), but at least find one who's willing to fight on his own. Give me a man with both fists clenched tight . . . and I'll give you a smile from here to next Thursday.

And there's another group you've gotta watch your food stamps around . . . "The Hopeless." They break down into three major categories: Married, "Just in for the Weekend," and terminally ill. Those affairs are the worst. You go into them with your eyes open, knowing all the limitations and accepting them maturely . . . then wham bam! . . . you're writing letters to Dear Abby and burning black candles at midnight and you ask yourself, "What happened?" I'll tell you what happened. You got just what you wanted! The person who thinks they's mature enough to handle an affair that's hopeless from the beginning is the very same person who keeps the publishers of Gothic Romances up to their tragic endings in mink; not to mention the reissuers of those twenties torch ditties . . . Music to be miserable by.

So, what's left? I don't know. But there are some. I found one once. His name was Charley. He was tall, handsome, rich, deaf. Everything you could want in an affair and more. The deafness was the more. He never screamed at me, all his friends were nice and quiet, I could play music as loud as I liked without ever disturbing his reading, and best of all I could snore. I even learned me some of that sign language. Wait, I still remember some. Like this here,

(He demonstrates)

it means cockroach. And this one

(Demonstrates)

means fuck. Here's my favorite.

(Demonstrates)

It means "I love you." And I did. But . . . not enough. I guess I bought them Gothic publishers a few minks of my own.

(Signing and speaking together)

For those of yis what ain't yet guessed I am an entertainer (or what's left of one), I go by the name Virginia Hamm. Ain't that a kick in the rubber parts? You should hear some of my former handles; Kitty Litter, Lorretta Dung, Bertha Venation . . . and I'm plenty tough too. I can afford to be; behind a phony name, face and figure. But that's alright.

(Back to his dressing)

See, I'm among the last of a dying breed. Once the E.R.A. and gay civil rights bills have been passed, me and mine will find ourselves swept under the carpets like the blacks done to Amos, Andy and Aunt Jemima. But that's alright too. With a voice and face like this I got nothing to worry about, I can always drive a cab. And that, chillun', is called power. Be it gay, black or flowered it always comes down to the survival of the majority.

Shit, I'd better get a move on it!

(He takes a roll of toilet paper and unwinds two huge wads.)

Would y'all mind turning your backs? . . . Well, could you at least close your eyes?

(He places the paper in his bra with his back to the audience, turns proudly with his chest held high, catches the unevenness of the sizes in the mirror and adjusts them.)

There are easier things in this life than being a drag queen. But, I ain't got no choice. Try as I may, I just can't walk in flats.

(Putting on his hat and shoes)

You know what I really want? I want the International Stud. No, not the bar. The man. A stud. A guy who knows what he wants and ain't a'scared to go out and get it. A guy who satisfies his every need, and don't mind if you get what you want in the bargain. Matter of fact, he aims to please. He'd be happy to be whatever you wanted him to be, 'cause you're happy bein' what he wants you to be. The more you put in, the more you get back. An honest man. The International Stud. One size fits all. But I wouldn't want no guy that wanted me like this here. No, I'd need him for the rest of the time. For the other part of me. The part that's not so well protected. Oh, there's plenty that want me like this. And I take their admiration gratefully. But, at a distance. I guess a drag queen's like bein' a oil painting! You gotta stand back from it to get the full effect.

(Standing)

Well, I think we're in business! My, how time flies when you's doin' all the talking.

(Tucking in the chair)

Who knows, maybe my Right Man is out there tonight, right? Y'all take care now, hear?

(He makes the "I love you" sign, turns to go, stops and comes back.)

Ya' know . . . In my life I have slept with more men than are named and/or numbered in the Bible (Old and New Testaments put together). But in all those beds not once has someone said, "Arnold, I love you . . ." that I could believe. So, I ask myself, "Do you really care?" And the only honest answer I can give myself is, "Yes, I care." I care be . . .

(Catches himself)

I care a great deal. But not enough.

(He smiles knowingly as the lights black out on him and up on the singer.)

SCENE 2: ED

As Lady Blues finishes her song, the sounds of a bar are heard faintly and the lights reveal Ed standing on the Stud platform, his back to the audience. He is tall, lean and very handsome. Although he is in his thirties his greatest charm is his boyishness.

> *(Suddenly stepping back onto someone's foot)*

Oh, excuse me. I'm sorry. I was just trying to duck that pool cue. Gets pretty crowded in here on a Saturday. Your foot O.K.? Good.

> *(He turns away, but then can't help sneaking a look at the stranger. He smiles and turns away embarrassed, then turns to him again)*

No permanent damage, I hope. To your foot I mean . . . Good.

> *(He turns away again, but still tries to sneak a look behind him. He gathers his courage and confronts the stranger with huge smile.)*

Look, the name's Ed Reiss. My friends call me Ed.

> *(No response)*

I'm Saggitarius . . . What's so funny? . . . Oh, well, some people like to know that stuff. I don't believe in any of it myself, but I have done some reading about it. See, I like to know what's expected of me.

> *(He stares with a huge grin.)*

You have a beautiful smile. . . . No, really, you do. Can I get you another beer? Alright, One Lite coming up.

(To bartender)

Can I have a Lite please?
No, not a match. I meant a Lite beer.

(To stranger)

Am I speaking English? I feel like I'm a Martian or something. I think it's that smile of yours. Say, what's your name?
Arnold? Your friends call you Arnie or Arna?
Arnold. Well, nice to meet you Arnold.

(Handing money to the bartender)

Here you go.

(Beer to Arnold)

And here you go.
Are you Italian?
Spanish?
Jewish!? I never would have guessed it. Not with those dark romantic eyes. I don't remember ever seeing you here before. I don't get in that often myself. I teach over in Brooklyn and so have to be up and out pretty early, so if I'm feeling horny this is where I come. I can be in and out of the backroom and home in bed within an hour.
No. I'm off tomorrow. That's why I'm out here instead of back there. You really do have beautiful eyes. Are you wearing make-up?
1 didn't think so. So, . . . uh . . . how's the backroom? Crowded, I'll bet.
Never?
No, it's just that you don't expect to meet someone in a backroom bar who's never been in the backroom. Are you here with a friend?
Is he your lover?
So, you're unattached. How lucky for me. Where you from?
Sure, I know where that is. Live alone?
Well, look, 1 have a car . . . I'd ask you back to my place but I have this straight roommate. He's got a hangup about gays. It's really his place. I only sublet from him.
Oh, well, I date women too. So . . . Anyway, I really live upstate. I've got a farm up about an hour from Montreal. That's my real home. I spend the weekends there during the school year and then all of my summer vacation. I own half of Walton Mountain.
No, that's really what it's called. Most of the land is trees, but there's a piece of flat farming land with an old barn and I work a half acre of that. I grow all my own vegetables. I've even got a small vineyard. The mountains have some great white water for canoeing, and in the winter . . . it's a skier's dream. You ski?
Would you like to learn?
Alright, it's a deal. You'll love the house, it's really great. One of those old Victorian farm houses with lots of ginger-bread and Franklin stoves. My father and I are restoring it.
Well, my parents winter in Florida but come north to stay with me in the warmer months. Hey, what'd'ya' say we continue this conversation in the car?
Great. By the way, what do you do?
No, I meant for a living.
Can you really make a living doing that?
I do believe you're the first one I've met . . . personally. Ready?

(Putting on his coat)

The car's just across the street. Anyone ever tell you you have a very sexy voice? You really do. Is it natural or do you have a cold?

(Gesturing)

After you.

(He turns as the lights go out on the platform and come up on the singer.)

RADIO SHOW BETWEEN

The following conversation should be tape recorded and played during Lady Blues' third song. She should listen to it as if it were part of the musical break. It is underscored by the piano.

ED:

(Excited)

Oh, wow. Your place is really great.

ARNOLD: I'm glad you like it.

ED: No, it's really fabulous. But, would you mind putting on a light?

ARNOLD: There's not much to see.

ED: There's you.

ARNOLD:

(Embarrassed giggle, sound of light switch)

Better?

ED: Better . . . and better. You're shaking.

ARNOLD: Nervous, I guess.

ED: Me too.

ARNOLD: Really?

ED: Really.

ARNOLD: I'm glad you asked me home.

ED: Me too.

ARNOLD: Ed?

ED: Yeah?

ARNOLD: I feel . . . I don't know . . . kind'a scared.

ED: Better?

ARNOLD: Better . . . and better.

(They both laugh intimately as Lady Blues continues her song.)

SCENE 3

The lights come up on Arnold in his apartment. He sits on the floor in shorts and a sweat-shirt with a paperback stuck in his mouth. It is The I Ching. He is throwing coins and marking the hexagram nervously. Reading . . .

ARNOLD: "Having completed the hexagram, compare it to the chart on page 228."

(He flips to the chart and compares his scratchings to it.)

Here it is. Number thirty-eight.

(He searches excitedly for the right page. He finds it.)

Here we go. "Hexagram Thirty-eight. Koo-eee-iiiii. The Estranged."

(He is struck by its meaning, and hides the book under the chair. He lights a cigarette while staring at the phone. He climbs into the chair, grabs the phone into his lap and dials.)

Hello, Murray? Call me back.

(He slams down the receiver and freezes, his hand perched over the phone ready to lift it as soon as it rings. It does not. Slowly his face begins to crack with worry. Still the phone does not ring. He is practically in frozen hysteria when suddenly it does ring.)

ARNOLD:

(Grabbing it angrily)

God dammit, Murray, what took you so long? . . . The shower could have waited Murray. . . . The shampoo in the shower could have waited, Murray. . . . The man with the shampoo in the shower could have waited, Murray. Anyway, I can't talk now. I gotta keep the line free.

(Starting to hang up)

What? . . . I just wanted to make sure the phone was working. . . . Ed. Alright? I'm expecting a call from Ed. . . . When? Well, it is now Tuesday, eight P.M. Well, Ed's gonna call sometime after Tuesday eight P.M. . . . Of course he's gonna call, Murray. You think I'd sit by the phone for six days if he wasn't gonna call? . . . You are getting on my nerves, Murray. Look he is a very busy man. With a great many responsibilities. He will call me when he is able. And I will understand. Got it! When you have been seeing someone for four months, Murray, you build a relationship based on trust and mutual respect. Something you and your Magic fingers shower massage would not understand. He will call, Murray. He knows when he's got a good thing going. He knows I ain't like those other cheap tricks he sees. He knows I got something that puts me above those runned up the mill, always on Sunday, anyplace I hang my crotch is home variety of homosexual commonly cruised in these here parts. I am important, Murray. I am impressive, Murray. But most of all, Murray, I am mysterious. Which is a quality you don't find on every bar stool.

(Getting slow and sexy)

Oh, no, Murray, he will call. And when he does. . . . And when he does . . . And when he does. . . .

(Jumping suddenly)

The phone's gonna be free!

(Slams down the phone)
(Pouting)

Oh ye of little faith!

(Arnold gets an idea. He puts out his cigarette, takes the phone in hand, takes two real deep breaths and holds them and dials. The phone in Ed's apartment rings as the lights come up revealing Ed dressed neatly for a date just about to open a bottle of red wine. There are two glasses on the table by the phone.)

ED:

(Lifting the receiver)

Hello?

ARNOLD:

(Letting out his breath in pants)

Hi. Was that you?

ED:

(Recognizing the voice. Slightly uneasy.)

Oh, hi. Was what me?

ARNOLD: Just now on the phone. Was that you trying to get me?

ED: No.

ARNOLD: Oh. Then I wonder who it was? See, I just walked in this second.

(Non-stop)

You know, I've been out of town all week. And I was fumbling at the door with my luggage and the keys when I heard the phone ringing, so of course I dropped the keys, and when I bent over to pick up the keys I dropped the luggage, so of course since I was nervous and the phone was ringing one of the cases uncaught and opened up and everything fell out all over the place. So, finally I got the door open and kicked everything inside, dove at the phone and picked it up just in time to hear whoever it was calling hang up.

(Slight nervous laugh, then quietly, almost sadly)

So, how are you?

ED:

(Gently)

I was going to call you real soon. I've just been really busy.

ARNOLD: What's the difference, we're talking now. By the way, you remember that Helen Morgan record I played last time you were here? Well, I was able to find another copy in a little secondhand shop uptown. It's almost like new. So I picked it up for you.

ED:

(Embarrassed)

Thanks.

ARNOLD: You're welcome.

ED: Look, Arnold, I can't talk right now. I've got a friend coming over for dinner and uh . . .

ARNOLD: That's O.K. I just called 'cause I thought it was you calling. So, give me a call when you're not so busy.

ED:

(Guilty)

I'm sorry. I'll call you tomorrow.

ARNOLD:

(Hurting)

Hey, no problem. I understand.

ED:

(Annoyed suddenly)

What do you understand? You never give me a chance to call you. Every time I'm just about to there you are calling me.

ARNOLD:

(Frightened)

E.S.P. maybe?

(No response)

Well, just think of all the money I save you on phone calls.

ED:

(Gently amused)

You're impossible. You know that?

ARNOLD:

(Relaxing a bit)

Yeah. It's a wonder you put up with me.

ED:

(Checks his watch)

So, how was your trip?

ARNOLD: My trip? Oh, my trip. O.K. Who's coming over for dinner?

ED: A friend. You don't know him.

ARNOLD: How do you know? I know lots of hymns: "Battle Hymn of the Republic," "Rock of Ages," "Oh Come Emmanuel". . . .

ED: You are impossible.

ARNOLD: So, is it an old him or a new him?

ED:

(Tightening)

Why do you do this to yourself?

ARNOLD: I'm just asking. Can't a person show a little interest in another person's life?

(Pause)

417

So?

ED: A new one.

ARNOLD:

> *(Definitely wounded but smiling through)*

Aha. Where'd you meet him? The Stud?

ED: I've really got to go now, Arnold. I'll call you soon, alright?

ARNOLD: That's what you said last week.

ED: Well maybe if you waited and gave me a chance to call . . .

ARNOLD:

> *(Letting go)*

That's all I'm asking *you* for; a chance. Why're you treating me like some trick you picked up last night?

ED:

> *(Angry)*

Arnold, I don't want a scene on the phone. I'll call you tomorrow and we'll get together and talk.

ARNOLD:

> *(Real soft)*

What's wrong? Until last week, I could've sworn things were going great for both of us. What's happening?

ED: Not now, Arnold.

ARNOLD: Yes. Now.

ED: Arnold, I'm just going to get angry.

ARNOLD: So get angry! Just talk to me!

> *(Silence)*

Hello? Are you there?

ED:

> *(Pause. Quietly.)*

I'm here.

ARNOLD:

> *(Soft)*

I miss you.

> *(Pause)*

I think about you all the time.

> *(Pause)*

I'm so damned horny.

ED:

> *(Slight laugh)*

You need a job.

ARNOLD: I've got a job. I need a lover.

ED:

(Hard)

Well, I don't. There. Is that what you wanted to hear?

ARNOLD: No. But it's a beginning. What *do* you need?

ED: A friend. I've said that all along. If you'd listen sometimes instead of . . .

ARNOLD: You've got a friend. And a lover too. All in one neat package. That's modern efficiency at work.

ED: It is not what I need.

ARNOLD: How do you know? Maybe it is. You'll never be sure unless you give it a try.

ED: I have tried, Arnold.

ARNOLD:

(Hard)

No you haven't!

(Softer)

You haven't. I wish to God you had, but you haven't.

ED: Arnold, this is not going to do any good for either one of us.

ARNOLD: What makes you so sure of what's good and what's not? Maybe it's just what we need. Maybe it's just what *I* need. You can't expect me to just sit around here waiting for you to call.

ED: I never asked you to. I told you to go out, have a good time, meet other people . . .

ARNOLD: I can't, alright? I'm not built that way.

ED: Well I'm just not ready to make that kind of a commitment.

ARNOLD: I'm not asking you to. But if I have to accept you going out then you have to accept that I'm not.

ED:

(Puzzled)

You really are crazy.

ARNOLD: I'm lonely.

ED: That's not my fault.

ARNOLD: Wanna bet?

ED: You've got no right to make me feel guilty.

ARNOLD: I happen to be in love with you. That must give me some kind of rights. And if that don't give me the right to see you, then at least I got the right to bitch about it.

(Long silence)

You said that you loved me. You do remember telling me that, don't you?

ED:

(Quietly)

Yes.

ARNOLD: Then, do you or don't you?

ED: You know how I feel about you.

ARNOLD: I don't. I wouldn't ask if I did.

ED: Yes. I love you.

ARNOLD: Then what's going on?

ED: What do you want me to say?

ARNOLD: I want you to say what's on your mind. That's what I want. I want you to tell me how in two short weeks we have gone from being lovers to whatever the hell you'd call this?

ED:

> (Trying to retain cool)

> You are being very difficult.

ARNOLD:

> (Mimicking)

> You are being very difficult.

> (Hard)

> Talk to me, goddammit!

> (Silence)

> Is it your parents coming north? Is that it? Are you ashamed of me?

ED: Of course not.

ARNOLD: Then what?

ED: Not on the phone. What if I come over straight from school tomorrow?

ARNOLD: No! I've got to hear it now. I know what'll happen if you come over, everything will be great just like it always is when we're together and we'll never even mention tonight. No, I want to hear it from this side of you.

ED:

> (Checking his watch nervously)

> Arnold, I really cannot talk to you now. She'll be here any minute. I'll see you after work tomorrow, O.K.?

> (No response)

> Arnold? Hello?

ARNOLD:

> (Disbelief)

> She? Did you say, SHE?

ED:

> (Mumbled)

> Shit.

ARNOLD: Oh, Shit! Thank God. For a minute I thought you said "She."

ED: I did say she. I am seeing a woman.

ARNOLD: And you called *me* crazy?

ED: Now you know why I didn't want to discuss it on the phone.

ARNOLD: Oh, sure. I can see how much more understandable it would be discussed calmly over a post-sexual cigarette.

(Long pause)

It *is* your parents.

ED: No it isn't!

ARNOLD: Then why all of a sudden like this?

ED: It's not all of a sudden. I just happened to meet her now, that's all. Don't make believe I never told you about my relationships with women.

ARNOLD: Sure you told me about your woman relations. But I thought you meant sisters and aunts and nieces.

ED: That's not funny.

ARNOLD: I think it's hysterical.

(Long pause. He tries to remain calm.)

So, . . . how long has this been going on?

ED: Not long.

ARNOLD: How'd you meet her?

ED: My friends Bob and Janet asked me if I was seeing anyone because they knew this girl they thought I might like to meet.

ARNOLD: And what did you say when they asked if you were seeing anyone?

ED: I said that I wasn't.

(Guilty pause)

Well, I could hardly tell them about you, could I?

ARNOLD: God forbid!

ED: What are you thinking?

(Silence. Quietly.)

ARNOLD: I am thinking about how it feels to be a no one in the life of someone you love.

(Pause)

Tell me about her.

ED:

(Uneasy)

Why don't you call me a bastard and hang up?

ARNOLD: I want to understand. Talk to me.

ED: I can't . . .

ARNOLD: Please.

ED: Well, she's wonderful.

ARNOLD: Bastard!

ED: You asked!

ARNOLD: I did, didn't I. It's the masochist in me. What'd you tell her about me?

ED: Nothing.

ARNOLD: That does seem to be my name. You did tell her you were bisexual, didn't you?

ED: No. I didn't think it was important.

ARNOLD: Of course not. How silly of me to even mention it.

ED: I'm not so sure that some secrets aren't better kept that way.

ARNOLD: You don't feel that's just slightly dishonest?

ED: No. We have a more mature relationship than that.

ARNOLD: Pardon my naïveté. I didn't know that there really was such a thing as, "Love with the proper stranger." So, when are you taking her to meet your parents?

ED: This weekend.

ARNOLD: I don't believe a word of this. And you're still going to tell me that they have nothing to do with this sudden burst of heterosexuality?

(No response)

Look, Ed, I don't know much about the straight world, but I do know that when a guy takes a gal to meet his folks, for the weekend no less, that this is no casual affair.

(No response)

Don't you feel you're being unfair to lead her on that way?

(Not to mention what you're doing to me.)

Don't you think she has a right to know what she's letting herself in for?

(No response)

What's the matter? Catch your tongue in the closet door?

(No response)

ED: You're really dragging me over the coals.

ARNOLD: Why should I be the only one with a barbecued ass? If I may ask another stupid question: What am I supposed to do?

ED: That's up to you.

ARNOLD: Not entirely.

ED: I had hoped that we could go on seeing each other. You may not believe this, but I really don't want to lose you.

ARNOLD: That's hitting below the belt; appealing to my Susan Hayward fantasies. . . . "Arnold, Back Street Woman"!

ED: That's not the way it is at all!

ARNOLD: Then take me to meet your parents.

ED: I could if I wanted to. They'd understand.

ARNOLD: Oh, I know they'd understand. It's you that can't. At least you didn't lie when you said you weren't scared for them to meet me. You're scared they'll meet you!

ED: Thank you very much. Your kindness is appreciated.

ARNOLD: Listen, Mr. Reiss. At this moment I don't think you have a right to expect me to be kind.

(Pulling back)

I'm sorry. I just feel so helpless.

ED:

(Slight relaxing laugh)

You helpless?

ARNOLD:

(Laughing too)

Dumb, huh?

(Cracking)

I don't understand. I thought . . . we were so happy. That we were so special. The way we made love . . . The way you cried in my arms . . . You said you loved me . . .

ED: I do. I always will.

ARNOLD:

(Desperately)

Then what are we doing?

ED: I don't know. I'm confused . . . I'm frightened.

ARNOLD: Ed, come over.

ED: No, I can't. I have made up my mind. I know what I want. I'm doing what I have to do. I know that you are hurting, but that is my decision.

ARNOLD: You can't see what you're doing.

ED: Yes I can. I'm not like you, Arnold. I can't be happy living in a ghetto of gay bars and gay restaurants and backrooms, scared that someone will find out that I'm gay and maybe get me fired. I hate those queens with their bitchy remarks and Bette Davis imitations. I don't want any part of that.

ARNOLD: But that's not us . . .

ED: I want more. I've got to be proud of who I am.

ARNOLD: How can sleeping with a woman make you proud of yourself if you know you'd rather be with a man? How can you ever get any respect from anyone if you won't be yourself? There's no you to respect!

ED: And just where's your self-respect? Huh? I certainly don't see any here!

ARNOLD: You wanna see my self-respect? Here's my self-respect!

(He slams down the receiver as the light blacks out on Ed. Then . . . calmer.)

I fell right into that one.

(The lights fade out on Arnold, as the singer is once again brought into focus.)

SCENE 4: ARNOLD

The bar sounds are heard again as the lights reveal Arnold standing on the "Stud" platform dressed in denims and swigging from a beer can.

Look Murray, I am not that lonely! This here's as far as I go. My standards may lie just left of reactionary, but my limit in a backroom bar is the front room. Maybe I just better go home, huh? Thank you for taking me out but . . .

It just ain't my kind of thing, ya' know? I realize you may find this hard to comprehend, you bein' the way you are, but Murray, I am just not that way inclined. I mean I'm that way inclined, but I'm not that way inclined. Ya' know what I mean, Murray? I mean, maybe I'm old fashioned but I like my sex in a bed. I don't see sex as a spectator sport. I like that one sneaked kiss in the elevator on the way to a man's apartment. I like the apologies he makes for the mess the place is in. I dig the dainty tour and arty conversation while he's dimming the lights and pouring the drinks. I like never finishing those drinks. See Murray, to me a lap in the bed is worth three in a bar. 'Cause deep down in my heart I know they do not marry sluts. No, they don't Murray. And it hurts me, Murray, it truly does, to see this multitude of men so love starved that they resort to sex in a dirty backroom instead of the way God meant us to be. It is cheap, Murray. And I refuse on moral grounds to support the degradation these men have brought themselves to. Period.

Why is it so important to you that I go into that backroom? Are you a'scared to go in there by yourself? Is that it, Murray? Have I hit on the nail? C'mon, level it, Murray, are you a'scared?

I am not a'scared, Murray. Oh no I'm not.

Alright, I'll prove it to you. We'll go back there together. But I'm tellin' you now, I ain't doin' nothin'. O.K.?

O.K. Let's go.

(He starts to turn tentatively and suddenly spins back.)

Murray, quick, hold my hand. I'm a'scared! What if nobody back there wants me? It's one thing to go into a regular bar and not get picked up. I mean that happens all the time to lots of people for lots of reasons, but Murray, to go into a place like that and get rejected . . . I don't think I could take it. I know I got personal qualities that put me above and beyond the norm: quick mind, sharp wit, glowing personality. But Murray, what if I don't glow in the dark?

No, I'm O.K. Really. Look, it'll take more than a backroom to set me back. After all, I am an Advocate Experience graduate. Poise, confidence, an open mind . . . they'll never put me away! Lead on.

(He turns his back to the audience as the lights change to dark red. When he faces front again he is groping to find his way. Loud whisper.)

Murray? Where are you? Murray? Murray? Oh, there you are. Well, it certainly is dark back here. Hang on a second.

(He takes out a book of matches and lights one. He looks around slowly with gaping mouth.)

Oh, my God!

(He blows out the match.)

Murray, quick, let's get outta here. This ain't no place for someone who goes to confessional. I'd jam up the booth for months!

(He freezes. Whisper.)

Murray, Murray? Someone's got his hand on my crotch. What should I do?

(He tries to smile and look natural then he grabs the hand and shakes it.)

Hi there. My name is Arnold, what's yours? Where'd he go, Murray? Oh, Murray, I gotta get outta here. I should've never come.

No I didn't come, Murray! Let's just go, huh? Uh oh. Murray? Someone's got his hand on my heiney. Can you see what he looks like?

Yes it does make a difference, Murray! Murray? Murray? He's reaching around front and opening my belt. Murray? Murray? He's opening my zipper. Murray? Murray? . . . What do I do . . . with the beer can?

(He bends over to put the beer can on the ground when he is suddenly penetrated.)

MURRAYYYYYYY!!!!!!!

(At first Arnold's face is twisted in pain and embarrassment as he sways with the humping rhythm. He tries to smile and look comfortable. He feels out the rhythm and quietly enjoys himself for a moment, then he looks unattached, almost bored.)
(Conversationally)

You come here often?
You do?

(The stud hits him on the shoulder.)

No, I don't have to talk. No, that's perfectly alright. I mean, it's not part of my fantasy or anything, conversation that is. Though I must admit I am prone to sweet nothings deftly whispered. However, they are not essential to my enjoyment of the lovemaking experience. I much prefer to open my senses completely to the moment thereby retaining more of an impression whereon to draw on later dates. If you get my drift.

(He gets hit again.)

But you'd rather I shut up anyway. O.K. I'm not offended. I realize that it must take a lot of concentration for you to keep your . . . concentration in a situation like this so I won't say another word. O.K.? O.K.

(Long pause. He looks around. Adjusts his hands. Then fumbles for a cigarette.)

Cigarette? Oh, I'll save you one for later. Mind if I. . . . That's very understanding of you.

(He lights a match and tries to light the cigarette but can't because of the motion. He grabs the stud's rear and stops him, lights up then taps him to begin again. Arnold positions his hands in a casual smoker's pose and looks about, puffing deeply.)

Got a nice crowd tonight. Ya' know, this here's easier than I thought it would be. See, I don't usually do this sort of thing, but what with breaking from my lover and all . . . But it's not as bad as I thought it would be. I guess that has a lot to do with you. Your attitude, I mean. I find that being a sensitive person, as I am, that I pick up easily on people's vibrations and hence incorporate them into myself. See, I figured I'd be too uptight to allow for such things. But since you obviously don't care, then I don't care. Just another bar right? Just another night out? Very practical idea. I mean, say you'd picked me up in another bar, well, it might've taken an hour for us to get to this. Or maybe we wouldn't've gotten along and so never got to find out that we really were so compatible. But this way we can build a relationship the other way around, right? You know, I really like you. Maybe that's a stupid thing to say in a place like this. But if you think about it, it's not so stupid at a time like this, is it? I can't wait to see what you look like.

(Hit again)

Oh, I'm sorry. I was talking again, wasn't I? Gee, I'm really sorry. It must be my nerves. I guess I'm not as relaxed as I thought 'cause when I get nervous I just talk insistently. On any subject, it don't matter. You just name a subject when I'm nervous and I will talk on and on about it. It don't matter what; sex, drugs, religion, rummage sales, anything. Try it. You'll see. Name a subject.

(The stud pulls out suddenly.)

Oh, you're finished? That was quick. Must'a been hot to trot, huh?

(Miming pulling back on his clothes)

I'd like you to meet this friend of mine. His name is Murray. He must be right around here somewhere. Murray? Murray? Oh, there you are. Murray, I'd like you to meet . . . Hey, I never did catch your naa . . .

(He split.)

Yoo hoo! Hello? Where'd he go? See, Murray, that's what I've got against places like this. You meet someone nice and you lose him in the dark. I know, I'll light a match. Oh, I don't know what he looks like. Of course, how dumb of me, he's gone out front to wait for me 'cause of the crowd and the smell. C'mon Murray. Let's go find him. What'd'ya mean, he won't be there? I'm sure he really liked me. He made love to me, didn't he? Well, didn't he?

(Long pause)

Let's get outta here.

(Arnold turns his back as the normal bar lights return. He squints and tries to smile.)

Well, at least I don't have to cook him breakfast.

(Slow fade. Black.)

Lady Blues sings her final song.

SCENE 5

The lights come up on the dressing room set again. They're more general than before. Ed enters tentatively, looks around, checks his watch and then sits on the chair at the vanity. He looks at the cards and notes scattered around the mirror and table. He looks uncomfortable. He checks out the make-up on the table and picks up a powder puff as Arnold enters. He stops short in the doorway and stares at Ed who has not heard him come in. There is a great sadness in Arnold's face. He puts on a huge smile and enters. Arnold is in a dressing robe.

ARNOLD: Careful, some of that might rub off on you.
ED:

(Jumping up)

You scared me.

(Holding out his arms)

Hello, Arnold.

ARNOLD:

(Walking right past him)

Hello.

ED: Bet you thought you'd never see me again.

(Pause)

You look fantastic.

ARNOLD:

(In grand Bette Davis)

Well, aren't you a deah to say so!

ED: The stage manager said it'd be alright for me to wait for you in your dressing room. You don't mind, do you?

(No response. Arnold sits and begins to peel his face off)

When I asked for you as Arnold he didn't know who I meant.

(A little laugh)

You look beautiful . . . Really. Lost a little weight, I see.

(He reaches out to touch Arnold.)

ARNOLD:

(Stiffening)

Please . . .

ED:

(Pulling back)

Sorry. I guess you're still pretty angry, huh?

ARNOLD: No, I'm not *still* angry. This is brand new. What are you doing here?

ED: I wanted to see you. I've been worried about you.

(Arnold shoots him a look.)

I wanted to make sure that you were alright.

ARNOLD: How'd you know I was here?

ED: I saw an ad in the paper.

ARNOLD: That ad should have satisfied your curiosity.

ED: I had planned on seeing the show and just leaving, but when I saw you onstage I had to come back and talk to you.

(Pause)

Been a long time.

ARNOLD: Five months ago you checked out on me with a single phone call. You said that you knew what you wanted and that I wasn't it. I haven't heard a word from you since. What do you want?

ED: Just to see you.

ARNOLD: You've seen me. Get out.

ED: Arnold, please. I'd like to talk to you.

ARNOLD: No.

ED: Wait, just listen to me for a minute.

ARNOLD: NO!

ED: It's got nothing to do with us . . .

ARNOLD: I said no, goddammit! Now just go and leave me alone.

> (Softer)

The one nice thing I could say about you was when you left, you left. No matter what I thought of your reasons or lack of them, you kept your word . . .

ED: You knew I'd come back to see you. I told you that I wanted us to be friends. You mean a lot to me.

> (Pause. He makes the "I love you" sign and holds it up.)

Arnold? . . .

ARNOLD: Don't get cute with me.

ED: Maybe I shouldn't have come here, but as long as the harm's done can't I talk to you? Just until you're dressed? It's important to me.

ARNOLD:

> (Indicating a folding chair against the wall)

Sit down.

ED:

> (He gets the chair and sets it behind Arnold.)

So, how you been?

ARNOLD: Can we somehow manage to skip the little niceties and get right to the meat. I know you're here for something.

ED: There is something I have to tell you, but give me a little time. It's not the kind of thing I can blurt right out.

ARNOLD:

> (Resigned)

How are your folks?

ED: They're fine. My father had a little trouble with an inner ear infection, but it cleared up nicely.

ARNOLD: They go back south for the winter?

ED: They left two days ago.

ARNOLD: Two days!? What took you so long?

ED: What?

ARNOLD: Ed, you can forget it. It's over. You are not coming back.

ED: You don't understand . . .

ARNOLD: I have never done time in the closet and I sure as hell ain't gettin' in one for you.

ED: But, I don't want to come back.

(Arnold stares.)

Really. Things are going great with Laurel. I tried to tell you. I came to talk to you as a friend.

(Arnold turns back to the mirror. Ed continues merrily.)

We spent a really fantastic summer upstate. We stayed at my parents' place in Florida for a week then back up to the farm. I got a lot done on the house including a new chimney.

ARNOLD: And what'd you do with what's-her-face?

ED: Laurel. Well, at first things were sort of strained. She'd hang around me all the time wanting us to work together. But I talked to her and finally she began doing things on her own. It was hard for her to understand. She doesn't take criticism very well. She tenses up and gets very quiet. Mid-August my sister sent her two kids up for a few days and Laurel took care of them. It was really a marvelous experience for both of us. Sort of like having a family of our own.

ARNOLD: Sounds wonderful! Pa out in the fields, Ma tendin' the young'uns, granma and granpa rockin' on the porch. I'm just sorry you and Laurel couldn't have spent the summer together.

ED:

(Missing that)

You should have seen how Laurel cried when the kids left. But that was nothing compared to the way she carried on when we came back to the city.

ARNOLD: Sounds like she does a lot of crying.

ED: Not so much anymore. We had a talk about that.

ARNOLD: Sounds like you do a lot of talking.

ED: We have a very honest relationship.

ARNOLD: I can see that. You two living together now?

ED: No. We haven't made that kind of a commitment yet. To tell you the truth I'm not sure I could take being with her all the time. She has a way of closing in on me. Actually, it was much easier spending time with you. More relaxed. You're easier to talk to.

(Pause)

I thought about you a lot up there. We would have had a great time.

ARNOLD: I'm not the farm-girl type.

ED: No, you would have loved it.

(Pause)

I worried about you; how you were getting along.

ARNOLD: You could have called and found out.

ED: I thought about it. Once, when everyone was out of the house, I even started dialing.

ARNOLD: What happened?

ED: I didn't think it was fair to build up your hopes.

ARNOLD:

> (Dreamily)
>
> There's just one thing I regret about our affair.

ED:

> (Sincerely)
>
> What's that?

ARNOLD: That I never beat the shit out of you!

ED: You *are* still angry.

ARNOLD: Where's a tape recorder? No one would ever believe this.

ED: Maybe I'd better go.

ARNOLD: No, please, I'm sorry. Stay, we'll have some wine.

ED: What kind?

ARNOLD:

> (Producing a gallon and cups)
>
> House white. Buck-fifty a gallon! You do the honors.

ED:

> (Pouring)
>
> Kind'a warm, isn't it?

ARNOLD:

> (Taking his cup)
>
> But cooling off nicely. I'm glad you came.

ED: So am I.

> (Takes a sip and gags)
>
> God! How do you drink this stuff?

ARNOLD:

> (Taking his cup away from him and pouring the wine into his own)
>
> In large doses. So, tell me, how's your sex life?

ED

> (Caught off guard for a moment)
>
> . . . Great.

ARNOLD:

> (Sure of himself)
>
> As good as with me?

ED: You're doing it again! Asking questions that you really don't want the answers to.

ARNOLD: Maybe I do.

ED: Arnold, I'm not sure the sex we had was always as good for me as it was for you. Sometimes I felt it got out of control.

ARNOLD: Meaning what?

ED: I don't know. Those last few times, it was like losing myself. I remember once, I don't even think I was conscious. All I remember was kissing you and then nothing until waking in your arms, my body all wet . . .

ARNOLD: And that's bad?

ED: It's not what I want.

ARNOLD: Funny; it's what I pray for.

ED: Well, that's fine when you're twenty-four. But I'm going on thirty-four. I have other needs.

ARNOLD:

(Quietly)

Look at us together in the mirror. Now who would ever believe that you were ten years older than me? I'm aging about as well as a Beach Party movie.

ED: You're beautiful.

ARNOLD: Is *that* why you left?

ED: I didn't leave you because Laurel was prettier.

ARNOLD: I know that. I've seen her.

(Pause)

That morning, after the phone call, I waited in a cab across from your building and watched the two of you leave for work. I was pretty shocked.

ED: We can't all look like Virginia Hamm. I happen to think she's very beautiful.

ARNOLD: Where would you be now if I was a woman?

ED: What?

ARNOLD: If I was a woman. Who would you be with?

ED: But you're not.

ARNOLD: But if I was. Would you ever even have looked at her?

ED: I love her, Arnold.

ARNOLD: Like you loved me?

ED: Like I could never love you.

ARNOLD: Because you never did love me. You were too busy running scared to love me. You were scared I'd leave you. Scared . . . someone would find out about us. Scared . . . you'd let yourself free for once in your life. Oh, I'm vain enough to think you could have loved me, but I don't think you had the time.

ED:

(Quietly)

I did love you. Everything would be very easy for me if I didn't. But I do.

(Long silence)

Sometimes . . . Sometimes when I have trouble reaching orgasm I imagine you behind me just about to . . .

ARNOLD: Does she know?

(Ed shakes his head.)

Have you talked about me at all?

ED: She knows your name. She found one of the drawings you made. The one of the tree outside my dining-room window. She may know more. I saw her looking at that music book you gave me. She didn't say anything, but remember you wrote poems to me on half the pages.

(Long pause)

I couldn't, Arnold. It's not what I want.

ARNOLD: What did you want to tell me? Huh?

(Softly)

You can talk to me. I'll understand.

ED: It's nothing really. Just a dream I had last week. I dreamt that I was in my parents' house and I went down to my father's workshop and got an old rag and a can of turpentine. Then I went to the kitchen and got a plastic bag. I took all the stuff back up to my bedroom where I soaked the rag in the turpentine and put it into the plastic bag. Then I got into bed, made myself comfortable, pulled the covers right up to my neck and then put the plastic bag over my head. The strangest part was: as I gathered all the stuff, as I got into bed, as I began blacking out from the fumes . . . I was enjoying myself, laughing up a storm.

(Break)

The phone woke me in the morning. It was Laurel. I couldn't understand what she was saying. Half of me was trying to listen to her, the other half trying to figure out the dream. I felt dizzy so I went back to bed and there, on the pillow, was the plastic bag with the turpentine soaked rag.

(Long pause)

I couldn't tell anyone else about it.

(Taking Arnold's hand)

This is what I've always wanted: you and me together talking. I think I love you more now than ever.

(Arnold's eyes widen, he jumps up suddenly and begins punching Ed wildly. Ed grabs hold of Arnold's arms and stretches them out to either side, so that they stand face to face. They freeze for a moment searching each other's eyes, then suddenly they are in each other's arms, crying, holding each other tightly.)

ED: I'm so scared. I need you.

ARNOLD:

(Gently releasing himself)

O.K. Time out. Everybody back to his corner.

(Ed sits back down as Arnold crosses to the vanity. Arnold is in turmoil. Finally in mock of his opening speech.)

Wha' happened!?!

(He laughs instead of crying. Crosses behind Ed and tentatively puts his hands on Ed's shoulders. Ed quickly takes them into his. Indecision . . .)

You feel better?

ED:

(Happy to be home)

Yes.

ARNOLD: Good. Then get out!

(He grabs back his hands angrily.)

Do you have any idea of what the last five months have been like for me? I cried on so many shoulders . . . I'm sure I lost half my friends. But I always knew you'd be back. But I thought that when you did come back . . . I don't know, that you'd finally have your shit together. And here you are more fucked up than ever.

(Still indecision)

Have you got your car with you?

(Ed nods)

Go get it. I'll . . . I'll get dressed and meet you out front.

ED: Want me to drive you home?

ARNOLD: Huh?

ED:

(Rising)

I'll get the car.

(He exits.)
(Arnold watches him leave then suddenly snaps himself to work. He sits at the vanity and quickly brushes out his hair, clears the table top and begins to undress when just as suddenly he stops and stares at the audience, searching each face.)

ARNOLD:

(Slowly . . . innocently)

So, what now? Huh? If I take him back now, knowing all I do, maybe I could make it work. With a little understanding? Maybe even a shrink?

(Little laugh)

I *could* just let him drive me home. Then I'd say something like. . . . "The next time you feel you have to say 'I love you' to someone, say it to yourself and see if you believe it!" No, that'd go over his head. I think it went over mine.

(Another little laugh)

Of course I could just leave him waiting out there in the cold. Just slip out the back and really cross him out of my life. That way I'd be over him in a few more months. Give or take a few more friends. I don't know. I don't know. 'Cause if we do start in again, who'd say he won't keep this shit up? Right? I don't know. Maybe that's what I want. Maybe he's treating me just the way I want him to. Maybe I use him to give me that tragic torchsinger status that I admire so in others. If that's true . . . then he's my International Stud. Wouldn't that be a kick in the rubber parts? I love him. That's for sure.

(Fighting back tears)

But do I love him enough? What's enough? This is enough.

(Standing, chin up, confronting the audience)

Enough.

(Slow fade to black)

The End

FUGUE IN A NURSERY

Fugue in a Nursery premiered at La Mama E.T.C. on February 1, 1979 with the following cast:

LAUREL	Marilyn Hamlin
ED	Edward D. Griffith
ALAN	Christopher Marcantel
ARNOLD	Harvey Fierstein

Directed by Eric Concklin
Music by Ada Janik
Stage Design by Bill Stabile
Lighting by Charles Embry
Production Stage Manager: Richard Jakiel
The production was subsequently presented by Mitchell Maxwell at The Orpheum Theatre with Maria Cellario as Laurel, Will Jeffries as Ed and with lighting by Cheryl Thacker.

A Note on the Music
A full score for Clarinet, French Horn, Violin and Cello was created for the original production by Ada Janik. The music should never overshadow or cause melodramatic effect. Rather it is meant to harmonize the themes and clarify the moments. In Ms. Janik's original score each character was represented by an instrument: Arnold by the Cello, Alan by the Clarinet, Laurel by the Violin and Ed by the French Horn. The musical notations of the text corresponded to the ones of the score.

Characters

ED	Thirty-five. Very handsome, masculine with a boyish charm.
LAUREL	Thirty-five. Rather unfancy in appearance. Thoughtful and bright though she shows a girlish enthusiasm.
ALAN	Eighteen. Shamefully beautiful. A frightened child in hustler's clothing.
ARNOLD	Twenty-five (going on forty). A kvetch of great wit and want.

Time
One year after the action of *International Stud*.

Place
Arnold's apartment and various rooms of Ed's farmhouse. Only one set is used (see description after prologue).

Important
In reading this script it is imperative that close attention be paid to stage directions and character names as the text may become unclear without that information.

PROLOGUE

There will be no pre-show music and the stage should be curtained. (For the La Mama pro-duction a revolving stage was used to hide the set from the entering audience.) As the house-lights dim we hear a telephone ringing. During the following conversation (which should be tape-recorded), the audience sees the musicians entering the pit and hears them warming up their instruments. Simultaneously, slides are shown on a screen over the set. We see photos of Arnold in drag, Arnold and Ed walking and talking together, Ed and Laurel in similar leisure pastimes and finally Arnold and Alan together. A telephone rings three times. (A loud radio in the background)

ARNOLD: Happy home for the bewildered.

LAUREL: Hello? Is this Arnold?

ARNOLD: That's what they tell me.

LAUREL: Hi. I don't know where to start. We've never met . . .

ARNOLD: Sounds like my life story. Hang on a second, would you?

> *(Muffled slightly)*
>
> HEY! Could you turn that thing down?

ALAN:

> *(Far off)*
>
> Who is it?

ARNOLD: I don't know but if you'd turn that fakachtah thing down I'd find out!

ALAN: If it's Murray tell him I wanna speak to him.

> *(The radio noises fade out.)*

ARNOLD:

> *(Syrupy)*
>
> Hello. You still there?

LAUREL: Look, am I interrupting something?

ARNOLD: Nothing you'd warnna write home about.

> *(Sound of a toilet flushing)*
>
> Well, come on. Speak up. I'm a drag queen not a mind reader.

LAUREL:

> *(Flustered)*
>
> Well, like I said, you don't know me but we have a mutual friend. Ed Reiss.

ARNOLD:

> *(Pause)*
>
> Is that what you called to tell me?

LAUREL: No. I'd better start again. You and I have never met. But, I think you'll know who I am. My name's Laurel. Ed and I live together. We're . . . lovers. As you know, Ed has a farm upstate where we spend the weekends and our vacations. Anyway, we got to talking and thought it'd be nice to have you up to visit for a few days. Still with me?

ARNOLD: I'm way ahead of you! I'm sorry but I'm not into any of that kinky stuff.

LAUREL:

>*(Laughing)*

>That wasn't our intention at all. I just thought you might like to get out of the city for a few days. Ed's told me so much about you and I've wanted to meet you for the longest time . . .

ARNOLD: Whose idea was this?

LAUREL: We'd both like you to come.

ARNOLD: Yeah, but whose idea was this?

LAUREL: What's the difference? The point is, I know how much Ed values your friendship and that the two of you haven't seen that much of each other lately, which probably has to do with you and I not knowing each other, but hopefully this weekend will straighten all of that out. So, what do you say?

ARNOLD: I don't think so. I appreciate the invite, it was swell of you to call, but I don't think it's such a good idea. But look, maybe after the summer you and I could get together for lunch or something . . .

ALAN:

>*(Mumbled and muffled)*

>Wait a minute, I wanna go.

ARNOLD: Hang on a second, would you?

>*(Muffled conversation)*

>Listen, Laurel, do you think it'd be alright to bring a friend?

LAUREL: Of course. Please do. I'm sorry I didn't extend an invitation to your friends myself but Ed didn't tell me you were seeing anyone.

ARNOLD: He doesn't know about Alan.

LAUREL: Well, by all means bring him. That'll make the weekend nicer still; to have the both of you. So, we'll pick you up on the Friday train.

ARNOLD: No. We'll be driving up. Alan can borrow a car.

LAUREL: Great. Let me give you the directions.

ARNOLD: That's alright. I think I can remember how to get there.

LAUREL:

>*(Loaded)*

>Of course, you've been here before. So, we'll see you Friday. I can hardly wait.

ARNOLD: O.K. See you then.

LAUREL: Bye bye.

>*(Sound of phones clicking off)*

>*(As the taped conversation ends, a slide appears on the screen:*

>NURSERY: *a fugue*

>*The conductor raises the baton and the first music begins to play. The set is an eight foot by nine foot heavily raked bed. It is mounded with pillows, blankets and*

all the props needed in the course of the play. It will serve as all rooms in the house. The couples will be lit as separately as possible using color to indicate the pairings when the more complicated conversations begin. Special care should be taken that the four characters never appear to be in bed together. The desired effect is of vulnerability not obscenity.

As the music begins the lights reveal Laurel filing her nails and Ed reading a newspaper. The other couple should not be seen. The music ends. . . .)

LAUREL:

(With deep satisfaction)

Isn't this civilized?

(Pause)

Do you think they have enough blankets? Maybe I should . . .

ED:

(Sharply)

They'll be fine.

LAUREL: But it gets awfully cold . . .

ED:

(Final)

Laurel, they'll be fine.

LAUREL: Alright. Don't be so grouchy.

(Cuddling)

Wanna . . . ?

ED: Aren't you tired at all?

LAUREL: I'm too excited about having them here. Don't you wanna . . . ?

ED: Didn't you say you had some paperwork to do?

LAUREL: You're an old fart you know that.

(Grabbing away his paper)

ED: Where's that newspaper?

LAUREL:

(Handing it back. Bubbling.)

This is just so civilized! Guests up to our country home for the weekend. I can't tell you how excited I am.

ED: We *have* had guests before.

LAUREL: I'd hardly compare this to having your sister and her kids or your parents or even friends from school up. Imagine being hostess to your lover's ex and his new boyfriend. Now if that isn't civilized then what is? It's downright Noel Coward. How's your English accent?

ED: What?

LAUREL: It might be fun to use English accents all weekend.

ED: Would you stop.

LAUREL: What're you being so grouchy about? I'm just fooling around.

(Teasing)

Are my domestic fantasies making you nervous? Don't worry. I promise I won't propose to you.

ED: Very funny.

LAUREL: What is your problem?

ED: I don't see why they can't spend a few quiet days up here without all this rigmarole.

LAUREL: I'm excited. That's all.

ED: . . . Because this is not the weekend that I had planned.

LAUREL: I have no idea what you're talking about.

ED:

(Tossing off the newspaper)

Alan. That's what I'm talking about.

LAUREL: What about him? He seems really nice.

ED: I should've known Arnold would pull something like this.

LAUREL: Now look, I told you that Arnold asked me if he could bring a friend and that I told him he could.

ED: You had no right to. . . . This weekend was supposed to be just the three of us.

LAUREL: So what's the big deal? We've got enough food for four. I didn't have to open another room or anything. What'd you expect Arnold to do? Sit around with us all day then watch us toddle off to bed while he slept alone? It's better this way. You'll see.

ED: No, you'll see. Did you catch the way he fawned over him at dinner? He practically cut his steak for him.

LAUREL: No more than I fawned over you.

(Cuddling)

And I did cut your steak.

ED:

(Pouting)

I could've killed you for that.

LAUREL: You're being ridiculous. There are bound to be compensations on all four of our parts. After all, the two of you were lovers. So little games and jealousies are bound to pop up. But I'm positive it's going to be a great weekend.

ED: Did you see how he made such a point of running off to bed early? "Oh, I'm so tired. All that good food has done me in." His hands all over the boy.

LAUREL: Well, if I had something as pretty as that to go to bed with, I wouldn't stay up late either.

ED:

(Seriously considering)

You think he s pretty?

LAUREL:

(Baiting)

Uh huh.

ED: I don't like them that young.
LAUREL: I do.

> (No reaction)

> They make a nice couple. Don't you think?

> (No answer)

> I think Arnold's a very handsome man. Don't know why he'd want to put on a dress.

ED: You really like them that young?
LAUREL: What?
ED: As young as Alan.
LAUREL:

> (Considering)

> Sure. Why not? All that energy. Did you hear the way their bedsprings were squeaking?

ED: I think I do pretty well in the squeaking department.
LAUREL:

> (Teasing)

> You do, huh?

ED:

> (Moving closer)

> Well, making certain allowances for wear and tear . . .

LAUREL: It's too early in the race to make a plea for sympathy.
ED: You want to race?

> (Excited)

> Alright, we'll race. And may the best man win.

LAUREL: And now, ladies and gentlemen, in the center ring, driving a 1968 Serta Orthopedic . . . couple number 2 . . .
ED: Hey, no tickling before the gun.
LAUREL: On your marks . . . Get set . . . Go!

> (The lights quickly black out on them and snap on for Alan. He sits straight up in the bed as if frightened out of sleep by a bad dream. A slide appears:

> SUBJECT

> He takes a deep breath relaxing a bit then looks for Arnold who is hidden under the mountain of blankets. He finds him asleep.)

ALAN:

> (Shoving his face into Arnold's)

> Hello.

ARNOLD:

(Asleep)

If you can't say something nice, don't say nothin' at all.

(He rolls over.)

ALAN:

(Climbing over to the other side)

Get your fat ass out of bed and get me something to eat. I'm hungry.

ARNOLD: Talk dirty to me.

ALAN: What? . . . Are you asleep?

ARNOLD:

(Opening his eyes wide)

God, you're gorgeous.

(Rolling away)

Now, go away.

ALAN: Come on, wake up.

ARNOLD: But I'm having this flawless dream.

ALAN: About me?

ARNOLD: If it is, will you let me go back to sleep?

ALAN: Yes.

ARNOLD: It's all about you.

ALAN:

(Moving in close)

What about me?

ARNOLD:

(Feeling behind)

My God, you really are awake.

ALAN: That doesn't matter.

ARNOLD:

(Waking more fully)

Maybe not to you . . .

ALAN: Stop changing the subject.

ARNOLD:

(Attacking)

Waste not, want not.

ALAN: Tell me the dream.

(Holding him off)

ARNOLD: If you like it can we . . . ?

ALAN: No.

ARNOLD:

>   *(Rolling over)*

>   Then I'm going back to sleep.

ALAN: Then I'm going to see if anyone else is up.

ARNOLD: Give my best to the bisexuals.

ALAN: Only he's bisexual. She's straight.

ARNOLD: How do you know?

ALAN: She told me so.

ARNOLD: Too bad. Mixed marriages never work.

ALAN: Yeah, then what were you doing with him?

ARNOLD: Slumming.

ALAN:

>   *(Climbing on top of him)*

>   And what're you doing with me?

ARNOLD: Nothing. It's gone.

ALAN: It'll be back.

ARNOLD:

>   *(Sulking)*

>   But it won't be the same.

ALAN: Of course it will.

ARNOLD: Do you ever think before you speak?

ALAN: No. Do you?

ARNOLD: Frequently. It passes the time while you're speaking.

ALAN: Be nice.

ARNOLD: Go back to sleep and wake up horny.

ALAN: You still haven't told me your dream.

ARNOLD: Why'd you wanna come up here this weekend?

ALAN: What's this black shit on the pillow?

ARNOLD: What black shit on the pillow?

ALAN: This black shit on the pillow.

ARNOLD: It's black shit on the pillow.

ALAN: Bullshit.

ARNOLD: Bull shit, black shit, why'd you wanna come?

ALAN: What do you mean?

ARNOLD: Never mind. Talk dirty to me.

ALAN: Tell me the dream.

ARNOLD: I ain't tellin' you nothin'. You lied to me.

ALAN: About what?

ARNOLD: You said it would come back. What's it waiting for?

ALAN: It's waiting to hear the dream.

ARNOLD:

>   *(Peeking under the covers)*

>   Is it really into that sort of stuff?

ALAN: We're waiting.

ARNOLD: How old are you?

ALAN: You know how old I am.

ARNOLD: Tell me again, I need reassurance.

ALAN: The dream?

ARNOLD: I know who you are. You're the son I always avoided having. Why's the lamp on?

ALAN: It's still dark out.

ARNOLD: Is there a storm?

ALAN: No, the sun's not up yet.

ARNOLD: You woke me in the middle of the night again?

ALAN: Do you mind?

ARNOLD: Of course not.

(*Taking the boy into his arms like a child*)

Come on. What frightened you?

ALAN: Nothing. I just felt like talking.

ARNOLD: Comfortable?

ALAN: Tighter. Did Ed ever have bad dreams?

ARNOLD: Everyone does.

ALAN: Did you have to hold him?

ARNOLD: Talk dirty to me.

ALAN: Get me a dog.

ARNOLD: Why?

ALAN: I want one.

ARNOLD: I don't give you things.

ALAN: Yes you do.

(*Arnold stiffens.*)

No you don't. But, a dog's not a thing.

ARNOLD: All the more reason.

ALAN: C'mon, get me a dog.

ARNOLD: I have no money for a dog.

ALAN: You can get one at the pound. They're free.

ARNOLD: Then get one yourself.

ALAN: I will. Can I keep it at your place?

ARNOLD: You shouldn't wear cologne. It tastes terrible.

ALAN: Sometimes they have dogs up for adoption in the paper. Where's that other copy of the *Voice?*

ARNOLD: Under the bed.

(*Alan starts for it.*)

No, don't move. I want to remember me like this forever.

ALAN: I want a cigarette anyway.

ARNOLD:

(*Sulking*)

Is that what you tell the other models at the studio; that I buy you things and that's why you live with me?

ALAN: No. Of course not.

ARNOLD: You make more money modeling for an hour than I do in a week. I don't buy you things. Don't say I do.

ALAN: I don't.

ARNOLD: Good. 'Cause I don't. Not things. Cigarettes. That's all.

ALAN: Alright already. Want a cigarette?

ARNOLD: They're mine, aren't they?

ALAN: Then do you mind if I have one?

ARNOLD: That's why they're here. Don't do that to yourself; treat yourself like a piece of meat. It's what all them leering faggots do, so you don't have to do it to yourself.

ALAN:

(Lighting a cigarette)

I don't.

ARNOLD: At least stop enjoying it. You don't have to be a model.

ALAN: You don't have to be a drag queen.

ARNOLD: How ridiculous! They're not the same things at all.

ALAN: What's the difference?

ARNOLD: A model IS. A drag queen . . . Aspires.

ALAN: Great aspirations!

ARNOLD: Very funny. I'm serious, Alan. Fantasies are fine in the bedroom, but outside they're not fantasies, they're lies.

ALAN: What are you talking about?

ARNOLD: Your hustler trips.

ALAN:

(Stuffs cigarette in Arnold's mouth)

Would you stop? Where's that newspaper?

ARNOLD:

(Handing it over)

Here.

ALAN:

(Long look at Arnold)

I love you.

(Arnold rolls into Alan's arms as the lights fade down on them and up on Laurel and Ed. They are in each other's arms.)

LAUREL: I don't believe I've seen you this turned on in months. If that's Arnold's effect on you then I think I'll ask him to move in.

ED: It's not Arnold, it's you.

LAUREL: Is that why you called me Arnold?

ED: I did not.

LAUREL:

(Giggling)

Oh yes you did. Deep into loving you whispered into my ear, "I love you, Arnold."

ED: That's not funny. You shouldn't make up things like that.

LAUREL: I'm not. What're you getting so upset about? Minds wander during sex. It's like dreaming; all sorts of things pass through the mind. I once blurted out the phone number of the house I grew up in. I'm not upset you called me Arnold, so there's no reason for you to be.

ED: I never called you Arnold. That's something passing in *your* mind.

LAUREL: Alright. So I misheard you. Take it easy.

ED: It's that damned kid. This was going to be a beautiful weekend. The three of us together. I thought . . . that having the two of you here together . . . that I'd be able to put a period on that whole section of my life. But the second he walked through the door I knew that I'd put the period there long ago and this whole weekend was unnecessary.

LAUREL: Well, thanks a lot. I'm glad you've made up your mind.

ED: That's not what I meant. I wasn't planning on comparing the two of you. Christ! Everything was going to be so simple, I wanted us all to be friends. Then Arnold had to bring that kid.

LAUREL: He also brought a cake, a lace tablecloth and the *Village Voice*.

(Handing him the paper)

Enjoy them all.

ED:

(Trying to cuddle)

Come here and I'll read you the funny pages.

LAUREL: I have my own reading, thank you.

(She picks up some papers as the lights cross back to Arnold and Alan in each other's arms.)

ARNOLD: Feels so strange. I can't get over it; you and I in this room with them in there. This was my room, y'know. I mean, we slept together in there but I kept my clothes in here in case any neighbors or family dropped in and peeked around. He didn't want them to think we were queer or anything. I can't believe I put up with that.

ALAN: So, what do you think?

ARNOLD: About what?

ALAN: Ed. Seeing him again with me to compare him to.

ARNOLD: Is that what I'm supposed to be doing?

ALAN: Sure. I have.

ARNOLD: So, what do you think?

ALAN: He ain't so hot. Not hot enough to be "The Great Love of Your Life" anyway.

ARNOLD: I don't consider him "The Great Love of My Life." But, he's got his good points. He's good natured, good looking, good in bed . . .

ALAN: . . . Good and boring.

ARNOLD: He's not good and boring. He's just plain boring. But there's worse things to be. I once knew this guy who . . .

ALAN: There's a lot of that going around.

ARNOLD: Hey, who's the straight-man here?

ALAN: I'm at that impressionable age. You're rubbing off on me.

ARNOLD:

> *(Blanche du Bois)*
>
> I never touched the Gray boy.

ALAN:

> *(Laughs)*
>
> Feel better?

ARNOLD: Yeah. So anyway, I once knew this guy . . .

ALAN: Did you really love Ed?

ARNOLD: I guess so.

ALAN: And he loved you.

ARNOLD: I wouldn't say that.

ALAN: I would. I see how he looks at you. Why'd you two break up?

ARNOLD: We wanted different things.

ALAN: Like what?

ARNOLD: I wanted a husband and he wanted a wife.

ALAN: You ever think of going back with him?

ARNOLD: You can't go back.

ALAN: Why not?

ARNOLD: Because.

ALAN: Because why?

ARNOLD: Because . . . because . . . because people change. They're never the same twice. So how can you go back?

ALAN: Well, did you ever want to start out fresh again?

ARNOLD: Jesus Christ! Were you ever not true to form? Thank God I was not your mother. I could have denied you nothing. I am in awe of her that she denied you as much as she did for you to need to ask for so much now.

ALAN: When I said that I loved you before, you didn't answer me.

ARNOLD: I didn't realize that it was a question.

ALAN: Well?

ARNOLD:

> *(Throws it at him)*
>
> Here, read the newspaper.
>
> *(Alan rolls away)*
>
> Are you pouting? This child is unbelievable. Come, I'll read to you. O.K.? O.K.
>
> *(A slide appears on the screen:*
>
> CODETTA
>
> *The lights come up on Laurel and Ed reading the paper in the same position as the other couple. Both couples are visible but the separation is clear.)*

ED:

> *(Reading from the paper)*

Banes, Iowa. "That'll teach them folks not to mess around with true love," beamed eighty year old Sarah Fonedwell as she left the Iowa courtroom arm in arm with her fifteen year old boyfriend.

Miss Fonedwell was charged with statutory rape and impairing the morals of a minor after the young boy's parents learned that their son was having intimate relations with the great-grandmother of six. The couple had met when the boy took over a friend's paper route. Miss Fonedwell was a steady customer. Judge John Sirrocco dismissed the charges saying, "No real harm was done. It's all in the boy's education." But before adjourning court he shook a warning finger at the feisty lady saying, "From now on you'd better walk to the corner when you want a paper." To which she quipped, "I don't mind the added exercise, but I sure will miss them home deliveries."

(The couples keep the integrity of their pairing while building in rhythm.)

LAUREL: You made me stop working to listen to that?

ED: I think it's very funny. Don't you?

ARNOLD: That's disgusting.

LAUREL: Would you think it was so funny if it had been an eighty year old man seducing a fifteen year old girl? You think the judge would have said it was all in her education?

ED: But it wasn't.

ALAN: I don't know, I think it's kind of sexy.

LAUREL: Sexy?

ED: Yeah, sure. Imagine his feeling of power. The strength he must have felt: he young and virile, she old and withered drinking in his youth . . .

ALAN: Think of the pleasure he gave her. I bet she even thought she was fifteen again.

LAUREL: You see him as the giver and her as the taker? That's even more perverse than I'd imagined it. I saw her giving her last favor; passing on her last gift to the next generation. But you see it as a simple matter of lust.

ED: Well if you'd listened to the way she talked, you'd see she's obviously just a dirty old lady.

ARNOLD: I can't believe that anyone would be that self destructive. I mean, if she was eighty to begin with, how old was she when it was over?

ALAN: Obviously, she was rejuvenated in his arms. A miracle of modern sex.

ARNOLD: The only miraculous thing about modern sex is that it exists.

LAUREL: Did you ever sleep with someone then wonder who gave more; or who enjoyed it more?

ARNOLD: Could we change the subject?

ALAN:

(Pushing Arnold away)

They don't buy the milk if they can get the cow for free.

ARNOLD: That's what I like to hear: Good old American "not now."

LAUREL: At the risk of rendering you impotent for the remainder of "The Milkman's Matinee," could you make love to me if I was an eighty year old woman and you a fifteen year old boy?

ALAN: Fierce, passionate love.

ARNOLD: Ah, but would I make love to you?

ED: Why not?

LAUREL: You could really sleep with an eighty year old woman?

ED: Are we talking about me or me if I was fifteen?

ALAN: At least she was willing to give it a go.

ED: I give what I can and trust that it's enough.

ALAN: Not unless you can slip in a few one liners.

ED: I don't lie awake nights wondering whether I gave more or you gave more or about
how old you are or if you're pretty or not. And yes I could probably make love
to an eighty year old woman. I could make love to an eighty year old camel. I
could probably make love to anything . . . as long as it kept its mouth shut.

(The lights go out on Laurel and Ed.)

ALAN: Sssssshhh!
(Listening)
I thought I heard someone talking.

ARNOLD: It was probably Ed talking in his sleep.

ALAN: He talks in his sleep?

ARNOLD: Talks, screams, gnashes his teeth, kicks . . .

ALAN: Really? How'd you ever get any sleep?

ARNOLD: I never slept better.

ALAN: You really loved him, huh?

ARNOLD: We starting that again?

ALAN: I'm just curious. Why?

ARNOLD: What'd'ya mean, "Why?" Why does anyone love anyone? Because I did.
Because . . . I did. Because . . . he let me.

(A slide appears on the screen:

STRETTO

Alan appears alone in a light as Arnold and Ed prepare for the scene. During this
section both Alan and Laurel will appear in their own lights regardless to whom
they speak. Arnold and Ed will appear center stage together.)

ALAN: I'm not talking to you. Deserting me all afternoon like that. Where the hell did
the two of you disappear to anyway?

ARNOLD: We spent the afternoon in bed. Jealous?

ALAN: Why should I be? You didn't do anything.

ARNOLD: How do you know? We were alone for three hours.

LAUREL: If you say you only talked then I believe you. Though I can't say I understand
why you had to do it in bed.

ARNOLD: You remember that poem about sleep: That in sleep all men are equal, the
pauper and the king and all that?

ED: Something about there being no limitations on dreams?

ARNOLD: Yeah, that's the one. Well, I figure if everyone's equal in sleep then just lying down
makes you at least reachable. Besides, that's where I do my best thinking. Don't
have to worry about the body, it just relaxes leaving all the blood for the brain.

ED: I used to call your bedroom the Nursery, remember? It was always so warm and
comfortable and safe.

ARNOLD: I thought it was because we never went to bed without a bottle.

ED: And you saved every bottle we drank together. You still have them?

ARNOLD: Nah.

ED: You said you wanted to make something out of them.

ARNOLD: When we broke up I did. Quite a racket.

(Mimes throwing bottles)

And quite a mess. So tell me, what's new with you?

ED: Not much.

ARNOLD: Well, are you seeing anyone?

(Ed laughs)

That wasn't supposed to be funny. You have been known to sidestep on occasion.

ED: Not since we've been together.

ARNOLD: Give it time.

ED: I doubt it. I really do love her very much.

ARNOLD: I'm happy for you. What can I say? It's what you said you wanted and I'm glad it's working out.

ED: Are you jealous?

ARNOLD: No. Should I be?

ED: You don't love him.

ARNOLD: What's that got to do with anything?

ED: 'Cause I'm jealous of him anyway.

LAUREL:

(To Alan)

So, tell me about yourself.

ALAN:

(To Arnold)

I had to talk to her all afternoon. Nothing else to do with the two of you running off. Y'know she tried to make me? It's the truth. And not even me. I mean it wasn't me she was trying to make, particularly. She's just got this thing for faggots. It's true. Ask her. She'll tell you the whole story. I think she likes to tell the story as much as she likes to make the faggots. Anyway, she's proved you wrong. You said people only went after me because of my looks, but she went after me because of my likes.

ED:

(With Arnold in his arms)

This feels wonderful.

ALAN: You know, at first I was insulted; being wanted just because I'm gay. But, that's almost like being wanted for myself . . . I think I'm flattered.

ARNOLD:

(To Ed)

Hey, watch your hands. I'm a married man.

LAUREL:

> *(To Alan. They are now lit together.)*

So, tell me about yourself.

ALAN: I'm a model. Clothes, toothpaste . . . anything they can sell with an All-American puss. I'd like to be an actor, but I think I'll let that ride until I've made all I can out of being the American Dream.

LAUREL: And what about your childhood?

ALAN: According to Arnold, it's only just begun.

LAUREL: Arnold really is something else. You two must be very happy together.

ALAN: Believe me, there are easier things than living with Arnold. He thinks it's immoral, that it makes him a lesser person to love me because I'm good-looking.

LAUREL: Oh come on.

ALAN: No, really. He'd be much happier if I was his age, his size, his . . . size. Sometimes I'm not sure if he wants a lover or a bookend.

LAUREL: It's good that you have a sense of humor. Ed has none. But that's part of his charm.

ALAN: No wonder they didn't last.

LAUREL: Well, I think there's more to it than that. But I can't tell you how happy I am that Arnold has you. My reasons may be a little selfish. Y'know, they were still going together when I met Ed. I didn't know it of course. If I did I never would have started seeing Ed. See, I met him through a friend from group . . .

ALAN: Group? Like in therapy group?

LAUREL: That's right. It's kind of a story, I guess. I had just come through a rather bad affair with a guy who turned out to be bisexual. (The bi leaning toward his new boyfriend.) When he broke the news to me I was quite a mess. See, he wasn't the first man to pull that on me. All told there were three of that particular persuasion plus a pair of married men thrown in for good measure. Not the greatest track record for a "One Man Woman" type like myself. I became what you could call . . . depressed. And when I looked among my friends for a sympathetic ear I realized that every one of them was gay. That's when it began to dawn on me that I might just have gotten myself into a rut. So, off to therapy I went. That's where I met Janet who told me about a handsomely available teacher she knew named Ed. She set up the get together and that was that.

ALAN: A real live blind date. How exotic.

LAUREL:

> *(Amused)*

Blind indeed. We'd been dating for over a month before he ever told me about Arnold. But by then, it was too late to pull out without a fight.

ALAN: So you fought?

LAUREL: No, that's not what I meant. I mean, it wasn't a fight. I just pulled back enough to let Ed feel his freedom: No promises, no pressure, no commitments. Soon he was telling me that he wanted to end his relationship with Arnold. So, I suggested he speak to my therapist and he joined the group . . .

ARNOLD: You never told me about the shrink.

ED: Because I know how you feel about "Shrinks." But really, the group's been very supportive. They've never pushed me toward any decision that I didn't want to make.

ARNOLD: Now I know where all that, "I owe myself the chance to lead a normal life" bullshit came from. So, I suppose you're straight now?

ED: Not now. I always have been.

ARNOLD: And me? . . . and all the others, what were we; a phase you were going through?

ED:

(Laughing)

You always were a homosexual chauvinist. To you everyone's either gay or in the closet.

ARNOLD: What's sex like with her?

ED: It's very beautiful.

ARNOLD: Is it satisfying?

ED: I'm with her, aren't I?

ARNOLD: So, what does that mean? I could've kept you. You don't believe it, but it's true. I've done a lot of thinking about you and some of the others I've been through and I think I've found a pattern: When things get too good . . . I get out. Well, I guess to a degree we all do. But most pull out; ride off into the sunset with a wave and a wink and a "Heigh-o-Silver." But not me. I am a pusher. I nudge and kvetch and cry and demand until I leave my partner no possible alternative but for him to run for his life. That makes him the villain and leaves the victim role to me. And "Poor Pearl" is a role I really love to play.

ED: I never saw myself the villain.

ARNOLD: You never saw yourself period.

ED: I wouldn't have stayed. In the year that Laurel and I have been seeing each other I haven't once fooled around. And believe me, our relationship allows for that. No, I wouldn't have stayed.

(Thinks)

I bet you think you could get me back if you wanted to.

ARNOLD: I don't want to. That's precisely my point. Why waste all that energy? When an affair hits the skids you shed it like last year's fashion and head back to the streets. There are plenty more where that one came from. And that, my ex-husband, is what I call the miracle of modern sex.

LAUREL: We attend private sessions on Tuesdays and on Thursdays we have group. You and Arnold should try it. Maybe not the private sessions but a group's the ideal way to open up the lines of communication between two people and really solidify a relationship.

ALAN: Sounds inspiring.

ED: And what about you? You don't love that kid.

ARNOLD: You said that, not me.

ED: So, do you?

ARNOLD: Maybe. What makes you think I'm in love with anyone?

ED: Because we've been lying in bed together for over an hour in and out of each other's arms and you've yet to make a pass at me.

ARNOLD: That's not love. That's good taste.

ED: Come on, Arnold, who is it? No, let me guess . . . Could it be me?

ARNOLD:

(Jumping)

ED:

God, the EGO!!!!

(Pulling him back)

I was only kidding.

ARNOLD: You wouldn't know him anyway. I don't know him. Not really.

ED: You wouldn't love him if you did.

ARNOLD: You're really impossible.

ED:

(Genuine)

Who is he?

ARNOLD: Well, you know The International Stud Bar has this dark backroom where everyone goes to fool around . . . What am I telling you for? I wouldn't know about such things if it wasn't for you showing them to me. Anyway, I've been going there a lot lately. Two, three times a week.

ED: What does Alan have to say about that?

ARNOLD:

(Sarcastically)

We have a very honest and open relationship. So, there's this guy there that I meet every night and we always get it on together. We haven't talked about anything really and we meet there only by chance, I mean we haven't set it up that way or anything. It's just that he's always there waiting for me, or if I get there first I wait for him . . . Oh, never mind.

ED: No, go on, it sounds very romantic.

ARNOLD: Just forget it, alright?

ED: I'm sorry, but first you tell me you're in love. Then you tell me you can only get it on in a backroom . . .

ARNOLD: That's not it at all.

ED: Have you ever made love together alone?

ARNOLD: No, but . . .

ED: Have you ever had a drink together in the light of the front room?

ARNOLD: He's very shy.

ED:

(Laughing)

Arnold, I think you've reached a new plateau of perversity.

ARNOLD: Hey, wait a minute here, who gospelled to whom about the advantages of the backroom? I'd never seen a backroom until after you. . . .

ED: I never took you into one.

ARNOLD: But that's where you would rather have taken me. If we'd met and stayed in the backroom we never would have had the problems we did.

ED: Is that your answer now? Put the blame on me. "Ed, you hurt me so bad. I'll never trust to love again." So, you're going to play this one nice and safe.

ARNOLD: Look who's knocking safety! Mr. All-American Heterosexual! Locked your life up tight didn't you. Picked yourself a nice little wifey type, plain and lonely enough to never worry about her stepping out on you, pleasant and giving enough to boss her around to get her to do anything or go anywhere that you want. And you're gonna read my beads?

(Arnold makes a dive under the covers.)

ED: Hey! What are you doing?
ARNOLD:

(Emerging at the foot of the bed next to Ed's feet, his feet next to Ed's face)

Take it easy. I'm just looking for a second opinion.
ED: I thought you were trying to get to the bottom of me.
ARNOLD: Heterosexuality has done "nada" for your wit. Your feet stink.
ED: They weren't expecting company.
ARNOLD:

(Picking up a bottle)

What's this?
ED: My cologne.
ARNOLD:

(Sniffing)

What is it, "Ben Hur"?

(Sprinkles it about)

Now I'm in my element. Toss me a pillow.

(Ed does)

Thanks. And just what's wrong with playing it safe? I can sleep when I want, eat when I want, fuck when I want . . .
ED: . . . Want when you want.
ARNOLD: Cheap shot.
ED: Can I just ask you a question? If you don't love Alan, why do you stay with him?
ARNOLD: He needs me.
ED: Come on.
ARNOLD: Alright, I need him.
ED: Forget I asked.
ARNOLD: What the hell would you know about need? You're like a baby in a crib, hands and fingers flexing, "Gimme. Gimme." You're all want. So, maybe I don't love him, but I need that gorgeous imbecile and I like to think that he needs me.
ED: So, he's like a pet.
ARNOLD: You're a pig, you know that?
ED: Arnold, I am exhausted from trying to understand.
ARNOLD: It gets easier with practice. He ain't complaining.
ED: Don't you think he deserves to be loved?
ARNOLD: Of course he does. Who doesn't? But, who is?
ED: I am.
ARNOLD: What do you suppose it is that makes me want to shove a chair up your nose?

(Pause)

What the hell am I supposed to do: sit around crying over losing you?

ED: That's not what I meant. I'm very happy you have him, alright?

ARNOLD:

(Long pause)

You and Laurel working on having kids yet?

ED: We haven't really discussed it in detail.

ARNOLD: Don't you still want kids?

ED: Still? Who said anything about having kids?

ARNOLD: You did. Don't you remember?: At the party there was that woman who arranged for gay couples to adopt. You probably don't remember, you said you wanted a boy, but you were gay then.

ED: I remember. But that was just talk. You know, a fantasy.

ARNOLD: Is that what it was?

ED: Sure, like our airplane, and our island . . .

ARNOLD: . . . and our relationship.

ED: That was one of the things that made me love you: that I could fantasize about anything, let my mind go as far out as it could and there you were all caught up in the dream with me, making it almost real.

ARNOLD: 'Cause I didn't know it wasn't. Those things weren't fantasies to me. To me a fantasy is a Genie or a magic lamp, something impossible that you wouldn't really want even if you could have it. Our airplane, our island, our child . . . they weren't fantasies. They were possibilities. None of it was impossible. Y'know, I keep a ledger where I list things like that. And when I get an item that's on the list I put a checkmark next to it. The ledger's got more than one hundred pages filled with my possibilities. You'd be surprised how many checkmarks there are too. Oh, they're little things like an electric toothbrush, or an azalea bush or a subscription to *National Geographic*. But they each mark an achievement for me.

ED: What's the inflation ratio; items as opposed to checkmarks?

ARNOLD: Never counted.

ED: Am I on the list?

ARNOLD: Listed and checked off.

ED: That's cheating. You don't have me.

ARNOLD:

(Cocksure)

Don't I?

ED: No.

ARNOLD: I'll be sure to correct my ledger first thing Monday morning.

ED:

(Pause)

Tell me something, what would you do with a subscription to *National Geographic?*

ARNOLD:

(Hiding his insult)

Look at the dirty pictures.

ED:

(Agreeing)

Oh.

(Arnold pulls a pillow over his head in disgust as a slide appears on the screen:

COUNTER SUBJECT

Arnold and Alan are in each other's arms just waking. The other two remain in the dark until indicated.)

LAUREL:

(Calling out)

Hurry up, you two sleepyheads, breakfast is on the table.

ARNOLD: Sleepyheads?

ALAN:

(Ecstatic)

Breakfast? How'd you sleep?

ARNOLD: Awfully. I dreamt that I was walking down this twisting path and no matter how carefully I watched I kept stepping in cowpies . . .

ALAN: You mean cow-chips. Not pies. Chips.

ARNOLD: Whatever. Anyway, as I turned a corner around this big Camperdown Elm I saw Ed squatting down naked making the cowpies . . . or chips. Now what the hell do you suppose that was supposed to mean?

ALAN: Maybe it was prophetic dreaming.

ARNOLD: Prophesying what?

ALAN: Maybe the toilet's gonna bust.

LAUREL:

(Calling out)

C'mon you two. We'll be late for church.

ARNOLD: She say church?

ALAN: Didn't you know, Ed plays organ for the services every Sunday morning.

ARNOLD: Give me a break. And they say dreams are meaningless?

LAUREL:

(Now lit)

Aren't you two coming?

ARNOLD: Actually, Laurel, I'd love to go but my religion strictly forbids entering any church for other than historical purposes; looking at stained glass etc.

LAUREL: Nonsense. I have lots of Jewish friends that visit churches.

ARNOLD: Oh, but I'm not Jewish anymore. I've converted. I'm what you'd call a Scientific American. Yes. See . . . we believe that all of mankind's problems can be solved with vitamins.

ALAN:

> *(Under his breath)*

> Groan!

LAUREL: So, you have no need for prayer.

ARNOLD: I wouldn't say that. I'm often found on my knees.

ALAN:

> *(A bit louder)*

> Groan!

LAUREL: But if you can't enter a house of God, where do you pray?

ARNOLD: Harvard.

ALAN:

> *(Loud)*

> Groan!!!

> *(Arnold leaps on him laughing.)*

ED:

> *(Lights on him and Laurel)*

> What's the matter?

LAUREL: Nothing. Are you ready?

ED: Are they coming down?

LAUREL: No. They're sleeping in.

ED: What's the matter? Did Arnold say something?

LAUREL: I'm not upset. Are you coming?

ED: This weekend's not turning out the way you thought it would either. Is it? Just remember, it was your idea.

LAUREL: I like Arnold. I really do. It's just . . . When I thought about this weekend I knew it was a set-up for all sorts of competitions, comparisons . . . and I was ready for them. After all, I knew no matter what happened that I had you. I knew you'd made your choice between us and felt I could deal with anything knowing you had chosen me.

ED: That's what I've been saying all along.

LAUREL: Would you just listen? . . . That's not what's happening here. Arnold is so relaxed, as if he has nothing on his mind, like he's simply visiting friends for the weekend.

ED: What's wrong with that?

LAUREL: He's just too sure of himself. Like a kid all puffed up with a secret.

ED: Are you sorry they're here?

LAUREL: No. Just aware.

> *(Lights out on them)*

ALAN: You weren't very nice to her.

ARNOLD: I do have my limits and one of them happens to be Sunday morning Mountain Church services. Actually, I'm shocked that Ed let her ask us at all. He probably would have introduced us as long lost relatives. The charcoal-grey sheep of the family.

ALAN: Kissing cousins. So, what do you make of her?

ARNOLD: She's alright. A little too giving and gracious for my tastes, but deep down she's a survivor.

ALAN: How can you say that? She makes the same mistakes over and over.

ARNOLD: Once is a mistake. Twice a misfortunate coincidence. But three times and you can start writing your memoirs.

ALAN: He's number four.

ARNOLD: I wonder if maybe she's really gay? I know just the woman to bring her out too. Bet she'd make a great lesbian.

ALAN: And you'd make a great lamp.

ARNOLD: I'm afraid I'd make a great deal more than that.

ALAN:

> *(Climbing onto him)*

> I'll make do . . .

> *(Lights out on them as a slide appears on the screen:*

> *STRETTO*

> *Lights come up on all four holding plates and napkins as if they've just finished lunch. They begin to pass the plates to Laurel.)*

ED: Laurel, that was a delicious lunch. Isn't she a great cook, Arnold? Besides being beautiful.

ARNOLD:

> *(Snatching the pile of plates from Laurel)*

> Just delicious. And beautiful.

ALAN: I bet I've gained five pounds in the past two days.

ARNOLD: Here, let me help you with those dishes.

LAUREL:

> *(Grabbing the dishes back.)*

> No, I'm fine. Ed, why don't you take Arnold and Alan out to the barn and show them our new canning machine. We've been canning all our own vegetables, you know.

ARNOLD: Really? Ed, why don't you take Alan and show it to him. He's the real can connoisseur in the family. I'll stay and help Laurel. We've yet to have a moment alone to compare notes on you.

ED: Just what Laurel's been waiting for.

LAUREL:

> *(Embarrassed)*

> Ed!

ED:

> *(Taking two glasses)*

> Let's hit the road before the fur starts flying. Grab that bottle of brandy. No need for us to rough it.

(There is a sudden light change focusing on Arnold and Alan in the center of the bed. Ed moves to the upstage right corner of the bed as Laurel moves with her dishes and dishrag to the downstage left corner. When Ed speaks it is to Alan's next physical position.)

ALAN: Go start packing. We're getting out of here tonight.

ARNOLD: Would you stop.

ALAN: I suppose you're going to tell me you spent another innocent afternoon in bed. Only this time with her.

ARNOLD: It was not an afternoon, it was only an hour. And we spent it in the kitchen doing dishes. You knew where we were. If you were lonely you should have come in.

ALAN: Oh, I wasn't lonely. I had lots of company. He tried to make me.

ARNOLD: Would you please . . .

ALAN: I'd like to be able to spend two minutes in this house without someone trying to shove me onto a couch . . .

ED: Would you like another brandy?

ALAN: . . . And you put down the studio? At least when someone makes a pass at me there it's got a trip to Europe or a movie contract as part of the deal. Here it's "Alone at last!" and a dive for my zipper.

ED: Well, here we are: Alone at last.

ARNOLD: Alan, when we walk down the street and an old lady asks you for the time you swear she's trying to make you. Now I'd be the last to say you weren't irresistible, but, Angel, there are limits.

(Joins Laurel)

ED: We can sit on this haystack.

(Alan joins him.)

ARNOLD:

(Wiping a dish)

Isn't this civilized? Doing the dishes.

LAUREL: Stuck with the dishes. I feel like we went out to lunch, you thinking that I was treating and I thinking that you were treating and here we are: working off the bill.

ARNOLD: No, I know, we're in-laws on one of them detergent commercials.

LAUREL: "Why Marge, your dishes are so shiny. I can see myself!"

ARNOLD: "Well, so can I!" Platter, platter on the stack. Does she think I want him back?

(He winces a bit.)

LAUREL: You work fast. I thought we'd kind'a waltz around the table a few times first.

ARNOLD: Sorry, I thought we might as well get it out of the way.

LAUREL: So, do you?

ARNOLD: What do you think?

LAUREL: I think you do.

ARNOLD: Really. Why?

LAUREL: Well, you don't love Alan.

ARNOLD: I keep hearing that. What makes you think I don't love Alan?

LAUREL: How could you when you still love Ed?

ARNOLD: What makes you think I still love Ed?

LAUREL: Well, I know that from the start you loved Ed more than he loved you . . .

ARNOLD: He told you that?

LAUREL: It's nothing to be ashamed of.

ARNOLD: Of course not. If it's true that one person always loves more than the other, why not be the one who feels the most? But why would that make you think I'd want him back now?

LAUREL: You're here, aren't you?

ARNOLD: You asked me to come.

LAUREL: Still, you didn't have to.

> (Uncomfortably)

> Look, I know more about your relationship than you might think. We have few secrets and a great deal of openness. It's the kind of relationship we have. We share almost everything with complete freedom . . . What I'm trying to say is that I know a great deal of what was said between you . . .

ARNOLD: So?

LAUREL: Please. So, I know what it feels like to be in that position. You felt hurt, rejected, angry . . . Then you started to wonder if there was ever anything between you. Or maybe you'd made it all up? Who's to blame for that? Who's to blame for breaking up?

ARNOLD: Are we talking about you or me?

LAUREL: You told Ed that you could get him back if you wanted to.

ARNOLD: I also told him that I didn't want to.

LAUREL: Then why do you call him all the time? I know about your calls in the afternoon while I'm at work.

ARNOLD: He told you that I call him?

LAUREL:

> (Haughty)

> I told you, we have a very honest relationship.

ARNOLD: Laurel, I don't want you to misunderstand and think I'm calling Ed a liar, but I've never called him. Yes, we've spoken on the phone, but he has always called me. And I've made those conversations as brief as was politely possible. He'd call and tell me all about how happy the two of you were and all about his family (none of whom I've ever met) and I'd say a nice little good-bye and that was that.

LAUREL: Then why'd you come up here?

ARNOLD: To see how my paint job was holding up. Y'know, I painted this room. Took me days. I was scared shitless of dripping on the floor; you know what a fussbudget Ed can be . . .

LAUREL: I'm sorry. I have no right to talk to you this way. I'm pushing you to admit something that you're obviously not ready to face.

ARNOLD: You're pushing me alright! But I don't think you realize toward what. Laurel . . . Are you happy with Ed?

LAUREL: The happiest I've ever been in my life.

ARNOLD: So what else do you want?

ALAN: To own a disco.

(Lights out on Arnold and Laurel, leaving Alan and Ed quite alone.)

I knew this guy, he was a few years older than me, who'd met this older guy who set him up in business. I figured that I could do the same. But when I made my entrance into the Big Apple, and believe me, a blue eyed blond of fourteen makes quite an entrance into any apple, I found that no one was interested in hearing about my business skills. In fact no one was interested in anything much besides my price tag for an evening. See, people with tastes for blue eyed blonds of fourteen are used to paying for it and consider a freebee suspicious if not downright immoral. And so, I became a hustler. I figured that I needed the affection more than they needed the money. Now, of course, things are different. But then . . . Anyway, I got along. The hustling led to some connections, the connections to my career, and the career to . . .

ED: Arnold!

ALAN: No, Arnold was more of a detour.

ED: That's Arnold.

ALAN: One night, I went out drinking with a friend and got more than usually polluted. Somehow I ended up in a lower east-side bar that had a drag show. Anyway, I wound up in a fight with this big black guy who threw me down on a table, jumped up on my chest and put a knife to my neck. Everyone was screaming and crowding around to watch me get cut, when all of a sudden there was silence and the crowd parted to make an aisle, and up through it like Moses through the Red Sea came this Amazon woman. You never seen anything like it. She was beautiful! Not like "pretty" beautiful, but like "mountain" beautiful. You know what I mean?

ED: That's Arnold!

ALAN: She put her hand out to the black guy like this,

(He demonstrates the gesture with haughty glare)

and he just handed over the knife and disappeared. No words, no nothing, just like that.

ED: When did you realize it was a guy?

ALAN: I was too drunk that night to realize that *I* was a guy. I sort of . . . fell onto that discovery the next morning.

ED:

(Moving in closer)

How'd you feel about it?

ALAN: I'm with him, aren't I?

(Easing away. Holding up his glass.)

More please.

(Ed pours)

Now, you tell me about you. That's the whole reason we're here.

ED: Is it?

ALAN: Sure is. Arnold didn't want to come, but I wasn't going to let this chance to see my competition go by.

ED: I'm no competition.

(He moves closer again.)

ALAN: Well, then my predecessor. Stop changing the subject. Tell me about you.

ED: Why don't you ask Arnold to tell you. I'm sure he's got lots to say on the subject.

ALAN: He has.

ED: And?

ALAN: He says you're a self-centered, insensitive, boring fool who wouldn't know love if it wore wings, a diaper and shot heart-shaped arrows at your butt.

ED: Meaning himself?

ALAN: Meaning himself.

(Lying down triumphantly)

Anything you'd care to add?

ED: No, that'll do.

(Lying down next to him)

And what do you think?

ALAN: I'll reserve my judgment until I can make a closer inspection.

ED:

(Putting his arm around Alan)

Close enough?

ALAN:

(Sitting up quickly)

Too close for comfort. You asked me to sit in the hay, not roll in it.

ED:

(Coming up behind him)

It was a two part question. I think you're very beautiful.

ALAN: I thought you were reformed.

ED: I'm not proposing marriage to you.

(Gently pulling him back)

If you want me to stop just say so. Do you?

(No response)

I didn't think so.

(The lights go out on them immediately leaving Arnold alone at the downstage right corner of the bed.)

ARNOLD: I don't know when to stop. That's my problem. Me and my big fucking mouth. I didn't come up here to hurt her. I didn't even come up here to hurt him. (Though that would've been alright.) I was so proud of myself until now. I thought I was really handling this whole situation so maturely. I guess I was saving it all up for that.

(To Alan as if he were there)

I hope you're enjoying all this.

ALAN:

> *(From the dark)*

> Oh, I am.

ARNOLD: Good. 'Cause it's all your fault. Couldn't take no for an answer, you just had to come up here. Why couldn't I just keep my trap shut? I've always thought of myself as a kind person. Not saintly but generously thoughtful (in a bitchy sort of way). But since being here I have said nothing that hasn't hurt someone: you, Ed, Laurel, myself. Well, she asked for it. She begged for it . . . and boy did I give it to her. I was brilliant. Point after pointless point I proved beyond a shadow of a doubt that Ed has no idea that she even exists. That, to him, she's simply living proof of his normality.

ALAN:

> *(Joining Arnold, they fold clothing into a suitcase)*

> How many dishes did she break over your head?

ARNOLD: Not enough to keep me quiet.

ALAN: You elaborated?

ARNOLD: Ad infinitum. I quoted every report I could lay my brain on concerning bisexuality and its inherent unresolved immaturity, backing each prejudiced selection with a biased statistic . . .

ALAN: I love when you get technical.

ARNOLD: . . . . And finished her off with a quote from the man in question himself: That if all things were equal (she and I being the same sex), he never would have left me. Now, if that ain't dirty logic then what is?

ALAN:

> *(Feigning anguish)*

> Mercy! Mercy!

ARNOLD: Can that crap. This is for real.

ALAN: What're you getting so upset about? Who ever listens to you?

ARNOLD: There's always a first time. Come here and comfort me! Can't you see I'm disturbed?!?

ALAN: Why should I if you're such a rat?

ARNOLD: Because the innocent must suffer, not the guilty. This is America.

ALAN:

> *(Laughing)*

> You ain't so tough.

> *(Embracing)*

> That feel better?

ARNOLD: And she took it. Stood there staring me straight in the eye and listened to it all. Never argued, just nodded. God, you smell so good.

ALAN: Better than him?

ARNOLD: Now you're gonna start?

> *(Messing his hair)*

> He's jealous of you. Really. He told me so himself.

ALAN: Who isn't? I have you don't I?

(Embrace)

You shouldn't have disappeared with her all afternoon. How do you think I felt?

ARNOLD: How'd you feel?

ALAN: You just shouldn't've.

ARNOLD: What're you, a baby? I gotta sit and hold your hand?

ALAN: I came up here to be with you, not him. Let's get outta here.

(The lights lower as a slide appears:

CODA

Alan slips under the covers, Laurel sits in the center, the phone rings.)

ARNOLD:

(Answering in his sleep)

Hello?

ED: Hi. I woke you.

ARNOLD: Good guess. Hold on a second.

(He sits up and tries to shake the sleep.)

Hello? Listen I was gonna call you later to thank you for the weekend.

(Morning cough)

As you can hear, the country air's done wonders for me.

ED: I thought I'd call to make sure you two got home alright.

ARNOLD: Yeah, fine. We drove straight through.

ED: I really enjoyed having you here. So did Laurel.

ARNOLD: I'm glad. We did too.

ED: You know, we got a lot out of having you up here. We learned a lot about our relationship.

ARNOLD: You holding seminars?

ED: Couldn't you be nice?

ARNOLD: Sorry, morning breath and all.

ED: Is Alan there with you?

ARNOLD: No, he dropped me off then headed out to Queens to bring the car back to his mother. I guess he spent the night.

ED: Oh. But he'll be back tonight?

ARNOLD: I suppose. What's the difference?

ED: I was curious, that's all.

ARNOLD: Something wrong?

ED: Not at all.

ARNOLD: You sound funny.

ED: No. But I do have a favor to ask.

ARNOLD: Shoot.

ED: Well . . . Laurel went into the city this morning to spend a few days. Just to check on some classes . . . Anyway, I thought it'd be nice if you had her over to dinner or went out together for lunch or something. Just so she's not alone.

ARNOLD: Shit, look Ed, I'm really sorry I caused trouble . . .

ED: Oh, no. We didn't have words or anything. I just felt that it would be better if we both had time to think about our relationship.

ARNOLD: I understand.

ED: I know you do. I love her very much.

ARNOLD: Have you tried telling her that?

ED: She's not like you, Arnold. She doesn't need to be reassured every hour on the hour.

ARNOLD: An admirable quality; to be sure.

ED: Will you talk to her?

ARNOLD: Don't worry about a thing.

ED: I appreciate it.

ARNOLD: Anything else?

ED: There is one thing more.

ARNOLD: Don't stop now.

ED: Did you have a chance to correct that list yet?

ARNOLD: What list?

ED: Of the things you want. Remember, I told you to erase the checkmark next to my name.

ARNOLD:

(Exasperated)

As a matter of fact, I haven't had the time. But don't you worry, I'll take care of it.

ED: Don't. I mean . . . I'd like it if you left the checkmark where it is.

(Laurel pops into the scene as Ed disappears under the covers.)

LAUREL: So what'd you tell him?

ARNOLD: I told him I'd leave the checkmark but erase the name.

LAUREL: You didn't?!?

ARNOLD: No, I didn't. But I should've. I don't know, sometimes I get the feeling he's learning, but God, it's a struggle. You going back to him?

LAUREL: I don't think so. I don't know.

ARNOLD: What'd your shrink say?

LAUREL: Not much. Nothing, as a matter of fact, nothing. He just kept asking me what I want. Over and over again, "What do you want?", "What do you want?"

ARNOLD: And what did you tell him?

LAUREL: I told him I wanted him to shut up.

ARNOLD:

(Giggling)

You didn't.

LAUREL:

(Laughing too)

No, I didn't. But I should've. What do *you* want?

ARNOLD: I wanna beer.

LAUREL: You know what I mean.

ARNOLD: What do I want? What do I want? What do I want? Well, it would have to be something witty because you're depressed and it's not enough to be funny when talking to a depressed person. One must be cleverly diverting or at least playfully bawdy . . .

LAUREL: Your brain is hopelessly delinquent.

ARNOLD: That's what I want: A hopeless delinquent! No, I already got one of those.

LAUREL: Alan and you are wonderful together. I'm sure everything will work itself out.

ARNOLD: I didn't know there was anything that needed working out.

LAUREL: Didn't you two have words?

ARNOLD: None we haven't used before.

LAUREL: Oh. I thought that was why you returned last night instead of this morning.

ARNOLD: Not at all.

LAUREL: What happened between Alan and Ed doesn't bother you at all?

ED:

(Sitting up to one side)

You blurted it out just like that?

LAUREL:

(To Ed)

I thought he knew. I meant it as a friendly remark.

ARNOLD:

(To Alan)

With friends like her who needs newspapers?

ALAN: I tried to tell you . . .

ARNOLD: I must say, you picked a great time to start telling the truth.

LAUREL:

(To Arnold)

Why did you think I left?

ARNOLD:

(To Laurel)

I thought it was something I said.

LAUREL: Don't be silly.

ALAN:

(To Ed)

Are you going to tell Laurel?

ED:

(To Alan)

What I do is my own business.

LAUREL:

(To Arnold)

We respect each other's privacy.

ARNOLD: . . . and he still had energy for me. Oh, to be eighteen again! But, you and Alan didn't . . .

LAUREL: No! Why? He said we did?

ARNOLD: Well, I'm sure he meant it as a compliment. . . . to both of you.

ALAN:

> (To Ed)

> I thought an open relationship meant that you told each other everything.

ARNOLD: You saw them together?

LAUREL: No. Ed told me about it after you left. He came into the bedroom and said he had something to discuss . . . discuss!? And he told me. He was crying. He said he was sorry—not that he'd done it, but that he had to tell me about it. I was dumbfounded. I didn't know which of us to comfort; who was hurting more. So, I sat there. We didn't say a word, occasionally catching each other's eye and looking away again. After a while he went down to the kitchen and I packed a bag and left. I hadn't planned on leaving . . . But, it seemed the right thing to do. There I was, packed, at the door . . . so I left.

ARNOLD: That wasn't very bright.

LAUREL: And what would you have done?

ARNOLD: I'd've shoved him head first into a meat grinder. But I would've hung around to see what came out the other end.

LAUREL: Arnold, you don't seem to be getting the drift of this at all. He made love to someone; your lover, with me not fifty feet away. What more reason would a person possibly need to walk out on someone?

ARNOLD:

> (To Alan)

> I have never felt so used in my life! I wanted to put a pillow over her face and snuff her out.

> (Mocking)

> "I hadn't planned on leaving." The gall! "What more reason would a person possibly need to walk out?" The nerve!!

LAUREL: So, this is the nursery. It's not at all what I'd expected from Ed's description. I like it though. It's got a coziness . . . a warmth. I can feel it.

ARNOLD:

> (To Laurel)

> Thanks.

LAUREL: If this is the nursery, does that make you the nurse?

ARNOLD: Registered with the A.M.A. You need one?

> (Laurel nods and begins to cry)

> Nurse Arnold to the rescue.

> (He takes her in his arms like a baby.)

> I accept Blue Cross, Blue Shield and Blue Nun. Hurts, huh?

LAUREL: Like a claw in my stomach. Just once in my life I'd like to have an affair go on the rocks after the passion wears off; when I'm bored with the routine, the sex, the talk. I'd love to know what it feels like to have the flame rekindled by jealousy instead of this . . . having the rug pulled out from under me like this. Just once I'd like to be standing on sure ground when the blow hits instead of crawling around on my hands and knees like a baby.

ARNOLD: You want a hell of a lot out of life. Don't'cha'? I'd settle for being able to say to someone, "I love you," and whether I meant it or not, finding them still in bed the next morning.

ALAN: All you had to do was ask me.

ARNOLD: Ask you what?

ALAN: Not to fool around with anyone else, and I wouldn't have.

LAUREL: But you never asked me.

ED: Because I wanted you to feel that you could.

ALAN: You mean, you wanted me to feel that you could. All those nights you spent out in them backrooms: How do you think I felt?

ARNOLD: That's not the same thing at all. I didn't even know those people's names.

ALAN: That makes a difference?

LAUREL: You mean you want me to see other men?

ARNOLD: No. But I want you to feel free to.

ALAN: I do. And I did. So, what are you so upset about?

ED: It's the kind of relationship you said you wanted.

LAUREL: Just because I said that's what I want doesn't mean that's what I want. I mean, that's what I want but that doesn't mean that I'm necessarily ready for it.

ALAN: You're being ridiculous.

ARNOLD: You telling me that you don't see any difference between my innocent jaunts to the backroom and your vile debauchery this weekend?

ALAN: Not really.

ARNOLD: Well. There you have it!

ALAN: There I have what?

ARNOLD: Don't be such a smart ass!

LAUREL:

(To Arnold)

It's my own fault for expecting something different. The only thing different about each of the affairs in my life is the way they dumped me. Not even the way so much as the words.

ARNOLD: I know what you mean. My favorite kiss-offs are those little speeches: "I really dig you, baby. You're the kind that I could really fall for. But, I'm not ready to fall so Adios."

LAUREL: I much prefer the continental version: "We've got a good thing going; let's not mess it up by getting too involved."

ARNOLD: How about, "Let's not make any promises we'll regret later?"

LAUREL: You ever hear the one about the trial separation?

ARNOLD: As often as I've heard about their reconciliation.

LAUREL: "I've got to try my wings."

ARNOLD: "I've got to repark the car."

LAUREL: "I've got to live free!"

ARNOLD: "She meant nothing to me!" Oops. Sorry.

LAUREL: That's alright. It's nothing I haven't heard before.

ARNOLD: Gee but it's GREAT to have someone else to blame.

(They both laugh.)

LAUREL: I don't understand; how could Ed ever have let you get away?

ARNOLD: I'm lousy in bed. It's true. I don't relax enough. I guess I'm just an old fashioned kind of guy: I hardly ever enjoy sex with someone I know. So, you ready to call home?

LAUREL: I don't know. What do you think?

ARNOLD: I think I'm the wrong person to ask.

ALAN:

(Coupling with Arnold)

That's the first thing you've said all week that's made sense.

ARNOLD: Look who's talking.

LAUREL:

(Coupling with Ed)

I should at least give him a chance to explain.

ALAN: She'll stay with him. They were made for each other.

LAUREL: I owe him as much.

ARNOLD: It's wrong.

LAUREL: After all, what have I got to lose.

ARNOLD: It's all wrong.

LAUREL: Otherwise . . . What was it all for?

ARNOLD: I can't tell you how strongly I feel that it's wrong!

(They are alone in the light.)

You were wrong to do what you did! . . . though I know why you did. And Ed was wrong to do what he did! . . . though I know why he did. And Laurel was wrong to use what you two did!! . . . though I know why she did. And I was wrong to do everything I did! . . . but I did. I don't know, maybe it all evens out in the end. I mean, if two wrongs don't make a right . . . maybe four do.

ALAN: So the score's all evened up.

ARNOLD: I can't tell with these "Make 'em up as you go along" rules. Monogamy's a much easier system to keep track of.

ALAN: Well, look at it this way: Ed's got what he wants—a warm body in bed with a very attractive break in his routine. And Laurel's got what she wants—Ed in bed . . .

ARNOLD: With a million new fascinating problems to discuss with her shrink.

ALAN: And we've got what we want . . . each other.

ARNOLD: You're awful pushy for a kid who ain't old enough to pee straight.

ALAN:

(Lying back)

Come here and I'll show you how pushy.

ARNOLD:

(Delighted)

Just let me turn out the lights.

ALAN: Why do you wanna turn out the lights?

ARNOLD: Because, even in times like these one must retain a degree of the old cherished decorum.

ALAN: Well, aren't we civilized.

ARNOLD: Terribly!

ALAN: Wait. There's one more thing I'd like to ask you.

ARNOLD:

(Into his arms)

The answer is yes.

ALAN: But you don't know the question.

ARNOLD: Doesn't matter. I'm too tired to argue about anything so whatever it is the answer is yes.

ALAN: Good. Because I love you too.

ARNOLD:

(Pulling away)

Oh for God's sake, Alan, after everything we've been through this weekend . . .

ALAN: Oh, shut up!

(Embarrassed)

Can't you take a joke?

(The music begins to play as Arnold sits up staring straight ahead in bewildered shock. As the bed begins to leave the stage he lies back into Alan's arms in hopeless surrender. Alan feeds him a piece of cake as the bed disappears offstage.)

A slide:

EPILOGUE

The quartet music is joined by a piano. Upstage we see the small ornate stage and baby grand piano of a nightclub. The pianist is playing the introduction to a violent, angry love song. Arnold enters in rehearsal clothes carrying his music and sings the song. His is a passionate interpretation. The song ends.)

ARNOLD:

(To pianist. Making a note on the score.)

That ought'a fog up their glasses and empty their mugs. We'll use it between "Cry Me A River" and "Who's Sorry Now." Just as a change of pace.

LAUREL:

(She's been watching from the wings)

God, you're depressing.

ARNOLD: Laurel? Oh, no!

LAUREL: Thanks a lot.

ARNOLD: No, I didn't mean: Oh no: not you. I meant: Oh no: you two had another fight.

LAUREL: Oh, no: not at all.

ARNOLD: Really?

LAUREL: You say that like you don't believe it.

ARNOLD: Oh, no.

LAUREL: Let's not start that again. Aren't you going to say hello?

ARNOLD: Hello. Sorry, but this just ain't my day. My maid called in sick, my cleaning came in late, we've got these new numbers to rehearse . . .

LAUREL: Maybe I'd better not bother you.

ARNOLD: No, stay. I could use a little gossip in the midst of all this reality.

> *(To pianist)*

> Five minutes, hon.

> *(Taking a chair off a little table)*

> Here, make yourself at home.

LAUREL: Oh, the man in front asked me to give you this.

> *(She hands him a small parcel.)*

ARNOLD:

> *(Taking down a chair for himself)*

> Thanks. Here sit down.

LAUREL: You really like that?

ARNOLD:

> *(Opening the package)*

> What?

LAUREL: Songs about suicide, lost love, growing old disgracefully.

ARNOLD: Pays the rent.

LAUREL: Funny, but I always imagined you'd sing comic songs. Y'know, novelty numbers.

ARNOLD: I'm strictly Torch. While all the other kids were listening to the Beatles, Sam the Sham and the Dave Clark Five, I was home lip-synching Billie Holiday, Jane Froman and Helen Morgan. As I got older I switched to *Lucia di Lammemoor, Tosca* and *Manon*. But it was always tragic stuff. Something about taking all that misery and making it into something . . . Anyway, the audiences like it. I guess getting hurt is one thing we all have in common.

LAUREL: You sound like one of your songs.

ARNOLD: I am one of my songs.

> *(Taking out a leash and collar from the package)*

> Oh look, it's my wedding present to Alan.

LAUREL: And you told me you weren't into that stuff.

ARNOLD: It's for Alan's dog.

LAUREL: I didn't know he had a dog.

ARNOLD: He doesn't. But he will tomorrow when I give him one.

LAUREL: You got him a dog? What kind?

ARNOLD: Well, y'know they say that a dog grows to look like its master, or that a master grows to look like his dog . . . So, I got him a big, fat, home-loving St. Bernard. It should be quite a battle.

LAUREL: Perfect. So, you two are getting married?

ARNOLD: As married as two men can illegally get. Actually it's more of a contract signing party. After that weekend the four of us spent together we decided to draw up a few rules and regulations, just so we'd know where we stood with each other. Well, we've spent our every waking, non-working hour on this document and we're finally ready to sign it.

(Holds up a rolled up piece of parchment)

LAUREL: That's wonderful. May I see it?

(She opens it)

It's one sentence long.

ARNOLD: Well, we had a little trouble agreeing on some issues. This is sort of a basic working philosophy which we can amend and elaborate on as we feel necessary.

LAUREL:

(Reading)

We, Arnold and Alan, being of sound mind and social-diseaseless bodies hereby swear to take equal responsibility for walking and feeding the dog.

ARNOLD:

(Taking it away)

Like I said, it's just a basis. Anyway, the ceremony's tomorrow after the show and we'd love for you to come.

LAUREL: I wish we'd known. But we've already made plans to take care of a few important things. Which brings me to my reason for coming to see you.

ARNOLD: . . . always a reason.

LAUREL: You know, now that it's time I don't know how to say it.

ARNOLD: Sounds serious.

LAUREL: It is.

ARNOLD: Be blunt.

LAUREL: Ed and I are engaged to be married.

ARNOLD:

(Blank)

Oh.

LAUREL: You and Alan, Ed and me. Kind of ironic, huh?

ARNOLD: That's the word for it. Well, congratulations. I'm sure you two will be very happy together.

LAUREL: Thank you.

ARNOLD: When was all this decided?

LAUREL: I guess about the same time you were drawing up your contract. We talked a lot when I went back to the farm; about what we wanted out of a relationship, what we wanted from each other . . . and we figured after that weekend . . . Well, if we could get through a thing like that and still be together then we could get through anything. Even marriage.

ARNOLD: I could hardly say I didn't expect it, but I could hardly say I did expect it . . . What I could say is that I'm happy for you. Hey, I'm gonna call Ed right now . . .

LAUREL: I'd rather you didn't. Ed doesn't know I'm here. As a matter of fact he's planning on coming by tonight to tell you himself. And I'd like to ask you not to mention my visit. After all, he did want to tell you first.

ARNOLD: Then why did you tell me?

LAUREL: I don't know. That's not true. I was scared that you'd say something negative—make fun of him or try to talk him out of it. Arnold, everything's going so well between us, but Ed is still shaky. And the wrong word from you . . .

ARNOLD: That's ridiculous.

LAUREL: No, it's realistic.

ARNOLD: You're just being silly. Really you are. The two of you will get married and live happily ever after and I'm very happy for you. And just to prove it . . . I'll be a bridesmaid at the wedding. So, what color are we wearing?

LAUREL: Oh, it would mean so much to both of us to have you there, but the wedding is at my parents' home in Massachusetts and . . . it's really going to be small . . . so we're limiting the guests to just immediate family.

ARNOLD: That's alright; I look terrible in green.

LAUREL: I'm sorry, really. Well, I'd better let you get back to your rehearsal. I've kept you long enough. It was wonderful seeing you again. And as soon as we get set up we'll have you over for dinner or something.

ARNOLD: Sure. We'd love that.

LAUREL: You won't say anything to Ed?

ARNOLD: My wrists are sealed.

LAUREL: Pardon?

ARNOLD: An old fag joke.

LAUREL: Well, bye bye. Give my best to Alan.

(*Laurel exits and Arnold returns to piano*)

ARNOLD: Hey Max, you know the wedding march? Never mind. Let's try the closing number.

(*The pianist begins to play as Arnold climbs up onto the piano.*)

It's over, concluded, expired, that's it.
I've had it, been through it, my limit's been hit.
It's not that I doubt your love for me,
Your passion or sincerity,
Your faith, hope, trust or charity,
What I doubt . . . is you.

You cheated, you lied, dear. You two-timed me twice.
And that makes four times, dear. And that isn't nice.
And now you've the nerve to say to me,
Your wife likes being one of three.
So I'll genteely answer thee:
Go blow it out your shoe.

I can't live on love alone.
Want somebody all my own.
I can't live on love alone.
You can argue but it's true,

Three can't live as cheap as two.
I can't live on love alone.

Fidelity is out of fashion,
Variety is everybody's passion.
Drugs can keep you copulating 'til you cash in.
And when you're through they'll bury you with your wife.

One night stands are not my quarry,
I signed up for repertory.
No I won't live on love alone.
Keep my number by the phone
Call me if you should atone.
But I can't live, no I can't live . . . on love alone.

(The lights fade to black.)

The End

WIDOWS AND CHILDREN FIRST!

Widows and Children First! premiered at La Mama E.T.C. on October 25, 1979 with the following cast:

ARNOLD BECKOFF	Harvey Fierstein
DAVID	Frederick Allen
ED	Will Jeffries
MRS. BECKOFF	Estelle Getty

Directed by Eric Concklin
Stage Design by Bill Stabile
Lighting by Cheryl Thacker
Costumes by Carla Lawrence
Production Stage Manager: Richard Jakiel

Characters

ED REISS	Forty, handsome, with a disarming boyish charm and innocence.
DAVID	Fifteen going on thirty. A wonderfully bright and handsome boy.
ARNOLD	Thirties, witty, personable and pleasant in appearance.
MRS. BECKOFF	Arnold's mother. Sixtyish. A real Jewish mother. A fighter.

Time
Five years after the action of *Fugue in a Nursery*.

Synopsis of Scenes
1. Arnold's apartment, 7 a.m. on a Thursday in June.
2. Same. 5 p.m. that day.
3. A bench in the park below, immediately following.
4. The apartment. 6 a.m. the next morning.

Author's Note
PACE!!!!!!! and honesty.

SCENE 1

The stage is a realistically represented living/dining room and kitchenette. There is an entrance door, a bathroom door and a hallway which leads to two offstage bedrooms. It is the set of a conventional sit-com with a convertible sofa, windows overlooking Central Park, and assorted objects and props. There is also a mini-set for Scene 3 which is described herein. As the lights

come up, a radio is blaring Fanny Brice singing, "I'm Cooking Breakfast For The One I Love."
Ed is busily cooking. The song ends. . . .

RADIO: It's seven-eighteen in the Big Apple and this is Hi Tide wishin' you a good, good
Mornin'.

(*A chorus of singers twitter, "Good Morning, Good Morning, Good Morning*
to you!")

And now for all you sleepy-heads what just can't shake them nighttime
blues, number one on our hot-pick chart and guaranteed to raise the dead . . .
Edward O. Wilson's, "I Was Born This Way, What's Your Excuse."

(*Music begins.*)

ED:

(*Quickly changing to a mellower station*)

There's a thought to start the day.

DAVID:

(*From within the bathroom*)

Arnold? You got anything I could put on my eye?

ED:

(*Calling back*)

He's in the bedroom.

DAVID: What?

ED: Arnold's still in the bedroom.

DAVID: Never mind, I found somethin'.

ED:

(*Hollering down the hall*)

Arnold, you up? Breakfast is on the table.

DAVID: What?

ED: I was talking to Arnold.

(*An explosion in the kitchen*)

ARNOLD:

(*Offstage*)

What the hell was that?

ED:

(*Running to kitchen*)

I think the coffee's ready.

ARNOLD:

(*Enters in bathrobe and bunny-shaped slippers*)

And a "Good Morning, Good Morning, Good Morning to you." You're
making breakfast? Aren't you an angel. Smells terrible.

ED: My specialty: Eggs, onions and Kippered Herring en casserole.

ARNOLD: Toast for me, I'm on a diet.

ED: Since when?

ARNOLD: Since I heard the specialty.

> *(Yelling down hall)*

> David, you up yet?

ED: He's in the throne room.

ARNOLD:

> *(Knocks on door)*

> Hurry up, Sugar-Puss, you'll be late for school.

ED: You look well rested.

ARNOLD: I feel like freeze-dried death.

> *(Sees mess)*

> Ed, since when do you make coffee in a pressure cooker?

ED: The water boils faster.

DAVID:

> *(Through crack in door)*

> Everybody ready? Stand back from the door and hang onto your apron strings 'cause here I come.

> *(Enters modeling a three piece suit)*

> Well? What'cha think?

ARNOLD:

> *(As Ed whistles approval)*

> What's the occasion? Ms. Schnable isn't due till next week.

DAVID: But your mother is due today. Think she'll like me?

ARNOLD: Who'd dare not like my baby?

DAVID: And look, I put some gook on. You can't even see the black eye.

ARNOLD:

> *(Examining)*

> When I think of that kid hitting you, I wanna tear down to that school and beat the shit outta him.

ED:

> *(Serving the food)*

> Your maternal instincts are incredible.

DAVID: I can take care of myself.

ARNOLD: I see.

DAVID: Would you stop.

ED: What'd the two of you fight about anyway?

DAVID: He called me something I didn't like, so I slugged him.

> *(Helping Arnold fold the couch)*

ED: So how'd you end up with the black-eye?

DAVID: I didn't slug him fast enough.

ARNOLD: That's my son, The Champ.

DAVID:

    (Posing)

    That's me, Champ David.

ED: What was it he called you?

DAVID: A douche bag.

ARNOLD: How fifties.

ED: Soup's on!

ARNOLD:

    (Exiting to bathroom)

    You stay away from that kid today.
    I ain't got no money to buy no new suit.

DAVID: He's somethin' ain't he? What's with this dentist music?

    (Switches to rock station. It is the same song only discoed.)

    Much better.

ED:

    (Holding out chair)

    May I seat you, sir?

DAVID: Don't mind if you do.

    (Sits)

    What died in here?

ED: Breakfast.

    (Holding plate over David's head)

    I cooked it myself. Any complaints?

DAVID: From me? Are you kidding? You know me, always ready for a gastronomic adventure.

    (Ed sets down plate)

    Looks wonderful. Could you pass the salt? How'd you sleep?

ED: The couch and I aren't speaking.

DAVID: It's only your fourth night. You'll get used to it. Could you pass the pepper? I slept on it for weeks while we worked on my room, and I'm still walking.

ED: I'll probably be able to find a place by the weekend.

DAVID: What's your rush? Can I have the ketchup? It's great having you here. Could you pass the mustard?

ED: Something wrong with the food?

DAVID: Not at all. Very tasty. Can I have the mayo, please?

    (Ed shoots a look)

    Hold the mayo.

(Tastes it)

Mmmmmm. Delicious. Oh, I forgot, your wife called.

ED: When?

DAVID: Middle of the night. I tried to wake you but you were out of it. I told her you'd call back in the morning.

ED: What time did she call?

DAVID: Must'a been around two. Somethin' about some papers for you to sign.

ED: Thanks. I'd better call. Help yourself to seconds, there's plenty.

DAVID: And I was worried.

(Ed goes to phone)

You sure are a heavy sleeper. The phone rang five times.

ED: What were you doing up so late?

DAVID: Answering the phone.

ED:

(Into phone)

Hello, Laurel? What's up . . . Couldn't that have waited til morning? . . . I don't think it's fair to wake the whole house. . . .

ARNOLD:

(Entering)

Hey, Champ, remember to bring back your report card. I signed it.

DAVID: Where'd you put it?

ARNOLD: By the door.

DAVID: Is Ms. Schnable really coming next week?

ARNOLD: Every third Thursday for the next three months. So stay outta trouble and pray that eye heals. I wish this damned probation period was over already. Gives me the creeps havin' someone check up on us all the time.

DAVID: What's the rush? When the adoption papers come through we stop gettin' the Foster care checks and we need the money.

ARNOLD: You may find this hard to believe, but I didn't take you in for the money.

DAVID: Then you're the first.

ARNOLD:

(Seeing Ed)

Who's on the phone?

DAVID: Ed.

ARNOLD: I thought I recognized the voice.

ED: . . . Laurel, I wish you wouldn't. . . . Not on the phone!

ARNOLD: There's nothing more frustrating that a one-sided conversation.

DAVID: There's another kind?

ED: . . . I really don't want to discuss this now. . . . Because, there are other people in the room.

DAVID: Don't mind us.

(Arnold swats him.)

ED: . . . Can we please talk about this later? . . . Hello? . . . Laurel, are you there? . . . For God's sake, are you crying?

ARNOLD:

(Under his breath)

Animal.

ED: Laurel, please. I'll come over and we can talk. . . . I don't know when. This afternoon. I don't know . . . Alright, I'll see you then. . . . Bye Bye.

(Hangs up)

DAVID: She gave you a hard time, huh?

(Arnold swats him again.)

Ow! That hurt.

ARNOLD:

(Big smile)

Want some coffee?

ED: No, I'm fine. After four days of those calls I think I'm getting used to them. I mean, I understand why she calls; she's confused, alone . . . What I can't understand is her damned crying.

ARNOLD: Of course it's just a wild guess, but do you suppose it's because she's confused and alone?

ED: Well, I don't see why. This separation wasn't all my idea.

ARNOLD: Look, Ed, I realize this is a trying time for you and I'll gladly supply a place to sleep, a home-thrown meal and all the amoral support I can muster, but you've got to keep the gory details to yourself.

ED:

(Grandly)

Ah, what price compassion!?!

ARNOLD: Fifty bucks an hour and I don't take credit cards.

ED: Fifty?

ARNOLD: Hey, talk's cheap, but listening'll cost ya'. Buck up, Bronco, things are bound to get easier.

ED: Oh, I know. I just wish she wouldn't carry on like that. You wouldn't believe the crazy accusations she was making . . .

ARNOLD: Ed, I'm serious. I really don't want to hear about it.

ED:

(Mock pout)

Some friend you are.

ARNOLD: I'm your ex-lover, Ed, not your friend.

DAVID: Oooooh. The heavy stuff. And it ain't even eight o'clock.

ARNOLD:

(Turning David's head back to his plate)

Don't talk with your mouth full.

DAVID: But my mouth's . . .

> (Arnold glares.)

> Is full. Very full.

ARNOLD: I didn't say that to be mean. Really. But I can't help remembering a phone call not unlike that one from someone in this very room, if you get my drift.

ED: Didn't think of that.

ARNOLD: Well, do. Please do. And please don't ask for any advice, 'cause you don't want to hear what I have to say.

DAVID: Heartbreaker.

> (Arnold glares.)

> I'm eating. I'm eating.

ARNOLD: All this and my Mother too.

ED: Well, I'll see Laurel this afternoon and hopefully end these midnight calls.

ARNOLD: That would be lovely. And while you're there could you see if she'd mind letting you stay with her Wednesday night? The Department of Child Welfare will be arriving early in the person of Our Ms. Schnable and I've got enough to explain without you on the couch.

ED: I'm good enough for your mother but not for David's social worker?

ARNOLD: It has nothing to do with being good enough. Ms. Schnable frowns on casual cohabitation.

ED: Casual? We've known each other for six years.

ARNOLD: Four of which you spent married to another woman.

> (To David)

> Take a glass of milk.

ED:

> (Pouring David's milk)

> I get it, it's not me she'll object to but my bisexuality.

ARNOLD: Could we please leave your perverted preferences unpurported this joyous morn?

ED: Bigot!

ARNOLD: Reactionary Chicken shit!

DAVID: Please, not in front of the child.

ED: I could lie and tell her I'm gay.

ARNOLD: Come on.

ED: Don't you think I could make a convincing homosexual?

DAVID: You could make this convincing homosexual.

ARNOLD: David! Besides, if she thought you were gay, she'd never believe you slept on the couch.

ED: I could show you the scars.

ARNOLD: I could show you the door.

DAVID: I could show you a good time.

ED and ARNOLD: David!!

DAVID: Well, I'd love to sit and chat with you grown-up types, but we straight C students pride ourselves on our punk-tuality.

ARNOLD: Go brush your teeth.

DAVID: Oh, Maaaaaaaa!

ARNOLD: Don't you, "Oh, Ma," me. March. And don't call me Ma in front of my mother.

(David exits. Ed giggles.)

Having a good time?

ED: Sorry, but you do act like his mother.

ARNOLD: Guess I do. But this parent act's still new to me. I can't quite get the hang of being mother, father, friend and confessor all rolled into one.

ED: You're doin' great.

ARNOLD: Think so?

ED: You're the best Mother-father-friend-confessor I've ever seen. You've just got to let go a little more.

ARNOLD: I will. Geez, I can't wait for my mother to get here; I can Mother-smother David, she can Mother-smother me . . .

ED: And I can Mother-smother referee.

ARNOLD: Laugh now Leroy, but we're gonna need one. Y'know, this stuff smells awful, but it tastes much worse.

ED: Be nice or I'll tell people it's your recipe.

ARNOLD: You don't have to threaten me twice.

ED: I'm enjoying being here with you and David enormously. I want you to know that.

ARNOLD: Good.

ED: You ever wonder what things would be like if I'd never met Laurel?

ARNOLD: That all depends, did I meet Alan?

ED: Of course not. If I didn't meet Laurel you wouldn't have met Alan.

ARNOLD: Oh. So that's how it works. Well, did I adopt David?

ED: That's what I'm asking. Would we have stayed together and would we have adopted David?

ARNOLD: How should I know?

ED: Well, didn't you ever wonder?

ARNOLD: Ed, I have enough trouble with the "What now's" without starting in on the "What if's."

ED: Yeah, but haven't you ever thought about what things would be like if we'd stayed together?

ARNOLD: I guess so. When Alan died I thought about a lot of crazy things. I'm sure you were among them.

ED: And?

ARNOLD: I don't know. Why, what do you think?

ED: I think we might've been very happy together. It's possible.

ARNOLD: It's also possible that it could be me you just walked out on.

ED: I didn't just walk out. And who just said they didn't want to discuss this?

ARNOLD: Who's discussing? I'm simply pointing out a certain pattern a certain person seems to have fallen into.

ED: People do make mistakes.

ARNOLD: I wanna write that down.

ED: . . . And sometimes they are even forgiven for them.

ARNOLD: Oh, don't be so melodramatic. I forgave you years ago. I don't think I could've been happy with Alan if I hadn't.

ED: Maybe you and your Mother should spend some time alone. I can still find a hotel.

ARNOLD: You're staying here and that's an order. You wouldn't leave me unprotected at a time like this would you? Of course you would. But you ain't gonna. My mother isn't going to feature the idea of my becoming a father, and your professional opinion as an American educator will prove invaluable.

ED: She'll say I'm prejudiced.

ARNOLD: She'll say a lot of things. You'll learn not to listen. More coffee?

ED:

(Hands his cup)

Please.

ARNOLD:

(Making coffee and cleaning up)

My mother's alright. Basically. When I was a kid we had a healthy Mother/Son relationship. A delicate blend of love, concern and guilt. We never talked much but when we did we kept things on an honest level. I mean, I told her I was gay when I was thirteen.

ED: You knew when you were thirteen?

ARNOLD: When I was thirteen I knew everything. Senility set in sometime after. And look at me now: On the threshold of thirty I need a calculator to write a check, a cookbook to fry an egg and Dial a Prayer to do the rest.

(To David)

Hurry up in there you'll be late.

DAVID:

(Offstage)

Don't rush an artist.

ARNOLD: What was I saying?

ED: Something about your mother.

ARNOLD: My mother: The Rita Hayworth of Brighton Beach. We always kept an open line of communication, that is until my father died; then, I don't know, something happened, she clammed up. I mean, we saw each other more than ever, and we spoke daily on the phone, but somehow we managed to say less than ever. It became a contest to see who could talk most but say least.

ED: It's called Adult Conversation.

ARNOLD: Thank you Tom Snyder. Where was I?

ED: Your mother.

ARNOLD: My mother: The Sylvia Sydney of Bay Twenty-fifth street. I think the root of it was my father's death. She refused to talk about it, or about how she was coping alone. But Alan and I were living together then, so I always had a source of subject matter in him.

ED: She knew Alan?

ARNOLD: Oh, yeah. And they got along as long as I didn't call him my lover. She preferred to call him my "Friend." Anyway, she retired, moved to Florida which reduced our relationship to weekly phone calls and biannual visitations. And then Alan died and I was expected to observe the same vow of silence about him as she had about my father. So we've learned to make meaningful conversation from the weather, general health and my brother's marital status. I never even told her how Alan was killed. She assumed it was a car accident and I didn't bother correcting her.

ED: So now you don't know how to tell her about David.

ARNOLD: Oh she knows about David. But she assumed he was my roommate and I . . .

ED: . . . You didn't bother correcting her.

ARNOLD: It's not the telling that frightens me. But I shake when I think of the long muzzled floodgates of Motherly advice that will unleash when she gets wind of this.

ED: How bad could it possibly be?

ARNOLD: Stick around kid.

DAVID:

> (Entering)
>
> How's these?
>
> (Big smile)
>
> And look, I'm taking the brush with me so's I can give them a swipe before my big entrance. Think Granny'll be impressed?

ARNOLD: David, you can put your elbows on the table, use vile and abusive language, even pass gas loudly during conversation. But whatever you do . . . Don't call her Granny!

DAVID: You could save yourself a load of grief if you'd just let me break the good news to her.

ARNOLD: Thanks, but I've heard your subtle mouth at work.

DAVID: Don't say I didn't offer.

> (Phone rings)
>
> I'll get it.

ED:

> (To Arnold)
>
> You want tea?

ARNOLD: Why not?

DAVID:

> (Into phone)
>
> Sister Arnold's House of Hope. You pay, we pray. Brother David speaking.

ARNOLD:

> (Grabs phone)
>
> Give me that. Hello? . . . Oh, hi Murray . . . No, that was David's idea of discretion.

DAVID: Think I have a future in the Diplomatic Corps?

ARNOLD: Hang on a sec.

> (To David)
>
> Don't you ever answer the phone like that again. What if this was Ms. Schnable? Have you got a comb?

(He produces one.)

A handkerchief?

(He moans.)

March!

ED:

(Handing tea to Arnold as David reads report card)

A handkerchief? Really Arnold.

DAVID: What the hell is this?

(Reads from card)

"I'm proud of his improvement and am sure he'll do even better on his finals."

ARNOLD: It said "Parent's Comments" and I had to write something.

DAVID: No you didn't.

(Storms to bedroom)

ARNOLD: Murray, can I call you back after I get my little men off to work? OK, I'll call . . . David! Hang up that extension! . . . No, you can't have a divorce. We're not married. . . . Murray? I'll call you back.

(Hangs up)

Alright, what'd I do wrong now?

ED: The kids like to brag that they forged their parent's signatures. But if there's a sensible comment like that then everyone will know it's the real thing.

ARNOLD: How was I supposed to know? God, he makes me feel old.

ED: Don't worry about it. What time is the Great Arrival?

ARNOLD: I don't know. I figure around noon.

DAVID:

(Enters with hanky)

I'm gettin' outta here before you think of something else.

ARNOLD: Where are your school books?

DAVID: In school.

ARNOLD: How'd you do your homework?

DAVID: Astral projection.

ARNOLD: You forgetting something?

DAVID: What now?

ARNOLD: Don't I get a kiss goodbye?

DAVID:

(Laughs)

You're unreal.

(Warm hug and kiss)

I love you.

ARNOLD: Me too. Now get outta here. You're late.

DAVID:

> *(Exiting)*

> Have a nice day, Ed. You too . . . Ma.

> *(Out)*

ED: Men kissing. What's this world coming to?

ARNOLD: My father and brother and I all kissed. It's called affection. Aren't you going to work?

ED: It's Brooklyn Day. My school's closed.

ARNOLD: Only the Brooklyn schools?

ED: And Queens.

ARNOLD: Queens too? Sounds like Affirmative Action at work.

> *(Sees Ed clearing dishes)*

> That's alright. I'll do them.

ED: Then I'll go for the papers. Maybe I'll get a lead on an apartment.

ARNOLD: Hurry back. I ain't facin' her alone. Do you and your mother get along?

ED: Sure. No problem. That is as long as I remember to call her every now and then. And send her a card on her Birthday. And Mother's Day. And Christmas. Oh, and of course there's Valentine's Day, and St. Patrick's Day, Labor Day, Thanksgiving, Easter, Fourth of July, Election Day and Christopher Columbus' Birthday.

ARNOLD: You forgot Halloween.

ED: That's her Anniversary.

ARNOLD: How romantic.

ED: Where's my blue jacket?

ARNOLD: My room, left side.

> *(Ed exits.)*

> Ed? You ever tell your folks you were gay?

ED:

> *(Reentering)*

> But I'm not.

ARNOLD: Alright, bisexual. Don't be so technical. I ain't Kinsey.

ED: No.

ARNOLD: Never?

ED: You need anything from the store?

ARNOLD: Wait a minute. I mean, I know you were in the closet when we were together, but I figured once you got married you'd feel secure enough to tell them.

ED: Once I got married there was nothing to tell them.

> *(Defensive)*

> And I wasn't in the closet.

ARNOLD: Ed, when the only people who know you're gay are the ones you're gaying with, that's called in the closet.

ED: Arnold, you may enjoy broadcasting your sexual preferences but I happen to believe that who I sleep with is my business and not the world's.

ARNOLD: We'll discuss the world later, I'm asking about your mother.

ED: Why put them through that?

ARNOLD: Through what?

ED: Making them feel that in some way they failed me or did something wrong. You know the trip.

ARNOLD: But you could explain to them that they had nothing to do with it. Well, not that way, anyway.

ED: They'd still be miserable. Besides, I really don't think it's any of their business.

ARNOLD: You told them about Laurel didn't you?

ED: We were married.

ARNOLD: You lived together for a year first. You sayin' they didn't know about her 'til after the wedding?

ED: Arnold, you told your parents, they accepted it and I'm very happy for all of you. Alright? Jesus. Your mother flies in for a visit and I get a Gay Consciousness Raising lecture.

ARNOLD: You have a Prim-Evil attitude about your sexuality, Mr. Reiss.

ED: Enough?

ARNOLD: And they wonder why we broke up.

ED: Arnold, you have nothing to worry about. Believe me, your mother will see you and David together and will be pleased with both of you.

ARNOLD: You really think I'm doing good with him?

ED: You've taken a punk kid who's spent the last three years on the streets and in juvenile court and turned him into a home-living, fun-loving, school-going teenager in all of six months. Yes, I think you're doing good with him.

ARNOLD: I wish Alan was here. He would'a been great with the kid.

ED: I'll see you later.

ARNOLD: Don't be too long.

ED:

> *(Exiting)*

> Give me an hour.

ARNOLD: See ya.

> *(Runs to door)*

> Ed? We need milk! Skimmed!

> *(The phone rings. Arnold grunts and answers.)*

ARNOLD: Hello? . . . Oh, hi, Murray. . . . Not much. The usual assortment of early morning crises. What's up by you?

ED: Arnold, she's here!

> *(Tears back into the room)*

ARNOLD: Hang on, Murr.

> *(To Ed)*

> What?

ED: She's here. She's headed up the stairs.

ARNOLD: Can't be. It's too early.

ED: There's a woman on the stairs checking all the apartment numbers.

ARNOLD: What'd she look like?

ED:

> *(Indicating)*

This tall, this wide, carrying a suitcase and a shopping bag.

ARNOLD: May Day, Murray! I'll call you back.

ED:

> *(As Arnold runs around the room)*

Calm down Arnold.

ARNOLD: She can't see the place looking like this. She'll walk through the door and head straight for the vacuum cleaner.

MA: Well, I might change my shoes first.

> *(In the open doorway)*

ARNOLD: Ma. Hi. Come on in.

MA: Hello.

> *(Friendly to Ed)*

You must be David.

ED: No, I'm Ed.

MA:

> *(Taking back her extended hand)*

How do you do. I'm the mother.

ARNOLD:

> *(Taking her bags)*

I really didn't expect you this early.

MA: Obviously.

ED:

> *(Backing out)*

Well, I've got to be off. Lovely meeting you, Mrs. Beckoff. I'll remember the milk.

> *(Out. Then back in.)*

Skimmed.

> *(Out)*

MA: Nice looking boy. Who is he?

ARNOLD: That's Ed . . .

MA: That's enough.

> *(For now.)*

I'm sorry I snapped at him but that bus-ride from the airport. . . . I had to stand the whole way. There wasn't a man on that bus would give me his seat.

I'm telling you, Arnold, Women's Liberation is giving me varicose veins. So, let me look at you. How do you feel? You look good.

ARNOLD: Good compared to the last time you saw me.

MA: The last time I saw you was at your friend's funeral. You're supposed to look lousy at funerals; it shows respect. You could stand a shave.

ARNOLD: I just got up. Coffee?

MA: A glass of tea. And a can of Lysol. What's that stench?

ARNOLD: Ed cooked breakfast

MA: So I know he's not the cook. Pretty wallpaper.

ARNOLD: It's not wallpaper. I stenciled the design.

MA: Next time use wallpaper. Covers a multitude of sins. Looks nice enough, but why you'd give up that lovely place in Brooklyn to move to Manhattan, God only knows.

ARNOLD: The other place had one bedroom. We needed two.

MA: I thought your roommate's name was David.

ARNOLD: It is. He isn't here right now.

MA: Three men, two bedrooms . . . I'll have my tea first.

ARNOLD: Ed's transitory. The sofa's a convertible. Honey?

MA: Lemon. I brought my own Sweet and Low . . . from the plane. You don't get much light here.

ARNOLD: We get what you call "indirect semi-shade." It's good for the plants.

MA: So's manure. Looks comfortable. How do you find the roaches?

ARNOLD: I turn on the lights.

(A little laugh at his little joke)

MA: Arnold, when a man's with his friends he makes wife jokes. When he's with his wife he makes mother jokes. And when he's with his mother . . . he lets her make the jokes.

(Arnold gets the message.)

You speak to your brother?

ARNOLD: He was over for dinner last week.

MA: He brought a girl?

ARNOLD: Andrea.

MA: He's still seeing her? Any talk of marriage?

ARNOLD: You'll see him tomorrow, you can ask yourself.

MA: And be accused of meddling? Bite your tongue.

ARNOLD:

(Entering with tea tray, Ma is seated on sofa)

Are you getting shorter?

MA: No, I'm sitting down. So, who's this Ed?

ARNOLD: A friend. Tell me about Florida. Anyone special in your life?

MA: Not particularly. You mean Ed's a friend-friend or a euphemism friend?

ARNOLD: He used to be a euphemism, now he's just a friend. Why aren't you seeing anyone?

MA: Because the only ones who ask me out are old men and the one thing I don't need is to become a nursemaid for some *alta-kakah.*

ARNOLD: Don't you meet any men your own age?

MA: In Miami Beach? If he's not your friend why's he cooking your breakfast?

ARNOLD: You never cook for your friends?

MA: Not breakfast. Didn't you used to have a friend named Ed who got married?

ARNOLD: You've got a great tan.

MA: He's a teacher?

ARNOLD: And a great memory.

MA: The girl was too, right? They've got a house in the country.

ARNOLD: Incredible.

MA: I remember thinking, "Now there's a man with his head on straight" What's he doing cooking your breakfast?

ARNOLD: He and his wife have separated. He's staying here 'til he can find a place of his own.

MA: Separated? How come?

ARNOLD: I don't know.

MA: Come on, the man's living with you. He must've said something.

ARNOLD: I didn't ask and he didn't volunteer.

MA: You're involved?

ARNOLD: No!

MA: Arnold?

ARNOLD: Ma?

MA: So why's he staying here?

ARNOLD: Because he asked if he could and I said yes.

MA: You must admit, it sounds a little queer: A man leaves his wife to move in with his old . . . friend.

ARNOLD: He's spending a few nights on my couch. What's the big deal?

MA: No big deal. But, you'd think he'd stay by friends that have more in common.

ARNOLD: What does that mean?

MA: You know; someone he met after the marriage.

ARNOLD: Maybe he needed to get away from all of that.

MA: You mean he's still . . . ?

(Makes a motion with her hand)

ARNOLD: Can we talk about the weather now?

MA: I'm glad you reminded me.

(Heads for her shopping bag)

Your mother! If I didn't have my head screwed on . . . I baked you some cookies.

(Produces a tin)

Fresh from the Sunshiney State. Take a whiff; you can smell Miami.

ARNOLD: David'll love these.

MA: I didn't know what to bring. I hadn't seen the place to know what you need.

ARNOLD:

(Friendly and confident now)

Oh, I didn't show you . . .

(Takes out an afghan)

Look what I'm making.I took a class in weaving and crocheting at night school. Isn't it beautiful?

MA: I'm telling you . . . !

ARNOLD: I made it for out here. Y'know, for taking a nap on the couch. I wanna make one for my bedroom too. You like it?

MA:

(Trying to look away)

Nice.

ARNOLD: Pretty design, huh?

MA: It's fairy nice.

ARNOLD:

(The wind knocked out of him)

Well, maybe you should go unpack. You can put your things in my room.

MA: How are we arranging all of this?

ARNOLD: You'll sleep in my room, David in his room and Ed and I can share the couch.

MA: Wouldn't it be easier if I slept on the couch? That way you'll have your privacy.

ARNOLD: We don't need privacy.

MA: How about if you shared David's room?

ARNOLD: Did you see my cigarettes around?

MA: You still smoke? Shame on you.

(Arnold heaves a heavy sigh)

What's the matter, *sheyna boyalah?* You didn't sleep good?

ARNOLD: I'm fine. Just give me a minute to get myself together.

MA: Go on, get yourself together. I could use a get together myself.

(Deep breath)

Arnold, where's the dog? He didn't come to say hello.

ARNOLD: I had to give him away. He used to sit by the door and whine all day and night, waiting for Alan to come home. I couldn't take it so I gave him to Murray.

(Referring to stack of papers she has unpacked)

What's all that?

MA: Don't ask me why, they forwarded some of your mail to me.

ARNOLD: Anything I should know about?

MA: Garbage. But there's a letter from Ernie the insurance man. You canceled your policy?

ARNOLD: One of them.

MA: You need money? You know I'm always good for a loan.

ARNOLD: Thanks but things are fine.

MA: Meanwhile you lost out on a very good deal. You wouldn't see a policy like that again.

ARNOLD: What do I need with a twenty-five thousand dollar life insurance policy?

MA: Now you don't need it, but someday . . . ? You never know; you might meet a nice girl . . .

ARNOLD: Maaaa!

MA: You never know. Look at your friend Ed.

ARNOLD: I'm looking. He's separated.

MA: Separated, but not divorced. Believe me, you never know.

ARNOLD: Believe me. I know.

MA: What's the matter; you don't want children?

ARNOLD: Not the kind you mean.

MA: The kind I mean have two arms, two legs, a mother, father and Chicken Pox. How many kinds are there?

ARNOLD: You'd be surprised.

MA: Arnold, you and your brother are the last of the Beckoffs.

ARNOLD: So?

MA: Don't you feel you have a duty to continue the family name?

ARNOLD: Not particularly. Anyway, there's always my brother. I'm sure there'll be lots of little Beckoffs running around.

MA: And what if he only has girls?

ARNOLD:

(Thinks a moment)

I know a good surgeon.

MA: I don't get you?

ARNOLD: Why don't you unpack while I take a shower and shave. And when I'm dressed we can sit and have a lonng talk.

MA: A "Lonnng" talk? I feel a gray hair growing in.

ARNOLD: It's not that bad. Let me help with your bags.

MA: I can manage.

ARNOLD: It's the room on the right. Shit, I didn't have time to make the bed.

MA: Take your shower. I'll do it.

ARNOLD: There's fresh linen in the closet at the end of the hall.

MA:

(Waving him on)

Go. I'll get by.

ARNOLD: I won't be long.

(Exits)

MA:

(Gathering her things)

You see, Jack? They still need the old Mama.

(Exiting)

Just think, if I wasn't here . . . who would make the beds?

(David enters through the front door, slowly, peeking in first. Seeing a deserted room, he enters fully and looks around. He spots the shopping bag.)

DAVID: She has arrived. But where are she?

(Looks in kitchen, under table, goes to bathroom door and listens)

491

We got us a live one.

(Arnold hums a bit of something.)

Wrong one.

(He is having fun. He tiptoes to the hall and exits . . . A moment of silence, then a shriek. David runs out of the hall pursued by Ma who is swinging at him with her purse.)

Mrs. Beckoff, please. I'm not a burglar!

MA: Then what are you; some kind of weirdo who gets a kick watching middle-aged women strip beds?

DAVID: I'm not a weirdo. Believe me.

MA: Then you're a rapist.

(She screams again.)

DAVID: What would a rapist be doing in a three-piece suit?

MA: How should I know? Maybe you got a wedding after.

ARNOLD:

(Entering, dripping in a robe)

What the . . . David! What are you doing out of school?

MA: This is your roommate?

DAVID: Charmed I'm sure.

MA: You know that "lonnng" talk we're gonna have? It just got lonnnnnnnger.

ARNOLD: What are you doing home?

DAVID: I forgot, I had a double period of gym and no uniform. So I tole' Mr. Kelley about your mother comin' and he said I could come home 'till after lunch.

ARNOLD: Just like that?

DAVID: Well, . . . you gotta call and say it's O.K. Wasn't that nice of him?

ARNOLD:

(Sees his mother's puzzled face)

We'll discuss this later.

(Trying to smile)

Ma, this is David.

MA: So I gathered.

ARNOLD:

(Long uncomfortable pause)

O.K. So, now we all know each other.

MA: Arnold, you're dripping on my shoe.

ARNOLD: Oh. How about this: You go finish unpacking, I'll go finish my shower, and you go start lunch . . . ?

DAVID: It's only nine o'clock.

ARNOLD:

(Parental order)

When I tell you to do something . . .

(Catches mother staring)

Well, I'm going to dry off now.

MA: You do that.

ARNOLD:

(Slowly backing out)

So, you'll unpack right? you'll make lunch, right? and I'll . . .

MA: Dry up.

ARNOLD: Right.

(Takes a last look, crosses himself and exits.)

DAVID:

(Pause)

Would you like a drink?

MA: Maybe later. I'm sorry I hit you.

DAVID: No sweat. I usually charge, but seein' how you're family . . .

(He laughs.)

MA: You have quite a little sense of humor. Shall we sit down?

DAVID: Sure.

(They do.)

MA: Tell me, David, you go to school?

DAVID: Yeah.

(Sees cookies)

You make these?

MA: Help yourself.

(He does, by the handful)

So, you go to college.

DAVID: High school.

MA:

(Her heart!)

High School. How nice.

(Hopeful)

Senior year?

DAVID: Freshman.

MA: That's very sweet. Tell me, David, just how old are you?

DAVID: Sixteen. . . . in two months.

(Sees her dying)

Something wrong?

MA: Not at all. Sixteen . . . in two months . . . that's wonderful. You have your whole life ahead of you . . . while mine's flashing before my eyes.

DAVID:

> (Chomping away)

> Good stuff.

MA: Thank you. David, it's none of my business, of course, but don't you think you're a little young to be out in the world all alone?

> (At first she thinks he referred to her life then . . .)

DAVID: No. But, the judge did, so here I am.

ARNOLD:

> (Sticking his head out)

> Everything alright out here?

MA:

> (Choking)

> Fine, dear. Keep drying.

> (Arnold withdraws.)

DAVID: You like the place? We cleaned all week for you. Sorry I didn't get back to see your face when you got here.

MA: That face couldn't compare to this one.

DAVID: I would'a taken the whole morning off, but you know Arnold . . . Hey, he better hurry up and call the school. Mr. Kelley'll think I was jivin' him.

MA: Does Arnold make all your excuses at school?

DAVID:

> (Enjoying the game)

> Sure. Who else?

MA: Who else, indeed. I've got an idea: Why don't I call the school while you change your clothes?

DAVID: Hey, I wore this special for you.

MA: I've seen it, it's cute, now put it away.

DAVID: Yeah, but . . .

MA:

> (Pointing)

> March.

DAVID:

> (Exiting)

> Now I know where Arnold got his technique.

MA: Cute kid.

> (Calling out)

> David? Where do you keep the phone numbers?

DAVID:

> (Off)

> In the phone book.

MA: A little too cute. Oy, Arnold, what have you got yourself into now?

> (Finds book)

> Here it is. Right on top. Must get used a lot.

> (Starts to dial . . .)

> David? What name shall I give them?

DAVID: What?

MA: Who shall I say is being excused?

> (No response)

> Your last name!

DAVID:

> (Sticking his head in)

> Beckoff, of course.

MA: Really? That's quite a coincidence. Have you and Arnold ever compared notes to see if there's any family relation?

DAVID: I'm his son. What more relation could there be?

> (Arnold steps out of the bathroom.)

MA: You're his what?

DAVID: His son.

> (Arnold goes right back into the bathroom.)

> Would you like that drink now?

> (The lights black out, music plays in the dark for a moment. It should be the Hartz Mountain Canaries singing "The Blue Danube Waltz.")

SCENE 2

Later that afternoon. The stage is exactly as it was before (except deserted). Ed lets himself in with his key. He enters carrying a small paper bag and newspaper.

ED: Hello? Anybody home?

> (A platter flies across the room from the hallway and just misses his head, smashing on the wall. It is followed by Arnold.)

ARNOLD: Deserter! Defector! Duty dodger! Ditching your post at the first sign of battle, you backstabbing, betraying, ball-breaking, Buttercup! How could you leave me unprotected? You Avoider! Abstainer! Abandoner! Absconderer!

ED: Absconderer?

ARNOLD: If the shoe fits . . . Where have you been?

ED: Buying milk.

ARNOLD: For nine hours?

ED: I was on the express line. What happened?

ARNOLD: Happened? What could possibly have happened? My mother walked through that door and within three minutes managed to insult the plane ride, the bus ride, Women's Lib, the apartment, Manhattan, my personal hygiene, sense of humor, afghan, smoking, stenciling and cockroaches. And, oh, you'll love this: She accused me of breaking up your marriage.

ED: You're kidding?

ARNOLD: She practically called me a homewrecker. O.K., so far so good. We finally sat down to chat when who should walk through the door, but the Patron Saint of Truants himself: Champ David. My mother gets a gander at him and goes, "What a sweet child. And whose little boy are you?" Giving the long awaited cue to my sweet little angel lamb to turncoat 'round and point his every available finger at me.

ED: Oops.

ARNOLD: Did you say, "Oops"? No, Ed, "Oops" is when you fall down an elevator shaft. Oops is when you skinny-dip in a school of piranha. Oops is for accidentally douching with Drano. No, Ed, this was not an "Oops". This was a (STRANGLED SCREAM)!

ED: Cut the dramatics and tell me what happened.

ARNOLD: I'm telling you, nothing happened.

ED: Nothing?

ARNOLD: As in, "Not a thing." Dear David went atwitter to his room, mother went to my room, and I sat in the bathroom making toilet paper flowers and flushing them down the drain. Three hours I flowered and flushed, flowered and flushed, till Thank God, I ran out of paper. Forced from my Autumn Beige Tiled retreat, I called a truce for lunch. It was eaten in silence. No one even chewed. (You ever gum down a hamburger?) After lunch David announced he was going back to school and my mother volunteered to walk him.

ED: Where are they now?

ARNOLD: I haven't the smoggiest. Knowing David, he's probably fuming over some pin-ball machine. I was gonna look for him but it's better if he makes it home on his own.

ED: That's very sensible.

ARNOLD: Not at all. But what would I say if I did find him? And the mother? . . . I don't know where she could be.

ED: "Leave them alone and they'll come home . . ."

ARNOLD: ". . . Dragging a noose behind them." Help me with dinner.

ED: A quick trip to the men's room and I'll set the table.

ARNOLD: You'll have to borrow a plunger from next-door, first. A thousand sheets really do last longer.

(Picking up the broken china)

Look at this, you broke my favorite platter.

ED: I broke?

ARNOLD: Come on, get going. And don't go disappearing on me again.

ED: I'll be right back.

(Exits)

(The phone rings. Arnold rushes to it.)

ARNOLD: Hello? . . . Oh, hi, Murray. . . . No, I've been home all day. . . . Because I was in the bathroom . . . Yes, all day. You wanna sue me? . . . Look, Murr, I ain't got time to tear a herring with you now. You got somethin' to say? Say it. . . . Rocco who? Rocco DiGemma? The one with the leatherette tee-shirts? . . . Yeah, I know him. What about him? . . . You told him I'd do what?!!!?. . . . uh huh. . . . uh huh. . . . uh huh . . . uh huh . . . and then?. . . . uh huh. . . . uh huh . . . uh huh . . . uh huh . . . uh huh . . . Listen, Marie,

(At this point Ma and David enter happily),

you can call that poor excuse for a rubber creep back and tell him . . .

(He sees them.)

. . . tell him I've got a previous engagement. Thanks for calling. Bye bye.

(Hangs up)

MA:

(Removing her jacket)

Who was that, dear?

ARNOLD:

(Puzzled)

It was Murray. He wanted me to do a favor for a friend.

MA: What did he want you to do?

ARNOLD: . . . Babysit. You were together?

DAVID: I took your mother to school with me.

MA: They were very nice. They let me sit in the back. He does very well; when he stays awake.

DAVID: Then I took her to play pinball.

MA: You weren't worried, were you?

ARNOLD: What, me worry?

DAVID: Hey, Alfred E., what's for dinner?

(Heads to kitchen)

MA: Would you like to go out? My treat.

ARNOLD: I've started dinner here. But if you'd rather . . .

MA: No, we'll go out tomorrow. Besides, my feet are screaming for my slippers.

ED:

(Enters with plunger)

Well, look who's here.

MA: Hello, Ed. How was your day?

ED: Fine . . . thank you, Mrs. Beckoff. And yours?

MA: Surprisingly pleasant, once it was settled into.

(Exiting. To David)

DAVID:

After you do your homework I'll teach you how to play chess.

(With a can of soda)

Homework? Is she kidding? Hey, Arnold, we got a chess set?

ARNOLD: Top shelf of your closet.

DAVID: Thanks. Hi Ed.

(Exits)

ED: And you were worried.

(Goes toward bathroom)

ARNOLD: I wasn't worried. I was concerned.

(Ed exits.)

MA:

(Enters in bunny slippers like Arnold's)

Give me an apron and put me to work.

ARNOLD: That's alright, Ma. Ed's gonna help.

MA: Oh, I wondered what the plunger was for. Listen, if I'm gonna die of ptomaine, it'll be from something I made myself.

(Holding up a potato)

What do you want done with these?

ARNOLD: I was going to bake them, but if I could twist your arm . . . ?

MA: You want my Latkes?

ARNOLD: I'd love your Latkes.

MA: Then you'll get my Latkes.

ED:

(Entering)

All fixed.

ARNOLD: Thanks, Ed.

DAVID:

(Off)

Hey, Arnold? I can't find the chess board.

ARNOLD: Coming

(Exits)

Be back.

MA:

(Trying to draw Ed in)

You like Latkes, Ed?

ED: I don't know. I never had it.

MA: Them. You're in for a treat.

ED: I couldn't help noticing, you've got slippers like Arnold's. Mind if I ask who gave them to whom?

MA:

(Modeling them)

You like my slippers? Aren't they Chick? Arnold gave them to me. You know what they say; In matters of taste, there is none.

ED: I see where Arnold gets his wit.

MA: That and his appetite are from me. But the face?; he's his father's son. He's got his heart too. Always a soft touch. Tell me, Ed, what do you think of Arnold taking in this boy?

ED: I think it's wonderful.

MA: You do? Frankly, I'm not wild for it. But look, it's only for a few more weeks, so what harm could it do?

EO Ooops.

MA:

(Calling to Arnold)

Arnold? You have Matzoh Meal?

ARNOLD:

(Enters)

Yeah, I'll get it for you.

MA:

(Proud)

He has Matzoh Meal. Did I bring him up right?

(David enters with a book, sits down on the couch and begins to read.)

ARNOLD: Here you go, Ma. You need eggs?

MA: Two please. And an onion?

ED:

(Looking agog at David)

Are you doing homework?

DAVID: Nah. I'm just readin' somethin' from school.

MA: Arnold's father used to love my Latkes. But his favorite was my Potato Soup. You remember how he liked it, Arnold?

ARNOLD: I remember.

MA: It wasn't potato soup like you think; made with vegetables and cream. What he liked was: You took a potato, boiled it in water, threw in a bissel salt and pepper and that was Potato Soup. Arnold used to call it, "Daddy's Potato Water." You remember?

ARNOLD: Yes, Ma.

MA: We were Depression babies. You understand? Whether you have to or not, you carry that through your life. The tastes, the smells . . . They bring back a cozy feeling of a time you don't quite remember. You know what I'm talking?

ED: I think so.

MA: Good. 'Cause I don't.

> *(Arnold hugs her.)*

What's that for?

ARNOLD: I'm glad you're here.

MA: Me too, Tatalah.

ED:

> *(To David)*

I didn't know you could read.

DAVID: I just look at the pictures.

ED: What is it?

DAVID: Some garbage for English.

ED: What?

DAVID: A poem. I don't know.

> *(Reading and mispronouncing the word "Gaol")*

"The Ballad of Reading Gaol" by Oscar Wilde.

ED: That's gaol, like in j-a-i-l.

> *(Correcting)*

DAVID: That ain't what it says.

ED: That's the British spelling.

ARNOLD: "Yet each man kills the thing he loves, By each let this be heard, Some do it with a bitter look, Some with a flattering word, The coward does it with a kiss, The brave man with a sword."

> *(From memory)*

ED: Very good.

MA: What? You think I raised a dope?

ARNOLD: We had to learn it in High School. Y'know, I still get shivers when I think of that poor man going through all that pain and torment just to write a cliche.

DAVID: What's a cliche?

ARNOLD: The sincerest form of flattery.

DAVID:

> *(To Ed)*

Was that a joke?

ARNOLD:

> *(Coming out of kitchen)*

Did your teacher happen to mention how Oscar Wilde came to be imprisoned?

DAVID: Maybe. Who listens?

ARNOLD: He was in jail for being gay.

DAVID: No, I think I would'a remembered that.

MA:

> *(Embarrassed)*

Arnold, I can't find the oil.

ARNOLD: In a minute, Ma. See, ten years earlier, the Parliament passed a law against homosexuality. And Oscar Wilde had this young lover named . . .

MA: Arnold, could you please give me a hand?

ARNOLD: Just a second. His name was Lord Alfred.

DAVID: Royalty, huh?

ED: Anything I can help you with?

(To Ma)

MA: No, thank you, Ed.

ARNOLD: Now, Lord Alfred's father found out about them and started causing scenes in public; chasin' 'em outta hotels and stuff. But the straw that broke the dam was a note sent to Wilde's hotel. It said, "To Oscar Wilde who poses as a Sodomite."

MA: For God's sake, Arnold. Could you change the subject?

ARNOLD:

(Annoyed)

I'll finish later.

(Goes back to kitchen)

ED: Here, we'll read the poem together and I'll explain anything you don't understand.

DAVID: I want the rest of the dish.

(Ed kicks him.)

Ouch, that hurt.

(David and Ed read quietly and we hear the conversation from the kitchen.)

ARNOLD: I wish you wouldn't interfere like that; it's very embarrassing.

MA: Excuse me, but listening to that is very embarrassing.

ARNOLD: I'm sorry you feel that way, but I have a responsibility to his education.

MA: I am sure that the people who put him here did not have that kind of education in mind.

ARNOLD: The people who put him here had exactly that kind of education in mind. And I'll thank you not to interfere.

MA: I am only suggesting that you should consider the huge responsibility you've taken on here.

ARNOLD: You think I'm unaware of it?

MA: Then act like it. You should be setting an example for the boy.

ARNOLD: And I'm not?

MA: Not when you talk like that, you're not. You've got to consider what you say to him for the remaining time. He's at an impressionable age. After all it's only for a few more months.

ARNOLD: What's for a few more months?

(Ed and David stop.)

MA: He's here on a nine-month program, right? And he's already been here six months, so . . .

ARNOLD: And what do you think happens then?

MA: He leaves.

DAVID: No, you misunderstoo . . .

> *(Ed kicks him again.)*

> Ow! This is getting serious.

ARNOLD: There seems to be misinterpretation afoot. Yes, David is here on a nine-month program, but after that, if we agree and the Bureau of Child Welfare allows, I will legally adopt David. And believe me, Ma, if I have anything to say about it, he's not leaving.

> *(Ma tries to say something, she is angry, confused, frustrated. She throws down whatever is in her hands and storms out. We hear the door slam.)*

ARNOLD: That was an "Ooops."

ED: I thought so.

ARNOLD:

> *(To David)*

> What'd you tell her?

DAVID: I didn't say nothin'.

ARNOLD: You certainly got a way without words. Well, kids, wish me luck.

DAVID: You goin' in there?

ARNOLD: Anybody got any suggestions?

DAVID: Don't look at me.

ED: Sorry, I'm just the babysitter.

ARNOLD: Somber times inspire your whimsicality. I'll remember that.

ED: And don't forget to write.

DAVID: We'll be in the next room; so talk loud.

ARNOLD: Thanks.

> *(Deep breath)*

> Well, here goes everything.

> *(He exits, we hear a knock on the door, then the door opens and closes. Ed and David jump up and rush to hallway.)*

DAVID: You hear anything?

ED: Sssshhhh.

DAVID: Ah, he stalled too long. They're gonna need time to warm up again. Let's eat.

> *(Going to kitchen)*

ED: I can't hear a thing. This is ridiculous; a grown man listening at a hallway. I should go right up to the door.

> *(He exits.)*

DAVID: You want a sandwich?

> *(Shouting)*

ED: Could you not yell like that?

(Runs back in)

DAVID: Hear anything?

(Whispers)

ED: No.

DAVID: Told ya'. Have a sandwich. We'll know when they get goin'.

ED: You're taking this very calmly. I'm more curious than you, it seems.

DAVID: Looks that way, don't it.

ED: What'd you tell her, anyway?

DAVID: A little of this, a little of that. What's the difference? You know how it is with grown-ups: They only hear what they wanna.

(He listens.)

Hang on, we're about to get a bulletin.

(Ma enters as if she rushed away. She sits on couch. Arnold follows and stands staring at her.)

DAVID: Care to repose and repast?

ED: Come on, Kissinger. I'll teach you how to play chess.

(Grabs David)

DAVID: Wait, my sandwich.

ED: You'll concentrate better on an empty stomach.

(Pulling him off)

ARNOLD: Is this it? We gonna sit and stare into space?

(Sits next to her. Pause)

MA: You want I should do a Bubble Dance?

ARNOLD: I need a cigarette.

(He gets one.)

MA: Frankly, Arnold, you've done a lot of crazy things, but this . . . ?

ARNOLD: Adopting David is not a crazy thing. It's a wonderful thing that I'm very proud of.

MA: If you're so proud how come you were too ashamed to tell your mother? Everything else you tell me. You shove your sex-life down my throat like aspirin; every hour on the hour. But six months he's been here and not a word. Why?

ARNOLD: I don't know.

MA: So what's new?

ARNOLD: Ma . . . Y'know, you're not the easiest person in the world to talk to.

MA: What did I say? Do I tell you how to run your life? Let me tell you something, my son: I learned long ago that no matter what I said or how I felt you and your brother were going to do just as you pleased anyway. So, I wouldn't say a word. On purpose! You want to know why you didn't tell me about this? I'll tell you why: Because you knew it was wrong.

ARNOLD: That's not true.

MA: No?

ARNOLD: No!

MA: Why then?

ARNOLD: . . . I don't know.

MA: You would if you'd listened.

ARNOLD: This isn't something I decided to do overnight. We put in our application more than two years ago.

MA: Who "we"?

ARNOLD: Alan and I.

MA: The two of you were going to do this together?

ARNOLD: That was the idea.

MA: Now I've heard everything.

ARNOLD: That's what I love about you; you're so open minded.

MA: Alright. So, Alan's not here. Why's the kid?

ARNOLD: Because with everything else I forgot about the application. Then, one day, the phone rang. It was the foster parent program and they had David for us. I told them what happened to Alan and they said I could probably take David anyway.

MA: And you said, "send him on over."

ARNOLD: Not at first. But then I thought it all through, called them back and said yes. . . . On a trial basis.

MA: I'm glad you got a money-back guarantee, but you still haven't told me why you wanted him.

ARNOLD: Because I was tired of widowing.

MA: Wida-whating?

ARNOLD: Widowing. Widow-ing. It's a word of Murray's.

MA: And a nice one at that. What does it mean?

ARNOLD: You know.

MA: No, I don't know.

ARNOLD: Widowing . . . feeling sorry for myself, cursing everytime I passed a couple walking hand in hand, watching Tear Jerkers on T.V. knowing they could only cheer me up. Christ, of all the things going down here, I was sure that was the one thing I wouldn't have to explain.

MA: How should I know about Whatchamacallit? Did you ever say a word to me?

ARNOLD: I didn't think I had to. Christ, it's only been three years since daddy died.

MA: Wait, wait, wait, wait, wait. Are you trying to compare my marriage with you and Alan?

(Haughty and incensed)

Your father and I were married for thirty-five years, had two children and a wonderful life together. You have the nerve to compare yourself to that?

ARNOLD:

(Scared)

That's not what I mean, I'm talking about the loss.

MA: What loss did you have? You fooled around with some boy . . . ? Where do you come to compare that to a marriage of thirty-five years?

ARNOLD: You think it doesn't?

MA: Come on, Arnold. You think you're talking to one of your pals?

ARNOLD: Ma, I lost someone that I loved very much . . .

MA: So you felt bad. Maybe you cried a little. But what would you know about what I went through? Thirty-five years I lived with that man. He got sick, I brought him to the hospital and you know what they gave me back? I gave them a man . . . they gave me a paper bag with his watch, wallet and wedding ring. How could you possibly know what that felt like? It took me two months until I could sleep in our bed alone, a year to learn to say "I" instead of "we." And you're going to tell me you were "widowing." How dare you!

ARNOLD: You're right, Ma. How dare I. I couldn't possibly know how it feels to pack someone's clothes in plastic bags and watch the garbage pickers carry them away. Or what it feels like to forget and set his place at the table. How about the food that rots in the refrigerator because you forgot how to shop for one? How dare I? Right, Ma? How dare I?

MA:

(Starting over his speech and continuing until her exit)

May God strike me dead! Whatever I did to my mother to deserve a child speaking to me this way. The disrespect! I only pray that one day you have a son and that he'll talk to you like this. The way you talk to me.

ARNOLD:

(Over her speech)

Listen, Ma, you had it easy. You have thirty-five years to remember, I have five. You had your children and friends to comfort you, I had me! My friends didn't want to hear about it. They said, "What're you gripin' about? At least you had a lover." 'Cause everybody knows that queers don't feel nothin'. How dare I say I loved him? You had it easy, Ma. You lost your husband in a nice clean hospital, I lost mine out there. They killed him there on the street. Twenty-three years old laying dead on the street. Killed by a bunch of kids with baseball bats.

(Ma has fled the room. Arnold continues to rant.)

Children. Children taught by people like you. 'Cause everybody knows that queers don't matter! Queers don't love! And those that do deserve what they get!

(He stops, catches his breath, sits down)

Whatever happened to good ole' American Momism and apple pie?

DAVID:

(Sticking his head out from the hall)

Could you keep it down? There's people tryin' to concentrate.

ARNOLD:

(Laughing)

Sorry.

DAVID: Round one over?

ARNOLD: I really lost control. I didn't mean to say any of that. But it came pouring out; I felt like I was fighting for my life.

DAVID:

> *(Coming close)*

This is highly flattering: A duel to the death over li'l ole me.

ARNOLD: Don't overdramatize. I do enough of that for both of us.

DAVID: I think you're wonderful.

> *(Hug)*

ARNOLD: Where's Uncle Ed?

ED:

> *(Sticking his head out)*

Present. Is round one over?

ARNOLD: We've called a cease fire to re-group.

DAVID: Can we eat now?

ARNOLD: Why don't you two go out for something?

ED: How about you?

ARNOLD: Don't know why, but I ain't hungry. Go on.

ED: You're not going back in there, are you?

ARNOLD: I can't leave things like this.

ED: You're very brave.

ARNOLD: I'm very stupid. None of this would've happened if I'd been honest all along.

ED: Or dishonest all along.

ARNOLD: That's not for me. Get going.

ED:

> *(Intimate)*

Let me stay. We can all talk together.

DAVID: You want us to bring something back for you?

ARNOLD:

> *(To David)*

No, thanks.

> *(To Ed)*

No, thanks.

DAVID:

> *(His jacket on)*

Put a candle in the window when it's clear to come home. We'll wait on the bench.

ARNOLD:

> *(Hugging him)*

I'll do that.

ED:

> *(At the door)*

What'll it be; pizza?

DAVID: You paying?

ED: Sure.

DAVID: Then I know this intimate little French restaurant . . .

(Exit)

ARNOLD:

(Takes a deep breath)

Round two.

(Sits on couch, feet up)

Yoo hoo, Mrs. Bloom! It's safe to come out. David and Ed went for a walk and we've got the whole place to fight in.

MA:

(Off)

Enjoy yourself. I'm going to bed.

ARNOLD: Ma, I'm sorry I lost my temper.

MA: Ha! I'm glad you're sorry.

ARNOLD: Please come out here. We can't talk like this.

MA:

(In doorway)

You don't want to talk, you want to fight. But I don't fight with my children. In your life did you ever hear your father and I fight? No. And do you know why? I'll tell you why: Because all my childhood I listened to fights. My father fought with my mother, my mother fought with my brother, my mother fought with me . . . When I married your father I told him, "Jack, I'll talk, but I won't fight." And did you ever hear us fight? No. And now you know why.

ARNOLD: You wanna sit down?

MA:

(Wandering over to the couch)

I'm sitting.

ARNOLD: Alright . . .

MA:

(Warning)

And don't holler at me. People say things they don't mean when they holler and you've already said quite enough.

ARNOLD: I won't holler. You just hit a raw nerve. We won't discuss Alan. Only David.

MA: So discuss.

ARNOLD: Why don't you tell me what you already know, and we'll go on from there.

MA:

(Trying)

I don't know anything.

ARNOLD: You spent the day with him. He must've said something.

MA: Let me think. He's an orphan . . .

ARNOLD: He's not an orphan.

MA: He said he was an orphan.

ARNOLD: Well, he's not. He was a battered child. They took him away from his parents. This is his third foster home. The first brought him back. The second he ran away from. So. . . .

MA: So, he's a liar.

ARNOLD: He's not a liar . . .

MA: This isn't going to work.

ARNOLD: Come on, we're finally getting somewhere . . .

MA: How do you expect me to sit here and discuss this insanity?

ARNOLD: You're right, this isn't going to work.

MA: Arnold, Arnold, what do you know from raising a child?

ARNOLD: What's to know? Whenever I have a problem I simply imagine how you would solve it, and do the opposite.

MA:

> (Standing)

> Is this what you invited me up here for? To insult me and spit on your father's grave?

ARNOLD: For cryin' out . . . Will you please sit down?

MA:

> (Sitting)

> Don't holler. I'm sitting. I don't know why, but I'm sitting.

ARNOLD: Alright. Now we're going to talk about David. Not Alan, not daddy, just David. And we're going to stay calm.

MA: Ha!

ARNOLD: I give up.

MA: Arnold, darling, open your eyes. Don't you see how ridiculous this is? I've been here less than a day, already I've seen you let him miss school, hang out on the street, go out without dinner . . .

ARNOLD: This is hardly a typical day.

MA: You wanna talk or make excuses?

ARNOLD: This isn't Little Lord Fauntleroy we're talking about here. If this kid decided I was coming down too hard on him, he'd pack and take off and I'd never get him back again. That sweet looking little boy knows how to make more money in a night than you and I could make in a week.

MA: So you let him run wild?

ARNOLD: No. But I don't beat him up either. I teach him. I advise him, I try to set an example for him . . .

MA: Some example. Arnold, look, you live the life you want. I put my fist in my mouth, I don't say a word. This is what you want. But think about the boy. He likes you. He told me he loves you. He sees you living like this . . . don't you think it's going to affect him?

ARNOLD: Ma, David is gay.

MA: But he's only been here six months!

ARNOLD: He came that way.

MA: No one comes that way.

ARNOLD: What an opening.

MA: By you everything is a joke.

ARNOLD: Don't you understand: the whole purpose of placing him here was for him to grow up with a positive attitude about his homosexuality.

MA: That's it.

(Stands)

I'm finished. The world has gone completely mad and I'm heading south for the summer.

ARNOLD: You make it very difficult to have an intelligent conversation.

MA: You want an intelligent conversation? Do what I do: talk to yourself. It's the only way.

ARNOLD: You think this is easy for me? Look; my hands are shaking. I've been like this for days knowing you'd be coming and we'd have to talk about this.

MA: Because you knew I'd show you how wrong you are.

ARNOLD: I'm not wrong.

MA: No? Tell me something: How old was your friend Alan when you met him?

ARNOLD: Seventeen.

MA: Seventeen. Seventeen and you were doing God knows what together. Now tell me; how old is this "son" of yours?

ARNOLD: I have no intention of sleeping with him if that's what you're driving at.

MA: I had no intention of having a homosexual for a son. So, look where intentions get you. Arnold, do what you want. You want to live like this? *Gay gezzintah hait.* I don't care anymore. You're not going to make me sick like you did your father.

ARNOLD: I made my father sick?

MA: No; he was thrilled to have a fairy for a son! You took a lifetime of dreams and threw them back in his face.

ARNOLD: What lifetime of dreams? He knew I was gay for fourteen years.

MA: What? You think you walk into a room, say, "Hi Dad, I'm queer," and that's that? You think that's what we brought you into the world for? Believe me, if I'd known I wouldn't have bothered. God should tear out my tongue, I should talk to my child this way. Arnold, you're my son, you're a good person, a sensitive person with a heart, *kennohorrah*, like your father and I try to love you for that and forget this. But you won't let me. You've got to throw me on the ground and rub my face in it. You haven't spoken a sentence since I got here without the word "Gay" in it.

ARNOLD: Because that's what I am.

MA: If that were all you could leave it in there

(Points to bedroom)

where it belongs; in private. No, you're obsessed by it. You're not happy unless everyone is talking about it. I don't know why you don't just wear a big sign and get it over with.

ARNOLD:

(Bordering on hysteria)

I don't know what to say to you. I really don't. I'm not trying to throw it in your face but it is what I am and it's not just a matter of who I sleep with.

(Crosses to her)

Ma, try to imagine the world the other way around. Imagine that every movie, book, magazine, T.V. show, newspaper, commercial, billboard told you that you should be homosexual. But you know you're not and you know that for you this is right . . .

MA: Arnold, stop already. You're talking crazy.

ARNOLD: You want to know what's crazy? That after all these years I'm still sitting here justifying my life. That's what's crazy.

MA: You call this a life? This is a sickness! But this is what you've chosen for yourself.

ARNOLD:

(Deep breath, one last try)

Ma, look: I'm gay. I don't know why. I don't think anyone does. But that's what I am. For as far back as I can remember. Back before I knew it was different or wrong . . .

MA: You have not heard a word I've said.

ARNOLD:

(Losing control)

I know you'd rather I was straight but I am not! Would you also rather I had lied to you? My friends all think I'm crazy for telling you. They'd never dream of telling their parents. Instead they cut their parents out of their lives. And the parents wonder, "Why are my children so distant?" Is this what you'd rather?

MA: But it doesn't have to be our every conversation either.

ARNOLD: You want a part in my life? I am not going to edit out the things you don't like!

MA:

(Scared)

Can we end this conversation?

ARNOLD: No. There's one more thing you've got to understand. You made fun of my crocheting before. You think it's a cute little effeminate thing I do. Let me tell you something; I have taught myself to sew, cook, fix plumbing, do taxes, build furniture . . . I can even pat myself on the back when necessary. All so I don't have to ask anyone for anything. There is nothing I need from anyone except love and respect. And anyone who can't give me those two things has no place in my life.

(Breath)

You are my mother, and I love you. I do. But if you can't respect me . . . Then you've got no business being here.

MA: You're throwing me out?

ARNOLD: What I'm trying to . . .

MA: You're throwing me out! Isn't that nice? Listen Mister, you get one mother in this world. Only one. Wait. Just you wait.

(Ma exits to bedroom. Arnold is still as the next scene begins. The lights slowly crossfade.)

510

SCENE 3

A bench in the park below. Immediately following. If possible the bench should be played on the couch. Through the use of Gobos and projections it is conceivable to create the night-time park atmosphere on the apartment set. David and Ed enter talking, eating hotdogs.

DAVID: How's your hotdog, Big Spender?
ED: Been years since I bought one of these off the street. I just remembered why.
DAVID: Teach you to forget your wallet.

> *(David sits on bench.)*

ED: C'mon, lazy. I gotta walk this thing off.
DAVID: We're supposed to wait here.

> *(Pointing up)*

> Look. You can see our windows from here. Almost didn't take the apartment because of it.

ED: You lost me.
DAVID: Arnold never brung you here? This is where it happened.
ED: I didn't know.
DAVID: Yeah, here. They were walking back toward the street, Alan and the other guy when the kids jumped out from behind these bushes. You can see; no way to run. Must've happened too quick anyway. Alan died right off, but the other guy crawled out to the street.
ED: I know.
DAVID: You can see a stain on the sidewalk in the daytime.
ED: Arnold showed you this?
DAVID: The day I moved in. At first I figured he was tryin' to scare me outta goin' into the park at night. I mean, I didn't know him from shit and here he takes me out, first day, and shows me some dried up blood on the sidewalk. I figured him for a nutcase. Like maybe he had a case against the world or somethin'. I mean, havin' a bunch of piss-offs take out your lover for kicks . . . I could understand him bein' crazy. So, I felt sorry for him, but just passed it off. Then about a week later we were watchin' the news on T.V. and there was this protest march; a bunch of Jews marchin' against Nazis. They had these signs that said, "Never Again" and "We Remember." And I looked over at Arnold and he was like cryin' real soft, and just like that I connected. I knew why he showed me this.
ED: No candle in the window yet.
DAVID: Give 'em time, they got a lotta yellin' to catch up on.
ED: That's one thing I can do without hearing any more of today. I saw Laurel this afternoon.
DAVID: Oh, yeah? What'd she want?
ED:

> *(Realizing to whom he's talking)*

> Oh, nothing.

DAVID: Sure.
ED: Really.

DAVID: You don't have to tell me.

ED: It was nothing. Really.

DAVID: Hey, it's cool. You don't have to tell me. It ain't like we're old friends or nothing. After all, what am I to you?

ED: It was nothing. She just wanted to know if I was thinking of coming back.

DAVID: And you told her no.

ED: How do you know?

DAVID: I know.

ED: Frankly, I haven't made up my mind yet.

DAVID: You won't go back.

ED: Can we change the subject?

DAVID: Sure. So, now that you and Laurel are washed up, you gonna start shoppin' around?

ED: Well, since I haven't yet decided, then I haven't yet decided.

DAVID: Don't think about it too long or you'll wind up like Arnold.

ED: And that's bad?

DAVID: Arnold goes out to work and shop. That's all and that ain't healthy.

ED: You say that like you mean it.

DAVID: Who knows more about sex and its effect on mental health than me? Got any idea how many couches I've been laid out on?

> (Ed smirks.)

> Psychiatrically speaking. Starting when they turned my folks in I've had Freudian Analysis, Primal Analysis, Gestalt Analysis, Handwriting Analysis, Scream Therapy, Dream Therapy, Aversion Therapy and EST. When they finally ran outta cures to put me through, they stamped my file "Hopelessly Homo," shook my hand, wished me luck and shipped me off to Arnold. So I picked up plenty of know how on my journey down the "Leatherette Road."

ED: Knowing and doing are two different things. You're only fifteen.

DAVID: Guess you don't read the *New York Times*. Seems no matter how many petitions they sign, they just can't get God to raise the age of puberty to eighteen. Kids have sex. But that's another subject.

ED: It certainly is.

DAVID: Bottom line is, here's Arnold: Attractive, sensitive, intelligent, a great conversationalist, pretty good cook, and he's living like an old Italian widow.

ED: So?

DAVID: So it's time for a change. Don't you think?

ED: Maybe.

DAVID: Got any suggestions?

ED: None I'd care to discuss with a fifteen-year-old.

DAVID: And you called him a bigot? Look, I ain't askin' for no miracles. Though I must say I'd be proud to call you Daddy. I'm simply suggestin' you could both use a little T.E.N.

ED: T.E.N.?

DAVID: Tension Easing Nookie. Sex is very therapeutic.

ED: So you've said.

DAVID: What do you say?

(Arnold enters carrying two hot dogs like a wedding bouquet)

ARNOLD:

(a la Kate Hepburn)

Hello Mother. Hello Father. The frankfurters are in bloom again.

(Examines them)

Such a strange flower. Suitable for any occasion. I wore one on my wedding day, and now I place them here in memory of something that has . . . I don't know when to stop, do I? I brought supplies.

ED: We had the same idea. They're poison.

(Holding his stomach)

DAVID:

(Grabbing two)

And so unfilling.

ARNOLD: Found your wallet on the table. Thought you might be hungry.

DAVID: Round two over?

ARNOLD: Two, three, four, five . . .

DAVID: Who won?

ARNOLD: When I left we both knew who won. Now only Robert Browning does. Ed, would you mind if I spoke to Champ alone?

ED:

(Embarrassed)

Oh, sure.

DAVID: No, stay. I want witnesses.

ED: It's O.K. Is it clear on the front?

ARNOLD: Should be. Got your key?

ED:

(Checks)

Yeah. I'll see you both later, then.

ARNOLD: Thanks, Ed.

(He exits.)

DAVID: That was lousy. He wanted to help.

ARNOLD: I don't need his help, thank you.

(Pause)

Things got pretty "padded cell" up there.

DAVID: Yeah?

(Aloof)

ARNOLD: You had to sit here, didn't you? I'm sorry I didn't tell her about you before. But believe me, it's not 'cause I was ashamed.

DAVID: Glad to hear it.

ARNOLD: My mother has a certain picture of what I should be doing with my life, and it's very hard for her to adjust to all the curves I throw in.

DAVID: Forge on.

ARNOLD: Alright. I knew that even if I told her about you, even before you came to live with me, that sooner or later we'd have this showdown. It has nothing to do with you. It's just her last go-for-broke campaign to straighten out my life.

DAVID: And?

ARNOLD: I asked her to leave.

DAVID: You're good at that.

ARNOLD: But you've got to understand that whatever happens between my mother and me has nothing to do with us.

DAVID: Come on, Arnold. This ain't Ed you're talking to. Whatever goes down with you two is exactly what will happen with us.

ARNOLD: How do you figure that?

DAVID: 'Cause you're just like her.

ARNOLD: You wouldn't say that if you'd heard what went on up there.

DAVID: I know what goes on with mothers. Remember, you're my fourth. You think it's different 'cause we're both gay. But it's the same trip.

ARNOLD: No offense, Angel Puss, but you're mistaken.

DAVID: Think so? What would you do if I met a girl, came home and told you I was straight?

ARNOLD: If you were happy, I'd be happy.

DAVID: Bull-China! Here you are, workin' your butt off showin' me all the joys of gay life, givin' me the line on dignity and self-respect . . . You tellin' me you wouldn't wonder where you went wrong?

ARNOLD: Not if you were sure that that's what you wanted.

DAVID: Yeah, I see the way you treat Ed. The guy keeps tellin' you he's Bi and all you keep doin' is callin' him a Closet Case.

ARNOLD: See, you don't know what you're talking about. I'd be perfectly willing to believe he's Bi if just once he thought about the person he was with before he considered what sex that person was.

DAVID: How could anybody do that? You ever meet someone and not know what sex they were?

ARNOLD: That's not what I mean . . .

DAVID: I know what you mean and it's just as dumb.

(Arnold tries to speak)

Shut up and let me finish. I stay with you because I want to. Dig? I really like living with you. I even like the way you try to mother me. But you can really be a shithead about things. But, you make me feel like I got a home. And a bunch of other assorted mushy stuff I don't want to get into here. But, Arnold, I'm tellin' you now: I'll walk if you try to use me as an excuse for sitting home alone, or to pick a fight with your mother or with Ed. Hey, you do what you gotta do. I ain't judgin'. Just don't blame anybody but yourself if you get my drift.

(Pause)

You get my drift?

(*Arnold nods.*)

I come down too heavy?

(*Shakes his head*)

Still want me to stay?

(*Arnold nods.*)

Alright. Now we're dancin'.

ARNOLD: I ever tell you, I think you're swell?

DAVID:

(*Standing*)

Break this up. I got school tomorrow.

ARNOLD:

(*Standing*)

You go on ahead. I need an airing.

DAVID: Want company?

ARNOLD: Go on. I'll be up.

DAVID: O.K. See you later.

ARNOLD: David? You're not, are you?

DAVID: What?

ARNOLD:

(*Embarrassed*)

Straight?

DAVID: What would you do if I was?

ARNOLD: Kill you.

DAVID:

(*Laughs*)

Nice to know you care.

(*Starts to leave*)

ARNOLD: Watch how you cross the street.

(*The lights fade down and out.*)

SCENE 4

Several hours later. The apartment. The lights are out, the couch unfolded and Ed is asleep in it. Arnold enters in a robe from the bathroom heading toward the kitchen, weaving, with an empty glass in his hand.

ED:

(*Waking*)

Huh? What?

ARNOLD: It's me. Go to sleep.

ED: Arnold? Oh.

(Trying to wake)

What time is it?

ARNOLD: Almost six. Go to sleep.

ED: I waited up for you.

ARNOLD: I see.

ED: You want to talk?

ARNOLD: No. Go to sleep.

ED: I don't want to go to sleep.

ARNOLD: So don't go to sleep.

ED: You just get home?

ARNOLD: A while ago.

ED: I didn't hear you. Where'd you go?

(No response)

She said she's leaving.

ARNOLD: I know. I tripped over her bags on my way in.

ED: She didn't want to stay the night, but she couldn't get a flight out until morning. When I came in she was walking out to spend the night in the airport. I got her calmed down a little.

(Pause)

She'd stay if you asked her.

ARNOLD: Go to sleep.

ED: Stop telling me to go to sleep.

ARNOLD: Alright, go to hell!

(Sorry)

Want a drink?

ED: Sure, white wine.

(Arnold shoots a look.)

Juice.

(As Arnold makes the drinks)

You know, I saw Laurel today. That's where I went. I don't think she's overjoyed with the separation. She told me she's pregnant. She's not, but she said she was to see if I'd go back to her . . . if she was. God. The things that ran through my mind. Baby carriages, walks in the park, my folks playin' with it . . . Quite a sensation. I guess I would've gone back if she was. But then . . . I don't know.

ARNOLD: I hope you didn't tell her that.

ED: Of course I did. After five years of marriage, I'm not going to start lying to her now.

ARNOLD:

(Numb)

What'd she say?

ED: She said she could be . . . if I came back.

(Pause)

She thinks we're sleeping together. Funny, huh? Laurel and your mother thinking the same thing. Maybe they know something we don't.

(Clears his throat)

I suppose it's her way of expressing anger. Laurel. Not your mother. Though I have seen happier women than her. Your mother, that is.

(Arnold is now sitting on the bed. He snickers.)

What's so funny?

ARNOLD: Seems like everytime I turn around here we are: Arnold and Ed in bed together.

ED: Talking.

ARNOLD: Talking. Me with a lump in my throat and you with a foot in your mouth.

ED: Why? What'd I say?

ARNOLD: Don't ask me. I stopped listening years ago.

ED: I don't see what I said that's . . .

ARNOLD: It was nothing. Pay me no mind; I'm drunk.

ED: Look, I know I'm not the most sensitive person in the world . . .

ARNOLD: Ed, take a note: Never fish for compliments in polluted waters.

ED: Are you really drunk?

ARNOLD: I hold it well, don't I? A trick I learned in finishing school. It's done with mirrors. You think I'm here in bed next to you but actually I'm asleep under a table in a bar on Forty-third.

ED:

(Amused)

This is the first time I've ever seen you drunk.

ARNOLD: Well get a good look, Leon, 'cause I'm dryin' out in the morning.

ED: Arnold Beckoff drunk.

ARNOLD: Blottoed, plastered and plotzed . . . incorporated.

ED: Why'd you get drunk?

ARNOLD:

(Knocking on Ed's head)

Hello? Anybody home? Sometimes you really frighten me.

ED:

(Offering his arms and shoulder)

Care to talk about it?

ARNOLD: Sure. Why should the neighbors have all the fun?

(Lies back)

I had a genuinely superior motive for drinking this much. Don't tell nobody, but I'm a pushover when I'm drunk. And I thought that if I got good and looped I'd repent and ask my mother to stay. It worked, too. Until I got a peek at her sitting in there on the bed with her "Holier Than Thou" attitude and her

"Merry Martyr" smile. The way she acts you'd think she and God went to school together. She thinks I hate her. I know the way her mind works and she thinks I hate her.

ED: I'm sure she knows you don't.

ARNOLD: Oh, no, she does. She thinks I hate her and everything she stands for. And I don't, for the life of me, know how to tell her that what I want more than anything is to have exactly the life she had. With a few minor alterations. My parents . . . They were something together. In all the years they were married the only time they were separated was for two days while my mother was in the hospital. And my father . . . He wouldn't even get into bed without her. He spent both nights on a chair in the living room. And the way they made my brother and me feel; like we were the smartest, handsomest, most talented, most important two people in the world. Didn't matter what we did, good or bad, it was the best. And she thinks she did something wrong.

ED: Are you really a pushover when you're drunk?

ARNOLD: Earth to Ed. Earth to Ed. Come in please.

(Ed giggles.)

You've got your own problems don't'cha? C'mon, spill your guts.

ED: David said you haven't gone out since Alan died.

ARNOLD: We're talking about you now.

ED: I can understand you not wanting to at first, but still. You could at least go out for a few drinks, take a quick trip to the backroom. No harm in that.

ARNOLD: You may not understand this, but I want more out of life than meeting a pretty face and sitting down on it. That answer your question?

ED: Graphically.

ARNOLD: I do my best.

ED: If I made a pass at you now . . . Would you let me?

ARNOLD: Alright, who spiked the orange juice?

ED: Actually, it's David's idea. He thinks you're pushing chastity too far. He says it's unhealthy.

ARNOLD: This is the first time I've been seduced in the guise of preventive medicine.

ED: I told him I'd consider it.

ARNOLD: What a friend.

ED: I didn't mean it that way.

ARNOLD: You never do.

ED: I mean, this is not exactly what I want.

ARNOLD: I came to the same conclusion myself. I think it was the wedding that gave you away.

ED: I didn't want that either. I mean, I did, but it turned out not to be what I want. In fact, it made me less sure than ever about what it is I do want.

ARNOLD: No problem. I've got a Sears catalogue you can flip through. If you see it there give a primal scream and I'll get it for your birthday.

ED: You're not being fair.

ARNOLD: I'm upset, uptight, and up to my nipples in Southern Comfort. I'm sorry.

ED: Never mind.

ARNOLD: I said I'm sorry. You're trying to say something and I've got diarrhea of the mouth. Come on, I'll behave. I promise.

(*No response*)

Hey, this is Arnold here. You can tell me anything.

ED: I want another chance with you.

ARNOLD: Anything but that.

ED: Wait. Just think about it for a minute. It makes a lot of sense. We know each other so well, there'd be no surprises. We know what to expect from each other. You said yourself we have no secrets.

ARNOLD: What'd that kid of mine say to you?

ED: Just listen for a second. Laurel and I together . . . It wasn't enough. Obviously or I wouldn't be here. And that's the point: I am here. No matter what I do, I always end up back here, with you, in bed . . .

ARNOLD: Talking!

ED: Talking. But here. Arnold, the time I've spent here with you and David . . . it's been the closest thing to whatever it is I want. I feel wonderful here . . .

ARNOLD: "Don't care if the kid ain't mine, I wanna be the father of your baby." I saw that movie. I even read the book.

ED: Are you finished?

ARNOLD: Ed, please.

ED: Not five minutes ago it's what you said you wanted.

ARNOLD: I thought you weren't listening.

ED: I know you're upset about your mother.

ARNOLD: That's not it . . .

ED: O.K. so maybe it's too soon after Alan . . .

ARNOLD: Oh, Puh-lease!

ED: I'm asking you to think about it. That's all. Just think.

ARNOLD: Don't you know that I have? How thick can you possibly be? Can't you see that since you called that's all I've thought about? Five days ago you walked through the door and from that moment I've been playing the dutiful wife and mother to your understanding if distant father. And David? He's been having the time of his life playing baby.

ED: And it's been wonderful.

ARNOLD: It's been preposterous. It's a joke. Three grown men playing house!

ED: You think this is playing house? You have no idea what playing house is. Arnold, I love Laurel. That may sound a little strange considering the circumstances, but my feelings for her are genuine and just as strong now as when we got married. It has, however, become apparent that what we have is a friendship, not a marriage.

ARNOLD: That's a hell of a lot more than most people have.

ED: I'm almost forty, Arnold. Can you understand what that means? It means it's time for me to stop jerkin' around. I want more than a marriage which is at best purposeless, unfulfilling but perfectly acceptable. Now, whatever you think of us, you could never describe us like that.

ARNOLD: Not the perfect part anyway.

ED: Are you through making cracks?

ARNOLD: I just don't see what you think is here that you can't have with Laurel.

ED: To tell you the truth I'm not sure either. But there's something that's kept me coming back . . .

ARNOLD: Are you forgetting why we broke up in the first place? You really think you could bring your friends here? You ready to introduce me to your parents as your lover and to David as *our* son? Ed. Angel, I just threw my mother—my *mother*—out of my house and all she wanted was to not talk about it. You think I'll ask less from you?

ED: I think it's time to find out.

ARNOLD: I don't know, Ed. Christ, I mean, I don't even know what this is supposed to be. I can't exactly buy a book or study some *Reader's Digest* article that's gonna tell me. All I know is whatever this is, it's not a Grade B imitation of a heterosexual marriage. See, I thought that Alan and David and I could find out together . . . so now . . .

ED: Let me help you find out. You, me and David.

ARNOLD: I can't.

ED: Why? You scared I'll walk out again? Of course I can't guarantee anything . . .

ARNOLD: That's not it.

ED: Then is it David? You afraid I'll hurt him?

ARNOLD: I know how you feel about him, I know you wouldn't.

ED: Then what, Arnold?

ARNOLD:

> *(Deep breath)*
>
> I am not Laurel.

ED: I'm counting on that.

ARNOLD: Go home, Ed.

ED: Are you crying?

ARNOLD: Leave me alone.

ED: I can't. Not with you like this. You need someone to talk to.

ARNOLD:

> *(Striking out)*
>
> I don't need anyone. Thank you.

ED: Well, maybe I do.

ARNOLD: Then go home. You've got a lovely wife who'd do anything for you. She can give you a home, a two-car garage, a child of your own, white picket fence . . . the whole shebang double dipped in chocolate and government approved. Go home, Ed. I ain't got nothin' like that here.

ED: You really believe that?

> *(Arnold nods.)*
>
> Your mother did quite a job on you.
>
> *(Teasing)*
>
> Hello? Anybody home? You're gonna make me say it, aren't you? Undemonstrative soul that I am, you're gonna make me say it.

ARNOLD: I don't want you to say anything.

ED: Oh no, I'll say it. I'm not ashamed, embarrassed maybe, but not ashamed. But I'll be damned if I say it to your back.

(Pulls Arnold over and pins him down)

ARNOLD: Ed! For Chrissake!

ED: You ready? Now you better listen good 'cause I don't know when I'll get the guts to say it again.

ARNOLD: Ed, you're gonna wake my mother.

ED: So, let her hear. I hope they're both listening. Might as well let everyone know. Is everybody listening? O.K. Here goes. Arnold Beckoff . . . I love . . .

DAVID:

(Interrupting as he enters)

What the hell's going on in here?

ED: Perfect timing.

DAVID:

(Throwing on the lights: We can now see his black and blue eye.)

Oh, am I interrupting something? I hope, I hope, I hope.

ARNOLD:

(Straightening up his appearance)

You're not, you're not. What're you doing up at this hour?

DAVID: My alarm went off ten minutes ago. In case you lovebirds haven't noticed, it's morning.

ED: Jesus!

DAVID: Is this a closed marriage or can anybody join in?

ARNOLD:

(As David climbs into bed between them)

And baby makes three.

ED: My first pajama party.

DAVID:

(To Arnold)

You look awful. Didn't you sleep?

ARNOLD: Nary a wink, blink or nod.

ED: . . . Incorporated.

ARNOLD: Thank you.

ED: Don't mention it.

ARNOLD: Any news from the other camp?

DAVID: I heard shuffling. I think she's ready to leave.

ARNOLD: I'd better splash my face and get ready for the grand exit.

ED:

(As Arnold struggles to rise)

Need help?

ARNOLD: I think my battery's dead. Gimme a boost.

(They shove from behind, Arnold flies to his feet. Then, a la Mae West)

Thanks, boys.

(Exits into bathroom)

DAVID:

(Anxiously)

Well?

ED: I struck out. He said no.

DAVID: You asked first? Don't you know anything? It don't mean nothin', anyway. Arnold always says no when you ask him a question. Then he thinks about it and . . . Watch.

(Calling out)

Hey, Arnold? You want breakfast?

ARNOLD:

(Off)

No, thanks.

DAVID:

(Counts to ten on his fingers.)

Now . . .

ARNOLD:

(Off)

David? Maybe I'll have an egg.

DAVID: Most contrary person I've ever met.

ED:

(Getting out of bed)

We better get dressed. They should be alone for the final round.

DAVID: I am dressed.

ED: Show off. Well, start the coffee while I catch up.

(Exits)

DAVID:

(Heading to the kitchen)

Do you like pancakes?

ED:

(Off)

I love pancakes.

DAVID: Great. I'll make you some . . . when I learn to cook.

(He turns on the radio.)

RADIO: Plaza 6-6654 with your requests. It's six fifty-four in the Big Apple on what looks to be a beautiful June day. And I'm here, with you, dedicated to the one you love. Now an Oldie by request, from Beulah to Robert and Michael. Guess she just can't make up her mind. Ha, ha. Alright, Beulah, here it is with love.

(Music begins)

Our number's Plaza 6-6654 and I'm waiting to play one for you.

(Music continues into the scene.)

ARNOLD:

(Entering)

What're you listening to?

DAVID: One of those call-in shows, I think. Want me to change it?

ARNOLD: No, leave it. I ever tell you about the time Alan phoned in a request to one of those shows? They read the dedication wrong. He announced, "From Ellen to Arnold." He must'a thought it was a typo or somethin'.

DAVID: What song was it?

ARNOLD: "My Funny Valentine."

(David wretches.)

It was very Romantic.

DAVID: Is your mother staying for breakfast?

ARNOLD: Ask her, not me. Has she shown her face yet?

DAVID: Nope.

ARNOLD: Go on in and see if she needs any help.

DAVID:

(Dramatically)

"Into the jaws of Death, Into the mouth of Hell!" Any message?

ARNOLD: No.

(David exits. Arnold folds the couch. Mother screams offstage.)

Not again.

MA:

(Enters with David)

Arnold, did you see this eye? How could you let him walk around with a face like this?

(Drags him to the kitchen)

Come over here. I'm going to put some ice on it.

DAVID: Mrs. Beckoff, it's alright.

MA: Alright? You look like an ad for "I'd rather fight than switch."

ARNOLD:

(To David's rescue as Ed enters)

Ma, leave him alone. Ice won't help. He's had it for two days.

MA: What're you talking? I saw him yesterday . . .

ARNOLD: He covered it with make-up so he'd look nice for you.

DAVID: I'm O.K. Really. But thanks, anyway.

ED: C'mon, Champ. I'll buy you breakfast out.

DAVID:

(Surveying the scene)

Great. But I gotta do somethin' first.

(Towards bedroom)

I'll be out in a minute.

ED:

(Putting on his jacket)

I guess I'll see you later.

(To Ma)

It was a pleasure meeting you, Mrs. Beckoff.

MA: The pleasure was mine, Ed. I hope you and your wife come to your senses. Couples must learn to live with conflict. After all, a problem is never as permanent as a solution.

ED: Uh . . . Thank you.

(Shouting)

David? Hurry up.

ARNOLD: Aren't you going to wash up first?

ED: That's alright. I'm alright.

(Pause. Desperate)

David!!!

DAVID:

(Off)

I'm comin', already!

ARNOLD:

(Taking Ed aside)

Ed? What we were talking about before? Y'know, six years is a long time . . . I don't know. But we can talk.

ED: That's all I'm asking.

(Trying to control himself)

Good. Good.

DAVID:

(Enters with a big grin)

Here I is.

MA: You take care of that eye.

DAVID: I will. It was nice meeting you.

(To Ed)

Remember your wallet this time?

(Ed checks)

See you later, Arnold.

(*Gives him a peck on the cheek*)

ARNOLD: Have a nice day. And don't come home before school's over!

DAVID:

(*To Ed*)

You look like someone kicked you in the head.

(*They exit. David sticks his head back in*)

And you two play like nice children.

(*Out*)

ED:

(*Off*)

Yahoo!

ARNOLD:

(*Holding back a laugh*)

He likes the wallpaper. Covers a multitude of sins.

MA:

(*Bringing her bags to the door*)

I'll be leaving myself, now.

ARNOLD: You don't have to fly back to Florida. You could stay . . .

MA: With your brother? No. It's better if he doesn't know about this. I'll call him from Miami, tell him I changed my plans and couldn't make it up this week.

ARNOLD: I'm going to tell him what happened.

MA:

(*Angry*)

Do what you want. I don't care.

ARNOLD: Ma, it's important that he knows. He's part of this family too.

MA: What else do you want to do to me? What, Arnold, what? You want me to leave? I'm leaving. You want me to fight? I'm too tired. You want me to change? I'm too old and I can't. I can't, I can't, I can't. So you do what you have to do, and I'll do what I have to do and I hope you're satisfied.

(*Arnold groans*)

If I had ever opened a mouth to my mother like you did to me, you'd be talking to a woman with a size six wedgie sticking out of her forehead. But I didn't raise my children like that. I wanted them to respect me because they wanted to. Not because I beat it in to them. Go now.

ARNOLD: Do we have to start this again?

MA: Yes. Because you can't put all the blame on me. It's not fair. Some of it was my fault, but not all. You think I didn't know about you, Arnold? Believe me, I knew. And not because you told me. I didn't need you to tell me. I knew but I said no. I hoped . . . What's the difference, I knew and I turned my back. But I wasn't the only one. There are other things you should have told me. You opened a mouth to me about your friend Alan . . . How was I supposed to know?

ARNOLD: Why? You would have understood?

MA: Maybe. Maybe not. You can't know for sure. But I flew up for the funeral and you never said a word.

ARNOLD: So you could've done what?: Tell me he's better off dead?

MA: Or maybe I could've comforted you. Told you what to expect. You and your "widowing."

(She turns to leave, stops, takes a breath. One last try.)

And about this Ed: You love him?

ARNOLD: I don't know. I think so.

MA: Like you loved Alan?

ARNOLD: No. They're very different. Alan loved all my faults; my temper, my bitchiness, my fat . . . He looked for faults to love. And Ed? Ed loves the rest. And really, who needs to be loved for their virtues? Anyway, it's easier to love someone who's dead; they make so few mistakes.

MA: You've got an unusual way of looking at things, Arnold Beckoff.

ARNOLD: Runs in the family. Ma, I miss him so much.

MA: Give yourself time, Arnold. It gets better. But, Arnold, it won't ever go away. You can work longer hours, adopt a son, fight with me . . . whatever, it'll still be there. But that's alright. It becomes part of you, like wearing a ring or a pair of glasses. You get used to it and it's good . . . because it makes sure you don't forget. You don't want to forget him, do you?

(Arnold shakes his head)

So, it's good.

(Pause)

I guess that's what I would have said . . .

(The phone rings)

if I'd known. You'd better answer that. It may be something with that . . . son of yours.

(Arnold goes to the phone. As soon as he's turned his back, Ma slips out the door with her bags. Arnold doesn't notice.)

ARNOLD:

(Answering)

Hello . . . Hi Murray . . . What? . . . The radio? It's on. . . . Alright, hang on.

(He puts the phone down and goes to the radio, turning up the volume.)

It's Murray, something about the radio.

RADIO:

(Mid-sentence)

. . . no, I've just checked with my producer who took the call and he's confirmed it. What a morning. Whatever is this world coming to? So, here it is, a dedication from David to Arnold with all his love . . .

(Music begins to play. It is Big Maybelle singing, "I Will Never Turn My Back On You.")

ARNOLD: How do you like that? That's some kid I got there, huh?

(Turning)

You hear that, Ma?

(Sees she's gone)

Ma?

(Goes to door)

Ma?

(Runs to window and looks out as the music plays. He turns toward the audience and listens to the song calmly. As the music ends, the lights fade and the curtain falls.)

The End

Richard Thompson (Carl), Cherry Jones (Anna), and Joe Mantello
(Third Man) in the 1992 Off-Broadway premier of
Paula Vogel's *The Baltimore Waltz*.
(Photograph reprinted with permission from the Billy Rose Theatre Collection,
The New York Public Library for the Performing Arts,
Astor, Lennox, and Tilden Foundations)

The Baltimore Waltz

BY PAULA VOGEL

To the memory of Carl—because I cannot sew.

Ron Vawter: . . . I always saw myself as a surrogate who, in the absence of anyone else, would stand in for him. And even now, when I'm in front of an audience and I feel good, I hearken back to that feeling, that I'm standing in for them.

—*"Breaking the Rules," David Savran*

The Baltimore Waltz was produced at the Circle Repertory Company (Tanya Berezin, Artistic Director; Terrence Dwyer, Managing Director), in New York City, in February, 1992. It was directed by Anne Bogart; the set design was by Loy Arcenas; the costume design was by Walker Hicklin; the lighting design was by Dennis Parichy; the sound design and score was by John Gromada; the dramaturg was Ronn Smith and the production stage manager was Denise Yaney. The cast was as follows:

ANNA	Cherry Jones
CARL	Richard Thompson
THIRD MAN/DOCTOR	Joe Mantello

The Baltimore Waltz was produced at the Perseverance Theatre (Molly D. Smith, Artistic Director; Deborah B. Baley, Producing Director), in Douglas, Alaska, on October 18, 1990. The workshop production was directed by Annie Stokes-Hutchinson; the set design was by Bill Hudson; the costume design was by Barbara Casement and Kari Minnick; the lighting design was by John E. Miller; the sound design was by Katie Jensen and the stage manager was Carolyn Peck. The cast was as follows:

ANNA	Deborah Holbrook
CARL	Rick Bundy
THE THIRD MAN/DOCTOR	Charles Cardwell

In 1986, my brother Carl invited me to join him in a joint excursion to Europe. Due to pressures of time and money, I declined, never dreaming that he was HIV positive. This is the letter he wrote me after his first bout with pneumonia at Johns Hopkins Hospital in Baltimore, Maryland. He died on January 9, 1988.

As executor of his estate, I give permission to all future productions to reprint Carl's letter in the accompanying program. I would appreciate letting him speak to us in his own words.

The Baltimore Waltz—a journey with Carl to a Europe that exists only in the imagination—was written during the summer of 1989 at the MacDowell Colony, New Hampshire.

—Paula Vogel

March 1987

Dear Paula:

I thought I would jot down some of my thoughts about the (shall we say) production values of my ceremony. Oh God—I can hear you groaning—everybody wants to direct. Well, I want a good show, even though my role has been reduced involuntarily from player to prop.

First, concerning the choice between a religious ceremony and a memorial service. I know the family considers my Anglican observances as irrelevant as Shinto. However, I wish prayers in some recognizably traditional form to be said, prayers that give thanks to the Creator for the gift of life and the hope of reunion. For reasons which you appreciate, I prefer a woman cleric, if possible, to lead the prayers. Here are two names: Phebe Coe, Epiphany Church; the Rev. Doris Mote, Holy Evangelists. Be sure to make a generous contribution from the estate for the cleric.

As for the piece of me I leave behind, here are your options:

1. Open casket, full drag.
2. Open casket, bum up (you'll know where to place the calla lillies, won't you?).
3. Closed casket, interment with the grandparents.
4. Cremation and burial of my ashes.
5. Cremation and dispersion of my ashes in some sylvan spot.

I would really like good music. My tastes in these matters run to the highbrow: Fauré's "Pie Jesu" from his *Requiem,* Gluck's "Dance of the Blessed Spirits" from *Orfeo,* "La Vergine degli Angeli" from Verdi's *Forza.* But my favorite song is "I Dream of Jeannie," and I wouldn't mind a spiritual like "Steal Away." Also perhaps "Nearer My God to Thee." Didn't Jeannette MacDonald sing that di-vinely in *San Francisco?*
Finally, would you read or have read A.E. Housman's "Loveliest of Trees"?

Well, my dear, that's that. Should I be lain with Grandma and Papa Ben, do stop by for a visit from year to year. And feel free to chat. You'll find me a good listener.

Love,
Brother

Characters

ANNA
CARL, her brother
THE THIRD MAN/DOCTOR, who also plays:
    Harry Lime
    Airport Security Guard
    Public Health Official
    Garçon
    Customs Official
    The Little Dutch Boy at Age 50
    Munich Virgin
    Radical Student Activist
    Concierge
    Dr. Todesrocheln
    and all other parts

The Baltimore Waltz takes place in a hospital (perhaps in a lounge, corridor or waiting room) in Baltimore, Maryland.

Notes

The lighting should be highly stylized, lush, dark and imaginative, in contrast to the hospital white silence of the last scene. Wherever possible, prior to the last scene, the director is encouraged to score the production with music—every cliché of the European experience as imagined by Hollywood.

Anna might be dressed in a full slip/negligee and a trench coat. Carl is dressed in flannel pajamas and a blazer or jacket. The stuffed rabbit should be in every scene with Carl after Scene 6. The Third Man should wear latex gloves throughout the entire play.

SCENE 1

Three distinct areas on stage: Anna, stage right, in her trench coat, clutching the Berlitz Pocket Guide to Europe; Carl, stage left, wearing pajamas and blazer; The Third Man/Doctor, in his lab coat and with stethoscope, is center.

(Anna reads from her book. Her accents are execrable.)

ANNA: "Help me please."

> *(Anna recites from memory.)*
>
> Dutch: "Kunt U mij helpen, alstublieft?" "There's nothing I can do." French—
>
> *(Anna searches in vain.)*
>
> I have no memory.
>
> *(Anna reads from Berlitz.)*
>
> "Il n'y a rien à faire." "Where are the toilets?" "Wo sind die Toiletten?" I've never been abroad. It's not that I don't want to—but the language terrifies me. I was traumatized by a junior high school French teacher, and after that, it was a lost cause. I think that's the reason I went into elementary education. Words like brioche, bidet, bildungsroman raise a sweat. Oh, I want to go. Carl—he's my brother, you'll meet him shortly—he desperately wants to go. But then, he can speak six languages. He's the head librarian of literature and languages at the San Francisco Public. It's a very important position. The thought of eight-hundred-year-old houses perched on the sides of mountains and rivers whose names you've only seen in the Sunday *Times* crossword puzzles—all of that is exciting. But I'm not going without him. He's read so much. I couldn't possibly go without him. You see, I've never been abroad—unless you count Baltimore, Maryland.

CARL: Good morning, boys and girls. It's Monday morning, and it's time for "Reading Hour with Uncle Carl" once again, here at the North Branch of the San Francisco Public Library. This is going to be a special reading hour. It's my very last reading hour with you. Friday will be my very last day with the San Francisco Public as children's librarian. Why? Do any of you know what a pink slip is?

(Carl holds up a rectangle of pink.)

It means I'm going on a paid leave of absence for two weeks. Shelley Bizio, the branch supervisor, has given me my very own pink slip. I got a pink slip because I wear this—

(He points to a pink triangle on his lapel.)

A pink triangle. Now, I want you all to take the pink construction paper in front of you, and take your scissors, and cut out pink triangles. There's tape at every table, so you can wear them too! Make some for Mom and Dad, and your brothers and sisters. Very good. Very good, Fabio. Oh, that's a beautiful pink triangle, Tse Heng. Now before we read our last story together, I thought we might have a sing-along. Your parents can join in, if they'd like to. Oh, don't be shy. Let's do "Here We Go Round the Mulberry Bush." Remember that one?

(He begins to sing. He also demonstrates.)

"Here we go round the mulberry bush, the mulberry bush, the mulberry bush:/ Here we go round the mulberry bush, so early in the morning." "This is the way we pick our nose, pick our nose, pick our nose:/ This is the way we pick our nose, so early in the morning." Third verse!

(He makes a rude gesture with his middle finger.)

"This is the way we go on strike, go on strike, go on strike:/ this is the way we go on strike, so early in the—" What, Mrs. Bizio? I may leave immediately? I do not have to wait until Friday to collect unemployment? Why, thank you, Mrs. Bizio. Well, boys and girls, Mrs. Bizio will take over now. Bear with her, she's personality-impaired. I want you to be very good and remember me. I'm leaving for an immediate vacation with my sister on the east coast, and I'll think of you as I travel. Remember to wear those pink triangles.

(To his supervisor.)

I'm going. I'm going. You don't have to be rude. They enjoyed it. We'll take it up with the union.

(Shouting.)

In a language you might understand, up-pay ours-yay!

ANNA: It's the language that terrifies me.

CARL: Lesson Number One: Subject position. I. Je. Ich. Ik. I'm sorry. Je regrette. Es tut mir leid.

ANNA: But we decided to go when the doctor gave us his verdict.

DOCTOR: I'm sorry.

CARL: I'm sorry.

DOCTOR: There's nothing we can do.

ANNA: But what?

CARL: How long?

ANNA: Explain it to me. Very slowly. So I can understand. Excuse me, could you tell me again?

DOCTOR: There are exudative and proliferative inflammatory alterations of the endocardium, consisting of necrotic debris, fibrinoid material, and disintegrating fibroblastic cells.

CARL: Oh, sweet Jesus.

DOCTOR: It may be acute or subacute, caused by various bacteria: streptococci, staphylococci, enterococci, gonococci, gram negative bacilli, etc. It may be due to other micro-organisms, of course, but there is a high mortality rate with or without treatment. And there is usually rapid destruction and metastases.

CARL: Anna—

ANNA: I'm right here, darling. Right here.

CARL: Could you explain it very slowly?

DOCTOR: Also known as Loffler's syndrome, i.e., eosinophilia, resulting in fibroblastic thickening, persistent tachycardia, hepatomegaly, splenomegaly, serious effusions into the pleural cavity with edema. It may be Brugia malayi or Wuchereria bancofti—also known as Weingarten's syndrome. Often seen with effusions, either exudate or transudate.

ANNA: Carl—

CARL: I'm here, darling. Right here.

ANNA: It's the language that terrifies me.

SCENE 2

CARL: Medical Straight Talk: Part One.

ANNA: So you're telling me that you really don't know?

DOCTOR: I'm afraid that medical science has only a small foothold in this area. But of course, it would be of great benefit to our knowledge if you would consent to observation here at Johns Hopkins—

CARL: Why? Running out of laboratory rats?!

ANNA: Oh, no. I'm sorry. I can't do that. Can you tell me at least how it was . . . contracted?

DOCTOR: Well—we're not sure, yet. It's only a theory at this stage, but one that seems in great favor at the World Health Organization. We think it comes from the old cultus ornatus—

CARL: Toilet seats?

ANNA: Toilet seats! My God. Mother was right. She always said—

CARL: And never, ever, in any circumstances, in bus stations—

ANNA: Toilet seats? Cut down in the prime of youth by a toilet seat?

DOCTOR: Anna—I may call you Anna?—you teach school, I believe?

ANNA: Yes, first grade. What does that have—

DOCTOR: Ah, yes. We're beginning to see a lot of this in elementary schools. Anna—I may call you Anna? With assurances of complete confidentiality—we need to ask you very specific questions about the body, body fluids, and body functions. As mature adults, as scientists and educators. To speak frankly— when you needed to relieve yourself—where did you make wa-wa?

ANNA: There's a faculty room. But why—how—?

DOCTOR: You never, ever used the johnny in your classroom?

ANNA: Well, maybe once or twice. There's no lock, and Robbie Matthews always tries to barge in. Sometimes I just can't get the time to—surely you're not suggesting that—

DOCTOR: You did use the facilities in your classroom?

(The Doctor makes notes from this.)

CARL: Is that a crime? When you've got to go, you've got to—

ANNA: I can't believe that my students would transmit something like this—

DOCTOR: You have no idea. Five-year-olds can be deadly. It seems to be an affliction, so far, of single schoolteachers. Schoolteachers with children of their own develop an immunity to ATD . . . Acquired Toilet Disease.

ANNA: I see. Why hasn't anybody heard of this disease?

DOCTOR: Well, first of all, the Center for Disease Control doesn't wish to inspire an all-out panic in communities. Secondly, we think education on this topic is the responsibility of the NEA, not the government. And if word of this pestilence gets out inappropriately, the PTA is going to be all over the school system demanding mandatory testing of every toilet seat in every lavatory. It's kindling for a political disaster.

ANNA:

(Taking the Doctor aside.)

I want to ask you something confidentially. Something that my brother doesn't need to hear. What's the danger of transmission?

DOCTOR: There's really no danger to anyone in the immediate family. You must use precautions.

ANNA: Because what I want to know is . . . can you transmit this thing by . . . by doing—what exactly do you mean by precautions?

DOCTOR: Well, I guess you should do what your mother always told you. You know, wash your hands before and after going to the bathroom. And never lick paper money or coins in any currency.

ANNA: So there's no danger to anyone by . . . what I mean, Doctor, is that I can't infect anyone by—

DOCTOR: Just use precautions.

ANNA: Because, in whatever time this schoolteacher has left, I intend to fuck my brains out.

DOCTOR: Which means, in whatever time is left, she can fuck her brains out.

SCENE 3

Carl and the Doctor.

CARL:

(Agitated.)

I'll tell you what. If Sandra Day O'Connor sat on just one infected potty, the media would be clamoring to do articles on ATD. If just one grandchild of George Bush caught this thing during toilet training, that would be the last we'd hear about the space program. Why isn't someone doing something?! I'm sorry. I know you're one of the converted. You're doing . . . well, everything you can. I'd like to ask you something in confidence, something my sister doesn't need to hear. Is there any hope at all?

DOCTOR: Well, I suppose there's . . . always hope.

CARL: Any experimental drugs? Treatments?

DOCTOR: Well, they're trying all sorts of things abroad. Our hands are tied here by NIH and the FDA, you understand. There is a long-shot avenue to explore, nothing, you understand, that I personally endorse, but there is an eighty-year-old urologist overseas who's been working in this field for some time—

CARL: We'll try anything.

DOCTOR: His name is Dr. Todesrocheln. He's somewhat unorthodox, outside the medical community in Vienna. It's gonna cost you. Mind you, this is not an endorsement.

ANNA: You hear the doctor through a long-distance corridor. Your ears are functioning, but the mind is numb. You try to listen as you swim towards his sentences in the flourescent light in his office. But you don't believe it at first. This is how I'd like to die: with dignity. No body secretions—like Merle Oberon in *Wuthering Heights*. With a somewhat becoming flush, and a transcendental gaze. Luminous eyes piercing the veil of mortal existence. The windows are open to the fresh breeze blowing off the moors. Oh. And violins in the background would be nice, too.

> (*Music: violins playing Strauss swell in the background.*)

SCENE 4

The Phone Call.

THE THIRD MAN: Lesson Number Two: Basic dialogue. The phone call. Hello. I would like to speak to Mr. Lime, please.

CARL: Entschuldigen Sie, bitte—operator? Operator? Hello? Guten Tag? Kann ich bitte mit Herr Lime sprechen? Harry? Harry? Wie geht es dir?! Listen, I . . . can you hear . . . no, I'm in Baltimore . . . yeah, not since Hopkins . . . no, there's—well, there is something up. No, dear boy, that hasn't been up in a long time—no, seriously—it's my sister. ATD.

THE THIRD MAN: ATD? Jesus, that's tough, old man. You've got to watch where you sit these days. She's a sweet kid. Yeah. Yeah. Wait a second.

> (*Offstage.*)

Inge? Inge, baby? Ein Bier, bitte, baby. Ja. Ja. You too, baby.

> (*Pause.*)

Okay. Dr. Todesrocheln? Yeah, you might say I know him. But don't tell anybody I said that. There's also a new drug they've got over here. Black market. I might be able to help you. I said might. But it's gonna cost you.

> (*Cautiously, ominously.*)

Do you still have the rabbit?

CARL: I'll bring the rabbit.

THE THIRD MAN: Good. A friend of mine will be in touch. And listen, old man . . . if anybody asks you, you don't know me. I'll see you in a month. You know where to find me.

THE THIRD MAN and CARL:

> (Simultaneously.)

> Click.

SCENE 5

THE THIRD MAN: Lesson Number Three: Pronouns and the possessive case. I, you, he, she and it. Me, you, their. Yours, mine, and ours.

VOICE OF ANNA: There's nothing I can do. There's nothing you can do. There's nothing he, she or it can do. There's nothing we can do. There's nothing they can do.

ANNA: So what are we going to do?

CARL: Start packing, sister dear.

ANNA: Europe? You mean it?

CARL: We'll mosey about France and Germany, and then work our way down to Vienna.

ANNA: What about your job?

CARL: It's only a job.

ANNA: It's a very important job! Head of the entire San Francisco Public—

CARL: They'll hold my job for me. I'm due for a leave.

ANNA: Oh, honey. Can we afford this?

CARL: It's only money.

ANNA: It's your money.

CARL: It's our money.

SCENE 6

THE THIRD MAN: Lesson Four: Present tense of faire. What are we going to do? Qu'est-ce qu'on va faire.

ANNA: So what are we going to do?

CARL: We'll see this doctor in Vienna.

ANNA: Dr. Todesrocheln?

CARL: We have to try.

ANNA: A urologist?

CARL: He's working on a new drug.

ANNA: A European urologist?

CARL: What options do we have?

ANNA: Wait a minute. What are his credentials? Who is this guy?

CARL: He was trained at the Allgemeines Krankenhaus during the Empire.

ANNA: Yeah? Just what was he doing from, say, 1938 to 1945? Research?

CARL: It's best not to ask too many questions. There are people who swear by his work.

ANNA: What's his specialty?

CARL: Well, actually, he's a practitioner of uriposia.

ANNA: He writes poems about urine?

CARL: No. He drinks it.

ANNA: I'm not going.

CARL: Let's put off judgement until we arrange a consultation . . . my god, you're so messy. Look at how neat my suitcase is in comparison. You'll never find a thing in there.

ANNA: I refuse to drink my own piss for medical science.

> *(Carl grabs a stuffed rabbit and thrusts it in Anna's suitcase.)*

What are you doing?

CARL: We can't leave bunny behind.

ANNA: What is a grown man like you doing with a stuffed rabbit?

CARL: I can't sleep without bunny.

ANNA: I didn't know you slept with . . . stuffed animals.

CARL: There's a lot you don't know about me.

SCENE 7

THE THIRD MAN: Lesson Five: Basic dialogue. At the airport. We are going to Paris. What time does our flight leave? Nous allons à Paris. A quelle heure depart notre vol?

> *(The Third Man becomes an Airport Security Guard.)*

AIRPORT SECURITY GUARD: Okay. Next. Please remove your keys and all other metallic items. Place all belongings on the belt. Next.

> *(Carl and Anna carry heavy luggage. Carl halts.)*

CARL: Wait. I need your suitcase.

> *(He opens Anna's luggage and begins to rummage around.)*

ANNA: Hey!

CARL: It was a mess to begin with. Ah—

> *(He retrieves the stuffed rabbit.)*

There.

ANNA: Are you having an anxiety attack?

CARL: You hold it.

> *(He and Anna stamp, sit and stand on the baggage. Carl manages to relock the bag.)*

ANNA: What is wrong with you?

CARL: X-rays are bad for bunny.

AIRPORT SECURITY GUARD: Next. Please remove all metallic objects. Keys. Eyeglasses. Gold Fillings.

CARL: Go on. You first.

AIRPORT SECURITY GUARD: Metallic objects?

> *(Anna passes through, holding the stuffed rabbit. Carl sighs, relieved. Carl passes through. The Airport Security Guard stops him.)*

One moment, please.

(The Airport Security Guard almost strip searches him. He uses a metallic wand which makes loud, clicking noises. Finally, he nods. He hands Anna and Carl their bags, still suspiciously looking at Carl.)

ANNA: Okay, bunny—Paris, here we come!

SCENE 8

THE THIRD MAN: At the hotel.

(Simultaneously with Carl's next lines.)

Lesson Six. Direct pronouns. I am tired. And my sister looks at herself in the mirror.

CARL: Sixieme Leçon: Pronoms—complements directs. Je suis fatigué. Et ma soeur—elle se regarde dans la glace.

(Carl climbs into a double bed with the stuffed rabbit. Anna stares into a mirror. The Third man, apart, stands in their bedroom.)

THE THIRD MAN: The first separation—your first sense of loss. You were five—your brother was seven. Your parents would not let you sleep in the same bed anymore. They removed you to your own bedroom. You were too old, they said. But every now and then, when they turned off the lights and went downstairs—when the dark scared you, you would rise and go to him. And he would let you nestle under his arm, under the covers, where you would fall to sleep, breathing in the scent of your own breath and his seven-year-old body.

CARL: Come to bed, sweetie. Bunny and I are waiting. We're going to be jet-lagged for a while.

ANNA: It doesn't show yet.

(Anna continues to stare in the mirror.)

CARL: No one can tell. Let's get some sleep, honey.
ANNA: I don't want anyone to know.
CARL: It's not a crime. It's an illness.
ANNA: I don't want anybody to know.
CARL: It's your decision. Just don't tell anyone . . . what . . . you do for a living.

(Anna joins Carl in the bed. He holds her hand.)

ANNA: Well, there's one good thing about traveling in Europe . . . and about dying.
CARL: What's that?
ANNA: I get to sleep with you again.

SCENE 9

CARL: Medical Straight Talk: Part Two.

(The Third Man becomes a Public Health Official.)

PUBLIC HEALTH OFFICIAL: Here at the Department of Health and Human Services we are announcing Operation Squat. There is no known cure for ATD right now, and we are acknowledging the urgency of this dread disease by recognizing it as our 82nd national health priority. Right now ATD is the fourth major cause of death of single schoolteachers, ages 24 to 40 . . . behind school buses, lockjaw and playground accidents. The best policy, until a cure can be found, is of education and prevention.

> (Anna and Carl hold up posters of a toilet seat in a circle with a red diagonal slash.)

If you are in the high risk category—single elementary school teachers, classroom aides, custodians and playground drug pushers—follow these simple guides.

> (Anna and Carl hold up copies of the educational pamphlets.)

Do: Use the facilities in your own home before departing for school.
Do: Use the facilities in your own home as soon as you return from school.
Do: Hold it.
Don't: Eat meals in public restrooms.
Don't: Flush lavatory equipment and then suck your digits. If absolutely necessary to relieve yourself at work, please remember the Department of Health and Human Services ATD slogan: Do squat, don't sit.

SCENE 10

Music: accordion playing a song like "La Vie en Rose." Anna and Carl stroll.

CARL: Of course, the Left Bank has always been a haven for outcasts, foreigners and students, since the time that Abélard fled the Ile de La Cité to found the university here—
ANNA: Oh, look. Is that the Eiffel Tower? It looks so . . . phallic.
CARL: And it continued to serve as a haven for the avant-garde of the Twenties, the American expatriate community that could no longer afford Montparnesse—
ANNA: My god, they really do smoke Gauloise here.
CARL: And, of course, the Dada and Surrealists who set up camp here after World War I and their return from Switzerland—

> (The Third Man, in a trench coat and red beret, crosses the stage.)

ANNA: Are we being followed?
CARL: Is your medication making you paranoid?

> (Pause.)

Now, over here is the famous spot where Gertrude supposedly said to her brother Leo—

> (The Third Man follows them.)

ANNA: I know. "God is the answer. What is the question?"—I'm not imagining it. That man has been trailing us from the Boulevard St. Michel.

CARL: Are you getting hungry?

ANNA: I'm getting tired.

CARL: Wait. Let's just whip around the corner to the Cafe St. Michel where Hemingway, after an all-night bout, threw up his shrimp heads all over Scott's new suede shoes—which really was a moveable feast.

(*The Third Man is holding an identical stuffed rabbit and looks at them.*)

ANNA: Carl! Carl! Look! That man over there!

CARL: So? They have stuffed rabbits over here, too. Let's go.

ANNA: Why is he following us? He's got the same—

CARL: It's your imagination. How about a little déjeuner?

(*Anna and Carl walk to a small table and chairs.*)

SCENE 11

GARÇON:

(*With a thick Peter Sellers French.*)

It was a simple bistro affair by French standards. He had le veau Prince Orloff, she le boeuf à la mode—a simple dish of haricots verts, and a médoc to accompany it all. He barely touched his meal. She mopped the sauces with the bread. As their meal progressed, Anna thought of the lunches she packed back home. For the past ten years, hunched over in the faculty room at McCormick Elementary, this is what Anna ate: on Mondays, pressed chipped chicken sandwiches with mayonnaise on white; on Tuesdays, soggy tuna sandwiches; on Wednesdays, Velveeta cheese and baloney; on Thursdays, drier pressed chicken on the now stale white bread; on Fridays, Velveeta and tuna. She always had a small wax envelope of carrot sticks or celery, and a can of Diet Pepsi. Anna, as she ate in the bistro, wept. What could she know of love?

CARL: Why are you weeping?

ANNA: It's just so wonderful.

CARL: You're a goose.

ANNA: I've wasted over thirty years on convenience foods.

(*The Garçon approaches the table.*)

GARÇON: Is everything all right?

ANNA: Oh god. Yes—yes—it's wonderful.

CARL: My sister would like to see the dessert tray.

(*Anna breaks out in tears again. The Garçon shrugs and exits. He reappears two seconds later as The Third Man, this time with a trench coat and blue beret. He sits at an adjacent table and stares in their direction.*)

ANNA: Who is that man? Do you know him?

CARL:

(*Carl hastily looks at The Third Man.*)

No, I've never seen him before.

(The Third Man brings the stuffed rabbit out of his trench coat.)

ANNA: He's flashing his rabbit at you.

CARL:

   (Carl rises.)

   Excuse me. I think I'll go to les toilettes.

ANNA: Carl! Be careful! Don't sit!

   (Carl exits. The Third Man waits a few seconds, looks at Anna, and then follows Carl without expression.)

   What is it they do with those rabbits?

   (A split second later, the Garçon reenters with the dessert tray. Anna ogles him.)

GARÇON: O-kay. We have la crème plombière pralinée, un bavarois à l'orange, et ici we have une Charlotte Malakoff aux Framboises. Our specialité is le gâteau de crêpes à la Normande. What would mademoiselle like?

   (Anna has obviously not been looking at the dessert tray.)

ANNA:

   (Sighing.)

   Ah, yes.

GARÇON: Vous êtes Américaîne? This is your first trip to Paris?

   (The Garçon smiles.)

ANNA: Yes.

GARÇON: And you do not speak at all French?

ANNA: No.

   (The Garçon smiles.)

GARÇON:

   (Suggestively.)

   Bon. Would you like la specialité de la maison?

SCENE 12

CARL: Exercise: La Carte. La specialité de la maison. Back at the hotel, Anna sampled the Garçon's specialité de la maison while her brother browsed the Louvre.

   (Anna and the Garçon are shapes beneath the covers of the bed. Carl clutches his stuffed rabbit.)

   Jean Baptiste Camille Corot lived from 1796 to 1875. Although he began his career by studying in the classical tradition, his later paintings reveal the influence of the Italian style.

ANNA:

(Muffled.)

Ah! Yes!

GARÇON:

(Also muffled.)

Ah! Oui!

CARL: He traveled extensively around the world, and in the salon of 1827 his privately lauded techniques were displayed in public.

ANNA: Yes—oh, yes, yes!

GARÇON: Mais oui!

CARL: Before the Academy had accepted realism, Corot's progressive paintings, his clear sighted observations of nature, revealed a fresh almost spritely quality of light, tone and composition.

ANNA: Yes—that's right—faster—

GARÇON: Plus vite?

ANNA: Faster—

GARÇON: Encore! Plus vite!

ANNA: Wait!

GARÇON: Attends?

CARL: It was his simplicity, and his awareness of color that brought a fresh wind into the staid academy—

GARÇON: Maintenant?

ANNA: Lower—faster—lower—

GARCON: Plus bas—plus vite—plus bas—

CARL: He was particularly remembered and beloved for his championing the cause of younger artists with more experimental techniques, bringing the generosity of his advancing reputation to their careers.

ANNA: Yes—I—I—I—I—!

GARÇON: Je—je! Je!! Je!

(Pause.)

CARL: In art, as in life, some things need no translation.

GARÇON: Gauloise?

CARL: For those of you who are interested, in the next room are some stunning works by Delacroix.

SCENE 13

Back at the Hotel.

CARL: Lesson Seven: Basic vocabulary. Parts of the body.

(Carl, slightly out of the next scene, watches them. Anna sits up in bed. The Garçon is asleep beneath the sheet.)

ANNA: I did read one book once in French. *Le Petit Prince.* Lying here, watching him sleep, I look at his breast and remember the Rose with its single, pathetic thorn for protection. And here—his puckered red nipple, lying poor and vulnerable on top of his blustering breast plate. It's really so sweet about men.

(She kisses the Garçon's breast. The Garçon stirs.)

GARÇON: Encore?

ANNA: What is the word—in French—for this?

(She fingers his breast.)

GARÇON: For un homme—le sein. For une femme—la mamelle.

ANNA: Le sein?

GARÇON: Oui. Le sein.

ANNA: And this?

(She kisses his neck.)

GARÇON: Le Cou.

ANNA: Et ici?

GARÇON: Bon. Décolleté—

(Anna begins to touch him under the sheet.)

ANNA: And this?

GARÇON:

(The Garçon laughs.)

S'il vous plâit . . . I am tickling there. Ah. Couille.

ANNA: Culle?

GARÇON: Non. Couille. Le cul is something much different. Ici c'est le cul.

ANNA: Oh, yes. That's very different.

GARÇON:

(Taking her hand under the sheet.)

We sometimes call these also Le Quatrième État. The Fourth Estate.

ANNA: Really? Because they enjoy being "scooped"?

GARÇON: Bien sûr.

ANNA: And this?

GARÇON:

(With pride.)

Ah. Ma Tour Eiffel. I call it aussi my Charles DeGalle.

ANNA: Wow.

GARÇON: My grandfather called his Napoleon.

ANNA: I see. I guess it runs in your family.

GARÇON:

(Modestly.)

Oui. Grand-mère—qu'est-ce que c'est le mot en anglais? Her con—here—ici—do you know what I am meaning?

ANNA: You're making yourself completely clear—

GARÇON: We called hers the Waterloo de mon grand-père—

(Anna digs under the sheet more.)

ANNA: And this?

GARÇON:

> *(The Garçon is scandalized.)*

> Non. There is no word en français. Pas du tout.

ANNA: For this? There must be—

GARÇON: Non! Only the Germans have a word for that.

> *(Carl enters and casually converses with Anna. Startled, the Garçon covers himself with the sheet.)*

CARL: Hello, darling. Are you feeling better?

> *(Carl walks to the chair beside the bed and removes the Garçon's clothing.)*

ANNA: Yes, much. I needed to lie down. How was the Louvre?

> *(The Garçon carefully rises from the bed and takes his clothing from Carl, who is holding them out. He creeps cautiously stage left and begins to pull on his clothes.)*

CARL: Oh, Anna. I'm so sorry you missed it. The paintings of David were amazing. The way his paintbrush embraced the body—it was just incredible to stand there and see them in the flesh.

ANNA: Ah yes—in the flesh.

> *(She smiles at the confused Garçon.)*

CARL: Well, sweetie. It's been a thoroughly rewarding day for both of us. I'm for turning in. How about you?

> *(The Garçon is now fully dressed.)*

ANNA: Yes, I'm tired. Here—I've warmed the bed for you.

> *(She throws back the sheet.)*

CARL: Garçon—l'addition!

ANNA:

> *(To the Garçon.)*

> Merci beaucoup.

> *(Anna blows him a kiss. The Garçon takes a few steps out of the scene as Carl climbs into bed.)*

SCENE 14

THE THIRD MAN: Anna has a difficult time sleeping. She is afflicted with night thoughts. According to Elizabeth Kübler-Ross, there are six stages the terminal patient travels in the course of her illness. The first stage: Denial and Isolation.

(The Third Man stays in the hotel room and watches Carl and Anna in the bed. They are sleeping, when Anna sits upright.)

ANNA: I feel so alone. The ceiling is pressing down on me. I can't believe I am dying. Only at night. Only at night. In the morning, when I open my eyes, I feel absolutely well—without a body. And then the thought comes crashing in my mind. This is the last spring I may see. This is the last summer. It can't be. There must be a mistake. They mixed the specimens up in the hospital. Some poor person is walking around, dying, with the false confidence of my prognosis, thinking themselves well. It's a clerical error. Carl! I can't sleep. Do you think they made a mistake?

CARL: Come back to sleep—

(Carl pulls Anna down on the bed to him, and strokes her brow. They change positions on the bed.)

THE THIRD MAN: The second stage: Anger.

ANNA:

(Anna sits bolt upright in bed, angry.)

How could this happen to me! I did my lesson plans faithfully for the past ten years! I've taught in classrooms without walls—kept up on new audio-visual aids—I read Summerhill! And I believed it! When the principal assigned me the job of the talent show—and nobody wants to do the talent show—I pleaded for cafeteria duty, bus duty—but no, I got stuck with the talent show. And those kids put on the best darn show that school has ever seen! Which one of them did this to me? Emily Baker? For slugging Johnnie MacIntosh? Johnnie MacIntosh? Because I sent him home for exposing himself to Susy Higgins? Susy Higgins? Because I called her out on her nosepicking? Or those Nader twins? I've spent the best years of my life giving to those kids—it's not—

CARL: Calm down, sweetie. You're angry. It's only natural to be angry. Elizabeth Kübler-Ross says that—

ANNA: What does she know about what it feels like to die?! Elizabeth Kübler-Ross can sit on my face!

(Carl and Anna change positions on the bed.)

THE THIRD MAN: The third stage: Bargaining.

ANNA: Do you think if I let Elizabeth Kübler-Ross sit on my face I'll get well?

(Carl and Anna change positions on the bed.)

THE THIRD MAN: The fourth stage: Depression.

(Carl sits on the side of the bed beside Anna.)

CARL: Anna—honey—come on, wake up.

ANNA: Leave me alone.

CARL: Come on, sweetie . . . you've been sleeping all day now, and you slept all yesterday. Do you want to sleep away our last day in France?

ANNA: Why bother?

CARL: You've got to eat something. You've got to fight this. For me.

ANNA: Leave me alone.

(Carl lies down beside Anna. They change positions.)

THE THIRD MAN: The fifth stage: Acceptance.

(Anna and Carl are lying in bed, awake. They hold hands.)

ANNA: When I'm gone, I want you to find someone.

CARL: Let's not talk about me.

ANNA: No, I want to. It's important to me to know that you'll be happy and taken care of after . . . when I'm gone.

CARL: Please.

ANNA: I've got to talk about it. We've shared everything else. I want you to know how it feels . . . what I'm thinking . . . when I hold your hand, and I kiss it . . . I try to memorize what it looks like, your hand . . . I wonder if there's any memory in the grave?

THE THIRD MAN: And then there's the sixth stage: Hope.

(Anna and Carl rise from the bed.)

CARL: How are you feeling?

ANNA: I feel good today.

CARL: Do you feel like traveling?

ANNA: Yes. It would be nice to see Amsterdam. Together. We might as well see as much as we can while I'm well—

CARL: That's right, sweetie. And maybe you can eat something—

ANNA: I'm hungry. That's a good sign, don't you think?

CARL: That's a wonderful sign. You'll see. You'll feel better when you eat.

ANNA: Maybe the doctor in Vienna can help.

CARL: That's right.

ANNA: What's drinking a little piss? It can't hurt you.

CARL: Right. Who knows? We've got to try.

ANNA: I'll think of it as . . . European lager.

CARL: Golden Heidelberg.

> *(Carl and Anna hum/sing a song such as the drinking song from* The Student Prince.*)*

SCENE 15

THE THIRD MAN: And as Anna and Carl took the train into Holland, the seductive swaying of the TEE-train aroused another sensation. Unbeknownst to Elizabeth Kübler-Ross, there is a seventh stage for the dying. There is a growing urge to fight the sickness of the body with the health of the body. The seventh stage: Lust.

> *(Anna and Carl are seated in a train compartment. Carl holds the stuffed rabbit out to Anna.)*

ANNA: Why?

CARL: Just take it. Hold it for me. Just through customs.

ANNA: Only if you tell me why.

CARL: Don't play games right now. Or we'll be in deep, deep do-do.

>*(Anna reluctantly takes the stuffed rabbit and holds it.)*

ANNA: You're scaring me.

CARL: I'm sorry, sweetie. You're the only one I can trust to hold my rabbit. Trust me. It's important.

ANNA: Then why won't you tell me—?

CARL: There are some some things you're better off not knowing.

ANNA: Are you smuggling drugs? Jewels?

CARL:

>*(Whispers.)*

>It's beyond measure. It's invaluable to me. That's all I'll say.

>*(In a louder tone.)*

>Just act normal now.

CUSTOMS OFFICIAL: Uw paspoort, alstublieft.

>*(Anna and Carl give him their passports. Carl is nervous. Anna smiles at the Customs Official a bit laciviously.)*

>Have you anything to declare?

ANNA:

>*(Whispering.)*

>Yes—captain, I'm smuggling contraband. I demand to be searched. In private.

CUSTOMS OFFICIAL:

>*(The Customs Official blushes.)*

>Excuse me?

ANNA: Yes. I said—waar is het damestoilet?

CUSTOMS OFFICIAL: Oh . . . I thought . . .

>*(The Customs Official giggles.)*

ANNA: Yes?

CUSTOMS OFFICIAL: First left.

>*(The Customs Official returns their passports.)*

>Have a very pleasant stay.

>*(Anna waves bunny's arm goodbye. The Customs Official looks at her, blushes again, and retreats. Carl relaxes.)*

CARL: You're good at this. Very good.

ANNA: When in Holland, do like the Dutch . . . Mata Hari was Dutch, you know.

SCENE 16

CARL: Questions sur le Dialogue. Est-ce que les hommes Hollandais sont comme les Français? Are Dutch men like the French?

(Anna and The Little Dutch Boy at Age 50. He wears traditional wooden shoes, trousers and vest. His Buster Brown haircut and hat make him look dissipated.)

THE LITTLE DUTCH BOY AT AGE 50: It was kermis-time, the festival in my village. And I had too much bier with my school friends, Piet and Jan. Ja. Soo—Piet thought we should go to the outer dyke with cans of spray paint, after the kermis. So we went.

Here in Noord Brabant there are three walls of defenses against the cruelty of the North Sea. The first dyke is called the Waker—the Watcher; the second dyke is de Slaper—the Sleeper; and the last dyke, which had never before been tested, is known as the Dromer—the Dreamer.

And when we got to the Dreamer, Piet said to me: "Willem, you do it." Meaning I was to write on the walls of the Dreamer. This is why I was always in trouble in school—Piet and Jan would say, "Willem, you do it," and whatever it was—I would do it.

Soo—I took up a can of the paint and in very big letters, I wrote in Dutch that our schoolmaster, Mijnheer Van Doorn, was a gas-passer. Everyone could read the letters from far away. And just as I was finishing this, and Piet and Jan were laughing behind me, I looked—I was on my knees, pressed up against the dyke—and I could see that the wall of the Dreamer was cracking its surface, very fine little lines, like a goose egg when it breaks from within.

And I yelled to my friends—Look! And they came a bit closer, and as we looked, right above my head, a little hole began to peck its way through the clay. And there was just a small trickle of water. And Jan said: "Willem, put your thumb in that hole." And by that time, the hole in the dyke was just big enough to put my thumb in. "Why?" I asked of Jan. "Just do it," he said. And so I did.

And once I put my thumb in, I could not get it out. Suddenly we could hear the waves crashing as The Sleeper began to collapse. Only the Dreamer remained to hold off the savage water. "Help me!" I yelled to Jan and Piet—but they ran away. "Vlug!" I cried—but no one could hear me. And I stayed there, crouching, with my thumb stuck into the clay. And I thought what if the Dreamer should give in, too. How the waves would bear my body like a messenger to the village. How no one would survive the flood. Only the church steeple would remain to mark the spot where we had lived. How young we were to die.

(Pause.)

Have you ever imagined what it would be like to be face to face with death?

ANNA: Yes—yes I have.

THE LITTLE DUTCH BOY AT AGE 50: And have you ever prayed for deliverance against all hope?

ANNA: I—no. I haven't been able to get to that stage. Yet.

THE LITTLE DUTCH BOY AT AGE 50: But the Dreamer held. And finally there came wagons with men from the village, holding lanterns and sand and straw. And they found me there, strung up by my thumb, beside the big black letters: Mijnheer Van Doorn is een gas-passer. And they freed me and said I was a hero, and I became the boy who held back the sea with his thumb.

ANNA: Golly. You were very brave.

THE LITTLE DUTCH BOY AT AGE 50: I was stupid. Wrong place, wrong time.

ANNA: How long ago did this happen?

THE LITTLE DUTCH BOY AT AGE 50:

(Sadly.)

Let us just say it happened a long time ago.

ANNA: You've faced death. I wish my brother were here to meet you.

THE LITTLE DUTCH BOY AT AGE 50: Where is he? Wo ist dein bruder?

ANNA: Oh, he stayed in Amsterdam to see the Rijksmuseum and the Van Gogh Museum.

THE LITTLE DUTCH BOY AT AGE 50: And you did not go? You should see them, they are really fantastic.

ANNA: Why? What's the use? I won't remember them, I'll have no memory.

THE LITTLE DUTCH BOY AT AGE 50: So you are an American?

ANNA: Yes.

THE LITTLE DUTCH BOY AT AGE 50: So do you want to sleep with me? All the women toeristen want to sleep with the little Dutch boy who put his thumb in the dyke.

ANNA: Do you mind so much?

THE LITTLE DUTCH BOY AT AGE 50: Nee. It's a way to make a living, is it niet?

(Shrugs.)

ANNA:

(Quietly.)

Let's go then.

SCENE 17

CARL: Répétez. En Français. Where is my brother going? Où va mon frère? Bien.

ANNA: I had just returned from my day trip and left the Centraal Station. The sun sparkled on the waters of the canal, and I decided to walk back to the hotel. Just then I saw my brother.

(Carl enters in a trench coat, sunglasses, holding the stuffed rabbit.)

I tried to catch up with Carl, dodging bicycles and pedestrians. And then, crossing the Amstel on the Magere Brug, he appeared.

(The Third Man enters, in a trench coat, sunglasses, and with black gloves, holding a stuffed rabbit.)

I trailed them from a discrete distance.

(The Third Man and Carl walk rapidly, not glancing at each other. Carl stops; The Third Man stops a few paces behind. Carl walks; The Third Man walks. Carl

stops; The Third Man stops. Finally, they face each other and meet. Quickly, looking surreptitiously around, Carl and The Third Man stroke each other's stuffed rabbits. They quickly part and walk off in opposite directions, but not before the Third Man attempts to grab Carl's rabbit and run. Anna rushes to C., looking in both directions.)

I tried to follow the man in the trench coat, and crossed behind him over the Amstel, but I lost sight of him in the crowd of men wearing trench coats and sunglasses. I want some answers from my brother. Whatever trouble he's in, he has to share it with me. I want some answers back at the hotel. He's going to talk.

SCENE 18

CARL: Questions sur le dialogue. You must learn. Sie müssen lernen.

(Anna enters the empty hotel room. On the bed, propped up on pillows, lies a stuffed rabbit.)

ANNA: Carl? Carl? Are you back? Carl?

(Anna stops and looks at the stuffed rabbit.)

CARL: You were not permitted to play with dolls; dolls are for girls. You played with your sister's dolls until your parents found out. They gave you a stuffed animal—a thin line was drawn. Rabbits were an acceptable surrogate for little boys. You named him Jo-Jo. You could not sleep without him. Jo-Jo traveled with you to the seashore, to the hotel in New York City when you were seven, to your first summer camp. He did not have the flaxen plastic hair of your sister's Betsey-Wetsy, but he had long, furry ears, soft white on one side, pink satin inside. He let you stroke them. He never betrayed you. He taught you to trust in contact. You will love him always.

(From the side.)

ANNA: My brother left you behind, did he? Alone at last. Okay, bunny, now you're going to talk. I want some answers. What have you got that's so important?

(Anna moves towards the stuffed rabbit.)
(Just as Anna reaches for the stuffed rabbit, The Third Man—in trench coat, sunglasses and black gloves—steps out into the room.)

THE THIRD MAN: I wouldn't do that, if I were you.

(Threateningly.)
(Anna screams in surprise.)

Now listen. Where is your brother? I have a message for him. Tell him he's running out of time. Do you understand?

(Anna, scared, nods.)

Good. He'd better not try to dupe us. We're willing to arrange a swap—his sister for the rabbit. Tell him we're waiting for him in Vienna. And tell him he'd better bring the rabbit to the other side.

(The Third Man disappears. Anna, shaken, sits on the bed and holds the stuffed rabbit. She strokes it for comfort. Carl enters, in a frenzy. He carries his stuffed rabbit. Anna stares as Carl tosses the decoy rabbit away.)

CARL: Don't ask me any questions. I can't tell you what's happening. Are you able to travel? Good. We have to leave Amsterdam tonight. There's a train in an hour. We'll go to Germany. Are you packed?

SCENE 19

ANNA and THE THIRD MAN:

(Simultaneously.)

Wann fahrt der nächste Zug nach Hamburg?

(German band music swells as Anna and Carl sit in their railroad compartment, side by side. Anna, pale, holds the stuffed rabbit in her lap.)

CARL: Ah, Saxony, Bavaria, the Black Forest, the Rhineland . . . I love them all. I think perhaps now would be a good time to show the slides.

ANNA: I'm so sorry. I hate it when people do this to me.

CARL: Nonsense. People like to see slides of other people's trips. These are in no particular order. We'll only show a few, just to give a taste of the German countryside.

ANNA: Carl took over two hour's worth of slides.

CARL: If you'll just dim the lights, please.

(The Third Man wheels in the projector and operates it throughout the travelogue.)

Well. Bonn's as good a place to start as anywhere. This is the view from the snug little hotel we stayed in. The gateway to the Rhine, the birthplace of Beethoven, and the resting place of Schumann.

(Slide: the view of downtown Baltimore from the Ramada Inn near Johns Hopkins Hospital, overlooking the industrial harbor.)

ANNA: Looks a lot like Baltimore to me.

CARL: My sister jests. As you can see in the slide, one night we splurged and stayed in a rather dear inn near the Drachenfels mountains, where Lord Byron had sported.

(Slide: a close-up of the balcony railing looking into the Ramada Inn hotel room.)

ANNA:

(Dead-panned.)

This is the room I slept in while I stayed with my brother Carl.

(Slide: gutted ruins of inner-city Baltimore near the Jones-Fall Expressway; rubble and obvious urban blight.)

CARL: Alas, poor Köln. Practically wiped out by airplane raids during World War II, and yet, out of this destruction, the cathedral of Köln managed to survive—one of the most beautiful Gothic churches in the world, with a superb altar painted by the master artist of Köln, Stefan Lochner.

(Slide: an impoverished storefront church, a black evangelical sect in Baltimore.)

Let's see—what do we have next?

(Slide: a Sabrett's hotdog cart with its blue and orange umbrella in front of Johns Hopkins Hospital.)

Oh, yes. Let's talk about the food. Whereas I snapped momentos of the regal pines of the Black Forest, Anna insisted on taking photos of everything she ate.

ANNA: I can remember things I feel.

CARL: Well, then, let's talk about the food. Germany has a more robust gustatory outlook than the delicate palate of France. The Germans positively celebrate the pig from snout to tail. I could not convince Anna to sample the Sulperknochen, which is a Rheingau concoction of ears, snout, tail and feet.

ANNA: Ugh.

(Slide: a close-up of vendor placing a hot-dog on a bun and lathering it with mustard; there are canned sodas in a wide variety.)

CARL: And of course, everything is washed down with beer.

(Slide: Anna sipping a Bud Lite.)

ANNA: It was delicious.

CARL: Enough of food. May we talk about culture, sister, dear? Next slide, please.

(Slide: the Maryland National Armory, the state penitentiary.)

Ah, Heidelberg. Dueling scars and castles. Spectacular ruin which serves as the locale for open-air concerts and fireworks . . .

(Slide: the Baltimore smokestack.)

. . . and by a quaint cable car, you can reach the peak at Königstuhl, 2,000 feet high, with its breathtaking view of the Neckar Valley.

(Slide: the Bromo Seltzer tower in Baltimore. Slide: the interstate highways viewed from the tower.)

Every cobblestoned street, every alleyway, was so pristine and clean.

(Slide: the row-houses on Monument Street. Slide: a corridor of Johns Hopkins Hospital, outside the basement laboratories.)

Wasn't it, Anna?

ANNA:

(Dead-pan.)

Yes. Sterile.

(Slide: a hospital aide washing the floor.)

CARL: Even the Black Forest looked swept. We splurged once again and stayed at the Waldhorn Post here, outside of Wildbad.

(Slide: exterior of Johns Hopkins Hospital.)

The hotel dates back to 1145—the chef there is renown for his game dishes.

(Slide: Anna in front of a vending machine dispensing wrapped sandwiches in the Johns Hopkins Hospital cafeteria.)

ANNA: I wasn't too hungry.

CARL: I was ravenous.

(Slides: Route 95 outside the harbor tunnel; the large toll signs are visible.)

Let's see—the Romantic Road . . . die Romantishe Strasse . . . a trek through picture-book Bavaria and the Allgau Alpen . . . Füssen to Wurzburg.

ANNA: Honey, perhaps they've seen enough. It's hard to sit through this many—

CARL: Wait. Just one more. They've got to see Neuschwanstein, built by mad King Ludwig II. It's so rococo it's Las Vegas.

(Slide: the castle at Disneyland.)

I believe that Ludwig was reincarnated in the twentieth century as Liberace. Wait a moment, that's not the castle.

ANNA: Yes, it is.

CARL:

(Upset.)

It looks like—how did that get in here?

ANNA: I don't know which castle you're referring to, but it's definitely a castle.

(Slide: a close-up of the castle, with a large Mickey Mouse in the picture.)

CARL: That's not funny, Anna! Are you making fun of me?

ANNA: Don't get upset.

(Slide: Donald Duck has joined Mickey Mouse with tourists.)

CARL: I went to Europe. I walked through Bavaria and the Black Forest. I combed through Neuschwanstein! I did these things, and I will remember the beauty of it all my life! I don't appreciate your mockery!

ANNA: It's just a little—

CARL: You went through Germany on your back. All you'll remember are hotel ceilings. You can show them your Germany—

(He rushes off, angry.)

ANNA: Sometimes my brother gets upset for no apparent reason. Some wires cross in his brain and he—I'm sorry. Lights, please.

(The Third Man wheels the projector off-stage.)

I would like to show you my impressions of Germany. They were something like this—

SCENE 20

In Munich. Anna is under the sheet beside the Munich Virgin, who is very young.

ANNA: Are you comfortable?
MUNICH VIRGIN: Ja, ja . . . danke.
ANNA: Good. Have you been the bellhop here for a long time?
MUNICH VIRGIN: Not so very long a time. My vater owns the hotel, and says I must learn and work very hard. Soon I will be given the responsibility of the front desk.
ANNA: My. That's exciting.

(*Pause.*)

Are you cold?
MUNICH VIRGIN: Nein. Just a . . . klein nervös. My English is not so very good.
ANNA: Is this your first time? You always remember your first time.

(*Pause.*)

I'm very honored.

(*Pause.*)

Listen. I'm a schoolteacher. May I tell you something? A little lesson? When you're a much older man, and you've loved many women, you'll be a wonderful lover if you're just a little bit nervous . . . like you are right now. Because it will always be the first time.
MUNICH VIRGIN: You are a very nice woman.
ANNA: The human body is a wonderful thing. Like yours. Like mine. The beauty of the body heals all the sickness, all the bad things that happen to it. And I really want you to feel this. Because if you feel it, you'll remember it. And then maybe you'll remember me.

SCENE 21

Anna and the Munich Virgin rise. Carl gets into the bed with his stuffed rabbit. Anna gets ready to leave.

THE THIRD MAN: Conjugations of the verb "verlassen." To leave, to abandon, to forsake. The present tense.
CARL: Are you leaving me alone?
ANNA: Yes. Just for a little while. I need to take a walk. I'm restless. It's perfectly safe.
CARL: Okay, sweetie. Don't be too long. Bunny and I are ready for bed.
ANNA: I won't stay out long. I'll be right back.
THE THIRD MAN: The future tense of the verb "verlassen."
CARL: Will you be leaving me alone again tonight? I'm ready for bed.
ANNA: I will be leaving you alone. Just for a little while.
CARL: Who will it be tonight? The bellhop? The deskclerk? Or the maitre d'?
ANNA: Don't be mean. You said you didn't make judgements.
CARL: I don't. I just want to spend time with you.
ANNA: I'll be back in time for a bedtime story.

THE THIRD MAN: The past tense of the verb "verlassen."

CARL: Again? Again? You left me alone last night. And the night before.

ANNA: I can't help it. I've been a good girl for the past thirty years. Now I want to make up for lost time.

CARL: And what am I supposed to do while you're out traipsing around with every Thomas, Deiter und Heinrich?

ANNA: Hug bunny.

THE THIRD MAN: There are three moods of the verb "verlassen": the indicative, the imperative, and the subjunctive. Anna and Carl are never in the same mood.

CARL: Leave me alone.

ANNA: Carl, don't be like that.

CARL: Why? It doesn't matter what I want. You are going to leave.

ANNA: I never stay out very long.

CARL: All I can say is if this establishment charges us for room service, they've got some nerve—

ANNA: I've got to take what opportunities come along—

CARL: I wish you wouldn't go—

ANNA: Please understand. I don't have much time. I spend as much time with you as I can, but while I still have my health . . . please?

SCENE 22

THE THIRD MAN: As children they fought.

CARL: We never fought, really.

ANNA: Not in a physical way. He was a sickly child.

CARL: She was very willful.

ANNA: No rough-housing. But he knew all of my weak points. My secret openings. He could be ruthless.

CARL: She'd cry at the slightest thing.

ANNA: He has a very sharp tongue.

CARL: But when one of you is very, very sick, you can't fight. It's not fair. You've got to hold it in. We never fight.

ANNA: But we had a doozy in the hotel room in Berlin.

CARL: Well, my god, Anna, even though you're sick, I have the right to get angry.

ANNA: We'd been traveling too long. We were cranky. The rooms were closing in.

CARL: I'm just saying that we should spend a little more time together. I don't get to see you alone enough. You're always restless.

ANNA: Fine. You go out without me for a change.

CARL: I'm going out for a walk.

ANNA:

> (Starting to weep.)

> I don't care.

CARL: When she was little, this would be the time I'd bribe her. With a comic book or an ice cream. I always had pennies saved up for these little contingencies.

ANNA: But sometimes, for the sake of my pride, I would be inconsolable. I would rush off and then feel just awful alone. Why didn't I take the bribe?

(To Carl.)

I'm going out.

CARL: To fuck?

ANNA: No, dear. The passive voice is used to emphasize the subject, to indicate the truth of the generalization. I'm going out. To get fucked.

SCENE 23

Music Kurt Weill. Anna goes over to a small cabaret table. There is a telephone on the table. The Radical Student Activist sits at another identical table, smoking, watching her.

ANNA: I'm going to enjoy Berlin without him. I'll show him. I'm going to be carefree, totally without scruples. I'll pretend I've never taught first-graders.

(Beat.)

I'm going to have a perfectly miserable time.

(The Radical Student Activist picks up the telephone. The telephone at Anna's table rings.)

Oh my goodness. My miserable time is calling me.

(Anna picks up the phone.)

Yes?

RADICAL STUDENT ACTIVIST: Are you alone, Fraülein?

ANNA: Well, uh, actually—yes, I am.

RADICAL STUDENT ACTIVIST: Gut. Du willst mal richtig durchgefickt werden, ja?

ANNA: I'm sorry. I don't speak a word of German.

(The Radical Student Activist laughs.)

RADICAL STUDENT ACTIVIST: Ja. Even better. I said, would you like to get fucked?

ANNA: Do you always come on to single women like that?

RADICAL STUDENT ACTIVIST: Would you like it better if I bought you tall drinks with umbrellas? Told to you the stories of how hard a time my parents had during the war? Tell you how exciting I find foreign women, how they are the real women, not like the pale northern mädchen here at home? How absolutely bourgeois.

ANNA: I see. Why do you come here?

RADICAL STUDENT ACTIVIST: I don't come here for the overpriced drinks. I come here because of the bored western women who come here, who leave their tired businessmen husbands in the hotel rooms behind.

ANNA: You're cute. In a hostile way.

RADICAL STUDENT ACTIVIST: Fucking is a revolutionary act.

ANNA: Your hovel or my hotel?

SCENE 24

In the Hotel Room. Anna, awake, lies in the middle of the bed. To her left, Carl sleeps, curled up. To her right, the Radical Student Activist, curled on her breast, slumbers. Anna is awake with an insomniacal desperation.

ANNA:

(Singing softly.)

Two and two are four; four and four are eight; eight and eight are sixteen; sixteen and sixteen are thirty-two—

RADICAL STUDENT ACTIVIST:

(Groggy.)

Wo ist die Toilette?

(The Radical Student Activist rises and stumbles off.)

ANNA: In love-making, he's all fury and heat. His North Sea pounding against your Dreamer. And when you look up and see his face, red and huffing, it's hard to imagine him ever having been a newborn, tiny, wrinkled, and seven pounds. That is, until afterwards. When he rises from sleep and he walks into the bathroom. And there he exposes his soft little derrière, and you can still see the soft baby flesh.

(As the Radical Student Activist comes back into the room.)

I've got a put a name to that behind. What's your name? Wie heissen Sie?

RADICAL STUDENT ACTIVIST:

(The Radical Student Activist starts dressing in a hurry.)

Auf Wiedersehn. Next thing you'll ask for my telephone number.

ANNA: No, I won't. I was just curious—

RADICAL STUDENT ACTIVIST: Ja, ja . . . und then my sign of the zodiac. I'll get cards from Hallmark und little scribblings like "I'll never forget the night we shared."

ANNA: Forget it.

RADICAL STUDENT ACTIVIST: There is something radical in two complete strangers committing biological necessity without having to give into bourgeois conventions of love, without breeding to produce workers for a capitalist system, without the benediction of the church, the family, the bosses—

ANNA: I have something to confess to you. I lied to you.

RADICAL STUDENT ACTIVIST: About what?

ANNA: I'm not here on business. I don't specialize in corporate takeovers. I don't work on Wall Street. I only told you that because I thought that was what you wanted to hear.

RADICAL STUDENT ACTIVIST: Okay. So you do estate planning? Income tax?

ANNA: No. You just committed a revolutionary act with a first-grade schoolteacher who lives in low-income housing. And I'm tired. I think you should go.

RADICAL STUDENT ACTIVIST: And your husband?

ANNA: Not too loud. And he's not my husband. He's my brother. A maiden librarian for the San Francisco Public.

(As the Radical Student Activist starts to leave.)

And by the way—the missionary position does not a revolution make.

(The Radical Student Activist leaves. Anna, depressed, lies down. Carl rises from the bed.)

SCENE 25

CARL: And as she lay in the bed, sleepless, it swept over her—the way her classroom smelled early in the morning, before the children came. It smelled of chalk dust—

THE THIRD MAN: It smelled of Crayola wax, crushed purple and green—

CARL: The cedar of hamster cage shavings—

THE THIRD MAN: The sweet wintergreen of LePage's paste—

CARL: The wooden smell of the thick construction paper—

THE THIRD MAN: The spillings of sticky orange drink and sour milk—

THE THIRD MAN and CARL:

(Simultaneously.)

And the insidious smell of first-grader pee.

CARL: It smelled like heaven.

ANNA: And the first thing I did each morning was put up the weather map for today on the board under the flag. A bright, smiling sun, or Miss Cloud or Mr. Umbrella. On special days I put up Suzy Snowflake. And when I opened my desk drawer, scattered like diamonds on the bottom were red, silver and gold stars.

(Beat.)

I want to go home. Carl, I want to go home.

CARL: Soon, sweetie. Very soon.

ANNA: I've had enough. I've seen all of the world I want to see. I want to wake up in my own bed. I want to sit with you at home and we'll watch the weather. And we'll wait.

CARL: We've come so far. We have to at least go to Vienna. Do you think you can hold out long enough to meet Dr. Todesrocheln?

(Anna, miserable and homesick, nods.)

That a girl. I promise you don't have to undertake his . . . hydrotherapy unless you decide to. I have a friend in Vienna, a college chum, who might be able to get us some of blackmarket stuff. It's worth a shot.

ANNA: Then you'll take me home?

CARL: Then I'll take you home.

SCENE 26

Music: A song such as the zither theme from The Third Man. *Carl and Anna stand, with their luggage, in front of a door buzzer.*

CARL: First we'll just look up Harry. Then we'll cab over to Dr. Todesrocheln.

> (*Carl rings the buzzer. They wait. Carl rings the buzzer again. They wait. An aging Concierge comes out.*)

> Entschuldigung. Wir suchen Harry Lime? Do you speak English?

CONCIERGE: Nein. Ich spreche kein Englisch.

> (*Carl and the Concierge start to shout as if the other one was deaf.*)

CARL: Herr Lime? Do you know him? Herr Harry Lime?

CONCIERGE: Ach. Ach. Ja, Herr Harry Lime. You come . . . too spät.

CARL: He's gone? Too spät?

CONCIERGE: Fünf minuten too spät. Er ist tot—

CARL: What?

CONCIERGE: Ja. Ein auto mit Harry splatz-machen auf der Strasse. Splatz!

ANNA: Splatz!?

CARL: Splatz?!

> (*It dawns on Carl and Anna what the Concierge is saying.*)

CONCIERGE: Ja, ja. Er geht über die strasse, und ein auto . . . spppllllaattz!

ANNA.: Oh, my god.

CONCIERGE:

> (*Gesturing with hands.*)

> Ja. Er hat auch eine rabbit. Herr Rabbit auch—sppllaattz! They are . . . diggen ein grab in den Boden. Jetz.

CARL: Now? You saw this happen?

CONCIERGE: Ja. I . . . saw it mit meinen own Augen. Splatz.

> (*As he exits.*)

> "Splatzen, splatzen, über alles . . ."

CARL: Listen, darling. I want you to take a cab to the doctor's office.

ANNA: Where are you going?

CARL: Ich verlasse. I'll find out what happened to Harry.

ANNA: I wish you wouldn't leave. . . .

CARL: I'll come back. Okay?

SCENE 27

Anna climbs onto a table and gathers a white paper sheet around her. She huddles.

ANNA: Some things are the same in every country. You're scared when you see the doctor, here in Vienna just like in Baltimore. And they hand you the same paper cup to fill, just like in America. Then you climb up onto the same cold metal table, and they throw a sheet around you and you feel very small. And just like at home, they tell you to wait. And you wait.

> (*As Anna waits, dwarfed on the table, the scene with Harry Lime and Carl unfolds. Music, such as* The Third Man *theme, up.*)

SCENE 28

On the Ferris Wheel in the Prater. Carl holds the stuffed rabbit closely.

CARL: Why are we meeting here?

HARRY LIME: Have you looked at the view from up here? It's quite inspiring. No matter how old I get, I always love the ferris wheel.

CARL: I just came from your funeral.

HARRY LIME: I'm touched, old man. Was it a nice funeral?

CARL: What are you doing?

HARRY LIME: It's best not to ask too many questions. The police were beginning to do that. It's extremely convenient, now and then in a man's career, to die. I've gone underground. So if you want to meet me, you have to come here. No one asks questions here.

CARL: Can you help us?

(Harry Lime at first does not answer. He looks at the view.)

HARRY LIME: Where is your sister? She left you alone?

CARL: She's—she needs her rest. You were my closest friend in college.

HARRY LIME: I'll be straight with you. I can give you the drugs—but it won't help. It won't help at all. Your sister's better off with that quack Todesrocheln—we call him the Yellow Queen of Vienna—she might end up drinking her own piss, but it won't kill her.

CARL: But I thought you had the drugs—

HARRY LIME: Oh, I do. And they cost a pretty penny. For a price, I can give them to you. At a discount for old times. But you have to know, we make them up in my kitchen.

CARL: Jesus.

HARRY LIME: Why not? People will pay for these things. When they're desperate people will eat peach pits, or aloe, or egg protein—they'll even drink their own piss. It gives them hope.

CARL: How can you do this?

HARRY LIME: Listen, old man, if you want to be a millionaire, you go into real estate. If you want to be a billionaire, you sell hope. Nowadays the only place a fellow can make a decent career of it is in Mexico and Europe.

CARL: That's . . . disgusting.

HARRY LIME: Look. I thought you weren't going to be . . . sentimental about this. It's a business. You have to have the right perspective. Like from up here . . . the people down on the street are just tiny little dots. And if you could charge $1,000, wouldn't you push the drugs? I could use a friend I can trust to help me.

CARL: When we were at Hopkins together, I thought you were God. You could hypnotize us into doing anything, and it would seem . . . charming. Carl, old man, you'd say, "Just do it." Cutting classes, cribbing exams, shop-lifting, stupid undergraduate things—and I would do it. Without knowing the consequences. I would do it.

HARRY LIME: Oh, you knew the consequences, old man. You knew. You chose not to think about them.

CARL: I've grown old before my time from the consequences. I'm turning you in.

HARRY LIME: I wouldn't do that, old man.

> (Harry Lime pats a bulge on the inside of his trench coat.)

By the time you hit the ground, you'll be just a tiny little dot.

> (Carl and Harry Lime look at each other, waiting.)

And I think you have something I want. The rabbit, bitte.

CARL: No. You're not getting it. I'm taking it with me.

> (Harry Lime puts his arms in position for a waltz and begins to sway, seductively.)

HARRY LIME: Come on, give it up. Come to my arms, my only one. Dance with me, my beloved, my sweet—

> (Carl takes the stuffed rabbit and threatens to throw it out the window of the ferris wheel. A Strauss waltz plays very loudly, and Harry Lime and Carl waltz-struggle for the rabbit. Carl is pushed and Harry Lime waltzes off with the rabbit.)

SCENE 29

Meanwhile, back at Doctor Todesrocheln.

ANNA: You begin to hope that the wait is proportionate to the medical expertise. My God. My feet are turning blue. Where am I? An HMO?

> (Anna waits.)

The problem with being an adult is that you never forget why you're waiting. When I was a child, I could wait blissfully unaware for hours. I used to read signs and transpose letters, or count tiles in the floor. And in the days before I could read, I would make up stories about my hands—Mr. Left and Mr. Right.

> (Beat.)

Mr. Left would provoke Mr. Right. Mr. Right would ignore it. The trouble would escalate, until my hands were battling each other to the death.

> (Beat. Anna demonstrates.)

Then one of them would weep. Finally, they became friends again, and they'd dance—

> (Anna's two hands dance together; she is unaware that Dr. Todesrocheln has entered and is watching her. He clears his throat. He wears a very dirty lab coat with pockets filled with paper and a stale doughnut. He wears a white fright wig and glasses. He also wears one sinister black glove. With relish, he carries a flask of a golden liquid.)

Oh, thank goodness.

DR. TODESROCHELN: Ja. So happy to meet you. Such an interesting specimen. I congratulate you. Very, very interesting.

ANNA: Thank you.

DR. TODESROCHELN: We must have many more such specimens from you—for the urinocryoscopy, the urinometer, the urinoglucosometer, the uroacidimeter, uroazotometer, and mein new acquirement in der laboratorium—ein urophosphometer.

ANNA: My goodness.

> *(Dr. Todesrocheln has put the flask down on a table. Quietly, his left hand reaches for it; the right hand stops the left.)*

DR. TODESROCHELN: Ja. Nowadays, we have learned to discover the uncharted mysteries of the fluids discharged through the urethra. We have been so primitive in the past. Doctors once could only analyze by taste and smell—but thanks to the advancement of medical science, there are no limits to our thirst for knowledge.

ANNA: Uh-huh.

> *(Dr. Todesrocheln's left hand seizes the flask. Trembling, with authority, his right hand replaces the flask on the table, and soothes the left hand into quietude.)*

DR. TODESROCHELN: So much data has been needlessly, carelessly destroyed in the past—the medical collections of Ravensbruck senselessly annihilated—and that is why as a scientist, I must be exacting in our measurements and recordings.

ANNA: What can I hope to find out from these . . . specimens?

DR. TODESROCHELN: Ah, yes—the layman must have his due! Too much pure research und no application makes Jack . . . macht Jack . . .

> *(Dr. Todesrocheln loses his train of thought.)*

> Fraülein Anna—I may call you Fraülein Anna?—Let us look at the body as an alchemist, taking in straw and mud und schweinefleisch and processing it into liquid gold which purifies the body. You might say that the sickness of the body can only be cured by the health of the body. To your health!

> *(His left hand seizes the flask in a salute, and raises the flask to his lips. In time, the right hand brings the flask down. A brief struggle. It appears the flask might spill, but at last the right hand triumphs.)*

ANNA: You know, even though I really grew up in the suburbs of Baltimore, I like to think of myself as an open-minded person—

DR. TODESROCHELN: The ancient Greeks knew that the aromatic properties of the fluid could reveal the imbalances of the soul itself. . . .

> *(The left hand sneaks towards the flask.)*

ANNA: I'm always very eager to try new foods, or see the latest John Waters film—

DR. TODESROCHELN: —its use in the purification rites of the Aztecs is, of course, so well known that it need not be mentioned—

> *(The hand has grasped the flask and begins to inch it off the table.)*

ANNA: And whenever I meet someone who cross-dresses, I always, compliment him on his shoes or her earrings—

DR. TODESROCHELN: It is the first golden drop that marks the infant's identity separate from the womb—

> *(The hand has slipped the flask beneath the table. His right hand is puzzled.)*

ANNA: But still, it's important to know where your threshhold is . . . and I think we're coming dangerously close to mine. . . .

DR. TODESROCHELN: Until the last precious amber releases the soul from the body—ashes to ashes, drop to drop—excuse me—

(His left hand, with the flask, swings in an arc behind his body; he swivels his body to the flask, his back turned to us. We can hear him drink in secrecy. With his back turned.)

Ahhh. . . .

(He orders himself. Composed, he turns around to face Anna again, and demurely sets down the flask. Its level is noticeably lower. Anna is aghast.)

I can sense your concern. I have been prattling on without regard to questions you must surely have—

ANNA: Is that your real hair?

DR. TODESROCHELN: Of course, I can not promise results, but first we must proceed by securing more samples—

ANNA: I don't believe that's your real hair.

DR. TODESROCHELN: I will need first of all twenty-four hours of your time for a urononcometry—

ANNA: You look familiar to me—

(Increasingly scared.)

DR. TODESROCHELN: Although I can tell you from a first taste—er, test, that your uroammonica level is high—not unpleasantly so, but full-bodied—

ANNA: Oh, my god . . . I think I know who you are . . . you're . . . you're . . .

(Anna rises to snatch his toupée. Dr. Todesrocheln suddenly stands, menacing. And the light changes.)

DR. TODESROCHELN.: WO IST DEIN BRUDER?

(He takes off his wig and glasses and appears as the Doctor in the first scene, peeling off the black glove to reveal latex gloves underneath.)

You fool! You left your brother in the room alone! WO IST DEIN BRUDER?

(Music: The Emperor Waltz plays at a very loud volume. Anna, frightened, races from the doctor's office to the hotel room. We see Carl, lying stiff beneath a white sheet. To the tempo of the Strauss, Anna tries to wake him. He does not respond. Anna takes off the sheet and forces him into a sitting position, the stuffed rabbit clenched beneath his arm. Carl remains sitting, stiff, eyes open, wooden; he is still in his pajamas. Then he slumps. Anna raises him again. He remains upright for a beat, and begins to fall. Anna stops him, presses his body against hers, pulls his legs over the bed, tries to stand him up. Frozen, his body tilts against hers. She tries to make him cross the floor, his arms around her neck. She positions him in a chair, but his legs are locked in a perpendicular angle and will not touch the floor. She presses his legs to the floor. He mechanically springs forward. Then suddenly, like the doll in "E.T.A. Hoffmann," the body of Carl becomes animated, but with a strange, automatic life of its own. Carl begins to waltz with Anna. Gradually, he winds down, and faltering, falls back to the bed. There is the sound of a loud alarm clock; the

Doctor enters, and covers Carl with a sheet. Then he pulls a white curtain in front of the scene, as the stage lights become, for the first time, harsh, stark and white.)

SCENE 30

In the Hospital Lounge. The Doctor holds the stuffed rabbit and travel brochures in his hands. He awkwardly peels off his latex gloves.

DOCTOR: I'm sorry. There was nothing we could do.
ANNA: Yes. I know.
DOCTOR: I thought you might want to take this along with you.

> *(The Doctor hands Anna the stuffed rabbit.)*

ANNA:

> *(To the stuffed rabbit.)*
>
> There you are!
>
> *(Anna hugs the stuffed rabbit and sees the Doctor watching her.)*
>
> It's Jo-Jo. My brother's childhood rabbit. I brought it to the hospital as a little surprise. I thought it might make him feel better.

DOCTOR: Sometimes little things become important, when nothing else will help—
ANNA: Yes.

> *(They pause and stand together awkwardly.)*
>
> At least Carl went in his sleep. I guess that's a blessing.

DOCTOR: If one has to die from this particular disease, there are worse ways to go than pneumonia.
ANNA: I never would have believed what sickness can do to the body.

> *(Pause.)*
>
> Well, Doctor, I want to thank you for all you've done for my brother.

DOCTOR: I wish I could do more. By the way, housekeeping found these brochures in your brother's bedside table. I didn't know if they were important.
ANNA:

> *(Anna takes the brochures.)*
>
> Ah, yes. The brochures for Europe. I've never been abroad. We're going to go when he gets—
>
> *(Anna stops herself. With control.)*
>
> I must learn to use the past tense. We would have gone had he gotten better.

DOCTOR: Anna—may I call you Anna?—I, uh, if there's anything I can do—
ANNA: Thank you, but there's nothing you can do—
DOCTOR: I mean, I really would like it if you'd call me for coffee, or if you just want to talk about all this—

> *(The Doctor trails off. Anna looks at him. She smiles. He squirms.)*

ANNA: You're very sweet. But no, I don't think so. Not now. I feel it's simply not safe for me right now to see anyone. Thanks again and goodbye.

> (Anna starts to exit. The Doctor, wistful, watches her go. The lighting begins to change back to the dreamy atmosphere of the first scene. Softly, a Strauss waltz begins. Carl, perfectly well, waits for Anna. He is dressed in Austrian military regalia. They waltz off as the lights dim.)

End of Play

ABOUT THE AUTHORS

Jane Chambers (*Last Summer at Bluefish Cove*) began her career in the 1950s as both an actress and a playwright. Her plays have been produced Off-Broadway, in regional and community theatre in the United States and abroad, and on television. She was the recipient of a number of awards including the Connecticut Educational Television Award (1971), a Eugene O'Neill fellowship (1972), a National Writer's Guild Award (1973), and from 1980–83, The Villager Award, the New York Dramalogue Critics Circle Award, the Alliance for Gay and Lesbian Artists Media Award, the Robby Award, the Oscar Wilde Award, the Los Angeles Drama Critics Circle Award, and a proclamation from Los Angeles, California, for "outstanding theatre." She has won the Betty Award twice, and in 1982 she was presented with the Human Dignity Award.

Her published novels include *Burning* and *Chasin' Jason*. Her articles have appeared in publications such as *The New York Times* and *Harper's*. Published plays are *My Blue Heaven, A Late Snow, Last Summer at Bluefish Cove,* and *Eye of the Gull* (Heinmann Books). Published poetry includes a volume of works, *Warrior at Rest*, and selected poems in *Gay and Lesbian Poetry of Our Time* (St. Martin's Press).

A founding member of the New Jersey Women's Political Caucus and Interart Theatre, NYC, she was on the planning committee of the Women's Project of the American Theatre Association and a member of the Writer's Guild East and East End Gay Organization for Human Rights. She taught in women's study, writing, and acting programs in universities throughout the United States. On February 18, 1983, she died of a brain tumor at her Greenport, Long Island, home, survived by her mother, two stepbrothers, and her life companion, Beth Allen. In 1983, the Jane Chambers Memorial Playwriting Award was established.

Mart Crowley (*The Boys in the Band*) was born in Vicksburg, Mississippi, and educated at the Catholic University of America in Washington, D.C. Plays and Film: *The Boys in the Band* (New York, 1968; London, 1969); produced and adapted CBS-Fox feature film of *The Boys in the Band* (1970); *Remote Asylum* (Los Angeles, Ahmanson Theatre, 1970); *A Breeze from the Gulf* (New York, 1973; London, 1991); produced the ABC-TV series *Hart to Hart* (1979–83); *Avec Schmaltz*, Williamstown, Massachusetts Theatre Festival (1984); *For Reasons That Remain Unclear* (Olney Theatre, Olney, Maryland); Anthologies: *3 Plays by Mart Crowley* (Alyson Books, 1996); *Selected Plays of Mart Crowley* (Applause Theatre and Cinema Books, 1996). Children's literature: edited Kay Thompson's *Eloise Takes a Bawth*, drawings by Hilary Knight (Simon & Schuster, 2002). *The Men from the Boys* (San Francisco, 2002; Los Angeles, 2003). Revivals: *The Boys in the Band* (New York, 1996; London, 1997).

Harvey Fierstein (*Torch Song Trilogy*) made his debut at the La Mama Experimental Theater Club in 1971 in Andy Warhol's only play, *Pork*. He followed that with appearances in more than sixty Off-Off-Broadway plays, writing and performing in many of his own productions. His *Torch Song Trilogy* opened Off-Off-Broadway in 1980, transferred Off-Broadway in 1981, and then went on to Broadway. For that three-act play, Fierstein won two Tony Awards, two Drama Desk Awards, an Obie Award, a Theatre

World Award, and a Dramatist Guild Award. *Torch Song Trilogy* was also nominated for the Olivier Award. Fierstein won his third Tony Award for the book of *La Cage aux Folles.* His other plays include *Safe Sex, Spookhouse,* and *Forget Him.*

He has appeared in thirty films, including *Independence Day, Mrs. Doubtfire,* and Woody Allen's *Bullets over Broadway.* His television appearances have included stints on *Cheers*, for which he received an Emmy nomination. Fierstein also provided the voice of Homer Simpson's executive secretary on *The Simpsons*, and he is a regular commentator on PBS's *In the Life.* His children's book, *The Sissy Duckling* (Simon & Shuster) garnered an Ace Award. For his performance as Edna Turnblad in the smash hit musical *Hairspray*, Mr. Fierstein received the 2003 Drama Desk Award (Best Actor in a Musical), Drama League Award (Outstanding Performance of the Year), and the New York Magazine Award. He also received the 2003 Tony Award (Best Actor in a Musical), making him only the second person in history to win Tonys in four different categories. Mr. Fierstein's most recent appearance on Broadway was as Tevye in the record breaking revival of *Fiddler on the Roof*. He returns to Broadway in spring 2008 in the new musical *A Catered Affair*, for which he wrote the book.

John R. Hopkins *(Find Your Way Home)* began writing for television in the early 1960s in England. A selection of his work produced includes the original television plays *Break-up* (Granada TV, 1958); *A Woman Comes Home* (BBC, 1961); *A Chance of Thunder* (BBC six-part thriller serial, 1961); *Z Cars* (BBC police series, fifty-four episodes, 1962–64); *Walk a Tight Circle* (BBC, 1962); *I Took My Little World Away* (ATV, 1963); *Horror of Darkness* (BBC, 1963); *Some Place of Safety* (BBC opera for television, 1964); *A Man Like Orpheus* (BBC ballet for television, 1964); *Fable* (BBC, 1964); *A Game-like-Only a Game* (BBC, 1965); *Talking to a Stranger* (BBC four plays for television, 1965); *Beyond the Sunrise* (BBC, 1967); *Walk into the Dark* (BBC, 1971); *Some Distant Shadow* (Granada TV, 1971); *That Quiet Earth* (BBC, 1971); *Fathers and Families* (BBC six plays for television, 1976); *A Story to Frighten the Children* (BBC, 1978); and *Hiroshima* (Showtime, 1995). Adaptations include *The Small Back Room* (BBC play for television from the novel by Nigel Balchin, 1958); *Mine Own Executioner* (BBC play for television from the novel by Nigel Balchin, 1959); *Dancers in Mourning* (BBC six-part serial from the novel by Margery Allingham, 1959); *Death of a Ghost* (BBC six-part mystery serial from the novel by Margery Allingham, 1960); *Parade's End* (BBC three plays for television from the novels by Ford Madox Ford, 1964); *The Gambler* (BBC two-part serial from the novel by Fyodor Dostoevsky, 1963); *Smiley's People* (BBC six-part serial from the novel written by John le Carré, 1984); and *Codename Kyril* (Thames Television four-hour miniseries from the novel by John Trenhaile, 1987). Films include *Two Left Feet* (British Lion [shared credit], 1963); *Thunderball* (United Artists [shared credit], 1965); *Virgin Soldiers* [shared credit], 1967); *The Offence* (United Artists, 1972); *Murder by Decree* (Avco Embassy, 1978); and *The Holcroft Covenant* [shared credit], 1985). Plays include *This Story of Yours* (London premiere Royal Court Theatre, 1968; Stuttgart, 1969; New Haven, 1982; Hampstead Theatre Club, 1987; Buenos Aires, 1995); *Find Your Way Home* (London premiere Open Space, 1970; New York premiere Brooks Atkinson Theatre, 1973; Frankfurt premiere Kleist Theatre, 1995); *Economic Necessity* (Leicester premiere Haymarket Theatre, 1973); *Next of Kin* (London premiere National Theatre, 1974); *Valedictorian* (Williston Northampton School premiere, 1978); *Losing Time* (New York premiere Manhattan Theatre Club, 1979; Hamburg [Berlin and Vienna, 1983]), and *Absent Forever* (premiere Great Lakes Theatre Festival, 1987).

Born in London, John R. Hopkins spent his early years in Wimbledon. After national service, he went up to St. Catharine's College, Cambridge to read English. After graduation he joined the BBC as a studio manager, and subsequently, as a producer. He left the BBC and went to Granada Television for two years, where he began to write, at first for television, subsequently for the cinema, and eventually, for the theatre. Hopkins won the British Screen Writer's Guild Award for his work on dramatic series two years in succession for *Z Cars*, in 1962 and 1963; the British Director's Guild Award for his miniseries *Talking to a Stranger* in 1966; and in 1969, for his contribution to *Masterpiece Theatre*, an Emmy Award. He was nominated for an Edgar Allen Poe Award for his screenplay *Murder by Decree* in 1978; and nominated twice for a Cable Ace Award in 1995 for his television movie *Hiroshima* on Showtime. He also received the Writer's Guild of America's Humanitas Prize and the Penn Literary Prize for *Hiroshima*.

Albert Innaurato (*Gemini*) wrote the play *Gemini*, one of the longest running non-musical plays in Broadway history. It opened the same week as his play *The Transfiguration of Benno Blimpie*, establishing his reputation as one of the more prominent baby boomer playwrights. He had a long association with Andre Bishop, while Bishop was the artistic director of Playwrights' Horizons. Innaurato's *Passione* played successfully there, before moving to the Morosco Theater on Broadway, where it became the last play given in that historical theater. Bishop also produced Innaurato's *Earthworms, Herself as Lust, Gus and Al* (twice), and an acclaimed production of *The Transfiguration of Benno Blimpie*, directed by Innaurato and starring the late, great Peter Evans. Innaurato also worked closely with Joe Papp at the Public Theater on his play *Coming of Age in Soho*.

According to Lyn Meadow, Innaurato, along with classmate Christopher Durang from Yale School of Drama, opened the Manhattan Theatre Club with their two one acts, *I don't normally like poetry but have you read Trees?* and *GYP, the Real Life Story of Mitzi Gaynor*. These works were performed by Innaurato and Durang in priests' vestments. Also with Durang, Innaurato wrote *The Idiots Karamazov*, which starred their classmates Meryl Streep and Sigourney Weaver, and played at the Yale School of Drama, Yale Rep, and twenty-five years later at ACT at Harvard. Innaurato won the Emmy Award for his teleplay *Verna the USO Girl*, wrote episodes for *The Days and Nights of Molly Dodd*, and many half hours for PBS, including the Emmy nominated *Death and Taxes* (which actually frightened the IRS). He has won three Obies and has been awarded the Guggenheim Grant, the Rockefeller Grant, and three NEA grants.

His journalism has appeared in *The New York Times, Vogue, Vanity Fair, Forbes, New York Magazine*, and his background as a musician allowed him to write for *Opera News* (many issues in the 1990s were written almost entirely by Innaurato). For the Metropolitan Opera Guild he recorded lectures about fourteen operas, wrote for the British magazines *Gramophone, BBC*, and in German for *Opernwelt*. He has taught at Columbia University, Princeton University, Rutgers University, and now teaches at the University of the Arts in Philadelphia, PA.

Terrence McNally's (*The Ritz*) most recent work *Chita Rivera: The Dancer's Life*, recently played on Broadway. His newest play *Dedication* or *The Stuff of Dreams* had its premiere at Primary Stages. *Crucifixion* had its world premiere at the New Conservatory Theatre in San Francisco in September 2006. *The Stendhal Syndrome* was also produced by Primary Stages as its inaugural attraction at the new 59E59 Theatre in 2004. Mr. McNally also recently wrote the book for the musical *A Man of No Importance*, which was produced at

Lincoln Center. Recent Broadway credits include the revival of his play *Frankie and Johnny in the Clair de Lune* and the book for the musical *The Full Monty*. He won his fourth Tony Award for Best Book of a Musical for *Ragtime* (music and lyrics by Stephen Flaherty and Lynn Ahrens). He is currently working on the book for *The Visit* with score by John Kander and Fred Ebb. McNally won the Tony in 1996 for his play *Master Class*, in which Zoe Caldwell created the role of Maria Callas; the 1995 Tony, Drama Desk, and Outer Critics Circle Awards for Best Play as well as the New York Drama Critics' Circle Award for Best American Play for *Love! Valour! Compassion!;* and the 1993 Tony for his book of the musical *Kiss of the Spiderwoman* (music and lyrics by Kander and Ebb). His other plays include *Corpus Christi, A Perfect Ganesh, Lips Together, Teeth Apart, The Lisbon Traviata,* and *It's Only a Play*, all of which began at the Manhattan Theatre Club. Earlier stage works include *Bad Habits, The Ritz, Where Has Tommy Flowers Gone? Things That Go Bump in the Night, Next*, and the book for the musical *The Rink* (music and lyrics by Kander and Ebb). For the Central Park Opera trilogy presented at the New York City Opera in the fall of 1999, he wrote the libretto for *The Food of Love*, with music by Robert Beaser. The San Francisco Opera presented *Dead Man Walking* with McNally's libretto and music by Jake Heggie.

McNally has written a number of scripts for television, including *Andre's Mother*, for which he won an Emmy Award. He has received two Guggenheim Fellowships, a Rockefeller Grant, a Lucille Lortel Award, and a citation from the American Academy of Arts and Letters. He has been a member of the Dramatists Guild since 1970.

Paula Vogel's *(The Baltimore Waltz)* play *How I Learned How to Drive* is the recipient of the 1998 Pulitzer Prize for Drama, the 1997 Lortel, Drama Desk, and Outer Critics Circle Awards for Best Play, and won her a second Obie. Productions were slated in 1998 in San Francisco, Seattle, Alaska, Providence, Houston, Baltimore, Toronto, Los Angeles, and London, making it the most produced American play of 1998 (according to *American Theatre Magazine*). Twice before nominated for a Pulitzer, her plays have been performed at theatres such as the Lortel Theatre and Circle Repertory in New York, the American Repertory Theatre, the Goodman Theatre, the Magic Theatre, Center Stage, and Alley Theatre, as well as throughout Canada, England, Brazil, and Spain. Her play *The Long Christmas Ride Home* debuted Off-Broadway in 2003 at the Vineyard Theatre, and received three 2004 Lucille Lortel Award nominations.

The Roundabout Theatre produced her play *The Mineola Twins* in 1999. It was published in 1997 by American Theatre. Both *Mineola Twins* and *How I Learned to Drive* are published by Theatre Communications Group in 1998 as the anthology *The Mammary Plays. The Mineola Twins* was produced at Perseverance Theatre in November 1996 and Trinity Repertory in 1997, both directed by Molly Smith. *The Baltimore Waltz* won the Obie for Best Play in 1992, and her anthology *The Baltimore Waltz and Other Plays* was published in 1996 by Theatre Communications Group. Other plays included in the anthology are *Hot and Throbbing, Desdemona, And Baby Makes Seven,* and *The Oldest Profession*. Other awards include the Pew Charitable Trust Senior Residency Award, a 1995 Guggenheim, an AT&T New Plays Award, the Fund for New American Plays, the Rockefeller Foundation's Bellagio Center Fellowship, several National Endowment for the Arts Fellowships, the McKnight Fellowship, Radcliffe College's Bunting Fellowship, the Governor's Award for the Arts, and in 2004, the Award for Literature from the American Academy of Arts and Letters. She is a member of New Dramatists. She has been the Adele Kellenberg Seaver Professor of Literary Arts at Brown University, a position she has held since 2003, having been on the faculty there since 1985.

Lanford Wilson (*Fifth of July*) is the author of the full length plays *Balm in Gilead*, *The Rimers of Eldritch* (Vernon Rice Award), *The Gingham Dog, Lemon Sky, Serenading Louie, Hot L Baltimore* (New York Drama Critics Circle Award, Best American Play; Obie Award, Best Play; Outer Critics Circle Award), *The Mound Builders* (Obie Award), *Angels Fall* (Tony nomination), *Talley's Folly* (Drama Logue Award, Los Angeles; New York Drama Critics Circle Award for Best Play; Pulitzer Prize for Drama), *Talley & Son, A Sense of Place or Virgil Is Still the Frogboy, Sympathetic Magic* (Obie Award), *Book of Days;* (American Theatre Critics Association Award, Best Play), *Rain Dance,* and some twenty produced one act plays including *Brontosaurus, The Great Nebula in Orion,* the paired evening of *A Poster of the Cosmos* and *Moonshot Tape,* and the entry *Noon* for the evening of three one acts; *By the Sea, By the Sea, By the Beautiful Sea.* He has written new translations of Chekov's *Three Sisters* and Ibsen's *Ghosts.* For television he has written *Taxi!* (not the series), and *The Migrants* (Emmy nomination, from a story by Tennessee Williams). He has also written the libretto for Lee Hoiby's opera of Williams's *Summer and Smoke.* Other awards include the Brandeis University Creative Arts Award in Theatre Arts, The Institute of Arts and Letters Award, The Edward Albee Last Frontier Award, The John Steinbeck Award, an Obie Award, Guild Hall Award, Lucille Lortel Award for Lifetime Achievement, the State of Missouri Outstanding Artist Award, American Academy of Achievement Award, and the Christopher Award. He has been inducted into the Missouri Writers Hall of Fame and the American Theater Hall of Fame. Wilson is founder (with Tanya Berezin, Rob Thirkield, and Marshall W. Mason) of The Circle Repertory Company in New York City and was resident playwright there from 1969 to 1995. He is a member emeritus of the Dramatists Guild Council and has made his home in Sag Harbor since 1970.

ABOUT THE EDITOR

Ben Hodges is an actor, director, producer, writer, and editor. He has had a wide-ranging involvement in the New York Theater world, including work with The Barrow Group Theater Company, Origin Theater Company, Daedalus Theater Company, Monday Morning Productions, Jet Productions, New York Actors' Alliance, Outcast Productions, Fat Chance Productions Inc., and the Ground Floor Theatre, as well as the New Off-Off-Broadway Association. He is the editor in chief of the annual *Theatre World* publications, and contributes to *.dot* magazine. On the silver screen, he can be seen in *Macbeth: The Comedy*. His radio and television appearances include *The Joey Reynolds Show* and *Philly Live*. *Forbidden Acts,* the first collected anthology of gay and lesbian plays of the twentieth century, edited and with an introduction by Hodges, was published, to acclaim, by Applause Theatre and Cinema Books in 2003. His *The Commercial Theater Institute Guide to Producing Plays and Musicals,* also warmly received, was released by Applause Theatre and Cinema Books in 2007. Originally from Morristown, Tennessee, he holds a B.F.A. in Theater from Otterbein College in Westerville, Ohio, and is an alumnus of the Commercial Theater Institute.

CREDITS

576

William Morris Agency, LLC
1325 Avenue of the Americas
New York, NY 10019
Attn: Eric Lupfer